What is Wrong with Islamic Economics?

STUDIES IN ISLAMIC FINANCE, ACCOUNTING AND GOVERNANCE

Series Editor: Mervyn K. Lewis, *Professor of Banking and Finance, South Australia and Fellow, Academy of the Social Sciences, Australia*

There is a considerable and growing interest both in Muslim countries and in the West surrounding Islamic finance and the Islamic position on accounting and governance. This important new series is designed to enhance understanding of these disciplines and shape the development of thinking about the theory and practice of Islamic finance, accounting and governance.

Edited by one of the leading writers in the field, the series aims to bring together both Muslim and non-Muslim authors and to present a distinctive East–West perspective on these topics. Rigorous and authoritative, it will provide a focal point for new studies that seek to analyse, interpret and resolve issues in finance, accounting and governance with reference to the methodology of Islam.

Titles in this series include:

Islamic Banking and Finance in the European Union
A Challenge
Edited by M. Fahim Khan and Mario Porzio

Islamic Capitalism and Finance
Origins, Evolution and the Future
Murat Çizakça

What is Wrong with Islamic Economics?
Analysing the Present State and Future Agenda
Muhammad Akram Khan

What is Wrong with Islamic Economics?

Analysing the Present State and
Future Agenda

Muhammad Akram Khan

*Former Deputy Auditor General of Pakistan (until 2003),
Chief Resident Auditor, UN Peacekeeping Missions
(2003–2007)*

STUDIES IN ISLAMIC FINANCE, ACCOUNTING AND
GOVERNANCE

Edward Elgar
Cheltenham, UK • Northampton, MA, USA

Published by
Edward Elgar Publishing Limited
The Lypiatts
15 Lansdown Road
Cheltenham
Glos GL50 2JA
UK

Edward Elgar Publishing, Inc.
William Pratt House
9 Dewey Court
Northampton
Massachusetts 01060
USA

A catalogue record for this book
is available from the British Library

Library of Congress Control Number: 2012951776

This book is available electronically in the ElgarOnline.com
Economics Subject Collection, E-ISBN 978 1 78254 415 9

ISBN 978 1 78254 414 2 (cased)

Typeset by Servis Filmsetting Ltd, Stockport, Cheshire
Printed and bound by MPG Books Group, UK

I dedicate this work to the seekers of knowledge who sincerely search for truth and are willing to transcend their own self.

Contents

PART IV   *ZAKAH* IN THE PRESENT AGE

Figures and tables

FIGURES

TABLES

Preface

REALIZATION OF THE NEED TO RETHINK THE AGREED PREMISES

During the last few decades, Muslim scholars and jurists have made significant efforts at reviewing and reinterpreting the generally accepted doctrines of Islamic law and culture. M.N. Siddiqi (2007-a) has catalogued some of these efforts to emphasize the point that socio-political developments in Muslim societies and large-scale movement of Muslims to non-Muslim lands have necessitated the rethinking of various agreed religious premises. He has illustrated the point by way of cases. For example, it has been held so far almost unanimously that if a woman married to a non-Muslim converts to Islam her marriage will be annulled immediately. She should, if she so likes, now find a Muslim husband. However, the revised opinion expressed by, among others, the European Council of Fatwa and Research, and Hasan Turabi, a Sudanese Islamic scholar, is that such a decree would discourage non-Muslim women from converting to Islam and also overshadow the possibility of non-Muslim husbands turning toward Islam. Similarly, it has been generally considered that Muslims residing in non-Muslim states should not join the military of those countries, as it might require them to fight against Muslim brethren. The recent decree is that Muslims should act as citizens of the countries where they normally live. It would not be against Islamic principles if they joined the military of those countries. It would only enhance the respect for the Muslim community in those countries and provide opportunities for interacting with non-Muslims at various levels. Raashid Ghanouchi, a Tunisian Islamic scholar, even considers that it is obligatory for Muslims residing in non-Muslim states to do so. Another example is the reaction of Muslim scholars toward the role of the Muslim woman in society. While there has been a general consensus on the restriction of women moving out, interacting with men and taking part in political and official institutions, recent thinking is that all this has no Islamic basis. It has only local cultural roots. In sum, argues Siddiqi, with the evolution of human society and owing to demographic and socio-economic changes, Muslim scholars are rethinking the given positions on various contemporary issues. In some cases, the rethinking has been a complete somersault from the previous position. It shows that, if Islam is to be relevant for all times and for all societies, it should remain open to rethinking by people of all ages.

INTELLECTUAL CONTEXT OF ISLAMIC ECONOMICS

Efforts to Develop Islamic Economics as a Social Science Emanated from the Islamic Revivalist Movements

The contemporary evolution of Islamic economics during the last half a century or so was deeply motivated by the Muslim desire to assert itself as a living *ummah*,[1] capable of organizing all its affairs in light of Islam, which is not a religion in the traditional sense but is considered by Muslims as a way of life. The need for developing Islamic economics as a social science is an offshoot of the Islamic revivalist movements of the nineteenth and first half of the twentieth century. We can clearly see two distinct streams of thought in this period which persuaded Muslim scholars to develop Islamic economics as a branch of knowledge that is distinct from conventional economics. The first movement can be called the 'modernist movement'. It pleaded for revival of *ijtehad*[2] and reinterpretation of the Qur'an and Traditions (*Sunnah*) of the Prophet in light of socio-economic developments that had taken place since the early days of Islam. The modernists argued that the literal application of the Qur'an and the *Sunnah* would not fit well into changed circumstances, as it would create practical difficulties and defeat the broader socio-economic objectives of Islam. They pleaded for selective use of the *Sunnah* and maintained a distinction between the *Shari'ah* and Islamic jurisprudence (*fiqh*), the former being divine and God-given and the latter a product of human thinking. They argued for the revision and rewriting of Islamic jurisprudence in light of changed circumstances. Syed Ahmad Khan (1817–98), Jamaluddin Afghani (1839–97), Shibli Nu'mani (1857–1914), Muhammad Abduh (1849–1905), Rashid Rida (1865–1935), Muhammad Iqbal (1876–1938), Muhammd Asad (1900–92), Mahmoud Abu Saud (1911–93), Khalifa Abdul Hakim (1896–1959) and Fazalur Rahman (1919–88) could be treated as some of the prominent scholars who promoted a modernist interpretation of Islam. They forcefully argued that Islam believes in the unity of life. There is no duality between matter and spirit. Whatever we do in the mundane affairs of life, if carried out in light of the Qur'an and *Sunnah*, is also religious action and is entitled to reward in the hereafter. The pursuit of business and economic affairs is very much a religious duty.

Muslims should perform this duty according to the teachings of Islam and while doing so they would only be engaged in an act of worship.

The second revivalist movement can be termed as 'neo-revivalist'. Hasan al-Banna (d. 1949), Syed Qutb (d. 1966), Muhammad Rafiuddin (d. 1969), Abu al-'Ala Mawdudi (1903–79), Muhammad Baqir al-Sadr (1931–80), Isma'il Raji al-Faruqi (1921–86), Ahmed al-Najjar, Nejatullah Siddiqi, Khurshid Ahmad, Umer Chapra, Anas Zarqa and Monzer Kahf are leaders in this school of thought. The neo-revivalists argued that Muslims can progress and regain their bygone glory by literally reviving teachings of the Qur'an and the *Sunnah* as they are without any reinterpretation. The *Sunnah* of the Prophet is as good a source of Islamic teachings as the Qur'an and should be implemented in letter and spirit. Western civilization is an onslaught on Islamic civilization, and there is a need to resist it, including at intellectual forums. Islam is a complete way of life, and Muslims need not borrow anything from the West. However, they agreed on a limited *ijtehad* in areas where there were no explicit teachings of the Qur'an or *Sunnah*. The neo-revivalist school of thought argues that Islam has a distinct economic system. It treats all forms of interest as *riba*. Western economic thought is not compatible with Islamic teachings, as it is based on assumptions which are in conflict with Islam's explicit teachings (see e.g. Mannan 2008: 63). It is, therefore, necessary that Muslims develop their own science of economics. Islamic banking is also a logical corollary of this thinking. The debate between the two streams of scholars is still going on. However, the neo-revivalist scholars had greater success in attracting the attention of the Muslim intelligentsia and Muslim people in general. Islamic financial institutions in the world at present owe their existence to the interpretation of Islam presented and pleaded by the neo-revivalist scholars.

The enterprise of Islamic economics derives its inspiration from Muslim yearnings for reassertion during the late nineteenth and early twentieth century. Muslims had been subjugated by the West all over the globe for more than three centuries. In the nineteenth century they awoke from a deep slumber to reassert themselves with a distinct identity. Muslim leaders took up the task of establishing the Muslim *ummah* as an entity. To realize this objective they conceived the idea of creating Islamic sciences, distinct from mainstream sciences. They talked about 'Islamic science', 'Islamic education', 'Islamic psychology', 'Islamic anthropology', 'Islamic economics' and so on. They tried to argue that Muslims are a distinct people from other religious communities and should preserve the original and pristine version of their civilization, culture and knowledge.

The Approach for Developing Islamic Economics as a Distinct Social Science was Misplaced; It Deterred the Wider Community of Social Scientists from Participating in its Development

One of the main arguments of the present book is that the enterprise of developing Islamic versions of mainstream economics was misplaced. It tried to convey the impression that Muslims are different from other human beings. The fact remains that they are not. They are very much like other human beings. In their assertion of being 'different', they tried to coin assumptions that appeared to be different from those of mainstream economics. For example, they argued that Islamic economics is couched in altruism, cooperation, sacrifice, justice, fraternity and brotherhood (see e.g. Zaman and Asutay 2009: 76–77). They further argued that since mainstream economics does not accept these assumptions there was a need to develop Islamic economics as a distinct social science. While this was an imprecise understanding of mainstream economics, the set of assumptions pushed the Muslim economists into the blind alley of an ideal Islamic society which did not exist anywhere. The postulates of Islamic economics could not be tested for want of empirical data. The new social science was still-born.

Instead of making a contribution in the mainstream sciences and thus remaining within the ambit of ever-developing human knowledge, the neo-revivalists embarked upon the creation of Islamic versions of knowledge, but had very little success. Despite lofty claims for developing Islamic economics as a distinct social science they were unable to break any new ground. Most of what has emerged under the rubric of Islamic economics is a restatement of mainstream economics decorated with Islamic terminology or a collection of religious injunctions or a set of fond assertions which can be neither verified nor falsified. The objective of creating a distinct discipline of Islamic economics is still a dream. The enterprise failed to achieve its objective. There was negative fallout, however. The prefix 'Islamic' to economics deterred professional economists from participating in development of the subject. They were simply put off getting into a religious debate. Had the Muslim intellectuals attempted to make a contribution in economics on rational grounds, they might have succeeded in attracting the attention of the wider community of social scientists toward a new dimension of knowledge that is inspired by divine revelation besides human reason.

It might appear that the above assessment is too sweeping to be reliable in the face of rapidly developing Islamic finance and related institutions. We shall argue in this book that even this development is more in name than substance. Most of what goes under the name of 'Islamic finance' is either camouflaged conventional finance or 're-marketing of capitalist debt-peddling model' (Zaman and Asutay 2009: 77) or a more inefficient and uneconomical alternative to it. Islamic finance started with the avowed objective of creating an alternative method of providing finance that is distinct from interest-based conventional finance. It has ended up in converging with conventional finance. All Islamic financial institutions are racing to prove that they can do everything that the conventional banks are doing. Their pride is in being similar rather than being different. They have arrived at a different destination from the one at which they planned to arrive. Perhaps the whole exercise of developing Islamic financial institutions is unnecessary or superfluous.

Despite all the sincerity and desire to develop a distinct branch of knowledge capable of enhancing our understanding of contemporary economic reality and guiding us to a welfare state as visualized by Islamic principles, the end product is not significantly different from mainstream economics. The present book is an attempt to persuade the reader that there is a need to rethink the given Islamic economic doctrine and to review its basis to align it with the broader socio-economic objectives of Islam. The book should not put off a contemporary reader as an attempt to introduce alien ideologies and thought-content into the pristine doctrine of Islam. Muslim intellectual history has always seen scholars and jurists who were bold enough to raise a voice for innovative thinking within the broader framework of Islamic teachings. It is with the same urge and with all humility that we are making the present effort.

The Book is a Departure from Mainstream Thinking on Islamic Economics and is an Attempt at Self-Rebuttal

The present book is an attempt at self-rebuttal. I have been actively involved in thinking about, writing about and advocating Islamic economics as a distinct branch of knowledge for over four decades. However, over the last decade, my thinking has gradually moved away from mainstream thinking on the subject. My thinking has led me to entirely different conclusions from what I had been writing and pleading for as an activist. I am now able to see the whole question of developing Islamic economics as a distinct discipline and its practical manifestation in the form of Islamic finance in a broader perspective. The evolutionary development in my thought has freed me from the grip of the establishment thinking on the subject. Most of the conclusions in this book would refute my own ideas. I am presenting these ideas with all the humility of a student who is willing to learn and modify his position in light of more rational, objective and persuasive arguments. My objective is not to argue that all that goes under the name of Islamic economics is rubbish and should be discarded. Instead, I aim to present my criticism of these ideas with suggestions for moving forward so that the message of Islam relating to economics attracts the attention of the wider contemporary scholarship.

OVERVIEW OF THE MAIN CONCLUSIONS

a.   Most of what goes under the rubric of Islamic economics is a crude mimicry of conventional economics embellished with verses of the Qur'an and Traditions of the Prophet. Muslim scholars have failed to delineate Islamic economic teaching (which is part of theology) and Islamic economics (which should be a social and behavioural science). A proper discipline of Islamic economics should consist of hypotheses, theories and laws that are verifiable or falsifiable. However, most of the knowledge content in the body of Islamic economics does not meet the criteria. At best we can treat that material as restatement of Islamic economic teachings stated in modern economic jargon. It remains, by and large, theology and cannot be termed a social science, as it has not been formulated in a format that can be tested, nor is there any Islamic society where it can be verified.

b.   An oft-pleaded justification for the developing of Islamic economics as a distinct discipline is the need to study the Islamic economic system. However, Muslim scholars have not adequately documented the real differences between Islamic and other economic systems. The Islamic economic system is a type of capitalism with a spiritual dimension. Muslim scholars have not properly highlighted this aspect of the Islamic economic system.

c.   The main plank of Islamic economics is the theory of *riba* (interest on loans). There is no disagreement among Muslim scholars about the prohibition of *riba* in Islam. However, the debate about the exact meaning of *riba* and its application in the present age is still going on. The orthodox interpretation that treats the commercial interest of conventional financial institutions as *riba* is a human effort to expand the meaning of the term. The expansion of the meaning of *riba* has created insurmountable problems in enforcing its prohibition in the present age. There is a need to revert to the original and pristine definition of the term '*riba*' and keep it restricted to loan transactions. Interest on transactions of financing and investment should not be covered by the term '*riba*'.

d.   The contemporary movement of Islamic finance that has manifested itself in the form of Islamic financial institutions is based on the assumption that all forms of interest are *riba* and hence prohibited. It professes to have put its business on a basis other than interest. However, in practice these institutions have devised a whole host of ruses and subterfuges to conceal interest. The entire effort in the name of Islamic finance requires rethinking on the criteria of economic efficiency and risk mitigation. In the name of Islamic finance, Muslims have devised a mechanism of banking which does exactly what conventional banks are doing but in more inefficient and riskier ways. The same is true for Islamic insurance (*takaful*).

e. Another landmark of Islamic economics is the Islamic system of *zakah*, a tax on the wealth and income of the rich for transfer to the poor and the needy. Despite the fact that the system is unique in several respects the insistence of Muslim scholars in implementing it in the same form in which it was in vogue in the days of the Prophet and his first four caliphs (up to AD 662) has made it irrelevant to the needs of a contemporary society. There is a need for rethinking the entire system of *zakah* in light of present-day requirements.

A NOTE ON CITATIONS

I have made references to Qur'anic verses by placing 'Q.' before the verse number. The verse number consists of two parts separated by a colon. The number preceding the colon refers to the chapter of the Qur'an and the number succeeding refers to the verse number of the chapter. For example Q. 2:275 means chapter 2 and verse 275. I have used Muhammad Asad's *The Message of the Qur'an* (1980) for translation of the Qur'an except where indicated specifically.

In the text, 'the Prophet' refers to the Prophet Muhammad. 'Traditions' refer to the written record of the saying, actions and approvals of the Prophet.

Generally, I have used the Chicago style system of citation (*Chicago Manual of Style*, 15th edition). When quoting another author who has given a further reference, I have tried for the sake of consistency to convert that reference also on the pattern of the Chicago style system.

Most of the literature extracted from the Internet does not mention the date on which I extracted it as the period of this research spreads over several years and I could not keep track of the dates of all the downloads.

NOTES

1. A community based on the common faith of Islam irrespective of the place of origin and residence.
2. *Ijtehad* refers to fresh thinking in light of the Qur'an and Traditions of the Prophet to find Islamic solutions relevant to the present times. Also see Glossary.

Acknowledgements

I started active research on this book in September 2006, but it has been a work-in-progress for the last four decades. It synthesizes various revisions in my thinking on the subject during this period. All along I have benefited from writings, discussions, correspondence and personal interactions with various scholars. I have also benefited from question–answer sessions at numerous presentations where I put forward my ideas. During the process I have learnt from the ideas and criticism of numerous writers, thinkers and participants at my lecture-sessions. It is impossible to name all of them. However, I am deeply indebted to them all.

Several scholars spared the time to review a draft of the book. I consider myself fortunate that Professor Muhammad Nejatullah Siddiqi, the undisputed *imam* and widely acclaimed founding father of Islamic economics, found time to review the manuscript. He made several critical comments and valuable suggestions. I have benefited from his comments and suggestions immensely and express my heart-felt gratitude to him. Professor Rodney Wilson (Adjunct Professor, Durham University, UK) gave encouraging remarks after reviewing parts of the book. Professor Volker Nienhaus (former President of Marburg University, Germany and Adjunct Professor, INCEIF, Malaysia) made a number of highly insightful comments about my overall thesis and on the presentation and format of the book. I have benefited from his comments and thank him from the core of my heart. Professor Muhammad Anwar (Adjunct Professor, Framingham State University, USA) spared the time to review about half of the manuscript. He made several incisive comments and gave thought-provoking criticism. I have taken note of his comments and criticism and express my deep appreciation. Professor Syed Abdul Hamid al-Junaid (INCEIF, Malaysia), despite his extremely busy schedule, was able to review a draft of the book and made several significant remarks. In finalizing the draft I have kept his suggestions in view. I am thankful to him. My thanks are also due to Professor Iram Khan of COMSATS Institute of Information and Technology (Islamabad, Pakistan), who took pains to go through the whole manuscript in detail and pointed out several changes. He challenged some of my thoughts and obliged me to refine my presentation at various places.

I express my thanks to my friend, the scientist and Islamic scholar Tahir Saleem Dogar, who reviewed parts of the draft and raised serious questions on some of my formulations. I am indebted to my elder brother, scientist and mentor, Dr Mushtaq Ahmed, who has always been a source of inspiration and encouragement for me. He took extraordinary pains to review the entire draft minutely and spotted several editorial and formatting errors, besides questioning some of my ideas. His criticism obliged me to make several changes in the manuscript.

During the years I was working on this book (2006–11), Mr Dost Muhammad and his illustrious son Mr Nasrullah, proprietors of the largest book store in Pakistan, Allied Book Company, were of great help. They not only always gave me an alert on any new resource on Islamic economics and finance but also provided prompt access to it with smiling faces. I thank them for their generosity.

I need not say that only I am responsible for any errors, omissions or weaknesses in the book.

Abbreviations

AAOIFI	Accounting and Auditing Organization for Islamic Financial Institutions
ABS	asset-backed securities
AD	*anno Domini* (in the year of Jesus Christ)
ADB	Asian Development Bank
AH	after the *Hijra* (to indicate the year in the Islamic calendar)
AIM	Amana Ikhtiar Malaysia (an Islamic microfinance NGO)
b.	born (followed by year)
BBA	*bai' bithaman 'ajil*
BCCI	Bank of Credit and Commerce International
BIBF	Bahrain Institute of Banking and Finance
BIMB	Bank Islam Malaysia Berhad
BIS	Bank of International Settlements
BMA	Bahrain Monetary Agency
BMI	Bank Muamalat Indonesia
BMMB	Bank Muamalat Malaysia Berhad
BMT	Bait al-Maal wa al-Tamwil
BNM	Bank Negara Malaysia (central bank of Malaysia)
BNMN-I	Bank Negara Monetary Note–Islamic
BNMN-M	Bank Negara Malaysia Note–*Murabaha*
BRM	Bank Rakyat Malaysia
CBB	Central Bank of Bahrain
CGAP	Consultative Group to Assist the Poor
ch.	chapter
CIE	Commission for Islamization of Economy (Pakistan)
CII	Council of Islamic Ideology, Pakistan
CMF	commodity *murabaha* financing (Malaysia)
CMLF	commodity *murabaha* for liquid funds (Malaysia)
CMOF	commodity *murabaha* for obtaining funds (Malaysia)
CMP	commodity *murabaha* programme (Malaysia)
CRIE	Centre for Research in Islamic Economics
CSR	corporate social responsibility
d.	died (followed by year)
DIB	Dubai Islamic Bank

DJIMI	Dow Jones Islamic Market Index
DT	deposits *takaful* (deposit insurance)
ed.	edited by/editor
eds	editors
e.g.	for example (Latin *exampli gratia*)
ESIB	Egypt–Saudi Investment Bank
et al.	and other people or things (Latin *et alii*)
etc.	and so on (Latin *et cetera*)
EUROBOR	euro interbank offered rate
FIBE	Faysal Islamic Bank of Egypt
FSC	Federal Shari'at Court of Pakistan
FTSE	Financial Times Stock Exchange
GCC	Gulf Cooperation Council
GGCCI	Global Gulf Cooperation Council Index
GII	Government Investment Issues (Malaysia)
h.	*hadith*
HBFC	House Building Finance Corporation (Pakistan)
IBBL	Islami Bank Bangladesh Limited
ibid.	in the same book, article, passage, etc. (previously mentioned) (Latin *ibidem*)
IDB	Islamic Development Bank (Jeddah)
IFP	Islamic Finance Project
IFRN	Islamic floating rate note
IFSB	Islamic Financial Services Board
IIBID	International Islamic Bank for Investment and Development (Egypt)
IIFM	International Islamic Financial Market
IIIBF	International Institute of Islamic Business and Finance
IIIE	International Institute of Islamic Economics (Pakistan)
IILM	International Islamic Liquidity Management
IIMM	Islamic Interbank Money Market (Malaysia)
IIRA	Islamic International Rating Agency
IIUM	International Islamic University Malaysia
IMF	International Monetary Fund
IMFN	Islamic Microfinance Network
INCEIF	International Centre for Education in Islamic Finance (Malaysia)
INID	Islamic negotiable instrument of debt (Malaysia)
IPO	initial purchase offer
IPDS	Islamic private debt securities
I-REIT	Islamic real estate investment trust
IRTI	Islamic Research and Training Institute (Jeddah)

LIBOR	London interbank offered rate
lit.	literally
LMC	Liquidity Management Centre
LOFSA	Labuan Offshore Services Authority (Malaysia)
MFI	microfinance institution
n.	note
n.d.	not dated
NICD	negotiable Islamic certificate of deposit
NIDC	negotiable Islamic debt certificate (Malaysia)
NGO	non-governmental organization
no.	number
OIC	Organisation of the Islamic Conference
p.	page
pp.	pages
PPs	participation papers (Iran)
PEP	politically exposed persons
PLS	profit–loss sharing
PTF	participants' *takaful* fund
Q.	Qur'an
RDS	Rural Development Scheme (of Islamic Bank Bangladesh)
SAMA	Saudi Arabian Monetary Agency
SBP	State Bank of Pakistan
SFH	special finance house
SSB	*Shari'ah* supervisory board
SSED	Small Scale Enterprise Development (Pakistan)
TFC	term finance certificate
TO	*takaful* operator
trans.	translator/translated by
UIA	unrestricted investment accountholder
vol.	volume
vols	volumes

PART I

Islamic economics

1. Islamic economics: state of the art

1.1 EVOLUTION OF ISLAMIC ECONOMICS

Interest in the economic teachings of Islam emerged with the general awakening about political independence and the right to self-determination of Muslim countries at the end of the nineteenth and beginning of the twentieth century. Muslim leaders like Jamaluddin Afghani (1839–97), Muhammad Abduh (1849–1905), Syed Ahmad Khan (1817–98) and Muhammad Iqbal (1876–1938), to name a few, were at the forefront of creating this awakening. However, we do not see the use of terms like 'Islamic economics' or 'Islamic finance' explicitly in their writings and speeches. It was with the work of Mawdudi (1903–79), Baqir al-Sadr (1931–80) and a later generation of scholars like Nejatullah Siddiqi, Khurshid Ahmad, Umer Chapra, Anas Zarqa and Monzer Kahf that these terms became popular among Muslim scholars and economists.

The earlier writings on Islamic economics by such religious scholars as Manazir Ahsan Gilani (1947), Haiderzaman Siddiqi (1950), Muhammad Yusufuddin (1950), Sheikh Mahmud Ahmad (1952), Muhammad Mazaharuddin Siddiqi (1955), Naeem Siddiqi (1958), Abu al-'Ala Mawdudi (1969), Muhammad Nejatullah Siddiqi (1970), Baqir al-Sadr (1971), Ghulam Sarwar Qadri (1978) and so on mainly discussed principles of Islamic economics as derived from the primary sources of Islam. These principles dealt with such subjects as the Islamic worldview, property and inheritance law, consumer behaviour, finance and interest, and *zakah* law. Soon these writings caught the imagination of Muslim economists who were educated in modern universities and trained as professional economists. They started questioning the methodology, assumptions and scope of conventional economics and expressed dissatisfaction with it. They tried to build a case for developing Islamic economics as a social science that is based on the worldview of Islam with an entirely different set of assumptions and analytical approach. The objective was to use the economic teachings of Islam as stated in its primary sources and the historical records of Muslim thinking during the last 14 centuries as the raw material for developing a new academic discipline parallel to conventional economics. Muslim economists started writing on such subjects as microeconomics and macroeconomics and the methodology and scope of the new discipline in light of Islamic teachings. However, the exact scope of the new subject was not yet clear. Some scholars defined Islamic economics as the study of an Islamic economy which abides by the rules of the *Shari'ah*. Others thought of Islamic economics as a discipline that is guided by the *Shari'ah* and studies all human societies (Zarqa 2008: 30).

There was a lot of discussion and ambiguity about the exact method for developing the new discipline. Without arriving at a conscious consensus on this question, some research institutions, exclusively devoted to Islamic economics and finance, took the lead. They employed Western-trained professional economists with some background in Islamic studies. Unwittingly, the development of Islamic economics at the hands of these economists adopted a path that did not take them to the original goal of developing a distinct discipline. Muslim economists, the majority of whom had an education and training in conventional economics, took up the task of developing a separate branch of knowledge under the rubric of Islamic economics. However, their limitation and challenge were to develop a social science about a model economy that did not exist in the real world. They could not test and establish the veracity of their postulates. In the absence of such an opportunity, they engaged themselves in elaborating various concepts of Islamic economics as found in the primary texts of Islam, in particular Islamic jurisprudence. They tried to present the legal content of Islam in the language of conventional economics to make it intelligible for modern economists. By itself it was a commendable effort. Islamic economic teachings were lying buried in pithy and difficult Arabic texts, most of which would not be intelligible even to Muslims, not to talk of non-Muslims. The Muslim economists did a yeoman's job in presenting these teachings in modern jargon that made sense to Muslims and non-Muslims. However, the original objective of developing a social science parallel to conventional economics escaped their achievements.

1.2 ACHIEVEMENTS OF ISLAMIC ECONOMICS

1.2.1 An Overview

During the first half of the twentieth century whatever appeared in the name of Islamic economics was part of the writings of Muslim religious scholars. In those days there was no exclusive platform or journals for publishing contributions on Islamic economics. Sporadic writings appeared in various types of scholarly and general-purpose magazines.

The turning point came with the establishment of the Centre for Research in Islamic Economics (CRIE) in 1976 in King Abdulaziz University, Jeddah. Within a short span of a few years several financial institutions also came into being, with the avowed purpose of doing business on the basis of Islamic principles. For the last three decades now, there have been significant developments in the production and circulation of research documents, books and journal articles on Islamic economics and finance. Nazim Ali (2008) analyses in detail the research work and publications in Islamic economics and shows the pace of development and various sources of material in the field on the basis of Harvard's Islamic Finance Project Databank (IFP databank). Prior to 1979, there were only 238 publications relating to Islamic economics and finance. In 1999, the number was 2722. In 2006, the number of publications in the databank was 6484. At the time of writing in 2011, there are some researches and refereed journals exclusively devoted to Islamic economics and finance,[1] besides a number of websites which host research material on Islamic economics.[2] Ali (2008: 155) presents a selected list of eight magazines which have recently started publication and are exclusively devoted to Islamic economics and finance. A number of universities in Muslim and Western countries have completed or registered Ph.D. dissertations on Islamic economics and finance. For example, Nazim Ali (2008: 157) mentions 484 research projects and 75 Ph.D. dissertations in various universities of 10 countries including the US, the UK and Germany. Besides, IFP databank contains information on 200 Ph.D. dissertations completed at different universities of the world (Ali 2008: 164). A number of institutions are now offering courses and degrees in Islamic finance.[3] A number of bibliographies of books, journal articles and dissertations have also come out pertaining to literature published in English, Arabic, Urdu, Bhasa Malaysia, Turkish and other regional languages. The IFP databank contains over a thousand unique titles on Islamic economics and finance (Ali 2008: 164). The Islamic Foundation (UK) and Centre for Maghreb and Islamic Studies are preparing a five-volume encyclopedia of Islamic economics and finance. A lot of literature on Islamic economics and finance has appeared in conference proceedings. Ali (2008: 164) mentions that the IFP databank contains a record of the proceedings of 1500 conferences.

During the two decades 1990–2010 literally thousands of publications, hundreds of seminars, conferences and symposia, and scores of websites hosting literature on Islamic economics and finance have appeared. Most of this literature is sponsored by the Islamic finance industry and does not add much to the knowledge base on Islamic economics and finance. It is repetitive and monotonous. Writer after writer is drumming in the same ideas without listening to the voice from the other side that is critical to it. Warde (2010: 11) makes a general survey of the literature on Islamic finance. He expresses his disappointment as follows:

> In sum, the literature on finance is deeply disappointing principally because it is neither empirical (that is based on evidence) – nor interdisciplinary (that is looking at all the facets of the complex and multidimensional phenomenon). The most learned volumes tend to wallow in endless hair-splitting: a proclivity common to jurists and theologians. The others tend to be shallow and faddish, focusing on the 'emerging market' of the day, and on Islamic finance as either a hot or fizzling new trend. Hence, their catechism-like flavour, offering a simple – often simplistic – perspective on complex topics.

1.2.2 International Conferences on Islamic Economics

King Abdulaziz University, Jeddah hosted the first international conference on Islamic economics in 1976. Thereafter the International Association for Islamic Economics in collaboration with the Islamic Development Bank has held conferences in Islamabad (1983), Kuala Lumpur (1992), Loughborough (2000), Bahrain (2003), Jakarta (2005) and Jeddah (2008) (Iqbal 2008). This is besides hundreds of seminars, workshops and discussion groups held all over the globe on Islamic economics and finance. Universities, Islamic financial institutions and various NGOs in the field hosted these events.

1.2.3 Accounting and Auditing Organization for Islamic Financial Institutions

The Accounting and Auditing Organization for Islamic Financial Institutions (AAOIFI) was established in Algiers in 1990 by a group of Islamic financial institutions. Its original name was Financial Accounting Organization for the Islamic Banks and Financial Institutions. It later made Bahrain its headquarters. It has been publishing standards and norms for Islamic financial institutions since 1993. The standards issued by AAOIFI are mandatory for Islamic financial institutions in Bahrain, Sudan, Jordan and Saudi Arabia. For other Muslim countries and Islamic financial institutions they are recommendatory. By 2010, it had issued 25 accounting standards, seven auditing standards, six governance standards, 41 *Shari'ah* standards and two codes of ethics.

1.2.4 Teaching of Islamic Economics in Universities

A number of universities and institutes of higher learning now offer courses on Islamic economics and finance. However, most of the courses offered by these institutions pertain to Islamic finance rather than Islamic economics. Kayed (2008: 190–191) has tabulated interesting data about courses on Islamic economics and finance being offered by 14 universities in Muslim countries. These universities offer 551 courses in conventional economics and finance and only 12 courses in Islamic economics and finance (a mere 2 per cent). He further asserts (2008: 193):

> The magnitude of negligence that Islamic economics has endured by the majority of universities in various Islamic countries is appalling and intolerable. A closer look at what is being offered reaffirms the perception that curriculum developers attempt to squeeze as much abstract information as they can in one paper (course) without debating the issues or giving due thought to the wider implications of provided information for the individual Muslim novice and consequently for the future development of Islamic financial industry in general.

The real problem is that, despite efforts for developing a separate discipline of Islamic economics, there is not much that can be genuinely called 'economics'. Most of Islamic economics consists of theology on economic matters. The difficulty in developing Islamic economics as a social science has become gradually apparent to Muslim economists as well. Some of them have expressed dissatisfaction with the approach for developing Islamic economics as a distinct Islamic economics. They realize that the task is beyond completion. For example, Haneef (2009: 4) says that, despite the Kulliyyah of Economics and Management Sciences of International Islamic University Malaysia (IIUM) having produced over 2000 graduates in 25 years, the record in the area of Islamic economics is still in its infancy.

As a way out, Muslim economists now recommend that Islamic economics should be taught as an adjunct of conventional economics and the focus should be on transferring knowledge of Islamic teachings relating to economics along with the education in conventional economics. For example, Hasan (2005: 30) says:

> Economics as currently taught in Islamic institutions is mostly anchored in the mainstream tradition with reference to curricula frames, course structures, reading materials, and the researches made. The phenomenon is likely to continue far into the future for a variety of reasons. Indeed, there is now realization that greater attention has to be paid to 'teaching of economics in Islamic perspective' than to the 'teaching of Islamic economics'.

In a later writing, Hasan is more vocal in his dissatisfaction about education in Islamic economics. He says (2009: 81):

> The situation at the post-graduate level leaves even more to attend. Educational programs including research in Islamic finance are in disarray. In general, there

is lack of sufficiency, depth, coordination and direction. The teaching faculties in many cases are found short of the needed knowledge, scholarship, and commitment.

1.2.5   Reading Material in Courses on Islamic Economics

The difficulty in developing a distinct branch of knowledge of Islamic economics is obvious to those who are involved in this enterprise as front-line activists. They have realized, quite candidly, that teaching Islamic economics requires distinct textbooks and teaching material which neither exist nor are easy to create. As a proxy for the whole concept they have started teaching conventional economics from an Islamic perspective (see e.g. Siddiqi 1996). They are still a few steps short of admitting frankly that they cannot develop Islamic economics as a distinct academic discipline.

About the quality of the teaching material for Islamic economics, Hasan (2009: 92–93) writes:

1. Most of the books are not cohesive and their authors tend to sidetrack the contributions of other writers unless the same are in line with the classical stream of thought. They often attempt to cover vast and varied topics in the same volume. The result is that most of them are found harping from one topic to another without coming to grips with any.
2. At times the writings suffer from serious internal inconsistencies, and erroneous formulations (Hasan 1998: 27).[4] The reviews of them published in academic journals have been rather prosaic, not evaluative. Even when weaker spots of any work were highlighted, the subsequent literature took little notice of the comments, however valid, as though they never existed. One must know that a body of knowledge cannot develop on the right course in the absence of constructive evaluations and the cognizance of what they are worth. The response from authors to the comments in the literature on Islamic economics is surprisingly rare.
3. Many of the publications treated as 'books' by their authors and publishers alike are at best no more than extended papers on specific topics. Individually, they seldom wear the format of a course covering text for students. Publications from IRTI especially tend to fall in this category. They are useful but are generally more informative than analytical or evaluative. Their utility for graduate level students is quite limited.

Briefly, the teaching material for courses on Islamic economics is either scant or of poor quality. The Islamic economic courses are taught as an adjunct to conventional economic courses.

1.2.6 The Problem of a Textbook

Muslim economists have been struggling to create a standard textbook on Islamic economics that incorporates the main segments of the received doctrine. Some scholars have also attempted to produce a sort of text-book. However, they are not yet clear how to handle the subject. The main problem is that the conventional economics textbooks deal or at least claim to deal with positive statements, i.e. the economic theory *as it is* and not as *it should be*. For Muslim economists, formulating a positive economic theory is a difficult task in the absence of any real-life evidence or empirical data. Moreover, they are not yet sure whether Islamic economics is positive or normative. However, we came across some exceptions. For example, El-Din (2008: 74) hints at the nature of an Islamic economics textbook in the following words:

> the structure and subject flow of a fully-fledged textbook of Islamic economics must respond to a completely different motivation; one that emanates from a *normative* Islamic worldview. In this sense, Islamic economics emerges as a system of *moral* policy rather than just a pure statement of *positive* economics. (Emphasis in original)

However, he also confuses the issue when he says that Islamic economics can use the analytical tools of conventional economics without realizing that the tools cannot help a normative discipline. He says (ibid.: 74–75):

> The problem, however, does not relate to the truth or falsity of focal concepts and analytical tools embedded in the mainstream positive economics (the law of scarcity, utility theory, behavioural rationality, equilibrium analysis, etc). Such tools are in fact largely relevant to a textbook in Islamic economics if it sets out from the right questions on moral policy. The eventual textbook must therefore differ from the mainstream economics in terms of structure and curricular flow that reflect the Islamic moral thrust, but not necessarily in terms of different underlying analytical tools.

One can excuse El-Din for not elaborating the point, as it was a book review and not a position paper. However, it is not clear how Islamic economics can use the analytical tools of mainstream economics if it does not have empirical data.

The realization that Islamic economics does not have a textbook looms large for Muslim economists and scholars. On 29–30 November 2010 the International Institute of Islamic Thought (London) organized a work-shop to arrange the writing of a textbook on Islamic economics. A number of eminent Muslim economists participated. At the end of the workshop, Dr Fahim Khan, a noted Muslim economist, was made coordinator for producing the textbook.[5] As of June 2011 no standard textbook of Islamic economics was available.

1.2.7   Research and Training Institutions

There are now several research and training institutions exclusively devoted to Islamic economics and finance. A list of the most prominent ones is as follows in random order:

a.   International Centre for Research in Islamic Economics, King Abdulaziz University, Jeddah, since renamed as the Islamic Economics Research Centre, and since 2011 further renamed as the Islamic Economic Institute;
b.   Islamic Research and Training Institute (IRTI), Islamic Development Bank (IDB), Jeddah;
c.   International Institute of Islamic Economics, Islamabad (IIUI), now renamed as the School of Islamic Banking and Finance;
d.   Institute of Islamic Banking and Insurance, London;
e.   International Centre for Education in Islamic Finance (INCEIF), Malaysia;
f.   Islamic Finance Training, Kuala Lumpur;
g.   Ethica Institute of Islamic Finance, Dubai;
h.   Islamic Finance Academy, Dubai;
i.   Centre for Islamic Banking and Finance Training, Kuala Lumpur;
j.   Institute of Islamic Finance, London;
k.   Islamic Finance Advisory and Assurance Services, Birmingham (UK);
l.   Islamic Finance Institute of South Africa;
m.   Centre for Islamic Finance of Bahrain, Institute of Banking and Finance (BIBF);
n.   Centre for Banking and Financial Studies, Qatar.

Besides these organizations, which are exclusively devoted to Islamic finance, a large number of consultancy services and other educational organizations offer courses on Islamic finance beyond their other business. Most of the research and training organizations in Islamic economics and finance offer courses for developing human resources for the Islamic finance industry. These courses have very little content relating to Islamic economics as a mother discipline.

1.3   RESEARCH IN ISLAMIC ECONOMICS AND FINANCE

1.3.1   Intellectual Freedom

On the institutional level, Islamic economic institutes or centres of research are hardly the places for free intellectual activity. The governments or other influential people who provide finance would like to keep these organizations within the constraints of defined freedom of thinking. For example, it is hardly conceivable that IRTI would allow research that criticizes the Islamic Development Bank or any policy of the government of Saudi Arabia. Similarly, no publication of the Islamic Foundation (Leicester) could allow criticism of the ideas of Mawdudi. Moreover, scholars on Islamic economics seem to be afraid of the clergy for fear of severe opposition. They feel shy of suggesting innovative ideas despite tall talk about *ijtehad*. For example, the CRIE as an organ of Jeddah University cannot allow publication of any work that goes against the orthodox thinking of the influential religious leadership of the country. The approach stifles all intellectual and innovative work. It keeps free-thinking minds away from such places.

1.3.2   The Audience of Islamic Economics

As the movement to develop Islamic economics built momentum, Muslim economists consciously started using Arabic words and phrases to discuss various concepts. The idea was that, as it was a separate branch of knowledge, they should use their own terminology and phraseology. The conventional economics terms are value-laden, and using them would keep the new discipline subservient to it. It was also argued that there are concepts and terms in Islamic economics which cannot be adequately translated into English and must be written in the original Islamic phrases. To a certain extent both points had a valid basis. However, the manner in which Muslim economists started using Arabic words indiscriminately in their writings actually restricted the access of their intellectual outputs to a wider international audience. At present most of the literature on Islamic economics addresses the Muslim audience only. It uses the idioms and jargon, the terms and phrases and the legal dicta that can be understood easily by the Muslim audience only. Non-Muslims are effectively barred.

It is true that every branch of knowledge has its own terminology and a distinct jargon. Anyone who likes to understand the discipline has to understand the specific meaning and connotation in which a particular phrase or term is used. The development of this terminology takes a natural course. As the knowledge grows and new concepts are elaborated, different terms come to be used and understood by scholars of the discipline. This is true for Islamic economics as well. It is quite understandable that such terms as *riba, zakah, Shari'ah, mudaraba, musharaka* and so on have peculiar connotations in Islamic economics. However, Muslim economists use Arabic words and phrases to express even those concepts that do not have any specific Islamic connotation. For example, they use *'adl* (for justice), *shura* (for mutual consultation), *ihsan* (for benevolence), *faqr* (for poverty), *hukuma* (for government), *daula* (for state), *ihtisab* (for accountability) and so on. Such concepts can be easily expressed in ordinary English. Frequent use of Arabic words and phrases in English writings to express those concepts that can be expressed in the ordinary idiom has led to at least two consequences:

a.   Muslim economists have successfully locked out the non-Muslim non-Arabic-speaking audience from the content of Islamic economics. The larger academic readership does not find Islamic economics an easy discipline to follow and pursue. Trying to 'show off' as torch-bearers of an independent discipline, Muslim economists have ended up talking to one another to the exclusion of 'others'. Unwittingly, they have made Islamic economics a closed discipline which no one but hard-boiled Muslims should study. Even ordinary Muslims should not try to dabble in it.
b.   It has given legitimacy to some sort of pedantry, ignoring the requirement of genuine scholarship that can persuade and win over others. Instead of deepening the content rationally and making a formidable case for Islamic economics, the Muslim economists are content in appearing to be scholarly by the use of 'distinct' vocabulary.

Islamic economics should be developed as a discipline for all human beings. The Muslim economists should have addressed humanity at large. Their agenda for research, the level of argument, the terminology of the subject and the style of discussion would undergo a change if they adopted this approach,

1.3.3   The Shift Away from Islamic Economics to Islamic Finance

A number of Muslim economists have realized that the direction of research in Islamic economics has shifted away from Islamic economics to Islamic finance. Islamic finance was originally a subset of Islamic economics but now sits in the driver's seat. It has practically taken over the whole enterprise of Islamic economics. The Islamic financial institutions are racing to develop new products that are compliant with the *Shari'ah*. The researchers have the task of engineering such products. In the process Islamic economics, which created the justification and need for Islamic finance, has been shifted to the back burner (Kayed 2008: 193). Haneef (2009: 2) laments that, despite all the fanfare about Islamic finance, research in pure Islamic economics has declined. The initial enthusiasm has waned. The second and third generations of Islamic economists have become a rare breed. He argues that the Islamic finance industry has taken over the field of research in Islamic economics. The industry determines the agenda for research and funds it. As a result, most of the research is in Islamic finance and not in Islamic economics. Funding for theoretical research in Islamic economics is quite meagre and is not a priority of the Islamic finance industry. Practically, Islamic finance has hijacked Islamic economics, which was supposed to provide it with its theoretical foundations. He wonders how even Islamic finance can flourish without solid research on its foundation, that is, Islamic economics.

Iqbal (2008: 80) expresses a similar dissatisfaction on the path that the movement of Islamic economics has taken. He says:

> The renaissance initiated by the Makkah Conference (1976) created many institutions as mentioned above either directly or indirectly. However, with the passage of time the movement has lost steam and commercial interests have taken precedence over academic excellence. Some institutions have lost their real direction and some have even been closed.

Tahir (2009: 71) joins the group of unhappy Muslim economists and says:

> While there is a niche in the form of Islamic banking and Islamic finance, there is little scientific knowledge to back it. There is hardly any theory that provides a unifying link between the existing positions on various issues. This is the biggest hurdle in the way of Islamic finance education.

Shamim Siddiqui (2008: 236) argues that, since the Islamic banks have adopted most of the techniques of financing which are similar to interest-based finance, the need for research in a different monetary policy has subsided.

Muhammad Nejatullah Siddiqi (2008-b) laments:

> All is not well with Islamic economic research. The enthusiasm of the early decades has gone. The surge in enrolment in Islamic economics courses, especially at the post-graduate level, observed during the eighties of the last century, has all but subsided. In its place we have kids looking for appropriate

qualifications in 'Islamic Finance', and sprouting of institutions offering such courses 'on line', to meet the growing needs of the 'industry'. Nothing bad. No regrets. The question is what about the grand idea of providing an alternative to capitalism and socialism that is informed by moral purpose and inspired by a spiritual vision. Has it yielded to a desire to join the flock at its own terms? I suspect it is so, and that this is rooted, among other things, in the change of times.

Systematic and organized research in Islamic economics has now entered its fourth decade. However, there is no concerted effort to evaluate the discipline. Hundreds of seminars, workshops and conferences have been held during this period. However, there is no assessment of where Islamic economics stands as a discipline and what the agenda for future research is. There is no strategic thinking on the subject (Haneef 2008: 372).

1.3.4 Narrow Focus

The focus of Islamic economics has been on a narrow range of subjects. Most of the researchers and scholars have written on Islamic banking and finance or *zakah* to the neglect of other areas. For example, Javed Ahmad Khan's bibliography (1995) has 1621 entries. Out of this, 936 pertain to interest and *zakah*. A similar picture emerges if we review other bibliographies on the subject. To an uninitiated reader, it gives an impression that Islamic economics consists of mostly interest-free banking and *zakah*. Even when these two subjects are the focus, the angle of research is extremely limited, leaving out fundamental questions. For example, there is hardly any study that discusses in a rigorous and conclusive manner the negative effects of interest, although the data on the developed capitalist economies are available and it should be possible to show, as alleged, that this institution is a source of injustice for humanity. Similarly, as we shall argue subsequently, the discussions relating to *zakah* are based on outdated juridical (*fiqhi*) premises which cannot withstand cross-examination even for a short time.[6]

1.3.5 Islamic Economics and Human Economic Problems

Has Islamic economics enhanced understanding of human economic problems such as poverty, underdevelopment, distribution of income and wealth, unemployment, inflation, environmental balance and so on? Muslim economists have discussed these issues and have cited various primary sources of Islam to highlight solutions to these problems. However, if we go deeply into the suggested solutions, besides references to the primary sources of Islam there is hardly anything that is different from mainstream economics. The suggested Islamic solutions do not stray significantly from what humanity already knows. The maximum one can say is that the Muslim economists have tried to relate some of these problems to interest on finance. But most of these discussions remain conceptual and are not based on real-life data. The literature on Islamic economics has not been able to substantiate these claims with fool-proof analysis to establish a causal relationship between interest and the economic problems of humanity. In sum, Islamic economics has not enhanced human understanding of economic problems and has not led to any innovative solutions. The question arises, if Islamic economics is unable to break new ground, then why do we have a new discipline to begin with?

There is some realization among the Muslim economists as well that they have not been able to address the real economic problems of humanity. For example, the Centre of Research in Islamic Economics, Jeddah (2008: 49) says:

> All religions have been poor-friendly, Islam particularly so. But this cannot be claimed for Islamic economics, so far. The attention paid to *zakat*, *sadaqat* and *awqaf*, the most poor-friendly of Islamic institutions, has been sporadic and feeble. The jewel in the crown of Islamic economics – Islamic banking and finance – proved to be largely irrelevant for the poor.
>
> Islamic economics focuses on man as well as on matter. It inculcates values conducive to mutuality without discouraging entrepreneurship. But this message made little headway during the past half century. It was hardly heeded by economic agents. It was rarely picked up by statesmen, even by those bent on 'Islamizing'. There is little by way of research and publication to show on that count.

1.3.6 Islamic Economics and Muslim Economies

It is amazing that Muslim economists have shown scant interest in the study of Muslim economies. Except for Islamic banking and finance most of the literature on Islamic economics is conceptual and theoretical. It is not related to real-life conditions of any Muslim country. According to Muslim economists these economies are secular in nature and not organized on the pristine principles of Islam. They are not 'Islamic economies' in the strict sense of the term. The study of these economies is the subject matter of conventional economics. However, to be relevant to the contemporary world Islamic economics should undertake in-depth study of Muslim economies and propose Islamic solutions to their problems. Brushing aside this potential area of study makes Islamic economics irrelevant for the people of these countries, who can genuinely ask: if Islamic economics is not concerned with our problems why bother to create this branch of knowledge?

Siddiqi (2008-b) acknowledges this shortcoming of Islamic economics. He writes:

> We know very little about contemporary Muslim economic behaviour. There is a lot of work on what Muslims should be doing as consumers, producers, employers, traders and managers. But what they actually do, and whether it is any different from what others are doing in similar situations, we hardly ever investigated. The same applies to our distinctive institutions like *awqaf*, *zakah* funds, and even Islamic financial institutions. The question: What to do if and when a Muslim behaves differently from the way he or she should behave cannot be addressed without knowing what actual Muslim behaviour is. Similarly, we need to know whether our institutions are actually playing the role claimed for them in Islamic economic literature.

Chapra (2007: 112) also laments the same indifference of Muslim economists about problems such as corruption, extravagance, waste, budgetary deficits, inflation, low savings, low investment, unemployment, poverty and extreme inequalities of income and wealth in Muslim countries. He proposes (ibid.: 114) that data should be collected on various economic and social variables of Muslim societies. Only when the baseline data are available can the impact of Islamic values and institutions on these societies be measured and evaluated. These are good suggestions. In reality there is nothing in the literature on Islamic economics that can be presented as the study and analysis of Muslim economies from an Islamic perspective.

1.3.7   Absence of a Theory of Prosperity and Misery

Muslim economists have been trying to fine-tune or 'Islamize' theories of development economics in their zeal for proving the superiority of the Islamic economic system over capitalism. They have neglected the Qur'anic verses relating to economic prosperity and misery in human societies. The Qur'an deals with this subject extensively. There are at least 24 places where the Qur'an mentions divine laws of prosperity and misery. For example, it says that observance of what God has revealed from on high in the Qur'an, the Torah and the Gospel leads to an increase in human prosperity (Q. 5:66, 7:96, 72:16). Adversity and material deprivation are a reminder from God for humankind to turn to Him (Q. 7:130, 7:94–96, 7:168, 9:126). Natural disasters are manifestations of God's wrath on those who lead a life of sin (Q. 6:6, 9:126, 13:31, 34:15–17). The grant of worldly bounties to those who deny the Truth is a divine strategy for giving rein to them and catching them later when they are deeply entrenched in sins (Q. 3:178, 6:6, 6:42–44, 22:48, 23:55–56, 26:205–207). Misery follows disobedience of God for teaching a lesson. It is changed to prosperity again as a means for testing human behaviour. Persistence in disobedience leads to final destruction (Q. 6:42–44 and also 7:130, 7:94–95, 7:168, 17:16, 18:7, 23:55–56, 23:75–77, 26:205–207, 39:49, 89:15–20, 90:4). Misery ensues from the behaviour of human beings (Q. 30:41, 34:15–17, 68:17–27). Injustice and exploitation lead to the wrath of God, who destroys communities where injustice is rampant (Q. 22:45, 22:48, 28:58–59).

The message of these verses, in brief, is that there are deeper, imperceptible and long-term currents of events taking place in the universe as a result of human actions and under the divine will of God. These currents affect the process of wealth creation in ways that cannot be explained easily in a simple cause–effect framework. The factors of production combine in the production process for creating wealth. Over and above the visible cause–effect relationship there are laws of blessing and deprivation that influence the ultimate result of the production process. These laws operate in response to certain traits of character and the nature of human behaviour. The implication is that human behaviour leads to prosperity and misery. A normative change in human behaviour can transform the state of misery into prosperity and vice versa. The conventional economic analysis also has a similar diagnosis. However, it does not relate the outcome of economic variables to the ethical and moral behaviour of human beings. It relates the outcome of the production process to practices such as planning, controls, management, leadership, hard work and so on. The Qur'an points toward ethical behaviour, which gets translated into prosperity and misery. The divine will of God operates through and in response to human action. The precise mechanism through which it operates is as yet not fully known. The meanings and interpretations of the Qur'anic texts on the subject require further thinking and deeper understanding. The absence of any research by Muslim economists in this field gives an impression that they have never noticed these verses of the Qur'an.

1.3.8 No Theory of Income and Wealth Distribution

The literature on Islamic economics is replete with what the Qur'an has enjoined with reference to the equitable distribution of wealth so that it does not circulate among the rich only (Q. 41:7). Beyond this reference Muslim economists have not ventured to develop a theory of income and wealth distribution in human societies. The Qur'an mentions God's scheme of distribution of sustenance (*rizq*) in numerous places. For example, it

says that, if people spend in charity, God increases their sustenance manifoldly (Q. 2:245). If people implement the divine injunctions in practical
life God endows them with worldly prosperity (Q. 5:66). God is responsible for providing a livelihood to all creatures (Q. 11:6). God expands and
contracts the livelihood of people as He wills (Q. 13:26, 17:30, 28:82, 30:37,
34:36–37), 34:39, 39:52, 42:12). The livelihood of every creature has been
provided by God on this earth in a precise measure (Q. 15:19–20, 41:10,
42:27). Inequality in income and wealth is a natural phenomenon of God
(Q. 16:71, 43:32). Abundance in material possessions is only a test from
God (20:131). Thanksgiving to God leads to material prosperity (Q. 14:7).
Seeking repentance from God for one's sins is the means to material well-
being (Q. 11:3, 71:10–12). God-consciousness (*taqwa*) results in a happy
state of life in this world and a source of blessings (Q. 10:63–64, 39:10,
65:2–3). However, the Muslim economists did not pay much heed to these
verses of the Qur'an, as is evident from their neglect to develop a theory of
income distribution in Islam, although the content of these verses suggests
a great potential for doing so.

1.3.9 No Islamic Theory of Economic Development

Some Muslim economists have written on the concept of economic
development in Islam (for example: Khurshid Ahmad 1980, 2007; Sadeq
1990; Akhtar 1993; Ansari 1994; Nienhaus 1995; Mannan and Ahmad
1996; and Chapra 2008-b). These writings, though valuable in their own
right, do not break new ground from an Islamic perspective. The Islamic
concept of development (not a theory) propounded in these writings generally matches quite closely with the concept of development in capitalist
economies. Both concepts deal with such economic variables as savings,
investment, employment, the competitive market, the oversight role of
governments, and a private property regime protected by the rule of law.
If we take out references to the divine texts and the assumption of an
ideal Islamic economy, the Islamic concept turns out to be so close to the
capitalist concept of development that it becomes difficult to tell one from
the other.

Muslim writers on economic development did not develop the concept
of man's vicegerency and his role in development. If man is God's vicegerent, what is his role on the earth? Most probably, he is charged with the
task of developing the resources of the earth. The activities that promote
development of the resources match well with the role of man as God's
vicegerent. The activities which lead to destruction of resources, such as
the burning of crops, killing of human beings, pollution of the environment, destroying of buildings and infrastructure in the physical sense,

cutting asunder of kinship ties, internecine wars, mutual exploitation, and fraud and cheating in dealings in an economic and social sense, defeat the primary role of man. The Qur'an terms such activities corruption on earth (*fasad fil ard*).

The Qur'an condemns corruption on earth as a major factor in the divine scheme for human deprivation and social misery. It discusses the concept and consequences of corruption on earth in a number of verses (for example, Q. 2:27, 2:205, 5:32, 7:56, 7:74, 7:85, 10:88, 11:85, 11:116, 13:25, 26:183, 28:4, 28:77, 30:41, 47:22). It traces the emergence of corruption to human behaviour arising out of the exclusive pursuit of materialism and the reckless accumulation of wealth without regard for moral values. The accumulation of wealth and material assets induces some people to adopt an arrogant lifestyle that is devoid of moral obligations towards human beings, the natural environment and other creatures. The Qur'an says that, if a society experiences corruption because of the unnatural behaviour of certain individuals and the society neither resists nor raises a voice against it, God destroys such societies (Q. 11:116). However, if a sizeable number of people resist corruption by at least raising a voice against it, God grants some time for fighting and controlling the corruption and realigning the society with the natural path of construction, love and compassion. If the society tolerates corruption for a long time the divine remedy unfolds. God either destroys the society or creates circumstances which are painful as punishment for not fighting the corruption. It comes as the divine response to social indifference toward corruption. God's punishment can take various forms. For example:

a. As a means to restore orderliness on earth God enables some people to repel others and thus cleanse some of the mess (Q. 2:251).
b. Unending strife for material gains takes place, leading to internecine wars, mutual destruction, banishing each other from the face of the earth, mutilating one another, wiping out whole communities, and so on (Q. 5:33; Asad 1980: n. 45).
c. A continuous state of enmity and hatred for each other among various communities emerges, never allowing anyone to have a final victory (Q. 5:64; Asad 1980: n. 83).

In brief, according to the Qur'an the primary role of man is to develop the resources of the earth. Any activity that defeats this role is against the very concept of development in Islam. The Muslim economists did not try to propound an Islamic theory of development on the basis of these fundamental concepts. An analysis of man's role as God's vicegerent, and the Qur'anic condemnation of corruption on earth can lead to new dimensions in the theory of development. It would be a much wider concept of economic development than the one presented by conventional economics, from which most of the Muslim economists tried to borrow the Islamic concept of development.

1.3.10 No Macroeconomic Theory

The literature on Islamic economics practically does not have an Islamic macroeconomic theory. The macroeconomic theory of conventional economics remains the basis for all discussions and teaching in the classroom. However, it is modified by replacing interest with a profit-sharing ratio. Since there is no way to verify the results of doing so, owing to the lack of empirical data, there is no generally accepted macroeconomic theory in Islamic economics. It is only a fine-tuned theory of conventional economics presented in an 'Islamic perspective'.

Chapra (2001: 48) writes:

> The attempts made so far simply replace interest by profit-sharing ratio and introduce *zakah* as a tax without assuming any substantial change in the behaviour of the economic agents. An appropriate macroeconomic policy structure in the light of Islamic economics has not developed and the *maqasid* (objectives of the *Shari'ah*) remain unrealized in the Muslim world.

1.3.11 No Microeconomic Theory

We come across discussion of microeconomic theory in Islamic economics in an ideal Islamic economy where everyone behaves as a true Muslim: honest, frugal, productive, sacrificing, generous, content, altruistic and righteous in all respects. Such human beings do not exist anywhere in the world. Therefore, whatever theoretical implications are derived from this behaviour are more of an intellectual excursion than a theory for understanding the economy and its actors.

Chapra (2001: 49) writes:

> Islamic economics has thus to establish the relationship between its macro-economic goals and the behavior of different economic agents through the development of a more realistic microeconomics. This may take place if there is a separate theory of consumer behavior and a separate theory of firm in the context of Islamic economics.

Addas (2008: 35), after analysing the work of several Muslim economists on microeconomic theory, laments that none of them has paid any heed to the development of an Islamic law of demand. He says:

In view of the above, we are surprised to note how a most fundamental concept in microeconomics such as *Law of Demand* could totally be missed out by Muslim scholars. One would even argue that the whole economic discipline hinges on this basic concept. And without a solid scientific explanation of the central concept of demand, the whole or even the best of economics would cease to exist. Consequently, the absence of an acceptable scientific explanation or the dissociation from a prevailing one, *albeit* secular, may render it extremely difficult to even pronounce oneself as an *economist* – Islamic or otherwise.

Hussein (2008: 56) writes:

With the exception of a very scanty work on factors of production, forms of business enterprises and capital structure of business enterprises, no attempt has been made to develop an integrated coherent Theory of Firm that will help understand how Islam views production process and its objectives and its interaction with Islamic ethics of business; factors of production, their markets and their rewards. If Islamic economics has to be offered as a different paradigm, distinct micro foundations of Islamic economics have to be discovered. The concepts related to consumption and consumer behavior highlighted in *Qur'an* and *Sunnah* require developing an altogether different paradigm for the analysis of these concepts so that economics of the teachings of *Qur'an* and *Sunnah* relating to consumption could be understood appropriately and policy implications can be drawn on how a society can achieve consumption pattern desired by Islam.

1.3.12   Economic History of the Muslim People is Not Documented

Muslim economists have not paid much heed to the economic history of the Muslim people. Despite the fact that in the political arena the Muslims deviated from the pristine teachings of Islam, most of the Islamic socio-economic institutions during the first eight centuries of their history functioned according to the Islamic law and social norms. These centuries were their golden period in terms of economic prosperity and material well-being. A deeper study of this period can bring to light the state of economic policies and economic institutions in the Muslim societies of those days (Siddiqi 2008-b). The period of decline that followed (which led to colonization of most of the Muslim lands) also contains lessons. How did it happen that a prosperous and booming economic civilization came to such devastating misery? A close and deep study of the economic history of the Muslim people could unfold some important insights. However, Muslim economists have not done much to explore this area. It would have required systematic reading and editing of thousands of manuscripts lying in various libraries of the world.

In some cases, Muslim scholars have ventured to explore their early history for the purpose of learning lessons. However, they were unable to exercise due caution in romanticizing the practices of the early days in light of human developments since then. One example of such blind following of the past is the occupation of Muslim scholars with the concepts of land tax (*kharaj*) as practised in the early days of Islam. Muslim jurists in the early days were extremely sensitive about the possibility of oppression through excessive taxation and extravagance with public funds by unscrupulous rulers. They were reluctant to consider the permissibility of taxes beyond *zakah, ushr, kharaj* and so on. Those were the times when the role of the state was quite restricted. The state did not have a mandatory role in providing public services or promoting economic development. These developments in public administration have taken place in recent human history. Trying to copy blindly the financial policies of Islamic states of the early days would be counterproductive now, as it would not generate enough resources for the state to achieve its objectives. Insisting on these policies would make the Islamic state fail even before it takes root.

1.3.13   Role of Government in the Islamic Economy

The literature on Islamic economics does not clearly define the role of government in the economy. Most of the Muslim economists consider that the government would do everything to undo injustice and smooth out inequalities from the economy. They paint a picture of a welfare state where the state takes care of the poor and the weak and provides a comprehensive social security net. They invoke the institutions of *zakah* and *awqaf* to argue that an Islamic economy would have ample resources to meet the needs of the poor. The discussion is based on a romantic view of early-day Islamic society and ignores the ground reality of Muslim economies in the present age. The Muslim economists have not attempted a well-grounded theory of the role of government and its interrelationship with private and non-government sector organizations in the Islamic framework. At best they have presented ideas similar to contemporary capitalist economies, with some fine-tuning to give the discussion an Islamic flavour. It seems that Muslim economists who delve into the romantic view of Islamic government do not have any perception of the capacity and will of government functionaries in present-day Muslim societies. They have not realized properly that Muslim economies are steeped in corruption and fraud and have moved away from the pristine values of Islam. Empowering government functionaries with resources and authorizing them to play an extended role may play havoc with whatever small amount is still being performed by secular institutions for the welfare of the poor and delivery of public goods and services.

1.3.14   What is an Islamic Economy?

Muslim economists have not so far tackled the basic question: what are the minimum and sufficient conditions for an economy to be called 'Islamic'? Are there any degrees of 'Islamicity' when it comes to defining an economy in these terms? Shall we say that prohibition of commercial interest will make an economy Islamic or that implementation of *zakah* will do so? What will transform the present-day Muslim economies into 'Islamic economies'? Taking the present-day Muslim economies, why are they not treated as 'Islamic'? In the absence of such a basic definition it becomes difficult to place the economic analysis in any perspective. Mirakhor (2007: 8–9) has also pointed out this gap in current research on Islamic economics. He points out that Muslim economists should define precisely the individual and collective behaviour expected in an ideal Islamic economic system which can be translated into a testable proposition for empirical verification.

1.3.15   A Common Language of Islamic Economics

To develop Islamic economics as a social science it is important that its terminology, phraseology, key words and concepts are defined in a standard manner which should mean the same thing to everyone. At present, all books on Islamic economics or related subjects have to have a glossary of terms. But no two glossaries will have exactly the same meanings for the key concepts. A certain 'degree of fuzziness and imprecision' permeates the discipline. Mirakhor (2007: 8–9) urges that, for Islamic economics to make progress, it should have a common language with agreed definitions of words, terms and concepts among the researchers.

1.3.16   Overall Assessment of the Work in Islamic Economics

The Islamic economics movement started with the avowed objective of developing a distinct branch of knowledge that studies the economic problems of humanity within the framework of the *Shari'ah*. However, actually, Islamic economics has achieved very little of this objective. The literature on Islamic economics does not cover all facets of economics as a discipline. Most of the work is conceptual, not even theoretical in the strict sense of the term, since there does not exist an Islamic economy where these concepts can be verified. The centripetal pull of conventional economics has been so strong that whatever has emerged in the name of Islamic economics is actually a rephrasing of conventional economics with a flavour of the Islamic *Shari'ah* introduced through references and quotes from primary sources of Islam. Peeling off the layer of these quotations and references leaves the literature on Islamic economics more or less similar to what conventional economics has presented. Substantively, Islamic economics has not addressed the human problems. It has not even studied the economic problems of Muslims. Islamic economics uses the tools of analysis of conventional economics but has not been able to develop its own macroeconomic or microeconomic theories. It even does not have its own law of demand, which is so basic to the knowledge of economics. Muslim economists have not pondered deeply over the Qur'anic guidance relating to economic prosperity and misery, income and wealth distribution, economic development and the economic role of the government. Some of the Muslim economists are aware of these shortcomings. However, they have not yet ventured to think out of the box. Is it that the original premise to develop a distinct discipline in the name of Islamic economics was not well founded? Asking this question requires intellectual courage and freedom from establishment thinking. It is not yet in sight.

NOTES

1. For example: the Islamic Development Bank's IRTI journal *Islamic Economic Studies*; the King Abdulaziz University journal *KAAU Journal: Islamic Economics*; the journal of the International Association of Islamic Economics *Review of Islamic Economics*; the International Islamic University Malaysia *Journal of Economics and Management*; the *International Journal of Islamic Financial Services*, India (online); the *Journal of Muamalat and Islamic Financial Research* (Malaysia); *Thoughts on Economics* (Bangladesh); the *Journal of Islamic Accounting and Business Research* (since 2010); the *International Journal of Islamic and Middle Eastern Finance and Management* (since 2008); the *Journal of Islamic Marketing* (since 2010); etc.
2. For example: http://inceif.org; http://www.islamic-banking.com; http://www.netversity.org/index1.html; http://financeinislam.com; http://www.islamic-world.net/economics/index.htm; http://scholar.google.com; http://alhudacibe.com; http://insif.org; www.ief-pedia.com.
3. For example: Postgraduate Diploma in Islamic Finance, Certified Islamic Banker, Certified Islamic Insurance Professional and Certified Islamic Investment Analyst programmes by the International Institute of Islamic Business and Finance (IIIBF); Certified Islamic Finance Professional by the International Centre for Education in Islamic Finance (Malaysia); Islamic Finance Qualification by the Securities and Investment Institute of the UK; Certified Islamic Public Accounting, and *Shari'ah* Auditor Advisor Certificate by the Accounting and Auditing Organization for Islamic Financial Institutions, Bahrain; Islamic Finance Programme by the Oxford Centre for Islamic Studies; etc. Some universities in the UK, such as Cass Business School, Reading University, Durham University, Loughborough University and Surrey University, International Islamic University, Islamabad (Pakistan) and Ripha International University, Islamabad (Pakistan) offer courses in Islamic economics and finance and also conduct regular research in these fields. The universities of Harvard (USA) and Bochum (Germany) have launched departments or programmes for the study of Islamic economics. Universiti Teknologi MARA, Malaysia (UiTM), University Utara Malaysia (UUM) and Yarmouk University, Jordan offer bachelor's courses in Islamic

economics. Imam Muhammad University of Riyadh offers courses on Islamic economics as part of its courses on conventional economics. On 4 July 2011, Durham University (UK) launched a new doctoral training centre named the Durham Centre for Islamic Economics and Finance (DCIEF).

4. [As in original] Zubair Hasan, Islamization of knowledge in economics: Issues and agenda, *IIUM Journal of Economics and Management* (Special issue) 6 (11) (1998), pp. 1–40.
5. For details visit www.iiit.org.
6. For elaboration of this argument see Chapter 22.

2. The 'why' of Islamic economics

The present chapter tries to explore the justification given by Muslim economists and scholars for developing an independent discipline of 'Islamic economics'. We shall give our assessment of the justification as we proceed and conclude that the reasons given for developing a separate branch of knowledge in the name of 'Islamic economics' are not well founded.

2.1 NON-COMPATIBILITY OF CONVENTIONAL ECONOMICS WITH ISLAMIC FUNDAMENTALS

In developing Islamic economics as a separate and distinct branch of knowledge, Muslim economists should answer the fundamental question: what is wrong with conventional economics from the Islamic point of view? The answer to this question should show that the study of conventional economics would lead to a significant compromise in the faith or practice of Islam. Alternatively, it should show that conventional economics does not illuminate our path to solving the economic problems of humanity in a manner that is acceptable to Islam. In the absence of such an exposition, the justification for developing Islamic economics as a parallel social science would remain weak and unpersuasive.

Some Muslim economists have accepted this challenge. For example, Siddiqi (2004) points out the non-compatibility of conventional economics with Islamic fundamentals. He says:

> Islam conceives individual as a component of society and his behavior is colored by social considerations. Therefore, social implications of individual behavior have to be built into the study of individual economic behavior from the very beginning. . . . So the first modification called for is to view the individual as a member of society. This amounts to introduction of social good and public interest in the model at the very outset. Secondly, care for others tempers self-interest. Pursuit of private gain must avoid harming others. Both remain in focus without endangering survival of individual decision-maker in which case the desirability of helping others becomes ineffectual. . . . [Lastly] maximization is largely replaced by balancing of various interests: the self, the society and the physical environment. . . . One may well remark that some of these can be

discerned at the policy making level even in conventional economics. But the important point is that for Islamic economics these are core considerations.

Chapra (2001: 16–17) has also emphasized similar reasons for developing Islamic economics as a distinct discipline. According to him, conventional economics has three fundamental concepts:

- Economics is neutral about social or ethical values. It studies what is and does not tell what ought to be.
- All human beings are selfish. However, individual selfishness becomes socially desirable through the invisible hand of the free market.
- The free market leads to the most efficient allocation of resources.

Chapra has written extensively on the subject. An oversimplified and crude summary of his views is as follows. He thinks that the basic assumptions of conventional economics are not realistic. As social scientists we cannot remain indifferent to what is good for the general public. We cannot remain content by just studying what is and leaving aside what ought to be. Human beings are not selfish in all cases. They do demonstrate traits of altruism or at least they can be educated to imbibe these traits. Free markets lead to distortions in income distribution owing to the misuse or abuse of economic power. We need to have a system of supervised free markets that ensure justice and equity. Because of these inadequacies we need to develop Islamic economics as a social science that has assumptions, methods and objectives different from conventional economics.

Let us examine the above arguments and see how far they justify another social science in the name of Islamic economics.

2.1.1 The Question of Social Positives and Social Negatives

In conventional economics the economy is assumed to achieve equity in resource allocation not through ethical or social values but through the operation of the free market. Any criteria other than market prices and the ability to pay would involve value judgements and do not fit well into the paradigm of conventional economics. The observation is valid. However, it ignores recent changes taking place in the management of capitalist economies. For example, it is now generally accepted that pollution is a 'social negative' and environmental protection is a 'social positive'. The polluter should pay the cost of keeping the environment safe and clean. To the extent that polluters are now required to internalize the cost of pollution, raising the prices of goods and reducing their net profits, the economic paradigm has shifted toward accepting some normative values as legitimate economic variables. Another example of integrating ethical values into economics is the general acceptance that business firms would not pay bribes to get contracts. Years ago, business firms were free to maximize their profits in any manner they could even though it meant bribing public functionaries. The situation has changed now. Several developed countries have passed laws banning such bribes and punishing the bribers. The economic analysis now internalizes the values of integrity and honesty in business dealings. In this case also, economic theory has conceded ground to ethical values despite its claim for neutrality. Still another example of accepting higher moral values as dominant is the acceptance of a social security system in all developed countries. The social security system, strictly speaking, is a distortion of market operations. Despite that, concerns about poverty, deprivation and extreme forms of inequality have led developed countries to install some form of social security system. Developing countries also concede the need for such a system, but do not have the resources and capacity. In brief, there is now a general acceptance of the need to integrate moral and social values in the economic paradigm even though the theory of mainstream economics may not have moved fast enough to adopt these concepts. Hasan (2011: 6) says that interest in ethical practices in corporate governance is surfacing and a lot of literature is coming out on the subject. Warde (2010: 108) points to recent developments in business and finance. There is a renewed emphasis on the ethical dimension of capitalism. He says:

> Ethics is now a fixture on business school curricula. Companies play up their philanthropic efforts and their 'social responsibility'. 'Socially responsible' funds are booming. Individualism or materialism have come under attack, and ideas about 'communitarianism', 'civic virtues', 'corporate citizenship', and 'stakeholding' have been widely promoted by intellectuals and also political figures, including the likes of Bill Clinton and Tony Blair. The underlying theme is that rights cannot exist in the absence of corresponding obligations, and that aggressive individualism is not a sustainable basis for any society. Individuals are called on to give their time and effort to their communities. Corporations are called on to acknowledge a wider range of responsibilities than maximization of shareholder value.

The critique of Muslim economists on conventional economics to the extent that it does not integrate moral and social values is not well founded. There is a growing realization among conventional economists that they must consider these values in economic analysis and economic policies.

2.1.2   Beyond the Integration of Ethics in Economic Models

Some Muslim economists are not satisfied with the integration of ethics into economics and think it is inadequate. A true Islamic economics would and should go even further from that. For example, M.F. Khan (2007: 65) writes:

> Marriage of ethics and Neoclassical Economics is only a marriage of convenience to get something to be called Islamic economics but not a new paradigm in Economics. . . . If we are talking of a scientific paradigm and want to present Islamic economics as a distinct scientific discipline, then we need our own framework for positive analysis of economic behaviour of man and use that framework to show the scientific nature of Islamic economics. This framework should be comprehensive enough so that it can allow us not only to analyze all (positive) economic aspects of the human life but also enable us to incorporate Islamic ethics in the analysis to study the impact of these ethics on individual society. Our framework should be able to help us, not only in analyzing economic behavior more scientifically but also help us explaining the economics of the normative concepts like *Israf*,[1] *Tabzir*,[2] *Tayyibat*[3] of goods, poverty, rights of others in individual property rights *etc.* . . . . [D]uring the last thirty years we took a path which did not take us anywhere in identifying Islamic economics as a distinct scientific paradigm.

M.F. Khan (2007) mentions a number of alternative approaches to neoclassical economics, such as post-autistic economics, new institutional economics, evolutionary economics, complexity economics, sustainable development, and altruistic economics. He thinks that Muslim economists should join hands with the proponents of these approaches to economics and try to develop their own analytical framework that is distinct from neoclassical economics. But, as yet, he thinks, this work is still undone. None of the Muslim economists, including M.F. Khan himself, have actually demonstrated how these thoughts can be actually translated into economic theory.

2.1.3   The Question of Self-Interest

According to Siddiqi (2004) Islam tempers the basic assumption of conventional economics about human selfishness and teaches caring for others. Pursuit of individual private interests must not harm others. The economic model should incorporate this assumption about human behaviour from the outset. We think the point is overplayed by Muslim economists. They have criticized the assumption of self-interest in conventional economics as something alien to the altruism of Islam. This criticism is not wholly valid. It is based on a flawed and biased understanding of self-interest used as an assumption in conventional economics. For example, Milton Friedman and Rose Friedman (1980: 27) write:

> Narrow preoccupation with the economic market has led to a narrow inter-pretation of self-interest as myopic selfishness, as exclusive concern with immediate material rewards. Economics has been berated for allegedly drawing far-reaching conclusions from a wholly unrealistic 'economic man' who is little more than a calculating machine, responding only to monetary stimuli. That is a great mistake. Self-interest is not myopic selfishness. It is whatever it is that interests the participants, whatever they value, whatever goals they pursue. The scientist seeking to advance the frontiers of his discipline, the missionary seeking to convert infidels to the true faith, the philanthropist seeking to bring comfort to the needy – all are pursuing their interests, as they see them, as they judge them by their own values.[4]

Nobel laureate Amartya Sen (2000: 261–262) has forcefully argued about a wider interpretation of self-interest in capitalism. He says:

> Self-interest is, of course, an extremely important motive. . . . [A]nd yet we also see actions – day in and day out – that reflect values which have clear social components that take us well beyond the narrow confines of purely selfish behavior. Social values can play – and have played – an important part in the success of various forms of social organization, including the market mecha-nism, democratic politics, elementary civil and political rights, provision of basic public goods, and institutions for public action and protest . . . the basic ideas of justice are not alien to social beings, who worry about their own inter-ests but are also able to think about family members, neighbors, fellow citizens and about other people in the world.

He continues:

> While capitalism is often seen as an arrangement that works only on the basis of the greed of everyone, the efficient working of capitalist economy is, in fact, dependent on powerful systems of values and norms. . . . Successful markets operate the way they do not just on the basis of exchanges being 'allowed', but also on the solid foundation of institutions (such as effective legal structures that support the rights ensuing from contracts) and behavioral ethics (which makes the negotiated contracts viable without the need for constant litigation to achieve compliance). The development and use of trust in one another's words and promises can be a very important ingredient of market success. (Ibid.: 262)

> We have to understand and interpret the peculiar fact that one of the most suc-cessful capitalist nations in the world [i.e. Japan] flourishes economically with a motivation structure that departs, in some significant spheres, from simple pursuit of self-interest, which – we have been told – is the bedrock of capitalism. Japan does not, by any means, provide the only example of a special business

ethics in promoting capitalist success. The merits of selfless work and devotion to enterprise in raising productivity have been seen as important for economic achievements in many countries in the world, and there are many variations in these behavioral codes even among the most developed industrial nations. (Ibid.: 266)

If rational behavior includes canny advancement of our objectives, there is no reason why the canny pursuit of sympathy, or canny promotion of justice, cannot be seen as exercises in a rational choice. . . . First, our conception of self-interest may itself include our concern for others, and sympathy may thus be incorporated within the notion of person's own well-being, broadly defined. Secondly, going beyond our broadly defined well-being, or self-interest, we may be willing to make sacrifices in pursuit of other values, such as social justice or nationalism or communal welfare (even at some personal cost). . . . But in dealing with other problems – those of distribution and equity and of rule-following for generating productive efficiency – Smith emphasized broader motivation. In these broader contexts, while prudence remained 'of all virtues that which is most helpful to the individual', he explained why 'humanity, generosity, and public spirit, are the qualities most useful to others'. (Ibid.: 272)

The above quotations from eminent economists show that conventional economics does not equate self-interest with selfishness, which is a deficiency in human behaviour. To that extent, it is quite similar to the basic assumption of Islamic economics which professes altruistic behaviour as an important dimension of human behaviour. It is also obvious from the above quotation that the concepts of cooperation, brotherhood and fraternity are not alien to conventional economics. They can be accommodated within the basic assumption of self-interest. The lengthy quotations from works of eminent economists amply demonstrate that the criticism of conventional economics by Muslim economists is not well founded. They have tried to justify the development of Islamic economics on flimsy grounds. There is no dispute that Islam teaches altruism and sacrifice for others. However, the Qur'an explicitly states that human beings are selfish by nature unless they follow the divine guidance. They are greedy, short-sighted, maximizers of private gains and motivated by material attainments. Islam would like to modify this behaviour. However, if we have to study human behaviour as it is, we cannot adopt the assumption of a behaviour which is as yet to be inculcated. To the extent we want to show that Islamic teachings modify inherent human selfishness to altruism and sacrifice, it is a desirable goal for Islamic theology and not for a social science like Islamic economics.

2.2   CONVENTIONAL ECONOMICS AND AN UNJUST ECONOMIC SYSTEM

One of the favourite pastimes of Muslim economists is to criticize dysfunctional aspects of capitalist economies. The basis of criticism is that conventional economics has led to the establishment of an unjust and unstable economic system in the form of capitalism. Muslim economists (e.g. Khan and Bhatti 2008: 7–37) would often cite data to argue that capitalist economies have extremes of wealth and income, a tendency toward equilibrium with unemployment, an unstable banking structure, speculative activity on the stock exchange, exploitation of the consumer by mega-corporations, environmental pollution, excessive depletion of natural resources, and so on. The list of highlighted weaknesses varies from author to author. Based on this criticism, they argue that we need an ethics-based system which is humane, just and stable. Such a system, the argument goes, is presented by Islam. From then on, the superiority of Islamic economic system is taken up as a popular theme.

Muslim economists are often persuaded by the assumption of an ideal Islamic society whose population is spiritually trained and morally guided in the norms of Islamic law (Kuran 1983). The assumption leads to oversimplified hypotheses about the Islamic economy. For example, while discussing the theory of the firm in the Islamic economy, Muslim economists hypothesize that disputes between business firms and customers would be resolved at a lesser cost and with greater efficiency as compared to the capitalist system (e.g. Azid, Asutay and Burki 2007: 12). Similarly, Muslim economists contend that the Islamic firm would maximize profit but would be constrained by the moral filter and keep these profits to a reasonable limit (ibid.).

Azid *et al.* (2007: 14), like many others, have tried to infer the principles of corporate social responsibility and environmental balance from various Islamic terms such as *rububiyya*,[5] *khilafa*,[6] *tazkiya*[7] and so on. The fact is that these concepts have emerged in the Islamic economic literature in an effort to catch up with conventional economics. There is heaps of literature available now on corporate social responsibility, business ethics and environmental protection. Trying to score a point that Islam has a similar or 'even better' framework for these concepts is only superfluous. These concepts have been well developed and well argued by conventional economists and social scientists. Trying to use Arabic words and phrases and forcing the meanings from these words to prove Islam's superiority does not impress anyone.

Zaman and Zaman (2000: 5) contend that a transition to Islamic finance will increase the level of investment in the Islamic economy, as many practising Muslims do not keep their surplus funds in banks because of commercial interest, which they consider unlawful. Once interest is banned, these devout Muslims will also tend to keep their savings in the banks. It would raise the level of available funds for investment in society. For the study of such a system we need Islamic economics, so the argument goes. The problem with this line of reasoning is that the Muslim scholars compare an actual situation (the capitalist system) with a hypothetical system (the Islamic one). The Muslim economists avoid the most obvious question: how many people in the Muslim population do actually behave according to these moral norms? If the answer is 'only minimal', then on what basis are they trying to construct an ideal moral marketplace? The fact is that most Muslims are equally motivated by profit maximization. Only an insignificant few devoutly religious persons may be following the moral standards propounded by the Muslim economists. Some of the Muslim economists are also critical of the above approach. For example, Hasan (2005: 30) says:

> But not a few writings in the area, including consumption, take a rather puritan approach, assuming as if an Islamic social order is already in place. They derive their inspiration from past and often lose sight of the great irreversible changes that have been taking place in social ethos over the centuries.

Hasan (2011: 7) has been quite candid in commenting that one must compare the ideal of one system with the ideal of the other. However, Muslim economists often try to score a point by comparing the reality of capitalist societies with an ideal Islamic society that does not exist anywhere. Siddiqi (2008-b) concurs with this conclusion when he says:

> We claim a Muslim would behave ethically. That there are higher spiritual horizons he or she is looking at in the conduct of business. But how far they do so, and what explains the discrepancy? Does the fault always lie with human perfidy? Or, someone may have overshot in defining the norms and developing the concepts. There is also the problem that inheres in comparing today's Muslims with the idealized image of Muslims during the days of the Prophet and the caliphs. The present we know and observe, but the past is partly a mental construct. The reports that form the basis for that construction are neither exhaustive nor all authentic. But their romantic spell is capable of clouding judgment and suppressing rational evaluation.

There is no way to verify claims for the superiority of the Islamic economic system. At best, we can say these are the teachings of Islam in the economic domain. Whether it will actually lead to a more benevolent and superior economic system than capitalism would depend on the extent to which society actually practises these teachings. At present, there is no country in the world that has implemented Islamic economic teachings in their pristine form. In the absence of such a system, and resultant lack of empirical data, any discussion about the superiority of the Islamic economic system is irrelevant and unpersuasive. The question of studying this system does not arise, as it does not exist anywhere.

2.3 THE QUESTION OF A MORAL FILTER IN RESOURCE ALLOCATION

Conventional economics recognizes the market as the only arbiter of resources. Through expression of demand for luxuries and socially less desirable goods the rich can distort the allocation of resources. The market may not allocate resources for the production of goods that are required by the masses. The welfare of the greater number of people can be jeopardized. There is no moral filter to ensure that the resources are allocated to socially desirable products and services. Chapra is the main presenter of the idea of a moral filter. He argues (2001: 28–29) that the Islamic marketplace has a mechanism of dual filters: moral and market. As a first step, each individual desire passes through a moral filter before it is expressed in the market. The moral filter reduces human claims on those goods and services that are not morally justified or socially desirable. At the second stage, the morally or socially justified desires are expressed in the market. It helps in synchronizing self- and social interests and reduces the effect of economic power in the allocation of resources. It is assumed that a Muslim would be motivated by the desire to achieve success in the hereafter. As a result, he or she would like to give preference to social obligations and moral requirements over self-interest, should there be a conflict between the two. This is complemented by an enabling environment created through a system of education and spiritual uplift. Spiritual education induces individuals to adopt a simple lifestyle, avoid conspicuous spending and save resources for investment. Collectively, the system promotes growth and employment. The state will have an active and dynamic role in promoting moral education, transforming human behaviour and creating an enabling environment for the moral filter.

The argument is plausible. However, it has at least three snags. Firstly, it is obvious that inequality of income and wealth is a natural phenomenon and would always be there in all societies. A society can adopt various policies to reduce these inequalities according to its worldview. But, if we have a free market, there is no foolproof method of suppressing human desires for comforts and luxuries. We cannot conceive of a system where, as a first step, all human beings are brought to a certain level of need fulfilment before some other people are allowed to express their desire for comforts and luxuries. This is possible only if we do not have a free market. With a free market, it would never be possible to restrain the rich from indulging in luxuries and comforts. The idea that Islam uses a moral filter to restrain or modify the demand is plausible. However, it would depend how many people accept these moral teachings and with what tenacity they do that.

Secondly, there is no way to define conclusively what is meant by 'luxury', 'comfort' and 'necessity'. What is a comfort for one person could be a luxury for another; what is a luxury for one may be only a necessity for another. These comparisons would require some arbiter to decide what is desirable and what is not. Who is that arbiter and how will it fit into the worldview of Islam? Chapra (2001: 14–15) discusses the question in detail and argues that, through proper upbringing, education and training and partly through government regulation, human behaviour can become its own arbiter. The argument is plausible provided we assume that the system of education, spiritual uplift and motivation is effective and would attain what is being claimed. It is possible, as has been the case throughout Islamic history, that the system of spiritual education revolves around outer procedures and mechanical practices, fossilizing the spirit of the *Shari'ah* and its goals. It is not possible to know if such a system would in effect transform human society in any significant manner in this age. Since there does not exist any such society where the system is in vogue, it is difficult to establish that the assumption would hold in practice.

Thirdly, it may be true that neoclassical economics does not recognize the role of moral education in transforming human behaviour, but it has conceded ground to certain factors that influence human behaviour in the market. An obvious example is advertising, which influences human behaviour in the market, yet it is accepted as a norm in all capitalist societies. Similarly, educational institutions impart some ethical education that teaches individuals how to lead life in a civilized society. These values transform human behaviour and inculcate values of sacrifice, cooperation, and voluntarism for helping the needy and the distressed. These are facts of life and can be observed even though the neoclassical paradigm may not recognize them.

The whole argument about a moral filter is valid provided we have an ideal Islamic society. However, we first need to create such a society before we girdle up to study it. We are trying to develop a social science for a society that has not yet been ushered in. The maximum we can say in support of Islamic economics is that it may play a role in transforming society – a fond hope, perhaps.

2.4   THE STUDY OF ISLAMIC SOCIETY

An argument for justifying Islamic economics as a distinct branch of knowledge is as follows. Capitalism being a free system does not have built-in controls to regulate human behaviour. Left to itself, the system does not achieve what Muslims would like to achieve as the 'good life'. It fails (i) to cater for universal need fulfilment; (ii) to achieve an equitable distribution of income; (iii) to grant dignity to human beings and regulate human behaviour by any ethical code because maximization of profit is the supreme value and everyone has an unbridled freedom to follow it. These are the objectives which Islam would like to achieve. The argument is that behaving in a moral way would lead to a social order that is egalitarian, just and prosperous. To validate the above assertion Muslim economists can use economic analysis. That justifies the development of a social science which would study Islamic society under a different set of norms and assumptions.

We think the argument is flawed on several counts. First, if we have to embed Islamic assumptions in economic analysis we will have to go back to the primary texts of Islam. Islamic assumptions cannot be derived from any empirical evidence, as we do not find any ideal Islamic society in the world. Doing so would take Muslim economists into the realm of unreality. They would get into the business of using an ideal Islamic society to prove their point. Empirical studies of the economies of Muslim countries are not likely to yield significantly different data as compared to non-Muslim societies. If that is the case, how will the analysis of Islamic economics be different from that of conventional economics?

Second, the assertion that Islamic economic teachings aim to achieve the above objectives while capitalism does not requires some clarification. The enormous amount of literature on economic development, poverty alleviation and income distribution shows that conventional economics also considers these as valid areas of inquiry. The proponents of capitalism are continually adjusting their position to achieve these objectives. How can we then blame capitalism for not caring for these sublime objectives? For example, how can we say that capitalism does not uphold human dignity when we know that the conditions in non-capitalist countries like China, Cuba and several Muslim countries are still worse? Similarly, the social security net of capitalist countries speaks volumes for their concern for universal need fulfilment. Further, the concept of progressive taxation has come with capitalism, and there is a lot of literature in support of a better and more equitable distribution of income. In brief, capitalist countries, in practice, do not lag far behind our objectives of the *Shari'ah* (*maqasid*). How do we make a case for Islamic economics in such a scenario?

Third, there is plenty of literature on corporate social responsibility, corporate governance, business ethics, business oversight, business regulation and control, and so on. The literature is based on moral principles and ethical values. Saying 'Capitalism has no values to impart' would require substantive evidence.

Fourth, Muslim economists assert that Islamic economics has a three-pronged approach: self-interest, social morality and state regulation. Gradually, conventional economics is also addressing these areas of human behaviour. For example, conventional economics does study the institutions of capitalist economies that make people adhere to some basic moral norms, ensure respect for private property, enforce honesty in dealings, protect standardization of products, regulate truth and fairness in advertisements, the economic power of business firms and consumer interests, and so on. In what sense, do they think, would Islamic economics make a difference?

Fifth, Muslim economists plead for the normative role of Islamic economic teachings when they argue that capitalism upholds unlimited freedom, which can hurt, and that only morality can help control this freedom. This is exactly what we can say: a code of best practice in economic matters. Islam provides that. Humanity needs to learn and follow it. There cannot be any serious difference of opinion about it. Does it justify a parallel social science known as 'Islamic economics'? Is it not in the domain of theology or ethics and so on? Will it not be more appropriate that we leave conventional economics as it is, write the economic teachings of Islam in modern jargon and train people in those teachings with the aim of transforming their behaviour? In that case, we shall end up with an economic theology of Islam stated in modern jargon and not Islamic economics as a social science.

2.5   CONCLUSION

Muslim economists have tried to make a case for Islamic economics as a social science on the basis of certain assertions about conventional economics and assumptions about the Islamic worldview. On both counts they have made an unconvincing case. The assertion that conventional economics does not integrate ethical considerations in economic modelling is by and large not attested by the facts. There is a lot of emphasis even in conventional economic analysis on ethical considerations. The welfare of society at large is one of the primary concerns of conventional economists as well. Analysis and cure of poverty, income distribution, environmental protection, debt relief to the least developed countries, and progressive taxation are some of the prime examples of the accommodation of ethical values in economic analysis. Of course, one can always say that economic theory does not integrate Islamic ethical values, which may be an overstated case if we note that Islamic ethical values are universal values and are generally accepted. However, if Muslim economists still feel that Islamic ethical values are not adequately integrated in economic analysis, they can do that in the analytical framework of conventional economics and enrich human understanding of economic reality. There are hardly any grounds for conceiving a new social science on the basis of this criticism of conventional economics.

The other reason offered by Muslim economists is that conventional economics assumes selfishness as the primary trait of the human character, while Islam teaches altruism and sacrifice. The fact is that even the Qur'an certifies that human beings are selfish, narrow-minded and maximizers of material gains unless they follow the divine guidance. There is no doubt that the Qur'an wants human beings to change this behaviour, but this is a subject of theology and not of economics.

Another reason for developing Islamic economics as a social science is couched in a romantic view of Islamic society based on the mental construct of historical society in the early days of Islam. Creating a new branch of knowledge to study such a society, which does not exist anywhere and which is only part of the wish list of Muslims, is not a realistic goal to pursue.

Some Muslim economists have also arrived at conclusions similar to our conclusion. For example, Shams (2004: 4) argues that Muslim economists should try to study how Muslim societies can develop. In the process if they consider that living according to Islamic teaching involves different laws, they should concentrate on those laws. But if the economic laws are the same and only the economic policies have a different emphasis they should clarify salient features of the Islamic economic order instead of creating a new science in the name of Islamic economics. He says:

> Economics is a science, meaning that it formulates laws of how an economy works. Islamic economics therefore, should study economic laws according to which a society in which Moslems [sic] live would develop economically. If these Moslems live according to the scripture and its ethical codes, will there exist laws different from those studied in the conventional economic analysis describing the functioning of a modern economy? In this case Islamic economics should scrutinize these laws. But in case the same laws as in a modern economy apply but there are differences in the economic order, where for example special care is taken for the poor or some investments are forbidden due to their unethical character and others are urged due to their moral value, there is no basis for an Islamic economics but only for a different economic order under the influence of Islam.

Haque (1992) is emphatic in arguing that the whole enterprise of Islamic economics is uncalled for. He thinks that it is an attempt to fuse religion with economics, which is a social science. The religion gives rules and injunctions that are final and have to be accepted without argument. Economics as a social science studies human and market behaviour and has the ability to examine, verify and falsify various ideas. That is the process of growth and development of ideas. If we merge religion with it, all progress in this branch of knowledge would stop, as religion is sacrosanct and cannot be questioned.

Should we conclude that there is no scope for developing Islamic economics as a social science? It would be a hasty conclusion. We shall argue in this book that, though the work done so far on Islamic economics is far from adequate, there is a sound basis for developing Islamic economics as a social science. Muslim economists would have to move away from the framework of theology and adopt the framework of social sciences to develop this discipline. We shall unfold the full argument in Chapter 5.

NOTES

1. Lit. excessive spending.
2. Lit. extravagance.
3. Lit. pure and nice things.
4. As quoted by Addas (2008: 42).
5. Lit. the power of God to nourish all creatures.
6. Lit. vicegerency of man on this earth.
7. Lit. purification of the soul.

3.   What is Islamic economics?

The present chapter tries to understand the nature of Islamic economics as defined by Muslim economists. The movement to develop Islamic economics as a social science parallel to conventional economics raised several questions in the minds of Muslim economists. Some of these questions were as follows:

- What exactly is meant by Islamic economics?
- What are the scope and objective of Islamic economics?
- How does it differ from conventional economics?
- Do we need to discard conventional economics?
- Should we create a discipline parallel to conventional economics?
- Should we teach conventional economics and present 'Islamic' criticism or an 'Islamic perspective' on it?
- Should we teach conventional economics but add Islamic economic teachings to widen the horizon of Muslim students of economics?
- Who are the audience of Islamic economics? Are they Muslims only or non-Muslims as well?

In the following discussion we shall take up these questions and see how Muslim economists have tackled them.

3.1   THE DEFINITION OF ISLAMIC ECONOMICS

There is no standard and generally accepted definition of Islamic economics, although several authors have tried to define it. However, we can trace some common threads to get a flavour of what is intended by most of the writers on the subject.

Akhtar (n.d.) explains that there are two categories of Muslim scholars who have addressed the question of the nature and scope of Islamic economics. The first category, represented by Laliwala,[1] Haque[2] and Siddiqi,[3] contend that Islamic injunctions should be studied within the framework of conventional economics by using the same methodology but incorporating different behavioural variables. Akhtar thinks that this position is not tenable, as 'the outlook, taste, and evaluation criteria of economic agents are essentially different from those of secular agents'. Akhtar quotes Haque, who considers efforts to develop Islamic economics as fruitless because of a dichotomy between religion and science. Religion consists of certain dogmas, while science deals with postulates which require verification or falsification. The effort to develop Islamic economics on the basis of religion would go unrewarded. Akhtar thinks that the position of Haque is misplaced, as it perceives Islam as a religion in a narrow sense while it is a complete way of life. However, Akhtar does not elaborate the features of the alternative framework in which the behaviour of Islamic economic agents can be studied.

Mannan (1992: 18) defines Islamic economics as follows: '[Islamic economics is a] Social science which studies the economic problems of people imbued with the values of Islam.' The definition revolves around the concept of ideal Muslims and economic problems as defined by conventional economists. While the assumption of ideal Muslims makes the definition irrelevant, the assumption of economic problems takes it back to the fold of conventional economics. How do we develop such a discipline when there is no such society where the majority of people are imbued with the values of Islam?

Hasanuzzaman (1984: 85) has defined Islamic economics as follows:

> Islamic economics is the knowledge and application of its functions and rules of *Shari'ah* that prevent injustice in the acquisition and disposal of material resources in order to provide satisfaction to human beings and enable them to perform their obligations to God and the society.

The definition is simply an expression of the writer's desire for people to practise Islam. It is not clear how it does become a social science. The definition is loaded with such phrases as 'injustice', 'satisfaction to human beings' and '*Shari'ah*', which require precise definitions. At present different people understand different things from these phrases.

Chapra (2001: 33) defines Islamic economics as follows:

> Islamic economics may be defined as that branch of knowledge which helps realize human well-being through an allocation and distribution of resources that is in conformity with Islamic teachings without unduly curbing individual freedom or creating continued macroeconomic and ecological imbalances.

Chapra has tried to accommodate the concept of scarcity of resources that we find in conventional economics but has left several other things ambiguous. For example: how to define and measure 'human well-being'? How do we determine that the allocation and distribution of resources are in conformity with Islamic teachings? What is precisely included in the term 'Islamic teachings' and what is excluded, as everything in the entire corpus of teachings is not of equal importance? What is meant by 'unduly curbing individual freedom'? Who will decide what is due with reference to a curb on freedom? Who is expected to curb freedom? What is meant by macroeconomic and ecological imbalances? How do all these concepts differ from the current thinking in conventional economics?

Hasan (1998) defines Islamic economics as follows: 'To formalize matters, we may define Islamic economics as that part of Islam's social doctrine that deals with the problems of choice in the face of uncertainty and resource scarcity so as to promote *falah* in a holistic framework.' Hasan endorses the definition of conventional economics presented by Robbins, with additional constraints from Islamic social doctrine. The definition requires elaboration about what is meant by 'Islamic social doctrine' and how the writer defines the term '*falah*'.

Zaim (1989) defines Islamic economics as follows:

> Islamic economics is a systematic effort to study the economic problem and man's behavior in relation to it from an Islamic perspective. It is also an effort to develop a scientific framework for theoretical understanding, as well as design appropriate institutions and policies pertaining to the processes of production, distribution and consumption, that will enable optimal satisfaction of human needs, enabling man to serve higher ideals in life.

He emphatically clarifies that Islamic economics is not theology. It is a social science that deals with economic problems and economic institutions. However, it is based on Islamic values, while conventional economics claims to be value-neutral. He questions the value-neutrality of conventional economics, which is deep-rooted in values, although most of the time these values are not made explicit. He emphasizes that it is unscientific to keep values hidden and claim to be value-neutral. It is much better to make the value framework explicit. That is exactly what Islamic economics intends to do. In this scenario, the values can be judged and the analysis can be assessed for its consistency with the values. He says that there is a growing realization among modern economists that economics cannot be value-neutral. According to Zaim, the other distinctive feature of Islamic economics is its comprehensive and integrated view of life, which studies economic problems in a holistic perspective. Further, Islamic economics studies economic reality not only as it is but also as it should be. We think the landmark contribution of Zaim is that he has successfully emphasized the separation of theology and social science. Most of the literature on Islamic economics confuses the two disciplines.

A.R. Yusri Ahmad (2002: 28) defines Islamic economics as follows:

Islamic economics is the science that studies the best possible use of all available economic resources, endowed by God, for the production of maximum possible output of *Halal*[4] goods and services that are needed by the community now and in future and just distribution of the output within the framework of the *Shari'ah* and its intents.

The author has tried to accommodate several ideas in this definition but has not been able to accomplish the job well. The definition raises several questions. For example:

a. Can we say Islamic economics is a science? If so, on what basis? The data for Islamic economics is supposed to come from the present-day Muslim societies, to make it a science. However, it is difficult to treat that data as Islamic and use it for analysis, as most Muslims do not adhere to the pristine standards of Islamic teachings. In the absence of real-life data, Islamic economics remains a description of Islamic teachings on economic issues. Can we call it a science?

b. The author has tried to replace 'scarce resources' by 'available resources' to avoid any controversy about scarcity of resources and the Qur'anic verse about adequacy of resources (Q. 41:10). But can we do that? Is not scarcity of resources a fact of life? Instead of finding a plausible interpretation of the Qur'anic verse the author has made the question of adequacy or scarcity of resources more ambiguous. For example, what is meant by *available* resources? Does it include the mineral resources estimated to be in the earth or not? Does it mean financial resources which are receivable but not in hand as yet? Does it include barren and undeveloped lands or not?

c. The expression 'endowed by God' is superfluous and unnecessary. There is no doubt that all resources are endowed by God. The expression can be easily dispensed with.

d. Production of maximum output implies that the objective is to utilize all resources, if possible, and produce whatever is possible, even though it may be wiser to set aside some resources for future generations. Does the author intend to say that?

e. The author includes the needs of the community in future just to avoid any blame for ignoring future generations. However, once you get maximum output with the resources, the question of preserving outputs for future needs becomes risky. Future generations can benefit better if all resources are not used in producing outputs but some are preserved for use later on.

f. The expression 'just distribution within the framework of the *Shari'ah* and its intents' introduces a lot of ambiguity about the actual form and mode of distribution. The concept of just distribution is also quite value-laden and is subject to varied definitions.

Zarqa (2008: 30) writes as follows:

> There are two approaches. One says that the scope of Islamic economics is to study the economic life of society which abides by the rules of the *Shari'ah*. Thus, according to this definition, Islamic economics in its scope does not cover non-Muslim societies. The second approach says that Islamic economics is economics, which is guided by the *Shari'ah*. So, it covers in its form all human beings (Muslims and non-Muslims) in their economic behavior, in their institutions and policies related to economic life, even when such behavior or policies are not *Shari'ah*-compatible. Briefly, Islamic economics is economics interacting with the *Shari'ah*. My preference is to choose the second definition. The main reason for this is that the universality of Islam leads to this definition requirement and then inviting other people to Islam requires again this more comprehensive definition.

The definition by Zarqa is quite comprehensive and clear. It says that Islamic economics consists of critical examination of conventional economics on the touchstone of *Shari'ah* and that it aims at inviting people to Islam. These are noble objectives. However, they effectively dissuade non-Muslims from taking any interest in the subject. They would have to accept *Shari'ah* as the criterion for examination. A person who does not believe in the *Shari'ah* cannot be expected to easily adopt it as a criterion. Moreover, when we say that our objective is to invite you into the fold of Islam, it puts off all non-Muslims. People in the modern world are afraid to get into the study of a social science that would ultimately invite them to accept a religious faith although they themselves are not firm believers in their own faith. Until we make rationality the touchstone of examination we cannot expect Islamic economics to have an appeal among all people in general.

Haque (1992) comments on the definition of Islamic economics as follows:

> There is unfortunately no clear-cut and unambiguous definition of Islamic economics available in the extant literature. This ambiguity in the definition is perhaps due to the reason that many concepts, notions, ideas, practices, customs and institutions like *riba*, *mudaraba*, *zakat*, *ushr* etc., which originated in early medieval times, are subject to different interpretations.

Haque (1992) says that Muslim economists often refer to Islamic values, but this is a vague term. He says:

> 'Values of Islam' is therefore a vague phraseology which requires clear definition and interpretation. Islam is a theological term in the sense of human

submission to the Divine Will. What does Islam mean in reference to a specific economic or political system of a given society? Values are ethical terms. There is the problem of preference of one value over the other in a given society. Is efficiency more important than equity? Must freedom be preferred to economic equality and justice? Is rationality a value? Which type of rationality is to be preferred?

Muhammad Ramzan Akhtar (n.d.) sums up the various definitions as follows:

> In spite of substantial growth of literature the questions relating to defini-
> tion, nature and scope of Islamic economics have not yet been satisfactorily
> answered. Most of the attempts on the question of definition are abstract. They
> also fail to connect the economic problems to the violations of particular eco-
> nomic injunctions. Similarly the discussions on the nature and scope of Islamic
> economics do not cover the whole spectrum of the issues involved.

After quoting various definitions of Islamic economics, Addas (2008: 108) concludes that it is still unclear as to what the discipline stands for, although we can see some common strands in all the definitions. It seems that Muslim economists are unable to agree on a general wording of the definition, although most of them want to say that Islamic economics deals with the economic problems of man from an Islamic perspective. If this understanding is correct, it would raise a further question as to whether such a social science can be made universally acceptable. Will it be possible to present Islamic economic analysis in such persuasive terms that even non-Muslims would like to consider its conclusions? If Islamic economics has to grow further, it is time that Muslim economists joined forces to develop a generally acceptable definition of the subject which would mean the same thing to everyone. The definition should also remain attractive for everyone, non-Muslims included. Developing a discipline of social science which requires belief in Islam simply locks out the majority of the scholarly community. Will not such an effort defeat the very purpose for which Islamic economics is being developed as a social science?

3.2 THE OBJECTIVES OF ISLAMIC ECONOMICS

Siddiqi (2007-b) delineates the objectives of Islamic economics. He thinks that Islamic economics integrates interests and values. Interests are time-bound and relate to the situation on the ground. Values are eternal and cosmopolitan. Islamic economics integrates interests and values and develops a vision of society in light of overall objectives of the *Shari'ah*. The vision is couched in a free social and economic environment where individuals are under no oppression to follow any values. Islamic economics studies the situation on the ground in light of the vision and defines the society that *should* be developed. Its ultimate objective is to show the path for moving from the existing state of the economy to the desired state. In doing so it does not prescribe any coercive measures. Instead, it relies on moral persuasion, ethical training, social norms and economic incentives in a free market environment. Unlike conventional economics, which is a mere spectator of the current situation, Islamic economics moves a step further and visualizes an action plan for moving from the existing to the desired state.

The desired society focuses on the welfare of others within a spiritual framework. It supplements the selfish motives of man with altruistic motives. It visualizes human beings who care for the welfare of others besides their own interests. To achieve this objective, Islamic economics relies partly on non-material incentives such as reward for good deeds in the hereafter. To establish this society some human behaviour would have to be regulated by law. But the law cannot regulate all human behaviour. A significant part of human behaviour would require guidance and regulation by moral values. Islamic economics can make a contribution by showing the cost–benefits of adhering to or deviating from the moral values. For example, it may be possible to show the cost of litigation if contracts are not adhered to and the benefits of meeting commitments voluntarily owing to a motivation derived from the Islamic moral code. Islamic economics upholds a free market economy. However, it recognizes the fact that markets cannot regulate themselves. Islamic economics visualizes a role for the state in regulating the markets to protect social welfare and promote the objectives of the *Shari'ah*. Although Islamic economics does not recognize dictatorship it also does not conceive of laissez-faire.

The above-mentioned objective of Islamic economics poses a serious challenge to Muslim economists. The knowledge relating to Islamic economics should be phrased in general, rational and objective terms so that it becomes plausible for everyone. If the knowledge of Islamic economics is formulated exclusively in religious terms it will put off the non-Muslim audience. They cannot participate in the discussion and examination of what Muslims are saying about Islamic economics until they also convert to Islam. Obviously, we cannot expect that all non-Muslims will be converted to Islam. To make Islamic economics a discipline that has an appeal to every human being, Muslim economists must couch all knowledge on the subject in general terms and on rational grounds so that it does not claim any religious sanctity. It should be available for examination, verification and even falsification by everyone. Once they accept the challenge, they will have to rewrite all that has been written so far in the name of Islamic economics.

Fortunately, the introspection among Muslim economists is leading them to shift the focus of their work from Muslims to the whole of humanity. For example, the Islamic Economics Research Centre, Jeddah presented a comprehensive strategy for future research in Islamic economics (2008). Some of the research areas identified by the Centre were as follows:

a. The benefits of globalization failed to reach the poor of the world owing to the moral deficit and self-centred approach of the rich. Islamic economics should study the relationship of globalization and poverty among nations.
b. Islamic economics needs to redefine its approach toward humanity so that global problems such as environmental pollution are solved in cooperation with others.
c. How should we live with capitalism and yet retain the Islamic mould of faith and ethics?
d. Islamic economics needs to address the problems of humanity rather than of Muslims only, seizing the opportunity presented by the failure of conventional economics.
e. What are the benefits of Islamic finance and monetary management for humanity, moving away from compliance with a strand of Islamic jurisprudence?
f. How can Islamic economics help alleviate poverty?

All these subjects have a common appeal to the whole of humanity. Research in these areas can lead to a breakthrough in Islamic economics. It will need to move on from finding a solution to *riba*-based financial institutions for Muslims to the broader issues being faced by humanity at large.

3.3 THE SCOPE OF ISLAMIC ECONOMICS

There is hardly any consensus among Muslim economists on what is included and what is excluded from the scope of Islamic economics. We find a wide canvas that includes the economic teachings of Islam as enunciated by the Qur'an, Traditions of the Prophet and Islamic jurisprudence (*fiqh*). It covers the writings of Muslim scholars on various economic subjects during the last 14 centuries. It also purports to study all those subjects which conventional economics does, like macroeconomics, microeconomics, money and banking, public finance, and so on. Some writers have even included the economic conditions of contemporary Muslim economies as part of Islamic economics. However, others feel uncomfortable about this, as they think that Islamic economics should include only those subjects which have something to do with Islamic teachings and not with the economic behaviour of present-day Muslims, which may not be in accordance with these teachings.

Haque (1992) criticizes the subject matter of Islamic economics. He says that a review of bibliographies of Islamic economics shows that the subject contains all sorts of stuff ranging from philosophy, law and ethics to history and commercial practices. It is very much like the scholastic economics of medieval times, which treated economics as a branch of moral theology. He reminds Muslim economists that economics, since then, has moved away from these rudimentary ideas. Economics now deals a lot more with the actual operations of the economic system rather than with the ethical and legal norms of behaviour. This is valid criticism. Muslim economists should draw a line about the scope and subject matter of Islamic economics. Until this is done, the subject will remain intermingled with theology, law, sociology, history and modern areas of economics such as macroeconomics, microeconomics and finance. Muslim economists often talk of a wider canvas of Islamic economics and also integration of various dimensions of life and of a holistic worldview. These are valid concepts. However, to contain Islamic economics within certain limits it is essential that the contours of the subject are defined more precisely.

3.4 THE RELATIONSHIP WITH CONVENTIONAL ECONOMICS

One of the early questions faced by Muslim economists was about the relationship of Islamic economics with conventional economics. There was a lot of discussion and ambiguity about the exact method to proceed in developing the new discipline. In the process several approaches developed. We shall discuss some of these that attracted most of the attention.

One approach was to reject everything that conventional economics offers, since its basic assumptions and worldview were not compatible with the *Shari'ah*. The idea was to develop a social science solely based on the primary sources of Islam. A.R. Yusri Ahmad (2002) can be treated as a representative of this school of thought. He argues (2002: 34) that the postulates, axioms and assumptions of conventional economics are either completely or mainly invalid from the *Shari'ah* perspective. However, we should keep the door open to benefiting from conventional economics. This can be done by reviewing the history of conventional economics and tracing links between its assumptions and philosophy and religion. We should try to understand the mechanics of the capitalist system and avoid its weaknesses. Islamic economics can also adopt some of the neutral concepts of conventional economics such as the theory of marginal productivity and the law of demand. It can also benefit from the analytical tools of conventional economics such as the distinction between microeconomics and macroeconomics, dependent and independent variables, endogenous and exogenous variables, the concepts of stock and flow, and so on. However, while explaining the nature of Islamic postulates he refers to the economic principles of Islam as reflected in its primary sources. That brings in an element of idealism to the discussion. There is no doubt that we can analyse the implications of the economic principles of Islam and show how they can lead to a better life in this world and in the hereafter. But the fundamental question remains: do these principles represent Muslims as they live today? If not, then the effort to formulate postulates from Islamic economic teachings ends up presenting the ideal Islamic society and the analysis becomes an attempt at showing that, if you follow the economic teachings of Islam, you will be better off. By itself it is a sublime objective. However, this cannot be treated as the science of Islamic economics, as A.R. Yusri Ahmad and many others of his ilk would like to have it. Besides having the blame of mimicking a well-established academic discipline, they are unable to proceed further in the absence of any real-life Islamic society. The result is an imaginary world with a hypothetical and unpersuasive pool of knowledge. There is no basis to prove or disprove what Islamic economics would be offering.

A similar response was to develop Islamic economics as a social science that replaces conventional economics. An example of this response is found in Addas (2008: 5) when he says:

> The *Islamization of Knowledge* process has, in economics, adopted what one may call a step-by-step approach. This *de facto* means that there has not been an attempt to entirely replace the mainstream concepts and theories with the pure Islamic ones but modify and integrate them with what Islam would allow. Part of the confusion on the methodological issues in Islamic economics can presumably be attributed to this sort of gradual and graded approach. . . . The subject under the name of *'Islamic economics'* is presently no more than the result of applying the Islamic rules and injunctions, i.e. *Islamic fiqh*, to secular economics: Islamic economics is not yet, contrary to what some scholars would want us to believe, a discipline that *replaces* secular economics.

Again, Muslim economists have lofty ideals, great claims and ambitious goals: replacing conventional economics with Islamic economics. Conventional economics with all its limitations has developed by the collective human efforts of centuries. It is built on human thinking that the West imbibed from Islamic civilization and thought. Aiming to replace it with Islamic economics that has as yet not even presented its first theorem is a ludicrous objective, to say the least. Muslim economists should realize that they cannot replace conventional economics. However, they can make a contribution by adding certain dimensions based on divine guidance. That too would be possible only if they adopted the generally accepted approach of presenting defensible ideas and postulates which can be tested independently by anyone, non-Muslims included, and in any society. If Muslim economists are not prepared to face this challenge squarely they should abandon the idea of developing Islamic economics as a social science.

Another approach to Islamic economics was to develop it on a similar basis to conventional economics by using the tools of the latter. Some Muslim economists took up the task of modifying conventional economics by incorporating 'Islamic' assumptions but using the same analytical tools as conventional economics does. During the last four decades a sizeable literature under the name of Islamic economics has appeared using this approach. However, a closer look at the literature will show that most of it is a poor caricature of contemporary economics stated in an Islamic idiom and sprinkled with verses of the Qur'an, and Traditions of the Prophet (*ahadith*) and law (*fiqh*) of Islam. It becomes difficult to tell Islamic economics from conventional economics if we peel off its Islamic idiom and turn to the substantive part. The literature thus produced does not make any major difference to our understanding of human behaviour or the functioning of markets and economies. What could actually make a difference is the Islamic belief in life after death and treating divine guidance as a source of knowledge. Conventional economics denies both of these assumptions. Muslim economists did not develop these differences further to understand human economic behaviour. El-Ashker (2006) comments on this approach as follows:

> Though the endeavor has been a success, it has led to generating a considerable amount of Islamic economic literature in the form of western economics 'from an Islamic perspective'. While the benefits of doing so are numerous, the danger is that this may lead to alienating both Islamic economics as an independent discipline that ought to have its own identity and built-in means of survival, and Muslims as the main supporters and agents of Islamic economic institutions.

If we have to develop Islamic economics as a social science, and we think it is a potentially feasible enterprise, we should not attempt to modify conventional economics[5] from an Islamic perspective. Instead, we should study conventional economics as it is but develop Islamic economics as a

social science from its theological foundations. It should not be an attempt
to transform conventional economics into Islamic economics.

Let us accept that in its core most of the Islamic economic principles
and assumptions about human behaviour are in line with capitalism,
for example private property, the free market economy, the welfare and
regulatory role of government, objectives of full employment and social
security, and so on. Therefore most of the conventional economic analysis can fit quite well into the Islamic framework. Since there is no ideal
Islamic society in existence, the economic behaviour of Muslims is quite
similar to the economic behaviour of non-Muslims. There is no reason to
have different assumptions with regard to human behaviour. Thus most
of the conventional economic analysis will apply to Muslims as well. We
need not quote Islamic injunctions to 'Islamize' conventional economics.
However, while studying conventional economics, if we find some of its
content non-compatible with Islamic teachings we should examine it on
rational grounds. Economics has been developed through human reasoning. If we are able to argue our case on rational grounds we shall be able
to create intellectual space for our ideas. For example, suppose we are
studying the law of demand in conventional economics. We find that the
law of demand may not function as it is if, for example, a person is motivated by Islamic values. He may decide not to buy liquor, for example,
even though it may be cheaper than fruit juice. The reason could be his
religious inclination or belief. We can then argue that the law of demand
would be modified if individual behaviour were motivated by some special
considerations such as Islam. In this manner we shall be able to argue with
the economists of the world, who will have the opportunity to react to
our point of view. Economics is a human heritage and we should accept it
as such. We shall be able to extend the scope of conventional economics
by building into it Islamic assumptions, wherever necessary. The rest of
conventional economic theory can exist as it is and should be acceptable to
everyone, including Muslims. But all this effort will not lead to the development of Islamic economics. It will be our contribution to conventional
economics.

We find a degree of confusion in the minds of Muslim scholars about
the method of approaching conventional economics and other social sciences. For example, Haneef (2010: 33) says:

> As far as modern economics is concerned, genuine and meaningful Islamization
> cannot occur without some level of 'critical' understanding of the functioning
> of the modern economy, its system and constituent elements. We state 'critical'
> because the modern system has to be evaluated from an Islamic framework
> or perspective. Knowledge in this category would include areas such as eco-
> nomic history (both of thought and practice), statistics (including today's

econometrics), theory (both macroeconomics and microeconomics) and economic sociology (which may include other social sciences). One must also be prepared to include elements of sociology, logic, psychology and philosophy in its connection to economics. In the context of developing Islamic economics, it would be necessary for us to 'master' these areas of western knowledge, but always with reference to the Islamic perspective. In terms of economics, banking and finance, this would mean understanding contemporary advances in these areas *critically*.

It is not clear what is meant precisely by the 'mastering of western knowledge with reference to the Islamic perspective'. Does it mean: taking a critical look at Western knowledge using Islamic teachings as criteria? If that is so, the effort will effectively banish the non-Muslim scholarship from the efforts that Muslims would thus be making. This defeats the grand purpose of developing Islamic economics as a social science in the first place. If we are trying to forbid non-Muslims from studying Islam, why are we making all the effort of creating a new discipline? The only sensible approach to the 'mastering of western knowledge' would be to study it critically from a rational point of view. That would mean challenging Western knowledge on the human plane, and everyone would be willing to look at the position that Muslims were taking. In fact, in this sphere the question of Muslim and non-Muslim should not arise. The knowledge developed by humanity is the common heritage of all human beings. If we find some of its postulates weak and questionable we should argue against them on rational grounds. There is no question of an 'Islamic perspective' in this context.

As a contribution to human knowledge, we should develop Islamic economics as a social science which is distinct from a collection of Islamic economic teachings. Most of the extant literature on Islamic economics actually consists of Islamic teachings on economic issues. It is a valuable effort and has a role to play, but by no means can it be termed a social science in familiar terms. Such a collection of Islamic teachings is only a presentation of Islamic theology in modern language. It cannot be treated as a social science. To become a social science, Islamic theological teachings must be presented in the format of a social science and subjected to the same rigorous examination as conventional economic postulates. We shall discuss the methodology of Islamic economics in the next chapter.

NOTES

1. [As in original] I.J. Laliwala, Islamic economics: Some issues in definition and methodology, *Journal of King Abdulaziz University: Islamic Economics*, 1 (1) (1989), pp. 129–131.

2. [As in original] Z. Haque, Nature and methodology of Islamic economics: An appraisal, paper presented at 8th Annual General Meeting of the Pakistan Society of Development Economists, 7–10 January 1992.
3. Akhtar (n.d.) has not given a reference to Siddiqi's work.
4. Lit. permissible by Islamic law.
5. We are using conventional economics as a proxy for whatever is known as 'economics' in the contemporary world. It includes those 'non-orthodox' approaches to economics which disagree with mainstream neoclassical economics.

4. Methodology of Islamic economics

There is a general consensus among Muslim scholars that the Qur'an and the *Sunnah* of the Prophet are two divine sources of Islamic economics. These sources are immutable and have to be accepted as given. The ordinances given in these two sources relating to Islamic economics provide high-level assumptions and cannot be questioned. Subject to that, Islamic economics derives its subject matter from the study and analysis of human society. Developing Islamic economics as a social science poses various methodological challenges. Some of these are as follows:

a. What is the methodology of Islamic economics?
b. What is the role of reason and revelation in Islamic economics?
c. How does the methodology of Islamic economics differ from that of conventional economics?
d. Should Islamic economics use the tools of analysis developed by conventional economics? If so, would it still retain its identity?
e. What are the assumptions of Islamic economics?
f. What is the concept of *Shari'ah* and the objectives (*maqasid*) of the *Shari'ah* and how are they relevant to Islamic economics?
g. What is the relationship of Islamic law (*fiqh*) and Islamic economics?

The present chapter aims at presenting the methodology of Islamic economics as understood by Muslim economists. In the process we shall highlight the areas that require clarity or rethinking.

4.1 CONFUSION ABOUT THE METHODOLOGY

Some Muslim economists (e.g. Chapra 2001; Siddiqi 2008) have quite ably made a case for Islamic economics by analysing the inadequacies of conventional economics. The essence of their arguments is that the basic philosophy, assumptions and methodology of conventional economics do not align well with the values and norms of Islam. Conventional economics focuses merely on the materialistic secular worldview. However, in the writings of most other Muslim scholars we find some confusion about the methodology of Islamic economics. Firstly, there are economists who are trained only in conventional economics but are now fascinated to write on Islamic economics. They think Islamic economics is, perhaps, stating what secular economics has said. To them adding some verses of the Qur'an or Traditions of the Prophet would transform conventional economics into Islamic economics. They have not been able to appreciate the reason why they are in the business of developing Islamic economics as a separate branch of knowledge.

Secondly, quite a large number of researchers have not been able to firm up their response to conventional economics. It seems that Muslim economists feel shy of entering into a dialogue with conventional economists. The very rationale for developing another academic discipline is the difference of the worldview, which is likely to affect the postulates, hypotheses, theories and laws of conventional economics. Muslim economists should have engaged in examining conventional economics and in pointing out similarities or differences between the two disciplines. They should have gone over them postulate by postulate, hypothesis by hypothesis, theory by theory and institution by institution and discussed the position of Islamic economics in each case. It means that an appropriate research approach should have led to the critique of conventional economics. In the process a large volume of literature would have emerged in the realm of Islamic economics. One reason that Islamic economists did not move in this direction, perhaps, could be that they were trained in conventional economics and did not find themselves equal to the challenge. It required a deeper understanding of the two worldviews and years of patient thinking to undertake such a venture. Most of the Muslim economists have not been trained for this type of innovative work. Haneef (2010: 35) has summed up the point quite aptly:

> In academia, modern western trained Muslim social scientists are not able to appreciate the philosophical and methodological issues underlying their own disciplines, let alone having any meaningful exposure to the Islamic legacy. Their training has created, in many cases, 'second class' western scientists, who sometimes even fail to grasp the essence of their disciplines, not to mention any ambition of 'mastering' their disciplines as demanded by the Islamization of Knowledge agenda.

4.2 MIXING UP THE DIVINE AND THE HUMAN

Muslim economists are confused about their response to the methodology of conventional economics. A crude and oversimplified gist of the methodology of conventional economics is as follows. Conventional economics studies human behaviour or constructs its mental image through abstract thinking. In either case, the thought is presented as a postulate in a language which is either verifiable[1] or falsifiable.[2] If it is verified by empirical evidence or if it is not falsified by any method the postulate becomes an economic theorem and remains available for further examination. Over a prolonged period economists make repeated attempts to verify or falsify it. It is either verified or at least cannot be falsified. At that stage, it becomes an economic law. Muslim economists faced this methodology with a certain degree of suspicion. They thought that verification or falsification of Islamic postulates would expose the divine ordinances to human verification or falsification, which would be committing a sacrilege. Therefore the methodology was not suitable for Islamic economics. For example Addas (2008: 29) writes:

> To be sure, Islamic economists have little interest in the *falsificationism* or *verificationism* criterion to evaluate the efficacy of economic theories: they scrutinize their validity just from an Islamic perspective anchored in a set of beliefs and rules derived from *Revelation*. Muslims would *falsify* or *verify* what is to be considered as true knowledge or otherwise on that criterion alone. In this sense, the methodology of Islamic economics is based neither on 'falsification' nor on 'verification'. It uses both.

It is a highly confusing statement. It mixes up divine ordinances with their human interpretation and understanding. To say Islamic economics would falsify and verify theories on the basis of revelation only does not recognize the fact that the divine ordinances are only a few in number and cover only some of the key situations in social reality. The functioning of economies and markets and the related human behaviour, in most of the cases, remain within the domain of human reasoning and understanding. Giving human thinking the status of immutable divine guidance is utterly misplaced and confusing. Siddiqi (2008-b) aptly made this point when he said:

> But one should not be constrained by the sayings and doings of other humans. The divine is binding but the human is not. Additional constraints thwart fresh thinking and innovation. Sacralization of the non-sacred has been a great source of degeneration in human history. It is one thing to treat history as help and inspiration. It is very different when we try to recreate it in a changed world and that too in economic affairs. History, even Islamic history, is not sacred. We run a great risk by giving it that status.

Islamic economics and conventional economics agree on the role of reason and rationality in human life. The Qur'an is replete with references to thinking, rational understanding and the pursuit of reason in all matters. There cannot be any conflict between the injunctions of the Qur'an and human rationality. However, it is possible that human understanding of the Qur'an or the *Sunnah* is deficient and may appear to contradict rationality. Such a situation only calls for a deeper thinking and reflection both in understanding the Qur'an and the *Sunnah* and in understanding the objective reality. Some Muslim scholars have tried to create a methodological breach between Islamic economics and conventional economics on the plea that the former is based on divine knowledge which cannot be questioned or subjected to enquiry or investigation (e.g. Addas 2008: 66, 115). This is a flawed understanding of Islamic economics. The basic injunctions of Islam as derived from the Qur'an and the *Sunnah* are divine and immutable, but that is the domain of theology. When it comes to developing a social science like Islamic economics these very injunctions have to be reformulated into verifiable or falsifiable postulates. For example, the law of *zakah* presents various limits and rates. Once the law is enforced, economists can come forward and frame postulates in the following manner: (a) the enforcement of *zakah* has led to a more (or less) equitable distribution of wealth in the economy; (b) enforcement of the *zakah* law has reduced (increased) the incidence of poverty; (c) *zakah* has encouraged (discouraged) investment in the economy; and so on. Such postulates can be tested and verified by empirical evidence. It would not require an ideal Islamic society. Once they are verified by empirical evidence or cannot be falsified in any manner they will become theories of Islamic economics. The process of postulate-making is a human endeavour and is subject to examination and correction. When Muslim economists are able to translate Islamic economic teachings into economic postulates they will take the first step toward creating a social science in the name of 'Islamic economics'.

4.3 THE TOOLS OF ANALYSIS

Muslim economists have debated over the legitimacy of borrowing the tools of analysis from conventional economics. Some of them have expressed their reservations about adopting these tools as, according to them, these tools are based on certain assumptions that are not compatible with Islam. For example, they have argued that using marginal utility analysis in Islamic economics would compromise the 'Islamicity' of the discipline. The marginal utility analysis assumes a behaviour where the individual always maximizes his or her utility. This is against the behaviour of '*homo Islamicus*' or an ideal practising Muslim. There were, however, other Muslim economists who argued in favour of adopting the tools of conventional analysis. A representative of this line of reasoning is Chapra.

A crude paraphrase of Chapra's (2007: 108) argument is that the development of knowledge in human history has been like a stream. Muslims never felt shy of borrowing ideas from other civilizations and cultures and adapting them to their own worldview. They passed on these ideas and knowledge to the West during the period of the Renaissance. The West has made an immense contribution and taken knowledge to new heights, but all knowledge is the common heritage of humanity. There is nothing wrong with benefiting from the collective knowledge of humanity and building upon it. There is no need to reinvent the wheel. Islam believes in the unity of mankind and encourages the cross-fertilization of ideas among all people. However, we should remain discerning about what the West in general, and conventional economics in particular, has developed. Not all ideas, percepts, methods and theories of conventional economics are compatible with the Islamic worldview. Even among conventional economists there have been protests against the divorce of economics from ethics. That gives us hope that the ideas of Islamic economics may become a going concern of economics in future as humanity examines these ideas and finds them more beneficial than conventional economics.

In our opinion, while adopting the tools of analysis from conventional economics, Muslim economists should not suffer from any prejudice. At the same time, this borrowing should not be reckless. Some Muslim economists have presented mathematical models and econometric analysis on economic issues. While the effort itself is commendable for enhancing the intellectual status of the subject, it is somewhat naïve and simplistic at the same time. In the absence of any real-life data about Islamic economies these models do not make a real contribution to human understanding of economic problems from the Islamic perspective. At the present stage of learning the issues of Islamic economics can, perhaps, be discussed more persuasively in everyday language. The use of mathematical models may be more of an exercise in pedantry. It seems that Muslim economists, over-awed by the grandeur of conventional economics, are preoccupied with the idea of showing that 'we are not far behind'. The original objective of finding Islamic solutions to the economic problems of humanity has dwindled to 'catching up' with conventional economics. This preoccupation of 'catching up' is premature. Recognition will come if Muslim economists are able to provide viable answers to the economic problems of humanity.

Borrowing the tools of analysis from conventional economics should not compromise the identity of Islamic economics. Using these tools indiscriminately may lead to a destination that cannot be distinguished as 'Islamic', thus defeating the very purpose for which Islamic economics has to be developed as a distinct social science. El-Gamal (2006: 137–138) points to the danger as follows:

[Although] Islamic economics was conceived as an independent Islamic social science, it quickly lost that emphasis on independence and redefined its identity in terms of normative ethical and social values. However, once researchers started using conventional economic tools, their discipline was quickly subsumed in the larger field of economics. . . . Similar to the convergence of Islamic economics with mainstream economic thought, Islamic finance also quickly turned to mimicking the (interest-based) conventional finance it set out to replace.

The point is well taken, but in practice where do we draw the line? The practical question is: which tools of analysis should be used and how do we use them and still maintain the identity of Islamic economics? Muslim economists have not addressed this question.

4.4 DEDUCTIVE VERSUS INDUCTIVE REASONING

Another question that has attracted the attention of Muslim economists is about the preferred method of Islamic economics with reference to deductive and inductive reasoning. There is no final answer to this discussion in the literature. However, the most reasonable approach seems to be one adopted by Zaim (1989) when he says:

Now, the methodology that Islamic economics uses is, to use a contemporary mathematical term, an axiological approach where the values and the principles that Islam gives go to make up a set of axioms. Once we have been able to formulate this set of axioms, the rest of the economics has to follow from this by true, deductive logic. And in this respect, a Muslim economist or a non-Muslim economist can both play a role because once the axioms are there, then it should be possible even for a non-Muslim economist to make contributions in the field of Islamic economics.

Zaim (1989) adds:

But together with the deductive method, Islamic economics also implies the inductive and empirical method – the study of the phenomenon as it is and the testing of the theories in practice, and a feedback from that for theoretical analysis. This is an integral part of the methodology of Islamic economics. But what I would like to emphasize is that while adopting the axiological, deductive and empirical approaches, the uniqueness of the Islamic approach lies in the comprehensiveness of these approaches – they do not run as parallel streams. Instead, they are fused together; there is interaction between them.

These are welcome ideas. However, it is not clear how they will be translated into practice. Until Muslim economists are able to demonstrate the application of these ideas, they will remain fond hopes.

4.5   THE ASSUMPTIONS OF ISLAMIC ECONOMICS

4.5.1   Scarcity of Resources

Muslim economists find themselves uncomfortable with Lionel Robbins's famous definition of economics (*An essay on the nature and significance of economic science,* 1932) that deals with the study of economic problems arising from scarcity of means that have alternative uses and multiple ends (e.g. Zaman 2005). They are confused about the concept of scarcity and often refer to the Qur'anic verse that refers to adequacy of resources (Q. 41:10). They find themselves at odds with the Qur'anic declaration of adequacy of resources for all creatures and acceptance of scarcity as a basis for studying Islamic economics (e.g. Wahabalbari Amir Ahmed 2010). The confusion arises from their understanding of the Qur'an. Actually, the verse refers to the total ownership and command of God over all resources and indicates that God has created this universe in a well-planned manner that has enough resources for all creatures. However, the Qur'an does not mention the mechanism by which these resources become available. It is the responsibility of man to search and develop the resources by applying knowledge and effort (Hasan 2011: 10). This does not mean that man will always be able to find all the required resources in the right quantities. There can and will always remain some gap between demand and supply that creates the economic problem. There is no conflict between an economic problem arising out of scarcity and the Qur'anic verse that speaks of the adequacy of resources.

4.5.2   Self-Interest or Human Selfishness

Muslim economists are not comfortable with the assumption of conventional economics about the selfishness of human beings. Muslim economists observe that the basic assumption of selfishness in human behaviour is not always true. They quote examples of altruistic and selfless behaviour among human beings. On the basis of this observation they think that the assumption of selfishness is unrealistic. It must be replaced by human beings who have a caring attitude, a sense of brotherhood and fraternity, a feeling of sincerity and well-wishing and an attitude of cooperation and sacrifice. However, these Muslim economists miss an important point. These are traits of behaviour that Islam promotes and inculcates. It encourages people to change their selfish behaviour to adopt altruistic behaviour. In other words, it is *what ought to be*. Islam does not say that human beings are altruistic by nature. Instead, the Qur'an observes quite emphatically that human beings are selfish, narrow-minded and niggardly by nature (e.g. Q. 4:128, 17:100, 59:9, 100:6, 102:1–2). Islam draws a fine line between selfishness and self-interest. Selfishness may mean concentration on one's own interest to the detriment of others. Self-interest is to care for one's own interest without harming others. But Islam does extend the meaning of self-interest to the human desire to attain success in the *hereafter* as well. That is the whole rationale for the Islamic way of life that encourages people to behave ethically and altruistically because it will be in their self-interest to do so. Such behaviour will lead them to Paradise – an appeal to the self-interest of human beings.

Conventional economics studies the market mechanism and response of other institutions such as government and non-government bodies, other governments and so on. It does not focus on the human beings behind the market response. As opposed to this Islam treats human beings as major economic actors and human behaviour as an endogenous factor of economic analysis. Human beings respond to various laws and economic conditions. Their behaviour is influenced by a large number of selfish as well as altruistic motives. Conventional economics, if at all, considers human behaviour as a variable and assumes that in all cases the response will be solely based on the maximization of profit. Besides, it considers that the uninterrupted market response always leads to human good. Both postulates are true to some extent. However, there is no doubt that human beings also have spiritual and moral inclinations and at times their behaviour is influenced by spiritual motives. This is entirely possible if we influence and transform human behaviour through education and training. The Islamic vision of human societies takes into account this possibility. Similarly, the existence of economic misery in the world as a whole and in market economies in particular falsifies the notion that the market response always leads to human good. It does not do so in all cases. Muslim economists can make a strong case for transforming human behaviour on spiritual lines so that the avowed human good is actually realized in practice. However, for this purpose, it would not be enough to assume that all Muslims or all human beings behave in a spiritual manner. Perhaps Muslim economists can argue that, if humanity agrees and tries to transform human behaviour in a spiritual sense, the market response of these human beings could be different and that would be better on measurable economic indicators.

4.5.3 Some Unique Assumptions of Islamic Economics

Some Muslim economists, in their enthusiasm to show the possibility and genuineness of developing Islamic economics as a distinct social science, have tried to impute unique assumptions to it. M.F. Khan (2002:

70), for example, quotes Rafic al-Masri (1998)[3] that certain Islamic concepts provide parallel assumptions for Islamic economics. For example, as compared to rationality in conventional economics the concept of *rushd* (able-mindedness, sound-mindedness, rationality with an element of responsibility) can be a valid basic assumption for human behaviour. On the basis of this assumption, he thinks, permission can be denied to a person to use his private property if he or she does not possess *rushd*. The point drags Islamic economics into an area of public policy where the state can become a monster in the name of implementing *rushd*. Such ideas betray a complete ignorance of the manner in which state functionaries work and what they can do to human freedom.

Another example given by M.F. Khan (2002: 72) of the distinctive nature of Islamic economics is about the assumption of the scarcity of resources. He agrees that resources are scarce, but conventional economics treats them as scarce with reference to wants, while Islamic economics treats them as scarce with respect to needs. This hair-splitting is an academic luxury. To the extent the resources are scarce, whether with reference to wants or with reference to needs, there is an economic problem. Moreover, conventional economics also studies the scarcity of resources with respect to needs. To that extent where is the distinction between the two? Furthermore, where is the limit to needs? Fulfil one and another will appear. You can hardly find one person who has met all his or her needs. There is no doubt that Islam teaches people to make sacrifices and spend on the needs of others. This is a behavioural norm and meant to change human behaviour. This does not mean that we need to have a distinct branch of knowledge that studies the scarcity of resources with reference to needs. M.F. Khan can argue that the concept of scarcity of resources with reference to needs can be a basis for public policy for income support or a social safety net, but these types of public policies exist even in those countries which do not profess any adherence to Islam or Islamic economics. The assumptions mentioned above are neither sufficiently distinct nor enough to support the development of the social science of Islamic economics.

Another unique assumption of conventional economics is maximization of utility. Although some Muslim economists think that maximizing behaviour is against Islamic norms (e.g. Siddiqi 1996: xiii, 17, 56), others are careful not to use the term 'utility' even when they agree that Islam endorses maximization behaviour (M.F. Khan 2002: 74). They have been at pains to derive the same principle from the primary sources of Islam although this was unnecessary. A respectable exception is Hasan (2005: 32), who argues that maximization behaviour has to be seen in the context of 'what' and 'how' before a final verdict can be given about it.

Another point of distinction between Islamic economics and conventional economics mentioned by M.F. Khan (2002: 79) is the question of *gharar* (uncertainty) in economic transactions. He considers that the Islamic law on *gharar* would make several types of transactions unlawful in the Islamic context and we should enquire about the implications of alternative modes of conducting those transactions. The most obvious examples are interest, insurance, and contracts of future and forward trading. While we have argued in this book that the very basis for treating interest and insurance as forbidden is of dubious validity, the other types of *gharar* also have many question marks.[4] In the light of such doubtful concepts, the argument for developing a distinct branch of knowledge that discusses alternatives to these concepts makes the whole venture of Islamic economics something of a non-starter.

M.F. Khan (2002: 81) also mentions other principles of Islamic law such as *maslaha mursala* and *istihsan* that can provide bases for public policy. There cannot be a dispute on these questions. Public policy is a democratic concept and it can take any form that the people of a country desire. In a country with a majority Muslim population the principles mentioned by M.F. Khan can become the basis of public policy. That does not prove that we need to have such a distinct branch of knowledge as Islamic economics.

4.6 SOURCES OF ISLAMIC ECONOMICS

4.6.1 The Qur'an and the *Sunnah*

Conventional economics considers human rationality and empirical evidence as the sole source of knowledge. As compared to this, Islam considers another source of information as a valid basis for studying economic problems and understanding human and market behaviour. The other source is the divine knowledge revealed by God to His prophets, the last of whom was the Prophet Muhammad. It means that Islam has the potential to enrich and expand the frontiers of conventional economics. Muslim economists can start from conventional economics as a given pool of knowledge, adopt the same methodology as conventional economics, but formulate economic postulates based on understanding, interpretation and implementation of Islamic economic injunctions. If they are able to do that, the whole of humanity will benefit from the Islamic injunctions.

4.6.2   Islamic Jurisprudence

In this perspective another important question is the relationship of Islamic economics with Islamic jurisprudence (*fiqh*). Some economists have drawn heavily on Islamic jurisprudence as a source of Islamic economics and while doing so have treated this source as an immutable body of knowledge. There is no doubt that Islamic jurisprudence is a reservoir of human wisdom on various religious questions, but it is human in origin and temporal in nature. Without questioning the value of this pool of knowledge it is obvious that no human thought could be valid for all times and all phases of social development. Jurists have expressed opinions in the context of their respective times. Borrowing from Islamic jurisprudence heavily and then making it an integral part of Islamic economics is a great source of confusion. A prominent example of this confusion is the slogan of 'profit–loss sharing'. It has been presented as an 'Islamic' alternative to *riba*. Profit–loss sharing is a human device and has no 'Islamic' basis in the strict sense of the term. Presenting it as an 'Islamic' alternative shows how human thought has been given a divine status. Various universities offering courses on Islamic economics teach Islamic jurisprudence relating to economic matters without giving thought to the fact that this is a body of Islamic legal knowledge and falls in the domain of Islamic theology and not economics (see e.g. Haneef 2010: 34–35).

In fact, Siddiqi thinks that the foremost reason for the stagnation of Islamic economics is the confusion caused by treating Islamic law (*fiqh*) as a divine source of guidance. Siddiqi (2004) says:

> Exercise in Islamic economics has been too much focused on *fiqh*. Although *fiqh* is a collection of human thought and is time-bound, the Muslim economists treated it as inviolable as the divine message of the Qur'an and followed it in letter and spirit. . . . It is, therefore, safe to conclude that a finite body of rules framed over earlier centuries of Islam to enable Muslims live as God wanted them to live could not be used to derive from them general rules applicable in later times without first checking their background in socioeconomic conditions, etc. But the fact is many of us proceeded to do precisely that. That some went beyond and tried to apply the rules themselves to situations entirely different from those in which they framed is also true.

The Islamic economics evolved from a statement of Islamic principles by religious scholars who spelt out the Islamic position on various economic issues. As a first step this was perhaps necessary. Unfortunately, Islamic economics has not been able to evolve further from this initial position. The present body of knowledge under the name of Islamic economics has a high level of legal content and too low a level of economic analysis. Even the legal content is not relevant to present-day social reality. It pertains to the periods of Islamic history when these ideas were developed. Even if the statement of the legal position was considered necessary for the development of Islamic economics it should have covered contemporary practices. For example, by adopting the Islamic law of sale as compiled by early jurists Muslim economists have also delimited the frontiers of Islamic economics. They have foreclosed the doors of contemporary commercial practices or are unsure of their relevance in an Islamic context.

Even when adopting Islamic law as a point of reference, Muslim economists are not quite sure how to integrate it with economics in developing Islamic economics as a discipline. They think that Islamic economics studies ground reality and applies criteria of Islamic law to determine whether the reality is compatible with Islam and if not how it can be brought closer to the Islamic position. An example of this strand of reasoning can be seen in Addas (2008: 97):

> It is, therefore, valid to say, as we have done, that Islamic economics is in a measure generated through the application of Islamic *fiqh* to the prevalent secular theoretical structures to separate the permissible from the non-permissible, *as well as to ascertain the position of the Shari'ah on economic acts and current business events.* One important difference here is that under Islamic economics performance of economic activities has much more weight than the predictions of such activities. By analyzing the current economic problems facing the *Ummah*,[5] then the position of the *Shari'ah* can be inferred on what most suitable economic policy to take to achieve *falah*.[6] Thus, performance assessment of economic variables has precedence over the prediction of such economic variables – the main motive behind secular economics.

What it boils down to is that the methodology of Islamic economics is to observe an objective reality and then assess the extent to which it deviates from the principles or verdicts of Islamic *fiqh*. This approach by itself professes to remain within the domain of theology. Religious scholars throughout the ages, in all religions, have been doing that. This has been the basis of preaching in all religions. If we adopt this approach we can never develop Islamic economics as a social science. We shall only be refining theology.

Secondly, if Islamic economics does not help in the prediction of future outcomes of a policy, how shall we know that a certain policy has achieved its objective? It will only mean that we shall have to live with whatever outcomes we encounter from our policies, which were adopted as instruments for human *falah* to begin with, never knowing that we have actually attained the *falah* or not.

Thirdly, the above approach does not accept the hard fact that Islamic economics has to be developed and used in this very world in which we live, where most people are leading their lives in an imperfectly Islamic way. This will always be the case. In such a situation, should we dispense with the need for testing our hypotheses? Muslim economists should accept the reality. They should present the hypotheses with reference to the real-life situation and test the hypotheses. If the ideas and postulates of Islamic economics are robust, they will withstand the usual tests for economics and survive. They will open up new vistas of knowledge for humanity. However, if they remain content with comparison of the situation with the *fiqh* rules they will never be able to persuade humanity at large to accept or adopt Islamic economics ideas. By adopting the above approach Muslim economists are presenting a recipe of gradual extinction from the realm of knowledge.

4.6.3   Juridical Maxims and Islamic Economics

Some Muslim economists have highlighted juridical maxims as a source of Islamic economics. Although these maxims are available in basic juridical sources, yet the most recent and comprehensive source is the *Majallah Ahkam al-Adaliyya*.[7] Examples of the maxims are: 'Repelling an evil is preferable to securing a benefit', 'A private injury is tolerated to ward off a public injury' and so on. The *Majallah* has compiled those maxims which are relevant to the social-economic dimensions of life. While there is no dispute about the value of these maxims, most are guidelines for juridical inference and are based on common sense and rationality. There would be hardly any maxim in this treasure house that could not be explained and defended on rational grounds. If Muslim economists insist on having a separate branch of knowledge that uses these or similar maxims they should demonstrate how they are different from the rational principles of public policy and what difference it would make if we adopted them.

4.7   THE *SHARI'AH* AND ITS OBJECTIVES

4.7.1   Definition of the *Shari'ah*

There is some confusion among Muslim scholars about the precise definition of the *Shari'ah*. For example, Hasanuzzaman (1984: 52) says: 'The *Shari'ah* comprises two things: injunctions and rules. The first signifies the do's and don'ts in the Qur'an and the *Sunnah* while the second are those set of principles which the *fuqaha* (jurists) have derived from the first (injunctions).' It means that human thinking over the historical past which was conditioned by the socio-economic conditions of its respective time becomes part of the *Shari'ah* and thus binding on succeeding generations.

This definition makes the *Shari'ah* irrelevant to the present age, as socio-economic conditions have changed since the earlier jurists gave their verdicts on certain questions.

Muslim economists have used the term '*Shari'ah*' recklessly. Whatever came to hand in the name of Islam from any source found a place in Islamic economics under the overriding phrase of 'injunctions of the *Shari'ah*'. Almost all scholars agree that there is no one written or codified source which could be identified as the *Shari'ah*. While all of them stress that the *Shari'ah* is a primary source of Islamic economics, none of them can point out what precisely is its content. Some Muslim scholars think that the sources of the *Shari'ah* are the Qur'an, *hadith* and various jurisprudential sources. Thus they mix up the divine with the human. The fact is that, if the *Shari'ah* has to be a source of Islamic economics, it should be precise and agreed and not a fluid concept. It cannot be accepted as reasonable that something on which Islamic economics depends is not precisely known and agreed upon. For this purpose we need to distinguish between the divine and the human content of religious knowledge. Since the *Shari'ah* has to be followed by all Muslims and since accountability in the hereafter is based on compliance with the *Shari'ah*, it is inconceivable that God would leave it ambiguous or fluid.

The *Shari'ah*, actually, consists of a small number of injunctions stated in the Qur'an or available in the *Sunnah* of the Prophet. It consists of dos and don'ts, what is permissible and what is prohibited, and rights and wrongs. They are termed ordinances (*nusus*). These injunctions are few in number but are quite clear and unambiguous. All these ordinances are divine, immutable and binding on Muslims. There cannot be any dispute, difference of opinion or second interpretation of these ordinances. Whatever does not meet this criterion falls out of the domain of the *Shari'ah*. It could be human thinking on the *Shari'ah* but not the *Shari'ah* per se.

Muhammad Asad (1947: 942) has elaborated this point quite aptly. He says:

> Only the uncontrovertible, self-evident *nass* injunctions of Qur'an and *Sunnah* – 'do this', 'don't do this', 'such-and-such a thing is right', 'such-and-such a thing is wrong' – only these injunctions constitute the eternal, unchangeable *Shari'ah* of Islam ... the *Shari'ah* concerns itself exclusively with what the Law-Giver has ordained in unmistakable terms as an obligation (*fard*) or put out of bounds as unlawful (*haram*); while the far larger area of things and activities which the Law-Giver has left unspecified – neither enjoining nor forbidding them in *nass* terms – is to be regarded as allowed (*mubah*) from the religious point of view: and this is the legitimate sphere of the Muslim law.

> There is no question of 'drafting' *Shar'i* laws, or 'deducing' them by the *fiqhi* process. No law can be regarded as a *Shar'i* law unless it is clearly laid down as

such, in terms of command, prohibition, or positive statement, in either of the Two Sources: that is to say, laid down in such a way that there can be no possibility of misunderstanding or interpreting it in various ways. This, indeed, is the definition of *nass*; and no passage of the Qur'an or of a *hadith* which does not conform to this definition can possibly have been intended by the Law-Giver to enunciate a law in the *Shar'i* sense. (Ibid.: 949)

Unfortunately, some Muslim economists while writing on Islamic economics have not maintained this difference between the *Shari'ah* and the human interpretation of the *Shari'ah*. They have mixed up the divine with the human. As a result, a lot of human thought is treated as the *Shari'ah* when it is not. The approach has embedded a sort of inflexibility and rigidity in the body content of Islamic economics. It creates a methodological problem. If, for example, there is an injunction of the Qur'an, what can an economist do except to preach its merits so that people should follow it? This is, effectively, the domain of Islamic preaching (*da'wah*). By itself it may be a lofty objective, but it cannot be termed Islamic economics, which if developed properly would require examination of various postulates derived from, besides other sources, Islamic theology. Until we clearly demarcate these two disciplines (i.e. economics and theology) the path of growth for Islamic economics is blocked. The development of Islamic economics as a social science has to be based on human understanding and application of the *Shari'ah* and not on the *Shari'ah* itself, which cannot be further developed. It has been revealed by God as a final word and requires no further development.

4.8   THE OBJECTIVES OF THE *SHARI'AH*

The literature on Islamic economics is replete with references to the objectives of the *Shari'ah* (*maqasid al-Shari'ah*). The concept of the objectives of the *Shari'ah* was systematically presented by al-Ghazali (d. AH 505/ AD 1111) and then refined by al-Shatibi (d. AH 790/AD 1388). The gist of the concept is that the objectives of the *Shari'ah* consist of protecting life, religion, progeny, reason and property. While discussing the direction of innovative thinking (*ijtehad*) on new issues, Muslim economists have often referred to these objectives but have not critically examined their relevance to the present age. It was Siddiqi (2004) who for the first time raised a voice on this issue. He considers blind resort to the objectives as one of the reasons for the stagnation of Islamic economics:

The Muslim economists restricted themselves to the *maqasid*[8] of the Islamic law and did not go beyond to think within the broader framework of Islam as it is. They did not try to think beyond the box in the light of new developments. There was a need to expand the scope of the *maqasid* to include such issues as justice and equity, protection of environments, eradication of poverty, human dignity, and sustenance for all, freedom of choice, peace and progress, and distribution of income and wealth. If the Muslim economists had included these issues in the list of *maqasid*, they would have expanded their horizon and resultantly the scope of Islamic economics.

A dispassionate look at the original or the expanded lists of objectives would leave one wondering about any possible conflict with conventional economics. The challenge before Muslim economists is to demonstrate that conventional economics comes into conflict with the objectives of the *Shari'ah*. Until that is done the relevance of the objectives to developing Islamic economics would remain a question mark. What is in these objectives that would not occur to a person of common prudence while thinking about any postulate of Islamic economics?

4.9 SOME UNRESOLVED ISSUES IN THE METHODOLOGY OF ISLAMIC ECONOMICS

Habib Ahmed (2002-a: 125) argues that there are some unresolved methodological issues in Islamic economics. For example, how are the fundamental problems of choice and scarcity addressed analytically in the value-laden framework of Islamic economics? There are no unique Islamic tools for economic analysis. For the sake of illustration he cites the oft-quoted example of the objectives of the *Shari'ah* (the *maqasid*) and the hierarchy of needs as necessities (*daruriat*), conveniences (*hajiat*) and refinements (*tahsiniat*) in the Islamic economy. It is often suggested that in the Islamic economy resources should be allocated according to this hierarchy. But at the same time it is asserted that Islam has a market economy. It is not clear how a market economy will allocate resources according to this hierarchy. Besides, even the definitions of necessities, conveniences and refinements are ambiguous. They will differ for each individual and between different times. The concepts cannot be used for any analysis. Similarly, it is asserted by some writers that a Muslim producer would like to maximize profit but would also take into account social considerations. How can this be shown analytically? Moreover, shall we call it an efficient level of production? If so, do we have a different definition of efficiency? How will demand and supply curves be derived in the Islamic market economy? He argues that the marginalist analytical tools can be integrated in the value-laden framework of Islamic economics because they do not contradict the Islamic paradigm. For example, a rational Muslim will also maximize utility but will have an additional constraint (besides the budget constraint), that is, the moral constraint. Assuming this is a valid method of analysing consumer behaviour in an Islamic society the method assumes an ideal practising Muslim. In practical life such individuals are in an absolute minority. Economic analysis thus carried out has only one value: it may persuade people to behave in an Islamic manner. But, for this purpose, all this effort to develop analytical tools and a separate branch of knowledge under the title of Islamic economics is unnecessary. This is basically a task in spreading the message of Islam and can be done in a simpler manner.

4.10   CONCLUDING REMARKS

Muslim economists need to distinguish between the divine and the human. The divine is eternal, immutable and given, but that is part of theology and not economics. Most of what has been presented in the name of Islamic economics so far consists of Islamic teachings and can be legitimately termed as theology. However, from these theological roots a distinct discipline of Islamic economics can be developed. Conventional economics should be studied as a branch of knowledge in its own right. It should not be treated as an adversary of Islamic economics. Human wisdom and analytical insights that consist of conventional economics are the common heritage of all humanity. Muslims should benefit from it and should not shy away from it.

Islamic economics has its roots in the worldview of Islam. It does not revolt against conventional economics. Instead, it informs conventional economic analysis with spiritual concerns. Human beings have a spiritual dimension. Conventional economics should recognize this reality. For example, Islamic economics does not reject rationality in decision making. It only extends the meaning of rationality to include human well-being both in this life and in the hereafter. It does not reject maximization of utility as normal human behaviour but redefines the meanings of 'utility'. Utility in Islamic parlance encompasses gain in the hereafter as well. It does not contradict the fact that human beings behave in self-interest, but it extends the meanings of self-interest, which could also include spiritual uplift, philanthropic spending, work for the well-being of one's family, neighbours and society at large, and so on. Economic analysis should integrate these wider meanings of self-interest. Islamic economics can potentially enrich economic analysis as understood in common parlance. The challenge is to integrate Islamic economic assumptions in the economic postulates and present them for verification or falsification. The divine roots of Islamic economics should not stand in the way of Muslim economists pursuing this course, nor should Muslim economists insist on embedding their postulates in an ideal Islamic society and among ideal Muslims. They should formulate Islamic economic postulates in such a manner that they can be tested in this mundane world.

NOTES

1. For a detailed exposition see for example Hausman (1985).
2. For a detailed exposition see for example Blaug (1992: xiii).
3. [As in original] IDB prize winner's lecture 14. Arabic. Jeddah: IRTI.
4. For example: How do we define excessive *gharar*? Whose opinion will be final in this regard? From whose perspective is *gharar* to be determined: buyer or seller, debtor or creditor? Over which period: for example, in a sharecropping contract, immediately at the time of contract, after the fruit is apparent but not fully ripe or after harvesting? And if it is to be on the ripening of the fruit, does it matter if the fruit has a certain level of juiciness, pulp and vitamins or not, and how will that be determined? On the basis of what evidence is *gharar* to be finally determined: visual observation, scientific examination or laboratory reports?
5. Lit. Muslim community or Muslim people as a collectivity.
6. Lit. success. Technically, prosperity and success in the present life as well as in the life after death.
7. *The Mejelle*, trans. C.R. Tyser, D.G. Demetriades and Ismail Haqqi Effendi (Kuala Lumpur: The Other Press, n.d.).
8. Lit. objectives.

5. From Islamic theology to Islamic economics

In the last two chapters we have repeatedly referred to the methodology of Islamic economics that takes it out of the realm of theology and moves toward making it a genuine social science. In this chapter we shall try to illustrate this point with examples from the Qur'an. We shall show how the divine and immutable statements of the Qur'an can be translated into economic postulates which can be presented for testing and verification. For this purpose first we shall summarize some of the economic statements of the Qur'an and then explain how they can be made the basis for developing Islamic economics. A similar methodology will be possible for authentic Traditions of the Prophet.

5.1 THE ECONOMIC STATEMENTS OF THE QUR'AN

The Qur'an is the Word of God. Muslims believe that whatever it says is immutable and true beyond any doubt. The Qur'an makes several statements about the economic aspect of life. These statements are nothing short of divine laws stated by God. Muslims believe that these laws in fact operate in this life through the divine will of God. But how these laws actually take effect is not evident from the Qur'an directly. We are unable to find explanations for these statements in the familiar cause–effect format. The text of the Qur'an uses such words and phrases as can have multiple meanings. The exegetes of the Qur'an have been interpreting these verses over centuries in different ways. But a conclusive interpretation which can be tested empirically is not available in most cases. We need to determine the meanings of the Qur'anic economic statements in a manner that allows verification of our understanding in the light of real-life data. Below are some examples that illustrate the point:

a.   Q. 2:155 says: *'And most certainly shall We try you by means of danger, and hunger, and loss of worldly goods, of lives and of fruits. . . .'* Q. 7:130 says: *'And indeed We punished the people of Pharaoh with years of* drought and shortness of fruits (crop, etc.) that they might remember (take heed).' There are other verses in the Qur'an that have a similar message (e.g. Q. 7:168, Q. 9:26). These verses indicate that poverty and misery could be either a trial to judge human conduct at times of adversity or a form of divine punishment for past human sins. The question arises: how can we differentiate between hunger and insecurity imposed by God as a trial and the misery ensuing as punishment for the past sins? Is there any relationship between human behaviour and human misery? If so, what is that and how do we measure it? If human behaviour has certain consequences that invite the trial of God in the form of misery, how does it operate in real life? When we see poverty and misery how should we conclude? Is it a trial from God or is it a punishment for the sins of the people? If it is punishment for sins, which particular sins are relevant in this context?

b.   Q. 2:276 says that God diminishes *riba* and increases charity (*yamhaqu Allah al-riba wa yurbi al-sadaqaat*). The verse mentions the decrease (*mahq*) caused by *riba*. We need to determine the exact meanings of the words *riba* and *mahq* in this verse. It is not obvious how in real life God diminishes *riba*. The common understanding that *riba* means interest of all kinds leads to several questions. What does a decrease in wealth as a result of an interest-based system mean exactly in physical terms, as the obvious situation is contrary to it? The lender on interest gets back a higher sum. In physical terms it is not a decrease in wealth. Some people think it refers to a decrease in social wealth, but such reasoning would require empirical evidence, which is otherwise. Capitalist economies where interest is deeply embedded in the entire economic fabric have progressed in leaps and bounds. In brief, there could be more than one meaning for the phrases *riba* and *mahq*, but the conclusive meanings should be verifiable. We need to have a methodology to arrive at the conclusive meanings of such verses of the Qur'an.

c.   Q. 3:178 says: '*And they should not think – they who are bent on denying the truth – that Our giving them rein is good for them: We give them rein only to let them grow in sinfulness; and shameful suffering awaits them.*' How do we know that the wealth of people who deny the truth (*alladhina kafaru*) is a rein and not a bounty of God? Should we say that all the wealth owned by all non-Muslims is only a Godly strategy to allow them to indulge in sins and thus earn hell in the hereafter? Does the wealth have a relationship with the faith of a person? If so, how does this relationship actually operate?

d.   Q. 5:66 says: '*and if they (followers of the Bible) would but truly observe the Torah and Gospel and all [the revelation] that has been bestowed from on high upon them by their Sustainer, they would indeed partake of all the blessings of heaven and earth. . . .'* The verse relates material prosperity to observance of the divine guidance. What is exactly meant by the phrase 'observance of the Torah and Gospel' (*iqmatu Torat wal Injil*)? And what is meant by 'all that is bestowed from on high upon them' (*wa ma unzila 'ilaihim*)? How does material prosperity flow from the observance of these divine books?

e.   Q. 6:6 says: *'Do they not see how many a generation We have destroyed before their time – [people] whom We had given [a bountiful] place on earth, like of which We never gave unto you, and upon whom We showered heavenly blessings abundant, and at whose feet We made running waters flow? And yet We destroyed them for their sins, and gave rise to other people in their stead.'* What is meant by generation (*qarn*)? Which were those people in history who were powerful but then destroyed? What exactly were those sins (*zunub*) that led to the destruction and misery of past nations? What is the nature of the behaviour that leads to destruction and misery? What is the cause–effect sequence that transforms prosperity into misery?

f.   Q. 6:42–44 say: *'And, indeed, We sent Our messages unto people before thy time, [O Prophet,] and visited them with misfortune and hardship so that they might humble themselves: yet when the misfortune decreed by Us befell them, they did not humble themselves, but rather their hearts grew hard, for Satan had made all their doings seem goodly to them. Then, when they had forgotten all that they had been told to take to heart, We threw open to them the gates of all [good] things, until – even as they were rejoicing in what they had been granted – We suddenly took them to task: lo! They were broken in spirit.'* The verse states that there could be hardship upon a people as a trial, but, if they do not humble themselves, God sends a wave of prosperity but takes them to task suddenly. A new period of hardship starts. This is a three-stage phenomenon. Do these verses state general principles for cycles of misery and prosperity? If so, can we explain this understanding with reference to empirical evidence? Can we analyse cycles of prosperity and hardships for various people throughout history and relate them to the ethical behaviour of the people as indicated in these verses? What is the cause–effect relationship? What exactly is meant by 'so that they humble themselves' (*yatadarra'un*)? What is the hardening of hearts (*qasat qulubuhum*)? What is meant by 'they had forgotten' (*nasu*)? What are the indicators of forgetfulness in this case? What are the good things which are bestowed as a trial from God? (See also Q. 7:94–95, 13:31, 26:205–207 for similar laws.)

g.   Q. 7:96 says: *'Yet if the people of those communities had but attained to faith and been conscious of Us, We would indeed have opened up for them blessings out of heaven and earth: but they gave the lie to the truth – and so We took them to task through what they had been doing.'* What is meant here by God-consciousness (*taqwa*) that leads to prosperity? What are the indicators of God-consciousness (*taqwa*)? What is meant by 'people of those communities' (*ahl-al-qura*)? Do we mean every person or the majority of the people or the leaders of the communities? Is this verse applicable in the reverse case as well, that is, if people do not profess faith (*iman*) and God-consciousness (*taqwa*) they would be materially ruined? What is the cause–effect sequence in the case of God-consciousness and prosperity? What changes in human actions are stimulated by faith (*iman*) and God-consciousness (*taqwa*) that lead to prosperity? (Also see Q. 10:63–64, 39:10, 65:2–3.)

h.   Q. 8:53 says: *'This, because God would never change the blessings with which He has graced a people unless they change their inner selves: and [know] that God is all-hearing, all-seeing.'* The verse mentions that God never changes (a state of) prosperity (*ni'mah*) that He has bestowed on a people unless they change what is in their own selves. What changes in the behaviour of a people lead to transformation of prosperity into misery or vice versa? (Also see Q. 10:44, 13:11.)

i.   Q. 11:3 says: *'Ask your Sustainer to forgive your sins, and then turn towards Him in repentance – [whereupon] He will grant you a goodly enjoyment of life [in this world] until a term set [by Him is fulfilled]; and [in the life to come] He will bestow upon everyone possessed of merit [a reward for] his merit. But if you turn away, then, verily, I dread for you the suffering [which is bound to befall you] on that awesome Day.'* Q. 11:52 says: *'Ask your Sustainer to forgive your sins, and then turn towards Him in repentance – [whereupon] He will shower upon you heavenly blessings abundant, and will add strength to your strength: only do not turn away [from Me] as lost in sin. . . .'* In physical terms, what is the relationship of repentance (*tauba* and *istighfar*) with material abundance (*mata'an hasana*)? Is it a general principle applicable to all human beings in all times? Is there any empirical evidence for this? God says that there is a relationship between rainfall and repentance. How can we explain this concept in physical terms? At some places in the Qur'an, God says that material prosperity should not be taken as an indicator of God's blessing. Here He implies that *tauba* and *istighfar* please Him and he makes people prosperous as a result. How do we differentiate between the two types of prosperity? God sends rains even to those lands where people do not believe in Him let alone talk of *tauba* and *istighfar*.

Then how can it be determined that *tauba* and *istighfar* have led to any rainfall? What is meant by the repentance (*tauba*) of a nation (*quam*) or community? What are essential and sufficient conditions for collective repentance (*tauba and istighfar*)? (Also see Q. 71:10–12.)

j.   Q. 11:116 says: *'But, alas, among those generations [whom We destroyed] before your time there were no people endowed with any virtue – [people] who would speak out against the spread of corruption on earth – except the few of them whom We saved [because of their righteousness], whereas those who were bent on evil doing only pursued pleasures which corrupted their whole being and so lost themselves in sinning.'* Can we trace, in empirical terms, the relationship of the destruction of communities with a lack of voice against corruption or with quiet tolerance of corruption? Is there any relationship between the destruction of communities and the luxurious and sinful lifestyle of rich people? If so, can we show empirically that those who suffer as a result of destruction are rich people? Perhaps the evidence is otherwise. Most of the victims of natural disasters like floods and earthquakes are poor people. What exactly is the correlation of richness and corruption on earth on one hand and the destruction of communities with lack of voice against corruption on the other? (Also see Q.17:16.)

k.   Q. 14:7 says: *'And [remember the time] when your Sustainer made [this promise] known: "If you are grateful [to Me], I shall most certainly give you more and more; but if you are ungrateful, verily, My chastisement will be severe indeed."'* What exactly is meant by gratitude (*shukr*) in this verse? In physical terms how does gratitude (*shukr*) lead to material abundance? Are there any implications for public policy or is it merely for individuals? What does ingratitude (*kufran*) mean in this context and how does it translate into God's punishment?

l.   Q. 16:30 says: *'Good fortune awaits, in this world, all who persevere in doing good.'* What is meant by good fortune (*hasana*)? What are its indicators? What are the good deeds in this context that lead to good fortune and how do we measure them? (Also see Q. 16:97, 22:50, 39:10, 72:16.)

m.   Q. 16:112 says: *'And God propounds [to you] a parable: [Imagine] a town which was [once] secure and at ease, with its sustenance coming to it abundantly from all quarters, and which thereupon blasphemously refused to show gratitude for God's blessings: and therefore God caused it to taste the all-embracing misery (*libas al-ju' wal khauf*) of hunger and fear in result of all [the evil] that its people had so persistently wrought.'* What is meant by ingratitude (*kafarat*) in this verse? What exactly did they do that led them to hunger and fear? How did the transformation take place in physical terms? Does it refer to any particular community specifically or is it a general rule? Can we say that those nations that are suffering from hunger (like many countries in Africa and Asia) or those that are in a state of fear (like Iraq and Afghanistan these days) are only facing the consequences of their ingratitude (*kufran*) in the past and God has now imposed this rule upon them?

n. Q. 20:124 says: *'But as for him who shall turn away from remembering Me – his shall be a life of narrow scope (*maeesha danka*)'.* What are the indicators of a life of narrow scope (*maeesha danka*)? What is meant by turning away from remembrance of God?

o. Q. 22:45 says: *'And how many a township have We destroyed because it had been immersed in evildoing (*heeya zalimatun*) – and now they [all] lie deserted, with their roofs caved in! And how many a well lies abandoned, and how many a castle that [once] stood high!'* And Q. 22:48 says: *'And to how many a community that was immersed in evildoing (*heeya zalimatun*) that I have given rein for a while! But then I took it to task: for with Me is all journey's end!'* What is exactly meant by evildoing (*zulm*) in these verses? What traits of character and human behaviour can be called evildoing (*zulm*)? How does it translate into destruction and ruin in physical terms? (Also see Q. 28:58–59 where the Qur'an uses the term 'communities that exulted in wanton wealth and life of ease' as a cause of destruction.)

p. Q. 24:55 says: *'God has promised those of you who have attained to faith and do righteous deeds that, of a certainty, He will cause them to accede to power on earth . . . and that of a certainty, He will cause their erstwhile state of fear to be replaced by a sense of security. . . .'* Is this verse quite categorical about God's grant of power and security as the result of faith in Him and righteous deeds? What are the indicators of faith and righteous deeds (*iman and a'amal al-saliha*)? Can we say that power, peace and security are indicators of a nation being on the divine path? If not, how do we know when the grant of power, peace and security is a gift of God and when it is not?

q. Q. 30:39 says that the '*riba* that you give so that it increases in the wealth of people does not increase in the sight of God'.[1] The verse mentions the 'giving of *riba*' with the purpose of getting it increased by commingling with other people's property. This is unusual, as the common understanding is that it is the *taking* of *riba* that involves exploitation and injustice. Why does this verse talk of the 'giving of *riba*'? What is the nature of this transaction? The verse talks of the property of the people (*amwal al-naas*). Why does it use the phrase 'the people' (*al-naas*), which usually connotes a community, nation or even humanity at large? The verse compares *riba* with *zakah* and not with an interest-free loan (*qard hasan*), although the reverse of a *riba*-based loan is an interest-free loan (*qard hasan*) and not *zakah*. Why is it so?

r.   Q. 30:41 says: *'[Since they have become oblivious of God] corruption has appeared on land and in sea as an outcome of what men's hands have wrought: and so He will let them taste [the evil of] some of their doings, so that they might return [to the right path].'* Some commentators, like Muhammad Asad, think that the verse refers to the environmental pollution caused by human actions. If that is so, what is the relationship of man's indifference toward God and environmental pollution? What is the cause–effect relationship of human actions and pollution of the environment? What type of behaviour would avert God's punishment in this case?

s.   Q. 34:15–17 say: *'Indeed, in [luxuriant beauty of] their homeland, the people of Sheba had an evidence [of God's grace] – two [vast expanses of] gardens, to the right and to the left, [calling out to them, as it were:] "Eat of what your Sustainer has provided for you, and render thanks unto Him: a land most goodly, and a Sustainer much-forgiving." But they turned away [from Us], and so We let loose upon them a flood that overwhelmed the dams, and changed their two [expanses of luxuriant] gardens yielding bitter fruit and tamarisk, and some few [wild] lote-trees: thus We requited them for their having denied the truth. But do We requite [thus] any but the utterly ingrate?'* The verses relate the transformation of prosperity of an agricultural community through floods which burst even the dams and destroyed all the agricultural infrastructure as a punishment for the ingratitude of the people. What are the indicators of ingratitude in this case? Can we say that heavy floods are always an indication of God's punishment for ingratitude? What exactly was the nature of the sins of the people of Sheba? What are the implications for human behaviour in this case? What are the implications for macro-level policy?

We can cite more examples from the Qur'an which refer to such laws of material prosperity and misery, distribution of income and wealth (*rizq*), the effects of charitable spending (*infaq*), and so on. The moot point is that these ethical laws are statements of facts, but we do not understand exactly how these laws operate in physical terms.

Conventional economics would treat these statements as exogenous factors and exclude them from analysis. That simplifies the task of economists no doubt but does not allow a comprehensive understanding of the economic phenomena or human economic behaviour in a wider cosmic framework. One of the contributions of Islamic economics to human knowledge could be to develop a methodology for making these exogenous factors endogenous to the analysis. If we are able to measure and analyse the effects of these factors we shall be able to have a much better understanding of the economic functions. Since the Qur'anic economic laws manifest themselves in human situations, the effects of these laws are measurable. Only the process is not visible. We need to 'discover' that process. We need to define the variables in measurable terms so that our understanding of the laws is confirmed or falsified by empirical evidence.

5.2 THE METHODOLOGY FOR DEVELOPING ISLAMIC ECONOMICS FROM QUR'ANIC STATEMENTS

Muslim economists (and religious scholars alike) have kept verses of the Qur'an dealing with economic laws in the domain of faith or treated them as matters relating to the hereafter. We do not see any discussion on these verses in the literature. However, we think there is a method that can help us understand these verses. It may take decades or even longer to understand all of these verses. Some may remain beyond human comprehension even after centuries. The Qur'an is a book that has been unfolding over centuries, and the process will continue for ever. Many facts which were referred to in the Qur'an over 1400 years ago but were beyond the reach of human intellect at that time became intelligible with developments in various sciences in later times. In a similar vein, the Qur'anic economic laws will unfold over the coming decades and centuries. The suggested method for extending our understanding is as follows:

a. Muslim economists should take the verses of the Qur'an as immutable and unchangeable. The objective should be to understand the cause–effect mechanism for the operation of these verses and not to test the truth of these verses.
b. Since each of the verses dealing with divine economic laws can be interpreted in more than one way the challenge is to arrive at an interpretation which can be tested and verified empirically. It is not that we need to test the Qur'anic statements. It is the human interpretation and explanation of these statements that we need to test empirically to understand these statements. The second step in the methodology, therefore, is to identify the key terms in each statement.
c. By a process of research, discussion, brainstorming and intensive thinking we can list all possible meanings of the key terms. The

meanings of the terms would remain subject to revision as more people think around them.

d. It would be possible to have numerous combinations and permutations of meanings of the key terms. Based on these combinations we can develop postulates relating to each Qur'anic statement. There could be several postulates for each statement, and these could increase or decrease with the passage of time.

e. We should prepare a short-list of these postulates based on the criteria of verifiability and falsifiability. It means that postulates on which data cannot be collected should be eliminated from the list at this stage.

f. We should collect empirical data on each postulate for certain geographical areas and for specified periods. The objective should be to falsify each postulate. The postulate that cannot be falsified would stand as the proven understanding of the statement of the Qur'an under study. Alternatively, we should try to verify the truth of our postulates in light of empirical evidence. The truth established in this manner will be the true understanding of the verse or set of verses on which the particular postulate was based.

The following example illustrates the above procedure. Since there is a continuing debate on the precise meaning of *riba*, we take verse 2:276 as an example to illustrate the procedure for arriving at a conclusive understanding of the term '*riba*'.

Q. 2:276 says: '*God deprives* riba *of all blessings (*yamhaqu Allah al-riba*) whereas He blesses charities (*yurbi al-sadaqaat*) manifoldly.*' This statement has two parts: deprivation of blessings (*mahq*) in *riba* and enhancement of blessings in charity. We take only the first part in illustrating the above procedure:

a. The key terms in the first part of the statement are (i) *riba* and (ii) decrease (*yamhaqu*). The challenge for us is to determine an interpretation of the term '*riba*' that meets the Qur'anic criteria of *mahq*, that is, deprivation of blessings. For this purpose we also need to interpret the term '*mahq*'.

b. Tables 5.1 and 5.2 list the meanings of the terms '*riba*' and '*mahq*' that come to mind for this illustration. A similar exercise by other people may lead to different sets of meanings.

The lists in Tables 5.1 and 5.2 can lead to a large number of postulates ($12 \times 12 = 144$) based on combinations and permutations of the items in each list. A review of these combinations can help in short-listing the most

Table 5.1   Possible meanings of the term 'riba'

'*Riba*' means:
1   Interest on all types of loans
2   Interest on consumption loans only
3   Compound interest only
4   Exorbitant rates of interest
5   Interest from poor and needy borrowers
6   Interest on institutional loans to individuals
7   Interest on inter-governmental loans (bilateral governmental loans)
8   Interest on loans from multilateral institutions
9   Interest on deferred payment in a sales contract
10 Interest on bonds and *sukuk*
11 Interest in a financing lease
12 Interest in an operating lease

Table 5.2   Possible meanings of the term 'mahq'

'*Mahq*' means:
1   Physical destruction of assets
2   Reduction in the income of the lender over time
3   The lender subject to losses and accidents apparently unrelated to the lending business
4   Reduction in social wealth
5   Reduction in satisfaction from the use of wealth
6   Social strife and hostilities among various sections of the population
7   Lack of happiness and peace of mind
8   Level of earnings from interest being lower than profit from trade for the same capital
9   Higher levels of wastage and inefficiencies in the production process employing interest-based capital as compared to equity capital
10 Interest-bearing international loans increasing the level of poverty in borrowing countries
11 Interest adding to the cost of production and causing inflation and hardship for the poor
12 Interest leading to the accumulation of wealth in a few hands, leading to deprivation of the masses

plausible of the combinations. For example, we can short-list the following postulates:

a. Interest on all types of loans ultimately leads to a reduction in the
    social wealth of a country.
b. The interest on consumption loans ultimately leads to a reduction in
    the wealth of the lender
c. The interest on deferred payment in a sales contract leads to a reduc-
    tion in the wealth of the seller over the long term.
d. Interest on international loans leads to the increased poverty of the
    borrowing country.

The above list of postulates is only for the sake of illustration. Many more
postulates can be short-listed in a similar manner.

We can now proceed to test these postulates in the familiar method
of testing and arrive at a theory that cannot be falsified or which can be
verified with empirical evidence. The postulate that cannot be falsified
will give us the conclusive meanings of the Qur'anic statement and also
inform us about the true meanings of the terms '*riba*' and '*mahq*'. The
usual procedure to draw policy implications from this understanding can
then take place.

In this way a mechanism to unfold the true and undeniable meanings
of the verses of the Qur'an relating to economic laws can start. Scholars
and students in universities and research institutions can endeavour to
find the true meanings of the economic laws of the Qur'an which cannot
be falsified in light of empirical data or which can be verified on the basis
of empirical data. Until we are able to prove such postulates the meanings
of the economic statements of the Qur'an will not be truly apparent to
us. We shall keep on making generalized interpretations, as the exegetes
have done, and will not be able to find the operational meanings of the
economic laws of the Qur'an.

We think that the method will be a breakthrough in the development of
Islamic economics as a social science. Instead of trying to copy the postulates of conventional economics and presenting them as 'Islamic' versions,
it will be better to present the laws of the Qur'an as given statements, with
a challenge for economists to discover the cause–effect mechanism for
these laws. It will generate a lot of intellectual activity, and the result will
be beneficial for humanity at large. It will give us a clue to the behaviour
pattern that leads to prosperity and blessings and also indicate the behaviour pattern that leads to misery. One can say that these behaviour patterns are already well known to Muslims. What is the use of getting into
the process of postulate testing? It is true that humanity is aware of good

and bad behaviour in ethical terms, but humanity cannot see the linkages of this behaviour with the creation and destruction of wealth as stated in the Qur'an. One of the strong points of this methodology is that it does not require an Islamic society to be in existence. These postulates can be tested in any society.

5.3 THE QUR'AN SUPPORTS THE SUGGESTED METHODOLOGY

The methodology suggested above is in line with what the Qur'an itself has suggested as valid for acquiring sure knowledge. It is evident from the following:

a. In Q. 2:258, the Qur'an mentions an encounter of the Prophet Abraham with a king who claimed divinity. Abraham argued that God makes the sun rise in the east and if the king thought he was a god he should make the sun rise in the west. On this the king was confused and had no answer. Thus Abraham invoked empirical evidence for the existence of God and also for falsifying the king's claim to divinity.
b. In Q. 2:259, the Qur'an narrates the story of a person who doubted the possibility of life after death. God made that person die for one hundred years and then resurrected him. On resurrection he saw the process of his donkey coming back to life, which was empirical evidence beyond doubt. God also showed him the state of his food, which had remained intact over the hundred years. Thus God showed by empirical evidence the possibility of life after death.
c. In Q. 2:260, God mentions the Prophet Abraham's curiosity about life after death. In response God asked Abraham to develop an affinity with four birds, kill and spread their parts on different hillocks and then call back these birds. Abraham followed the procedure. The birds came alive, running to Abraham. The event points to God's preference for empirical evidence.
d. Q. 3:137 says: *'Go then around the world and see the ultimate fate of those who rejected the Truth.'* Chapra (2001: 39) says: 'This verse as well as a number of other verses is a clear indication that the Qur'an considers its normative theories to be testable against facts.'
e. Q. 10:36 says: *'Behold, conjecture can never be a substitute for truth.'* [Lit. *'Conjecture can in no wise make [anyone] independent (*la yughni*) of the truth.'*] It is conclusive about establishing the truth of any statement. The statement must be based on facts and not on mere conjectures.

f.   Q. 17:36 says: *'And never concern thyself with anything of which thou has no knowledge.'* The verse clearly points to the criteria for establishing truth. It must be based on sure knowledge and not a mere thought.

g.   Q. 53:28–30 say: *'and [since] they have no knowledge whatever thereof, they follow nothing but surmise: yet, behold, never can surmise take the place of truth. Avoid thou, therefore, those who turn away from all remembrance of Us and care no more than the life of this world, which, to them, is the only thing worth knowing.'*

These verses clearly emphasize the following:

a.   All knowledge should be based on valid and indefensible evidence. The evidence can be either empirical or based on a divine source. If the evidence is not based on either of these two sources, it may be more of a conjecture and surmise than truth.

b.   The knowledge should not be focused merely on the life of this world but should also have a spiritual dimension that reminds man about God and life in the hereafter. It defines the scope of intellectual investigation. It should not be restricted merely to life in this world but should extend to the life in the hereafter as well.

5.4   CONCLUDING REMARKS

Most of the literature on Islamic economics consists of explanations and interpretations of the Qur'anic verses, Traditions of the Prophet, Islamic law, Islamic history and Islamic public policy during the last 14 centuries or so. There is no argument about the value of this literature, but most of it falls in the domain of theology and not economics. It is time that Islamic economics came out of the cocoon of theology and developed into a social science. The methodology suggested in this chapter is a way forward. The future of Islamic economics lies in this methodology.

NOTE

1.   Translation of the verse is by the present writer.

6. Expanding the frontiers of economics

6.1 THE NEED TO DISCOVER MORAL LAWS RELATING TO THE ECONOMIC PROBLEM

Conventional economics studies the economic problem of man arising from scarcity of resources in a market economy perspective. The economic analysis focuses on the behaviour of consumers, producers, business firms, government and non-government organizations, and so on. However, to keep the analysis simple and understandable, it treats a large number of factors such as individual differences due to genetic and hereditary factors, environmental pollution, climate change, international legal developments, political changes across the globe and so on as exogenous, although they influence the economic problem. Economics considers the effect of exogenous factors on economic variables but assumes them away as 'other things being equal'. Muslim economists have adopted the same frame of reference for the development of Islamic economics. They are also trying to develop microeconomics, macroeconomics, public finance and so forth on the same pattern as in conventional economics. In addition they treat extra-market factors as exogenous.

Developing Islamic economics as a social science presents immense possibilities for expanding the frontiers of economics. Besides the factors that are generally treated as exogenous a number of moral laws operate in the universe. Some of these laws affect the creation of wealth, distribution of income and state of material prosperity and deprivation. The moral laws influence the nature of the economic problem faced by man. Without studying the influence of these laws, the study of the economic problem remains partial and incomplete. It does not provide a comprehensive explanation of the differences between material possessions and the causes of prosperity and misery. Conventional economics does not recognize the operation of any moral laws that influence the economic problem of man. The methodology cannot help in understanding the moral laws, because they are invisible and non-measurable and operate in a complicated manner. They are not amenable to economic analysis in the usual manner. Mere human thinking cannot make them manifest.

It requires divine guidance to understand the existence and operation of these laws.

The human understanding does not take into account invisible factors that influence the process of generation and distribution of wealth. Our present knowledge does not go much beyond what the text of the Qur'an says about certain moral laws that affect the distribution of resources on earth. Although the moral laws influence the material conditions significantly, man has not as yet discovered these laws. An illustration from the field of physical sciences will explain the point. The law of gravity was operational in the universe even before Isaac Newton (1642–1727) discovered it. Bacteria caused infection even before Louis Pasteur (1822–95) discovered their existence and the treatment of certain diseases caused by the bacteria. Similarly all developments in physical sciences explain various natural phenomena which existed even before they were discovered. Human beings struggled hard to unfold the mysteries of nature and understand the physical laws. In the process various physical sciences have also developed methodologies to confirm or refute hypotheses propounded by scientists. In the field of moral laws, this work is yet to be done. Firstly, human beings are not quite aware of the moral laws that are operating in the universe. These laws are difficult to discern by the physical senses and material experimentation. They require divine guidance to begin with. Secondly, they are extremely complicated and have backward and forward linkages with the physical world. Thirdly, the divine time scale is much longer than the usual human time scale. The Qur'an mentions the length of one divine day as equal to one thousand years by our reckoning (Q. 22:47). The moral laws may have linkages with human behaviour at points of time which are not discernible easily at the present moment. Fourthly, the moral laws deal with human behaviour, but changes in human behaviour can also influence the operation of these laws. Thus it is a two-way relationship. The moral laws influence and are in turn influenced by changes in human behaviour. That complicates the situation further.

Since it is not possible for human beings to discover these moral laws by direct sensory perceptions, God has pointed to these laws in the Qur'an. Some of these laws have also been hinted at by the Prophet Muhammad. The two primary sources of Islamic economics refer to certain moral laws that affect our material well-being. However, the exact functioning of these laws is not yet known. We need to discover it by introspection, experimentation and dialogue. For example, the Qur'an points to the moral law of prosperity and misery but does not explain its exact operation in a cause–effect framework. Human beings have to discover that relationship as they discovered the relationship of various facts in the physical sciences. The task in the social sciences has yet to start. This should be the main task before Muslim economists if they are to develop Islamic economics as a distinct social science. Instead of trying to prepare an 'Islamic' copy of conventional economics they should take up the task of expanding the frontiers of economics by discovering the moral economic laws and enriching the pool of knowledge for the benefit of humanity. This can be done in the following manner:

a. Prepare a list of moral laws as discerned from the Qur'an and Traditions of the Prophet relating to economics.
b. Try to understand and interpret the moral laws in a cause–effect framework and present them in the format of postulates that can be tested and verified.
c. Publish the results of postulate testing and invite the community of economists to examine the results.
d. Engage the economists of the world in understanding, interpreting and undertaking further research into these laws.

Over a long period of time and after years of research and introspection some of these moral laws would be discovered in a format that can be used in economic analysis. The whole idea may look like a wild-goose chase at this stage. But the statements of the Qur'an are immutable and true. They have direct relevance to the life of contemporary man as they have throughout the ages. It should be possible to interpret the moral laws mentioned in these statements. The above-mentioned course of action will enable Islamic economics to extend the frontiers of conventional economics. It will have a distinct research agenda for itself and have no dispute with conventional economics. Both social sciences can complement the findings of the other and live side by side.

In this chapter we shall try to present the moral law of the Qur'an about prosperity and misery for the sake of illustration. We shall present a synthesis of the Qur'anic verses relating to resource endowment, prosperity and misery. The chapter will set the stage for starting a process of postulate formulation for subsequent empirical verification and conclusive understanding of the divine laws relating to prosperity and misery. It is only through Qur'anic guidance and a dispassionate observance of reality that we can get a true understanding of the process of creation and destruction of wealth. A similar exercise can be done for the authentic Traditions of the Prophet. Besides the law of prosperity and misery, there are other moral laws. For example, we find the moral laws of income distribution (*rizq*) and charitable spending (*infaq*). We need to build a comprehensive inventory of such laws that would provide a research agenda to Islamic economics for several years to come. At this stage of learning it is not clear how these laws are actually operating in the real world. The challenge for humanity is to discover the actual operation of these laws in a cause–effect framework.

6.2   THE QUR'ANIC LAW OF PROSPERITY AND MISERY

The ultimate objective of economic development is to create an enabling environment for a prosperous and fulfilling life and to minimize human deprivation and misery. We are using 'prosperity' here as a broad and comprehensive concept that transcends the boundaries of material wealth and encompasses economic, social and political freedom[1] and spiritually peaceful living. By the same token by 'misery' we mean, besides material deprivation, a state of fear, insecurity and socio-political dependence. The issue of prosperity and misery is so basic to human life that the Qur'an has used it as an argument for persuading people toward faith in God and the Day of Judgement. Throughout history, human beings have been concerned about finding the most appropriate means for leading a happy and prosperous life and avoiding the pain of deprivation and misery. The Qur'an addresses this issue and draws attention, over and above material variables, to certain moral positives that lead to a prosperous life and also certain moral negatives that add to human misery.

The creation of wealth takes place when the factors of production interact successfully. The inputs lead to outputs after going through a process of transformation. It is possible to predict almost with mathematical precision the output of a production process in a given situation in light of physical, financial, human, environmental and technological factors. However, in practice the results are not always according to the prediction because exogenous factors may affect the actual output. It is generally possible to analyse the reasons for the variance between the predicted and the actual output. The analysis can identify the exogenous factors in generating the variance, but it does not take us very far in understanding the deeper and more long-term causes of the variance. For example, it may be possible to relate the variance to market conditions, political factors, legal and technological changes, global trends in trade and so on, but the analysis does not tell us why these exogenous factors took place at this point in time or at this place.

The Qur'an discusses prosperity and misery in general terms. It refers to deeper, imperceptible and long-term currents of events taking place in the cosmos as a result of human actions and under the will of God. These currents affect the process of wealth creation in ways that cannot be explained easily in a simple cause–effect framework. The factors of production combine in a production process and create wealth. Over and above the visible cause–effect relationship of the factors of production there are moral laws of blessings (*baraka*) and deprivation (*mahq*) which influence the ultimate result. These laws operate in response to certain traits of human character and behaviour which influence the state of prosperity and misery. A normative change in human behaviour can transform misery into prosperity and vice versa. The precise mechanism through which the laws operate is as yet not known, because the meanings and interpretations of the Qur'anic texts on the subject require further thinking and deeper understanding. Now we shall present various elements of the Qur'anic Law of Prosperity and Misery.

6.3 THE INVISIBLE HAND OF GOD

An element of the Law of Prosperity and Misery is the Invisible Hand of God (the Hand), which controls the generation and distribution of resources. Beyond a certain limit, it overshadows the physical laws of creation and distribution of wealth. The Hand operates through myriad factors. It is not possible in the present state of our learning to comprehend all of these factors and thus arrive at a mathematically precise model of the generation and distribution of wealth. Some examples of the phenomena through which the Hand operates are as follows:

a. differences in individual physical, mental and psychological abilities endowed by God at the time of birth;
b. differences in the endowment of physical resources such as landscape, mineral wealth, water resources and so on to different geographical entities;
c. differences in climate such as patterns of rainfall, snowfall, drought and so on, causing differences in economic wealth and time-bound differences in food and other resources;
d. the creation of opportunities through innovation, technological developments and the creativity of human beings at appropriate times in human development according to a grand divine plan which coordinates the discoveries and innovations in a remarkably timely manner;[2]
e. long-term demographic trends in birth and death rates, leading to extensive implications for investment, enterprise, development, industry, markets, resources, consumption patterns and so on;
f. changes in leadership through the electoral process, conspiracies, violence, wars or natural deaths at specific moments of history, with wide-ranging implications for economies;

g. the emergence and general acceptance of certain ideas, percepts, ideologies and philosophies, leading to vast implications for resource distribution among individuals and nations;
h. the increase or decrease in social peace as a result of changes in human interaction, global practices, prejudices, tolerance, mutual respect and so on;
i   the emergence of certain trends and fashions in consumer behaviour, having vast implications for production, distribution, raw material, labour, technology and so on;
j. the discovery of certain physical laws or remedies for certain diseases, with immense implications for human behaviour, consumption, production and industrial growth.

In sum, innumerable factors that influence individual and collective lives and lead to differences in the distribution of resources keep on happening at each moment of time around the world.[3] Most of these factors are also beyond human control. It is not humanly possible at this stage of our learning to comprehend all that is happening through the operation of the Hand. Different branches of knowledge may explain only some of the visible phenomena, but the divine plans remain hidden from human observation.

6.4   THE INVISIBLE HAND OF GOD: A METAPHYSICAL EXPLANATION

Shah Waliullah (1703–62), the renowned Indian sage and mystic, has given an explanation of the operation of the Invisible Hand of God in metaphysical terms in his *magnum opus, Hujjatullah al-Baligha*. According to him, God manages the affairs of this world through two Councils: the Higher Council and the Lower Council. Both Councils consist of angels and the human souls of selected pious persons. These Councils do not have the authority to take any decision, but God gives information about His decisions to the Higher Council, where the angels and pious souls keep praying for the welfare of humanity. God's decisions are then transferred to the Lower Council in such a form that the angels are able to take them to the material world for implementation. The members of the Lower Council execute the divine decrees through the inspiration, motivation and influencing of minds, thoughts, desires, likes, dislikes and options of individuals and other creatures. For example, Waliullah explains (2003: 48):

> They [the members of the Lower Council] can influence the hearts of men and animals so that their wills and their inner promptings are transformed into

something compatible with carrying out of the desired object, and they influence certain natural phenomena by augmenting their movements or transformations. For example, a great stone may roll away and some powerful angel may help increase its motion so that it rolls along the ground with greater velocity than normal. Sometimes a fisherman may cast a net in the river and armies of angels will inspire instincts in certain fish to plunge into the net, and in some others to flee, and they will contract one rope of the net and loosen another, and they do not know why they do that, but they follow what they are inspired to do. Sometimes two armies may be warring with each other, and then angels come and create visions of courage and perseverance in the hearts of one side through inner voices or images as the situation requires.

The above explanation indicates that once God decides to increase the resources for someone (a human being or entity) He creates an enabling environment for it. For example, if it is a company, its products may become popular so that people throng to buy them. If it requires some raw material its deposit may become available abundantly and cheaply. Or a certain breakthrough may take place in technology that leads to windfall gains. Similarly, if God decides to contract the means of sustenance for someone the reverse might happen. People may discontinue buying a certain product, a certain raw material may become unavailable, or a change in the global environment may make production, sale and distribution of the product expensive, leading to contraction of its market. In brief, besides the human factors that can be analysed, the Invisible Hand of God is also working, which leads to expansion and contraction of the material resources.

Shall we say that the Invisible Hand of God operates in an arbitrary and unsystematic manner? The Qur'an refers to several traits of the human character and modes of human behaviour which invite operation of the divine will in a certain direction. The mechanics of the divine will, not fully understood at this stage of human knowledge, enhance human resources beyond what is expected by a process termed '*baraka*' (blessings) in the Qur'an. We shall, first, explain the concept of *baraka* before we take up the traits of character leading to prosperity.

6.5   THE CONCEPT OF *BARAKA* (BLESSINGS)

The Qur'an uses the concept of *baraka* at several places. It is generally translated as 'blessings'. However, there is no exact word that can translate this comprehensive concept.

While explaining the concept of *baraka*, Iqbal and Mirakhor (2008: 43) write:

The concept [of *baraka*] maintains that righteous conduct, i.e. behaviour whose motivation and objective is to please God,[4] will have returns with an increasing rate. This concept asserts that expending one's wealth 'in the cause of God' (without expecting a return from the receiver directly) will not lead to diminution but to its expansion. Such actions will, in fact, bring manifold returns to the giver. The concept establishes a positive correlation between the system's conduct and prosperity. It encourages Muslims to go beyond the minimum requirements of the *Shari'ah* in 'pleasing God'. The converse of the concept holds as well. That is, unrighteous conduct in earning, possessing, and disposing of wealth will rob its holder of its *baraka*. It not only applies to individual behaviour, but also holds true for the community as a whole: a society prospers if it preserves a keen perception of the Message (and acts according to its rules); its prosperity departs if it declines in morality (and acts against the rules of the *Shari'ah*).

Baraka manifests itself in material terms. Some examples are as follows:

a.   output exceeding the sum total of inputs or 'synergy';
b.   minimization of cost for obtaining a certain output or 'efficiency';
c.   reduction or minimization of waste and redundancies;
d.   safety from accidents and untoward occurrences or 'mitigation of risks';
e.   lower depreciation leading to a longer-than-expected life of assets;
f.   a slower rate of obsolescence than expected despite innovation in technology;
g.   higher-than-expected demand for the products of an enterprise;
h.   staff cooperation in providing services with diligence and sincerity;
i.   developments in the neighbourhood providing a safer environment, better infrastructure and so on;
j.   public policies that boost the prospects of business;
k.   international developments that extend the frontiers of the business market;
l.   technological developments enabling production of better products at lower cost.

6.6   MEASUREMENT OF *BARAKA*

A possible method of measuring *baraka* is to take two business enterprises engaged in the production and marketing of similar products. The enterprises should be of similar size in terms of investment and line of products. Their operation base should also be the same area. Then over a period it should be observed how the two firms perform. The difference in their performance could be attributed to *baraka*.

The first step should be to conduct a baseline study for both firms for a given set of indicators. The second step will be to conduct the same study for a given period and measure the difference in performance on each indicator. The difference in performance for each indicator should be analysed. Some of it would be due to ostensible reasons such as business plans and management practices, but some difference in the performance would be due only to '*baraka*' in the case of the higher performer. For example, suppose both firms make almost similar efforts to expand into the overseas market, but the market of one enterprise expands overseas while the other remains concentrated in the local market. This can be explained by *baraka* that acted upon the first business through expansion in the market to overseas. One can always counter-argue that there is no reason to bring in a discussion of *baraka*, as the growth can be explained in terms of marketing effort. The answer is that both firms made similar efforts to expand in the overseas market with similar products, but one could get a foothold and the other could not. Why did it happen like that? Why could the other not succeed? The answer is that because of *baraka* in the efforts of the one it could do so. The other did not have a similar *baraka* in its efforts.

The Qur'an relates *baraka* to human behaviour. Certain types of human behaviour lead to prosperity and other types lead to deprivation. The Qur'an says that God bestows certain types of behaviour with *baraka* and enhances the wealth as a result, while for certain other types of behaviour God deprives the production process of His blessings, which leads to misery and destruction. It is not known, at this stage of human knowledge, how human behaviour translates into blessings or deprivation. To understand the operation of *baraka* in a cause–effect framework, we need to follow the methodology suggested in the previous chapter. The objective of the present discussion is to demonstrate that the Qur'an makes several statements relating to human prosperity and misery which have normative implications for human behaviour. Although we do not fully understand how each factor actually operates, the discussion can throw some light on the fact that human prosperity cannot be fully explained by material input–output models alone. These factors add a spiritual dimension to the theory of economic growth and development.

After the above digression on *baraka* and its measurement, we now revert to the Qur'anic law and discuss some of the traits of character that contribute to prosperity.

6.6.1 Gratitude (*Shukr*)

Gratitude (*shukr*), besides an expression of thanksgiving through word of mouth, involves an attitude of mind. The Qur'an says that an attitude of gratitude (*shukr*) leads to prosperity (e.g. Q. 14:7). That raises the question: what is meant by *shukr*? How does it lead to prosperity? An exact understanding of this term would require an excursion into the path of postulate formulation and its empirical verification. A tentative understanding of the concept and its relationship with prosperity at this stage of learning could be as follows:

a. A person who expresses *shukr* also recognizes that the resources are bounties of God and should be preserved and put to the best use by maximizing their utility.[5] Thus a person who expresses *shukr* makes the most efficient use of resources, minimizing waste and getting maximum benefit out of them. *Shukr* becomes an engine of efficiency. The attitude brings in a whole host of internal controls, cost accounting, and good management practices for safeguarding assets and reducing waste and mismanagement.

b. An attitude of *shukr* leads to contentment with what one gets through honest means and shuns illegal means. Besides creating a state of inner peace (which in fact is a state of perennial happiness, joy and prosperity), contentment creates respect for the property of others, reduces jealousies and minimizes negative strife. From the reverse side, it means all avenues of injustice and exploitation (*zulm*) are closed for a person who expresses *shukr*. Once institutionalized, it creates an enabling environment for economic activity through which markets flourish and material prosperity abounds.

c. A person with an attitude of *shukr* would not be indifferent to productive opportunities and would treat them as bounties of God. *Shukr* generates a sort of dynamism in character which is the soul of all enterprise.

d. *Shukr* creates awareness that everything belongs to God and human beings are only trustees (Q. 102:8). The concept creates a culture of accountability, which is woven in the entire economic fabric of society. It governs all institutions as a basic value. It is the soul of a good code of conduct.

e. *Shukr* generates the realization that resources are bounties of God and not the mere result of hard work or the ability of the owner. It infuses a sense of humility that encourages a caring attitude towards other creatures and environments. It motivates the owner of the resources towards charitable spending on those who are unable to take care of themselves. *Shukr* becomes the engine of prosperity through an injection of purchasing power and boosting consumption.

6.6.2   Repentance (*Tauba*)

The Qur'an says that repentance (*tauba*) for past sins leads to prosperity. A tentative understanding of repentance and its relationship with prosperity is as follows:

a.   Repentance (*tauba*) for past mistakes indicates an attitude of self-analysis. It bestows the person with some sort of inner benchmark for distinguishing good from evil, positive from negative, right from wrong, and so on. At the macro-level, if a society adopts this value as a normal behaviour, it is likely to make better choices in its socio-economic and political life.

b.   The habit of self-analysis inculcates the ability to review one's past and the heritage from one's parents and earlier generations and then decide the extent to which they made appropriate choices during their lifetime. Invisibly, this trait of character takes away the tendency of following one's forefathers blindly (*taqlid*). A generation that is endowed with this faculty is enriched with creativity and innovation and the ability to develop appropriate responses to the developments of their own times. The creativity, ultimately, is the engine of all development and progress. In brief, the habit of seeking God's forgiveness through self-analysis endows society with a treasure of creativity that leads to growth, development and prosperity.

c.   Willingness to amend past mistakes is an indicator of humility. An arrogant person never feels sorry for his or her behaviour and will seldom bow down to seek forgiveness. Humility, in turn, is the source of all learning. A humble person is likely to excel in learning, as he or she likes to acquire it, as compared to an arrogant person, who displays indifference toward learning.

d.   Repentance (*tauba*) introduces a person to a behaviour pattern that gives the courage to try new ideas. The fear of making mistakes does not deter him or her. The possibility of making amends remains open. The tendency to venture into new fields with the ability and hope to get oneself right if one goes wrong is the soul of all enterprise. It encourages a person to take risks and remain ready to commit mistakes but hopeful to reap dividends in the form of the right course.

e.   The attitude of repentance (*tauba*) has a built-in ambition: 'I can improve in the future if I retract from my past mistakes.' This ambition accelerates the engine of progress and growth. If people as a whole have this positive attitude they are likely to perform better in future.

f.   In interpersonal relations if a person causes some harm or injury to someone else and then seeks God's forgiveness, he or she also has to undo the damage done to the other person before the repentance (*tauba*) is accepted by God. Thus it creates willingness to give back what one has taken wrongly. The attitude of 'giving' what is due to others adds harmony to social life and creates a society of 'givers' rather than 'takers'.

g. Q. 25:71 says that one who repents actually turns towards God. It means he or she enjoys the company of God, who guides the person to the right path. The right path does not mean only religious rituals. It means the right path in professional matters as well. A politician on the right path will make the right policy choices with God's guidance. A scientist gets God's guidance in finding solutions to research problems, and so on. Repentance (*tauba*) shortens the path to success, as God's help comes quickly. It saves the circuitous route of a person who is trying all by him- or herself.

6.6.3 God-Consciousness (*Taqwa*)

Generally, scholars have translated the term *taqwa* as piety or fear of God. It is not the precise meaning of the term. A tentative explanation of the concept is, however, as follows: *taqwa* refers to belief in the Oneness of God, angels and prophets and being aware that God is omnipotent and omnipresent, being constant in prayers, being mindful of accountability on the Day of Judgement, behaving ethically in all situations, showing magnanimity toward others in mutual dealings, being patient at times of adversity, fulfilling commitments and promises, being fair and just in dealings, and refraining from *riba*. *Taqwa* is consciousness of God the Omnipresent that restrains an individual from committing acts forbidden by God. It is an inner state of heart that demands unflinching obedience to God. The Qur'an mentions a number of virtues that cultivate *taqwa* in a person: the keeping of trusts (*amana*) (Q. 2:283); faithfulness (*al-wafa*) (Q. 3:76); and patience (*al-sabr*) (Q. 3:186). The Qur'an relates *taqwa* to the good life (*hasanat*) on this earth besides rich rewards in the hereafter (Q. 7:96, 10:63–64, 39:10). God relates *taqwa* to material ease in this life and creates circumstances favourable to one's sustenance in a manner that one does not even expect (Q. 65–63). However, the exact mechanism for how it happens is not conclusively known. It would require an understanding of the concept of *taqwa* that allows empirical verification.

6.6.4 Spending on Others (*Infaq*)

Like all religions Islam places a great emphasis on spending to meet the needs of others. It is technically known as '*infaq*'. It refers to spending willingly and voluntarily on the needs of family members, friends, relatives and the community and to promote the common good or social welfare. Spending on others is equal to spending in the cause of God. It must be with the intention of getting a reward from God in the hereafter and not expecting anything in return from the beneficiary (Q. 92:18–19). God treats *infaq* as a loan upon Himself and promises to return it with manifold increase (Q. 2:245, 2:262, 8:60, 57:11, 57:18, 64:17, 73:20). While spending on others is a desirable trait of character, it is closely linked to the resource endowment of the person spending on others. The *infaq* should be from what a person can spare from his or her resources (Q. 2:219) and should be at a moderate level so that there are no regrets later on (Q. 17:26–27, 25:67, 47:36–37). The Qur'an stipulates that *infaq* is a vehicle for an increase in wealth at the individual and social levels. A society that withholds *infaq* treads a path of destruction (Q. 2:195). The mechanism of the increase in social wealth is now quite well understood after Keynesian theory. It operates through the consumption multiplier effect. When the rich (who have a lower propensity to consume) spend on the poor (who have a higher propensity to consume), the poor increase aggregate demand, which stimulates investment. However, the mechanism by which the individual wealth of the giver also increases is not quite well understood at this time. It would require the formulation of various hypotheses and the testing of those hypotheses to arrive at a conclusive understanding of the process of the increase in individual wealth as a result of *infaq*.

Parallel to the Qur'anic Law of Prosperity is the Qur'anic Law of Misery (*mahq*) (see Figure 6.1), which manifests itself in the form of unusual losses, unexpected breakdowns, and unmanageable situations, leading to a diminution in wealth. The following traits of character and human behaviour lead to deprivation and misery.

6.6.5 Injustice, Exploitation and Inequity (*Zulm*)

The Qur'an uses a comprehensive term, *zulm*, to denote behaviour that is unjust, exploitative and inequitable. It could take the form of bribery, corruption, fraud, cheating, theft, undue usurpation of another's property, taking undue advantage of another's weakness, lending money on *riba*, or hoarding foodstuff at times of shortages, to name a few of the practices involving injustice. The Qur'an says that God destroys or ruins a society that tolerates *zulm* and does not resist it. How it actually happens has to be determined in light of empirical evidence as proposed earlier.

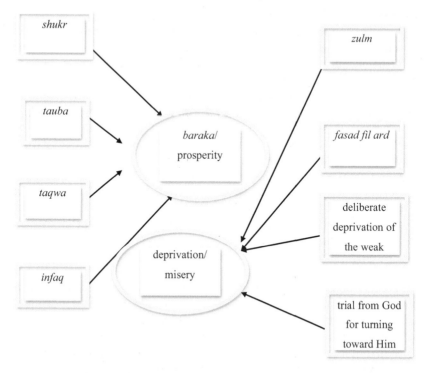

Figure 6.1   The Qur'anic Law of Prosperity and Misery

6.6.6   Corruption on Earth (*Fasad fil Ard*)

Man is God's vicegerent on earth. His mandate is to develop and maintain the earth for the good of mankind and all other creatures. Trying to live by this mandate brings peace and harmony with other human beings and the environment. Pickthall (2008) wrote:

> His [man's] duty is not one of devastation or oppression, but of cultivation and improvement. He is entrusted with the power of judgment and free-will; and guidance has been given to him again and again in the world's history. All the Prophets came with the same message of Man's responsibility to God, and human brotherhood. Man's duty of improvement, when fulfilled, leads to *falah* (success through full development). (p. 532)

> Cultivation, development, improvement of himself and his surroundings, assisting the development of others: that is the duty of Man as Allah's viceroy in the spiritual, ethical and material spheres, according to the teaching of Islam. (p. 533)

Neglecting the role of God's vicegerent creates frictions with other human beings, other creatures and the environment. Behaviour that ignores this primary role leads to corruption on earth (*fasad fil ard*), which is a source of misery for society. Some elements of corruption are quite evident and relate to misery quite obviously. For example, one can easily see that destruction of crops, infrastructures, human beings and the environment and internecine wars lead to human misery. But other elements such as breaking kinship ties, mutual hatred and exploitation, reckless materialism, tolerance of evil and so on are not quite obvious and require further research to relate them to misery. See Figure 6.2.

6.6.7 Deliberate Action to Deprive the Poor

The Qur'an narrates (Q. 68:17–27) an anecdote of a household that planned to keep away the poor at the time of the harvest to deprive them of a share from the crop. God destroyed the crop before they could harvest it. Some people have derived a general principle from this anecdote that if a society plans to keep the poor people deprived consciously God punishes it through the destruction of resources by natural calamities. However, before we generalize this conclusion from the anecdote, we would need to verify it in light of empirical evidence. But one thing is obvious: that God encourages people to set aside some resources for the well-being of the poor. Not doing so is a source of social misery. How this principle actually operates is yet to be discovered. At least one strand of the principle is obvious. If a society frames policies and laws that favour only the rich and the wealthy to the exclusion of the poor, it is certainly going to face extremes of income and wealth distribution which lead to socio-economic destabilization in the long term. However, more extensive empirical evidence would be required to establish a general principle.

6.6.8 Deprivation as a Reminder from God

Several verses of the Qur'an mention that material deprivation is a divine strategy to divert the attention of the people toward God, their Creator and Provider (e.g. Q. 7:94–96, 7:130, 7:168, 9:126). It is quite natural that people look up for some solace and comfort when they are in trouble. Economic deprivation is one of the most painful experiences. God uses it to remind people that they should turn toward Him and discard other entities that they could be worshipping or looking up to. Interestingly, the Qur'an also says that such reminders benefit only those who are God-conscious and other people tend to remain oblivious. A natural corollary is that the hardship should turn into ease when people turn to God with

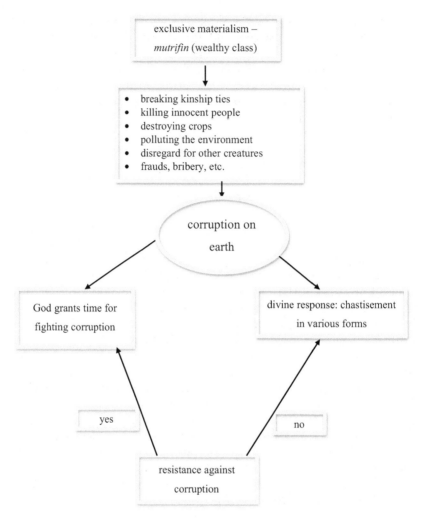

Figure 6.2   The Qur'anic Law of Corruption on Earth

repentance. The understanding would require verification in light of empirical evidence.

6.7   CONCLUDING REMARKS

We have tried to sum up the Qur'anic Law of Prosperity and Misery, which relates human behaviour to divine response, which in turn leads to material well-being or deprivation. We have given some explanation of the human behaviour in both cases. However, the true and conclusive understanding of the law must wait until we are able to formulate appropriate postulates and test them to confirm our understanding. God's laws of prosperity and misery provide only an example of the moral laws of God that human beings should discover. Islamic economics can take a lead in inviting the attention of humanity towards these laws. Discovery of the exact *modus operandi* of these laws should constitute a major part of the research agenda for Islamic economics for several years to come.

NOTES

1. 'Freedom' here refers to the 'set of capabilities' as defined by Amartya Sen (2000), but much more than that when we supplement it with spiritual peace and optimism for success in the hereafter.
2. For example, it was not a mere coincidence of history that the invention of the steam engine, discovery of vast coal reserves, discovery of rubber technology for wheels of vehicles, telecommunication signalling and electricity were discovered in the same span of human history. It seems it was part of a grand plan of the Creator to coordinate all these happenings in a specific period of human development.
3. Al-Qur'an (55:29).
4. The original text uses the word 'Allah (swt)', but I have translated it to 'God' to make it comprehensible for a wider audience.
5. *Shukr* does not mean maximizing utility in the sense in which it is used in neoclassical economics, which refers to maximizing utility for *acquiring* resources. Here it is being used for maximizing utility in the *use* of whatever resources one has.

7. An Islamic economic system or spiritual capitalism?

7.1 JUSTIFICATION FOR AN ISLAMIC ECONOMIC SYSTEM

Several Muslim scholars have tried to argue that Islam has a distinct economic system. From amongst the most influential voices, Muhammad Iqbal (1877–1938) through his poetry tried to create awareness that Islam gives a distinct economic system as compared to capitalism and socialism. Several others, notable among them Abu al-'Ala Mawdudi (1903–79), Syed Qutb (1906–66), Baqir al-Sadr (1929–80) and, from the second generation, Khurshid Ahmad, Nejatullah Siddiqi, Umer Chapra, Anas Zarqa, Monzer Kahf and Fahim Khan, to name a few, produced an extensive literature in support of this slogan. These scholars cited prohibition of interest, the obligation of *zakah*, the concept of lawful and unlawful (*al-halal wal haram*) regulation of consumer and commercial behaviour, the limitation of private property and so on as distinctive features of the Islamic economic system. The movement for developing Islamic economics as a distinct social science was driven by the objective of studying the Islamic economic system and implementing it in the present age. Since socialism has almost died with the break-up of the USSR and the adoption of capitalism by all the former socialist states except China, the dominant system now in the world is capitalism. Even the Chinese are making modifications in their economic system to get closer to capitalism at a gradual pace. The real parallel, if there is any, of the Islamic economic system is capitalism. Let us examine the arguments presented in favour of an Islamic economic system to make it distinct from capitalism.

7.2 THE OBJECTIVES OF AN ISLAMIC ECONOMIC SYSTEM

The fundamental difference between an Islamic economic system and capitalism is said to stem from the objectives of the Islamic economic system. Zarqa (2008: 25) defines the objectives of an Islamic economic system as follows:

a. guarantee of a minimum level of living to every member of society;
b. achievement of economic power in the sense of the ability to achieve goals and economic independence from the need to ask others for assistance and a reasonable independence of economic decisions;
c. reduction of disparity in income and wealth among people.

A closer look at these objectives will show that they are so similar to the capitalist system or at least to the capitalist economies of the present day that it is difficult to tell what is particularly distinctive in these objectives that makes them 'Islamic'. All developed capitalist economies of the present day have some form of social security system that aims at guaranteeing the basic minimum level of living for everyone. Similarly, the capitalist economies also aim at achieving economic independence. Most of them have some form of progressive taxation for redistributing income and wealth. Thus the objectives of the Islamic economic system are met, to a large extent, in capitalism as well. Zarqa (2008: 25) has also identified institutions of the Islamic economic system as follows:

a. individual ownership with corresponding social responsibility;
b. communal and state ownership;
c. open competitive markets observant of *Shari'ah* rules;
d. the family as a basic building block both economically and socially;
e. a state or social authority that upholds justice, helps the weak and the poor, keeps security and intervenes to ensure the social and mandatory duties in Islam.

It is obvious from the above list of institutions that they are basic ingredients of a well-functioning capitalist system. Capitalism has individual and communal ownership. It supports open competitive markets, though it does not follow the *Shari'ah* rules. But the *Shari'ah* rules revolve around justice and fairness, which capitalism also supports. There is no doubt that the family system has become weak in capitalist societies, but that is not because of capitalism. There are wider socio-ethical reasons for that. The role of the state as an upholder of justice and protector of the weak is very much manifest in capitalist societies as well. The question arises: why do we insist on a distinct system if at the end of the day we have to adopt what capitalism is offering?

7.3   PROPERTY RIGHTS IN ISLAM

One of the oft-repeated assertions of Muslim economists is that Islam has a distinct law of property that is more just and equitable than that of capitalism. The basis of this assertion is the theory of man's vicegerency (*khilafa*) on the earth. The theory contends that the real owner of all resources is God, and man is only a trustee with defined rights and obligations for acquiring and using the resources. As a trustee, man is not sovereign in earning and consuming the resources. He has an obligation to share the resources with others if there is a need. In case an individual fails to do so, the state has the authority to intervene and ensure the sharing of resources. An example of this assertion can be seen in Iqbal and Mirakhor (2008: 35–42).

If an individual is not willing to share private property and if the public interest requires such sharing, the Islamic government has a right to intervene. No rational person can deny the supremacy of social needs over the individual interest, in particular if it means averting some social harm. However, the idea is embedded in the following assumptions:

a. The government is perfectly just and would never commit any injustice.
b. The state machinery is honest and free from corruption.
c. The government has perfect information on social and individual needs and has the capacity of striking a balance between the two.
d. The system of justice and rule of law is foolproof and intervenes if the state authority transgresses its limits.
e. The state uses authority with transparency, and its functionaries are fully accountable.
f. Citizens have a right to information where the state employees exercise discretion.

In practice these assumptions would seldom hold. Intervention of the state machinery in private property rights will open the floodgates of coercion, abuse of authority, and bad governance.

It is, perhaps, for such reasons that the Qur'an and the Traditions are silent on this extended authority of the state. We do not find anything in these primary sources about the right of the state to intervene and infringe upon private property. In contrast, we find examples from the Prophet's conduct that are contrary to this principle. When the Prophet had to construct the first mosque in Medina after the Migration he bought a piece of land from two orphans and paid them the price (Lings 2005: 124). There was no takeover of the private property in the name of communal or social interest. We do not find any example in his life of having used this authority to force individuals to share private property in the name of public interest. In his sermon of the Last Pilgrimage, the Prophet categorically said that the property of an individual is inviolable. The idea of state intervention in the name of the public interest comes in later thinking. The sharing of property rights with others, whether these others are individuals, the community or society at large, is a voluntary act. Islam encourages people to do so to earn a reward in the hereafter. It does not give the state or government authority to appropriate lawful private property in the name of the public interest.

Iqbal and Mirakhor (2008: 42) have mentioned the possibility of the state's right to restrain the use of private property if an individual is indulging in extravagance (*israf*) or reckless spending (*tabdhir*). The concept is plausible but is inherently subjective, as it is not possible to determine conclusive benchmarks for appropriate spending styles. A level of spending that is extravagant (*israf*) for one may be necessary for another. It is only the moral training of an individual that guides to proper spending in a given situation. It is impossible to define these concepts in operational terms. These are moral instructions and require voluntary compliance. Giving state functionaries a right to limit the freedom of individuals would introduce an element of discretion that could be abused. A society can have extremes of income and wealth distribution where the masses are grinding in poverty and a small minority are rolling in luxuries. In such situations the legislature of a country may pass laws to enhance distributive justice. Such laws would have no divine sanctity, however. The Islamic injunctions against extravagance (*israf*) and reckless spending (*tabdhir*) would remain moral principles for individual compliance and not for state intervention.

The other features of property law often stated by Muslim scholars (e.g. Iqbal and Mirakhor 2004: 52) focus on the following:

a. The property should be acquired by lawful means.
b. The property should not cause damage to others.
c. The property should not validate an invalid claim nor should it establish an invalid claim.

Subject to the above general rules, Islam does not place an upper limit on the acquisition of property.

The above law is not significantly different from the property law of capitalism. For example, both laws require that property should be acquired through lawful means. Both laws do not accept property rights if they are acquired through corruption, fraud, bribery, deception, usurpation, coercion or forgery. Both laws accept that the private property of an individual should not cause damage to others. Both laws agree not to validate an invalid claim. However, there are some differences as well. For example, under the capitalist system, it is lawful to acquire property through prostitution, pornography, gambling and the sale of weapons of mass destruction,[1] all of which are not permitted in Islam. Subject to this overriding moral nexus of lawful–unlawful (*al-halal wa al-haram*) in Islam, most of the other elements of property law are similar in Islam and capitalism. Under capitalism, it is legitimate if people acquire certain resources in any manner if they do not violate the law of the land. Remaining within the law they can also dispose of their resources freely. However, in Islam the acquisition and disposal of resources are guided and controlled by ethical principles as well. The economic criteria of profitability, prudence, risk and so on may support a decision, and the law may also allow it, but if the Islamic moral law does not permit it the property cannot be acquired or disposed of. The Qur'an (Q. 5:100) categorically lays down this criterion. The maximization of profit would be modified to the extent it clashes with the moral teachings of Islam. It is only to this extent that the Islamic law of property differs with the law of property in capitalism. Should we say that this difference in the property laws of capitalism and Islam calls for a distinct Islamic economic system?

7.4   WASTE, DESTRUCTION, ABUSE AND MISUSE OF RESOURCES

It is also often contended by Muslim scholars (e.g. Iqbal and Mirakhor 2004: 52) that a distinctive feature of Islamic property law is its prohibition of waste, destruction, abuse and misuse of resources. While Islam regulates consumer behaviour in the use of resources, capitalism gives a free hand to do whatever one likes. In this sense Islam creates conditions that are more conducive to social welfare. The argument ignores the hard fact that, despite the freedom to use or abuse property, capitalism does create conditions which force every rational person not to waste or destroy his or her own property. The practice of capitalism dilutes the conceptual difference between Islam and capitalism. To that extent, the two systems do not differ significantly. Similarly, Iqbal and Mirakhor (2004: 56) argue that Islam visualizes property rights as a contract between an individual and society. The Qur'anic emphasis on fulfilment of contracts (e.g. Q. 5:2) extends over the individual's obligation toward society as well. Again, the argument is overplayed. Though not in the same sacred way, yet in a very similar vein, the capitalist system also imposes social obligations upon individuals. In the case of contracts between private parties, capitalism also ensures that contracts are enforced in a true spirit. Conceived in this perspective, laws exist in all societies, non-Muslim in particular, to protect and promote social interests. Representatives of the people have passed these laws. There does not seem to be any substantive difference in the concept of private property under Islam and capitalism. There could be differences in details, of course. However, those differences do not define a distinct economic system for Islam.

7.5 SELF-INTEREST, MORALITY AND STATE OVERSIGHT

Muslim economists assert that the Islamic economic system has three foundations: self-interest, individual morality and state regulation. By this they mean that, while Islam recognizes self-interest, it encourages a moral sense among people that modifies their behaviour. However, if the moral sense does not operate effectively, the state has an oversight role to regulate the market in the best social interest. They argue that capitalism operates under stark self-interest. There are no modifiers of the market outcome as in the case of Islam. We think that the argument oversimplifies the actual operation of capitalist economies, which have similar foundations. There could be differences of degree and emphasis. For example, capitalist economies have developed an institutionalized arrangement for making people adhere to some basic moral norms such as respect for private property, honesty in dealings, standardization of products, truth and fairness in advertisements, and so on. Similarly, regulation of the private sector and control of monopolies and excessive economic power by strong regulatory bodies are quite common in all developed capitalist economies. In which practical sense is Islam different? It could be argued that Islam declares a definite right of poor people in the wealth of the rich, and that is the distinguishing feature of Islam. True, but capitalism has also instituted it through progressive taxation and the allocation of a chunk of resources for the social security of the poor.

7.6 JUSTICE AND BENEVOLENCE

Muslim economists argue for a distinctive Islamic economic system because it upholds justice and benevolence (*al-adl wa al-ihsan*). It means the Islamic economic system is not based on market operations only. It is guided by the principles of justice and benevolence as well. If the economic system is allowed to operate freely, the holders of economic power can exploit the weak and the poor in the name of competition. As compared to this the Islamic economic system, so goes the argument, modifies the operation of the market on the basis of justice and benevolence. If market forces lead to an obviously unjust outcome, the state intervenes and regulates the market. Similarly, if the poor are too weak to participate in the market the system encourages other people to show benevolence to them. Capitalism does not have these features. The argument is valid if we take capitalism in its ideal state. In practice, capitalism has moved away from this state. There is hardly any argument about the existence of the rule of law and justice in all capitalist societies. Almost all developed capitalist societies have now some form of social security and organized private philanthropy. Capitalism is no longer devoid of benevolence. Arguing that Islam has a distinct economic system which overrides market forces is ignoring the fact that capitalism has also adjusted itself to the demands of justice and benevolence over time. It is no longer a system that protects the 'Shylock' and his pound of flesh.

7.7   CORPORATE SOCIAL RESPONSIBILITY

Another strand of argument in favour of an Islamic economic system is the concept of corporate social responsibility. The argument, in brief, is that Islam requires business firms to be sensitive to social needs and to allocate resources to meet social obligations. One of the early justifications for Islamic banking was to develop institutions which could provide financing to the poor on benevolent terms. It is argued that Islam is distinct in obliging its corporate sector to play an overt role in promoting social welfare. We think even this point is overplayed, as most of what is being presented under the rubric of an Islamic economic system also exists in capitalist economies and that too in a more developed form.

There is an upsurge of literature on corporate social responsibility (CSR) in conventional economics and finance. The literature emphasizes the role of corporations in promoting social welfare, protecting consumer interests, safeguarding the environment, creating gender balance, and enhancing individual skills through education and training, besides promotion of cultural activities and so on.[2] The upholders of corporate social responsibility plead for enlightened self-interest, which stands for the original vision of Adam Smith about capitalism. It is no longer valid to say that capitalism stands for an amoral business environment. The questions that are being debated are: should business firms volunteer to behave responsibly or should government enact laws to enforce socially responsible behaviour or should civil society put pressure on business firms? It means that making morality and ethics an integral part of business operations is not under dispute. Only the mechanics of doing so are being debated. Noel Purcell (2008) notes that business firms are already moving toward more socially responsible behaviour. He writes:

> A growing number of companies have shifted or are shifting their mindsets and rediscovering the true role of business in society. Progressive companies are out there raising the bar through new coalitions, groupings and initiatives, such as the Extractive Industry Transparency Initiative, the Equator Principles, the Forestry Stewardship Council, the Principles for Responsible Investment, the Ethical Trading Initiative, and the Australian Business Roundtable on Climate Change, to name a few. . . . Encouragingly, there is now a growing view in equity and investment markets that this is the right strategy. The message is becoming increasingly clear: the pursuit of excellence in business does not require companies to forget their moral sense and the related risks. . . . A decade ago, the Caux Round Table codified a set of principles and guidelines for activating a moral sense in business. The Caux Round Table's *Principles for Business* initiative was followed in 1999 by the United Nations' *Global Compact* – ten principles defining responsible corporate citizenship covering the areas of human rights, labor, the environment and anti-corruption. Today, around 4,000 corporations have signed up to such principles. (pp. 15–17)

The slant of the argument has found favour among Muslim economists because it seems very natural for Islamic economics to handle the issue of CSR (e.g. Dusuki and Dar 2007: 254). They have tried to trace the roots of CSR to Islam's basic concepts such as human vicegerency of God (*khilafa*), obligation to perform acts of collective good (*fard kifaya*), the general rule of promoting good and forbidding evil (*'amr bil maruf wa nahi anil munkar*), and so on. There does not seem to be any problem in tracing the concept of CSR to Islamic divine roots. However, it is not clear from the Islamic economic literature how the Islamic concept of CSR differs from the concept in the capitalist economy so that it is treated as a justification for a distinct economic system.

7.8   DIMENSIONS OF ACCEPTABLE AND HARMFUL SPECULATION

The literature on Islamic economics criticizes capitalism on the role of speculation in initiating a process of economic instability. Several Muslim scholars have argued vehemently that speculation is the fundamental characteristic of capitalism and that the Islamic economic system is against all types of speculation (e.g. Toutounchian 2009). We think the point is overplayed. There is no doubt that speculation has the tendency to dwindle into gambling. However, in its generic form, speculation is an essential ingredient of decision making in commercial activities. Whenever a commercial decision is made it has some form of speculation inherent in it. The buyer or seller speculates on the future, which is unknown. To that extent no one, including Muslim scholars, has anything against speculation. That gives rise to the next question: what are the Islamic criteria for differentiating between lawful and unlawful speculation? Muslim scholars have not as yet faced this question squarely. A consensus on the answer to this question would enable Muslim scholars to take a decisive position on speculation in options trading, forward and futures markets and various types of foreign exchange transactions. These are as yet grey areas in Islamic commercial law. Once the issue is settled, the dimensions of speculation acceptable to Islam will also become clear. Only at that time will it be possible to see if the presence or absence of speculation is a necessary condition of the Islamic economic system.

7.9   THE MUSLIM CONTRIBUTION TO CAPITALISM

The literature on Islamic economics argues that Islam has a distinct economic system parallel to capitalism. It is interesting to note that present-day capitalism has Islamic roots. The Muslims were the pioneers in creating capitalism as it exists today from the ashes of the medieval economies of Europe.

Heck (2006: 6–7, 77) has argued that the Muslim 'key economic demands' of European goods during the Crusades and 'key commercial instruments' developed during the eleventh to thirteenth centuries, and the integrated commercial network helped the European continent to pull out from the 'Dark Ages'. The roots of present-day capitalism lie in Muslim commercial practices. The source of Islamic prosperity in those days lay in the skill of Muslim jurists to adapt juridical principles for accommodating 'interest-bearing' commercial transactions, while their Christian counterparts were slow in doing that, although both Muslims and Christians believed in the prohibition of usury. The emergence of the European continent from the Dark Ages, and its ushering into modern capitalism, is due to the borrowing of business structures and instruments from the Muslims by European merchants. The Muslim concepts of a free market and profit motivation deeply transformed the European tools of trade and business vocabulary. These concepts were a marked improvement over medieval Europe's Christian concepts, which stifled the profit motive, devalued material gains, held poverty and asceticism in high esteem and preached contentment and 'other-worldliness' in preference to the material gains of life. Many commercial terms used by the Muslim merchants were adopted and adapted by the European merchants (ibid.: 24).

7.10   THE SOCIAL AGENDA OF ISLAM

A deeper look at the economic teachings of Islam shows that the Prophet did not have an economic agenda. Instead, he had a social agenda. The salient features of his social agenda were as follows:

a.   establishing a faith-based society that transcends tribalism;
b.   promoting the rule of law and equality of all human beings before the law;
c.   protecting human dignity and universal rights of freedom for all;
d.   inculcating brotherhood and fraternity among the people;
e.   eliminating injustice and exploitation in mutual dealings, including commercial transactions;
f.   promoting justice, fairness and equity among the people;
g.   providing social security to the poor and the weak.

In brief, he intended to develop a society on the basis of the unity of faith, universal ethical values, justice, benevolence and mutual fellow-feeling. The law of *zakah*, for example, aims at transferring wealth from the rich to the poor. The business law of Islam focuses on private property, the free market, and justice and fairness. All his instructions about business dealings focus on minimizing disputes, injustice and exploitation. The tenancy contract reform in agriculture also focuses on fairness and equity. The essence of the commercial and business law of Islam is to discourage excessive uncertainty and risk (*gharar*), deception, fraud, bribery, and the usurpation of another's wealth. Prohibition of *riba*, the cornerstone of modern Islamic finance, also rests on the same principle. It aims at promoting brotherhood and fraternity among fellow members of society. The wealthy are supposed to provide loans to the needy on an interest-free basis and allow leniency and extension in the recovery of the loans.

As head of the Islamic state, the Prophet did not announce any economic agenda. We do not find any public policy by the Prophet relating to savings, investment, financing, economic development, employment, technology, environmental protection and so on. He did not propound any macroeconomic guidelines or policy for reform. He left these matters to the free will of the people. Whatever economic reforms we see in his teachings are focused on social well-being or on establishing an ethical, coherent and just society. Islamic scholars who have tried to derive macroeconomic policy guidelines from Islamic teachings are actually reading contemporary capitalist economics into Islam. By itself, there is nothing objectionable to it. However, they need to recognize that such a reading is human and not divine and does not lend itself to the definition of a distinct economic system.

The Islamic economic system propounded by Muslim scholars has all the features of capitalism. The basic concepts of capitalism such as private property, the profit motive, freedom to maximize utility, regulation of economic behaviour by the state, redistribution of income through progressive taxation, public investment, economic development, full employment, provision of basic needs through social security, and so on are features we find in some form in Islam as well. For example, Islam recognizes private property and allows the maximization of profits. There is no upper limit on profit set by Islam. The Islamic law of *zakah* is quite similar to the social security system of capitalism. The prohibition of *riba*, involving exploitation of the poor, is visible in the anti-usury laws of capitalism. The distribution of income through the law of inheritance in Islam has a parallel in capitalism in the form of progressive taxation. The concepts of social well-being and reform (*islah*) in Islam are present in capitalism in the form of economic development and full employment policies. The Islamic concept of enjoining good and forbidding evil (*'amr bil maruf wa nahi anil munkar*) translated in the institution of ombudsman (*hisba*) in the early days of Islam can be seen in present-day capitalist societies in the form of state regulation of the private sector. The objective of market regulation in both capitalism and Islam is to ensure free competitive markets and to forestall deliberate manipulation by market players (Oran 2010: 134). The Islamic emphasis on fair business dealings, free from fraud, deception and uncertainty, is taken care of in capitalism by organized and regulated markets. We see the Islamic emphasis on dispute-free commercial activity in the elaborate dispute resolution mechanisms that exist in capitalist societies.

7.11   THE BUILDING BLOCKS OF SPIRITUAL CAPITALISM

7.11.1   The Need for Spiritual Capitalism

M.N. Siddiqi has stressed the moral and spiritual aspects of economics in several of his writings. He has argued that the failure of capitalism is basically a moral failure (2008-c) and that Islam aims at creating a society that upholds moral values for the welfare of humanity. He writes (2007-c):

[C]apitalism in its motivational or human aspect cannot continue without getting transformed in a basic way. Neither pure self-interest nor the exclusive pursuit of economic growth has a future. We have learnt enough about the consequences of both these motivations to continue adhering to them. . . . For the present I offer the tip that the possibility of this transformation opens a door for Islamic finance too. You would appreciate that a religion-mandated, morally-oriented way of life would never entertain self-centered profit-seeking behavior or/and pursuit of limitless growth as public policy. As long as these behavioral norms and policy goals dominated, as they do under capitalism, Islamic finance had little chance. Now that humanity seems to be growing out of those self-destructive stances it may well give Islamic finance a hearing.

He further writes (2008-c: 131):

All the technical flaws and tactical mistakes leading us to the current crisis are rooted in a moral failure. If we are given or able to create a society in which individuals care about public good and cooperate with one another to promote it, even after securing their self-interest in order to ensure survival, we could escape much of the troubles currently facing us. Only such a society of individuals who care for public good can opt for the right mix of state intervention and private initiatives. Such a society is possible. Let us first shed the illusion that we have been living for decades now under the best of all arrangements, social, political, economic and financial. We have not. However, let all join the search for such an alternative.

Certainly, he points to Islam as an alternative. Islam has basic features of capitalism such as private property, the profit motive, free and open markets and selfish human beings driven by greed and love of wealth. However, Islam aims to modify the system by the education, training and persuasion of individuals and by installing a regulatory framework for society. The objective of this change is to persuade human beings to achieve *falah* in this world as well as in the life to come. This is what, for want of a better term, we call *spiritual capitalism*.

7.11.2   What is Spiritual Capitalism?

The primary features of spiritual capitalism are the same as those of capitalism in contemporary societies. However, capitalism has not given people a spiritually satisfying lifestyle owing to its over-indulgence in materialism, unending economic strife and over-stretched struggle to 'keep up with the Joneses'. With the advent of adolescence, almost every young man or woman in a modern capitalist society gets into a debt trap to acquire various assets to meet the necessities and enjoy the comforts and luxuries. The rest of his or her life is spent in paying off these debts and settling down in life. In the process the anxiety and stress of the economic struggle to meet financial commitments eat inner peace and tranquillity. The modern man needs economic prosperity with inner solace and spiritual peace. The spiritual capitalism presented by Islam promises to present that opportunity to humanity.

If we like to sum up the whole point, we can say:

$$\text{Spiritual capitalism} = \text{capitalism} + falah,$$

where *falah* is success in this life and in the hereafter.

7.11.3   Stages of Spiritual Capitalism

Spiritual capitalism is a dynamic concept. A society that aims at establishing spiritual capitalism will need to pass through the following five stages. However, during the process of transformation a society can be at any one of these stages, which are hierarchical, and every later stage is built on the former:

a.   spiritual foundations;
b.   spiritual development;
c.   spiritual consciousness;
d.   regulation and oversight;
e.   *falah*.

Spiritual foundations
The spiritual foundations of spiritual capitalism consist of three main ingredients:

a.   **Faith:** It consists of unconditional belief in the Oneness of God, prophethood of Muhammad and all past prophets, and belief in resurrection and accountability. Faith in the Oneness of God means that God is the creator of everything. He is Almighty, Ever-Present, All-Knowing, All-Hearing, Lord of the universe. He has created human beings to develop earth and its environment according to His guidance that He communicated through various prophets and through the use of reason if there is no direct divine guidance. Human beings are the trustees of God on this earth and must observe His rules. The life after death is a reality, when God will resurrect all human beings for accountability in acquisition and use of resources and other acts and omissions.
b.   **Righteous acts:** Righteous acts consist of five daily prayers, fasting during the month of Ramadan, paying *zakah*, performing *hajj* once in

one's lifetime and following the restrictions of *halal–haram*. Besides, all voluntary acts for the well-being of the self, family and society, the struggle to earn an honest livelihood, and all positive acts such as seeking knowledge, research, exploration and so on are also considered righteous acts.

c.   **Interpersonal relations:** Interpersonal relations should be based on principles of justice and fairness (*'adl*) and benevolence (*'ihsan*). Besides, individual behaviour should conform to mutual respect, truthfulness, the keeping of promises, the joining of kinship ties, and respect for the honour and property of others. It presumes a conscious effort to subdue selfishness and unbridled materialism.

Spiritual development (*tazkiya*)

Spiritual development is the second level for building a society of individuals who are pursuing *falah* as their goal. Spiritual development (*tazkiya*) refers to the development of human character and behaviour once the basic conditions of faith and righteous acts are met. At this level of development, human beings are motivated to adopt the following traits of character through training, education and social pressure. These traits of character are ethical and moral values on which Islam likes to build human society:

a.   **Social spending (*infaq*):** This is spending on members of the family, relatives, dependants and the poor and needy without any expectation of getting a reward. The individual must allocate some resources for this purpose. Social spending (*infaq*) can be for institution building such as hospitals, schools and so on, or spending on needy individuals.

b.   **Gratitude (*shukr*):** This means being thankful to God for all resources, realizing that whatever is available to human beings is through the mercy and blessings of God. Thankfulness to God in all circumstances presumes that there would be no room for complaining, crying and impatience should a person face adversity.

c.   **Repentance (*tauba*):** This means expressing repentance for one's sins, but in a wider sense it refers to an attitude of willingness to make amends and learn from the past and a determination to remain alert in the future. It is an attitude of humility and willingness to seek knowledge that opens the gates to research, experimentation and enterprise.

d.   **Trust in God (*tawakkul*):** This means keeping trust in God for results after human efforts are made to achieve an objective. In a wider sense it refers to an attitude of experimentation, struggle, strife and enterprise to explore newer fields and to keep trust in God for results. It inspires a sense of optimism and hope and an attitude of hard work and high achievements.

e. **Patience (*sabr*):** This refers to remaining steadfast against heavy odds and against all adverse circumstances. It also means keeping hope in the mercy and blessings of God. It includes showing a brave face against losses, adverse situations and a hostile environment.

f. **Contentment (*qana'a*):** This means an attitude that fights greed and unbridled materialism and creates balance and harmony in life. It helps contain the desire for excessive materialism, which at times also poses a risk to health and a happy social life.

g. **Sacrifice (*ithar*):** This is an attitude of generosity and well-wishing for others while one is also in need – an attitude of giving rather than taking. The concept is embedded in the broader and deeper social value of brotherhood or fraternity (*ukhuwa*).

h. **Moderation (*iqtisad*):** With respect to consumption, it refers to a moderate approach between extravagance and miserliness. In the case of the acquisition of resources, it means a balance between covetousness, greed and ruthless materialism on one hand and monasticism and asceticism on the other. In public policy, it would mean adopting policies that maintain the balance in urban–rural, rich–poor, young–old and men–women, and among different regions of the country.

Spiritual consciousness (*taqwa*)

The third level of spiritual capitalism is building a human personality to achieve spiritual consciousness (*taqwa*). Once individuals are trained in spiritual development (*tazkiya*), they should then be trained in spiritual consciousness. Spiritual consciousness consists of three segments:

a. **Consciousness about the Ever-Present, All-Knowing, and All-Seeing God:** Although faith in the Oneness of God teaches belief in these attributes, to achieve *taqwa* human beings should be conscious of God at all times. Human behaviour should be guided by this consciousness. If a person is oblivious of this fact even for a while he or she should immediately turn to God with repentance (*tauba*) for guidance.

b. **Consciousness about accountability to God:** This means that we should remain conscious that the present life is a trial and we shall be accountable for our acts and omissions in the hereafter. Although this is part of the faith as well, spiritual consciousness requires that the feeling should be present at all times. One should always remember that the life in this world is transitory and soon we shall depart for our permanent abode. All wealth and material resources will be left behind and we shall have to account for the manner in which we earned and spent our wealth.

c. **Consciousness toward the rights of others:** This refers to consciousness of obligations and a balanced attitude toward society, the environment and other creatures in such actions as the payment of taxes, truthfulness in dealings, and the maintenance of trust and promises (Q. 5:1, 9:4). It keeps one satisfied with what one gets through lawful means with reasonable effort and restrains one from an unfair attitude toward others. Justice and fairness are essential ingredients of God-consciousness (*taqwa*) (Q. 5:8).

Regulation and oversight

The above-mentioned three elements of spiritual capitalism deal with individual behavioural norms. Human beings have an inherent tendency to deviate from these norms. To regulate human behaviour Islam visualizes an active role for the state and society through motivation, education, guidance, training and legal action. However, oversight and regulation do not provide government functionaries with freedom to encroach upon private property and the privacy of individuals. They only give the state the role of a referee to maintain justice and fair play.

It can be argued that capitalist economies also have a role for government intervention, in particular where the market fails, monopolies emerge or business entities collude to the detriment of the public interest. To this extent, the Islamic position is close to capitalism. However, the essential difference between the two approaches lies in the wider socio-economic objectives of the two societies. Islamic society places a premium on the spiritual development of human beings. It justifies government intervention in the economy where, despite spiritual training, human behaviour deviates from the social norms. For example, the Islamic government will regulate investment decisions on the basis of ethical norms. It will intervene to block investment in gambling houses, liquor production, pornography and so on, divert the resources toward more compelling needs and promote the spiritual environment in society. Governments in capitalist countries do not intervene in these matters and consider the intervention as detrimental to the economic objectives of society. Subject to these broad interventions, state functionaries in Islamic society will not have any authority to control or manipulate private property.

Falah

The goal of spiritual capitalism is to attain '*falah*'. The term '*falah*' means to thrive, become happy and have luck or success. In Islamic parlance, the concept pertains to both worlds. It refers to conditions which manifest success both in the life of this world and in the hereafter. In the present life it means physical survival, freedom from want, and military power.

In the hereafter, it means eternal survival, everlasting prosperity and everlasting glory. Although the ultimate objective of spiritual capitalism is to invite people to achieve *falah* in the hereafter yet that can be achieved only as a result of actions and behaviour during life in this world. The *falah* would be manifest both at the individual and at the social level. At the individual level the *falah* would mean a state in which an individual has the means for biological survival, employment for a livelihood, inner peace and basic human rights. At the social level, the *falah* would be manifest in a hygienic environment, management of natural resources for the benefit of the entire population, inner social cohesion, independence and self-determination, and military power for protection from enemies. The ultimate objective of spiritual capitalism is to achieve the *falah*, whereas capitalism aims only at the material well-being of human beings. See Figure 7.1.

7.12   MOVING TOWARD SPIRITUAL CAPITALISM

How do we usher in an era of spiritual capitalism? Can we rely on human good sense and individual initiative to bring spiritual capitalism into being? Human nature is ridden by several influences: inborn tendencies of selfishness, love of wealth, greed, envy, jealousy and wickedness, besides the influences of the society, government, global forces and so on. Left to it, individuals are not likely to adopt the moral and spiritual principles of Islam and we may be left with the stark capitalism that we have in existence at the moment in all capitalist economies. Therefore, to usher in an era of spiritual capitalism we shall need to ensure that the following are put in place:

a.   the education and training of individuals both at home and in educational institutions in the faith and spiritual practices of Islam, leading to a state of *tazkiya* in a voluntary manner;
b.   the development of codes of ethics for business firms relating to all stakeholders, such as customers, employees, owners, creditors, financiers, communities and so on;
c.   the development of a system of monitoring the behaviour of individuals and business firms relating to compliance with spiritual and moral codes of practices;
d.   the creation and strengthening of institutions to regulate organizations so that power is decentralized, the rule of law is ensured, the interests of the various stakeholders are protected, monopolies are avoided and waste, corruption and fraud are restrained;

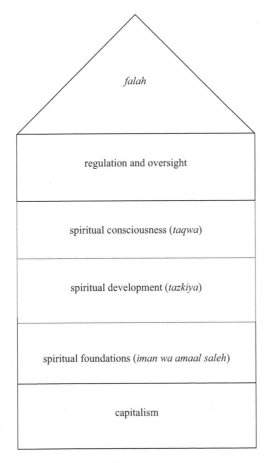

Figure 7.1 The building blocks of spiritual capitalism

e. the ensuring of a systematic development of leadership so that competent and honest people hold all the positions of power and influence.

A long educational process that aims at reforming human conduct and building regulatory institutions is necessary to move toward spiritual capitalism. Islamic economics should aim at the study of spiritual capitalism and develop a theory for its establishment in existing capitalist societies, which are, by themselves, at different stages of socio-economic development. Pursuing this goal will set the agenda for Islamic economics for several decades to come.

NOTES

1. Although there is no explicit law prohibiting the sale of weapons of mass destruction, it is covered under the general prohibition of spreading corruption and destruction (*fasad*) on earth.
2. It has led to a movement on socially responsible investment. Several indices have appeared which quote the performance of companies that adhere to pre-specified ethical criteria for investment. Examples are the Business in the Community Index (BITC), FTSE4Good, Dow Jones Sustainability Index (DJSI), Domini 400 Social Index and so on.

PART II

Prohibition of *riba*

8. Elimination of interest: from divine prohibition to human interpretation

8.1 NO LEARNING OF LESSONS

The divine texts of the three main monotheistic religions, namely Judaism, Christianity and Islam, prohibit interest on loans. However, the way the religious scholars of all three religions have interpreted the prohibition did not succeed in eliminating interest on loans. Human history is thus a history of failure to implement the human interpretation of divine prohibition of interest on loans. Throughout history, there has been a temptation among the religious elite, reformers and social workers to devise some legal mechanism for abolishing interest. Some of them launched a relentless struggle to achieve this objective. Unfortunately, almost always, legal solutions of the problem led to two outcomes. First, there developed a black market for interest-bearing credit, pushing the rates of interest even higher and thus defeating the very purpose for which interest was banned by the law. Second, people were induced to devise series of subterfuges to camouflage interest so as to bypass the legal sanctions. Evidence of this latter outcome can be seen in the form of a long list of subterfuges which Islamic financial institutions have devised in the present time.[1]

At the beginning the religious leaders of Judaism and Christianity tried to harness political support to implement the ban on interest. However, subsequently, the pressures of socio-economic developments and everyday business needs compelled them to concede ground. Gradually, they created room to accommodate some forms of interest. In the process, first the political support weakened and then gradually it vanished altogether. The secular laws of Western countries recognized interest on loans as legitimate, though excessive rates of interest are still considered usurious and unlawful.

Orthodox Muslim scholars were aware of the history of Judaism and Christianity relating to the prohibition of interest. However, they looked down on these developments as efforts to distort the divine law by the clergy. The orthodox scholars alerted Muslims to be vigilant against any slippage toward a distortion of the divine law as with the followers of the other two religions. The Qur'an prohibits dealings in *riba* categorically.

However, when it comes to translating or interpreting the term '*riba*' several basic and deeper questions emerge. We shall be discussing those questions in later chapters and see how Muslim scholars have handled them. For now, we want to argue that orthodox Muslim scholars have interpreted '*riba*' as interest on funds provided by one party to another irrespective of whether the funds were provided as an investment or as a loan. They did not distinguish between a loan and a financing transaction. To the extent the provider of the funds determined a rate of return in advance it was treated as *riba* because it resembled a loan transaction. Thus orthodox Muslim scholars treated all types of interest as *riba* if the contract fixed it in advance. Following this line of argument they pronounced any predetermined rate of return on funds (normally called interest) as *riba*. In the process orthodox Muslim scholars arrived at a definition of *riba* which was almost the same as that which Jewish and Christian scholars had presented centuries earlier. They did not notice that, after centuries of struggle to implement this definition in practice, the followers of the two older religions had to abandon it.

The above-mentioned definition of *riba* came under severe pressure with the advent of modern commercial banking. The question about the legality of commercial interest came up for discussion among the Muslim intelligentsia. The immediate and almost unanimous response of orthodox scholars was that commercial interest was *riba* and prohibited in Islam. The interpretation found a ready audience. The last quarter of the twentieth century saw the emergence of several Islamic financial institutions with the basic concept that all types of interest are *riba* and that banking business must be organized on a basis other than interest. The most prominent theory for the alternative basis was to develop the medieval-age concepts of the principal–agent (*mudaraba*) relationship and partnership (*musharaka*) and commission them to the service of present-day banking. However, the Islamic financial institutions soon discovered that banking business on the basis of *mudaraba* and *musharaka* was full of unacceptable risks. They started developing methods which could bring them a predetermined and secure stream of income (very much like commercial interest) and that were also acceptable to the *Shari'ah* scholars. To satisfy religious scholars, the Islamic financial institutions set up *Shari'ah* supervisory boards (SSBs). As the business developed and as they faced new challenges, the SSBs were presented with ever new problems. In most of the cases, they were able to accommodate interest on bank funds in one form or another, using different nomenclatures and roundabout legal procedures. As we shall show later, a whole lot of legal tricks and ruses were invented by Islamic financial institutions and supported by SSBs that accommodated interest on bank funds.

The moral of the story is that the religious leaders of Judaism and Christianity had to yield ground to interest on investible funds. Muslim religious scholars have done the same. The difference is that the religious scholars of Judaism and Christianity reconciled their interpretation with reality. Muslim religious scholars are still trying to maintain their 'official' position. However, in practice they have yielded ground to interest. Muslim scholars have not learnt any lesson from human history in implementing the prohibition of interest on investible funds. They are still insisting on their definition but in practice accommodating interest of various types in the dealings of Islamic financial institutions.

The present chapter sums up how Judaism and Christianity reacted to the human response to the religious interpretation of the divine texts relating to the prohibition of interest. The later chapters of this book will sum up the arguments of orthodox Muslim scholars and practical responses on the definition of *riba*. We shall also show how Islamic financial institutions have in practice accommodated various forms of interest. We do not blame the Islamic financial institutions for that. They have adopted a path that human need and ingenuity would recommend. However, their *raison d'être* as 'Islamic' financial institutions has become doubtful. The whole effort to create these institutions on the basis of an orthodox interpretation of *riba* that says that all types of interest are *riba* becomes redundant once we note that they are practically dealing in interest in more complex and perhaps more inefficient ways than conventional financial institutions.

8.2   THE PROHIBITION OF INTEREST IN JUDAISM

El-Gamal (2007: 1–2) summarizes the prohibition of interest on loans in Jewish law,[2] which is stricter than the contemporary Islamic juridical opinion on *riba*. For example, Jewish law prohibits a difference in cash and credit prices, treating the increase as akin to lending on interest,[3] but contemporary Islamic jurists have allowed this increase in price due to deferred payment of the sale price. The Jewish rabbis ruled that a business is not allowed to charge two prices, a lower cash price and a higher credit price, 'because someone who pays the higher price is actually paying an additional fee for credit. This is *Ribbis*.' The rabbinic alternative to the interest-based loan contract, however, appears to be the contract known as *heter iska* (investment contract), which may be customized for various purposes to re-characterize the interest as a profit share for the provider of the capital.[4] (Samples of various *iska* contracts for various business and consumer applications are provided in Reisman.[5]) The rabbinical law (*halaka*) disqualifies a person from being a witness if he indulges in interest-bearing lending. The lender is not allowed to live in or use the debtor's property on a rent-free basis, as it involves hidden interest (Abdul-Rahman 2010: 22).

8.2.1   The Evolution of Judaic Thought on Interest

Cornell (2006)[6] has discussed the approaches of Judaism to interest and usury. At the beginning Judaic thought considered all types of interest as prohibited and did not make any distinction between interest and usury (ibid.: 13–14). The prohibition was more a moral sin than an illegal act punishable by law (ibid.: 15). Subsequent discussions expanded this prohibition to those cases where there was even a slight resemblance to interest. It was considered as 'dust of interest'. The concept of interest covered transactions in commodities too. Sale of goods not in one's possession was also considered a form of interest. In addition, any contract that guaranteed a full value of an investor's capital was treated as interest (ibid.: 15).

There have been sporadic but unsuccessful efforts to implement a ban on interest throughout Jewish history. Hammurabi (2123–2081 BC), the ruler of Babylonia, in his Code prescribed maximum rates of interest for various types of loans and also suggested profit–loss sharing to avoid interest (Sheikh Mahmud Ahmad 1989: 13–14). The Jews in Babylonia established the earliest interest-free bank in 700 BC by the name of Agibi Bank on the basis of the mortgage of productive assets to get an interest-free loan. The bank was allowed to make use of the asset, like a house, a horse, land, a slave and so on. The bank was not sustained, as it did not have a mechanism for short-term loans and discounting of bills (ibid.).

In 594 BC, Solon (Greek statesman, lawmaker and poet, 638–558 BC) ameliorated the plight of debtors after an Athenian riot by debtors. He cancelled the debts and banned debt-slavery and the compounding of interest, but he did not ban interest altogether (Mills and Presley 1999: 103). In the Roman Empire in 450 BC the maximum rate of interest was fixed at 10 per cent and then reduced to zero per cent in 342 BC. But this ban on interest did not survive for long. In practice people started dealing in interest until in 88 BC the formally adopted rate of interest was 12 per cent. It continued until the fall of the Western Empire (Mills and Presley 1999: 103).

The way to various innovations and tricks (*hiyal*) to legitimize interest was opened by the twelfth-century Judaic scholar Maimonides (Jewish rabbi and scholar of Morocco and Egypt; Arabic: Musa bin Maymun, 1135–1204). He introduced several innovations through which interest could be taken without 'violating the Talmudic law'. For example, *contractus mohatrae* was allowed, 'which involved the arrangement of a sale below the present market price with immediate delivery and instantaneous resale at a higher market price with future delivery' (Cornell 2006: 17). Other innovations were:

> leasing to the debtor of a field taken by the creditor as security for his loan; extending to a neighbour a loan of certain sum of money in the form of merchandise according to its supposed market value and acquiring elsewhere the same amount of merchandise at wholesale prices. (Ibid.: 17)

The discounting of bills for immediate payment of cash was also allowed in the same vein. Another important innovation was the contract of *'iska*, recognized but not fully approved by Maimonides, which consisted of a particular type of 'silent partnership' (ibid.: 17). Maimonides also allowed the charging of interest from non-Jews when there was a dire need and in the amount necessary to provide the person with a basic living (Abdul-Rahman 2010: 23).

8.3 THE PROHIBITION OF INTEREST IN CHRISTIANITY

Christianity held fraternity and brotherhood in high esteem, and the prohibition of interest actually flowed from this very consideration. Visser (2009: 39) gives a short history of the prohibition of interest by the Church. One of the first to speak against interest was Clement of Alexandria[7] in 220. In 306, the Church fathers were unanimous in condemning interest on the grounds of greed and selfishness. The Council of Nicaea (AD 325) forbade interest among clergymen. The Council of Elvira enacted proscription of interest in that year. The First Council of Carthago (in 345) forbade interest payments by laymen. St Ambrose (d. 397), St Jerome (d. 420), St Augustine (d. 430), and Pope St Leo the Great (d. 461) all condemned usury, characteristically in connection with taking advantage of the needy and the poor. The term used for interest was *usura*, which is used for exorbitant rates of interest (Visser 2009). Father Augustine (d. 430) declared interest to be theft (Mills and Presley 1999).

Emperor Charlemagne[8] enforced a law in 789 to extend the ban on usury from clergymen to all Christians (Heck 2006: 27). Among Christians, the first medieval definition of usury was introduced in 806, which said that usury exists if more is asked than is given (ibid.: 18). In 809, Charlemagne levied a penalty of 60 *solidi* on anyone who indulged in the sin of usury (ibid.: 27). Until AD 1050, interest taking was considered by the Church to be a sin and lack of charity (Mills and Presley 1999). Heck (2006: 23) provides extensive evidence that the Church put an absolute ban on all types of interest. He quotes Monk Gratian (Italian monk, d. 1159) as having said that any excess on the amount borrowed whether in money or in kind would be usury and thus banned. The argument was that capital was sterile and could not fructify.[9] The Second Lateran Council (1139) excommunicated the usurers. The Third Lateran Council (1179) denied Christian burials to usurers. The Fourth Lateran Council (1215) condemned those who did business with Jewish usurers. The Council of Vienna (1311–12) issued a threat of excommunication to those authorities that permitted usury or protected usurers (Visser 2009: 43).

Abdul-Rahman (2010: 24–25) quotes from the Bible and St Thomas Aquinas (Catholic scholar, 1225–74) about the prohibition of interest in Christian law. St Thomas Aquinas argued that the rent of money on interest is like renting an apple, which is not possible because the apple is destroyed in the process of using it. The case of money is similar. It is also consumed, so it cannot be rented out on interest. Christian religious scholars also held that any increase in the sale price of a commodity due to deferment in price constitutes interest (usury). Saadullah (1994: 6) says:

> Le Goff (Jacques Le Goff, 1977, *Pour un autre Moyen Age, temps, travail et culture en Occident*, Paris: Gallimard, 46) quotes the answer given by a church-man in the fourteenth century to a question in this respect:
>
> Q. May the trader demand in the same transaction from the buyer who cannot pay immediately a higher price than from a buyer who can? The substantiated answer is No, because the tradesman is selling time, thus committing the sin of usury by selling what he does not own.
>   The text clearly indicates that the Church in the Middle Ages banned both loan usury and price increase in deferred payment. The Church, however, revised its position later and permitted both.

Pope Benedict XIV (1675–1758) issued the last encyclical against usury in 1745. Later developments gradually turned the direction of the Christian position on usury toward permissibility.

8.3.1   The Evolution of Christian Thought on Interest

Charlemagne's son Louis the Pious (778–840) exempted the Jews from the Christian ban on usury (Heck 2006: 27). This was the first step toward accommodating interest in commercial practice. Christian thought evolved to accommodate the charging of interest to enemies and criminals and for the preaching of the faith. This opened the door for the charging of interest to the Saracens during the Crusades (1080–1300). But Church officials found themselves caught between the need to provide justice to the poor and the requirements of finance arising from a rapidly happening Industrial Revolution. It persuaded them to devise several innovations for accommodating interest for the purpose of trade and industry (Heck 2006: 20). At about the same time the concept of *lucran cessans* (gain forgone by lending) appeared in the form of opportunity cost. Pope Alexander III (1105–81)[10] in a letter in 1176 accepted interest as legitimate if it was to compensate for an opportunity forgone. By the fifteenth century the concept was universally accepted by Christian theologians. The principle of *damnum emergens* allowed interest if the lender had to suffer a loss or had to borrow money because his own money was being used by someone else. It also covered situations where the borrower delayed the repayment of a loan (*poena conventionalis*). The principle of *periculum sortis* justified interest if there was a risk of default by the borrower. The Fifth Lateran Council (1515–16) sanctioned an exception to lend to the poor on a low rate of interest, such as 5 per cent, to protect them from the clutches of usurers (Visser 2009: 42–43).

Warde (2010: 63) mentions the trick of combining three contracts into one under the rubric of *contractum trinius*. The contract combined partnership, sale of profit and insurance. The lender would invest money with a merchant on a profit–loss-sharing basis, insure himself against a loss of capital, and sell back to the merchant any profit above a specified amount. Each component of the contract was legitimate, but led to the lending of money on interest.

In 1515 the Fifth Lateran Council legitimated interest on secured loans (Warde 2010: 63). Still it took a long time before interest was accepted as fully legitimate. The real breakthrough came when the Jewish rabbis of Poland and other countries in Eastern Europe drafted *heter iska*, which was refined several times and which redefined a loan as an investment contract and thus opened the door for charging interest (Abdul-Rahman 2010: 23).

Ultimately, the French Protestant theologian John Calvin (1509–64) made interest palatable to followers of the Church in 1545 by declaring that only excessive and biting usury is unlawful. The rest is lawful and acceptable. In the same vein, the Catholic Church allowed interest if it was for maintaining a household, helping the poor or for public benefit. By 1750 the scholastic theory approved the demanding of interest on loans (Abdul-Rahman 2010: 26). Professor Christopher Kaczor of Loyola Marymount University in Los Angeles, California quotes Jeremy Bentham in letters written in 1787 as saying: 'Church never taught that all charging of interest is wrong.' It seems that it is a recent development of Christian thought. In 1917 the Canon law required Church institutions such as hospitals, schools and orphanages to invest their surplus funds on interest (Abdul-Rahman 2010: 26).

In England, the last Act condemning all interest as contrary to God's law was passed in 1571. However, punishments enacted were very severe for charging interest over 10 per cent. This set the natural rate of interest at that level. After 1600 the debate was whether interest should be banned altogether or a maximum rate be fixed. Parliament periodically reduced the maximum rate until it had reached 5 per cent by 1714. Ultimately, the argument emerged that a cap on the interest rate subsidized rich borrowers, raised black market rates and constituted a paternalistic restriction on economic freedom. In 1854 the Moneylenders Act in the UK abolished the 5 per cent interest law. However, in 1927 a limit of 48 per cent was again imposed. But since 1974, when the Consumer Credit Act was passed, there has been no such restriction. The onus is now on the borrower to prove in a court of law that he or she has been a victim of exploitation (Mills and Presley 1999: 103).

8.4   THE EVOLUTION OF MUSLIM THOUGHT ON INTEREST

Muslim thought on Islamic finance in recent decades has passed through similar stages to Jewish and Christian thought in their respective times. The orthodox position is that all types of interest are *riba* and thus unlawful. Some modernist writers have argued that only usurious rates of interest and interest on consumption loans from the poor were *riba*. However, modernist opinion could not get many adherents. Orthodox opinion that officially treats all interest as *riba* and thus unlawful still prevails. With the development of Islamic financial institutions many orthodox Muslim scholars have accommodated interest in one guise or another. The most significant concession is the permission to charge a higher price for a good if sold on credit as compared to its cash price. Similarly, *murabaha* is now generally accepted as a legitimate financing technique. It is also a significant step toward accommodating interest in commercial dealings. There are several other techniques which have made it possible for Islamic financial institutions to deal in interest in disguised forms. We think that Muslim practice has moved in the right direction except that the orthodox position that treats all forms of interest as *riba* needs to be modified. Orthodox scholars need to recognize that not all forms of interest are *riba*. Some business transactions, such as the difference in cash and credit prices, the mark-up on credit sales, and so on, involve interest but are not *riba*. When this recognition comes, Muslim orthodox thought and the practice of Islamic financial institutions will be fully aligned.

NOTES

1. See Chapter 20 for details.
2. [As in original] Exodus [22:25], Leviticus [25:35–37] and Deuteronomy [23:19–20]; additional elaborations can be found in *Bava Metzia*, chapter 5, *Mishna* 2.
3. [As in original] Yisroel Reisman, *The laws of Ribbis: The laws of interest and their application to everyday life and business* (New York: Mesorah Publications, 1995), p. 112.
4. The *heter iska* was developed by the rabbis in order to structure business transactions in such a manner as to avoid running afoul of the prohibitions against *ribit*. The *heter iska* principle is based upon the borrower and lender agreeing to be partners in a business venture, whereby one partner invests money and the other uses his entrepreneurial skills to manage the venture. The investor-partner can thereby earn 'profit' attributable to his portion of the joint business venture, and the sharing of such profit by the manager-partner would not constitute payment of interest upon a loan. The arrangement thus has characteristics of both a loan and a trust. (Kenneth H. Ryesky, *Secular law enforcement of the heter iska*, http://www.jlaw.com/Articles/heter1.html.)
5. Reisman, *Laws of Ribbis*, pp. 124–129. Footnote 7 in El-Gamal (2007).
6. The paper was first presented to the Second International Conference on Islamic Economics, Republic of Trinidad and Tobago, 17 March 1990. The chapter appeared as 'In the shadow of Deuteronomy: Approaches to interest and usury in Judaism and Christianity', *al-Nahda* (Kuala Lumpur) 10 (1–2) (1991), pp. 39–43.
7. Titus Flavius Clemens (150–215), Christian theologian and head of the Catechetical School of Alexandria, popularly known as Clement of Alexandria.
8. King Charlemagne (747–814) was the King of the Franks and the Emperor of the Romans.
9. Interestingly, this very argument is often given by Muslim religious scholars for the prohibition of all types of interest.
10. He was pope in 1159–81.

9. Prohibition of *riba* in the primary sources of Islam

Without going into the technicalities of law we can say in everyday par-lance that the Qur'an uses the term '*riba*' for interest on loans. In this chapter we shall summarize the message of the Qur'an relating to the prohibition of interest on loans. We shall also present a summary view of various Traditions (*ahadith*) of the Prophet on the subject.

9.1 THE QUR'ANIC VERSES ON *RIBA*

The first verse in chronological order of the revelation relating to *riba* is Q. 30:39. It was revealed in the Makkan period.[1] The prohibition here is not categorical, as it only says that whatever you give by way of *riba* so that it increases in the wealth of other people does not increase in the sight of God. Only *zakah* increases in the sight of God. It is a persuasive verse declaring God's preference for *zakah* and His dislike for lending money on interest and making lending a business. Amin Ahsan Islahi (1904–97) in his *magnum opus Tadabbur e Qur'an* (1999, vol. 6) considers that the words 'the wealth that you give to others on basis of *riba*' are deliberately omitted (*mahdhuf*) and not mentioned in the text. According to him the phrase 'giving of *riba*' in this verse actually refers not to interest but to the capital lent on interest with the intention of increasing it by its intermingling with the wealth of other people. Seen in this context, the verse refers to the practice of adopting interest-based lending as business. This was in vogue among pre-Islam Arabs, and God showed His dislike for it. The practice flouted the norms of fraternity, fellow-feeling, mutual help and coopera-tion. The verse sets the tone for the subsequent total ban on interest-based lending (Q. 2:275–281).

Verse Q. 3:130 is the second revelation on *riba* in chronological order and clearly indicates that *riba* is something that multiplies with time and its prohibition is categorical. The verse was revealed in Medina sometime in AH 2. Most of the scholars think it clearly shows God's disapproval of usurious and compound rates of interest, which were quite common in those days and were exploitative in nature.

132

Verses Q. 2:275–281 are final, clear and emphatic about the prohibition of *riba*. These verses unambiguously declare that creditors are entitled to their principal sums only. Injustice and inequity are also clearly mentioned as the reason for the prohibition. Charity and spending in the way of God (*infaq*) are the alternative to *riba*-based lending.

Regarding the nature of *riba* practised during the times of the Prophet, Muhammad T. Uthmani (1999-b: 11) quotes Abu Bakr al-Jassas (d. AH 380) from *Ahkam al-Qur'an* as saying:

> And the *riba* which was known to and practiced by the Arabs was that they used to advance loan in the form of *dirhams* (silver coin) or *dinars* (gold coin) for a certain term with an agreed increase on the amount of the principal advanced.

Also by al-Jassas: 'The *riba* of pre-Islam Period of Ignorance (*Jahiliyya*) was a loan given for a stipulated period with a stipulated increase on the principal payable by the debtor' (ibid.).

Uthmani (ibid.) also quotes from Fakharuddin al-Razi (d. AH 606/AD 1209) as follows:

> As for the *riba an-nasi'ah* (i.e. interest on deferred payment), it was a transaction well-known and recognized in the Period of Ignorance (*Jahiliyya*). They used to give money with a condition that they will charge a particular amount monthly and the principal will remain due as it is. Then on the maturity date they demanded the debtor to pay the principal. If he could not pay, they would increase the term and the payable amount also. So it was the *riba* practiced by the people during Period of Ignorance (*Jahiliyya*).

The above explanation clearly states that in the days of the Prophet some people were in the business of lending money on interest. Usually they would give money as a loan for a stipulated period at a certain rate of interest. If the debtor was unable to repay the principal sum on the due date, the creditor would extend the period for repayment and also increase the claim by adding interest for the extended period. The rate of interest for the extended period could be the same as in the previous period or it could be a penal rate. In most cases the extensions were at usurious rates which would double or quadruple the principal sum. All excess on the principal sum of the loan was treated as *riba* by the Qur'an and was prohibited.

9.1.1 Prohibition of *Riba*: Not a Legal Issue

The Qur'anic prohibition of interest on loans is a moral restriction and not a public law for enforcement by the state. However, orthodox Muslim scholars have recently argued that the prohibition of *riba* is a legal offence and its violation should be punished by law. The basis of their argument is the following Qur'anic verse: 'O those who believe! Fear God and give up what still remains of the *"riba"* if you are believers' (Q. 2:278).[2] The argument says that, on the basis of this verse, the Prophet during his Last Pilgrimage sermon abolished all claims of interest on loans and first of all abolished the claims of his own uncle, Abbas bin 'Abdul Muttalib. This action of the Prophet, it is argued, makes claims relating to interest unlawful. On the basis of this action of the Prophet an Islamic state is supposed to enact laws against dealings in interest, and the courts should not entertain claims for recovery of interest in future (M.T. Uthmani 2000: 27). It is possible to impute the above interpretation to the Qur'anic verse and the action of the Prophet in this manner. However, we think it is an overzealous interpretation. The Prophet declared all claims of interest void and first of all those of his own uncle to set an example. However, he did not promulgate any law on it. The characteristic of the law is that it always has bite and its violation attracts some punishment. In this case, the Prophet could easily have announced the broad features of such a law. The fact is that neither the Prophet nor the Qur'an has announced any law relating to interest, as in the case of theft, adultery or murder. The attempts to convert these injunctions into a public law are quite recent.

Another verse that is often referred to support a public law against *riba* is Q. 2:279, where God gives an ultimatum of war against those who do not give up the practice of *riba*. On the basis of this verse orthodox scholars have argued that dealing in *riba* is like a revolt against the state and should be punished accordingly. Trying to interpret this verse in this manner is a recent effort. It has come in the wake of calls for the abolition of interest from the economy in the second half of the nineteenth and the first half of the twentieth century.

The interpretation would be plausible if we read the verse in isolation from the historical event which necessitated its revelation. The verse was revealed in the context of the peace treaty of the Prophet with the Banu Thaqifs of Taif, who were in the business of money lending. Muhammad T. Uthmani (2000) writes about the treaty as follows:

> One of the proposed clauses of treaty was that 'Banu Thaqifs would not forego the amounts of interest due on their debtors but their creditors would forego the amount of interest due from them'. The Prophet, instead of signing the treaty, simply dictated a sentence on the proposed draft of the treaty that 'Banu Thaqifs would have the same rights as the Muslims had'. Banu Thaqifs having the impression that their proposed treaty was accepted by the Prophet claimed the amount of interest from Banu Amr ibn al-Mughirah who declined to pay interest on the ground that *riba* had been prohibited after Islam. The matter was placed before 'Attab bin Usayd, the Governor of Makkah. Banu Thaqifs

argued that according to the treaty they were not bound to forego the amounts of interest. 'Attab bin Usayd referred the matter to the Prophet on which the following verses were revealed:

> O you who have attained to faith! Remain conscious of God, and give up all outstanding claims of *riba*, if you are truly believers. For if you do it not, then know that you are at war with God and His Apostle. But if you repent, then you shall be entitled to your principal. You will do no wrong, and neither will you be wronged. (Q.2:278–279)

The above explanation shows that this ultimatum was with specific reference to the historical situation. Since the Banu Thaqifs were intending to break the peace treaty they were told that if they did not honour the treaty the relationship with them would revert to the pre-treaty state. They would again face the war that was postponed because of the treaty. It was not because dealing in interest was by itself a crime requiring such an ultimatum. The Banu Thaqifs were given an armistice and a pact of peace on the condition that they would have the same rights and obligations as Muslims had. The treaty implied that interest on their loans was also abolished as it had been abolished on the loans of other Muslims. However, they tried to rescind the treaty and go back on their word and insisted on claiming interest. They were then reminded by the above verse of the Qur'an that if they went back on their treaty the ceasefire would also be annulled and they should get ready for war again – a situation that prevailed prior to the treaty. This was an ultimatum to the Banu Thaqifs from God and His Apostle, as they were trying to violate the treaty. This verse does not institute a law that could make dealings in *riba* a state crime.

Even after this neither the Prophet nor the first four caliphs nor any subsequent Islamic government ever enacted any law against *riba*. This has never been the understanding of Muslims of any age, and a law against *riba* has never been enacted to give effect to this warning. An exception, however, has been mentioned by Badawi (2000: 63, n. 67). He quotes Alusi (*Ruh al-Ma'ani*, 3, 53) that the majority of the commentators on the Qur'an hold the view that those who indulge in *riba* become apostates and should be executed. Badawi (2000: 68, n. 72) also quotes Zamakhshari as saying that the wealth of those who indulge in *riba* and also do not repent will be booty for Muslims (*al-Kashshaf*, 1, 108). We think these opinions of religious scholars have no divine sanction and have never been implemented in practice.

Similarly, Islamic jurisprudence discusses the subject of *riba*. None of the juridical sources prescribe any punishment against those who deal in *riba*. Jurists have defined the limits of transactions and warned against any deal that involves *riba*. The treasure of Islamic jurisprudence which has covered all facets of life, including imaginary situations, does not mention any punishment for one who indulges in *riba*. The most recent example of codified Islamic law is the *Majallah Ahkam al-Adliyyah*[3] enforced by the Ottoman caliphate. The law does not have a chapter on the law of *riba*. Similarly, a recent compilation of Islamic law, *Encyclopedia of Islamic Fiqh* (Ministry of Religious Affairs and Awqaf of Kuwait), does not contain any Islamic law on *riba*. None of the authentic books of Islamic jurisprudence *(fiqh)* produced throughout Islamic history have any law relating to *riba*. The sections dealing with *riba*, of course, discuss its nature and what makes a transaction lawful or unlawful but do not contain any public law for enforcement through state machinery. It is only in Tahir, Atiquzzafar, Ali and Waheed (1999: 141) that we come across a suggestion that dealing in *riba*-based transactions should be made a criminal offence and punishable by law. Even their idea has not been accepted by any Muslim state. In brief, these verses are being used as rhetoric against commercial interests by the religious lobby without going further to prescribe a legal punishment for indulging in *riba*-based transactions. These iconoclastic views have not been accepted by the Muslim people in general.

9.2   TRADITIONS OF THE PROPHET RELATING TO *RIBA*

There are three sets of Traditions relating to *riba*. The first set condemns *riba* as a heinous sin and emphasizes its prohibition. One prominent example is the sermon of the Prophet during his Last Pilgrimage when he declared all claims of *riba* null and void (e.g. Abu Dawud, *Sunan*, Kitab al-Buyu, ch. 5). In the same vein we find several Traditions that condemn the taking and giving of *riba* and the witnessing and writing of *riba* contracts. These Traditions have not been much discussed among religious scholars (e.g. Imam Muslim, *Sahih*, Kitab al-muzara'a, h. 126–127).

The second set of Traditions defines *riba* as something that accrues in loan or deferred payment transactions (*riba al-nasi'ah*) (e.g. Imam Muslim, ibid., h. 122–123). The position that *riba* arises only in loan transactions was held by several prominent companions of the Prophet such as Ibn Abbas, 'Urwa bin Zubayr and Zayd bin Arqam (Farooq 2006-c). This set of Traditions clearly relates *riba* to loan transactions and illustrates the Qur'anic prohibition of *riba*. There is not much discussion of this set of Traditions either.

The third set deals with *riba* that arises in the exchange of commodities. This has been termed in the literature *riba al-fadl* as distinct from *riba al-nasi'ah*, which arises from the loan of monetary assets. As an example, we quote below only one Tradition relating to *riba al-fadl*:

From 'Ubada ibn al-Samit: The Prophet said: Gold for gold, silver for silver, wheat for wheat, barley for barley, dates for dates, and salt for salt – like for like, equal for equal, and hand-to-hand; if the commodities differ, then you may sell as you wish, provided the exchange is hand-to-hand. (Imam Muslim, *Sahih*, Kitab al-muzara'a, h. 97)

The Traditions dealing with the above subject have created serious problems of interpretation. First, these Traditions say that six things should be exchanged in equal quantities and on the spot. Any excess or delay in exchange would involve *riba*. It raises the obvious question: why would a person having, for example, 100 kilograms of wheat like to exchange it with another person for the same quantity of wheat and at the same time? This obviously is an irrational situation. To rationalize this and similar other Traditions, jurists have tried to assign reasons for such exchanges and their prohibition. They did not think of questioning the text itself, because the Traditions had been transmitted by authentic companions of the Prophet and were reported in the most reliable compilations of the *hadith* literature. Instead, they tried to find some plausible explanation for the prohibition to rationalize the ambiguity in the text. However, they were not quite successful.

In the process further questions arose. For example, do we restrict the prohibition to these six commodities or can we extend it to other commodities as well? If we have to extend it, what would be the basis for such an extension? The discussion diverted to finding the characteristics which necessitated the prohibition of these six commodities. Some jurists thought it was because these commodities could be used as money. On this analogy, those commodities which have the characteristic of being used as money should also be covered by this prohibition. Others thought it was because four of these items could be used as food. Therefore any commodity which could be used as food would come under the law *of riba al-fadl*. Still others thought that the reason for prohibition was that these six commodities could be stored. On the basis of these discussions different juridical schools engaged in compiling lists of those items which could be exchanged on a deferred basis and which had to be exchanged on a cash basis. No one dared to raise the basic question about the reasons for prohibition of such an exchange in the first place.

The theory of *riba al-fadl* has created several problems. Some of these are as follows:

a. The Traditions relating to *riba al-fadl* prohibited the exchange of six commodities if there was an excess on one side or if payment was deferred by one or both parties. The exchange of these commodities had to be in equal quantities and on the spot. This made *riba* a subject of cash or spot exchange. The Qur'anic prohibition of *riba* related to excess in loans. Some other Traditions of the Prophet also declared that there was no *riba* except in loans (*nasi'ah*). The Traditions on *riba al-fadl* came into direct conflict with these injunctions. Jurists had to labour hard to reconcile the two sets of Traditions, with very little success.

b. The Traditions on *riba al-fadl* mention only six commodities on which the *riba* accrues if they are exchanged on a deferred basis. Even when we extend the application of these six commodities to others of the same genre and include food, those having the characteristics of money and those which can be stored, taking into account the extensions proposed by all juridical schools, millions of things would remain out of the pale of *riba al-fadl*. That makes the whole theory of *riba al-fadl* of dubious validity. It is difficult to rationalize this inconsistency.

c. The Traditions on *riba al-fadl* also created problems relating to such exchanges as gold and silver on one hand and ornaments made of these metals on the other. The strict application of the equivalence in exchange would make it impossible for the exchange of ornaments for the same metal except in equal weight, ignoring the labour and workmanship in making the ornaments. But this, obviously, is against common sense. Despite that, hobbled by the text of the Traditions, orthodox jurists opined that the ornaments and metals with which they are made must remain equal in quantity. Any excess would be *riba*.[4]

d. All schools of jurisprudence restrict the prohibition of exchange of commodities either to the six commodities mentioned explicitly in the Traditions or to those which, on the basis of analogical reasoning, have the characteristics of these six commodities. The question remains: if *riba al-fadl* is not conducive to human welfare or is a source of injustice, why should it not apply to the exchange of all commodities? Why should it be restricted to a few categories as reasoned by the jurists of different schools? Interestingly, the analogical reasoning of different schools is such that in one school a transaction is considered to be based on *riba al-fadl* and thus prohibited but in the opinion of another school it is permissible.[5]

e. The law of *riba al-fadl* does not take into account differences in the quality of commodities of the same genus. This is against common sense, since differences in quality are facts of life and it cannot be expected that the lawgiver will not recognize this everyday reality. How could the Prophet, the lawgiver himself who was under divine guidance all the time, ignore such a fact of life and oblige people to exchange goods of the same genus in equal quantity even though the quality was significantly different on each side?

f. *Riba al-fadl* may also create problems in applying the prohibition of *riba* to loans in present-day paper money. Saeed (1996: 37) writes:

> Coins like *fals*,[6] for instance, did not involve *riba*, according to Shaf'ites. Thus, one hundred *fals* could be exchanged for two hundred either on the spot or on a deferred delivery basis. If this is maintained, then obviously today's fiat [i.e. paper] money could also be put in this category, since it is neither gold nor silver currency. Commodities which were countable, like apples or eggs, did not involve *riba*, and hence could be exchanged less for more, according to some jurists. A piece of cloth could be exchanged for two pieces of the same quality and measure since it was neither 'currency' nor 'measurable' nor 'weighable', nor a 'foodstuff'.

g. Fazlur Rahman (1964: 20) undertakes a detailed examination of various Traditions relating to *riba al-fadl*. He points out contradictions and ambiguities in these Traditions. For example, while some Traditions prohibit the exchange of six commodities of the same genre on a deferred payment basis as well as when done on the spot, others allow exchange of animals of the same kind in different numbers even on a deferred payment basis. For example, the *Muwatta* of Imam Malik and the *Sahih* of Imam Bukhari allow excess in the exchange of cattle even when on a credit basis. Similarly, the *Sahih* of Imam Muslim allows the exchange of slaves and copper money in excess on a credit basis.

9.2.1   The Condition of Simultaneous Exchange

The most popular citations about *riba al-fadl* refer to Traditions of the Prophet that prohibit the exchange of six commodities except when they are equivalent and the exchange is simultaneous. This second condition of the exchange, being simultaneous (hand to hand), has made an understanding of the entire literature on *riba al-fadl* problematic, as it does not make any sense for two persons to exchange the equivalent quantities at the same time. Luckily we come across a Tradition from Said ibn Jubayr that Ibn Abbas said: "'*Riba* is not found at all in 'here you are' and 'here you are' [from hand to hand]." Said ibn Jubayr took an oath to the effect that he [Ibn Abbas] did not retract this view till he died.'[7]

A comprehensive review of Traditions on *riba al-fadl* shows that some Traditions on the subject do not mention the words 'the exchange should be on the spot' (*yadan bi yadin*). Tahir *et al.* (1999: 14–18) has compiled most of the Traditions relating to *riba*, including *riba al-fadl*. They quote seven Traditions from the *Sahih* of Imam Muslim and one from the *al-Jami'* of Imam Tirmidhi relating to *riba al-fadl*. Only one of these Traditions (Imam Muslim, 2971) mentions the words '*yadan bi yadin*' (i.e. the exchange should be on the spot). Others mention that the exchange between the goods should be equal in weight if they are the same genre or kind. On the basis of this evidence from the *hadith* literature itself, it seems quite plausible that the Traditions in which the words 'simultaneous exchange' (*yadan bi yadin*) are reported could have been an unintentional mistake of the narrator or transmitter of the Traditions, and the Prophet may not have uttered these words.

If we take this position then the famous Tradition on the authority of Usama bin Zayd (and also on the authority of Ibn Abbas) that 'there is no *riba* except in *nasi'ah*' (delay) will also reconcile with the Traditions relating to *riba al-fadl*.[8] It would mean that the Prophet wanted to say that, just as excess repayment in the case of cash loans involves *riba*, the excess repayment in the loan of commodities would also involve *riba*. It means that excess caused by delay in repayment would lead to *riba* in any case. This explanation removes the obvious conflict between those sets of Traditions which restrict *riba* to delay (*riba al-nasi'ah*) and those which deal with the exchange of commodities (*riba al-fadl*). *Riba* will take place if you borrow cash or commodities and return a higher amount or quantity after a period. The question of *riba* arising from spot exchange thus is ruled out. Seen in this light, the entire literature on *riba al-fadl* becomes redundant.

9.2.2 Difference of Fungibles and Non-Fungibles

A clear dichotomy exists in the theory of *riba* when treating fungible (*mithli*) and non-fungible (*qimi*) property. El-Gamal (2006: 39) writes:

> Thus, while a usurer is not allowed to trade one ounce of gold for two, he is allowed to trade one non-fungible item (e.g. a diamond) for two diamonds. Moreover, a usurer may legally sell a diamond worth $10,000 today for a deferred price of $20,000 tomorrow. The buyer may have no interest in the diamond and sell it for $10,000 in cash. Thus the usurer would legally collect overnight interest of 100 percent in a valid contract that avoids *riba* in form (though obviously usurious in substance). This clearly illustrates that the prohibition of *riba* cannot possibly be limited to questions of interest or exorbitant interest, since interest can be hidden in sale (as *murabaha* and *tawarruq*), and can easily be made exorbitant while avoiding the formalistic rules of *riba*.

Thus creating a difference between fungibles and non-fungibles picks a hole in the otherwise compact and all-embracing definition of *riba*.

9.3 SUMMING-UP

We think the Traditions of the Prophet relating to *riba al-fadl* need to be re-examined with reference to the prohibition of *riba* in the Qur'an and in other sets of Traditions that deal with interest on loans. Similarly, creating a distinction between fungible and non-fungible commodities confuses the absolute prohibition of *riba*. The simple and straightforward injunction is that any excess in the case of loans, whether taken in the form of cash or commodities, would be *riba* and thus unlawful.

NOTES

1. This refers to the first 13 years of the prophethood of Muhammad (609–22) before he migrated to Medina (AD 623).
2. Translation by the present writer.
3. *The Mejelle*, trans. C.R. Tyser, D.G. Demetriades and Ismail Haqqi Effendi (Kuala Lumpur: The Other Press, n.d.).
4. Based on Fazlur Rahman, *Islamic methodology in history* (Islamabad: Islamic Research Institute, 2009 reprint), p. 64.
5. For example, the Shaf'ites restrict *riba al-fadl* to items of foodstuff and gold and silver, while the Hanafites apply it to all items that are sold by weights and measures.
6. A unit of currency made of a metal which is not gold or silver and was used in some parts of the Muslim world.
7. Quoted by Farooq (2006-c) on the authority of Zaki Badawi, *Theory of prohibited riba* (1964), trans. Imran Ahsan Khan Nyazee, pp. 114–115 (available online, 2000), quoting Al-Subki, *Takmilat Majmu'*, Vol. I, 36. Subki mentioned that the report of Said ibn Jubayr is with *isnad*, that is, agreed upon for authenticity.
8. Badawi (2000: 50) reports that Ibn Abbas and his companions denied the existence of *riba al-fadl* in the *Shari'ah*.

10. Theory of *riba*: the orthodox interpretation

The Qur'an declares *riba* unlawful but does not define it (Q. 2:275–281) because ordinary people in the days of the Prophet were familiar with it. There were professional moneylenders who provided loans on interest. In the case of default, the creditor used to increase the amount payable either at an increased rate of interest or at the previous rate and give an extension in the period for payment. Thus interest payable on loans was equivalent to *riba*. Orthodox scholars of Islam have argued that *riba* stands for any excess on the principal sum of loan irrespective of the amount, purpose and duration of the loan. Although several commentators of the Qur'an understood similarly in the past, yet this interpretation of *riba* was presented to make a case for interest-free banking in the first half of the twentieth century. A large number of prominent scholars such as Mufti Muhammad Shafi (1896–1976), Muhammad Abu Zahra (1898–1974), Abu al-'Ala Mawdudi (1903–79), Syed Qutb (1906–66), Muhammad Hameedullah (1908–2002), Sheikh Jad al-Haqq Ali Jad al-Haqq (1917–96), Zaki Badawi (1922–2006), Baqir al-Sadr (1935–80), Hifzur Rahman Seoharvi, Sheikh Mahmud Ahmad (1918–90) and Anwar Iqbal Qureshi, to name a few, pleaded for this interpretation. Among the second generation of scholars Khurshid Ahmad, Nejatullah Siddiqi, Taqi Uthmani, Umer Chapra, Monzer Kahf, Anas Zarqa, Fahim Khan and a large number of other scholars have endorsed this interpretation. We present below some examples of the interpretation of the term '*riba*' by orthodox scholars for the sake of illustration. M.U. Chapra (1985: 56–57) says: '[*Riba*] refers to the 'premium' that must be paid by the borrower to the lender with the principal amount as a condition for the loan or for an extension in its maturity.' Siddiqi (2004-a: 38) says:

> The majority of scholars, however, think that it covers the interest stipulated at the time of the contract in case of loans as well as the subsequent increases in case the loan or the debt arising from sale if credit is rolled over because the debtor does not pay it at the time stipulated in the contract.

In 1964, Zaki Badawi, an Egyptian scholar and once right-hand man of Abd al-Razzaq al-Sanhuri (1895–1971), the architect of the Egyptian constitution, renounced his views of 1939 and took a traditional approach toward *riba*.[1] His revised position was that all forms of increase on loans were *riba* (Khalil and Thomas 2006: 77). Another Egyptian scholar, Muhammad Abu Zahra (1898–1974), also took the traditional line and declared all forms of interest as *riba* (ibid.: 77). In 1976, King Abdulaziz University, Jeddah organized the First International Conference on Islamic Economics in Makkah. Several hundred Muslim intellectuals, *Shari'ah* scholars and economists unequivocally declared in this conference that all forms of interest are *riba*. The Fiqh Academy of the OIC ruled in 1986 that all types of interest-bearing transactions were void as they involved *riba* (Warde 2010: 54). The Research Council of al-Azhar University ruled in 1965 as follows:

> Interest on all types of loans is forbidden *riba*. There is no difference in this regard between so-called consumption and production loans. Moreover, *riba* is forbidden (*haram*) in small as well as large quantities, whether it is affected through time deposits, demand (or checking) deposits, or any interest-bearing loan contract. All such dealings are among the forbidden *riba*. (El-Gamal 2000: 39)

Sheikh Jad al-Haqq Ali Jad al-Haqq, who served both as *mufti* and as Shaykh Al-'Azhar, ruled in his book *Al-Fatawa Al-'Islamiyyah* that depositing monies to collect a fixed rate of interest is forbidden in Islam, and borrowing with interest from government institutions or banks is forbidden *riba*. In this regard, it has long been established that deposits (e.g. with a bank) become loans as soon as they are used by the recipient of the deposit (El-Gamal 2000: 39).

Jordanian civil law (item 889) states:

> If the deposited item was an amount of money or something which perishes by usage, and if the depositor allows the recipient to use the deposited items, then the contract is considered a loan contract. In loan contracts, any increase, as we have seen, is forbidden *riba*. (El-Gamal 2000)

El-Gamal (ibid.) concludes: 'Therefore, the vast majority of jurists (including those of Al-'Azhar in Egypt) rule that bank deposits are loans and that the interest incurred on them is forbidden *riba*.' The *Federal Shari'ah Court of Pakistan (FSC) Judgment* (1991) defined *riba* as follows:

> The directions of the Holy Qur'an and the *Sunnah* are quite explicit on the point that any amount, however little, stipulated in addition to the principal in a transaction of loan is *riba*, hence prohibited. (paragraph 106)

> Any additional amount over the principal in a contract of loan or debt is the *riba* prohibited by the Holy Qur'an in several verses. (paragraph 242)

The FSC judgment also declared all forms of interest, whether simple or compound, on consumption loans or commercial loans, short-term or long-term, private or government, between Muslims and non-Muslims, between two states or between citizens and the state, as *riba*. It categorically included all forms of interest in the banking business as *riba*. The Supreme Court of Pakistan *Shari'ah* Appellate Bench decision (1999, paragraph 468) defined *riba* as follows:

> Any amount, big or small, in excess of the principal, in a contract of loan or debt, is *riba*, prohibited by the holy Qur'an, regardless of whether the loan is taken for the purpose of consumption or for some production activity.

Other paragraphs of the judgment fully endorsed the Federal *Shari'ah* Court's decision of 1991 so far as the definition of *riba* was concerned. In brief, the orthodox interpretation of *riba* holds all types of interest as *riba*. Any predetermined excess over the principal sum provided by one party for a certain period would be *riba* and thus unlawful in Islam. The most critical conditions in this definition are as follows:

a. It has to be a transaction of monetary exchange where the principal sum has to be returned with an increase.
b. The increase is predetermined either as an absolute sum or as a rate for a period.
c. It will not matter:
    i.   what the rate of interest is (high or low);
    ii. what the purpose of the loan or monetary exchange is (consumption or commercial);
    iii. what the period of the transaction is (any span of time);
    iv. who the parties to the contract are (individuals, institutions, governments, inter-governmental bodies, NGOs, etc.).

The prohibition is absolute for any fixed predetermined return on the principal sum over a period of time. It is based on this interpretation of *riba* that the whole movement of Islamic finance has started. The justification for establishing Islamic financial institutions also stems from this interpretation. Since conventional financial institutions deal in interest, their whole business was declared unlawful, and Islamic financial institutions were supposed to deal on some basis other than interest. In subsequent chapters we shall make an assessment of the interpretation of *riba* and the business of Islamic financial institutions and see to what extent they have adopted this interpretation in practice.

NOTE

1. In 1939, Badawi pleaded for the legitimizing of the modern interest of commercial banks. He provided the intellectual basis to Abd al-Razzaq al-Sanhuri to write the constitutions of Egypt, Syria, Iraq, Libya and Kuwait (Khalil and Thomas 2006: 76).

11. Assessment of the orthodox interpretation

There are two important strands of Muslim thinking on the nature and definition of *riba* and its relation with modern commercial banking and finance. The first and by far the most influential (the orthodox) considers all types of interest as *riba* and treats present-day commercial banking as unlawful in Islam. It pleads for an Islamic model of banking and finance that does not deal in interest. The thinking of orthodox scholars has fired the contemporary movement of Islamic finance. The second strand, consisting of liberals and modernists, considers that the interest of modern banks is not *riba*. Both strands have taken indefensible positions in facing questions on their respective points of view. The present chapter will make an assessment of the orthodox interpretation of *riba*. We shall assess the position of the modernists in the next chapter.

Once we equate *riba* with interest, the immediate question arises: why has God prohibited interest? There is no direct answer to this question either in the Qur'an or in the Traditions of the Prophet. However, Muslim scholars have dealt with this question in detail. A summary of the reasons for prohibition given by orthodox scholars with our comments is as follows.

11.1 RATIONALE FOR THE PROHIBITION OF INTEREST

Orthodox scholars have provided several explanations for the prohibition of interest. The following discussion presents their case with our comments.

11.1.1 Interest Leads to Injustice

A summary of the main argument presented by several writers (e.g. Chapra 2006: 98–99[1]) is as follows:

> The primary reason for the prohibition of interest is that interest-based loans are inherently exploitative. In the case of consumption loans the element of

exploitation is too obvious to require any evidence. In the case of commercial loans, the entrepreneur borrows funds at a fixed rate of interest, undertakes commercial activity and assumes all the risks. If at the end of the period the business suffers a loss the entrepreneur still has to pay interest on the borrowed funds. The party that undertook the commercial activity and assumed all the risks goes without any gain, but the financier who has done nothing except forward the money gets a return in the form of interest. This obviously is an unjust situation.

A second strand of this argument is that interest is a major tool for inequitable distribution of income and wealth. Interest transfers wealth from those who suffer losses to those who provide loan capital. For example, Siddiqi (2008-c: 129) says:

Repayment of the borrowed sum with interest added by those whose ventures failed to create wealth causes a transfer of wealth from the entrepreneurs to the owners of money capital, who would not share risk, yet want a return. Putting producers/innovators at a disadvantage as compared to those having money to spare does not bode well for the society.

Let us examine the argument.

a.   How real is the probability of loss?

It is pertinent to ask the question: how real is the probability of loss in a business enterprise? At the micro-level it will differ from business to business and its circumstances, and no general rule can be prescribed. However, at the macro- and global levels there is ample evidence to show that most of the businesses earn profits and that too at rates that are several multiples of the rates of interest.

Toutounchian (2009: 126) has provided data for the G-7, France, Italy and Canada for 19 years and for the US, Japan, Germany and the UK for 29 years. The data show that the rates of profits over these periods in these countries have been consistently higher by several multiples of the rates of interest. It means that business enterprises, in general, experience profit from their operations. There is no evidence to show that most businesses at most times suffer losses. Orthodox scholars have not presented any data for any society and for any period to show that most entrepreneurs suffered losses. Conceptually, it is not possible to imagine an economy where most of the business firms for most of the time are facing losses. It is against common sense. The economic rules are framed with respect to the situation prevailing in most of the cases in most of the times. It would not be fair to base the whole financial system on an assumption that holds in some cases and only at some times. It is time that some empirical research was conducted to verify the assertion of orthodox scholars for the prohibition of interest.

When a business firm suffers losses, it could be the result of multiple factors and in no way can always be imputed to capital. The management may have utilized the capital in less than an optimum manner. The management practices and controls may have been sloppy, and the business could have been a victim of government policies or of the international business environment. It cannot be simply attributed to capital.

Where business firms suffer losses a further question arises: who is responsible for the losses? Suppose this is a profit–loss-sharing finance case, shall we not make the entrepreneur suffer the entire loss if it has been due to his or her negligence? It means there is no blanket mechanism to make the financier bear the losses until we determine how the loss occurred and who was responsible for it. It introduces a controversial dimension to the whole financing deal: how to determine who is actually responsible for the loss and to what extent. No foolproof criteria exist for that.

b.   Wealth creation is a complex process
The question of justice and fairness in the distribution of profits and losses, despite being highly desirable, is extremely complex. It is not only financing on interest that may in some cases be unfair, but there could be a large number of socio-economic factors, including government policies, that lead to injustice and inequity in society. If we have to ensure justice, we would require a comprehensive policy package and implementation structure. The mere disbanding of interest might not be sufficient.

The concept of assigning loss to financial capital is based on a narrow definition of capital, which may have relevance to small-scale proprietor-managed businesses, most popular in the Middle Ages. In present-day complex and large-scale business corporations, capital does not consist of financial capital only. Business corporations create wealth through a social process that results from the interaction and collaboration of several factors. Business firms deploy various types of capital. Some of the more significant ones are: reputational capital, social capital, human capital, physical capital and, of course, financial capital. Reputational capital attracts customers, employees, investors, and knowledge workers for experimenting with their ideas. A business organization builds this capital by acting morally over extended periods of time. Social capital provides the business with its culture, leadership style and motivation for employees. Social capital also leads to smooth dealing with financial institutions, and mutual trust among customers, suppliers, competitors, government and civil society. Human capital provides competence and knowledge, a motivated work force, employee loyalty, and continuity through institutional memory. A business organization builds this capital through appropriate motivation, leadership style and transparent personnel policies. Physical capital consists of buildings, machines, equipment and technology. Financial capital provides cash for running the business, buying raw material and paying for various services. Owners, lenders and business partners contribute financial capital. Lenders and business partners provide financial capital on the basis of trust that the business will be able to fulfil its promises. External to the business organization are several factors, which can be termed the 'enabling environment', that contribute to the creation of wealth. Examples are physical infrastructure, telecommunications, the regulatory framework of the government, protection of private property, rights, privileges and trademarks, the rule of law and honest bureaucracy, to name some.

It is the interaction of all these types of capital that leads to the profit or loss in a firm. Conceiving business into simplified traditional factors of production and then assigning responsibility of loss to financial capital only is an oversimplified way of looking at the process of profit–loss creation. Even when honest people run business with all sincerity, loss can take place through the failure or malfunction of any of the multifarious factors stated above. It would not be reasonable to argue that capital had been responsible for the loss. Justice would demand, if we think at all that there should be a fair distribution of profits and losses among all factors of production, the devising of the means for delineating the contribution or lack of it by all the multifarious factors of production that may have contributed to the final results of the business endeavour. Assigning loss to financial capital, to the exclusion of other forms of capital, is not realistic.

The fact is that the classical Islamic juridical construct of treating financial capital as responsible for loss has become outmoded in this age of complex and large business firms. For this very reason, the oversimplified argument that, if there is a loss, capital should bear it, as the entrepreneur should not be the only party to bear the loss, requires reconsideration.

c. Some Islamic modes of finance can also lead to a situation similar to interest-based finance

Some Islamic modes of finance (about which we shall have a detailed discussion in Chapter 17) can lead to a situation quite similar to interest-based finance. Let us take the example of *bai' al-salam*, a contract where a farmer receives finance of $10 000 from a bank and agrees to sell 10 000 kilograms of wheat after the harvest at $1 per kilogram. Suppose further that because of bad weather the produce of the farm is merely 9000 kilograms. The farmer will make up the loss through personal means. In this contract, the entire loss is the liability of the farmer. The bank gets its share without any shortfall. The contract has obviously led to a situation quite similar to that of interest-based finance. However, orthodox scholars allow the former but disallow the latter.

Another example is that of a sharecropping contract (*muzara'a*) where a land-owner provides land for a fixed rent and the farmer is responsible for all inputs and labour. The farmer may not have enough harvest to pay the rent. However, the right of the land-owner is protected. Orthodox scholars allow the contracting of land for a fixed rent but do not allow financing on interest. The likelihood of loss is present in both cases. The orthodox scholars have no problem with fixed rent on land even though the yield of the land is not enough to pay the rent. However, they object to interest on capital if there is a loss in business. The two situations are similar, but the orthodox position on both is inconsistent. There is no plausible explanation for this inconsistency.

d. Fixed rent and fixed wages are acceptable but fixed interest is not

There is no difference of opinion about the permissibility of fixed wages for services and fixed rents on durable assets. Ibn Ashur (2006: 302), for example, justifies the contracts of wage and rents on the basis of the objectives of the *Shari'ah*:

> Labor-based transactions consist mainly of *ijara* (hire), *musaqa* (sharecropping), *mugharasa* (orchard sharecropping), *qirad* (commenda), *ju'l* (wages) and *muzara'a* (cultivation partnership). . . . The contracts based on these transactions are not free from some degree of ambiguity (*gharar*), owing to the difficulty of accurately assessing the amount of work required and the amount of profit for the workers from their labor and for the investors from their capital. Nevertheless, the *Shari'ah* has ignored all these types of risk, believing that greater harm would result from depriving so many people from the great benefits of work. Similarly, these contracts are not immune to certain harm that might befall the workers in many cases, such as when they participate in *musaqa* or *muzara'a* but the trees do not bear fruit, or when they work in *ju'l* but the stipulated benefit does not materialize, or when they work in *qirad* but no profit is made. Thus, the workers would have spent much of their time and suffered much hardship in fulfilling these contracts for nothing. Yet, the *Shari'ah* has again ignored these consequences because it considers that to remain unemployed is indeed more harmful for laborers than facing failure in one case or another.

The employee of a firm who works for a wage or the owner of premises who receives fixed rent periodically has a risk-free contract. Muslim scholars who object to interest because it is fixed and predetermined do not see any inconsistency when they allow fixed wages and fixed rents but disallow fixed interest. When a person offers a physical asset like a building or a machine for rent it is up to the person getting the asset to decide how and when to use it. If he or she keeps the asset idle, the provider is still entitled to the rent even though the asset has not been productive. Similarly, if an employer does not assign any duty, the employee is still entitled to wages. In the same vein, if a person obtains finance for business but is unable to use it productively, the provider of the finance still remains entitled to receive interest. It is not consistent to single out finance for sharing the results and risks of the business while other resources can receive a fixed return irrespective of the business results.

Muslim economists have, generally, not looked into this inconsistency. As an exception Toutounchian (2009: 88, 102, 106, 107) has faced this question partially. He argues that even wages should not be fixed. As for capital, the worker should also share in the profit or loss. The argument makes the return on two factors of production (i.e. capital and labour) consistent but does not show how it will function in practice. Also, the author does not say anything about the rent of land, which is also predetermined and fixed.

Zaman (2009: 546) mentions the argument of Zamir Iqbal and Mirakhor which says that 'labor-owned firms would express the spirit of Islam better'.[2] However, there is no extensive debate on the subject in the literature. Restricting the Islamic position to only labour-owned firms would introduce unnecessary rigidity in the economic system, while there is no strong basis for this in the *Shari'ah*. Profit sharing does not have any Islamic basis. It is a secular concept and has been in vogue since ancient times because of the commercial needs of the people. Islam has not prescribed it.

A person who provides finance makes available a more useful asset as compared to a person who is providing a physical asset like building or machinery. The finance has the flexibility of being put to any use and for any length of time, but the physical asset can be used only for the limited purpose for which it has been made available. Thus the person who provides finance has a claim for interest that is more compelling than the claim for rent of a person who provides a physical asset.

e.   It is unfair to assume the probability of loss in all cases

There is a complete consensus among scholars of all shades and persuasions in Islam that the rationale for the prohibition of *riba* lies in the Qur'anic injunction: 'you will do no wrong, neither will you be wronged' (Q. 2:279). Thus injustice (*zulm*) is the *raison d'être* for the prohibition of *riba*. On this point the orthodox as well as the modernists agree. But orthodox scholars assume that all kinds of interest involve injustice (*zulm*). However, the assumption does not hold in all cases. In some cases, interest could be a cause of injustice (*zulm*); in other cases, interest is not.

For example, when a person deposits his or her savings with a bank to earn interest and the bank pays interest, there is no occasion to believe that either party (i.e. the saver or the bank) has committed an act of injustice. Both parties are better off. Similarly, when a business firm takes funds from a bank for investment, the interest is part of the profit that it earns with the help of the bank's capital. The probability of loss is a special case and not covered by the general situation. To the extent a business earns profit and pays interest neither of the parties commits injustice on the other. It is only when the firm goes insolvent and is unable to pay back the principal with interest that the likelihood of injustice arises. But these are exceptions. They do not justify extension of the probability of loss to all situations and then declaring that interest in all cases would be unjust. Examples where capital obtained on interest leads to a win–win situation can be multiplied. Treating all such situations similarly to the one where capital on interest leads to loss is not reasonable. In brief, the orthodox view has extended the prohibition of interest from a situation of actual injustice to all situations where injustice is a mere probability. The real-life situation is not like that. Most of the situations involving finance from banks do not involve loss (and thus injustice on the payment of interest). Making a small number of cases the main plank of the argument against interest and equating it with the injustice of the moneylender is not realistic.

The only situation where interest is always a source of injustice is when a poor person borrows money but is unable to repay on the due date. The addition of interest to capital in such cases may lead to a scenario where the person, who is already hard pressed to pay the principal sum, pays back more than the principal in the form of interest and yet has to pay the principal. The Qur'an (Q. 3:130) has aptly termed it as *riba* that is multiplied by many times the principal ('*ad'afan mud'afa*'). In such situations, the element of injustice is quite obvious and predominant. There is no doubt that interest in such situations would be treated as *riba*. But treating all other situations of interest on capital where it is not possible to demonstrate that either the debtor or the creditor has caused any injustice to the other as *riba* on the basis of a 'probability' of loss would not be reasonable.

f.   Interest involves gain with liability for loss
One of the arguments in favour of the prohibition of *riba* is derived from the following Tradition of the Prophet:

> Amr b. Shu'aib reported on the authority of his father, who narrated on the authority of his father: The messenger of God said: 'The sale of something

which is not in your possession is not lawful, *nor is the profit arising from something which does not involve liability* (to accept loss). (Ibn Majah, Muhammad b. Yazid. Kitab al-tijarah, ch. 20. *Sunan*. Cairo. AH 1313)

The second part of the above Tradition, that is, the entitlement to gain co-extending with acceptance of a possible loss in a sale transaction, is often cited as an argument against interest. It is argued that the lender of money on interest for business purposes seeks to make a gain from lending but does not accept any risk of loss in the business. Interest, in this case, therefore falls in the category of prohibited gains and is a form of *riba*. (See, for example, Ghazi 2008: 461.)

We think that the inference from the above Tradition is consistent with neither the application of the juridical rules at other places nor a precise understanding of the nature of interest in business finance. For example, classical as well as contemporary jurists accept sale on mark-up (*bai' al-murabaha*) as legitimate. In this form of sale, the seller gets a predetermined profit without accepting the liability of loss. There is no possibility of loss in it, as the profit is ensured. Similarly, it is also generally accepted (now) that the credit price can be higher than the cash price for the same product (e.g. al-Masri 2004: 40). The extra gain due to the credit sale over the spot sale does not involve any risk of loss. If we say that the risk of loss in this case is that the buyer may not pay on time or may not pay at all, such risks are present in the case of an interest-bearing business loan as well.

Secondly, it is also not precise to say that business loans from present-day banks do not involve any risk. It is possible that they have different types of risks. But the risks of non-payment, delayed payment, erosion in the value of money and so on are present in these loans as well. Therefore, to say that the interest is a risk-free gain is not a precise statement. It seems to be a remote inference from the above Tradition of the Prophet.

g. Is there an Islamic theory of exploitation?

As Farooq (2007) has pointed out quite aptly, there is no empirical evidence to show that interest of all kinds is exploitative and thus would be covered by the Qur'anic prohibition of *riba*. Muslim scholars who assert that interest of all types is *riba* have not undertaken any research to validate their assertion. In fact, we do not have an Islamic theory of exploitation, by which we mean a rigorously defined concept of 'exploitation' which can help us distinguish various situations as exploitative. In the absence of any such definition the whole debate remains subjective and polemical and not objective and conclusive.

11.1.2   The Financier Gets Something for Nothing

The second justification for the prohibition of interest as presented by orthodox scholars is as follows:

> In an interest-based loan transaction the creditor gets something in the form of interest without giving anything in return. It is unjust and unfair.

The argument is fallacious even if we accept all types of interest as *riba*. It is not true that in an interest-based loan the creditor is getting something for nothing. The creditor provides funds to the debtor. The funds are useful and valuable, which is why the debtor borrows them in the first place. However, the Qur'an has prohibited the taking of interest on loans for another reason. Lending is a charitable act, and Muslims should not charge a price for it. The *riba* is prohibited not because the lender has provided something useless to the debtor. It is because the lender is helping the debtor and thus undertaking an act of brotherhood, fraternity and cooperation. It is against universal human ethics to charge a price for that. There is no difference of opinion among Muslim scholars that 'the main objective of the *Shari'ah* is to establish a strong community with a stable social system' (Ibn Ashur 2006: 220). The prohibition of *riba* is in line with this primary objective of the *Shari'ah*.

11.1.3   Interest Income Encourages Idleness and Creates a Class of Parasites

> Dependence on interest income dissuades people from work and encourages reliance on unearned income. It encourages idleness and creates a class of people who like to make money without doing anything.

The argument comes into conflict with several other Islamic legal principles. Islam accepts situations where a person can acquire wealth without working for it. An obvious example is the inheritance that a person gets from a deceased relative. *Mudaraba* is another example where a person provides capital and gets income without actively working for the business. Similarly, the *Shari'ah* recognizes that the wealth of children, widows and old persons is invested in business by other people and these categories get a share in the profit. The argument will not make any sense if we replace the individual lender with a bank. Lending money on interest by a bank does not make the bank a 'work-shirker'.

11.1.4   Interest Leads to Exploitation of the Poor by the Rich

> Interest-bearing loans, in most cases, are provided by the rich to the poor,
> who are vulnerable and weak. The rich can exploit the needy poor because of
> the economic weakness of the latter.

The argument is valid when a poor person gets an interest-bearing loan
from a rich person, but it does not apply to situations where rich businessmen seek finance from commercial banks. Orthodox scholars extend the
definition of *riba* to all situations of financing although they cannot show
exploitation of the poor by the rich. Secondly, in the case of commercial
banks ordinary depositors are definitely poorer than the bank that uses
those funds. The present argument does not hold. Thirdly, the argument
becomes least plausible when we see poor widows, orphans, pensioners
and invalids, persons on interest income without which they would eat
away their savings and become destitute or dependants. In such situations
the whole argument would boil down to saying that these poor savers are
exploiting the banks and the governments (if they are saving with government saving centres). Does it make sense?

11.1.5   The Interest-Based Loan Treats Money as a Commodity

> Money is not an asset or a commodity. It is only a medium of exchange. A
> unit of money cannot be exchanged except for an equal value of the same
> currency. In the case of a loan, the lender extends the loan and gets back a
> larger amount than the principal sum lent. It is as if the lender treated money
> as a commodity and sold it or exchanged it for a sum larger than its face value.

Although several economists have delved into the above argument, a
recent and perhaps the most comprehensive enunciation is available at
Toutounchian (2009). A summary of his presentation is as follows:

> The prohibition of all types of interest emanates from the peculiar concept
> of money in Islam, where money is only a medium of exchange and a unit of
> measurement and not a store of value. Money is not an asset and any return
> for the use of money cannot be justified. Nor can we justify any increase on
> exchange of money for money. Once we accept that money is not an asset, the
> demand for money for speculative purposes becomes zero as Keynes has most
> ably argued that liquidity preference or demand for money as an asset is only
> for speculative purposes. Thus, not only interest is not justified, all types of
> speculation also become unjustified and illegitimate in the Islamic framework.
> As a logical corollary we should prohibit all types of speculation as well. (p. 75)

The argument is misplaced at best and unnecessary at worst. First, the
problem that if we accept money as a store of value or an asset we shall

have to concede a reward for its utilization, and hence the legitimacy of interest, ensues from a foregone conclusion that we have to prove that all types of interest are unfair and have to be prohibited. If we discard this a priori conclusion, common sense rejects the idea that money is not an asset. Possession of money gives a sense of well-being, a sort of confidence and feeling of security and an ability to help others because it is an asset. Once we argue that money is not an asset, psychologically the person feels denuded of all wealth and social status. How do we make ordinary people believe that this argument is real and substantive?

Second, the notion that if we accept money as an asset we shall have to concede the legitimacy of an unequal exchange of money for money is a baseless apprehension. Such an exchange is unnecessary if it is on an on-the-spot basis. The exchange of money for money is relevant only when one party pays now to get it back at a later date. In that event, the exchange could be equal or unequal depending upon the terms of the contract. In the case of the parties agreeing to exchange money for money with one party delivering later but in an unequal quantity, the increase or decrease arises owing to the time involved and not because the money is an asset. It is the time value of money that leads to the inequality in the exchange of money for money. It is not because money is an asset.

Third, if money is not a store of value, the question arises: what is the justification for charging *zakah* on money? There has never been a difference of opinion among *Shari'ah* scholars that cash balances at the end of a year are subject to *zakah*. This is also supported by the text of Traditions of the Prophet on the subject. Once we argue that money is not an asset, we shall have to contrive some other justification for levying *zakah* on cash balances. This is an unnecessary effort and has no basis in the *Shari'ah*.

Fourth, in modern business accounting all values are one of these categories: assets, liabilities, incomes, expenses or funds. If cash balances of a business are not assets, how do we propose to record them in the accounts? We shall have to develop an entirely new accounting category just to accommodate our self-styled concept of money.

Fifth, the proponents of the argument have to take the primary assertion to its logical conclusion and declare all types of speculation unjustified and un-Islamic. However, declaring speculation as unlawful in Islam does not have any basis. Speculation is the basis of all business decisions. All acts of buying and selling are based on some form of speculation. The buyer or seller speculates on some gain or profit from a transaction before deciding to deal in it. Once we declare all speculation un-Islamic we have the unpleasant job of differentiating between speculation and business decisions. At this point, the argument against speculation becomes fuzzy and involved, leaving the reader wondering where trade ends and speculation starts.

In sum, the argument of declaring money as not being a store of value is misplaced, leading from one baseless assertion to the next and ending in a quagmire of fuzzy thoughts. We think the argument is unnecessary. There is no need to contrive it, as it is based on an assertion that is against common sense as well as other injunctions of Islam. Money is an asset (or a store of value) and a unit of measurement, and its primary function is also to serve as a medium of exchange. To establish that interest on loans is prohibited we need not get into the definition and functions of money. Interest on loans is prohibited for ethical reasons and not because money has a different function in the Islamic economy as against the capitalist economy.

11.1.6 Money is Unproductive; Charging a Price for its Use is Unfair

> Money is sterile and unproductive. By itself it is of no use until it is transformed into real assets. Charging a price for a sterile asset is unfair.

This argument has its roots in Christian Catholic thinking, which itself was based on the Aristotelian theory of the 'sterile commodity' and has no basis in the *Shari'ah*. In the Islamic *Shari'ah* only productive or 'potentially productive' wealth (*mal nami*) is subject to *zakah*. There is a consensus that idle cash is subject to *zakah*. How could this be justified if money is sterile?

11.1.7 A Return is Justified When Money is Productive

An oft-quoted argument of orthodox scholars is that money lent on interest is only potentially productive. It will become productive only when it is actually converted into physical assets and put to use. Until that stage comes, it is premature to ask a return on the finance provided by a bank. Only when money is actually invested and turns out to be productive can the bank claim a return on it. Many orthodox scholars have made this point. A recent and comprehensive exposition is available at Toutounchian (2009). He writes: 'The sum of money supplied to benefit from interest in the money market may or may not go into the "adventure" of investment' (p. 136).

It is true that the results of business operations can be seen only after some time and not at the time of getting finance from the bank. However, as in everyday life, most business decisions are made in the present; the results will ensue only in the future, which is uncertain and unknown.

When a business firm purchases a product for sale, it is unknown whether the product will sell for a profit or not. Yet business firms take hundreds of decisions on a daily basis and are unsure about their outcome. They take these decisions after calculating the risks. The same is the case when a business enterprise approaches a bank with a request for finance. The firm must have calculated its risk. Saying that finance so obtained may not go into actual investment raises the question: why would a firm request finance from a bank if it did not intend to invest it? Business firms request finance from a bank only after calculating all the risks and with the confidence of making gains. They would never try to get finance from a bank if the probability of loss were higher than the probability of gain. It is very much like hundreds of other business decisions that firms make. All those decisions have the approval of orthodox scholars except the decision to obtain finance from the bank. The argument is not consistent.

11.1.8   The Debt Does Not Grow

> Since the debt does not grow there is no justification for returning a higher amount after a period.

An oft-repeated argument against interest is that by its very nature the debt cannot grow. For example, Kahf (2005: 4) says: 'A debt is, by definition and by its nature, incapable of growing or increasing because it is purely conceptual; it is a relationship between a person and another person.'

The argument is shallow. The debt can grow. A person can borrow money and then use it productively to earn a profit on it. There is nothing inherently impossible about this. If Islam prohibits the charging of interest on a loan it is not because the loan cannot grow. It is because interest on a loan flouts the Islamic spirit of brotherhood and social harmony.

11.2   THE DYSFUNCTIONAL ROLE OF INTEREST

Orthodox scholars take another route to justify the prohibition of interest. They try to argue that the *Shari'ah* has prohibited interest because it plays a negative role in the economy. We do not want to discuss the advantages and disadvantages of interest in the economy. However, we would present the arguments of orthodox scholars against interest and see how far they are based on robust reasoning.

11.2.1 Interest and Need Fulfilment

> Interest through a route of easy access to credit for unproductive purposes
> squeezes the availability of resources for need fulfilment.

Chapra (2006: 99) has discussed this point at length. Briefly the argument is that interest-based credit enables borrowing with ease for unproductive and wasteful purposes, which reduces the available funds for development and thus the basic needs of the population remain unfulfilled. There is no doubt that improper priority in the use of resources can lead to such a situation, but blaming it on interest is rather far-fetched. There is no way to show, in the absence of any empirical evidence, that financing on the basis of profit–loss sharing would not lead to this mismatch of priorities. Public sector planning is not driven by considerations of interest and availability of funds from banks. It is a complex mechanism and has to do with a large number of political, economic, social, cultural and, of course, financial considerations. It is a gross oversimplification to argue that, since there is interest in the banking system, so funds are being squeezed for development and hence needs are not being fulfilled.

The contrary evidence is more compelling. The developed countries of the OECD are deeply entrenched in interest-based finance. These countries are meeting the basic needs of their citizens in an adequate manner. The percentage of poor people in these countries is quite small. If interest had played its avowed role in these countries, there would have been an acute mismatch of public priorities and financing by banks, and the level of poverty would have been significantly higher. The facts are quite different and speak loudly for the superficiality of the argument about the alleged negative role of interest.

A related strand of this argument is that the burden of debt servicing in poor and developing countries takes away a significant segment of public resources, leaving inadequate funds for development and need fulfilment. Rich countries and multilateral lending institutions like the World Bank, the International Monetary Fund and so on lend money on interest to poor countries, which keep repaying the loans but the burden does not decrease. Ultimately, the poor countries start borrowing money to repay the existing loans, creating a situation where the net flow of funds is from poor to rich countries. The argument is supported by statistics of negative fund flows, which have been aptly phrased as a 'financial haemorrhage'. The argument is plausible so far as the burden of interest payments is concerned. However, it is not known, owing to lack of adequate empirical evidence, what would be the burden of Islamic finance if a country resorted to financing through Islamic modes. There is a consensus among

Muslim economists that Islamic finance would not be free. It would also have a cost, determined in whatever manner. Would this cost not burden the public exchequers of the countries availing themselves of this finance? What would be its impact on the overall allocation of resources and on the availability of these resources for need fulfilment? These questions lack answers, as empirical data do not yet exist.

A deeper issue is the whole mechanism of borrowing funds from international donors for development purposes and then wasting those resources through mismanagement, fraud and corruption. It is now well known that the leaders and bureaucracy of poor countries are the actual beneficiaries of the public debt, leaving their economies in a state that cannot discharge their obligations. Had the borrowed funds been used with due diligence and honesty, they would have generated enough resources for repayment. In most cases, the poor countries borrowed money for the sake of development projects or to meet balance-of-payments needs. The ultimate aim was, and it was duly justified at the time of borrowing, that the funds would be used prudently, and would generate enough surplus to repay the principal with interest. Only when they make a plausible business case for such financing are they able to get money from the financiers. Now what happens to these funds? Many countries misuse these funds. Their leaders misappropriate the funds or siphon them off to their personal accounts. *The Economist* (London, 14 March 2009) quotes a report by Global Witness (11 March 2009) titled 'Undue diligence: How banks do business with corrupt regimes'. *The Economist* (ibid.) distils the report as follows:

> The authors note some striking cases of financiers colluding with tyrants. In 2001 Britain's banking regulator found that 23 banks in London had handled $1.3 billion of some $3 billion–$5 billion looted by Sani Abacha, a Nigerian despot. Five years ago a venerable American institution, Riggs Bank (where Abe Lincoln once banked), collapsed after a Senate inquiry revealed that Augusto Pinochet of Chile and Obiang Nguema, the long-serving president of Equatorial Guinea, had stashed millions in private accounts, with no proper questions asked. Mr Nguema admitted he had put state funds in a private account, but said he did so to keep it 'safe' from thieves. Barclays, which was shown by the report to be doing business with members of Mr Nguema's family, told Global Witness that it was not prepared to discuss its dealings with individual clients; the bank added, however, that it always takes care to follow 'globally applicable anti-money laundering policies'.

In sum, it is not fair to blame interest as the culprit. It is the corrupt regimes and their unscrupulous rulers who create situations of negative flow of funds.[3]

11.2.2   Interest Leads to Lower Investment and Higher Unemployment

The argument is summed up by Chapra (2006: 101) as follows:

> real high rates of interest . . . have been one of the major factors responsible
> for low rates of rise in investment and economic growth. These low rates
> have joined hands with structural rigidities and some other factors to raise
> unemployment.

An oversimplified translation of the above argument is as follows. An increase in the rates of interest discourages entrepreneurs and dampens their perceptions about the profitability of investment. In response they cut down on new investment and on expansion and renovation of existing plant and equipment. Ultimately, it translates into lower employment rates. The theory, based on Keynesian economics, is generally accepted in macroeconomics. However, what is missing in this argument is the fact that even Islamic finance comes with a cost. We do not yet know with certainty the effect of Islamic finance on the level of investment and employment. Sufficient data are not yet available to show that the abolition of interest and implementation of Islamic finance will actually lead to optimum growth and full employment. In the absence of such evidence the argument that interest leads to unemployment, and Islamic finance would not, is merely an assertion.

Chapra (2006: 102) continues:

> A decline in government and private sector wasteful spending may, perhaps,
> be the most promising way of promoting savings and productive investment.
> This may not, however, be possible when the value system encourages both the
> public and private sectors to live beyond their means, and the interest-based
> financial intermediation makes this possible by making credit available rela-
> tively easily without sufficient regard to the end use.

It is obvious from the above that the causal relationship of interest and wasteful expenditure is not quite straightforward. It has much to do with the value system of the society as well. To support part of the argument made above by Chapra, we should like to add that developed countries maintain and display a high degree of financial discipline because of their value system and the institutional framework. Interest-based finance has not introduced financial indiscipline in these countries. It would be a gross oversimplification to assert that interest-based finance has been instrumental in promoting financial indiscipline in poor countries, where actually the political system, top management style, value system of the society and weak oversight and accountability mechanisms have been responsible for it. If interest-based finance has played any role in promoting financial indiscipline in poor countries, we need to validate the assertion with real-life data.

Implicitly, the argument presumes an ideal Islamic society where people would live according to their means and not indulge in excessive borrowing for consumption purposes. Most of the financing would be for productive purposes. It is difficult to pick an argument with this point of view on a theoretical basis, but obviously this is a romantic view of the world and has nothing to do with reality.

11.2.3   Interest Distorts the Distribution of Income and Wealth

Another rationale for the prohibition of interest presented by orthodox scholars is as follows. The major criterion for approving a financing request followed by financial institutions is the ability of the enterprise to present suitable collateral. They do not attach much weight to the profitability of the project if the enterprise is unable to present the collateral. Consequently, most commercial credit flows to rich people because they can present the collateral. The smaller and potentially more profitable projects are unable to get finance because of their inability to present the collateral. Ultimately, the resources flow to the already rich, neglecting the smaller firms which may have more promising business proposals (Chapra 2006: 103). The argument is quite plausible and the available data on the distribution of banks' funds, particularly in developing countries, supports the conclusion. However, the question as to whether Islamic finance would be available in larger quantities to smaller business firms in preference to the rich has yet to be answered on the basis of empirical evidence. There is nothing to show that this has happened in the case of Islamic banks, which have been in business now for over 35 years.

M.T. Uthmani (1999-b: 43) has framed the orthodox argument in another manner as stated below:

> If the entrepreneurs having only ten million of their own acquire 90 million from the banks and embark on a huge profitable enterprise, it means that 90 percent of the projects are created by the money of the depositors while only 10 percent was generated by their own capital. If these huge projects bring enormous profits, only a small proportion (of interest which normally ranges between two percent to ten percent in different countries) will go to the depositors whose input in the projects was 90 percent while all the rest will be secured by the big entrepreneurs whose real contribution to the projects was not more than 10 percent. Even this small proportion given to the depositors is taken back by these big entrepreneurs, because all the interest paid by them is included in the cost of their production and comes back to them through the increased prices. The net result in this case is that all the profits of the big enterprises are earned

by the persons whose own financial inputs do not exceed 10 percent of the total investment, while the people whose financial contribution was as high as 90 percent get nothing in real terms, because the amount of interest given to them is often repaid by them through increased prices of the products, and therefore, in a number of cases the return received by them becomes negative in real terms.

The above argument will make a valid case against interest-based finance and in support of profit–loss sharing if it can be shown that in the Islamic economy a similar situation would not happen. In the Islamic economy, what will stop the entrepreneurs from getting 90 per cent financing from the banks? What will stop the entrepreneurs from including the share of profit paid to the financier in the prices of goods? Will the Islamic economy have an ideal competitive market? The above is an example of simplistic arguments justifying the prohibition of interest and cannot hold in the absence of any empirical evidence. In fact, if there is empirical evidence at all, it is contrary to what Uthmani has speculated. Seibel (2007: 2–3) has documented the performance of an Islamic bank in Iran and has concluded that in 2003–04 most of the finance was provided to big borrowers.

The argument that interest leads to gross inequalities in the distribution of income and wealth is quite popular with Islamic scholars. However, empirical evidence to show that interest income does create these inequalities is notably lacking. There is no significant and rigorously argued study, of either Muslim or non-Muslim countries, showing that interest is causing or contributing to inequalities of income and wealth. In fact, the empirical evidence could even point in the reverse direction. For example, the interest income of small savers through national saving schemes in Pakistan helps alleviate poverty to some extent. If poor people do not have this avenue to invest their savings on interest, they would not be able to invest these savings on 'profit' in any business and would thus be worse off. Interest is making the existing inequality of income a little less painful.

11.2.4   Interest Leads to Economic Instability

Chapra (2006: 104) argues that interest-based finance is a major contributing factor in creating economic instability. He says:

> There are a number of internal and external factors that cause volatility in the financial markets. . . . One of these is the excessive build-up of public and private debt as a result of relatively easy access to credit, particularly short-term credit, in an interest-based system of financial intermediation, where the lender tends to rely more on the crutches of collateral than on the strength of the project.

In a later paper Chapra (2008-b: 122) expands this argument. He contends that, in an ideal situation, Islamic finance promotes greater financial discipline, as the financier and the entrepreneur both assess the risk in a profit–loss-sharing environment. The argument would hold only if we were to replace interest by profit–loss sharing. In practice, Islamic financial institutions have not found it feasible to do so. Chapra argues that the fixed-return modes of finance like *murabaha* and *ijara* also promote greater stability because they are tied to real assets and are not merely the sale of debts. To the extent that a debt created by *murabaha* or *ijara* terminates at its maturity with the first creditor and debtor, the argument is sound and realistic. However, the whole cycle of sale of debt will emerge in the Islamic economy as well when we allow the sale of debt created by *murabaha* or *ijara*. If we do not allow it there will be no secondary market for these debts in the Islamic economy. It means we are conceiving a rigid market where investors will not like to tie their funds. In this age, no economy can function without a secondary market for financial assets. How do we solve that problem in the Islamic economy?

Secondly, it is yet to be established that the availability of short-term finance in the Islamic framework would be more restrictive than under the interest-based system, since multiple factors, other than the rate of interest, shape the perceptions of the bank and influence its decision-making process. Moreover, if under the Islamic system it is more difficult to get short-term finance, we need to study how it would affect the economy as a whole. Will it not introduce rigidities in commerce and trade?

Thirdly, Chapra's position that interest leads to economic instability can be defended only if it is shown that an economy that is not based on interest is more stable than one based on interest. However, it is not possible to do so, as we do not have empirical evidence for that. On the contrary, we can say that the rate of interest in Japan has been close to zero during the last decade or so. But the Japanese economy met with similar financial jerks to the economies of the US and Europe during the financial breakdowns of 2008 and 2009. Being interest-free did not help Japan in the least in this regard (Askari, Iqbal, Krichene and Mirakhor 2010: 39).

The fact is that volatility in the financial markets takes place because of the speculation and perceptions of market players. Interest could also be a contributing factor, though it would require more extensive research to prove the validity of this assertion. We would need to delineate the contribution of each factor in creating financial instability and determine precisely the role played by interest-based finance.

Mirakhor and Krichene (2009: 40–50) forcefully build a case on the basis of Keynesian theory that the capitalist system propelled by interest-based credit is inherently unstable. Business firms contract debt on interest. To the extent that they deploy the debt capital in business and generate an income stream, the system remains stable. However, in practice it does not stop at that. The debt instruments are traded in the secondary market and create several layers of debt as they change hands. Consequently, the size of the debt multiplies with respect to the underlying asset which generates income, but all the other layers of the debt are not income-generating. The multiplication of debt as compared to the underlying real asset generates credit bubbles, which burst when it becomes unsustainable to service all the debts.

The above explanation by Mirakhor and Krichene is realistic. However, the culprit in this mechanism is not interest-based debt but secondary markets for financial instruments. If the financial instruments are held till maturity the debt bubbles would not emerge. However, the secondary market for financial instruments is a real-life need of the business. Even if we eliminate interest, as the proponents of Islamic finances profess, the alternative instruments of finance such as *sukuk* and other Islamic bonds would also require a secondary market. But Islamic finance in its pristine form does not have and cannot have a secondary market. Efforts to create a secondary market for Islamic financial instruments have ended up in a host of ruses, compromises and stratagems.[4] It is not financing on interest that is the source of instability. It is the secondary market of financial instruments that creates instability. The question arises: are Muslim economists recommending that in this age they would like to compete with conventional finance without having recourse to a secondary market for Islamic financial instruments? If so, they will have to create some mechanism to persuade genuine investors to offer capital on Islamic terms. Most of the investors will not be willing to bind themselves for long periods of time without a way to redeem the capital freely. Alternatively, the case of economic stability can be established if we are able to ensure a smooth-functioning economy without a secondary market for the financial assets.

Mirakhor and Krichene (2009: 40–50) argue that at least theoretically it is possible to say that the Islamic economic system, which is based on equity capital and not debt capital, is more stable than the capitalist system. However, they argue that for such a system to exist there has to be a strong institutional framework, which they call the 'scaffolding' of the system. The institutional framework that they refer to consists of various injunctions of the Qur'an and *Sunnah* relating to property rights, honesty, contract fulfilment, production and distribution of wealth, allocation of resources, and so on. They argue that the institutional framework of Islam ensures a stable economy. They write:

There can be little doubt that with such a strongly rules-based framework based on faithfulness to contracts and a strong prohibition against taking interest, lying, cheating and other fraudulent activities, the financial system of Islam would be transparent, efficient and informationally trouble-free. For example, consider the implications of full operationalization of only one element of Islam's institutional scaffolding – that is, the first verse of Chapter 5 of the *Qur'an*: the rule of faithfully abiding by the terms and conditions stipulated by a contract to which one is a party. Its full implications are nothing short of astounding. No one would need fear that a contract would not be performed as a result of lying, cheating, fraud or negligence. Imagine the efficiency gains in such a system; there would be no monitoring costs, no risk of moral hazard or adverse selection, and a minimal cost of transaction in contracting.

Implicitly, they are assuming a society that consists of ideal Muslims. Not only does such a society not exist anywhere, but the comparison with the capitalist system is also misplaced. Does the capitalist economy prescribe cheating, fraud, non-fulfilment of contracts, or injustice? We come across these practices in the behaviour of people. There cannot be any guarantee that Muslims would not behave in this manner. Thus it is an attempt to score a point without any basis in real life.

In another persuasive formulation, Askari, Iqbal and Mirakhor (2010: 89) argue that the concept of two-window operation in Islamic banking makes it more stable. The deposits of an Islamic bank consist of two types: (a) current account deposits backed by a 100 per cent reserve; (b) investment deposits for investment in the real sector with depositors sharing the return with the bank. There is no credit creation by a stroke of the pen and out of thin air. Each financing operation leads to the creation of real assets, goods and services. There is no creation and multiplication of debt from debt. Savings are equal to investment. Aggregate supply is equal to aggregate demand. Tangible real assets owned directly cover the financial liabilities of the financial institutions. Thus, theoretically, it is not possible for banks to proliferate debts and create a situation that is unsustainable, should there be a downturn in the economy. The argument is persuasive theoretically. However, it is based on the concept of profit sharing, which has serious limitations in practice, as we show in Chapter 18. The argument, therefore, despite being theoretically sound, has a limited practical application.

Habib Ahmed (2009: 18) has discussed the causes and impact of the 2008 financial crisis. He argues that the position of the proponents of Islamic finance regarding greater financial stability is not tenable. Islamic financial institutions have gradually moved toward practices which are quite similar to those of conventional finance. In doing so, they have exposed themselves to the same dangers of instability as conventional financial institutions have. He writes (p. 19):

When the practice of Islamic finance and the environment under which it operates are examined, one can identify trends that are similar to the ones that caused the current crisis. At the institutional level, the regulatory standards for the Islamic financial sector are in elementary stages, weak and still evolving. Thus, the regulatory restraints on Islamic financial institutions are expected to be no better than their conventional counterparts. At the organizational level, it is difficult to prevent excessive profit seeking and risk taking in Islamic banks unless their Boards of Directors and management impose prudent risk-management practices. In the recent past, the Gulf region has witnessed its own episodes of speculation in their stock and real estate markets. Finally, the Islamic financial industry has witnessed rapid growth with innovations of complex *Shari'ah* compliant financial products. Risks in these new Islamic financial products are complex, as the instruments have multiple types of risks, and they evolve and change at different stages of the transactions.

Hassan and Kayed (2009: 52) argue that the global financial crisis of 2008 has not left the Islamic economies unscathed. They write:

> Although Islamic finance has not felt 'the full impact' of the global credit crisis, the immediate fallout from the crisis is evidenced by the fall in equity valuations and the plunge in the real estate market across the Gulf States with all that entails for the Islamic banking sector – bearing in mind the intense engagement of the Islamic banking sector in the real estate industry (Richter, 2008;[5] Khalaf, 2009[6]). The fall in property prices in the Gulf States is therefore a cause of major concern for Islamic banking, given the asset-based nature of Islamic finance, where real estate is the preferred instrument to protect these investments (Singh, 2009[7]). According to Standard & Poor's (S&P), the Islamic financial sector has also suffered a sharp decrease in the value of *sukuk* ... issued in the year 2008 to the sum of about $15.5 billion, down from about $47.1 billion in 2007 (Khalaf, 2009; 'Malaysia leads in Islamic finance', 2009).

It shows that, if interest-based finance has seeds of instability, the Islamic alternative is no better.

11.2.5 The Enigma of a Zero Rate of Interest: The Japanese Case

After putting all the blame on credit expansion out of thin air and excessive expansion of credit, Askari *et al.* (2010) argue that low interest rates are the cause of financial instability, as they make credit available so easily. They cite the example of the Bank of Japan, which had kept the rates of interest close to zero since 1999 (p. 39), and also other major central banks which had kept interest rates low and even negative in real terms in 2001–06 (p. 48). They say:

> With respect to the role of central banks, the Bank of Japan has kept interest rates near zero since 1999. This was a source for the creation of international

liquidity, generously fed by the Japanese yen carry-trade (borrowing in yen and lending in higher yielding currency). The same policy of low interest rates and liquidity creation was adopted by both the European Union Central Bank and the Bank of England. This monetary laxity in leading industrial countries fueled commodity price inflation and housing speculation, pushed massive loans to subprime markets and finally precipitated a severe financial crisis in 2007. (p. 39)

During the years 2001–06, major central banks kept interest rates low, and, sometimes, even negative in real terms. For example, the US federal funds rate was rapidly lowered from 5.5 percent in early 2001 and set at 1 percent during the period 2003M7–2004M6; the Euro interbank rate was kept below 2.5 percent during the period 2003M5 to 2005M12; Japan's mcall-money rate was near zero, at 0.01 percent, during the period 2001M4–2006M6; and LIBOR fell below 1.5 percent during 2002M11–2004M4. (p. 48)

In brief, the argument is that the Bank of Japan artificially kept the monetary rate of interest below the natural rate of interest. In this argument, the culprit is a low or zero rate of interest. This is really a confusing situation. If Muslim economists stand for the elimination of interest they should welcome Japan's having done that. They should study the beneficial aspects of this policy. Instead, they are now arguing that the zero rate of interest in Japan has been a source of financial instability. What is their final position vis-à-vis interest? Do they want to eliminate it or retain it? Any reduction, even a percentage point, in the rate of interest should logically be closer to their objective of ushering in an interest-free era and they should welcome it. However, they are taking a topsy-turvy position by advocating higher rates of interest. This is highly confusing.

They are arguing that capital should come at a cost, and at a high cost, so that there is no uncontrolled expansion of credit in the economy. It means they would like to retain the natural rate of interest anyway,[8] even though they might, artificially, eliminate the monetary rate of interest. The so-called profit–loss-sharing rate[9] would replace the monetary rate of interest, and the economic effect of this rate vis-à-vis the natural rate of interest would be the same as that of the monetary rate of interest. It means that, if for any reason the profit-sharing rate goes below the natural rate of interest, the economy will experience expansion and inflation, and if it goes higher than the natural rate of interest it will set in motion deflation. If this is the line of argument, then they are only changing the semantics. They are only replacing the monetary rate of interest with the profit–loss-sharing rate without much insight as to how it will be determined and what will be its behaviour. The rest of the capitalist system stays.

11.2.6　*Riba*-Based Finance and Overuse of Natural Resources

One of the arguments against interest-based finance is that it leads to the deterioration of natural resources, as the poor countries overstretch themselves to service their debts. M.N. Siddiqi (2007: 5) explains how it works:

> On the level of the economy as a whole, the compulsion for economic growth is created by the fact that the total amount to be repaid is invariably larger than the total amount obtained through loans and this has devastating consequences. It leads to overuse of natural resources and is very destructive of the environment. Since the increased payment must also follow a timetable, it increases anxiety levels by enforcing rigid timetables all around. It is also one of the factors leading to commercialization of almost all spheres of life, including family relations, education and health care as these spheres too come under debt-financing with its compulsions of repayment with an addition at an appointed time.

This is about interest-based finance. However, the same question is valid about Islamic finance as well. An entrepreneur who gets money from an Islamic bank remains under pressure to create more than the amount he took from the bank. He cannot be comfortable at declaring losses. The profit motive and desire to create more wealth than one has invested are inherent in human nature. They are not generated by interest-based finance. Other effects of interest mentioned in the above quotation are also true for Islamic finance, as it does not come without a cost. There is no evidence to show that eliminating interest and adopting Islamic modes of finance will not create similar effects to those visualized by Siddiqi in an interest-based financial system.

11.2.7　Interest-Based Finance and Objectives of the *Shari'ah* (*Maqasid al-Shari'ah*)

Siddiqi (2009-a: 188–237) discusses the question of prohibition of *riba* in the broader context of the objectives of the *Shari'ah* (*maqasid al-Shari'ah*). It is not possible to reproduce the whole argument in as explicit detail as Siddiqi has done himself. A crude and oversimplified summary of the argument is as follows. According to him, the *Shari'ah* objectives focus on two main requirements: (a) fairness in financial dealings, eliminating all those practices which could lead to injustice to any party in a deal; (b) the return on capital being related to the performance of the capital. In the simplest form it means the capital and enterprise should be closely aligned. The finance provider should have a close and direct relationship with the economic activity. The finance should be utilized to procure assets which should lead to real economic activity.

However, the argument goes, in the capitalist system the direct relationship between finance and underlying assets soon gives way to sale and purchase of mere paper financial claims, not related to the actual business activity. In the first instance, though, the interest-bearing finance may be used to acquire assets, but soon the certificate of debt is sold in the money market for ready cash. The buyer of the certificate, in turn, sells the certificate to another party. Thus a sequence of sale and purchase of the debt certificates takes place, moving each subsequent buyer and seller away from the underlying asset which originated the debt in the first instance. As the activity gets going, the original debt which financed the asset generates many multiples of its value in the form of debts. An inverted pyramid of debts comes into being. The activity in the money market gets detached from the original capital that financed the underlying asset. The gains and losses of the buyers and sellers of the debt instruments lose all relationship with the performance of the underlying asset. People can lose or gain not as a result of any real business activity but by mere dynamics of the money market.

In addition to the detachment of gains and losses from the real business activity, the money market is a potential risk to the stability of the entire system. To the extent everyone honours his or her commitments in the money market, business continues as normal. But, as happens quite often, some stakeholders in this inverted pyramid default because of either their own bad management or market compulsions. The inverted pyramid comes crumbling down, leading to financial crisis which sometimes threatens the entire global financial system. The *Shari'ah* has forestalled such eventualities by aligning the return on finance with its actual performance. It does not allow the sale of debts at a value other than the face value, which eventually means it does not allow the sale of debts at all.

Siddiqi's case is formidable. It is difficult to disagree with his analysis. However, he turns an oblique eye toward an equally fundamental question. The discounting of trade debts is a business need. Practically, business firms cannot remain in business if they do not have a mechanism to get their accounts receivable discounted for cash. Given the situation that the debts cannot be sold, no financial institution would encash the accounts receivable. That creates a situation where a business firm genuinely needs cash but cannot get it as it has blocked its revenue in receivables. How can this firm convert its receivables into cash? It means there has to be some mechanism for encashing the receivables. But no bank would do it at par with the face value of the receivables. Once we open this door, we allow the entire cycle of the capitalist money market to enter the Islamic money market, leading to the same consequences as interest-bearing conventional finance would lead us to. If we do not allow discounting of the debts, we will make the Islamic business firms non-competitive as compared to their non-Muslim competitors. They would be beaten out of the global market. Obviously, this could also not be the objective of the *Shari'ah*.

11.3   CONCLUDING REMARKS

We have summarized various explanations presented by Muslim economists for prohibition of interest. One set of explanations attempts to rationalize the prohibition of interest but these explanations are weak and cannot be defended. The second set consists of arguments that highlight dysfunctional aspects of interest in the economy. There is no doubt that interest has several negative implications for the economy, but humanity has not been able to find a better solution for financing investments, as we shall explain later in this book. The criticism on interest stems from the fact that it is a fixed and predetermined charge on capital, irrespective of the fact that the business enterprise ends up in profit or loss after using the capital taken on interest. The argument would have weight if we could show that the Islamic alternative is significantly different from this. The profit–loss sharing which is the ideal alternative has inherent operational problems. Islamic financial institutions have devised a long list of financing techniques which end up in a fixed charge on capital. In pure economic terms the impact of interest and the so-called Islamic modes of finance remains the same. In both cases the business enterprise availing itself of finance from a financial institution bears a fixed cost, give it whatever name you will. The economic impact cannot be different in both cases. Therefore all the dysfunctional aspects of interest highlighted by Muslim economists would have a similar presence in the case of an Islamic economy where finance is available through various 'Islamic modes' of finance but with a fixed predetermined cost.

The question arises: what then is the rationale for prohibition of *riba* in Islam? Our answer is that *riba* has been prohibited on purely moral grounds. *Riba* discourages people from the ethical behaviour of helping others and encourages an attitude of selfishness and indifference. This is the primary reason for the prohibition of *riba*. It does not allow extension of the definition of *riba* to financing transactions bearing interest where both parties deal with a view to undertaking a profit-making deal. The party that obtains funds invests those funds and the party that gives those funds gets a return for providing those funds. There is no selfishness on the part of either of them. The argument provides little justification for extending the definition to interest on transactions of financing and investment.

Muhammad Asad (1980: 622–623) has illustrated this point quite aptly:

> Roughly speaking, the opprobrium of *riba* (in the sense in which this term is used in the Qur'an and in many sayings of the Prophet) attaches to profits obtained through interest-bearing loans involving an *exploitation of the economically weak by the strong and the resourceful*: an exploitation characterized by the fact that the lender, while retaining full ownership of the capital loaned and having no legal concern with the purpose for which it is to be used or with the manner of its use, remains *contractually* assured of gain irrespective of any losses which the borrower may suffer in consequence of this transaction. With this definition in mind, we realize that the question as to what kinds of financial transactions fall within the category of *riba* is, in the last resort, a moral one, closely connected with the socio-economic motivation underlying the mutual relationship of borrower and lender; and stated in purely economic terms, it is a question as to how profits and risks may be equitably shared by *both* partners to a loan transaction. It is, of course, impossible to answer this double question in a rigid, once-for-all manner: our answers must necessarily vary in accordance with the changes to which man's social and technological development – and, thus, his economic development – is subject.

In the final analysis, prohibition of *riba* is a moral question. The type of society Islam aimed to build rested on the foundations of unity of faith and mutual cooperation and brotherhood. In such a society lending is a charitable act by a Muslim brother for another Muslim. In this society, charging interest on a loan was a shame, an immoral act to be abhorred and abandoned. However, some people in the days of the Prophet had made lending on interest their business. That was prohibited by the Qur'an as *riba*. Lending should remain a charitable act, and the creditor should not earn a return on the sum lent. However, the Qur'an did not make it obligatory upon wealthy people to offer a loan in all cases. It was a purely voluntary act. But, if a loan was to be extended, it must be without interest. Whether the above straightforward explanation covers situations where capital is provided for financing and investment will be discussed in Chapter 16.

NOTES

1. The paper was originally presented to the *Shari'ah* Appellate Bench of the Supreme Court of Pakistan. It is a modified version of M.U. Chapra, *Future of economics: An Islamic perspective* (Leicester: Islamic Foundation, 2000), pp. 5–20.
2. Based on Zamir Iqbal and Abbas Mirakhor, The stakeholders' model of governance in an Islamic economic system, *Islamic Economic Studies* 11 (2) (2004), pp. 43–63.
3. For more information on the stolen wealth of corrupt rulers, visit the official website of the Basel Institute on Governance, which publishes information on stolen assets and their recovery (http://www.baselgovernance.org/big).

4. See Chapter 20 for details.
5. [As in original] F. Richter, Islamic finance is no longer immune to crisis, 2008, retrieved 8 January 2008 from www.reuters.com/article/ousiv/idUSTRE4B21UM 20081203.
6. [As in original] R. Khalaf, Islamic finance must resolve inner tensions, *Financial Times*, 5 April 2009, retrieved 10 April 2009 from www.sukuk.net/news/ articles/1/.
7. [As in original] H. Singh, Liquidity squeeze hits Islamic finance, *Islamic Finance Asia*, 6 May 2009, retrieved 19 May 2009 from http://islamicfinanceasia.blogspot.co.uk/2009/05/liquidity-squeeze-hits-islamic-finance.html.
8. Originally pleaded by H. Thornton, *An inquiry into the nature and effects of paper credit of Great Britain*, ed. F.R. von Hayek (New York: Rinehart, 1802). Later on Knut Wicksell (1898) expanded this theory in *Interest and prices*, trans. and ed. R.F. Kahn (London: Macmillan, 1936; reprinted New York: A.M. Kelly, 1965).
9. Rigorously speaking profit sharing is a ratio and not a rate, but intuitively it can be seen that whatever return capital earns through the profit-sharing ratio can be converted into a rate easily.

12. Modernist thinking on *riba*

12.1 VIEWS OF EGYPTIAN SCHOLARS

We find the earliest reference to modernist thinking on *riba* in the ideas of Muhammad Abduh (1849–1905), the Grand Mufti of Egypt in 1899–1905. Abduh issued certain verdicts during his lifetime on the question of *riba*. His pupil Rashid Rida (1865–1935) elaborated his writings, though at times it becomes difficult to tell if a certain idea derived from Muhammad Abduh or was a brainchild of the pupil. Rashid Rida held that the prohibition of *riba* in the Qur'an belonged to only a compound rate of interest and not to a simple rate of interest (Khalil and Thomas 2006: 71). Badawi (2000) has discussed the views of Muhammad Abduh and Rashid Rida in detail. His conclusion is that Muhammad Abduh never explicitly decreed that contemporary commercial interest is permissible. It was Rashid Rida who, after the death of Muhammad Abduh, elaborated his ideas and concluded that the prohibited *riba* was the one in vogue during the times of the Prophet. Contemporary interest on commercial loans was not *riba*, as it did not fall in the prohibited category.

Abd al-Razzaq al-Sanhuri (1895–1971), the architect of the Egyptian, Syrian, Iraqi, Libyan and Kuwaiti constitutions, thought that the prohibition of *riba* in the case of simple interest could be lifted if there was a need, but that the prohibition of compound interest was absolute and conclusive. He says:[1]

> So long as the need exists to obtain capital by means of loan or otherwise, and so long as capital is not owned by the state, but rather is the property of the individual who accumulates it by his work and his effort, then it is his right that he does not oppress concerning it and that he not be oppressed; as long as the need exists for all this, then interest on capital within the mentioned limits is permitted as an exception to the basic rule of prohibition. . . . Once the need is over, the prohibition of riba would revert to its original position. For this purpose, he held that the legislature should enact suitable laws about the rates, method of accrual and the total sum to be demanded. An example of the lifting of need was, according to him, the transformation of the capitalist system into a socialist system. In that case, even the simple rate of interest would be prohibited as riba. (Khalil and Thomas 2006: 73–74; also see Badawi 2000: 244)

Said al-Ashmawi (b. 1932), Chief Justice of Egypt in the 1980s, ruled that the interest of commercial banks did not come under the purview of *riba* (Visser 2009: 32). El-Gamal (2000: 39) has summarized modernist thinking on *riba* in modern Egypt as follows:

> Dr. 'Abd-Al-Mun'im Al-Nimr, an ex-Minister of 'Awqaf in Egypt, wrote an article in *Al-'Ahram* (June 1, 1989), in which he argued that the reason for the prohibition of *riba* (which he argued to be the harm caused to the debtor) does not apply to deposits with banks. Therefore, he argued, bank interest was not the forbidden *riba*. The past *mufti* of Egypt, and current Shaykh Al-'Azhar, Dr. Muhammad Sayyid Tantawi, issued a ruling (*fatwa*) (*Al-'Ahram*, 12 July 1989) permitting certain forms of interest, and in a series of five rulings (*fatwas*) in the same newspapers in May 1991, he permitted all banking interest. The current Egyptian *mufti*, Sh. Nasr Farid Wasil, reiterated this opinion in the UAE daily paper *Al-Ittihad* (August 22, 1997): 'I will give you a final and decisive ruling (*fatwa*). So long as banks invest the money in permissible avenues (*halal*), then the transaction is permissible (*halal*). . . . The issue is an investment from money. Otherwise, it is forbidden (*haram*) . . . there is no such thing as an Islamic or non-Islamic bank. So let us stop this controversy about bank interest.'

The decree of Sayyid Tantawi (1928–2010) deserves a special mention. Tantawi considers that there is nothing in the Qur'an or Traditions of the Prophet that prohibits the pre-fixing of the rate of return, as long as it occurs with mutual consent of the parties (Khalil and Thomas 2006: 83). His 2003 *fatwa* says: 'there is no canonical text (*nass*) in the Book of God or the Prophetic *Sunnah* that forbids this type of transaction, wherein the profit or return is pre-specified, as long as both sides mutually consent to this type of transaction' (ibid.: 89). Tantawi also gives an example of a person who engages a driver to ply a taxi for him at a fixed daily rate, leaving the residual earning to the driver. There is nothing, he considers, wrong in this arrangement, as it is easy to administer and also protects both parties from potential conflict (ibid.: 84). Tantawi observes that, in the case of investment certificates issued by a bank, 'it is the bank which is the borrower and the public the lender'. And he makes the very compelling point that it is difficult to argue that a bank is being exploited when it voluntarily offers a fixed interest rate in order to attract capital. On the contrary, Tantawi is saying, if the depositor is not assured a fixed return then it is he who is being exploited (ibid.: 84). He argued that 'determination of the profit in advance is for the sake of the owner of the capital (that is depositor) and is done to prevent a dispute between him and the bank'.[2]

Vogel and Hayes (1998: 46) also report about Tantawi:

> Later he went even further, saying that interest-bearing bank deposits are perfectly Islamic, and more so than 'Islamic' accounts that impose disadvantageous

terms on the customer. Laws should change the legal terminology used for bank interest and bank accounts to clarify their freedom from the stigma of *riba*.

The al-Azhar Institute of Islamic Jurisprudence issued a ruling (*fatwa*) in 2002. It says, *inter alia*, the following:

> Those who deal with the International Arab Banking Corporation – or any other bank – thus forwarding their funds and savings to the bank to be their investment agent in the bank's permissible dealings, in exchange for a predetermined profit that they receive at pre-specified time periods. . . . This transaction, taking this form, is permissible and beyond any suspicion, since there is no text in the Book of God and prophetic tradition that forbids such transactions wherein the profit or return is pre-specified, provided that both parties mutually consent to the transaction. (El-Gamal 2006: 9)

12.2   VIEWS OF SOME ASIAN SCHOLARS

There are several other scholars in the Indo-Pak subcontinent who contributed to the modernist interpretation of *riba*. Some of the prominent ones are Ja'afar Shah Phulwari (1959), Tamanna Imadi (1965), Rafiullah Shihab (1966), Yaqub Shah (1967), Abdul Ghafur Muslim (1974), Syed Ahmad (1977), Aqdas Ali Kazmi (1992) and Abdullah Saeed (1995, 1996).

Abdullah Yusufali (1882–1953), the famous commentator of the Qur'an, when explaining verse Q. 2:275 writes:

> The definition [of *riba*] I would accept would be: undue profit made, not in the way of legitimate trade, out of loans of gold and silver, and necessary articles of food, such as wheat, barley, dates, and salt (according to the list mentioned by the Holy Apostle himself). My definition would include profiteering of all kinds, but exclude economic credit, the creature of modern banking and finance. (1988, n. 324)

Another architect of modernist thought on *riba* was Fazlur Rahman (1911–88). He made a strong case for the permissibility of interest on commercial loans. His position (1964: 7) can be seen from the following extract:

> In short, the *riba* of pre-Islamic days, which was categorically declared illegitimate (*haram*) by the Qur'an, so that who indulged in it were threatened with war from God and His Prophet, was of an atrocious kind and went on multiplying in a manner that the poor debtor, in spite of his regular payments, could not pay off the usurious interest let alone the capital.

Fazlur Rahman (1964: 40) defined *riba* in the following terms: '*Riba* is an exorbitant increment whereby the capital sum is doubled several-fold, against a fixed extension of the term of payment of the debt.'

Nahdatul 'Ulema, the leading Muslim organization of Indonesia, ruled in 1938 that bank interest benefits society and is, therefore, permissible (Visser 2009: 33).

A recent exposition with a slight difference has come from Balala (2011: 62–95). She says that the Qur'an has prohibited inequity and inefficiency in commercial dealings. In the case of a commercial deal involving inequity it would come under the purview of prohibited *riba*. Short of that all interest-bearing transactions need not be treated as *riba*-based. The orthodox opinion that all types of interest are *riba* is not supported by either the Qur'an or the Traditions of the Prophet. Interest on loans is not prohibited *riba*, because the rate of interest is regulated by the market and the chances of it being inequitable are minimal. As compared to these loans, Islamic finance, which is by and large unregulated and operates in a non-competitive market, has the potential to be exploitative and inequitable. She argues (ibid.: 82) that the orthodox interpretation would recommend people to extend interest-free loans, which requires exceptional sacrifice and poses unbearable risks to creditors in terms of opportunity cost, erosion of value through inflation, risk of default by debtors, and so on. How, she argues, could the *Shari'ah* demand such an unnatural behaviour from creditors?

What then is *riba*? She answers that *riba* would be an inequitable and inefficient gain. How do we define an inequitable or inefficient gain? Her answer is that a regulated and competitive market defines it. Marking to the market would be equitable and efficient and deviating away from it would be inequitable and inefficient (ibid.: 87). Contemporary interest is not *riba*, as it is competitive and regulated by the market and thus equitable and efficient. However, financial transactions that do not have a commercial market or which are unregulated could involve *riba* in the form of a gain (which would be considered inequitable). The inequity in the transaction could be caused by either party, not necessarily the creditor.[3] It further means that only transactions of loans or other dealings among individuals which do not have a market or are unregulated could involve *riba* if there is a gain for one party. In sum, any gain in interpersonal loans would be *riba*, as it is taken and given in an unregulated environment. Conventional commercial bank interest-based transactions do not involve *riba*, because the interest on these loans is marked to the market. A logical conclusion of this line of argument is that there is no need for anything known as 'Islamic finance'. In fact, she herself arrives at the same conclusion, quite honestly (ibid.: 79).

The case built by Balala is an improvement on the traditional modernist standpoint. The modernist thinking always left the question of equity undefined. It also never answered the question about the criteria for distinction between consumption and commercial loans. Balala has done away with this controversy. All conventional loans by financial institutions are permissible, irrespective of purpose and nature, because they are regulated competitively by the market. Only interpersonal dealings (whether loans or otherwise) that give an increase to one party involve *riba*, because they are unregulated.

The problem with Balala's line of argument, however, is that it treats only financial transactions not routed through the financial market as susceptible to *riba*. The interpretation would treat interest on interpersonal loans, though for a commercial purpose, as *riba*. For illustration purposes, see the following. Businessman A requests finance from businessman B for investment and both agree that A would share profit with B but at a fixed rate of interest for the sake of accounting convenience. The rate of interest agreed is not the market rate. Now this is a commercial transaction between two businessmen. It is not a loan transaction. The interest in this transaction would be considered *riba* by Balala, as the rate has not been determined competitively by a regulated market. However, the fact is that it is a financing arrangement where one party is investing and the other party is agreeing to pay a share of the profit, though not determined by the market. For convenience of account keeping they agree on a fixed rate of interest. According to the orthodox view, this interest is *riba* because it is fixed *ex ante*. According to Balala it is *riba* because it is informal and not regulated by any market mechanism. Both interpretations fail to capture the fine point that it is an investment contract where the rate has been fixed only for the convenience of account keeping. The fact that it is not regulated by any market mechanism is an unnecessary condition imposed only by Balala and not by the *Shari'ah*. People should be free to enter into similar deals according to their convenience and calculations. We need not force them to move through the financial market. To the extent both parties deal freely and without deception and coercion the deal should be acceptable to the *Shari'ah*.

We can now sum up the modernist interpretation of *riba* as follows. The term *riba* must be understood with reference to the practice prevalent in Makkan society of the seventh century when the Qur'an decreed its prohibition. *Riba* pertains to interest on consumption loans, obtained by the poor from rich moneylenders to meet consumption needs. The rates of interest on these loans used to be exorbitant, and compound interest would accumulate to large sums despite periodical repayments by the debtor. It was a tyrannical system in which the poor were under financial slavery to the rich. The root causes were poverty and exorbitant rates of interest. The purpose and rates of these loans made them tyrannical. The purpose was to get loans to meet consumption needs. The rates were high and also compound. The commercial loans of banks prevalent in the present age are quite different. They are for the purpose of business, and both the borrower and the lender gain from such loans. The rates of interest on these loans are not exorbitant, as they are controlled and regulated by central banks or another state authority. Exploitation of the debtor arising from poverty and exorbitant rates of interest is absent in the case of commercial loans. For these reasons, interest on commercial loans is not *riba*, while interest on consumption loans is *riba*.

12.3   ASSESSMENT OF THE MODERNIST POSITION

The modernist interpretation of *riba* has some merit. It tries to define *riba* with the Qur'anic reference to exploitation (*zulm*). It opens the door for commercial interest and makes interest-based commercial transactions legitimate. It shows a path for developing business enterprises with the help of financial institutions. The interpretation restricts *riba* to situations where the interest rate is exorbitant and leads to exploitation and injustice. However, the interpretation has some problems:

a.   The modernists have tried to approach the problem from a social angle. According to them, the type of interest that causes hardship on the poor should be treated as *riba*, while interest on commercial loans is acceptable, as it promotes trade and industry. From a purely legalistic point of view, the argument is weak, as in a transaction the decision about permissibility and prohibition should depend on the intrinsic nature of the transaction and not on the financial position of the parties to the contract. For example, in a sales contract the transaction is valid if the two parties freely agree and are of majority age, the object of the trade itself is lawful, and so on. It will not matter whether the buyer or the seller is poor or rich. The same is the case for interest. If interest is lawful intrinsically, it should not matter if the borrower is rich or poor.

b.   Even if we concede that the purpose of prohibition was to protect the poor, the concept of poverty is relative and there is no conclusive method of knowing that parties to a transaction are poor or rich and if so against which benchmark.

c.   The term 'exorbitant rate of interest' is subjective. An interest rate that may seem to be exorbitant to one person could be justifiable to another. Leaving aside cases of such obvious rates of interest as 100 per cent or so, the question remains: how do we determine that a particular rate of interest is exorbitant or not? It obviously is related to the need and economic condition of the borrower, the purpose and period of the loan, and so on. These variables can differ in each situation. How can we determine, then, whether a rate of interest involves *riba*? A prominent example of this confusion is interest on loans provided by Grameen Bank, where the effective rate could be even higher than 80 per cent but the practitioners of microfinance consider it legitimate because, they say, Grameen Bank is providing the poor with access to capital which they otherwise would not have. If we accepted the definition of *riba* by the modernists we would always be arguing whether a certain rate of interest was exorbitant or not and the controversy would never end.

d. The interpretation also restricts *riba* to a situation where the principal sum is doubled and redoubled over time owing to interest payments. This, obviously, is a situation of injustice and can be termed *riba*. But the question arises: how do we know on an a priori basis that a certain rate of interest would lead to a situation of doubling and redoubling of the principal sum? If the borrower repays on time, even though the borrower is poor and the rate of interest is quite high, the principal sum of the loan will not double and redouble. How do we decide on an a priori basis that a certain interest-based loan is in fact *riba*-based?

e. The interpretation also restricts *riba* to a situation where the borrower seeks an extension and the lender grants it in lieu of an increase in the principal sum. But it does not say anything where interest is built into the agreement in the beginning and the question of extension does not arise. An obvious example is sale on mark-up, where the seller adds interest into the sale price and agrees to receive the price later on. Shall we term the interest added to the sale price in the beginning as *riba* or not?

f. The interpretation restricts *riba* to consumption loans and allows interest on commercial loans. In some cases the purpose of the loan is quite obvious. However, in other cases the distinction is blurred and it becomes difficult to tell whether the loan is for consumption or for a commercial purpose. An obvious example is a loan for education. Is it a loan for consumption or for a commercial purpose? Is a loan for health care a consumption loan or a production loan? No conclusive answers are possible. Another example is a loan for buying a car. What is the nature of this loan? It could be a commercial loan if the car increases the earning ability of the borrower and a consumption loan if it only helps the borrower run household errands. Binding *riba* with such a hazy variable makes the distinction between interest and *riba* blurred.

g. There is a legal objection to this definition. By saying that *riba* is restricted to consumption loans only, modernist thinkers exempt commercial loans from the purview of *riba*, while the Qur'anic prohibition is absolute and does not make any exception. The interpretation cannot find favour with the majority of Muslims on the grounds of methodology.

h. The modernist interpretation relates *riba* with the practice of interest-based loans prevalent in seventh-century Makkan society. That drags them into a historical debate which remains inconclusive. Those who disagree with the modernists have tried to search for evidence in the historical annals that commercial loans were prevalent in the days of the Prophet. Others have tried to challenge this evidence. All said and done, the evidence from both sides is thin and inconclusive and has generated endless debate with no consequence. Some people have also raised issues of epistemology relating to this method of argumentation. They think that restricting the Qur'anic prohibitions to the practice in the days of the Prophet is tantamount to delimiting the universality of the Qur'an, which is a Book for all times and for all societies.

For the above reasons we think that the modernist interpretation, despite having some merit, suffers from technical deficiencies. The modernist interpretation needs to be further refined to the following extent:

a. There is no need to distinguish between consumption and commercial loans. The purpose of the loan is immaterial. To the extent that there is a loan transaction, any excess on it should be treated as *riba*. The objection that the modernists are trying to create an exception in the Qur'an's absolute prohibition can be overcome by this refinement.

b. There is no need to restrict *riba* to higher or lower rates of interest. Any excess over the principal sum, whatever the rate, should be treated as *riba*. The problem of subjectivity of rates of interest can be resolved by this modification.

c. However, we need to distinguish that all financial transactions where a party gives money to another with the promise of taking it back are not loan transactions. An obvious example is the money provided by a person to another for business on the basis of *mudaraba*. The intention here is quite clear. The person giving the money intends to take it back with some profit. Some financial transactions appear to be loan transactions but, if the parties to the contract clarify that they are not giving or taking a loan but are entering into a financing and investing deal, any interest on the principal sum will be legitimate, whatever the rate and whatever the period. With this refinement, the modernist interpretation of *riba* will be a distinct departure from the orthodox interpretation and will also overcome all objections on their understanding.[4]

NOTES

1. Abd al-Razzaq al-Sanhuri, *Masadir al-haqq fil-fiqh al-Islami*, 6 parts in 2 volumes (Egypt: n.d.). Part 3, III, p.220. Also see Visser (2009: 21).
2. Quoted from Chibli Mallat, Tantawi on banking, in *Islamic legal interpretation: Muftis and their fatwas*, ed. Muhammad Khalid Masud, Brinkley Messick and David S. Powers (Cambridge, MA: Harvard University Press, 1996), pp.286–296.
3. For example, a debtor could cause inequity by not paying back the principal in full or by delaying the payment or by returning it in a currency which has a lower value at the time of payment as compared to the time of the loan.
4. Chapter 16, in particular sections 16.2 and 16.3, elaborates the difference between lending and financing in greater detail.

13. Prohibition of *riba*: the continuing debate

Orthodox scholars try to convey the impression that the debate about the definition of *riba* is finally settled. All types of interest come under the purview of *riba*. Commercial interest is illegitimate and so is the business of conventional financial institutions (e.g. Zaman 2009: 543). However, in fact the debate is still continuing. Nyazee, a renowned jurist, also contends that there is no general agreement about the exact definition of *riba* (Nyazee 2000: 5). In the following discussion we shall present the views of some scholars who have tried to modify the prevalent interpretation. The objective is to show that the debate on the exact meanings of *riba* is still going on and the issue is far from settled.

13.1 ORTHODOX SCHOLARS OF THE INDO-PAK SUBCONTINENT

Yusuf (2009) has chronicled in detail the opinions of scholars from the Indo-Pak subcontinent who treat all types of interest as *riba*. For example, Rashid Ahmad Gangohi (1829–97), Ashraf Ali Thanvi (1863–1943), Nazir Hussain Dehlvi (1805–1902), Thana Ullah Amritsari (1870–1948), Muhammad Shafi (1897–1976), Abu al-'Ala Mawdudi (1903–79) and Rashid Ahmad Ludhianwi (1922–2001) thought dealing in interest in all situations and with all persons (Muslim or Non-Muslim, citizens of enemy states or friendly states, etc.) is prohibited and falls under the definition of *riba*. According to these scholars keeping deposits in banks or working for banks is also prohibited. Similarly, housing finance from banks is prohibited. They also do not allow interest on deposits even if taken for charity.

However, some other scholars like Abdul Hayee Lucknawi (1848–86), Irshad Hussain Rampuri (d. 1892), Ahmad Rida Khan Breveli (1856–1921), Shah Muhammad Mazharullah (1886–1966), Mufti Kifayatullah (1875–1952), Mahmud Hasan Gangohi (1907–97), Muhammad Amjad Ali Azmi (1878–1948), Abu al-Khair Nurullah (1914–83), Iqtidar Ahmad Khan (b. 1945) and Jalaluddin Ahmad (b. 1933) think that dealing in interest with non-Muslims or in a warring state (*dar al-harb*) is permissible.

According to them, dealing with banks and interest income in non-Muslim countries is legitimate because taking the property of non-Muslims with their consent is lawful. Similarly, Muslims in these countries can keep the funds of mosques and other welfare organizations in banks and earn interest. They can also borrow on interest or purchase houses with mortgage-based finance in these countries. Interest on the saving deposits of present-day India is legitimate as it does not fall in the category of *riba*. The basis of this opinion is: (a) all verses of the Qur'an and all Traditions of the Prophet dealing with *riba* address only Muslims; they do not apply to non-Muslims; (b) there is a Tradition that says: 'There is no *riba* between Muslims and enemies (*ahl al-harb*) in a land that is in a state of war with the Muslims (*dar al-harb*).'[1] Imam Abu Hanifa (AH 703–67) thought that, if a Muslim travelled to a non-Muslim land and dealt in interest with another Muslim in that land, it would be permissible. Interestingly, some scholars think that dealing with banks owned solely by non-Muslims is lawful but dealing with banks owned by Muslims is unlawful.[2] In Pakistan, Mufti Muhammad Shafi (1973) decreed that it is legitimate for employees to accept interest on provident fund deposits provided that the deduction of the fund from the salary was compulsory. Thus he created some room for accepting interest in some form. Javed Ghamidi, another contemporary scholar of Pakistan, considers that the taking of interest on loans is *riba* but the giving of interest is not (*Isharq*, February 2009, p. 65).[3] Thus it is another effort to find a mechanism of reconciliation with the prevalent interest-based banking system.

13.2   INVOKING THE PRINCIPLE OF NECESSITY

Finding it difficult and at times impossible to do away with conventional interest, Islamic scholars have moved towards accommodating interest, bit by bit, in Islamic economic thought and the practice of Islamic finance. One of the excuses for allowing interest in some form has been 'the principle of necessity' that Islamic law recognizes in cases of dire need. Warde (2010: 41) explains how this principle was extended to legitimize some forms of interest:

> In financial matters, *darura*[4] has been invoked to justify many departures. For instance, when pricing their products by relying on interest-based benchmarks, the argument was that Islamic banks, given their small size relative to conventional banks were price-takers and not price-makers. Many other practices, including charging interest on certain loans, could be rationalized on the ground that Muslims had to be able to compete with other peoples who were not bound by the same strictures. Keeping interest-bearing balances in foreign

banks could also be justified since such were the norms and practices of the international economy.

Another excuse has been the difficulties faced by Muslims living in non-Muslim lands. El-Gamal (2006: 19) shows how the excuse was commissioned to legitimize some forms of interest:

> Some flexibility is given to Muslims living in non-Muslim lands. The *fatwa* issued by Ayatullah Sistani (Iraq's most prominent *Shi'i* cleric) seems to accommodate many forms of conventional finance for those Muslims. For instance, he allowed depositing funds with banks, and collecting interest thereof, on the basis of permissibility of charging interest to non-Muslims in those lands. Moreover, he allowed Muslims to take mortgage loans from non-Islamic banks – even with knowledge that they will pay principal plus interest – provided that they do so with an intention other than 'borrowing' in the classical sense of '*iqtirad*'.[5] Likewise, the prominent *Sunni* jurist Yusuf Al-Qardawi issued a similar *fatwa* allowing Muslims in North America to finance their home purchases with conventional mortgages.

13.3   MAHMOUD EL-GAMAL'S VIEWS ON *RIBA*

Mahmoud El-Gamal has contributed several important ideas to Islamic economics and Islamic finance. He has discussed the question of *riba* in detail in several of his writings. Broadly, he is in agreement with the orthodox interpretation. However, we find him indecisive when it comes to the rationale for the prohibition of *riba*. While discussing the difference between *riba* and trade, El-Gamal writes (2001: 21):

> The contemporary confusion is hardly new. In Ibn Al-'Arabi's *Ahkam Al-Qur'an*, he reports a specific argument given by the Arabs during the time of Prophet Muhammad to support their statement that '*trade is like riba*' (Q. 2:275). They argued as follows: Consider a credit sale with a price of 10 payable in a month. After a month, the buyer and seller agree to postpone for one more month, and increase the price to 11. The latter is forbidden *riba*. They then argued: Is this not the same as an initial sale with the price of 11 deferred for two months? The answer in Q. 2:275 was decisive '*but God has permitted trade and forbidden riba*'. The legal difference between the two is very clear: one is a sale in which price is increased for deferment and the other is an increase in the amount of a debt for deferment. The first is permitted and meets almost all the financing needs which can be met through forbidden *riba*-based lending. The second, however, is strictly forbidden. The permissibility of the first and the prohibition of the second are both quite clear and unequivocal. Therefore, we may use credit sales as a form of finance and we must categorically avoid interest-bearing loans. Why one is permitted while the other is forbidden can only be fully known by God and whomsoever he gave such knowledge. As a

practical matter, we should know what is permitted and use it to our advantage
and what is forbidden and avoid it.

El-Gamal has not faced the ultimate question about the rationale for
the prohibition of *riba* and permission of trade. He has left it to the knowledge and wisdom of God. He clearly sees that in both cases the increase is
due to deferment. Why is an increase due to deferment allowed in the case
of trade and why is it prohibited in the case of a loan? From the perspective of the person who takes advantage of the finance both situations have
a cost. Why is one prohibited and the other permissible? El-Gamal does
not answer this question.

13.4   JAVED GHAMIDI'S VIEWS ON *RIBA*

Javed Ghamidi, a Pakistani scholar and a follower of the Farahi school of
thought[6] with a reputation for a rational interpretation of Islam, has tried
to modify the orthodox position on *riba*. We shall discuss his views in the
following paragraphs.

13.4.1   Ghamidi on the Definition of Interest

Ghamidi (2008: 2) defines interest as follows: 'Interest refers to a predetermined increment on the principal of a loan.'[7] He treats interest as *riba*,
although he does not say so specifically. The definition makes predetermination a defining condition for interest. We think this is unnecessary.
In a loan transaction, if the lender seeks something over and above the
principal sum, it is *riba* and thus prohibited irrespective of the fact that
the demand for an excess was predetermined or not at the time of lending.
Ironically, a predetermined and stipulated excess over the principal sum
could be less exploitative than something that a creditor may seek later
on, as in the case of the pre-Islam days when the excess was often double
or quadruple the principal sum, which was condemned by the Qur'an.
Further, the above definition is not comprehensive. For example, it does
not cover situations where a person allows a cash discount on a credit sale.
There is no difference of opinion that such a discount is interest; whether
or not it is *riba* is a different question. Similarly, if a creditor charges a
penalty for delayed payment, it is interest, whether it is one-off or cumulative or increases with time or not. However, whether we should treat it as
riba is a different question.

13.4.2   Ghamidi on Interest and Rent

Ghamidi (2008: 2) writes:

> Apparently, interest and rent seem to be similar. But if we look deep into the
> two concepts we can see that the assets that are given on rent remain intact
> when in use while money has to be converted into some asset before it becomes
> useful and for repayment it has to be recreated. A demand of increment on
> such money thus becomes tyrannical. Since this difference of rent and inter-
> est is quite fine and human beings could commit mistakes in differentiating
> between the two, God has through his Prophets and Messengers, clarified in
> His *Shari'ah* that any increment on loan of money was not allowed. Interest
> has been illegal in every *Shari'ah* in human history and the Qur'an has also
> prohibited it categorically.

We think the above effort to distinguish between interest and rent is not
well founded. In both cases (rent of fixed assets and loan of liquid cash)
there is a provider of the asset and there is a user of the asset. It hardly
matters if the user of the asset has to transform the asset before using it.
In fact, if we look deep, we can appreciate that the provider of liquid cash
as a loan makes available a more useful asset. The user of liquid cash has
the flexibility of using the whole or part of the asset at any time and place.
The utility obtained from the liquid cash may be higher than the utility of a
fixed asset in most cases. Saying that the user of the cash having to recreate
the cash for repayment makes it tyrannical is not clear. How does it become
tyrannical? Does it mean that the reason for the tyranny is 'regeneration'?
If that is so, then the principal sum of the interest-free loan has also to be
regenerated by the borrower. But we do not treat an interest-free loan as
tyrannical. The only reason we can call it oppressive is that an increment
over the principal sum is demanded by the lender. If that is so, then the
argument about regeneration of the principal sum becomes redundant.

13.4.3   Ghamidi: Proposed Reforms in Commercial Banking

Ghamidi (2008: 3) seems inclined to accept the prevalent interest of commercial banks with three modifications. We think that the suggested
modifications are unnecessary or would complicate the matter without any
benefit. The following are the proposed modifications, with our comments.

a.   Restrict recovery of the loan to the principal sum if the business suffers losses or the business is closed

In the case where the client of the bank suffers losses or the business has to
be closed for any reason, Ghamidi proposes that the bank should restrict
recovery of the loan to the principal sum only and should not charge any

further interest. On the face of it, the proposal seems fair to the debtor, who is now facing straitened circumstances. But the matter is not that simple. Profit and loss in business, despite appearing to be quantitative, are subjective concepts. Even if we assume complete honesty and integrity in maintaining accounts, profits and losses can be manipulated by creative accounting acceptable to auditors. For example, losses can be shown by charging higher rates of depreciation, raising rates of amortization of intangible assets, spending enhanced amounts on repairs and maintenance in a particular period, contracting expensive funds for short terms, purchasing expensive foreign exchange from the money market, and so on. Such policies can lead to the reduction of profits or a declaration of losses. The user of funds can get back to the bank for relief under what Ghamidi has proposed as a reform of the banking system. If the bank provides the relief, there would be queues of free-riders and the banks might go broke.

Besides, we cannot rule out the possibility that an honest user of funds can also be negligent, imprudent, inefficient and so on. Such a person can get into serious trouble and ultimately enter into losses. There could also be users of funds who actually steal business assets and declare bankruptcy to get relief from the bank. Even Ghamidi would agree that, in each case when a business declares a loss, the bank would like to know the circumstances that led to the loss to make sure that the loss was beyond the business's control despite its best efforts and the most efficient business decisions. Arriving at such a judgement is no mean task. The bank would require expertise in all types of business to fix responsibility before accepting the declaration of a loss. Imagine, how much cost and effort would it involve? Would it be workable in practice?

b. The banks should remain partners to an asset until all instalments are paid off by the buyer of the asset

This is the second reform that Ghamidi proposes. In fact, this is also unnecessary. Commercial banks that deal in interest do not sell assets on instalments. They provide funds. The user can buy the assets and then repay the funds with interest. It is only through the ingenuity of so-called 'Islamic' finance that the banks are now into the instalment sales business, and that too in name only. Making them co-own the asset until all the instalments are paid off is not relevant to the commercial banks' business. The reform means that those who obtain funds for buying assets should not be sole owners until all the funds are paid off. The banks should remain co-owners and bear repair maintenance and insurance costs. Even though the proposal may seem fair, the cost to the banks would be prohibitive and make the whole business unviable. The users of funds would also not accept it, because it would restrict their sovereignty.

c. **In the case of non-commercial loans, the banks should demand compensation only for a decline in the value of money due to inflation**

This is the first time that a religious scholar has recognized the need to compensate the lender for a decline in the value of money during the loan period. We think that even this otherwise reasonable proposal is unnecessary. Lending in Islam is a charitable act. The verses of the Qur'an on *riba* (Q. 2:275–281, 30:39) mention charity (*sadaqa*) while prohibiting *riba*. These verses point to the fact that lending money on an interest-free basis is a form of charity. In the case of a loan the lender should understand that lending is a charitable act and that the charity is not only in terms of parting with the money. It may also involve a decline in its real value due to inflation. The lender can refuse to lend if he or she cannot 'afford' the total sacrifice. The *Shari'ah* has not made it obligatory upon everyone to extend interest-free loans in all cases. However, if a person does extend a loan, he or she should understand that the decline in value is part of the deal and should bear it. Seeking to compensate lenders to the extent of inflation opens the door for various problems. The first and foremost is the exact determination of inflation. It is not possible to determine it precisely so as to establish a fair relationship between the borrower and the lender. Secondly, economic theory generally upholds that indexation ignites the fire of inflation rather than subdues it. Such a reform despite being fair in its appearance is not without problems. The proposed reform is uncalled for.

13.5   IMRAN AHSAN NYAZEE'S VIEWS ON *RIBA*

Imran Ahsan Nyazee, a Pakistani jurist, has written extensively on various issues relating to Islamic economics. He has also given his opinion on interest and *riba*. Nyazee (2009) has tried to discuss the subject more rigorously than any other modern jurist. He has derived four basic rules, which led him to define *riba* as follows. He thinks that *riba* is either manifest or concealed. Manifest *riba* is (p. 12):

a. *riba al-fadl*, which is the excess stipulated in the exchange of two currency values of the same species whether the transaction is spot or delayed; and/or
b. *riba al-nasi'ah*, which is the potential benefit to be derived during the period of delay stipulated for either of the exchanged currency values.

Riba is concealed when the primary objective of two or more related transactions is the same as that of a single transaction of manifest *riba*.

He thinks that the primary objective for prohibition of *riba* is distributive justice – fair distribution of goods and services among people (p. 4). He has illustrated the above definition by several examples. Some of the examples state the familiar orthodox position. However, in some other cases he takes an iconoclastic position which will baffle even the orthodox scholars. For example:

a. A deposit into a bank and its withdrawal even without interest involves *riba*, as it provides a potential benefit to the bank. The only alternatives are either to give an interest-free loan to the bank or to keep the money as a deposit so that the bank has to return the same currency notes! Can anyone imagine how to run commercial banks in this age with this definition of *riba*?

b. A person lends money to another person on an interest-free basis for a stipulated period. According to Nyazee, it involves *riba*, as the money has been given for a stipulated period. It will be permissible if the loan is given without interest for an indefinite period. Does *Shari'ah* encourage unplanned and reckless social behaviour?

c. A person gets an advance equal to his three months' salary from a bank, to be paid back in 12 instalments. Even without interest, Nyazee thinks it involves *riba*, as it has a stipulated period during which the repayment has to be made. Does the *Shari'ah* require people's dealings to remain unplanned?

d. A person buys ordinary shares of a company at par value. After one year, the company declares a dividend. The shareholder takes the dividend and also redeems the capital by returning the shares to the company. According to Nyazee, it involves *riba*, as the transaction involves the exchange of two currency values with a period of delay. This is an extreme case where you cannot invest in ordinary share capital and subsequently redeem your capital. It would ban all transactions with open-ended investment trust funds and close the door to small savers investing their funds. In other words, it would defeat the very purpose which Nyazee thinks is behind the prohibition of *riba* – distributive justice.

e. There is no provision for cash loans in Islamic law. Credit can be raised only through the sale and purchase of goods and services. It means there cannot be any financing for business on the basis of debt (Nyazee 1998: 66).

Even the purpose of prohibition of *riba* as stated by Nyazee is quite illusive. What is fair distribution of income and wealth and how do we determine that? The general principle regarding distribution of wealth

(Q. 59:7) is stated in the Qur'an with reference to distribution of booty obtained without fighting (*fai'*) and not with reference to *riba*. How has he stretched that to the principle of *riba*?

13.6   SAYYID TAHIR: *BLUEPRINT OF ISLAMIC FINANCIAL SYSTEM*

In 1999, the International Institute of Islamic Economics, Islamabad published *IIIE's blueprint of Islamic financial system including strategy for elimination of riba* (*Blueprint*). The main driving force behind the *Blueprint* was Sayyid Tahir, professor of economics at the Institute. Some of his colleagues collaborated with him. The *Blueprint* gives the following definition of *riba*: '*Riba* is discrepancy which results from the contractual obligations of a party in the context of a direct exchange of items of the same general kind between two parties' (p. 39). This definition does not restrict the occurrence of *riba* to loan transactions only. It covers all types of exchanges, including those for investment and financing of business. It encompasses any contractual obligation. Moreover, by transforming excess on a loan to a 'discrepancy' the *Blueprint* has stretched the original meaning of *riba*. The definition also does not relate to deferment (*nasi'ah*), which is explicitly stated in a number of Traditions of the Prophet quoted in an earlier chapter of the *Blueprint* (p. 15). Some Traditions clearly state that there would be 'no *riba* except when there is a delay in repayment'. For example, the *Blueprint* presents the following Tradition from *Sunan* by Imam Nasai', a famous compiler of the Traditions: 'According to Obaidullah bin Abu Yazid, he heard Ibn Abbas saying that Usama bin Zayd told him as follows: "The Prophet said that there was no *riba* except in lending (*nasi'ah*)"' (p. 15).

The above Tradition and several others with similar meanings clearly state that the *riba* arises only when there is a loan transaction. There would not be any *riba* if there was a spot exchange. The *Blueprint* definition deviates from this explicit injunction of the Prophet. In fact, the authors are quite emphatic (p. 41, 5.1) in asserting that *riba* is 'time invariant', by which they mean *riba* can arise even when there is no loan transaction. The essence of *riba* is not price for time. It is contractual discrepancy in exchange of the same kind. However, the authors were unable to explain the above and similar other Traditions of the Prophet which explicitly state that *riba* arises only in the case of deferment (*nasi'ah*). The authors have taken refuge in a self-defined position later on (p. 41, 4.4.5) by saying that the Traditions relating to deferment (*nasi'ah*) should not be taken literally. The question arises: why do we ignore them? What other meanings should be given to these Traditions?

The authors of the *Blueprint* also contend (p. 38, 3.6) that in exchange transactions of the 'same general kind' the qualitative differences would be ignored. This conclusion flouts common sense. How could the divine guidance prescribe that two things of different quality should be treated as equal on the basis of quantity? The naivety of this conclusion becomes obvious if we tell a person with one kilogram of 24-carat gold to exchange it for an equal weight of 18-carat gold, as otherwise it will involve *riba*. If the person objects to that, we tell him or her to first sell the 24-carat gold on the market and then come back to buy the 18-carat-gold for cash. What an inefficient and roundabout method of handling a simple exchange transaction! The Tradition of the Prophet in which he advised his companion to sell lower-quality dates for cash and then buy higher-quality dates for cash only (p. 15) refers to a situation where it was not possible to determine the equivalence of two types of dates by mere judgement. In the case of other things, for example gold of 24 carats and 18 carats, no judgement is involved. It can be measured and calculated precisely. The qualitative differences can be ascertained precisely. How could the *Shari'ah* deny this? The advice of the Prophet indicated his preference for a fairer way of doing business. It does not mean that he advised ignoring the qualitative differences and artificially declared inferior and superior qualities as equal. Such simplistic and naïve conclusions go against common sense. It could not be the teaching of Islam.

The authors find themselves in a tight corner when explaining a Tradition of the Prophet in which he authorized his official to take one camel on the promise of giving two camels in return (p. 39, 3.8). Their explanation is that in the case of the camel loan, even when the same camel is returned, it is most likely to be better than before. So they mean to say that the quality of the same camel being returned would be better in any case and the Prophet tried to equalize the qualitative difference by giving a second one in lieu of the higher quality that would have been the case if the same camel was returned. The explanation is laboured. The authors deviate from their earlier position where the qualitative differences had to be ignored. They also deviate from their definition where the exchange has to be strictly equal if the exchange is between two items of the same kind.

The authors contend (p. 40, 4.4.2, 4.5 (iii)) that the exchange of jewellery and gold as metal must be exchanged in equal quantities. If the jeweller charges any money for labour it would amount to *riba*. The question arises: is it fair? How could the divine law prescribe that the jeweller who has spent his time and effort to convert gold into jewellery should not be compensated for the labour?

The authors have asserted that bank transactions involving interest come under the purview of loan transactions (p. 41, 5.3). Therefore the bank interest is *riba*. The position is in line with the literature produced by other orthodox scholars on the subject. The entire literature on the prohibition of interest from the orthodox perspective is based on this assumption. However, as an example the reader can refer to al-Jarhi and Iqbal (2001: 17). They keep on working at the problem of treating a deposit as a loan or a deposit for safekeeping (*wadi'a*) or trust (*amana*) but do not see the obvious position of the depositor who would like to keep the deposit with the bank to earn some money on it or to have the benefit of various banking services. In that case, it is neither a loan nor a deposit for safekeeping. Trying to fit it into one of the categories that the jurists of the medieval age devised is diverting attention from something quite obvious. Muslim economists fail to see what is quite obvious to an ordinary person. None of them has tried to find out the intention of the depositor, although all of them accept that in the Islamic *Shari'ah* the nature of each matter is determined by the intention of the doer, based on a Tradition of the Prophet reported as the opening Tradition in his *al-Jami al-Sahih* by Imam Bukhari. In the case of bank deposits, they should ask any depositor whether she or he is giving a loan to the bank or ask a bank if it is seeking a loan from the depositors. Most probably the reply in both cases would be in the negative. But somehow Muslim economists have not cared to determine the nature of the transaction with reference to the intention of the depositors and the banks.

Farooq (2006-a: 14) rightly points out: 'Definition and understanding of demand deposit are quite uniform around the world, and nowhere any idea of "loan" is attached to demand deposit.'

Mahmoud El-Gamal has quoted a decree (*fatwa*) of Syed Tantawi of al-Azhar University (Cairo, Egypt) as follows:

> Funds given to a bank cannot be considered a form of loan (*qard*), since the bank is not in need. . . . Thus, if the transaction is not a loan, the customer must be viewed as an investor who intentionally goes to the bank seeking profits.[8]

The question of *riba* arises only in the case of loan transactions. Once the deposits are not loans, the decree of *riba* on the interest on deposits does not remain relevant. El-Gamal (2001) argues that the Qur'anic prohibition of *riba* does not refer to the exploitation of the rich creditor by the poor debtor. Those who treat bank deposits as loans can see the irrelevance of their point of view. A person buys treasury bills of the US government and gets interest on them or a person gets interest on IBM bonds. In both cases the creditors are poorer than the debtors and there is no question of exploitation of the poor by the rich (El-Gamal 2001: 2). In the case of banks, the depositors with the banks are not richer than the banks in most cases. How can we say that the savers who receive interest on their savings are exploiting the 'poor' banks?

Orthodox scholars try to evade the above argument by saying that current account deposits are not in the nature of investment. They are not trust money (*amana*) either, as the banks can use this money. These deposits are loans to the bank and any interest paid by the bank would be *riba*. The argument is far-fetched. It arises from our insistence on remaining within the classical classification of all deposits into two main categories: (a) loan or (b) trust (*amana*). That is how classical jurists classified all deposits. We need to recognize that current account deposits need not fall into either of these classes. Let us accept that it is another category of deposits where the depositors keep their money with the bank to avail themselves of various banking services. The deposits are neither loans nor *amana*. They are deposits for benefiting from various banking services. A new juridical term needs to be coined for classifying current account deposits.

13.7   CONCLUDING REMARKS

In this chapter we have tried to show that the debate on prohibition of *riba* is far from settled. Orthodox opinion that equates interest with *riba* in all cases has made several scholars uncomfortable who have tried to propose changes in the orthodox position. Some of them have tried to create space for the permissibility of interest behind the veil of a Muslim–non-Muslim divide. Others have tried to accommodate it either in the name of compulsions (in the case of a provident fund) or the absence of an alternative (in the case of the non-availability of interest-free loans). Some have taken refuge in the law of necessity. Still others have toed an extremist line that would make life impossible in this age. We have examined the views of these scholars and shown how they also do not make a good case in support of their position. The definition of *riba* is still defying consensus, and the issue is far from settled.

NOTES

1. Imam Abu Hanifa based his opinion on this Tradition. This is a *mursal hadith*, which means that the last reporter in the chain of transmitters is not a companion (*sahabi*) of the Prophet but a student of the companion (*tabi'i*). But the student of the companion narrates the saying of the Prophet. Based on this Tradition Imam Abu Hanifa allowed the sale of one *dirham* for two *dirhams* in a non-Muslim country.
2. For example, Mufti Jalaluddin Ahmad Amjad holds this opinion. See Yusuf (2009: 39).

3. Quoted by Ghamidi's pupil M.R. Mufti.
4. Lit. necessity.
5. This means that they should treat it as a business and not a borrowing activity.
6. The Farahi school refers to the Qur'anic work by Hameedudin Farahi (1863–1930) and his pupil Amin Ahsan Islahi (1904–97). Farahi worked as a professor in Madrastul Islah, Serai Mir, Azamgarh, India (1925–30) and propounded the theory of Coherence of the Qur'an, which Amin Ahsan Islahi developed and refined. Ghamidi professes adherence to the Farahi school.
7. This is a free-flowing translation by the present writer of the author's Urdu note.
8. Mahmoud El-Gamal quotes this in his presentation 'The recent Azhar *fatwa*: Its logic, and historical background' (2003), as quoted by Farooq (2006-a: 17).

14. Unresolved issues in the orthodox interpretation of *riba*

The orthodox interpretation of *riba* is the dominant explanation among contemporary Muslims. However, Muslim scholars have not resolved all issues emerging from this interpretation. The present chapter will discuss some of these issues.

14.1 THE DIFFERENCE BETWEEN CASH AND CREDIT PRICES

One ticklish issue in Islamic finance is about the legitimacy of the difference in cash and credit prices for the same commodity. Orthodox scholars who contend that all types of interest are *riba* find themselves in a tight corner on this question. The seller who charges a higher price for a credit sale than a cash price charges the additional sum for the time allowed for payment. It is similar to getting a cash loan and repaying with interest. However, orthodox scholars do not accept this reasoning (e.g. M.T. Uthmani, n.d.-a: 10). According to them, it is a sale transaction, the price, whether cash or credit, is agreed, and the increase in the price on a deferred payment basis is not interest. Tahir, Atiquzzafar, Ali and Waheed (1999: 43, 9.1) justify the transaction because the difference in prices is only theoretical until the deal is done. The credit price is the agreed price and the question of difference between cash and credit prices becomes irrelevant. This is a legalistic explanation. The fact remains that the seller is charging a higher price for the time given for payment. This is interest in common economic parlance. Those who treat all types of interest as *riba* cannot provide a satisfactory economic explanation for this transaction.

Badawi (2000: 36ff.) says that, in fact, *riba* in the days of the Prophet mostly consisted of the increase in the price of a commodity at the time of sale if the payment was deferred. Only a few transactions were direct cash loans with interest. An increase in the price of the commodity sold on credit was interest in lieu of the initial period allowed and was concealed in the price. The second increase was done in lieu of further extension in time if the buyer was unable to pay on the due date. Badawi (2000: 216) refers to *al-Mabsut* (Vol. 14, 36) by the famous Hanafite jurist al-Sarkhasi (d. AD 899), who says that the Tradition forbidding two sales in one refers to the difference in cash and credit prices of the same commodity (Abu Dawud, *Sunan*, Kitab al-buyu', ch. 53). Al-Sarkhasi considered such a sale as unlawful because it involved *riba*.

Despite the fact that the element of interest is included in the price of the product and it is quite obvious to an ordinary person, orthodox scholars do not accept this common-sense situation. However, there are exceptions. For example, El-Diwani (1999) shows by using the discounted cash flow analysis technique that the difference between the cash and credit prices is due to interest on the money required for paying the price of the commodity. M.N. Siddiqi (2009-a: 194) tacitly recognizes on the basis of research by other scholars that the difference in the cash and credit prices plays the same role as interest in conventional finance.[1] Rafic al-Masri (2004) has explicitly recognized that the difference between cash and credit prices is a form of interest but is not *riba*. His argument is that not all forms of interest are *riba* and one such example is the difference between the cash and credit prices. The explanation by Rafic al-Masri resolves the issue for an ordinary person. However, it creates a problem for orthodox scholars who insist that all forms of interest are *riba*. They are captives of their own definition of *riba*. They find themselves in a situation of conflict. If they allow a difference between cash and credit prices, they will yield to the point that not all forms of interest are *riba* and thus their definition of *riba* is incorrect. If they disallow the practice, they confront a commercial situation which is not practicable. Business firms cannot survive where cash and credit prices are equal. To absolve themselves of this conflict, they have tried several explanations. We discuss some of these in the following paragraphs.

Toutounchian (2009: 116) has presented an economic rationale for the difference in cash and credit prices. According to him the mark-up on credit prices is not interest, as it involves the exchange of commodities for money, while interest, by definition, involves the exchange of money for money. From an economist's point of view this type of convoluted reasoning may be acceptable, but from the perspective of an ordinary person the increase in the credit price is nothing but interest. Let us explain the situation. Suppose a trader approaches a seller to sell a product and asks for the terms of sale. The seller says that the cash price is Rs10 000 while the credit price is Rs10 500 for payment after three months. Now the buyer approaches a bank and seeks a loan of Rs10 000 for three months at 20 per cent per annum and buys the product for cash. In what respect, from the perspective of the buyer, are the two deals different? It is only a veil of commodity that hides the interest. The buyer is taking advantage of the facility of finance for three months. In both cases, he is paying interest. In the first case it is included in the price of the commodity and in the latter case it is explicit in the terms of financing. From the buyer's perspective, it is the cost of getting finance for three months. It hardly matters, as the two rates are equal, whether the buyer gets the finance from the seller or a bank.

Kahf (2007) has argued that the Qur'anic verse (Q. 2:275) that refers to the objection of the pre-Islam Arabs about the similarity of trade and *riba* actually means situations where the cash and credit prices are different and they were confused by the similarity of the deal with an interest-based loan. He thinks the Qur'an legitimizes trade where the cash and credit prices are different. He argues, however, that there are similarities and differences between such a sale and interest. An example of the difference is that the main reason for the prohibition of interest on a loan is that 'a debt, because of its own nature, cannot produce any increment'. By this he means that, since a sale by its very nature creates an increment, the seller is entitled to share such an increment, but in the case of a loan there is no such inherent increment. The argument is not realistic. It cannot be argued with certainty that the buyer of goods on credit would certainly earn a profit. He could end up in a loss. What then is the justification of the seller getting a profit on this finance? On the other hand, a person who gets a loan on interest may be able to use the loan in a profitable manner and thus produce an increment. We cannot say that a loan in all cases is unable to create a surplus.

Kahf (2007) tries to show some further differences between a sale on credit and debt finance, but his discussion lacks realism. First, he argues that accepting the loan as having an increment also requires another unrealistic assumption about valuation of the increment, that is, the rate of interest. This argument applies as well to the rate of increase in the sale price of the commodity when sold on credit. How do we arrive at that rate? It would also require an unrealistic assumption. Second, he says that a loan requires operations of discounting and penalties for early or late repayments respectively. Such operations do not create any value, he argues. They only transfer wealth from one person to another. The argument is true to the extent that discounting and compounding do not create any value. But they are so important to financial deals that even Islamic economists are searching for alternatives to these operations. They also require some tools to discipline delinquent borrowers. Third, interest-based debts lead to trading in debts which only transfer wealth among people without adding any value to society. They create debt bubbles and thus instability in society. It is true that the trading of debts can create such a scenario. But, even in an Islamic society where people have accumulated large amounts of accounts receivable and require liquidity for further business, solutions are being sought to liquidate these debts. Trading of such debts is a business necessity, and no society can progress or benefit from economic opportunities if it does not find a solution to generate liquidity by the sale of debts. One of the weak points of the traditional interpretation of *riba* is that it has no solution for generating liquidity from accounts receivable. Fourth, loan-based finance does not allow moral and social screening without additional legal and administrative costs. Again, this applies to sale-based finance as well. No business firm will extend credit to a customer until it is satisfied with its credibility. It is not clear how the two situations differ. Fifth, the size of finance in the economy gets detached from the real sector. It presumes that those people who get finance from banks do not invest in business but use it in speculative pursuits. Is it realistic to make such an assertion in most cases? It is possible that some of the bank loans may flow to speculative pursuits, but we cannot say that for the majority of the cases.

In brief, the effort by Kahf to distinguish interest on credit sales from interest on loans is laboured and unrealistic. In both cases, there is capital and there is interest on the capital, whatever roundabout manner we adopt. That means that orthodox opinion on *riba* is unnecessarily labouring to prove that a difference between cash and credit prices is permissible while interest on loans is not. The position is inconsistent, and efforts to locate fine differences between the two are frivolous and laboured. The orthodox position that treats all types of interest as *riba* has created all these difficulties. If we accept that not all types of interest are *riba* but that only interest on loans is *riba*, we get out of this difficulty.

14.2   THE DISCOUNTING OF RECEIVABLES

The discounting of receivables or bills of exchange is a nagging problem, but orthodox scholars have not been able to find a conclusive solution. Tahir *et al.* (1999: 107) contend that bills of exchange can be encashed against discounted values, as they are not the sale of debt but the sale of property rights. Balala (2011: 114) has argued similarly. Balala justifies the discounting of bills on the basis of the Prophet's own action in the case of the Jewish community of Banu Nadir, when he asked them to accept a lower value of their debts for early payment (*da' wa ta'jjal*). But we can excuse Balala, as she does not consider conventional interest to be *riba*. Her argument that bills can be discounted at going interest rates fits squarely into her overall position. However, she took an unnecessarily circuitous route to establish the point that the discounting of debts is not the sale of debt but the sale of property rights.

If we do not get into legal niceties, we can easily see that the essence of the matter remains the same. Allowing discount in the name of 'the trading of property rights' and not 'the trading of debt' does not change the essence of the matter. Discounting is forgoing the value of the bill with reference to time and the rate of interest, call it by whatever name you like. The arrangement would be acceptable if we concede that not all forms of interest are *riba*. But if we insist that all forms of interest are *riba* (as for example Tahir *et al.* do) the arrangement is nothing but a disguised method of accepting the interest.

14.3   THE TIME VALUE OF MONEY

The question of the time value of money is unresolved in Islamic financial theory (Ahmad and Hassan 2006: 68). On one hand, Muslim jurists accept an increase in the price of goods when payment is deferred (as in *murabaha*) or when there is a fixed return on capital (as in financing *ijara*) and on the other they refuse to allow an increase on a cash loan, treating it as *riba*. The position is inconsistent and unsustainable on rational grounds (El-Gamal 2001: 3).

One of the most significant arguments for the justification of interest in conventional finance lies in the time value of money. The argument briefly states that, since the value of money in the present is higher than in the future, the lender must pay interest to compensate for the diminution in value over time. The argument is generally accepted by economists and financial analysts. Most projects are appraised on the basis of present value, determined by discounting the cost–benefit flows over time. The argument in favour of the time value of money is so persuasive that Muslim economists also feel deterred from arguing against it (see e.g. Obaidullah 2006: 10). They tend to forget that, by accepting the time value of money as a valid concept, they are actually conceding the ground in favour of interest as a rational payment. Instead of accepting this deeper implication, they adopt a simplistic stance and argue that the time value of money is a valid concept and so is discounting provided the rate of discount is the 'rate of return' on capital rather than the rate of interest (e.g. Zarqa 1983; M.F. Khan 1991). They forget that it is not the question of which rate you use, but the question of conceding the point that the value of money in the present is higher than its value in the future (by whatever amount). Once we accept this point, we also accept that we need to compensate the lender for the diminution in the value of money caused by the passage of time. This is the justification for interest in modern financial theory. Muslim economists and financial analysts do not face this question squarely.

Contemporary Islamic jurists recognize the time value of money when they legitimize a higher price for a credit sale than the cash price. The Islamic Fiqh Academy of the OIC has also approved it (Ahmad and Hassan 2006: 75). There is in addition a consensus that the delivery price of a commodity in a contract of *salam* can be lower than the price at the time of financing. Similarly, in a contract of *istisna'*, the price of the manu-factured asset can be higher than the market price at the time of signing the contract. In these cases, variations in prices arise from the time factor. By accepting these variations as legitimate, Muslim jurists tend to approve the reason for charging conventional interest. However, to escape the blame, they argue that Islam recognizes the time value of money in sales but not in debts.

For example, Iqbal and Mirakhor (2008: 61–62) say:

> According to the *Shari'ah*, compensation for the value of time in sales contracts is acknowledged, but in the case of lending, increase (interest) is prohibited as a means of material compensation for time. . . . Given a sum of money, it can be invested in a business venture or it can be lent for a given period of time. In case of investment, the investor will be compensated for any profit and loss earned during that time and Islam fully recognizes this return on investment as a result of an economic activity. On the other hand, if money is in the form of a loan, it is an act of charity where surplus funds are effectively being utilized to promote economic development and social well being. In response to the contemporary understanding that interest on a loan is a reward for the opportunity cost of the lender, Islamic scholars maintain that interest fixed *ex ante* is certain, while profits and losses are not and to take a **certain** as a compensation for the **uncertain** amounts to indulging in *riba* and is therefore unlawful.

The above argument has several fallacies:

a. There is hardly any disagreement now, after Böhm-Bawerk's (1890) seminal work on the theory of interest, that the prevalent commercial interest is a reward for time. Thus any increase in the value of capital due to the passing of time is interest. It is based on the common-sense observation that benefits received sooner in time are perceived to have a higher value than those received later in time. The more distant the time when you hope to receive some benefit the lower is the value of that benefit to you. Interest is considered to be a compensation for the diminution in the (perceived) value of money lent now and to be received later. There is no difference of opinion that this recognition of the time value of money is the *raison d'être* of interest in capital-ism. Saying that we recognize the time value of money but deny the rationale of interest is to argue two opposing points of view in the same breath.

b.   The argument that the time value of money is legitimate in investment but not in loans is plausible if we treat lending as a charitable activity (Ahmad and Hassan 2006: 86). In the case of lending, too, the time value of money exists. The lender would, however, be forgoing that value as a matter of sacrifice. It would be an ethically desirable act. However, the above explanation does not face the hard question: are banks in the business of charity? Obviously not. They are commercial institutions and are investing the funds of their customers. Those who are getting finance from the banks are also engaged in a commercial venture. Calling it by the name of 'loan' does not change its substantive nature. Most people who get money from banks are doing so for business and industry and other gainful activities. For them, Muslim economists recognize the time value of money. The only objection that remains is that it should not be fixed in advance. How does it change the nature of the whole transaction? It remains interest whether you fix the rate in advance or fix it later.

c.   The argument that fixing in advance is asking for a certain compensation for an uncertain amount (of profit) is also fallacious. Not all such transactions where one part of the compensation is uncertain and the other is certain are disallowed in Islam. Consider the case of a person who hires a driver to ply a taxi on a fixed daily rate from the driver, irrespective of his earnings. This is allowed in Islamic law. Another example is that the rent of land fixed in advance (*muzara'a*, contractual lease) is permissible although it is not certain that the peasant would be able to make a profit. A person visits a restaurant where meals are available for a fixed price at the buffet. However, the restaurant owner does not know how much a person would eat. You subscribe to a journal for one year. The price is fixed in advance but you do not know whether you will get the journal or what the contents will be or how many pages, and so on. In everyday life, we do not always enter into transactions where both sides are certain about their obligations 100 per cent. Some risk is always there. In the case of interest too, the various risks involved in the investment of funds are squeezed to some extent into the form of a single payable amount, and both sides are sure of their obligations and rights. In the case of profit–loss sharing the investor knows the amount of the capital but is unsure of the return. There is a greater amount of risk for the investor owing to this uncertainty.

In brief, the whole problem emanates from treating all forms of interest as *riba*. The fact is that an increase on the principal sum of a loan is both interest and *riba*, but other forms of interest, arising through myriad types of transactions, are interest but not *riba*. If we accept this argument, the confusion about the time value of money will dissipate.

14.4   REDUCTION IN DEBT ON EARLY PAYMENT

One of the manifestations of the time value of money is a reduction in debt if the debtor pays early. The four *Sunni* schools of jurisprudence do not allow it by consensus (Ahmad and Hassan 2006: 78). This is enigmatic. They allow an increase if the price is deferred but do not allow a reduction if the buyer pays sooner than promised. It means they do not allow a cash discount.

Saadullah (1994: 7) writes:

> Reduction of a debt in return for early repayment is a matter of contention among jurists. The juristic consensus is opposed to making such reduction of a deferred debt conditional on earlier repayment. This view is adopted by the four *imams* (leaders of the four major jurisprudential schools). Such reduction, however, has been permitted by some companions of the Prophet and some of their followers. This position has been advanced by Ibn Taymiyya[2] and Ibn al-Qayyim,[3] and it has, more recently, been adopted by the Islamic Fiqh Academy of the OIC. The Academy decided that 'reduction of a deferred debt in order to accelerate its repayment, whether at the request of the debtor or the creditor is permissible under *Shari'ah*. It does not constitute forbidden *riba* if it is not agreed upon in advance and as long as the creditor–debtor relationship remains bilateral. If, however, a third party is involved it becomes forbidden since it becomes similar to the discount of bills.' (Islamic Fiqh Academy, 7th session, 1992, Resolution 66/2/77)

The position taken by the Islamic Fiqh Academy regarding reduction of debt on early payment admits, though obliquely, the time value of money. Once we accept that, it becomes difficult to oppose interest, which is justified on the same basis. Moreover, accepting a reduction in debt if payment is expedited opens the door to the discounting of bills, which otherwise is opposed by all orthodox scholars. The position is inconsistent and unsustainable on rational grounds.

Badawi (2000: 206–207) has discussed this question at length. He has reported a difference of opinion among companions of the Prophet as well as jurists. His conclusion is that *riba* applies to an increase in debt. A reduction in debt is not *riba*. The conclusion recognizes the time value of money. However, it is not consistent with the orthodox interpretation of *riba*, which does not recognize it. How can we justify the time value of money for the discounting of debt but turn our face away while charging interest on debt?

14.5 RESCHEDULING OF PAYMENTS

In conventional finance, a client can request the bank to reschedule payments. The bank will generally agree to this on payment of interest. Generally, it will mean that interest will continue accruing beyond the earlier due date, if no additional or penal interest is added. In the case of *murabaha*, for example, the banks do not and cannot agree to reschedule, as it would not bring them any additional income. Rescheduling of payments is a real-life need for business firms. However, Muslim jurists have not, as yet, found a solution to this problem.

14.6 INDEXATION OF LOANS

The question of erosion of money value due to secular inflation has been vexing Islamic scholars. In the case of long-term and medium-term finance, the value of money depreciates in a regime of inflation. Once we make finance interest-free, the value of money at the time of repayment is diminished as compared to the time the finance was provided. It is an inequitable situation where the debtor is likely to impose hardship on the creditor. The question arises: once we prohibit interest, how do we compensate the creditor in an inflationary regime? One suggestion is to index the loans with inflation without legalizing interest. That does not resolve the dilemma of the orthodox scholars. If they agree to compensate the creditor for inflation, an additional sum over the principal amount will be due on the principal sum. It would be difficult to tell indexation from interest. By allowing indexation of loans, interest would enter the scene surreptitiously.

Even on economic grounds, Islamic economists have argued that indexation is not a viable option. For example, W.M. Khan (2002: 104) says:

> Full indexation is an invitation to galloping inflation. Adaptation to inflation thus contains a paradox. The more a society insulates its members from inflation, the more unstable inflation is likely to become. Countries that have thoroughly indexed their economies (such as Brazil) found it extremely costly to eradicate inflation even through such measures.

Iqbal and Mirakhor (2008: 58–61) summarize the arguments against indexation of loans as follows:

a. The prohibition of *riba* in the Qur'an is absolute. We cannot create exceptions to it on our own.
b. Even if a person does not lend money, its value would erode anyway

owing to inflation. Why should the borrower bear the loss due to inflation?

c.   There are several contributing factors and parties to inflation. It is unfair to hold one party (i.e. the borrower) responsible for it and make him bear the brunt.

d.   There is no perfect index by which inflation can be measured without causing injustice to other parties.

All said and done, these arguments do not face the ultimate question. The lender gave a certain value to the borrower, but he or she is getting a shorter measure of value in return. Is it fair? The nature of inflation is that people are being robbed of the value of their possessions (money) overnight through no fault of their own. In this scenario, if a person tries to take back some of the property, should we consider it blameworthy? The interest that the person gets on deposits is a sort of effort to save some of the property from being stolen. At times, the compensation may not even be equal to inflation. How can we blame the person for taking that interest on deposits? Asking to leave the deposits and allow them to erode over time will only be an unreasonable suggestion.

Some economists have suggested ways for getting out of this difficulty as follows. There has been a suggestion by some writers that compensation for inflation should not be construed as *riba*. According to W.M. Ballantyne (1986: 125–126):

> When an article loaned is neither weighed nor measured, there is a choice between requiring the return of the equivalent at the date of repayment or requiring a return of the article's value as at the date of the loan. Ibn Qudama[4] held that, with objects not measured or weighed, there could be no equivalents, so the debtor had to restore to the creditor the value of the article as it was when the obligation originally arose, that is, at the time of the loan contract. An argument could be constructed on this basis that a creditor should at least be able to recover a sum equivalent to the amount by which the original principal lent has depleted in real terms during the period of the loan. . . . Ibn Taymiyya,[5] an independent Hanbali whose views have been approved by legal modernists [also] . . . believed that the lender should recover the original value. . . . It would be possible to argue with some force that Ibn Taymiyya's view is the one which ought to be adopted, because the lender is not engaging in *riba* – he is not making a real profit out of the transaction. If he could not recover for losses sustained as a result of inflation, he would be much less inclined to grant a gratuitous loan.

Iqbal and Mirakhor (2008: 61) make the following suggestion:

> Irrespective of causes and sources of inflation, indexation is not accepted by scholars; however, other remedies have been suggested. For example, if the lender and the borrowers are concerned about inflation, then the loan can be

denominated in terms of a commodity, i.e. gold. The lender can lend a certain 'quantity of gold' to the borrower who is obligated to return the same quantity at the expiry of the loan.

Zaman (2008: 50–51) proposes the following:

> One idea would be to allow the depositor a range of possibilities through which some index of the value of deposits could be preserved. For example, deposits could be stored in a bundle of currencies optimized for stability, or in the form of a local indexed basket of consumer goods, or more specifically targeted towards particular future needs such as the education of children. The main arguments offered in favor of bank interest by Muslims have been the propensity of inflation to reduce the real value of deposits. An institution of the type proposed could overcome this problem without resorting to interest.

Noorzoy (1982: 10) also allows some sort of adjustment in the principal sum of the loan owing to a fluctuation in prices. He writes:

> But recent experience indicates that inflation will not be eliminated completely in the world at large. Under these conditions it seems equitable for the lender to obtain the same level of purchasing power at which a loan was initiated. It seems then, that the application of the law on *riba al-fadl* is more appropriate under inflationary and deflationary conditions. This in turn means that when *riba* is interpreted to mean interest the real rate of interest will be zero, which will permit nominal increases or decreases over the principal of the loan equivalent, respectively to the rate of variation in the price level under inflationary and deflationary conditions.

Tahir *et al.* (1999: 137) propose that the expected inflation should be built into the price of the goods sold on a deferred payment basis. This solution does not cater for cash loans. To that extent it is inadequate. Besides, this is a trick to cover up inflation in the form of a higher price, which in its essence is nothing but interest. The solution concedes some role to interest to compensate for the decrease in the value of deferred payments due to inflation.

There is no consensus on any of the above suggestions. In the final analysis any excess allowed on the principal sum to compensate for inflation would be so close to interest that it would be difficult to tell one from the other. Orthodox scholars have strong objections to any such arrangement. Uthmani (1999-b: 48) has finally surrendered to the position that more research is needed.

14.7 PENALTIES FOR DELAYS IN THE REPAYMENT OF LOANS

One of the vexing problems in Islamic finance is to control and manage delinquent clients who do not abide by the repayment schedule. In conventional finance, it is quite simple. Interest continues accumulating for the period of delay. In Islamic finance, the problem is how to ensure repayment on schedule. Muslim scholars have proposed several solutions, but none is satisfactory. For example, some jurists have proposed imprisonment, while others have suggested a financial penalty. Imprisonment involves criminal court proceedings and is inherently cumbersome. In the case of a penalty too, some have proposed that the penalty should be paid to the creditor as compensation for the loss of income while others think that it should be paid out as charity (e.g. Abu Ghuddah n.d.-a: 120; Uthmani n.d.-a: 22). M.S. Siddiqi and Khan (2010) discuss this issue at length. They conclude that Islamic law allows this type of contribution but think that the solution is not appropriate as a system. The solution is a legalist device to discipline delinquent clients. However, it has problems. Firstly, the contribution by the client will be compulsory and not voluntary. That flouts the basic Islamic principle that all charitable acts have to be voluntary. Secondly, it will have similar features to interest on delayed payment, as the amount of contribution will be decided with reference to the amount payable and the period of delay. Thirdly, the bank will not be able to solve its problem of liquidity with this technique. From the bank's perspective this type of contribution will be of no commercial consequence. That makes Islamic banks less competitive as compared to their conventional counterparts. Fourthly, it creates another dimension of management problem that relates to efficient management of the charity fund and its oversight. The probability of its misuse by the Islamic bank would always remain. The bank may use the fund to help its own poor employees, who otherwise would have been the responsibility of the bank. For all these reasons the solution is sub-optimal.

The amount of penalty has also been under debate. Some would like to restrict it to the creditor's cost; others suggest a flat fee. HSBC Amanah, for example, charges an administration fee for late payment. Some scholars allow a penalty in proportion to the creditor's capital and participation in the transaction (Visser 2009: 77).

Warde (2010: 163) writes:

> Islamic banks face a serious problem with late payments, not to speak of outright defaults, since some people take advantage of every dilatory legal and religious device. . . . In most Islamic countries, various forms of penalties and late

fees have been established, only to be outlawed or considered unenforceable. Late fees in particular have been assimilated to *riba*. As a result, 'debtors know that they can pay Islamic banks last since doing so involves no cost'.[6] . . . Many businessmen who had borrowed large amounts of money over long periods of time seized the opportunity of Islamicization to do away with accumulated interest of their debt, by repaying only the principal – usually a puny sum when years of double-digit inflation were taken into consideration.

Iqbal and Mirakhor (2008: 89) write:

> [In the case of the *murabaha* contract:] In the event of default by the end user, the financier only has recourse to the items financed and no further mark-up or penalty may be applied to the outstanding liability. . . . In some cases, *Shari'ah* scholars allow the financier to recover additional amounts to off-set any loss or damage due to default. . . . The financier is allowed to ask for security to protect itself against any non-payment in the future.

Uthmani (1999-a: 132–133) makes the penalty conditional on the dishonesty of the defaulter. It is not clear if a simple and manageable method for establishing dishonesty is available. A further question arises: is this additional amount not interest? Another suggestion by him is that the bank should repossess the goods sold to the client. From the perspective of the financial institution, repossession of goods is a cumbersome way of managing the contract. It may involve additional cost to the bank. Who will bear that cost? Is it an efficient way of managing the contract?

Al-Suwailem (2006: 125) proposes that the bank can have direct access to the income of the client and deduct its instalment at source. Obviously, it is of limited use, as not all clients would have such visible income streams that could be accessed by the bank and not all clients would be willing to provide access to the bank. Moreover, is this not a tyrannical method of recovering the debt: the same type of tyranny (*zulm*) against which we started our crusade of Islamic banking in the first place?

Even conventional banks obtain security from borrowers besides a clause of penal interest in the contract. The security taken by the banks is not an efficient manner of protecting themselves, as it involves valuation and legal problems and requires prolonged action. In Islamic finance, what is the parallel of interest that accumulates in the case of default? If there is no such parallel, what is the compulsion for the client to repay on time? There is an incentive for delaying the repayment in the absence of penal interest. How do we handle this problem?

Chapra (2008-a: 8) agrees that the problem of compensation for delay is still unresolved:

> Second, it is the price of the good or service sold, and not the rate of interest that is stipulated in the case of sales – or lease-based modes of finance. Once

the price has been set, it cannot be altered, even if there is a delay in payment due to unforeseen circumstances. This helps protect the interest of the buyer in strained circumstances. However, it may also lead to a liquidity problem for the banks if the buyer willfully delays the payment. This is a major unresolved problem in Islamic finance. Discussions are, however, in progress among the jurists to find a *Shari'ah*-compatible solution.

Sairally (2002: 80) says:

> Other scholars have, however, disapproved the concept of a financial penalty. They argue that it does not conform to the principles of the *Shari'ah* since it is similar to the charging of additional amounts (*riba*) during the days of *Jahiliyya*[7] when debtors were unable to effect payment at the due date. The ruling given by the Islamic Fiqh Academy of Jeddah, which had advised against the imposition of penalties, supports this argument (*Majma al-fiqh al-Islami.* Resolution No. 53, 5th Annual Session, Jeddah, Journal No. 6, V. 1, p. 447).

That takes us back to square one. If the banks cannot charge a penalty, how can they solve the problem of delinquent clients?

Muslim scholars have opened the door to allow penal interest in Islamic finance. Kamali (2007: 10) reports that the *Shari'ah* Advisory Council (SAC) of the Securities Commission of Malaysia in its resolution of 8 November 2000 agreed to impose a penalty with certain conditions. He writes:

> *Ta'wid* (compensation) can be imposed after it is found that deliberate delay in payment (*mumatalah*) is present on the part of the payee to settle the payment of principal or profit. The rate of *ta'wid* on late payment of profit is one per cent per annum of the arrears which may not be compounded. Where the *ta'wid* rate on payment of the principal is based on the prevailing market rate in the Islamic interbank money market, it too may not be compounded. The SAC resolution added that 'the imposition of *ta'wid*, or *shart jaza'i'* is penalty agreed upon by the *'aqd* parties as compensation that can rightfully be claimed by the creditor, when the debtor fails or is late in meeting his obligation to pay back the loan. Payment by way of *ta'wid* may not in any case exceed the total amount of the outstanding balance.[8]

With reference to the contract of *istisna'*, the Islamic Fiqh Academy of the OIC has also allowed imposition of a penalty with certain conditions. Kamali (2007: 11) writes:

> The Fiqh Academy of the Organization of Islamic Conference, in its resolution (1992) authorized imposition of liquidated damages and penalty in *istisna'* (manufacturing contract) on the basis of a prior agreement between the contracting parties. This is when the parties agree and stipulate in their contract a sum that shall be payable in the event one party fails to discharge or delay

his contractual obligation.[9] ... Mustafa al-Zarqa has observed concerning compensation (*ta'wid*) that it is payable for losses the parties incur in a business transaction due to waste or disruption of business. Due to the change of circumstances people may need to insert a condition on *ta'wid* in contracts to secure their economic interests in which case they are bound by their stipulations.[10]

The fact is that Muslim economists have not been able to find an equally efficient way to handle default in repayment. Despite various interim suggestions, the dilemma remains. Adhering to the orthodox interpretation of interest would not allow any penalty for late payment. How do we discipline delinquent clients?[11]

14.8   FEES FOR BANK GUARANTEES

Another unresolved issue in Islamic finance is fees for issuing bank guarantees. The generally accepted juridical position is that any fee that guarantees repayment of a debt is actually interest for the funds guaranteed. When the bank issues a guarantee it theoretically sets aside equivalent funds for honouring it, should the client fail. Issuing a guarantee is actually a form of loan on which the bank charges interest and calls it a 'guarantee fee'. The relationship between clients who seek guarantees and the bank is an arm's length one. It is not possible for a bank to issue guarantees for all clients without a fee to cover itself against the risks involved. That leads to a dilemma for orthodox scholars. If they allow the fee they take the blame for accepting interest as legitimate, and if they disallow it they create rigidities in commercial practice that are not tenable. Uthmani (n.d.-a: 19) says:

> [Some] *Shari'ah* scholars . . . say the prohibition of guarantee fee is not based on any specific injunction of the Qur'an or the *Sunnah* of the Prophet. It has been deduced from the prohibition of *riba* as one of its ancillary consequences. . . . In today's commercial activities, the guarantor sometimes needs a number of studies and a lot of secretarial work. Therefore, they opine, the prohibition of the guarantee fee should be reviewed in this perspective. The question still needs further research and should be placed before a larger forum of scholars.

14.9   THE PROMISE TO BUY OR SELL

The question whether, in a contract of *murabaha*, the promise to buy or sell is binding or optional has drawn the attention of Islamic jurists. *Murabaha* requires the financiers to buy or sell and undertake significant risks if the clients do not fulfil the promise. Although honouring a promise to buy and sell is a moral duty, the proponents of Islamic finance have argued that the S*hari'ah* would make such promises binding to alleviate the risks to the financial institutions. For example, Uthmani (n.d.-a: 16) says:

> But in commercial dealings, where a party has given an absolute promise to sell or purchase something and the other party has incurred liabilities on that basis, there is no reason why such a promise should not be enforced. Therefore, on the basis of the clear injunctions of Islam, if the parties have agreed that this particular promise will be binding on the promisor, it will be enforceable. This is not a question pertaining to *murabaha* alone. If promises are not enforceable in the commercial transactions, it may seriously jeopardize commercial activities.

The explanation is plausible. However, the effect of making the promise binding creates a situation where the banks do not take any business risk. Let us take an example. A client approaches the bank for finance to buy raw material. Since interest is prohibited, the bank agrees to supply the raw material from the market on a mark-up basis. The client promises to buy and the bank procures the raw material. But the client violates the promise, and refuses to take delivery and make payment. The bank has incurred significant costs. The above ruling by Uthmani says that in such cases the client would be forced by law to accept the delivery. This is a fair ruling. However, what is the essence of the deal? The bank has provided the raw material to the client on the basis of a mark-up. The client cannot refuse the merchandise. The business risk of the bank is zero, while the return on the finance is fixed and guaranteed. The situation in the case of interest-based finance is simpler and easy to administer, with the same economic consequences. The conventional bank provides funds at a fixed rate of interest. The client buys the raw material from the market and returns the principal with interest. In both cases the cost to the client is the same. However, if the bank provides the raw material it incurs extra costs (which is a deadweight on society) and undertakes activities which are unfamiliar to its regular business. The client also remains unsure about the quality and delivery of the raw material. The whole process is cumbersome and complex. Taking finance on the basis of interest and paying it back on the due date is simpler to administer. The fundamental reason for discarding interest-based finance is that the financier does not take any business risk. In the case of mark-up-based finance too, the financier does not take any risk. Why adopt a roundabout method of doing something that can be done in a simpler manner?

14.10   THE RESIDUAL VALUE OF THE ASSET IN FINANCIAL LEASES

There is no difference of opinion among Muslim scholars about the legitimacy of operational leases where the lessor remains the owner of the asset, which on termination of the lease reverts to the lessor. Islamic financial institutions have adopted financial leasing as a major technique for providing finance. In a financial lease, the intention is to provide finance to the lessee to purchase an asset. However, the legal mechanics are such that in theory the lessor, in this case an Islamic financial institution, remains the owner of the asset. When the lessee pays all the instalments and the lease terminates, theoretically the asset should return to the lessor. However, this creates legal and administrative problems for the financial institution. From an economic perspective, if the asset returns to the lessor, the cost of finance to the lessee becomes prohibitive. After paying the total price of the asset, the lessee should own the asset in whatever shape and condition it is. How can that be done in a legal manner? Some Islamic financial institutions donate the asset to the lessee, while others transfer it to the lessee at a token price. The question arises: why should the lessor donate the asset and that too as a matter of compulsion? If it is a token price, why is the lessor giving the concession? Actually, these methods are techniques to hide the reality of dealing in interest. Islamic financial institutions provide finance at a certain rate of interest through the mechanics of a financing lease. Once the lessee has repaid the entire amount with interest, the lessor has no right in the asset. That is so in conventional finance as well. However, to conclude the deal in a logical manner, Islamic finance has to adopt the circuitous route of either donating the asset or selling it for a token price, and so on. Simple interest-based finance would not create these problems.

14.11   THE QUESTION OF SUBLEASES

The practice of leasing and subleasing is quite common in the contemporary world. Large corporations lease their premises or other assets to a lessee, who is given the legal right to sublease the asset. The main lessee becomes a lessor for other lessees. The difference in the rent rates of the sublease and the main lease is income for the main lessee. The question arises: is a sublease contract permissible in the *Shari'ah*? The main lessee is passing on an asset to another party on sublease without adding any value to it. What is the justification for this income of the main lessee? If it is compensation for managing various small subleases, it should be related to the service being provided and not to the period of the lease. It is a case where the intermediary is getting something for nothing. According to a strict orthodox interpretation such earnings should be treated as *riba*, as they derive from the sale of debt for a higher price. However, orthodox scholars have not given any clear verdict on this. Kamali (2007: 11) is an exception. He concurs with some juristic schools that the subleasing contract is valid and is closer to market reality. However, he does not face the question: how far is the main lessee earning this income? What risk is he or she taking? What service is he or she providing? Is this not the sale of debt for a higher price?

14.12   FORWARDS, FUTURES AND OPTIONS TRADING

Contemporary financial markets deal in forwards, futures and options contracts on an extensive scale. Trading in these markets has evolved over centuries and is the result of commercial needs. For example, forwards contracts help business firms to lock in the price of a product or raw material or foreign exchange to be bought and sold in the future. It provides both sides with certainty about the price and helps in planning operations. However, even forwards have certain risks. For example, either party to the deal may default, causing losses to the other. Similarly, if a party wants to offload a forwards deal, it needs a party to accept the deal; it may not be easily available. To cover such risks, trading in futures has emerged. Futures are traded at an exchange where the management regulates the deals by standardizing the products, payment periods, settlement procedures, margin limits and so on. Transactions in a futures exchange overcome the risks of the forwards market. However, futures trading too has risks. For example, in a confirmed deal both parties are locked in, and the parties cannot revoke it in response to any movement in prices or other events in commercial dealings (such as acceptance or rejection of tender bids, developments in technology, and so on). To overcome such uncertainties, options trading emerged as an alternative. In options trading, the market players commit to buy or sell by paying a token sum as the price of the option. If the option is exercised, the deal will be executed. If the option holder decides not to proceed, the price of the option is forfeited. The mechanism minimizes the loss for reversing the deal as a whole. Markets in forwards, futures and options have evolved as business necessities. In the present-day competitive world, business firms which do not operate in these markets are exposed to higher risks and may become uncompetitive and be forced out of the market (based on Bacha 1999).

Despite the obvious advantages, orthodox scholars have expressed their disapproval for these markets (e.g. Uthmani 1999; Al-Suwailem 1999, 2000). However, Kamali (1995) is, perhaps, an exception, who thinks that these forms of business are permissible. A consensus has yet to emerge about the permissibility of trade in these markets. It is interesting that, despite the negative opinion, Muslim jurists are unable to suggest an alternative to cover the business risks for which these forms of trade have evolved over centuries.

14.13   EXCHANGE OF CURRENCIES

In the domain of international trade, exchange of currencies is a normal function. The buyers of goods and services have to make payments in foreign currencies that they may not hold. The Islamic law of currency exchange (*bai' al-sarf*) requires spot exchange, which may not be possible in some cases. It also requires some mechanism to insure against movements in the foreign exchange markets. Traders who conclude agreements on the basis of the prevailing exchange rates may face extremely adverse situations when making payments if foreign exchange rates have moved adversely. Owing to speculation in the international foreign exchange markets and arbitrage in the rates of exchange, trillions of dollars cross borders on a daily basis. Muslim traders cannot remain unconcerned with these developments. However, strict interpretation of the Islamic law making spot currency exchange compulsory creates practical difficulties. M.N. Siddiqi has realized this problem. He writes (1999):

> There remains the gray area of exchange between different monies, i.e. selling one currency for another. Islamic economic research in this area has yet to catch up with the times. I do not have any opinions to pronounce save noting that it is a necessary economic activity facilitating exchange of goods and services across borders. Fear of making financial transactions 'profitable' without there being any link whatsoever with exchange of real goods and services makes many Muslim scholars opt for the strictest interpretation of the relevant rules. But that carries the danger of restricting what may be really necessary. The challenge of finding the golden mean remains.

Contemporary jurists have relaxed the condition of simultaneous exchange of currencies in the case of some precious metals such as gold and silver. Their plea is that precious metals such as platinum are not the same thing as the gold or silver mentioned in the Traditions of the Prophet.[12] Thus Islamic banks can trade in these metals on a deferred exchange basis (El-Gamal 2006: 69). However, the matter remains unresolved in the case of paper currencies.

14.14 CONCLUDING REMARKS

We have summarized various unresolved issues arising from the orthodox interpretation of *riba*. Muslim scholars feel the compulsions of trade and commerce in the present age and also realize the facility with which conventional finance has handled these issues. They have either proposed methods to allow interest through the back door or expressed their helplessness. They are unable to grasp the moral courage to recognize that the problems have arisen only because of the peculiar interpretation of *riba* that they have adopted. If they reject this self-imposed interpretation, most of the problems will be solved and the way forward will be quite clear.

NOTES

1. [As in original] Abraham L. Udovitch, Reflections on the institutions of credit and banking in the medieval Islamic Near East, *Studia Islamica*, 41 (1–21) (1975), p. 9. Also, by the same author, Bankers without banks: Commerce, banking and the society in the Middle East, in *The dawn of modern banking*, ed. Abraham L. Udovitch (New Haven, CT: Yale University Press, 1979), pp. 255–273.
2. Ibn Taymiyya (d. 1328).
3. Ibn Qayyim al-Jauzi (d. 1350).
4. Ibn Qudama al-Maqdisi (d. AH 620).
5. Ibn Taymiyya (d. 1328).
6. [As in original] Quoted from F. al-Omar and M. Abdel-Haq, *Islamic banking: Theory, practice and challenges* (London: Zen Books, 1996).
7. Lit. Period of Ignorance. Technically, the pre-Islamic era in Arabia.
8. [As in original] Securities Commission of Malaysia, n. 10, 103.
9. [As in original] Majma'al-Fiqh li Rabitah al-'Alam al Islami, *Qararat Majma' al-Fiqh al-Islami* (Jeddah, 1975).
10. [As in original] Ali al-Khafif, *Ahkam al-Mu'amalat al-Shar'iyah* (Bahrain: Bank al-Baraka, n.d.), n. 2, 490–491.
11. Interestingly, Muslim scholars have not noticed the truce agreement signed by the Prophet with the people of Tai'f. The text of the agreement is available in Hameedullah (2009: 509–511). Clause 9 of the agreement says: 'Any unsecured debt that has become due but the debtor is defaulting, interest will be payable, though Allah does not sanction its legality.' Clause 19 further elaborates: 'Any mortgaged debt on which interest has not yet been paid would be repaid without interest. However, the debtor would get extension till the month of Jamad al-Awwal, if he does not have means to pay. If he does not pay the debt in the extended period, interest will be payable on it.'
12. This refers to Traditions of the Prophet relating to *bai' al-sarf* (exchange of precious metals and currency).

15. Practice of interest-based finance among Muslims

15.1 CLAIMS OF CONSENSUS ON THE ORTHODOX INTERPRETATION OF *RIBA*

Orthodox scholars claim a complete consensus (*ijma'*) about commercial interest being a form of *riba*. Farooq (2006-d) has quoted from a sample of 10 scholars who claim the consensus. Included in this list are Abu al-'Ala Mawdudi (1903–79), Yusuf al-Qardawi, Wahba Zuhayli, Tariq Talib al-Anjari, Thanvir Ahmed, Mabid al-Jarhi, M.N. Siddiqi, M.U. Chapra, Munawar Iqbal and Imran Ahsan Khan Nyazee. To refute the claim of consensus, he has given another list of scholars, which includes Syed Ahmad Khan (1819–98), Muhammad Abduh (1849–1905), Rashid Rida (1865–1935), Abdullah Yusufali (1872–1953), Abd al-Razzaq al-Sanhuri (1895–1971), Muhammad Asad (1900–92), Fazlur Rahman (1911–88), Mahmud Shaltut (1893–1963), Abdel Wahab Khallaf (1888–1956) and Ibrahim Shihata (1937–2001). Besides, some of the contemporary Islamic scholars hold similar views. Examples are Fathi Osman, Nawab Haider Naqvi, Salim Rashid, Imad al-Din Ahmed, Omar Afzal, Raquibuzzaman, Abdulaziz Sachedina, Abdullah Saeed, Mahmud El-Gamal and Mohammad Fadel.

A more fundamental question is: what is meant by consensus? We find a lot of confusion on the exact meaning and connotation of the term 'consensus' (*ijma'*) in Islamic law. There is no agreement about whose opinion, of which period, to what extent and on which subjects an opinion will be evaluated to determine the state of consensus. A general misconception is that consensus (*ijma'*) means a complete agreement of all scholars of all ages on a legal issue. If we accept this interpretation, it would mean there had never been consensus on any matter throughout Islamic history, as dissenting opinions are available on almost all subjects. Despite that, consensus is an accepted mode of the legal process in Islam. The question arises: what does consensus mean and is there a consensus on the definition of *riba*?

The subject requires detailed discussion that would drag us into the methodology and theory of Islamic law and displace the focus of the present discussion. For brevity's sake we are relying on the opinion of a scholar of our age, Muhammad Khalid Masud, former Chairman, Council of Islamic Ideology, Pakistan. The opinion tries to rationalize the entire debate on the subject and suggests a workable answer to the above question.

Masud (2007: 3) writes that consensus (*ijma'*) has never been equivalent to 'total agreement by all'. There have always been dissenting voices. A practical manifestation of the consensus (*ijma'*) on an opinion is the agreement of the majority (of scholars) that is also accepted by the people in general. Seen in this light, the orthodox claim of consensus on treating commercial interest as *riba* is not well founded. As we shall show further on, there is little evidence that the majority of the scholars and people in general have accepted the orthodox interpretation of *riba*. In 57 Muslim countries today, most of the financial institutions are based on interest, and the majority of Muslims deal with them without much qualm of conscience. The claim that there is consensus on the prohibition of all types of interest being *riba* is, thus, not supported by the evidence. We shall substantiate this conclusion by further evidence.

15.2   THE PRACTICE OF *RIBA* AMONG MUSLIMS

The economic history of Muslims is a thinly researched area. There are only a few authentic historical reports on the economic practices and policies of the Muslim people. Belief in the prohibition of *riba* was in vogue throughout Muslim history, but it cannot be asserted with any certainty that all Muslims avoided it in practice. Nor is there any authentic report that Muslims in general did not indulge in interest. There are fragmented reports, though, that some Muslims dealt in interest.

15.2.1   Historical Evidence

Warde (2010: 62) has quoted Abraham Udovitch as saying: 'The frequent and vehement reiteration of the prohibition against usury in medieval Islamic religious writings has been interpreted by some scholars as indirect testimony to its equally frequent violation in practice.'[1]

Nagaoka (2010) writes:

> Maxime Rodinson asserts that moneylenders lending at a usurious rate of interest was quite common in the pre-modern Islamic world; therefore, the prohibition of *Riba* became increasingly irrelevant at the time (Rodinson 1966[2]). Indeed, several empirical studies seem to exemplify Rodinson's proposition.

For example, Haim Gerber shows proof of the existence of interest-based loans known as *Istighlal* in Bursa during the seventeenth century (Gerber 1988: 128[3]). Further, Toru Miura considers litigation documents related to Damascus in the nineteenth century, and explains with the help of a case study interest bearing transactions between a guardian and a ward (Miura 1999: 322–326[4]). Nobuaki Kondo clarifies the prevalence of *Bey-i Shart* transactions in Tehran during the nineteenth century, which were similar to interest-based loans (Kondo 2005[5]).

However, Nagaoka (2010) concludes after discussion that the interest-based system was not universal even in the medieval ages. It was prevalent, though, in some regions. The *bai' al-'inah*-based financial instruments were embedded in the real sector of the economy in most parts of the world. There was no divergence between the financial sector and the real sectors of the economy. In that respect, the Islamic financial system was a universal system, and interest-based transactions were marginal in nature. However, it is also fair to say that a structured banking system without interest never existed even in the pre-modern age.

Noorzoy (1982: 6) writes:

> While this controversy continued in sixteenth century Ottoman Turkey, the actual practice of founding cash-*waqfs* apparently was established in the fifteenth century, and by the seventeenth century it was generally accepted in the Ottoman legal and economic systems.[6] Moreover, there is also evidence that a rate of interest of 10 percent was in common use in Egypt during the nineteenth century.[7]

Siddiqi (2009-a: 210) mentions that financing at a fixed rate of return was accepted side by side with other forms of financing during Muslim history. Abdul Azim Islahi (2011: 20) quotes al-Muhibbi (1651–99), who held a professorial chair in Damascus, in the following words:[8]

> Burhan al-Dimashqi known as Shaqlabaha, who used to sell silk before he traveled to Istanbul, occupied the positions of teacher and judge. Upon retirement, he returned to Damascus where he had dealings with farmers. He was famous for charging *riba* and in this way he increased his fortune to an unlimited extent. He used to deal with his borrowers very harshly (al-Muhibbi, I: 455). Al-Muhibbi (4:394) notes another incidence of loan on mortgage and the practice of interest.

There are opposing views as well. For example, Mirakhor (2007-a: 23) quotes Udovitch[9] that review of the Cairo Geniza scrolls shows there is little evidence of usurious loans in the medieval age. Chapra (2007: 108) quotes Udovitch (1981: 257, 268[10]) to support the opinion that interest-bearing loans and other usurious practices were not in vogue in the medieval age.

15.3 BANKING DURING THE ABBASID PERIOD

Chapra (2007: 107) says that, by the time of Abbasid Caliph Muqtadir (908–32), *sarrafs* had started performing most of the basic functions of modern banks to meet the financial needs of agriculture, industry and commerce within the constraints of the then prevailing technological environment. Ahmad Farras Oran and Ghaida Khaznehkatbi (n.d.) write in the *Encyclopedia of Islamic Economics and Finance*:

> Banking services included accepting deposits, these being the main source of funding, providing loans to individuals, traders, and governments, intermediating in internal and external commercial dealings, exchanging (discounting) financial instruments and monetary exchanges. The banks also had a number of practical problems to overcome, not least dealing with the different kinds and weights of *dirhams* given these were at variance with the official coinage, and the daily clearing of *sukuk* or cheques. All financial services were done in exchange for some amount of money or at some rate of interest. (p. 18)

> A *suftajah* could be exchanged, in one or several payments, when presented at its due date; otherwise it could be discounted in exchange for an amount of money or some interest rate, the latter often equating to as much as 10 per cent. (p. 19)

> To overcome shortages or delays in revenue, the state used to borrow, on an interest basis, from *jahbadh*. (p. 22)

> [*Wazir*] Ali bin Osi further convinced two *jahbadhs* to jointly become a continuous source of lending for the government in exchange for 1 per cent of the total tax collection of Al-Ahwaz province. On the first day of every month from 300 AH/912 AD – 316 AH/928 AD, 150,000 *dirhams* were borrowed consecutively from these *jahbadhs*. Given the continuity of this agreement, even after the death of the original lenders, this deal has been seen as equivalent to the establishment of an official bank. Similarly, *Wazir* Abdullah Kulwadhani borrowed 200,000 *dinars* in 319 AH/931 AD from some *jahbadh* house paying an equivalent of one *dirham* per *dinar*. There are no accounts of any external borrowing. (p. 28)

Tahir, Atiquzzafar, Ali and Waheed (1999: 82, 6.3) say:

> During the next three hundred years of Islamic history covering the period of the Umayyads and the Abbasids, there were some instances of debt incurred by field commanders and *wazirs* to tide over a temporary shortfall in funds. In some instances, the element of *riba* is also discernible.

The above is only fragmented evidence of the practice of interest-based finance. It would not be fair to conclude that this was the dominant form of financing throughout Muslim history. However, the existence of the practice to some extent cannot be denied.

15.4 CASH-*WAQFS* IN TURKEY

The practice of establishing *waqfs* (trusts) has been in vogue since the early days of Islam. The income from the property of the *waqf* was used for the defined beneficiaries. Later on, the custom of setting aside cash to establish a *waqf* got currency. The trusts created with cash were known as cash-*waqfs*. Cizakca (2000: 24ff.) explains the mechanics of the cash-*waqfs* in Ottoman Turkey. The institution of the cash-*waqf* was prevalent more prominently in sixteenth-century Ottoman Turkey. Cash-*waqfs* also existed in Syria, Egypt, Sudan, Aden, the Ural–Volga region, the Indo-Pak subcontinent, Iraq, Malaya and Singapore. The *waqfs* generally invested cash funds on interest. In a study based upon a sample of 1563 Bursa cash-*waqfs* and their respective profit/capital ratios covering the period 1667–1805, Cizakca (1993[11]) found that only four of these *waqfs* resorted to profit–loss sharing (*mudaraba or musharaka*), while the rest produced remarkably constant returns fluctuating within a narrow margin of 9 to 12 per cent per annum. This can be considered as sufficient proof that in most cases the Ottoman cash-*waqfs* lent money with a nearly constant return. Only rarely were these funds invested through *mudaraba* or *musharaka* (Cizakca 2000: 34). However, the return from the *mudaraba* was fixed in advance. Some jurists allowed this arrangement (see M.N. Siddiqi 2009-a: 210).

These *waqfs* also operated like rudimentary banks of the present day. Entrepreneurs were able to borrow from the *waqfs* at fixed rates of interest. Sometimes an indirect method of earning interest was used. The business or individual requiring finance would assign a property to the *waqf* to get an interest-free loan. The *waqf* was allowed to lease out the property and earn rent. This was more of a ruse to lend and borrow money on interest. With the passage of time, a class of money-changers, known as *sarrafs*, emerged, who used to borrow funds from the *waqfs* and re-lend at higher interest rates, keeping the difference as their income. This was the genesis of modern commercial banking. The moot point is that the cash-*waqfs* did not use the mechanics of *mudaraba* and *musharaka*, most probably, owing to the high risks involved in these methods of investment. Instead, the *waqfs* preferred to lend funds on fixed interest, which they termed '*istighlal*' rather than interest, to avoid any resemblance with the prohibited '*riba*'. Cizakca (2000: 36) further reports that most of the borrowers from the cash-*waqfs* were small consumers or trustees themselves. The *waqfs* provided loans on interest for consumption purposes as well.

15.5   INTEREST-BASED FINANCE FOR *JIHAD*

During the colonial period of India, Hanafite scholars allowed interest-based transactions on the plea that India is a land of enemies (*dar al-harb*) and the normal rules of prohibition do not apply. Jalal (2008: 68) reports the response of Shah Abdulaziz, an ardent upholder of traditional views, about taking interest on commercial transactions as follows: 'under the Islamic law interest on money invested for profitable purposes was legitimate for Muslims living in *dar al-harb*'. She also quotes (ibid.: 78, 93) the example of Sayyid Ahmad of Rai Breilli (1786–1831), who fought *jihad* against the Sikhs and was martyred in 1831 at Balakot. He paid hefty interest on money delivered to him by Hindu financiers for a military campaign against the Sikhs. He also entered into an agreement with Hindu moneylenders in Manara, a large commercial centre near Hund on the western side of the River Indus, to pay a 12 per cent rate of interest on the money borrowed.

15.6   RESPONSE OF THE MUSLIM PEOPLE TO ISLAMIC FINANCE

The establishment of hundreds of Islamic financial institutions in the short span of three decades is the response of Muslim governments and the wealthy class to the orthodox interpretation of *riba*. However, the general public in Muslim majority countries have not been quite so enthusiastic about Islamic finance. Orthodox scholars contend that the reason for the slow acceptance is lack of a sufficient number of such institutions. Muslim states inherited the financial systems and institutions developed by the colonial powers. The people are obliged to deal with interest-based institutions. They are simply helpless. It is difficult to refute this argument off the cuff, but a heart-to-heart talk with ordinary Muslims would testify that they are not fully convinced of the Islamicity of Islamic financial institutions. Besides, they suspect that Islamic finance is unprofitable, risky, imprudent and cumbersome. Because of these suspicions most Muslim countries have not adopted Islamic finance for their normal business. A large number of Muslim countries do not have even a minority presence of these institutions. Even in the countries where Islamic financial institutions have appeared, the most dominant part of the financial business is still based on interest. The most dominant form of banking and finance in Muslim countries, including such orthodox ones as Saudi Arabia, Pakistan and Sudan, is still based on interest. The conclusion is that Muslim people have not generally accepted the orthodox position, although few have raised a voice against it for fear of reprisals from the intolerant religious lobby.

The Economist, London (20 June 2009) wrote: 'Today $700 billion of global assets are said to comply with *sharia* law. Even so, traditional finance houses rather than Islamic institutions continue to handle most Gulf oil money and other Muslim wealth.'

Mills and Presley (1999: 50) write:

> Although religious sentiment has played a part in attracting deposits, Islamic banks have nevertheless offered competitive returns on investment deposits. Not only do they face competition for funds from other non-interest investment outlets (e.g., property) and other Islamic financial institutions, but they wish to attract the deposits of less zealous Muslims seeking a competitive return. The result has been strong pressure to provide returns at least commensurate with the conventional competition. This goal has generally been achieved, but at the expense of skewing investment policy towards short-term, secure and quick-returning outlets.

Warde (2010: 47) writes: 'Some Islamic institutions have stead-fastly refused to receive interest, whereas others, including the Islamic Development Bank and the Faisal Islamic Bank of Egypt (FIBE) have always placed their excess funds in interest-bearing accounts, usually overseas.'

M.M. Khan and Bhatti (2008: 49) present the results of an analysis of financing trends in a sample of bigger Islamic banks and found that, during 2004–06, only 6.34 per cent of the total financing was based on profit–loss-sharing instruments, which was down on 17 per cent during 1994–96. Ascarya and Yumanita (2008: 400) note that Islamic banking started in Indonesia in 1992. By July 2007, it had 25 Islamic bonds outstanding with a cumulative value of $336 million. It was merely 5 per cent of the total value of the bonds issued in the Indonesian capital market. Adnan and Muhamad (2007: 220–221) report that, by July 2006, Indonesia had three full-fledged Islamic banks, 10 Islamic banking units and 94 rural *shari'ah* banks. However, the total share of Islamic finance in the banking sector was merely 1.42 per cent in terms of deposits, 1.51 per cent in terms of assets and 2.58 per cent in terms of financing. Indonesia had a total population of 238 million, with over 80 per cent Muslims. Seibel (2005: 16–18) writes about the situation in Indonesia in 2003:

> There is no indication that the establishment of Islamic banks in Indonesia was preceded by a broad popular demand for *sharia*-based Islamic financial services. This situation appears to have changed little. According to surveys carried out in several provinces with an average Muslim population of 97%, only 11% were found to understand products and benefits of *sharia* banking. . . .

In terms of numbers, the two Islamic commercial banks represent 1.4% of all commercial banks. If we treat the eight commercial banking units like separate commercial banks and add them to the total number, then the Islamic commercial banks and commercial banking units account for 6.8% of the total number of 146 banks and banking units. The Islamic bank offices account for 3.3% of all commercial banking offices if the Bank Rakyat Indonesia (BRI) units are excluded and for 2.2% if they are included. In terms of total banking assets and financial activities, Islamic banks and banking units represent a mere 0.74% of total banking assets, 0.64% of total deposits and 1.16% of total loans outstanding. . . . During 1989–2003, the conventional rural banks have grown twenty times faster than the rural Islamic banks per year.

Jobst (2008: 111) notes that in Malaysia the size of Islamic *sukuk* issuance was \$27 billion in 2006, which was only 10 per cent that of conventional debt securities.

Wherever the religious lobby has exercised its influence, governments have adopted superficial and perfunctory measures to ease out the pressure. For example, in Pakistan, the national saving schemes of the government, which are based on interest, pay out interest but term it as 'profit' to make it palatable to ordinary persons. Similarly, the commercial banks in Pakistan accept fixed-term deposits and pay interest on them but call it 'expected rate of profit' when accepting the deposit. The fact is that Muslim people have generally not accepted the orthodox position on interest.

In Pakistan (Khan and Bhatti 2008: 178), in 2006, total Islamic banking assets were valued at \$1.3 billion, and the operations of the Islamic banks were merely 2.2 per cent of the overall financial market of Pakistan. This is because:

> the majority of people look on the existing government-led Islamic banks with deep suspicion and contempt. . . . Depositors may be emotionally attached to the cause of Islamization, but real support in terms of committing their funds under the profit-loss sharing (PLS) system was in desperately short supply. (Ibid.: 190)

Khan and Bhatti (2008: 67) report that, in Bangladesh in 2005, Islamic banking deposits accounted for 13 per cent of the total banking deposits, and Islamic investment represented 5 per cent of total investments in the banking sector.

Khan and Bhatti (2008: 72) quote Sheikh Lubna al-Qasimi, Minister for the Economy in the UAE, that 80 per cent of the US\$1.8 trillion of private wealth of the Gulf countries is invested abroad because there are insufficient Islamic-friendly investment opportunities in the region.

Kamali (2007: 15) reports with reference to the popularity of *sukuk* as

Table 15.1   Islamic banking market share by country, 2006 (percent)

	%
Saudi Arabia	19.54
Bahrain	18.97
Malaysia	16.30
Kuwait	14.64
UAE	14.39
Qatar	3.79
Egypt	2.83
Iran	2.82
Switzerland	1.86
Jordan	1.73
Bangladesh	1.24
Indonesia	1.11
Pakistan	0.35
UK	0.25
Palestine	0.09
Yemen	0.06
Rest	0.03

follows: 'It was further noted that only 20 per cent of Muslim population in GCC countries buy Islamic products.'

Askari, Iqbal and Mirakhor (2010: 139), on the authority of ISI Analytics in 2007, have provided the information in Table 15.1 indicating the market share of Islamic banks in the total assets of the banking system of these countries. The table shows that, except for four countries of the Middle East and Malaysia, where the share of banking assets held by Islamic banks was between 15 and 20 per cent, the rest of the Muslim world did not show any keen interest in this venture. For example, in countries with populations of over 90 per cent Muslims, such as Indonesia, Bangladesh, Pakistan, Iran, Egypt, the UAE and Qatar, the market share of Islamic banks was negligible. It was only 0.35 per cent in Pakistan and 0.06 per cent in Yemen. Overall, the response of Muslim people to Islamic banking has not been very encouraging.

15.7   INVESTMENT OF SURPLUS FUNDS BY THE ISLAMIC DEVELOPMENT BANK

The Islamic Development Bank, Jeddah is a lead Islamic financial institution. It faces the problem of finding interest-free avenues for investing its surplus funds. However, it has not been able to find a purely Islamic solution to this problem. Kahf (2005: 10) writes:

> The Islamic Development Bank in Jeddah, Saudi Arabia that is an Islamic inter-governmental bank with 57 Muslim countries in its membership, and some two billion US dollar as paid-up capital in the mid 1990s, accumulated about one billion US dollar in earned interest by the end of the last century and established the largest ever Islamic charitable endowment fund (*waqf*) for charitable services throughout the Muslim countries and communities.

Warde (2000: 50, 144) writes:

> Some Islamic institutions have steadfastly refused to receive interest, whereas others, including the Islamic Development Bank and the Faisal Islamic Bank of Egypt (FIBE), have always placed their excess funds in interest-bearing accounts, usually overseas. . . . The Saudi Arabian Monetary Agency (SAMA) acts as the depository institution for IDB funds. One occasional source of controversy has been the fact that those funds were receiving interest – in fact becoming the main source of profits for the bank. The bank's charter expressly permits it to invest excess funds 'in an appropriate manner', and the criterion of overriding necessity (of development in the Islamic world), in addition to the lack of suitable investments has been repeatedly used to defend the policy.

Aggarwal and Yousef (1996: 11) report that in 1981–90 FIBE kept an average of 46 per cent of its stock investment facilities with the Central Bank of Egypt on the basis of interest. They provide a list of 22 Islamic financial institutions as of 1990 which kept an average of about 65 per cent of their surplus funds in interest-based deposits.

15.8   CONCLUDING REMARKS

In this chapter we have tried to show that the claims of consensus on the prohibition of commercial interest are not well founded. There have been dissenting voices among Muslim scholars. The practice of Muslims through history does not conclusively vouch for the prohibition of interest on commercial transactions. Even the present movement of Islamic finance, despite all its fanfare, has not been able to attract support from most of the Muslim people. Leading Islamic financial institutions also place their funds as interest-bearing deposits with conventional banks. Most government business in Muslim majority countries is still being conducted on the basis of interest. The claim of consensus on the acceptance of the orthodox interpretation that treats all types of interest as *riba* is not supported by the ground reality.

NOTES

1. [As in original] Abraham L. Udovitch, 1979. Bankers without banks: Commerce, banking, and society in the Islamic world of the Middle Ages. In *The dawn of modern banking*, ed. Abraham L. Udovitch (New Haven, CT: Yale University Press, 1979), p. 257.
2. [As in original] M. Rodinson, *Islam et capitalisme* (Paris: Seuil, 1966).
3. [As in original] H. Gerber, *Economy and society in an Ottoman city: Bursa, 1600–1700* (Jerusalem: Hebrew University of Jerusalem, 1988).
4. [As in original] T. Miura, Socio-economic relations in the *Salihiya* quarter: *Sharia* court registers in 19th century Damascus (2), *The Memoirs of the Institute of Oriental Culture*, 137 (1999), pp. 295–349 (in Japanese).
5. [As in original] N. Kondo, Moneylenders in Tehran during the nineteenth century, *Bulletin of the Society for Western and Southern Asiatic Studies*, 63 (2005), pp. 14–40 (in Japanese).
6. [As in original] Jon E. Mandeville, Usurious piety: The cash *waqf* controversy in the Ottoman empire, *International Journal of Middle East Studies*, 10 (August) (1979), pp. 289–308.
7. [As in original] Peter Gran, *Islamic roots of capitalism* (Austin: University of Texas Press, 1919), esp. pp. 3–34.
8. [As in original] Al-Muhibbi, *Khulasat al-Athar fi a'yan al-Qarn al-Hadi 'Ashar* [A summary of history of the eleventh century] (Cairo: Dar al-Kitab al-Islami, n.d.), 4 vols.
9. [As in original] Abraham Udovitch, *Partnership and profit in medieval Islam* (Princeton, NJ: Princeton University Press, 1970).
10. [As in original] A. Udovitch, ed., *The Islamic Middle East, 700–1900: Studies in economic and social history* (Princeton, NJ: Darwin Press, 1981).
11. [As in original] *Risk Sermayesi, Özel Finans Kurumlari, ve Para Vakiflari* (Istanbul: ISAV, 1993).

16. Prohibition of *riba*: the way forward

The prohibition of *riba* is absolute and unequivocal in the Qur'an. However, Muslim scholars differ on the interpretation of the term '*riba*'. Chapters 10–15 have discussed the position of orthodox and modernist scholars. Our general conclusion is that none of the interpretations of *riba* is satisfactory. The orthodox interpretation that equates *riba* with all types of interest leaves several questions unanswered. For example, it does not have satisfactory answers for the difference between cash and credit prices, discounting of commercial papers, penalty for late payment, indexation of loans, determination of profit and loss, and so on. Modernist scholars also do not have a conclusive definition of *riba*. For example, they accept interest as legitimate if the rate is not 'exorbitant', without giving a benchmark for the exorbitant rate. They distinguish between interest on consumption and productive loans and treat the former as *riba* and accept the latter as legitimate. However, the demarcation between consumption and production loans is blurred. The general response of Muslim people is also confused. Most of them deal in interest-based transactions though they may believe in the prohibition of interest. The economies of most Muslim countries are also based on interest-based finance. The question arises: what, then, is the meaning of the prohibition of *riba* in the present age? The present chapter deals with this question.

16.1 CONFUSION BETWEEN LOANS AND INVESTMENT

The Qur'an quotes the objection of disbelievers on the prohibition of *riba*: 'they say: trading is like *riba*; while God has permitted trading and forbidden the *riba*' (Q. 2:275). The Qur'an quotes the objection but does not refute it directly. Instead it only says that trading is permissible while *riba* is not. The question arises: what is the difference between the two? What makes a transaction trading and another *riba*? Orthodox scholars tried to explain the difference. They concluded that *riba* had two characteristics: (i) it is predetermined as a rate of increase on a loan; and (ii) it does not share the risk of loss. As a logical corollary to this conclusion, they declared all types of interest to be *riba* and the practice of commercial banking unlawful.

However, for various useful functions that the banks perform, they needed to find an alternative basis for banking. That led to the contemporary movement of Islamic finance in the last quarter of the twentieth century.

There is no difference of opinion among Muslim scholars that an increment on the principal sum of a loan is *riba*. However, not all financial claims arise from loan transactions. Financial claims could arise through trade (e.g. credit sale), investment (e.g. share certificates), provision of services (e.g. transportation of goods, rent of buildings), recovery of an earlier overpayment (e.g. overpaid salaries), project financing (e.g. debentures) and so on. Financial claims could consist, partly if not wholly, of interest on capital provided for the acquisition of assets. Unfortunately, both orthodox and modernist scholars failed to see the difference in the nature of the underlying transaction leading to a financial claim. Both of them treated the financing of assets as loan transactions.

Before extending their conclusion to commercial banking, orthodox scholars should have asked the question: does the business of commercial banks involve the lending of money? If the answer is in the positive, interest on capital will be *riba* and thus prohibited. If the answer is in the negative, the interest on capital will not be *riba* and thus permissible. Although the banks appear to be in the lending business yet a deeper look would show that they are in the *financing* business. They charge interest on the finance they provide. Since they do not provide loans in the strict sense of the word, the interest charged by them cannot be termed *riba*. Anybody who requires finance for business or personal needs can get it from the banks on interest. The banks do not provide finance free of charge. Instead, they offer to finance the needs of their clients against a charge, which is interest. For interest-free finance, commercial banks are not the right forum. Anyone looking for interest-free finance should approach family or friends. Muslim scholars also recognize this fact. They know that anyone who needs finance for business purposes cannot get it free of charge. The finance will come with a cost even in an ideal Islamic society (see e.g. W.M. Khan 2002: 4). That is why, after declaring interest to be *riba*, Muslim scholars did not commence their search for free finance. They started with the avowed objective of finding a basis for finance other than conventional interest. That makes the whole issue of taking advantage of finance for business operations a matter of procedure and not substance. Once we understand that the nature of commercial banking is not to provide loans but to provide finance the question whether interest is *riba* or not does not arise. *Riba* is relevant only when there is a lending transaction. If there is no lending transaction, the question of interest charged by banks falls out of the domain of *riba*.

A person who deposits money does not lend it to the bank. The deposit is either for safe custody or for earning a return or for getting an entitlement to other services. Since it is not a loan to the bank, any return on the deposit is not *riba*. Similarly, when a person acquires finance from the bank for personal needs (like buying a house, a car, an air-conditioner and so on) or for commercial purposes, he or she is not seeking a loan. He or she needs finance to buy some assets. Any payment over and above the principal sum in all such cases would not be *riba*. However, if a person is seeking a loan from the bank any increase in the principal sum would be *riba*. It means the test of the transaction is whether both the parties consider the financial transaction to be a loan. If the answer is 'yes', the interest on the principal sum will be *riba*. If the answer is 'no', the interest will not be *riba*. It further means that not all types of interest will be *riba*. Interest will be *riba* when both parties consider the transaction a loan. It will also be *riba* if the party that takes advantage of the finance considers it a loan even though the other party considers it a commercial transaction. It would be a perfect example of the prohibited *riba* mentioned in the Qur'an where some people had adopted lending as a business.

The above explanation staves off several problems in financial transactions. For example, we need not worry about predetermination of the rate of interest. We need not wait for the results of the investment. We need not ask questions about the purpose of the finance. All these questions become irrelevant. The only relevant question is: is the financial transaction a loan from the perspective of both parties or at least from the perspective of the party making use of the finance? If the answer is in the affirmative, the interest will be *riba*, whatever the rate, fixed or variable, predetermined or post-determined. If the answer is in the negative, the interest will not be *riba*. The next important question is: what is the difference between a loan transaction and a financing transaction? We shall try to answer this question in the following discussion.

16.2   WHAT IS A LOAN TRANSACTION?

A loan can be defined as follows:

A loan is a financial claim arising out of a financial accommodation provided by a creditor to a debtor or to a third party on the debtor's behalf with the arrangement that the debtor will return the sum advanced with or without interest.

In the above definition, the most critical element of the loan transaction is the intention of the debtor and the creditor. Both enter into a loan arrangement. If this intention on the part of both is not present the transaction will not be a loan. We come across many examples of financial exchange in everyday life that are not treated as loans. Let us consider some examples:

a. A gives B Rs1000 as a gift on the marriage of A. As a social custom, and without making it explicit, A understands that B will, at an appropriate time, give a similar gift of Rs1000 or more on the marriage of B. It is a financial transaction but not a loan. The intention of both parties is to give and receive a return gift. Any increase in the amount of the gift will not be *riba*.

b. An employer deducts 5 per cent of the salary of his employee as a contribution to a provident fund. Both parties understand that the employer will return this amount at the time of retirement or resignation of the employee with some increment. It is a financial transaction but not a loan. The intention is not to give or take a loan. Any return on the principal sum (fixed and predetermined) will be interest but not *riba*.

c. A deposits one million rupees in a bank for safe custody. It is not a loan to the bank, as A does not intend to give a loan to the bank; the bank also does not consider it a loan. Any return on the principal sum (fixed and predetermined) will be interest but not *riba*.

d. A deposits one million rupees into a bank or gives the sum to a trader for the purpose of investment. It is not a loan. The intention is not to take or give a loan but to invest funds. Any return on the principal sum (fixed and predetermined) will be interest but not *riba*.

e. A bank gives money to a business firm for investment. The transaction is not a loan; neither the bank nor the client intends to lend or borrow money. Any return on the principal sum (fixed and predetermined) will be interest but not *riba*.

f. A bank gives money to a person to buy a car. The bank does not intend to lend; the client intends to get an interest-free loan. But since the bank is not willing to lend on an interest-free basis the client accepts it as a mode of finance for buying the car. Both parties agree on a financing transaction; it is not a loan. Any return on the principal sum (fixed and predetermined) will be interest but not *riba*.

g. A moneylender gives money as a loan. It is a loan transaction as both the parties have the similar intention to create a loan transaction. Any return on the principal sum (fixed and predetermined) will be interest and also *riba*.

h. A moneylender or a bank gives money to a client. The person who takes the money with the intention of returning it treats it as a loan. But the moneylender or the bank says that it is an investment. Is the transaction a loan? Yes. This is a loan transaction. The moneylender or the bank would charge interest on a loan, which is *riba*. In fact, this is precisely the situation in which the Qur'an says (Q. 2:275): 'Allah has permitted trade and prohibited *riba*.' This is the situation where a lender is trying to make lending a business and the Qur'an has prohibited that. If the person accepts the loan on interest under duress, he or she is accepting to pay *riba* and the moneylender or the bank is receiving *riba*. In Islamic parlance, it would be illegal (*haram*).

i. A moneylender or a bank lends money on an interest-free basis but the borrower returns the principal with some increment voluntarily and happily. Is this increment *riba*? No. It is established on the authority of the Prophet's own example. He himself said that, if a borrower returns something over and above the principal sum voluntarily, it is permissible (Imam Muslim, AH 1334, *al-Jami al-Sahih*, Kitab a-muzara'a, H. 142, Beirut).

j. A sells goods to B on credit. The price is higher than the spot price. The increase in the credit price is due to an element of interest which has been embedded into the price. However, it is a financing transaction; the seller is financing the purchase of the goods. The transaction generates a financial claim which has interest as an in-built element. But the interest embedded in the credit price is not *riba* since the underlying transaction is not a loan transaction.

k. A owns a property. B hires it for a defined rent. The rent is payable at the end of the period. The financial claim in the form of rent is not *riba* since the underlying transaction is not a loan transaction.

The above examples illustrate that the loan is only one form of exchange that generates a financial claim. The essence of the exchange is the intentions of the two parties. Financial claims arising out of sales, a lease or services are not loans. They are various forms of financing. Financial claims where a party clearly intends to provide a loan and the other party also considers it a loan is a lending transaction. The Qur'an forbids making lending a business. It should remain a charitable act.

16.3   WHAT IS A FINANCING TRANSACTION?

As discussed above, every transaction involving a financial exchange is not a loan. Some financial transactions are in the nature of financing or investment. Financing and investment (*tamwil*) are two sides of the same coin. The term 'financing' is used from the perspective of the one who takes advantage of the finance and 'investment' from the perspective of the one who provides the finance.

Financing is seeking a financial accommodation or obtaining the facility to defer payment for goods or services procured in the present with the intention of: (i) creating the ability to increase wealth; or (ii) enhancing the ability to increase wealth; or (iii) preserving resources; or (iv) increasing the earning potential of the user of the funds or resources.

Investment is making available cash or assets, goods or services on a deferred payment basis with the intention of: (i) creating the ability to increase wealth; or (ii) enhancing the ability to increase wealth; or (iii) preserving resources; or (iv) increasing the earning potential of the provider of the funds or resources.

The examples of a bank's client seeking funds to install industrial plant and a businessman buying goods on a deferred payment basis are quite obvious. The example of a person seeking funds to buy a car or a house or to pay educational expenses or to meet expenses on health also points to the potential of the finance in increasing the earning ability of the user of the funds or resources. In the process the bank that invests these funds also intends to increase its earnings.

Financing thus potentially creates or enhances the wealth or earning ability of the user of the resources. Whether the user of the resources would be able actually to realize this potential depends on a host of physical, social, cultural, legal, administrative, environmental and global factors. If the user is unable to realize the potential it is a failure of the user and not that of the financier. The financier provided the resources and created a potential ability in the user to enhance the wealth or earnings. The expectation of the finance for a return is, in fact, based on this very potential. It is because of this contribution of the finance in potentially increasing the ability of the user of funds to create more wealth that there is a consensus even among Muslim scholars that the finance has a legitimate right to demand a return on its use.

If, however, the user of funds is unable to increase the earnings for any reason, the finance should not be made to suffer. The finance performed its primary function: potentially increasing the ability to create or enhance wealth. Seen in this perspective Muslim economists have a weak case when they insist that finance should get a return only if the results of investment are profitable. The profit or loss arises not only from the use of funds. It is the result of a host of factors, none of which are controlled by the financier. The user of funds may not be able to realize the potential of creating or enhancing wealth owing to negligence, mismanagement, corruption, incompetence, legal tangles, unnecessary government intervention, adverse global economic currents, policies of other countries, adverse taxation policies and so on. It is, therefore, unfair to assert that the finance should also share the loss, if there is any. The finance performed its function as soon as it became available and should be entitled to its reward, irrespective of the result of the enterprise at the end of the period. If we insist that capital is partly responsible for the profit or loss, we need to demonstrate and delineate the part of the profit or loss that can be fairly assigned to finance. The role of finance is not to create wealth. It only creates the potential or ability for creating wealth. It neither creates wealth nor decreases it. It is the human use of these funds that leads to profit or loss. The role played by finance is certain and categorical, for which it can legitimately ask for a return. That leads us to a related question: what is the basis for an entitlement to profit in Islamic law?

16.4   WHAT IS THE BASIS FOR AN ENTITLEMENT TO PROFIT?

Classical Islamic law defines entitlement to profit for three reasons: (a) contribution of wealth (*mal*), as in a partnership contract; (b) providing services (labour) for a share in the profit; (c) accepting responsibility (*daman*), as in a partnership contract where the partners agree to bear liability for the goods bought on credit or for delivering services (Nyazee 1998: 53). These are valid bases for an entitlement to profit. The law further states that: the wealth should be contributed as capital; the partners must retain ownership of the capital; the partners must bear full liability for claims against the partnership; and the partnership should involve joint ownership and joint liability of the partners (Nyazee 1998: 54–55). These conditions effectively rule out any entitlement to profit for capital provided on a temporary basis. Thus it does not solve the most common problem of business firms which require finance for a short term or for specific purposes.

Fortunately, developments in commercial finance over the last three centuries or so have created possibilities for solving this problem. The banks as financial intermediaries can provide finance on a temporary basis. Business firms, by obtaining short-term finance, can enhance their ability to create wealth. However, these developments have not persuaded Muslim scholars to have a fresh look at Islamic law as developed in the Middle Ages.

Muslim scholars need to recognize the evolution of the social and economic environment for entitlement to profit. The new basis for entitlement to profit is the provision of resources to another person or entity which has the potential to enhance the ability of the recipient to create wealth, irrespective of the fact that the recipient is actually able to do that. This is an area for fresh thinking (*ijtehad*) in Islamic law. So far, Muslim scholars have been trying to rewrite classical Islamic commercial law in modern jargon without adopting an innovative approach to handle the emerging situations. Financing by the banks has created new avenues for thought. Remaining restricted to the classical moulds of business law hinders the path of business firms to overcome their daily financing needs.

16.5   WHAT IS DEBT FINANCING?

In the literature on business finance, the term 'debt financing' is often used to denote financing through debt from a financial institution or by floating bonds in the open market. Orthodox Muslim scholars also use this term and consider it prohibited as it involves interest which is *riba*.

We think that the term 'debt financing' is a misnomer, because it combines two distinct entities, that is, debt and financing. A financial claim can arise either through a debt or through financing. It cannot be both at the same time. A financial claim arising out of a debt transaction involves a lender, a borrower, a principal sum, and a time period for repayment with or without interest. In this transaction both parties agree that it is a debt. Any increment on the principal sum demanded by the creditor is interest. In Islamic parlance, it is *riba* and thus illegal (*haram*).

Financing involves a transfer of cash, goods or services, leading to a financial claim on the user of the resources, a period for repayment, and terms of repayment (including any increment on the principal sum as a fixed or variable return, whether fixed *ex ante* or not). Both parties agree that it is not a loan but a business deal with the purpose of providing resources to the recipient to enhance his or her ability to create wealth, irrespective of whether the wealth is actually created or not. Any increment received on the principal sum could be interest, if fixed in advance at a certain rate. However, since it is not a loan transaction, in the Islamic parlance the interest will not be *riba*. It will be permissible (*halal*). It is precisely on this reasoning that contemporary jurists have allowed an increment in the price of goods if they are sold on a deferred payment basis. El-Gamal (2000: 4) has quite aptly said: 'The best way to summarize the status of lending and *riba* in Islam is this: In Islam, one does not lend to make money, and one does not borrow to finance business.'

The prevalence of the term 'debt financing' is due to certain similarities between debt and financing. For example, both have a principal sum which has to be repaid, both involve a time period and both may have a rate of return fixed in advance. However, they are not the same. What distinguishes them is: (i) the intention of the parties; and (ii) the purpose for which the financial transaction takes place. In the case of a loan, the lender is not much concerned about the use of the funds. He or she is more concerned about the safe return of the funds with some interest, if it is an interest-bearing loan. In the case of financing, the purpose is to enhance the ability of the recipient of the funds to create more wealth. In the capitalist framework, there is no pressing compulsion to differentiate between the two terms. Whether a particular return on capital is *riba* is not the concern of conventional finance. However, in the Islamic framework, the question is important and cannot be ignored. Therefore we need to differentiate between what is *riba* and what is not. In Islamic parlance using the term 'debt financing' is confusing and does not reflect the reality.

Seen in this perspective, the questions relating to the permissibility of bill discounting and the sale of negotiable instruments in the Islamic framework are also answered. Trade bills are financial assets arising through business and not loan transactions. Because of their commercial origin, they are not debts. The sale and purchase of these assets at the going market price or discounting at a certain rate of interest is like the sale and purchase of any other asset. The interest rate only helps in arriving at a fair market price. It means, in essence, that the existing practices of bill discounting and bond flotation are permissible in the Islamic framework. If we do not accept this we face two problems:

a.   We tend to use the term '*riba*' inconsistently. For example, we allow a difference in the cash and credit prices (although it is interest beyond doubt) because it arises from a business deal, but we disallow the discounting of bills (which is also an interest-based transaction) and do not accept it although bills too arise from business deals. Another example is that we accept a penalty on the delayed payment of utility bills but not on the delayed payment of bank financing. Both involve interest, but we accept one and reject the other. The definition of *riba* becomes confusing.
b.   We enter into a blind alley where the solution to commercial requirements of liquidity, short-term financing and the freedom to buy and sell all assets, including financial assets, becomes extremely restricted.

16.6   WHAT IS INTEREST?

Any discussion about *riba* and interest would require us to define the term 'interest' if we are to understand its relationship with *riba*. We can define interest as follows:

Interest denotes: (i) an increase in the nominal value of a financial claim due to deferment of payment; or (ii) a decrease in the nominal value of a deferred financial claim due to an immediate cash payment.

Examples of interest are as follows:

a.   an increment on the principal sum of a loan;
b.   the difference between the cash and credit prices of the same product or service;
c.   an increase in the nominal value of a deposit irrespective of the nature of the deposit;
d.   a discount paid on a negotiable bill for immediate cash;
e.   a penalty on the late payment of utility bills or other financial claims;
f.   a cash discount on credit sales;
g.   charges paid on credit card expenses beyond the grace period.

Interest arises irrespective of:

a.   the amount of the financial claim;
b.   the length of the period of deferment;
c.   the purpose or source of the financial claim;
d.   whether or not the rate of the increase or decrease is predetermined;
e.   the rate or even if it is expressed as a lump sum;
f.   the purpose of the increase or decrease in the financial claim.

16.7   NOT ALL TYPES OF INTEREST ARE *RIBA*

There are three main ways that financial claims arise:

a.   **Loan:** A lends money to B. It is a loan transaction. Both parties agree that it is a loan. Any interest on the principal sum will be *riba*. The Qur'an promotes lending as an act of charity and condemns any compensation or reward in the form of interest on the loan. It treats interest on loans against the spirit of cooperation, fraternity and social cohesion that is necessary for the inner strength of the global Muslim community (*ummah*).[1]
b.   **Trading:** A and B are in a trade mode, exchanging goods and services. A's financial claim on B has resulted from trade. A allows B to pay later but claims interest on it. The interest is not *riba*, as it has resulted from a trade transaction, which in its very nature involves increasing one's capital. It is because of this consideration that *Shari'ah*

scholars have now recognized the difference in cash and credit prices as legitimate although the increase represents interest. But this interest, without naming it so, has been accepted as legitimate and is not treated as *riba*.

c. **Financing and investment:** A provides capital to finance B's business either directly or through a bank. A is not lending but investing the capital.[2] It is unanimously acceptable to invest capital through someone else. This is the basis of the permissibility of *mudaraba* and *musharaka*. It is permissible to provide one's capital to an intermediary (like a bank), which finds a *mudarib* and then uses the capital for *mudaraba*. Similarly, providing capital to buy shares of a company is permissible even though the provider of capital is not working for the business. Earning profit on such capital is also permissible. The only difference between conventional finance and 'Islamic finance' is on the timing of profit. According to the Islamic finance theory the rate of profit should not be predetermined. It means that there is no difference of opinion on the following points:

i. A person can provide his or her capital to another person directly or through an intermediary (bank) for investment purposes.
ii. The provider of capital can claim a return on this capital.

However, Islamic finance insists that the rate of profit on the capital should not be predetermined. Conventional finance does not see any problem in fixing the rate of return on an *ex ante* basis. It boils down to a procedural matter. Trying to found a new system (in the name of Islamic finance) on the basis of a procedural and not a substantive matter is not persuasive.

It can be argued that the other difference (of course, the main one) is that under Islamic finance the provider of capital agrees to bear the loss, if there is any, on the capital, while in conventional finance the principal sum of the capital provided by the bank is protected. This difference, on which the whole of Islamic finance rests, is only hypothetical in nature. No banking system would be practicable where most of the users of funds posted losses and banks as a whole suffered losses and tried to pass on those losses to providers of funds (depositors). Even the theoretical justification of Islamic banking vehemently pleads that the overall position of banks would never be in the red. The profits from various parties would cancel out any losses, leaving the banks in profit as a whole. Thus the possibility of losses and banks sharing them with the depositors is only hypothetical. Secondly, profit–loss sharing poses insurmountable problems of accounting and monitoring in practice, making it impossible to practise it on a global basis. In such circumstances, the theoretical concept of profit–loss sharing (which is not practicable) makes a weak case for Islamic finance and satisfies only the religious zealots. It neither makes a good business case nor persuades an ordinary person.

16.8   ACCEPTING INNOVATION IN FINANCIAL TRANSACTIONS

The traditional concept of Islamic jurisprudence says that financial exchange is restricted to two main categories: (a) the trust (*amanah*); and (b) the loan (*qard or dayn*). In the case of the trust, the person receiving the money is supposed to return it as it is on demand. The trustee may charge a fee for safekeeping. In the case of the loan, the debtor can use the money but has to return it at the appointed time. The creditor cannot charge any interest on the loan, as it would amount to *riba*. While developing the contemporary theory of Islamic finance, Muslim scholars retained these two categories of financial exchange. Every financial transaction should fit into one of the categories. Muslim scholars treated deposits as loans and then proceeded to find an alternative for interest on deposits. They had scant success, though they were able to develop a vast array of ruses and subterfuges.

Muslim scholars could have escaped the wild search for an alternative to interest if they had reviewed the classical classification of financial transactions. They should have recognized that, over time, another type of financial transaction has evolved. It is financing or investing capital potentially to enhance the earning ability of the user of the funds. Creating the ability to enhance wealth and earnings entitles the provider of funds to a return. People can now provide money to earn a return whether the person receiving the deposit uses the funds properly and does increase the wealth or misuses it and wastes the resources. If we recognize the third category as a legitimate form of financial exchange we can also accept an increment on the resources made available for this purpose. In fact, the concepts of *musharaka* and *mudaraba* accept this type of increment as legitimate. The only condition is that the return should be related to the actual outcome of the investment. The difference evolved during the last three centuries is that finance is now considered to place at the disposal of the user of finance a potential ability to create wealth. This development in human thought did not exist during the Middle Ages. Now funds can be made available, besides traditional trust and loan categories, for financing purposes as well, with the clear understanding that the third category creates a potential for increasing wealth and earnings. To the extent that finance has done its job, it is entitled to a return irrespective of whether or not the user was actually able to earn profit.

The above discussion solves several problems:

a. Once we accept that interest on loans is *riba* and interest on capital for financing is not *riba*, we do not get into the debate relating to the purpose of the loan, the rate of interest, its fixity or variability, its predetermination or post-determination or the duration of the loan.

b. We would not need to go to the trouble of adjusting medieval concepts of trade like *musharaka, mudaraba, ijara, salam, istisna'* and so on to our own times with limited success. We would get away from the problem of devising tricks, stratagems and ruses to legitimize fixed rates of return on capital. All fixed returns on financing would be interest but not *riba*.

c. We need not get into the business of promoting or developing a separate genre of banks or financial institutions in the name of Islamic financial institutions.

d. We shall open the door to all types of financing to Muslims from conventional banks without any qualm of conscience.

e. It solves the problem of the time value of money and all related problems such as: (i) the difference of cash and credit prices; (ii) the discounting of bills; (iii) fees for issuing bank guarantees; (iv) penalties for delayed payment; and so on.

f. The problem of indexation of loans is also solved. Once it is a loan agreement, the principal sum will be returned as it is. There will be no increment and no indexation. However, if it is a financing contract, the rate of interest will take care of inflation over time.

g. The question of delay in repayment is also covered. In loan contracts, the delay in payment will have to be treated as a gesture of benevolence by the creditor according to the Qur'anic injunctions. In the case of financing contracts, the rate of interest will take care of any delays.

h. It takes away all problems relating to the disclosure of accounts, sovereignty of business firms, banks' expertise to oversee the business where financing is done, and so on.

i. Since interest is a simple and straightforward mechanism for determining the return, it is less prone to disputes or value judgements.

16.9   WHY IS *RIBA* PROHIBITED?

Why is *riba* prohibited? The answer to this question stems from the social agenda of the Prophet. Although the cardinal doctrine of the Qur'an is

Tawhid (Unity of God), the Prophet aimed at transforming tribal Arabian society into a global community based on the fraternity and brotherhood of all human beings. This is visible from his mission in Makkah where he promoted mutual help, the joining of kinship ties, assisting the poor, patronizing slaves, uplifting the downtrodden and protecting the oppressed. The mission culminated by establishing *mawakhaat* (brotherhood) among the local people (*Ansar*) of Medina and the immigrants (*Muhajirun*) of Makkah. Other items of the social agenda were making *zakah* obligatory, encouraging charitable spending (*infaq*), emancipating slaves, establishing the rights of neighbours, relatives, travellers and non-Muslims in Medina, and so on. He had the vision of creating a well-knit society organized on values of justice, brotherhood, mutual help, benevolence, morality and sacrifice. He encouraged people to grant loans to the needy and fulfil their needs on a gratuitous basis. Interest on loans, against this background, was termed *riba*, an abominable practice and thus prohibited. The prohibition was a building block of a socially coherent community, which adhered to a common faith and common values. In such a society the charging of interest on loans would be an act of dire selfishness and even callousness if the borrower were a poor person.

Ibn al-Qayyim (d. AH 751/AD 1350) points out another reason for prohibition of *riba*. It was the Prophet's concern for protecting the poor and weak in society, as they were mostly the people who would require loans (Ahmad and Hassan 2006: 81). By prohibiting *riba*, the Prophet intended to provide relief to the poorer sections of society. The Qur'anic pointer to injustice (Q. 2:279) reinforces this understanding.

The Qur'anic verses prohibiting *riba* (Q. 2:275–280) emphasize the treatment of kindness and leniency toward the debtor. The Qur'an advises giving an extension to the debtor if he or she is hard pressed financially and even forgiving the loan, if possible. The Prophet said: 'The debtor is your captive; be, therefore, truly kind to your captive' (Asad 1980, n. 11, verse Q. 76:8).

By prohibiting *riba* on loans, the Prophet was not interfering with the prevalent economic practices. Economic activity was mainly financed, in those days, through private savings, partnerships (*shirka*) or sleeping partnerships (*mudaraba*). The Prophet did not interfere with these practices. There is scant evidence to show that loans were also a method of obtaining finance for business needs in those days.[3] The mechanism of using loans as a means for business finance came into existence much later in human history when, during medieval times, such commercial houses came into being and could act as intermediaries and provide finance for business.[4] Thus using external finance for business is a later development. The prohibition of *riba* was basically a social reform.

Mirakhor (2007-a: 21) mentions that during the eighth to fifteenth centuries (for more than 700 years) the world followed the risk-sharing methods of finance like *commenda* and *maona* (*mudaraba* and *musharaka* in Islamic terminology) introduced by the Muslims. These methods, which were basically trust-dominated, remained in vogue for eight centuries. He quotes (ibid.: 23) Goitein (1964: 317[5]) that interest-based commercial loans were of limited use during the Middle Ages. From the sixteenth century, interest-based loans began to be used in trade when Europe adopted loan-based finance owing to the systematic breakdown of trust caused by such traumatic events as the Crusades, Mongol invasion, and prolonged religious wars among European countries. Besides, there were several other factors which encouraged interest-based finance, such as gradual scholastic acceptance of interest, the emergence of the nation state, an inflow of large amounts of gold to Europe through colonization, the emergence of fractional reserve banking, specialization of banks as intermediaries, risk aversion by the wealthy classes, and so on. It was in the nineteenth and twentieth centuries that loan-based capital became the most dominant form of financing.

In brief, Muslim economists and religious scholars need to recognize that the financing of business needs on the basis of interest is a later development. The Prophet did not address this issue at all. His primary concern was to organize a socially well-knit society on the basis of brotherhood and mutual help. In such a society anyone who required a loan should get it from a fellow brother on an interest-free basis. The question of financing through loans had not arisen in that social set-up. We need to do innovative thinking on the subject. The innovative thinking would suggest that we need to differentiate between a loan transaction and a financing transaction. Interest on loan transactions would be *riba*, as it would fall in the same category of social estrangement which the Prophet intended to discourage. However, interest on financing would be legitimate, as it aims at creating and enhancing the ability of the user of the finance to increase wealth.

16.10 CONCLUDING REMARKS

The confusion about *riba* has emanated from the interpretation of Muslim scholars to extend meanings of *riba* from its original context. *Riba* in the days of the Prophet pertained to any increase on the principal sum of a loan. In those days, business finance in the form of loans was not widely practised for financing business needs. For the next seven centuries the same situation prevailed throughout the world. After the Industrial

Revolution and with other socio-economic developments, commercial banking developed and the question about the legitimacy of interest-based finance came up for discussion among Muslim scholars. Although a large number of modernist scholars argued that the prevalent commercial interest-based finance does not fall under the category of the prohibited *riba*, yet the view of orthodox scholars has prevailed. They stretched the meanings of *riba* to apply to commercial finance as well. The mistake in this interpretation was that the orthodox scholars confused financing transactions with loans. The way forward is to return to the original meanings of the term *riba*. Any increment on the principal sum of a loan should be treated as *riba*. All other types of interest should be acceptable. Taking this route would help solve all the problems that the orthodox interpretation has created. It would open the door to guilt-free dealings with conventional financial institutions. Islamic financial institutions would not be required in the strict sense of the term. However, they should be free to continue with their business if they so desire.

NOTES

1. This is the generally accepted position among Muslim economists. See for example al-Jarhi (2002: 89, footnote 1).
2. It is interesting to cite the example of *riba*-free banking practised and pleaded by the American Finance House in the name of *Lariba* banking. The bank uses the term 'finance' and not 'loan' for all its operations where it provides capital to a client (Abdul-Rahman 2010: 258).
3. Orthodox scholars have laboured hard to collect scattered pieces of evidence from historical sources to prove that commercial loans were in vogue in those days. See for example Muslehuddin (1969). However, despite all the pain taken the evidence is neither conclusive nor persuasive.
4. This is well documented in the history of modern banking. For fear of making the present discussion imbalanced, we are skipping further elaboration of this point.
5. [As in original] S.D. Goitein, Commercial and family partnerships in the countries of medieval Islam, *Islamic Studies* (3) (1964), pp. 316–319.

PART III

Islamic banking and finance

17. Theoretical basis of Islamic banking

17.1 ISLAMIC BANKING MODELS

The Islamic banking and finance movement started in response to the economic injustice of capitalism. Its avowed objective was to create a framework for economic development within the overall objectives of social justice and human well-being as visualized by Islam. This is abundantly obvious from the formation of the first Islamic bank in 1963 at Mit Ghamr (Egypt). Its main emphasis was on socio-economic development through interest-free finance. Orthodox scholars saw interest on commercial loans as a device of exploitation and declared interest-based banking illegal from the Islamic perspective. The main objection was that banks provided finance at fixed rates of interest and had no concern for actual profitability and productivity of the funds provided by them. Even when a client of the bank suffered loss, the principal had to be repaid with interest. To them it was a situation of inequity and injustice. To resolve this common-sense situation, they commissioned a simple idea. The banks should provide funds on the basis of *musharaka* or *mudaraba*. If at the end of the period the business made a profit, it should share the profit with the bank and, if it suffered a loss, the bank should also take part of the loss. The idea in its pristine simplicity was quite persuasive and seemed to be fair and just.

17.1.1 Two-Tier *Mudaraba* Model

The above idea of banking without interest had been in circulation in varying details in the writings of Muslim scholars such as Abu al-'Ala Mawdudi, Manazir Ahsan Gilani, Hifzur Rahman Seoharvi, Anwar Iqbal Qureshi, Muhammad Uzair, Sheikh Mahmud Ahmad and so on. Most of these writers either hinted at the possibility of interest-free banking or gave its bare skeleton. It was M.N. Siddiqi who in 1969 presented the first comprehensive model of interest-free banking in his Urdu book.[1] In 1983, an English version of the book also became available. Siddiqi based his model on the concept of two-tier *mudaraba*, while retaining the primary role of a financial intermediary operating on the basis of a fractional cash reserve. Siddiqi's model is quite comprehensive and covers all aspects of commercial banking. The bare bones of the model in a crude approximation are as follows.

The two-tier *mudaraba* model assumes that a commercial bank will be established as a corporate body with shareholders' capital. The savers (known as investment accountholders) deposit their savings with the bank on the basis of *mudaraba*, and the bank invests these savings in the real sector, again on the basis of *mudaraba*. The clients of the bank (business firms availing themselves of the bank's finance) share the net profit with the bank on the basis of a pre-agreed ratio, while the bank takes up all losses attributable to the bank's finance on a pro rata basis. The bank aggregates its profits and losses from all clients and shares the net profit with the investment accountholders on the basis of a pre-agreed ratio. If the bank suffers a net loss, it divides the loss among the shareholders and the investment accountholders in proportion to their respective capitals. The model also explains the operation of other banking services and central banking functions.

Thinking on the subject led to further suggestions for diversifying the basic model into various other modes of finance such as *bai' mu'ajjal, bai' murabaha, ijara, salam, istisna'*, and their combinations and permutations. The interested reader can peruse these ideas in any standard text on Islamic banking.[2] Here we are assuming that the reader is familiar with this work and repetition of these ideas would be an unnecessary digression. Several writers presented modified versions of the model as well as alternative models of Islamic banking. A good summary and critique of these models is available at Anjum (2007).

17.1.2 Two-Window Model

A significant variation of the two-tier *mudaraba* model is two-window Islamic banking. According to this model, the bank will open two types of deposit accounts: (a) demand deposits; (b) investment deposits. The demand deposits will be in the nature of a trust, and the bank will guarantee their return but will not pay any return. Instead, the bank may charge a fee to recover safekeeping and other administrative expenses. The bank will keep a 100 per cent cash reserve for the demand deposits. For investment deposits, the bank will invest the funds at the risk of depositors. There will be a zero per cent cash reserve for the investment deposits. Profit on the investment deposits will be shared by the bank with the depositors in agreed proportions. Justification for the bank's share emanates from the service that the bank provides in managing the investment. The net loss from the investment of deposits will be passed on to the depositors, as they are the owners of the funds and on their behalf and with their consent the bank invests the funds. The bank will not share the loss.

17.1.3 Three-Tier Model: Keeping Financial Intermediaries Away from the Real-Sector Business

There is a lot of confusion in the literature about the role of Islamic financial institutions. Some writers suggested that these institutions should enter the real sector as merchants, but they were unable to sell the idea. Another strand is that the Islamic financial institutions should not provide finance but try to provide real assets on the basis of *murabaha, salam, istisna'* and *ijara*. However, provision of goods and services, on whatever basis, pushes Islamic financial institutions into the real sector. They cannot perform these functions properly, as they do not have the necessary capacity and expertise. When they actually resorted to financing on the basis of these modes, they had to devise various tricks to remain true to their primary role of financial intermediation. Against this background, Siddiqi (2002) suggested a model of three-tier *mudaraba*. According to this model, Islamic financial institutions should act as financial intermediaries. Specialized companies dealing in *murabaha, salam, istisna'* or *ijara* should provide assets and services. The specialized companies should get finance from the Islamic financial institutions on the basis of *mudaraba*. Thus the two-tier model is converted into a three-tier model. The first tier consists of depositors and banks; the second consists of banks and specialized companies; the third consists of specialized companies and entrepreneurs who require finance. The profit–loss distribution follows the same principles as in the case of the two-tier model. Siddiqi makes a further refinement to this idea by suggesting that commercial banks and investment banks should be separated and speculation should be banned (Siddiqi 2009).

The proposed model meets the requirements of Islamic law. There is no empirical data from which to draw a final conclusion about its practicability, but conceptually it is easy to see that finance through this model would come at a higher cost. The third tier will also earn a return, which will be added to the cost of finance. In the long term, such an arrangement, if ever it is tried in practice, will not be able to compete with conventional finance.

17.2 ISLAMIC MODES OF FINANCE

After interest was declared unlawful, the challenge for Islamic banks was to provide finance on bases other than interest. Muslim economists presented various suggestions. However, the list of possible modes of Islamic finance presented by the State Bank of Pakistan was the most comprehensive. The list was as follows:

a. equity capital;
b. *musharaka* (partnership);
c. *mudaraba* (agency partnership);
d. *bai' mu'ajjal* (sale of assets on credit);
e. *bai' murabaha* (cost-plus asset financing);
f. *bai' salam* (advance payment for the purchase of agricultural produce);
g. *bai' istisna* (advance payment to purchase manufactured goods or constructed assets);
h. *ijara* (providing assets on lease);
i. *ijara wa iqtina'* (lease and purchase of assets);
j. rent sharing for housing finance;
k. purchase of property with a buyback agreement;
l. interest-free loans.

The so-called 'Islamic' modes of finance are actually secular concepts. Historically, people have used these modes all along; they are still in vogue even in non-Muslim societies. There is nothing 'Islamic' about them. These concepts have evolved through human thinking and commercial practice. Neither the Qur'an nor the *Sunnah* prescribes them. Presenting these modes as 'Islamic' is misleading. Even *mudaraba* and *musharaka*, which are touted as the most pristine forms of 'Islamic' finance, have no roots in the *Shari'ah*. Similarly, *murabaha* and *ijara*, the two most dominant practices of present-day Islamic finance, have no divine sanction. Whether we adopt or we don't, Islam has nothing to prescribe about these modes. Theoretically, equity finance, *musharaka, mudaraba, bai' salam, bai' istisna, ijara* and interest-free loans eliminate interest from the financing contract. However, the other modes have elements which make them similar to interest-based finance. We shall discuss this latter category in Chapter 20.

17.3   LIABILITIES OF ISLAMIC BANKS

17.3.1   Depositors as Temporary Shareholders

Theoretically, depositors of Islamic banks are treated as temporary shareholders with a stake in decisions of the bank. They cannot remain unconcerned about the way the bank uses their funds. The depositors share risk in the bank's business. Sharing of the risk between depositors and investors is a core justification for Islamic banking. It is considered to be more stable and conducive to the growth and development of the economy (Chapra 2007-a). However, the argument is removed from reality. Is it possible to conceive of a bank that would allow depositors to monitor its decisions? Would the depositors themselves be willing to get into the business of monitoring the bank's business? Normally, they would be interested in keeping their deposits safe and productive, leaving the headache of management to the bank as their agent. If we accept the argument that depositors should have a role in the bank's decision making, we are in fact arguing for a model where the bank would not be an agent of the depositors. The benefits of the agency services provided by conventional banks would dissipate. An ordinary depositor does not have the time or capacity to monitor a bank, nor will a bank allow this.

17.3.2 Deposits for Short Durations

According to the orthodox interpretation, a return on deposits can be calculated only after the actual results of the investment become known. That happens only a few months if not years after the deposit is made. The problem arises when the deposits are for short periods and the results of investment cannot be ascertained. The question has been vexing Muslim economists. They have not been able to find a solution to it. However, Tahir, Atiquzzafar, Ali and Waheed (1999: 62) make a suggestion: 'Fresh accounting conventions can be developed that are compatible with the *Shari'ah* and allow for weekly and even daily calculation of profits and losses.' They have not explained any further how this would actually operate if the deposits are on the basis of *mudaraba* and *musharaka*, which require that profits and losses are shared at the end of the period. If they think that daily or weekly calculation of profits is a reasonable economic need, why do they insist on calculation of profits after the end of an economic operation? Daily or weekly calculation of profits is a typical characteristic of interest-based finance, and the whole rigmarole of creating Islamic finance is to eliminate interest. If they are trying to create the essential features of interest-based finance somehow, why do they support such an elaborate effort to create Islamic financial institutions in the first instance?

Tahir *et al.* (1999: 62) also conceive of a possibility of perpetual *mudaraba* or perpetual *musharaka* accounts where the depositors can get into and out of these accounts at their convenience. The authors do not explain the methodology in detail. However, it becomes immensely clear that these accounts would be just like any saving accounts in a conventional bank. It is not clear from their discussion how these deposit accounts differ from conventional savings bank accounts.

17.3.3   *Ijara* Deposits

Another possible form of deposits suggested by Muslim economists is *ijara* deposits. This is prevalent in Iran. The concept of *ijara* deposits is summed up succinctly by Tahir (2007: 88) as follows:

> According to this option [i.e. *ijara* deposits], ownership of funds always remains with the depositors, and is at no stage shared with the banks (as opposed to the case of *mudaraba* or *musharaka*) or transferred to them (as in the case of a loan). The banks come in the picture as managers (or *ajeer*) of depositors to administer the funds. Under these circumstances, as owner of the funds all profits belong to the depositors. The banks would be entitled to a fee.

The above concept of deposit is more akin to safekeeping, for which Islamic banks can charge a fee. All decisions on investment would be made by the depositors at their own risk. Such deposits can be operated only by a few people who have spare time and expertise in leasing business. It is obviously an inferior concept to that of conventional savings bank deposits, where the savers get interest besides safekeeping of funds with no headaches about investment decisions.

17.3.4   General Savings Deposits

Islamic banking theory also visualizes general saving deposits on the pattern of conventional banks. A return on these deposits is possible in the name of a gift (*hiba*). In Iran, this return on foreign deposits is equal to LIBOR (Visser 2009: 83). How does it differ from interest on deposits in conventional banks?

17.3.5   Investment Deposits with Stable Income Flow

Islamic banking theory suggests that those people who like to have a regular stable income with safety of funds can open regular income investment deposit accounts. The Islamic bank will invest these funds in such modes of finance as will bring a fixed income such as *ijara* or *murabaha*. Besides, the banks can create an income equalization fund to meet the fixed income contract with depositors, should the return on the current investment fall below the contract. The end result is that the depositors will get a fixed regular income on their deposits very much like interest on conventional bank deposits. The rest is all law and accounting from the perspective of the depositors. There is hardly a method to tell the 'Islamic' from the 'un-Islamic'.

17.3.6   Grouping of *Mudaraba* Deposits

One of the concerns of Islamic economists has been to ensure that depositors share the profits and losses ensuing from their own capital and that
no one should be made to bear the burden of others. In this pursuit, they
tried to refine the concept further and suggested that Islamic banks can
accept deposits on the basis of *mudaraba* for investment in different types
of businesses specified by the depositors. Thus they can operate different
pools of investment funds, such as a pool of funds for investment in real
estate, a pool of funds for investment in raw material, and so on. They
must maintain separate accounts for each pool. While theoretically it is
possible to do so, in practice the likelihood of commingling profits and
losses from different pools is quite real. Tahir (2007: 93) expresses his
concern as follows:

> There always remains the possibility of profits actually belonging to one group
> of depositors being passed on to another and losses of one category of deposits
> shifted to another. This issue cannot be ignored as either trivial or irrelevant on
> grounds of no objection from the depositors.

The avowed objective of keeping the accounts separate for each group of
investment may not be achieved in practice. Also, in another strand of the
theory it is asserted that the banks should be able to net off their profits
and losses from different sources to arrive at a final figure, which would in
most cases be positive. Thus the suggestion of keeping separate accounts
does not fit well in mainstream thinking on Islamic banking.

17.4   SECURITIZATION

Raising external capital is an everyday need of business and industry. In
conventional finance, business firms raise capital by issuing securities. The
capital is repaid with interest. However, the mechanism is not acceptable
to orthodox Islamic scholars, as it involves interest. Islamic finance has
devised an alternative in the form of Islamic bonds (*sukuk*). AAOIFI
defines *sukuk* as 'securities of equal denomination representing individual
ownership interests in a portfolio of eligible existing or future assets, usufruct, services and business activities' (AAOIFI Standard 17). The Fiqh
Academy of the OIC legitimized the use of *sukuk* in February 1988 (Visser
2009: 63).[3] The mechanics of the *sukuk* are as follows.

The business firm that requires capital (the originator) creates a special
purpose vehicle (SPV), an independent entity. The SPV purchases assets

(like land, buildings, machinery and so on) from the originator. The SPV converts the value of the assets into securities (*sukuk*) and offers to sell the *sukuk* to investors. The sale proceeds are paid to the originator as the price of the assets. The SPV, acting as a trustee on behalf of the *sukuk*-holders, arranges to lease the assets back to the originator. The *sukuk*-holders, being effective owners of the assets, become entitled to lease income payable by the originator. The originator gives a binding undertaking to buy back the asset after the lease period.[4] The main difference is that, in conventional finance, the originator borrows funds through interest-based bonds to purchase an asset. In the case of Islamic finance, the originator already owns the asset and sells it to *sukuk*-holders through an SPV and leases it back with the promise to pay the lease money. The originator buys back the asset from the SVP at a nominal price on termination of the lease. The whole deal is different from conventional finance in form and formalities rather than substance. It may even be more expensive (Balala 2011: 145).

17.5   HOUSING FINANCE

Islamic finance has four models for housing finance. Iqbal and Mirakhor (2008: 122) summarize as follows:

> The first model is based on the *Ijara* (lease) contract, and is the closest to the structure of conventional mortgage. The second model is based on equity partnership (*musharaka*), where the mortgagee (lender) and the mortgagor (borrower) jointly share ownership, which, over a period of time, is transferred to the mortgagor who buys shares of ownership by contributing each month toward buying out the mortgagee's share in the property. Return to the lender is generated out of the rental value of the property. The third model is based on *murabaha* and is practiced in the UK, where property transfer tax (stamp duty) discriminates against the *ijara*- or *musharaka*-based mortgage. The fourth model is designed on the lines of cooperative societies, where members buy equity (*musharaka*) membership and help one another in purchasing property from the pool of the society's funds.

In these models, the first one is obviously the same one that the conventional banks are following except that Islamic finance uses the Arabic terms (*ijara*, etc.) to make it look Islamic. In practice, the banks revise the rate of 'rent' every year, in line with the prevailing market interest rate (El-Diwani 2003). The second model hides interest payments to the bank in the name of rent, as the joint ownership of property is only a legal way of protecting the lender; otherwise the house is owned by the borrower, who is responsible for repair maintenance and insurance payments. Moreover, it creates a dilemma about the sale price of the house.

On transfer to the client, if the price of the house has gone up significantly the banks do not find it profitable to transfer the property to the client at the old purchase price. They will prefer to sell it at the going market price. However, if the price of the property goes down, they are unwilling to accept the lower price. They prefer to sell it at the original price. The model is acceptable to the banks only if the client agrees to give a higher price when the market moves up and guarantees to pay the original price when the market goes down (El-Diwani 2003). The banks do not like to do real business. They are only after a sure profit, as conventional banks are. All this makes the whole arrangement a hidden mechanism for charging interest. The third model is a mark-up on the funds lent for the purchase of property. But even in this case the banks agree to finance property that is likely to increase substantially over a long period, and they are able to build in a proportionate mark-up in the sale price. They will not favour this deal if they expect the prices to go down in due course. The details of the fourth model and the extent of its use in practice are not yet known.

The fact is that Islamic finance has not faced the problem of housing as it exists on the ground. The problem rests on a real-life dilemma. A Muslim who is told that borrowing on interest, and thus taking a house on mortgage, is a sin has to save enough money to buy a house. Suppose the price of a house in 2008 is \$100000 and the Muslim saver requires 15 years to save this money. During this time, he or she will be living in rented accommodation. By the time the \$100000 has been saved, the prices of houses have gone up. Muslim savers can hardly ever win the race of rising prices with their private savings. As compared to this a person who borrows funds on a mortgage can acquire the capacity to earn enough rental income to pay for the price of the property. The advice to refrain from interest-based housing finance is obviously not prudent advice.

17.5.1 Cost of Islamic Home Finance

One important factor in accepting Islamic finance to buy a house is the cost of finance as compared to mortgage finance provided by conventional banks. Dar (2002: 65) concludes that the cost of Islamic finance is not attractive for ordinary Muslims and is one of the major causes for its lack of popularity. He writes:

> Close scrutiny of the Lease Contract used by Islamic Investment Banking Unit of UBK (IIUB)[5] reflects that, in fact, the bank takes into account LIBOR as an opportunity cost of the capital when calculating rent of the leased property. In practice, the monthly payments, however, are much higher than in the case of conventional mortgage. (Ibid.: 66)

Visser (2009: 112) reports that the cost of Islamic home finance in Canada is 100 to 300 basis points higher than conventional home finance, and 40 to 100 basis points higher in the USA.[6] The financial institution has to show the assets financed under *ijara* in its balance sheet as fixed assets, as it retains the title to these assets. Under Basel I and Basel II, conventional mortgages and *murabaha* financing have a risk weighting of 50 per cent, but *ijara* has a risk weighting of 100 per cent. It makes *ijara* financing more expensive for the financial institution, which would like to pass on these costs to clients (Visser 2009: 110).

17.6 CREDIT CARDS

Credit cards perform various useful functions in the present-day economy. For example, they are a means of getting short-term or long-term finance. They provide ease of spending without cash and in foreign countries without holding foreign currencies. The way credit cards function locks the holder of the cards, the seller of goods and services and financial institutions in binding relationships. However, all this is motivated by commercial gains. The financial institutions provide the credit card services to earn interest on capital. They are not in the business of charitable lending. The financial institutions charge interest at predetermined rates if the cardholder does not make the payment within the grace period. Charging interest, according to the orthodox interpretation, makes these cards unacceptable. However, Muslim scholars also find it a useful innovation. How are the two positions to be reconciled? They would like to get the benefits without indulging in interest. They have not been successful in finding a workable solution to this dilemma. However, the mechanics and operations of credit cards have come under discussion among Muslim scholars.

Manzur Ahmad (2008: 83–124) has discussed at length various opinions about the legality of credit cards. He concludes that various scholars have tried to give a favourable opinion about their legality by establishing a similarity with the classical concepts of *kafala*, *wakala*, *iqrad* and *ji'ala*. However, he shows adequately that all these efforts lack precision and legal robustness. Therefore, it is not possible to accept the prevalent credit card as permissible under the *Shari'ah*. However, he does not face the ultimate question about the mechanics of the credit card in the Islamic financial system. The difficulty arises from the fact that Muslim scholars are trying to locate a parallel of the credit card and its legal basis in classical jurisprudence but are unable to find one that will fit the prevalent credit card precisely. These difficulties will continue until they transcend the classical juridical basis. They must recognize changes that have taken place with the development of human society. Trying to find a precise equivalent in Islamic jurisprudence in each case cannot succeed. Askari, Iqbal and Mirakhor (2009: 135) admit that there is, as yet, no instrument that is compatible with *Shari'ah* that can offer the same service as the conventional credit card does, although attempts have been made to devise some sort of 'Islamic credit cards'. (See section 20.13.)

17.7   FINANCE FOR THE GOVERNMENT

Interest-based finance enables governments to borrow for all purposes, including those where the possibility of profit–loss sharing (PLS) does not exist. For example, a government may borrow short-term to pay salaries to employees. Under the PLS regime it is not possible to borrow for short durations. Muslim economists are aware of the limitations of PLS financing. They have made several proposals for government finance as discussed below.

Some Muslim economists do not face the question of government finance squarely and refer to an ideal Islamic economy where the need for government finance can be met through interest-free modes. For example, Zaman and Zaman (2000) hold that an Islamic government should not borrow at all, as it only increases the burden of future generations. In the interest of inter-generational equity, there should not be any government borrowing. To finance development projects which generate an income stream, such as power houses, roads, bridges, airports and so on, the government should raise funds on the basis of revenue sharing. For other projects the government should raise funds through *zakah*, zero-rate bonds or philanthropy. The proposals are naïve and do not need any further discussion. If only the authors had shown by empirical data that these proposals were practicable, it would have deserved some discussion. Zaman and Zaman oppose public debt because governments waste borrowed funds through inefficiency and corruption. The point is well taken, but what is the guarantee that the funds raised through so-called 'Islamic' modes would not meet the same fate?

Ziauddin Ahmad (1989: 21) suggests that the government can meet its deficit by obliging commercial banks to extend loans on an interest-free basis. This is reasonable, he thinks, since the banks will be expected not to pay any return to current accountholders. He did not develop the proposal any further. It is not clear whether such a proposal is practicable. We need to examine its feasibility with reference to the government deficit and the amount of funds available with banks. It raises questions of fiduciary obligations, risk management, inflationary impact, and the solvency of banks. In the absence of a deeper analysis, this proposal remains unpersuasive.

M.T. Uthmani (1995: 169) thinks that the government can raise funds from the general public against interest-free bonds for those projects which are not commercial and can give them allowances in income tax. The reduction in tax is not interest, he argues. The proposal changes the mechanics of financing. Instead of borrowing cash and paying interest, the government should give a rebate in income tax to take advantage of interest-free finance. The income forgone by the government would reduce the income stream of the government as payment of interest on a loan would have done, had the government borrowed cash on the basis of interest. From the perspective of economic impact, the proposal does not change much. It is only a change in the procedure and not the substance.

Kahf (n.d.-a: 17) spells out the conditions for public borrowing. The government debt should be exchanged at face value only, irrespective of the date of maturity. The government debt should not be exchanged for debts. The first condition makes it difficult to discount government debt certificates in the secondary market. However, Kahf (ibid.: 18) finds a way out. According to him, the government debt may be redeemed at face value or at a discount. The only condition is that such an arrangement should be part of the original contract of the loan. The question arises: if a government debt can be discounted at a value different from the face value, how does it differ from the conventional discounting of bills on the basis of the interest rate?

A similar accommodation for a hidden form of interest is possible by providing incentives to creditors if they lend money to the government. The incentives could be in the form of a mark-up on goods sold to the government, tax exemptions and relaxations in tax deadlines, reduction in future fees for education and medical services, protection against inflation, and so on. All these are indirect methods of providing compensation for interest on loans. The question arises: what is the net benefit to the public treasury in adopting these indirect and complex routes? In fact, such methods provide wider, unregulated access to the government to exploit or give undue benefits to lenders, since these benefits do not have a competitive market. Kahf (n.d.-a: 20) proposes that the government can issue *salam, istisna'* and leasing certificates and public utility warrants at a mark-down price on the face value, enabling the holder to get the face value at maturity, or, if the prices are likely to increase, issue the certificates at face value with the promise to pay the price of the certificates after adjusting for inflation. Are not these methods attempts to accommodate interest in an indirect manner? Kahf (n.d.-b: 15) says that the government may issue debt certificates on an interest-free basis. However, it can redeem the certificates before maturity and seek a discount on early redemption. Should we not call this discount interest?

17.7.1   Purchasing Assets on a Deferred Payment Basis

Tahir *et al.* (1999: 84) propose that, instead of borrowing cash, the government should buy assets and supplies from private business firms and issue promissory notes to acknowledge the debt. The price of the assets and supplies can be fixed in such a manner that the selling firm gets adequately compensated for the benefits that it is forgoing by tying its funds in the transaction. The selling firm can get the notes discounted at a discount rate that compensates the discounting bank for the cost of collection and for the profits forgone on the funds that the bank is providing. The discounting can take place at secondary and tertiary levels as well. Thus a secondary market for these notes will emerge. The authors have also mentioned certain additional conditions, but that does not change the essence of the above arrangement. It can be easily seen that the government is getting assets and supplies at a higher price than that at which it would buy for cash. It is tantamount to building interest into the cost of goods. The discounting of promissory notes also involves interest. The transaction differs from conventional borrowing on interest to the extent that it is more complicated and risky. It may even be more expensive, as the mark-up added in the sale price may be higher than the interest on borrowed funds. There is no competitive market for mark-up in the sale price of assets.

17.7.2   Certificates for Manufacturing Assets (*Istisna'* Certificates)

Tahir *et al.* (1999: 84) have also suggested that the government can get its assets manufactured by issuing certificates to be paid in the future. They say these certificates would not be tradable. The possibility of using this method of government finance cannot be popular with business firms, as they would not be able to sell their certificates in a secondary market.

17.7.3   Assets for Advance Payment Received (*Salam* Certificates)

Tahir *et al.* (1999: 85) have also suggested that the government can receive cash in advance as the sale price of assets to be delivered in the future. For example, if the government is expecting to find oil, it can sell the expected output for cash and issue certificates with a promise to deliver the oil on drilling. Later on, when the government delivers the oil, the certificate-holders will return the certificates. However, the authors also propose that the certificate-holders will be able to sell the certificates in the open market at the going price. They do not mention the discounting of these certificates. They also do not tell how the secondary market for these certificates will function. How will the price of the certificates be determined? They contend that this is not the sale of a debt, as the certificate-holders are not selling any debt. They are selling rights of ownership. The legal stance may be correct. However, in essence, it is nothing but the sale of receivables. The investors may want to redeem the certificates before maturity. The later in the day this happens, the smaller will be the difference in the sale price of a certificate and its face value. For all practical purposes, it is quite the same thing as the sale of interest-bearing bonds at a discount.

17.7.4   Asset-Lease Certificates (Asset-*Ijara* Certificates)

Tahir *et al.* (1999: 85–88) also suggest a detailed mechanism of issuing lease certificates for an asset that the government commits to take on lease. The asset can be constructed (like a school building) by issuing certificates through a financial intermediary. Those who buy the certificates would be entitled to rent that the government would pay for using the asset. They also suggest that the certificates would be openly saleable on the secondary market. In essence, it means that the certificate-holders would receive a stream of income which they could sell for a price on the secondary market. The buyer of that stream would obviously calculate the investment he or she was going to make and the return expected from it. The secondary market would operate similarly to the interest-based market for such certificates.

The authors also conceive a situation where a lessee pays the rent for the entire period in advance and then sublets the asset to a new lessee at a rent which is different from the original rent paid to the lessor. In essence it means the original lessee tries to redeem his or her investment through a sublease contract. The second contract could be for more or less than the original rate of rent paid by the lessee. They say that the *Shari'ah* does not have any objection to this arrangement. Without going into legal intricacies, it is easy to see that the arrangement would, in practice, boil down to an investment of cash for a certain period and then redeeming it later on, most probably at a rate of return that corresponds to the period for which the funds remained tied. This is nothing but discounting on the basis of interest.

The authors have also raised the question of resale of lease certificates for assets which have not yet been constructed or which are under construction. During the period, these assets do not have any usufruct. How can the usufruct of these assets be resold under the *Shari'ah*? Their answer is that we can treat them as *salam* certificates with certain legal guarantees. But what is the essence of the matter? A person is holding a leasing certificate for an asset which is not yet complete. He or she sells it on the secondary market. How would the buyer of the certificate assess its value? Obviously, it would be for the period the buyer's funds would be tied before it starts getting a return. The whole arrangement is nothing but buying and selling of conventional interest-bearing bonds, except that the Islamic alternative is more complex and riskier.

17.8   ISLAMIC CENTRAL BANKING

17.8.1   Managing the Money Supply in the Absence of an Interest Rate

The interest rate is the primary tool for regulating the money supply in a capitalist economy. Central banks use this tool on a routine basis. However, once we abandon interest as the basis for banking, the question of regulating the money supply by the central banks emerges as a challenge. Several Muslim economists have addressed this question. They have made certain proposals to cope with the situation in the absence of interest. For example, Uthman (2001: 111) says:

> The absence of financial debt instruments in our system calls for the design of alternative tools for monetary policy. One tool is for the central bank to auction, on profit-sharing basis, stocks of money to the financial institutions. The banks that offer the central bank a higher profit share shall get more funds. In other words, the sovereign profit-sharing rate (SPS) shall replace the discount rate as a tool of monetary policy.

Uzair (1980) and Siddiqi (1982) have argued that absence of interest will not cause much of a problem for monetary policy. Profit–loss-sharing ratios (between savers and bank and between bank and entrepreneur) can be used to manipulate the money supply. Without going into the intrinsic validity of this argument, it is obvious that, since profit–loss sharing as a basis for financing has not been widely accepted, the use of the ratios as mentioned is only a hypothetical possibility. However, Tahir *et al.* (1999: 118) argue that the central bank should not have authority to manipulate the profit–loss-sharing ratios of the banks with their *musharaka* partners, as that would go against the Tradition of the Prophet where he refused to interfere in the market when there was a general hike in prices in Medina. But they concede that the central bank may have the authority to determine the proportion of investment between a client and a bank in a *musharaka* agreement.

Uthman (2001: 112) has also proposed that the central bank can use 'rediscounting' as a tool for buying and selling non-fixed-income instruments of Islamic banks at over and above the market prices of these tools. Although the author has not explained, it seems that he means to say that if, for example, a bank has issued *musharaka sukuk*, which are tradable on the stock exchange, the central bank may offer to buy them at higher than the market price to induct money into the economy or at lower price to sell them to absorb the money supply. Uthman does not demonstrate how this type of 'rediscounting' would actually take place and whether it would be effective as a monetary policy tool. But the proposal presumes that there is an efficient capital market for non-fixed-income securities and the central bank can use this tool to achieve its objectives. However, there is no such market available where the idea could be practised.

Tahir *et al.* (1999: 119) argue that, though the existing bank rate instrument as a monetary policy tool will be irrelevant in the Islamic framework, the central bank will be able to influence the money supply by: (a) discounting bills of exchange in return for the transfer of collection rights directly; and (b) acquiring tradable securities such as *bai' mu'ajjal* securities and asset-*ijara* securities held by the banks to induct liquidity into the banking sector. They have not explained how this would actually be done and what the terms and conditions of these actions would be. Direct discounting of bills is obviously an interest-based activity. It is not obvious how the other option would be exercised and whether it would effectively avoid interest or not.

As a substitute for open market operations, Tahir *et al.* (1999: 119) contend that the central bank might issue *mudaraba* certificates to be purchased by the banks. The central bank could use these funds to finance government projects and share profits with the banks as they accrue. In practice, such certificates have not found favour because of the risks involved. Tahir *et al.* (1999: 120) have proposed another tool of monetary policy to inject liquidity into banks. They have suggested that the central bank might invest its funds in the share capital of the banks as *rabb al-mal* in a *mudaraba* contract. This means that the central bank would become an investor in the capital of the banks and get a share in the shareholders' profit. This proposal does not indicate what would be done if the central bank wanted to contract liquidity. Also, by this proposal some banks could be beneficiaries of the central bank's funds. What about others? How would the central bank's actions be regulated to safeguard against favouritism?

Another tool of monetary policy proposed by some Muslim economists (including Uthman 2001) is a 100 per cent reserve requirement for current accounts. The idea is that banks should not create money, which they do under the fractional reserve requirement regime. Capitalist economists have presented the idea as well. However, it is questionable whether this type of banking would be able to meet the financing needs of a present-day economy. Muslim economists have not shown beyond doubt that this is possible (see e.g. Uthman 2001). Tahir *et al.* (1999: 117) have argued that a 100 per cent reserve ratio would be against the objective of the *Shari'ah* that allows borrowers to use their funds as they like. Once we make 100 per cent of deposits the reserve requirement, the banks would not be able to use these funds and that would defeat the objective of the *Shari'ah*.

Sudan has issued central bank *musharaka* certificates (CMC) on the basis of central bank ownership of certificates in commercial banks and government *musharaka* certificates (GMC) to mobilize savings from the general public. It is possible to use both types of certificates for liquidity management, but the exact mechanism for doing that is not clear.

In brief, there is no final solution to the problem. Islamic finance has yet to develop practicable tools and methodology for managing the money supply in the absence of an interest rate.

17.9   RISKS IN ISLAMIC FINANCE

All banking business entails some risk. However, Islamic financial institutions face additional risks which make their business more challenging, more expensive and less efficient as compared to conventional financial institutions. Sundararajan (2007: 124) argues that Islamic financial institutions may be more vulnerable than their conventional counterparts partly because of 'the inadequate financial infrastructure including missing instruments and markets, a weak insolvency and creditor rights regime, factors that limit effective risk mitigation'.[7] Some of the additional risks that Islamic financial institutions face are as follows.

17.9.1   Credit Risk

It is a potential risk that banks' clients will fail to make payment on time, including the risk arising from the settlement and clearing of transactions. Islamic banks cannot charge interest for delay in payment. Further, there are additional risks in specific types of contracts. For example, in the case of non-binding *murabaha*, the client may refuse to take delivery of goods. In case of *salam* or *istisna'*, the client may fail to supply the commodity or asset on time or according to specification and quality. In the case of *mudaraba*, the bank cannot monitor or take part in management of the client's business but remains committed to accept the loss if there is any.

17.9.2 Mark-Up Risk

In the case of *murabaha* contracts, the mark-up rate is fixed, while the market rate of goods supplied may increase beyond the mark-up rate, forcing the bank to forgo any potential gain from the increase in the market rate.

17.9.3 Price Risk

In the case of *salam* or *istisna'* contracts, the market price of the underlying commodity or asset may go down when the bank receives them. The bank may suffer erosion in its profit or even losses. Another allied risk is that the commodity supplied will be substandard and not fetch the expected price.

17.9.4 Value of Leased Asset

In the case of an operating lease, the bank may suffer owing to a reduction in the residual value of the leased asset.

17.9.5 Foreign Exchange Risk

The value of the currency in which receivables are due may depreciate, and the value of the currency in which payment has to be made may appreciate. Since Islamic banks cannot enter into current-swap-future agreements, they face additional risks.

17.9.6 Security Price Risk

Islamic banks invest part of their surplus funds in marketable securities (*sukuk*). However, the prices of these securities are subject to yield risk. Moreover, as yet the *sukuk* market is not sufficiently mature. Islamic banks may face additional risks of illiquidity and distorted prices.

17.9.7 Equity Investment Risk

Islamic banks undertake risk by investing in equity or through financing on the basis of *mudaraba* and *musharaka*. They have to incur extra costs to monitor the business of clients against negligence, lack of transparency, weak integrity and poor management.

17.9.8 Rate of Return Risk

Islamic banks may earn a lower rate on investments than the estimated rate payable or expected by investors because in equity-based investment the return is not known *ex ante*. Islamic banks compete with conventional banks and offer 'expected rates' of return, which are almost as guaranteed as on interest-based investments. Islamic banks have more limited capacity to withstand the shocks due to fluctuations in their own returns.

17.9.9 Displaced Commercial Risk

This is a type of risk where the Islamic banks decide to distribute more profits among depositors than they themselves earn, with the objective of stopping depositors from displacing their deposits and taking them to other banks. In the anxiety to do so, they may not pay enough to shareholders and thus incur the risk of insolvency.

17.9.10 Liquidity Risk

This is the risk that Islamic banks might not have enough cash to meet their obligations. Non-availability of a *Shari'ah*-compatible money market and of an efficient interbank market and the shallow secondary market for its financial papers make liquidity risk most critical for Islamic banks.

17.9.11 Hedging Risk

Owing to the non-availability of a money market, and the shallow secondary market, Islamic banks have a limited capacity to hedge themselves against various types of risks.

17.9.12 Fiduciary Risk

Islamic banks often use current accountholders' funds for investment purposes. But, if the bank has heavy losses, the funds that were accepted on the basis of trust would become a burden and the bank might lose its business or reputation or both.

17.9.13 Transparency Risk

The reporting practices of Islamic financial instruments are yet not standardized. Islamic banks run a transparency risk in reporting on these instruments.

17.9.14   *Shari'ah* Risk

The practice of Islamic banks is still in its infancy. The number and versions of *Shari'ah* decrees are far from uniform. The staff of Islamic banks are also not fully trained in these practices. Islamic banks run the risk of non-compliance with the *Shari'ah*.

17.9.15   Reputation Risk

Islamic banks have adopted modes of finance that are akin to interest-based finance. They are running the risk of copying the conventional banks' business under Islamic names. This may affect their reputation.

17.10   COSTS OF ISLAMIC BANKS

Islamic banks have to incur certain additional costs as compared to conventional banks (Visser 2009: 99). For example:

a. They have to pay the *Shari'ah* board for legal services. The costs are significant, given the demand for *Shari'ah* scholars and their supply in the market.
b. In most financing schemes, they have to prepare more than one contract to justify the deal from an Islamic perspective, leading to additional legal costs.
c. Islamic banks have to monitor the business decisions of clients to protect their interests against corruption and fraud in those businesses. That involves additional costs.

Islamic banks and their clients have to pay a price for their adherence to the *Shari'ah*. However, we recognize that, with increasing standardization of Islamic financial products, the additional costs are declining sharply.

17.11   ISSUES IN ISLAMIC BANKING THEORY

17.11.1   Islamic Banking and the Stability of Financial Markets

Muslim economists have argued vehemently that Islamic banking is conducive to financial stability (see e.g. Scharf 1983; M.S. Khan 1986; Ayub 2002; Iqbal and Mirakhor 2008). The gist of their argument is that Islamic banking relates finance to real investment in trade and industry. It provides finance in one of three main categories: (a) capital for projects; (b) sale of goods; and (c) leasing of assets. In these cases, there is not any gap between the real sector and finance. Finance is not available for speculation in the money market. All financial claims are supported by real-sector assets.

Financial instability of conventional finance flows from proliferation of debts through sale and purchase of financial claims without any relationship with the underlying assets. In conventional finance, debts proliferate as new debts are created on the basis of earlier debts. There is no direct and visible link between the real sector and the financial sector. The debt-propelled system multiplies existing debts by several times the real assets, creating room for speculation and instability. The Islamic financial system, so goes the argument, aligns the real and financial sectors. Every financial transaction is based on some existing or potential real asset.

The above assertion overstates the merit of Islamic banking. In most cases clients of conventional banks are business firms, and they use the funds for commercial purposes in the real sector. To that extent the real sector and financial sector remain aligned even in the conventional system. However, some clients do divert these funds toward speculative financial investments. The possibility of diverting finance to speculative purposes arises from the existence of a secondary market for financial claims, which is a real-life need of business firms. The need for flexibility in cash flows compels business firms to get their notes receivable discounted at the going rate of interest. This is possible in conventional finance. Islamic finance has not been able to find a solution to this problem as yet, but the need for a secondary market for financial claims is so compelling that Islamic finance cannot postpone it for very long. Already Islamic banks have started finding back-door solutions to discounting Islamic financial instruments. Sooner or later a formal secondary market in the Islamic financial instrument will emerge. The whole argument that Islamic finance aligns the real and financial sectors would come to naught once Islamic finance developed a secondary market for financial instruments. In the final analysis the Islamic financial system will not settle down to a different situation to that of the conventional financial system. In light of the limited experience that we have of the actual functioning of Islamic financial institutions, we see that debts have proliferated in the Islamic financial market as well. On the *sukuk* market and *tawarruq*, Siddiqi (2006: 17) writes:

> Instead of moving away from debt proliferation and financing unrelated to real assets we are moving towards debt proliferation and asset unrelated financing. Islamic finance does need extension of Islamic financial services to all sectors of the economy, including consumer sector. But this is to be done within the

paradigm of Islamic economics focused on justice and human felicity not at the cost of it. That is the real challenge, not the replication of conventional debt instruments under Arabic names.

The claim that the Islamic financial system will be more stable than the conventional financial system does not have any empirical support. Siddiqi (2006: 6), the founding father of Islamic banking theory, acknowledges this as follows:

> It was shown that a financial system based on profit sharing will be more stable than one dominated by debts. This was in addition to the earlier argument in favour of an interest-free system based on profit sharing that focused on justice and fairness, one that had more resonance in a world experiencing great instability. By its very nature, the claim could not be supported by empirical evidence in a world where the conventional interest-based system held sway leaving no exceptions.

Muslim economists argue that conventional banks lend money for speculative purposes without due regard for financial prudence and are pushed solely by greed and profit maximization. A question arises: what is the guarantee that Islamic financial institutions will not behave in a similar manner to conventional banks? Islamic banks could also burn their fingers in real estate finance or in certificates of property developers. On this question Siddiqi (2006: 6–7) has quite aptly concluded:

> The theory is strong as a critique of the conventional system but it could not make a head way in supporting the hypothesis that Islamic system will be more stable due to integration of financial and real sectors. The empirical evidence needed to boost its credibility can possibly come only if people convinced of it demonstrate it in a country or region. But can they?

Iqbal and Mirakhor (2008: 20) say:

> The present international system is deficient in many ways, of which the two most important are as follows:
>
> - A debt-based system needs an effective lender of the last resort, and the present international financial system does not have and it is not likely that one will emerge anytime soon.
> - A debt-based system needs bankruptcy proceedings, debt restructuring and workout mechanism and processes that the present international financial system lacks.

It leads to several questions: are we sure that the Islamic financial system does not require an effective lender of last resort? The need is already being felt that Islamic financial institutions can compete with conventional banks only if they have a lender of last resort.[8] Will not the Islamic financial system require a framework for bankruptcy proceedings? Have Islamic financial institutions developed that framework?

Another argument for greater stability of the Islamic financial system is as follows. Conventional banking is based on interest, which is a fixed charge on the sum borrowed, irrespective of the actual productivity of the capital. Conventional banking is conducive to instability, as the banks' liability to depositors remains fixed, while the banks' income, owing to the possibility of defaults and bankruptcies in the business sector, may fluctuate, causing stresses and strains in the financial sector. A banking system based on profit sharing would create a mechanism of automatic adjustment of banks' liabilities with the shortfall in banks' income. Thus a banking system based on profit sharing would be more stable (Iqbal and Mirakhor 2008: 19–20). The assertion is valid if we have an ideal system of Islamic banking. In practice, all Islamic banks promise and pay fixed rates of return on term deposits. The liability of Islamic banks remains fixed even if their return is not. The claim of greater financial stability for Islamic banks is more wishful thinking than a reality.

17.11.2   The Question of Collateral

An oft-repeated rationale for interest-free finance presented by Muslim economists is that conventional banks agree to finance weak projects if the client is able to present collateral. As opposed to this, Islamic finance requires the bank to share in the profit and loss of the project financed. Hence Islamic banks will focus only on really profitable projects (see e.g. Zaman and Zaman 2000: 8) even though the client cannot present the collateral. The argument is oversimplified and shows that the writers do not have a deep understanding of the method of project appraisal, risk assessment and decision processes followed by conventional banks. If the point made by the writers were correct, most of the funding decisions by conventional banks would have turned into losses, leading to worldwide failures of banks. The empirical evidence is exactly opposite to that. Zaman and Zaman contend that, in the absence of mandatory collateral, Islamic banks would be willing to finance poor people as well, if their projects otherwise made sense. The question arises: what if the poor people do not repay the money taken from the bank? Also, with 35 years of Islamic banking in practice, in which country have Islamic banks actually provided greater access to poorer people?

The moot point is how we protect Islamic banks against the irresponsible behaviour of clients. The banks are trustees of other people's money.

How do we ensure that the clients of Islamic banks do not waste or misappropriate funds or siphon them off to other projects? What is the mechanism in Islamic finance to substitute for collateral? There is no final answer to this question. Some Muslim economists have tacitly conceded that collateral will be necessary. For example, Tahir *et al.* (1999: 57) and Chapra (2007-a: 43) contend that Islamic banks would require collateral as conventional banks do.

On this question, Islamic finance has other problems as well. Theoretically, entrepreneurs who obtain finance are supposed to be partners of the Islamic bank. In principle, there should be no requirement for collateral from the partners. By asking for collateral, Islamic banks behave as lenders and not as partners. Does this not weaken the case for Islamic banking? The justification for Islamic banking started from criticism of financing on the basis of collateral rather than the profitability of the project, but it has ended up in conceding that collateral is necessary in the case of Islamic finance as well. Where is the justification for Islamic banking then?

17.11.3 Deposit Insurance

Islamic banking theory has not been able to resolve satisfactorily the question of deposit insurance. In conventional banking, deposit-taking institutions guarantee the safety of deposits. However, in Islamic banking such an assurance is difficult to come by. Investment accountholders face the risk of loss on their deposits. Current accountholders, in theory, have the assurance of getting back their principal sum. However, in practice, Islamic banks use these funds for short-term investments. In the process, the banks may suffer losses and find that they are unable to repay the original deposits in full. The conventional solution of deposit insurance is not available to Islamic banks, as according to the orthodox theory conventional insurance is also unlawful. That leaves the depositors in limbo. They do not have the guarantee of getting back their deposits in full. This has led to various models of deposit *takaful* (DT). The idea is to develop a sort of deposit insurance parallel to conventional deposit insurance. However, certain questions are still unresolved. For example, should the deposit *takaful* cover all deposits or only demand deposits? Where and how should the deposit *takaful* funds be invested? How are the claims to be resolved if the bank actually fails (Solé 2007: 19)?

In practice, Islamic banks guarantee the return of the principal sum of investment deposits as conventional banks do. To overcome the problem of sharing losses and also guaranteeing the return of deposits, most Islamic banks use the mode of profit equalization reserves to smooth out fluctuations in earnings and to protect depositors. Islamic banks guarantee saving bank deposits by using a legal fiction that these deposits are a trust (*amanah*) and hence must be returned in full. But that creates a problem of interest on saving deposits. In theory, trust funds cannot earn interest. To overcome that, another legal fiction of the gift (*hiba*) is contrived that makes it perfectly lawful for a trustee to give something as a gift (like interest) to the depositor (Visser 2009: 82–83; and also M.F. Khan 2003). If that is how Islamic banks have tried to guarantee deposits, conventional banks also do the same. In this respect, Islamic banks come closer to conventional banks.

17.11.4   Hedging against a Variable Rate of Return

Conventional banks hedge against fluctuations in the rate of return by making the interest rate variable, adjusting it periodically as the market fluctuates. In the case of Islamic finance, this method is not available. Islamic banks also face the risk of a changing rate of return, owing to changes in the demand for and supply of finance. What are the Islamic options? Al-Suwailem (2006: 119) says that, in the case of *ijara* finance, the contract can provide for adjustment to the rent rate according to the market periodically, say biannually. However, in the case of *murabaha*, this option is not available, since the sale price is fixed finally and cannot be changed. Al-Suwailem suggests that banks can hedge against changes in the rate of return by changing the amount of instalment for the client. When the market rate of return increases, banks can increase the amount of instalment and reduce the number of instalments. When the market rate of return goes down, a reverse procedure can be adopted. The mechanism does provide some comfort to the bank, but is not flexible enough to match the conventional banks, which can adjust the rates for as short periods as a day or so. Moreover, it is as yet unknown what the response of Islamic bank clients to this mechanism will be. Will they prefer to do business with Islamic banks or shift to conventional banks?

17.11.5   Diversified Deferred Price

Islamic financial institutions can face the problem of liquidity in long-term finance. Al-Suwailem (2006: 128) has proposed a way out of this difficulty on a diversified deferred payment basis. For example, if a bank finances an oil company with $100 million at 5.2 per cent for 20 years on the basis of *murabaha*, its total revenue from the client will consist of 49 per cent principal and 51 per cent mark-up. The bank can agree with the oil company to receive back the principal in cash and mark-up in the form of an asset, say future oil output. (This can be a basket of assets as well.) The bank will have the flexibility of issuing *sukuk* on the basis of this oil revenue. The return on the *sukuk* will be linked to the market price of oil in the future. The bank can thus realize its amount of mark-up at an early date. The *sukuk*-holders will be able to sell the *sukuk* in the market at a price that will vary with the price of the oil. In this proposal, it is not clear at which price the quantity of oil will be defined in the first instance. Will it be the current oil price or a future oil price? If it is the current oil price, the risk for the bank is that when the output actually becomes available the price of oil may have gone down drastically, leading to heavy losses for the bank or for the *sukuk*-holders. If it is a future oil price, how shall we determine that for 20 years down the line? The whole process of conversion of mark-up into a commodity and then the commodity into *sukuk* and then *sukuk* into cash is so complicated and full of hazards and risks that very few people would dare to try such a solution.

17.11.6   Islamic Capital Markets

Capital markets are an integral part of any financial system. They help mobilize resources, provide investment avenues, help business and industry in seeking funds, provide a meeting ground for buyers and sellers of financial papers, and smooth out rates of return on capital. Islamic finance primarily relies on equity finance. Well-functioning capital markets where investors can offer and business firms can seek funds are a great need of Islamic finance. Islamic investors should have options of entry to and exit from the capital market that requires a secondary market in financial papers. However, profit–loss sharing or other modes of 'Islamic' finance do not allow the trading of financial papers at a price other than the face value. That inhibits the emergence of a secondary market in financial papers. Islamic financial institutions are obliged either to keep large pools of surplus funds to meet unexpected customer needs or conclude *murabaha*-based contracts with conventional banks, allowing them to draw funds on an emergent basis. In both cases, liquidity management by Islamic financial institutions is more costly than for conventional banks. Despite the rapid growth of the *sukuk* market globally, there is a negligible secondary market for these instruments, leading to a scenario of 'buy and hold'. The problem is that orthodox opinion treats the financial claims as debts and prohibits trading in them. Until a solution is found for trading in financial claims, the problem of a secondary market for financial instruments will persist. Askari, Iqbal and Mirakhor (2009: 131) admit that a *Shari'ah*-compatible capital market does not exist.

Another issue pertains to the sale and purchase of shares of companies that are still at the initial purchase offer (IPO) stage. These shares represent either cash or near cash. According to orthodox opinion, such shares cannot be traded at a price different from the par value. That restricts the emergence of a secondary market for shares at the IPO stage. Islamic finance has yet to find a mechanism to handle this issue.

17.11.7 Use of LIBOR-Based Rate of Return

Most Islamic bonds (*sukuk*) link the rate of return to the London interbank offered rate (LIBOR) or similar benchmarks. M.M. Khan and Bhatti (2008: 73) write:

> It is no secret that Islamic financial institutions always use the London-interbank offered rate (LIBOR), market interest rates, discounting tables and time value of money techniques to fix PLS ratios and returns on their *murabaha* and other investments. Moreover, *sukuk* are always issued on the basis of LIBOR.

Using LIBOR disentangles the *sukuk* from the assets in which the *sukuk* funds have been invested and attaches them to the financial market based on interest. It defeats the very purpose for which the Islamic financial products were designed and offered in the first instance. Contemporary jurists have accepted LIBOR as a valid basis for deciding the mark-up in transactions involving a fixed return such as *murabaha* and *ijara*. For example, Uthmani (n.d.-a: 13) condones the use of LIBOR as a benchmark, although he, too, agrees that Islamic banks should devise some other benchmark.

Abdul-Rahman (2010: 101) thinks that the short-term interest rate determined by the US Federal Reserve Board is not an interest rate prohibited by the *Shari'ah*, since it is merely a tool to manage money supply in the economy and does not involve the actual renting of money on interest. Iqbal and Mirakhor (2008: 131) have recommended that the government should support the development of primary and secondary markets for Islamic financial products, but they also do not have a proposal for replacing LIBOR as a benchmark for the rate of return. In brief, Islamic finance has yet to find a mechanism for determining the rate of return that satisfies investors, is reasonably risk-free and also complies with the *Shari'ah*. Omar *et al.* (2010) have surveyed various other rates of return proposed by Islamic scholars to replace the use of LIBOR or a rate of interest as the basis for bank profits. However, they have found all of them lacking in one or more respects. They have proposed a method to determine a pricing benchmark by taking into account the historical trends of profitability in different sectors of the economy based on stock exchange data and supplementing it with the unique risks of each firm. However, the validity of this proposal is yet to be tested in practice, because it is still at the conceptual stage.

17.11.8   Margin Trading of Shares and Stocks

In conventional finance, it is possible to trade shares and stocks by making marginal payment and settling the account on a net basis later on. Since it involves sale without possession, it does not conform to the *Shari'ah*. However, there is no alternative mechanism in Islamic finance that enables traders to deal in shares by paying the margin. The benefit of such trading is that it increases the liquidity of the market by increasing the trading capacity of the traders.

17.12   ISLAMIC MICROFINANCE

17.12.1   The Challenge

Conventional microfinance provides funds on the basis of interest, which is prohibited according to the orthodox interpretation. The generally accepted principles oppose any ceiling on the rate of interest, as it restrains the microfinance institutions from covering their costs and thus restricts the supply of funds to the poor (Obaidullah and Khan 2008: 5). The cost of funds in traditional microfinance is often significantly higher than the cost of other finance by the banks because of the higher cost of managing a microfinance institution. For example, the cost of managing 1000 small loans of $100 each would be significantly higher than the cost of a single loan of $100 000. A study published by the Consultative Group to Assist the Poor (CGAP)[9] (Rosenberg, Gonzalez and Narain 2009: 2) shows that the interest rates for conventional microfinance could be as high as 85 per cent plus taxes which the borrower has to pay. Obaidullah (2008: 14) quotes Mannan[10] that the effective rate of interest by Grameen Bank, Bangladesh could be as high as 86.41 per cent if we include the cost of documentation and method of accounting used by the bank. Wilson (2007: 200) reports that the Grameen Bank, Bangladesh interest rate for basic income-generating loans is 20 per cent, but 8 per cent on housing loans and 5 per cent on education loans. El-Hawary and Grais (2005: 2) report that mark-up rates range between 12 and 12.5 per cent, with a compound interest rate of 24–25 per cent on microfinance in Bangladesh. They also report on the microfinance project of Jabal al-Hoss in Syria (launched in

2000) and the Yemen Hodeidah microfinance project (launched in 1997). In both cases the financing was done on the basis of *murabaha*, but the rate of mark-up was higher than the market interest rate. The interest rates of non-institutional sources to small borrowers could even be as high as 120–140 per cent (Rahman 2010: 126).

Obviously, the objective of microfinance to help the poor is defeated by interest rates that are clearly exploitative. The challenge before Islamic microfinance is to find a solution to the high cost of funding which is also compatible with the *Shari'ah*. The experience in Muslim countries shows that microfinance institutions (MFIs) have overly resorted to *murabaha*-based finance, whether it is relevant to the type of loan or not. In plain words, the finance is provided by the MFIs on a fixed rate of mark-up, which is quite similar to interest. The authenticity of such types of loans on the strict benchmark of *Shari'ah*-compatibility is doubtful. The challenge of finding cheaper finance for the poor within the Islamic framework thus remains.

Obaidullah and Khan (2008) have discussed the whole range of institutional and management challenges that Islamic microfinance faces. They have made several useful recommendations for developing microfinance institutions in Muslim countries. However, the authors have not faced the question of the cost of finance and the method by which it can be made available to the poor in such a manner that it is cheaper than conventional finance.

Obaidullah and Khan (2008: 18) and Chapra (2008-b: 123) suggest that *zakah* and *awqaf* should provide the mainstay for Islamic microfinance. They think that conventional microfinance ignores or marginalizes the poorest of the poor, as they are not 'bankable' in the conventional sense. Further, they support the method of interest-free loans, purely as a charitable activity. Obviously, this type of finance is sustainable only among small communities and for reasons of social integrity and fraternity. It cannot be an alternative basis for microfinance institutions. Kahf (2008) has proposed a model of microfinance that draws funds from *waqf* and *zakah*. The funds have to be in two categories: (a) cash for interest-free loans or on the basis of the market rate through one of the Islamic modes of finance such as *murabaha* or *ijara*; (b) *awqaf* properties or other resources which can be used to generate profits to be used for subsidizing microfinance institutions. The expenses of microfinance institutions have to be met from both *zakah* and *awqaf*. Essentially, the model moves away from a commercial solution to microfinance. It commissions charity to handle the problem of microfinance.

NOTES

1. *Ghair sudi bankari* [Banking without interest] (Lahore: Islamic Publications, 1969) (in Urdu).
2. For example, Council of Islamic Ideology, Pakistan (1983); Ayub (2002, 2007).
3. However, Al-Amine (2008: 3) writes: 'For instance, the practical aspects of *ijara sukuk* or even the theoretical characteristics of the *musharaka sukuk*, and despite their existence in the market for a number of years, have not yet been discussed by the Fiqh Academy which is in reality the highest and most influential *Shari'ah* institution addressing financial issues. Thus, there is no *Shari'ah* resolution from these institutions determining what is *Shari'ah* compliant and what is not.'
4. The *Shari'ah* Board of AAOIFI has disallowed this guarantee, as it is against the *Shari'ah* rules.
5. United Bank of Kuwait (Islamic Investment Banking Unit).
6. Based on *Executive News*, 25 (2007), www.Islamicfinance.de.
7. The Islamic Financial Services Board (IFSB) has issued several standards to strengthen the risk-management regime of Islamic financial institutions.
8. Iqbal and Mirakhor (2008: 131) themselves feel the need for a lender of last resort for Islamic financial institutions.
9. This is a multi-donor consortium of 31 public and private development assistance organization agencies working together to expand access to financial services for the poor (Obaidullah and Khan 2008: 4).
10. [As in original] M.A. Mannan, *Alternative microcredit models in Bangladesh: A comparative analysis between Grameen Bank and Social Investment Bank and myths and realities*, paper presented in 1st International Islamic Conference on Inclusive Islamic Financial Sector Development: Enhancing Islamic Financial Services for Micro and Medium Sized Enterprises (MMES), Brunei, 17–19 April 2007, p. 3.

18. Problems of profit–loss sharing

The theory of Islamic banking visualizes profit–loss sharing (PLS) as an ideal form for financing. Several Muslim scholars have expressed dissatisfaction in the contemporary practice of Islamic banks because they do not follow profit–loss sharing as a dominant mode of finance. They have adopted other modes of finance, like mark-up (*murabaha*), leasing (*ijara*), cash advances for the purchase of agricultural produce (*salam*) and cash advances for the manufacture of assets (*istisna'*). These modes of finance provide a fixed return on banks' capital and are in compliance with Islamic law. We shall examine the practice of Islamic banks in the subsequent two chapters. In this chapter we aim to show that the pristine theory of Islamic banking that recommends PLS as an ideal form of financing has several insurmountable obstacles. Insistence on PLS may also defeat the very purpose for which Islamic banking was started in the first instance.

18.1 INTEGRITY IN FINANCIAL REPORTING

The problem of deliberate misreporting by clients of Islamic banks is, perhaps, the most significant deterrent to Islamic financial institutions adopting PLS. The general standards of morality and integrity in present-day Muslim societies are quite low. Even if we assume that these standards are compatible with non-Muslim societies, the inborn greed and materialistic temptations create natural inclinations to hide and misreport real profits with a view to reducing the share of the financier. Besides, clients of Islamic banks are reluctant to provide open access to their books. They would rather turn to conventional finance than allow Islamic financial institutions to intervene in their day-to-day business matters. Islamic financial institutions, on their part, would have to incur significant monitoring costs to ensure honest reporting by their clients. They might have to conduct spot checks and review important business decisions by the client firms. This would require additional staff and technical resources. These factors make PLS finance an unattractive proposition for Islamic banks as well as for their clients.

When we say that financial capital should share the loss (in the case of *musharaka*) and bear all the loss (in the case of *mudaraba*), are we not pleading for a moral-hazard-based regime? Mirakhor and Krichene (2009: 5) reply in the affirmative as follows:

> In financial transactions, the concept [of moral hazard] refers to a situation where the entrepreneur seeking financing intends to use the funds differently than agreed upon with the surplus funds holder, who either has insufficient information regarding the entrepreneur's intention or has no control over the entrepreneur's behavior to mitigate the risk of moral hazard. This leads to the need for monitoring mechanisms that ensure the entrepreneur's behavior is compatible with that expected at the time of the transaction. The associated costs are referred to as 'monitoring costs'.

Besides additional costs, the banks cannot monitor all types of businesses, as they do not have the necessary expertise. Once entrepreneurs know that their losses would be partly or wholly borne by the Islamic bank, they might become reckless in taking business decisions, be negligent in taking appropriate care or remain lax in implementing internal controls and risk-mitigating strategies. They would have the comfort of knowing that their losses would be partly or fully borne by the Islamic bank. PLS finance has a built-in incentive for business firms to obtain funds from Islamic banks for riskier projects, since the losses will be passed on, partly or wholly, to the financier. Visser (2009: 90) mentions a survey of 385 small firms in Sydney which confirmed that these firms would be more inclined to get Islamic finance if the investment proposal was risky.

18.1.1 Minimizing the Risk of Misreporting

One significant risk that Islamic financial institutions face in a *mudaraba*[1] contract is the possibility of misreporting by the *mudarib* (working agent). The risk is so real that most Islamic financial institutions avoid extending finance on the basis of *mudaraba*. However, Al-Suwailem (2006: 123) has proposed a method for minimizing this risk. Suppose a bank customer, A, requires finance on the basis of *mudaraba*. The bank encourages A to enter into a deal to buy certain products on short-term credit, with the option to cancel the contract within 48 hours. After making this deal, A sells the product in the market (presumably at a higher price). At this stage, A presents to the bank evidence of the two deals. The bank examines the evidence and provides finance to A to settle the first contract of purchase. A receives the sale price of the second contract from the purchaser and repays the bank. The bank receives back its original capital and also adjusts its share of profit, and the balance is left with the *mudarib*.

Technically, this is feasible and does minimize the chances of misreporting. However, it introduces several rigidities. It requires the *mudarib* to find a seller and a buyer within a short time and assumes that the transactions will close in profit. It also assumes that there will be no collusion between the *mudarib*, the seller and the buyer. With all these rigidities and naiveties, this procedure can make *mudaraba* financing a feasible option. But can this become a basis for banking business as a going concern? This remains an open question.

18.2   EFFICIENCY IN THE PLS SYSTEM

Under the PLS system there is a premium for being inefficient, since the client can partly pass on the price of inefficiency (loss) to the bank. There is relatively less pressure on the client of an Islamic bank to operate in the most efficient manner as compared to the client of a conventional bank, since the latter has to generate a surplus to repay the principal with interest. There is no equally compelling pressure on the client of an Islamic bank, as a loss will partly be borne by the bank. The client of the Islamic bank has leverage to be inefficient. The same is true for a contract between an Islamic bank and depositors. The Islamic bank passes on a net loss to the depositors. Its only loss would be the forgone share of the expected profit. As compared to this, a conventional bank is committed to repay the principal to the depositors with interest and has a compelling reason to operate efficiently. In both contracts, that is, between the client and the bank, and the bank and the depositors, efficiency takes a back seat under the PLS system.

Under the PLS regime, even if we assume that the entrepreneur is ideally honest and has the best intentions, losses can occur because of sub-optimal, negligent and inefficient business decisions. Each time a business entity declares a loss, the question arises: how did the loss occur? Did market conditions contribute to it? Was it the consequence of unforeseen technological changes or scientific innovations, which could not be predicted by the management? Was it the result of poor risk management, weaker internal controls, lack of a sense of urgency, deliberate loss of opportunities, a faulty communication and monitoring mechanism, or the outright theft and corruption of the operational management? Was it because of unethical practices or management overriding internal controls? If the loss was caused by the sheer negligence of the management or missed opportunities the bank would not want to share the loss. To determine the cause of the loss, an investigation would be necessary in each case. One can imagine the extent of disputes that would ensue, as business management is not yet a hard science like physical sciences and involves value judgements and subjective evaluation. Even if negligence is established, the loss caused by a missed opportunity when management could have acted more promptly or shown a greater sense of urgency cannot be established without dispute. There would be a large number of cases where disputes would linger on for years, leading to unnecessary cost for the business and the economy.

18.3 ACCOUNTING FOR PROFIT OR LOSS

The common-sense meaning of profit is any increase in the original capital as a result of business operations. Technically, it is determined as follows:

$$\text{Net profit} = [\text{Total assets}] - [\text{Total capital} + \text{Total liabilities}]$$

To arrive at the value of the assets, management takes several policy decisions such as the rate of depreciation, timing of the recognition of income, expenditure on assets and liabilities, rates of amortization for intangible assets, and so on. The valuation of assets, liabilities, income and expenditure, in the final analysis, depends upon management accounting policies and financial management decisions. That creates space for management to manipulate various accounting values. The management can, for example, decide to declare a lower level of profit by depreciating some of its assets at a higher rate than actual wear and tear. No amount of independent auditing or compliance with accounting standards can completely forestall this tendency. Profit–loss sharing can thus lead to situations that are potentially unfair for one or the other party, and there is no foolproof method to overcome it. In the case of PLS financing, detailed rules would be required for defining profits and losses that are in compliance with the international accounting standards. Ensuring compliance with the rules and forestalling manipulation would be cumbersome and expensive.

18.4 DETERMINATION OF THE PLS RATE

Interest-based financial transactions have a ready market where the rates of interest are determined by the demand and supply of funds. Also, generally, the central bank acts as a regulator of the money market and ensures that banks do not indulge in exploitation of borrowers. There is no such market for the rate for profit–loss sharing. A bank that enters into a PLS agreement to provide finance can exploit the client by charging exorbitant rates of profit sharing, with no one regulating the activity. This problem has been vexing Muslim economists as well. However, they are unable to suggest a solution to this problem. There is no market rate for PLS at present. Rafic al-Masri (2004: 38–39) writes:

Claiming that all forms of interest are categorically prohibited and that inter-est rate whatsoever is likewise prohibited, would lead to severing all relations with the literature on interest, central banks control authorities, interest rate tables, the scientific criteria for calculating interest rates and the control of central banks over such rates. Creditors would exploit the severance of all such relations to charge exorbitant interest rates from the public and weak among them on pretext that all interest rates are prohibited, although this is not a confirmed issue, neither from the *Shari'ah* nor the economic perspective, let alone the exploitation, blackmail and inequity this leads to. This is so because the increase in debt balances (whether in the form of a loan or an installment or any other names given to it) would not be based on a scientific yardstick or criteria. In other words, such increase would be chaotic and uncontrollable. Religious people should pay attention to this fact themselves against ignorance and inequity.

Kuran (1989: 178) highlights this problem as follows:

One writer who takes up the issue [of the PLS rate] states that the shares are to be determined by custom – as if a practice becomes fair by virtue of being customary.[2] Another writer, using a mathematical model, says that the shares are to be determined through the interaction of the supply and demand for contracts – as if, once again, an equilibrium allocation could never be lopsided.[3] Only one writer, as far as I am aware, recognizes that the literature effectively evades the issue.[4]

Balala (2011: 81–82) says:

It is, in fact, the potential of unregulated Islamic banks that structure loans and finance in the form of sale and leases or buy-backs that is of greater concern. Their potential to charge excessive rates of interest guises as 'fee' or 'gratuity' or 'profit sharing' and the inequity that results there from (being the 'essence of *riba*' Muhammad spoke of) has led practicing academics like El-Gamal to emphasize the appropriateness of Islamic banks' 'marking to market'.[5] This emphasis acknowledges that in a regulated financial market, interest is capped whereas profit making being unregulated, gives Islamic banks a blank cheque to charge uncapped fees on their financial products in the name of 'profit' that may in effect be unjustifiably high and inequitable. In other words, it is not excessive interest we should be concerned about, but the excessive 'profit' presently being made by the Islamic finance industry.

At present the fixed rates of return in the form of *ijara*, mark-up and so on are being used as a proxy or benchmark for the PLS rate. We think this is an area where further theoretical work needs to be done by Muslim economists. In the absence of a market rate for profit–loss sharing, there remains room for exploitation by either side.

18.5   UNCERTAINTY ABOUT THE AMOUNT OF CLAIMS AND LIABILITIES

The general stance of the *Shari'ah* is that parties to commercial contracts should know their rights and obligations clearly and unambiguously. It minimizes the occasion for disputes, injustice and exploitation. In the case of profit–loss sharing, the financier does not know what it will get at the end. Similarly, the client of the bank does not know the total liability at the time of final settlement. The contract creates a situation of gross uncertainty and generates problems of cash flow planning and the future course of action for both parties.

The problem assumes a serious dimension in the case of endowment funds. A large number of charitable institutions around the world are financed by the interest income of endowment funds. The idea is akin to the Islamic concept of *waqf*. But the orthodox interpretation of *riba* does not allow the creation of such funds which earn interest. The endowment funds provide resources for charitable educational, health and other welfare institutions. The question is: how can we use the mechanism of endowment funds to finance such institutions in the Islamic framework? Should we say, 'No trust funds should be created since Islam does not allow interest income?' This obviously is not in line with the objectives of the *Shari'ah*. If we say that the trust funds should rely on rental income or business income, we do not properly appreciate the risks involved in such arrangements. Interest income allows the institutions supported by these funds to have proper financial management. They can calculate their income and prepare budgets. In the absence of such arrangements, it becomes difficult to do so.[6] As compared to this, one can calculate expected income from fixed-term interest-based deposits. It is possible to plan operations in light of the expected financial flows. Under PLS, both users and providers of funds are agreeing on something that is uncertain. Thus it involves undefined and un-hedged risks for both parties.

18.6   OTHER LIMITATIONS OF PLS FINANCE

18.6.1   Education and Health Finance

Student loans are a big need of modern society. College education and training is costly. Islamic finance has yet to find a generally acceptable mechanism for education finance. Askari, Iqbal and Mirakhor (2009: 135) candidly confess that gaps exist in the area of education loans on a *Shari'ah*-compatible basis, since education loans do not create any tangible asset and do not have any collateral other than personal guarantees. A similar problem arises if the government requires money to fund projects relating to health. There are no profit-sharing possibilities in these projects unless these functions are transferred to the private sector, with serious implications for poverty, distribution of income, quality of service and coverage of the population. It could defeat the socio-economic objectives of Islam.

18.6.2   PLS Financing for Short Periods

Business firms require funds for working capital needs. There is no way to get finance for short periods such as a day, a week or a month under PLS, because profit or loss cannot be determined for these periods. Tahir, Atiquzzafar, Ali and Waheed (1999: 67) propose that, for working capital needs for short periods (such as the need of sugar companies to buy sugar cane), the banks may provide finance on the basis of *mudaraba* or *musharaka*. They also mention the possibility of using *salam* or *istisna'* modes for various situations. However, these are limited solutions. Business firms may also require funds to meet such expenses, which are not amenable to profit sharing. They also want to keep their flexibility in the use of funds. Muslim scholars have not found a satisfactory solution to this problem.

18.6.3   The Problem of Excess Liquidity

According to the orthodox interpretation of *riba*, Islamic financial institutions are not able to place their surplus funds on the basis of interest. If they do so, they violate the prohibition of *riba*. Some of them do violate this prohibition in the name of necessity (*darura*). In any case, they incur the guilt of violating the *Shari'ah*. M.M. Khan and Bhatti (2008: 71) write:

> Islamic financial institutions are haunted by the chronic problem of excess liquidity. On average, Islamic financial institutions carry 40 percent more liquidity than their conventional counterparts. . . . Islamic financial institutions cannot invest their funds in the conventional inter-bank market and other short-term instruments. They cannot accept interest accrued on the deposits they have in the central banks under statutory requirements.

18.6.4   PLS and Discounting of Bills

Discounting of trade bills requires a rate of discount, which is available in the case of interest-based finance. In the case of profit–loss sharing, no such rate is available. It is not possible to discount trade bills under this mode of finance. That restricts the application of PLS in business transactions.

18.6.5   PLS and Project Appraisal

The generally accepted method of project appraisal applies the technique of discounted cash flows by using the rate of interest as the discount rate. Since profit–loss sharing does not have such a rate, appraisal of projects under the PLS regime is not possible. Some writers (e.g. Zarqa 1983) have suggested that project appraisal can be done by using the expected rate of profit as a discount rate. But there is no market-expected rate of profit which can be used as a discount rate.

18.6.6   Investing with Guaranteed Capital and a Regular Income Stream

There is a consensus among Muslim scholars that the *Shari'ah* aims at alleviating poverty. The Islamic government is required to adopt policies that provide some sort of social security net. *Zakah* is the most prominent Islamic institution for alleviating poverty. However, profit–loss sharing does not provide a secure and guaranteed income stream to the poor by investing their savings. Pensioners, widows, orphans and other vulnerable groups of society do not have access to an Islamic mode of investment that protects their capital as well as guarantees a regular income. Profit–loss sharing exposes them to unbearable risks. Muslim economists have yet to find a solution to this problem.

18.6.7   Contingent Liabilities of Banks

Banks issue letters of guarantee to their clients for a fixed fee based on a percentage of the amount guaranteed. Should the client fail and the guarantee is called, the banks are liable to encash the guarantee. For that risk, they charge a fixed fee, which in fact is a sort of interest payment on the amount of the guarantee. In a situation where interest is prohibited, what will the arrangement be for issuing such guarantees? So far, Islamic scholars have not found a suitable substitute for the guarantee fee under a PLS regime. W.M. Khan (2002: 32) writes:

> the classical literature on the subject of guarantee is unanimous on the inadmissibility of charging any fee for providing such a service. . . . [S]cholars are of view that serious thinking is required on the subject particularly in view of the fact that context in which the classical Islamic legal thinking on the subject was developed has completely changed.

18.7 THE UNRESOLVED JURIDICAL (*FIQHI*) ISSUE IN PROFIT–LOSS SHARING

18.7.1 Limited Liability of the Joint Stock Company

The joint stock company provides a mechanism that limits the liability of shareholders for repayment of debts of the company to the extent of their share capital. The mechanism can potentially create a situation where the debts of the company exceed the asset value of the company. If that happens, the creditors will not get the full value of their loans. This is the generally accepted legal position in capitalist economies. However, it comes into conflict with the *Shari'ah* ruling that creditors must be repaid in full. In one case when a person had died without repaying his debt the Prophet refused to offer a funeral prayer until someone had assumed the responsibility for repayment.

The advantages of limited liability of the joint stock company are so obvious that Muslim scholars tend to accept it as a legitimate legal format. However, when it comes into conflict with the *Shari'ah* ruling of full settlement of debts, they are unable to take a final position. Muslim scholars have been discussing the issue. Scholars who allow limited liability as a valid legal device have also accepted the modern concept of incorporation, which means that the company is a legal person. As a legal person it borrows the money in the first instance and it is the company that is liable to repay it (e.g. Hasanuzzaman 1989; Uthmani 1992[7]). The liability of the shareholders of the company remains limited to their share capital. Without accepting the theory of incorporation, the concept of limited liability has no legs on which to stand. When a company borrows money, the question arises: who has borrowed the money? If the shareholders have borrowed it, then they should repay it until all their assets (invested in this company or lying elsewhere) are exhausted. If the company has borrowed the money it should repay until all its assets are exhausted. The assets of the company are nothing except what is represented by the share capital, reserves and liabilities. If the company goes bankrupt, it pays its lenders from its assets to the extent it can. If there is any residue, the shareholders will get it on a pro rata basis. But if the company does not have enough assets, the lenders will suffer the loss to the extent of the shortfall in the value of assets. The shareholders will lose their capital like the lenders. The legal fiction of accepting the company as a person is necessary to support the concept of limited liability.

Nyazee (1998: 83ff.) categorically contests this idea. He contends that the concept of a legal person may be acceptable. However, the manner in which it is applied in modern commercial law flouts the basics of Islamic law. He argues that the classical Islamic law does not accept the notion of incorporation and thus the concept of limited liability of shareholders. Nyazee (ibid.: 175ff.) considers that the contract of shareholders with the company is like that of lenders, who have provided it with money. He thinks that the shareholders, by purchasing shares, transfer funds to the company, which is a legal entity. Now the company owns all the assets and all the profits and losses. The shareholders have no ownership of the assets (ibid.: 195). The shareholders are like lenders on the basis of profit sharing rather than lenders on interest. The terms of the share certificate provide that the lenders (meaning thereby shareholders and creditors) will own all the profits. It is a mechanism to earn 'a relatively risk-free return' (ibid.: 197). The argument is fallacious, as shown below:

a. If the shareholders are lenders, then how come they become entitled to all the profits and losses? No loan contract entitles lenders to this type of return. This type of entitlement is not for lenders. It is for the owners of a business entity.

b. It is not fair to say that the shareholders are entitled to a risk-free return. If the shareholders have a contract similar to that of lenders, they should not be concerned with losses. But in a company losses are borne by the shareholders and not the lenders. How is this to be explained?

Nyazee (1998: 177) considers share capital to be similar to loan capital because, in the case of insolvency, the shareholders are like lenders with the lowest priority of claim. But he does not face the situation of losses short of insolvency. In such situations, the company's shares lose their market value. The shareholder selling shares at that time suffers loss in the form of a lower price. If the shareholder was like a lender, why should he or she suffer this loss? Even when there are no losses and the value of the shares goes down in the market for other reasons, the shareholders suffer. It is because they are the owners of the company. No lender will suffer because of the decline in the value of the shares of the company.

The point Nyazee misses is that shareholders by purchasing the shares of a company become its owners. They are not lenders to the company. As owners of the company, they are entitled to all the profits and losses. The actual anomaly in this situation is that the liability of the shareholders is limited, while their entitlement to profit is unlimited. If the shareholders, as owners of the company, are entitled to all the profits, they should also bear all the losses. Restricting their liability for losses to the extent of the capital is unfair. It is a mechanism to pass on the risk to creditors without giving them an equal entitlement to the return earned with their capital. The company earns profits on total capital, which is provided by shareholders as well as creditors. If there are profits, the creditors get only fixed interest and the shareholders are entitled to *all* the residual profits, even the surplus of the profit earned with the creditors' capital after paying the fixed interest. However, if there are losses which cannot be met by the assets of the company, the creditors lose their money. A fair deal will demand that the shareholders who are entitled to *all* the profits should also bear *all* the losses. But the concept of limited liability does not do precisely that. It makes the shareholders entitled to all the profits but restricts their liability for losses to share capital only.[8]

As soon as we arrive at this conclusion, we are back to square one. We end up with a situation where the shareholders of modern corporations should have unlimited liability. The need to have a legal person in the form of a joint stock company dissipates. We are again in a situation of partnership and not of a joint stock company. The argument is logical in the classical legal framework of Islam, for if we accept the limited liability of the joint stock company the lenders may find themselves in a situation where they cannot get back their money. This is despite the fact that the shareholders are entitled to all the residual profits but they are not obliged to repay the debt beyond their own capital if the company fails to do so.

At the same time, the need to have some mechanism by which the shareholders' liability remains limited to a certain extent is also necessary for present-day business. The matter has become significant in the light of Islamic banking, where investment accountholders (IAH) need to be protected somehow against losses caused by a bank's decision to acquire liabilities larger than its assets. Besides, the large amounts of capital for modern business firms can be raised only if the liability of the shareholders is limited to the extent of their capital. People will be diffident about providing finance to a company where their liability is unlimited. That creates a legal problem for Muslim scholars. On one hand, the lenders' rights are protected by Islamic law. They must get back their principal sums in any case. On the other, the shareholders cannot be made liable to an unlimited extent. Who is to pay the lenders if the company goes bankrupt?

Nyazee (1998) has tried to propose a solution that accommodates the concept of limited liability within the Islamic legal framework. He suggests that a modern company be created on the basis of the principal–agency (*wakala*) relationship. The shareholders will provide capital. They will be co-owners of the assets of the company along with the company as a legal person. The creditors will not provide any cash capital. Instead, creditors, like banks, will provide credit through the supply of goods and services on credit. This, he thinks, will restrain the company from over-borrowing. He thinks that, in a modern company, the management may raise credit to the extent of multiple times the share capital and, if the company goes insolvent, the company will not be able to meet the claims of the creditors. In the case of his proposed Islamic model, the company can never, according to him, contract credit beyond the limit of the capital. If the company goes bankrupt, there will always be assets to meet the claims of the creditors.

Now all this argument is based on a faulty understanding of business and finance. Firstly, in the modern age, restraining business firms from getting cash credit is creating an undue limitation that would make business impossible. It does not require too much business acumen to realize that such a restriction is unrealistic and impracticable and makes the proposed Islamic alternative unworkable. Secondly, once a company does not get cash credit and gets credit only through the supply of goods and services, what is to restrain such a company from buying goods and services which are much in excess of the share capital? It can keep expanding its business to any extent. Nyazee thinks it would never happen (1998: 197), but he does not say what would stop the business entity from doing that. Thirdly, the proposal does not fully comprehend how losses occur. Even if we do not get cash credit and get loans in the form of goods and services, losses can occur for a host of factors, some of which may be beyond the control of the company. Once that happens, the assets of the company lose value. The decline in the value can even be such as to eat up all the assets of the company, which were financed by both the capital of the shareholders and the capital of the creditors. In that case, the creditors have to be paid off anyway. Who will pay them? Obviously, the shareholders will pay them, as they are the co-owners of the company. They can be made to pay only when their liability is made unlimited. Thus we are back at square one. We are unable to find a solution to the limited liability of shareholders. Nyazee proposes that for such situations we should have business insurance. This is going beyond the theory of the firm and trying to find a crutch for the theory. This is the matter that still requires resolution. Muslim jurists have yet to find a satisfactory solution.

18.8   REVENUE SHARING AS AN ALTERNATIVE

Some writers (e.g. Al-Suwailem 1999: 89) propose revenue sharing as an alternative to profit sharing because of the difficulties involved in determining the profit. According to them, revenue sharing has precedence in Islamic law in the form of sharecropping (*muzara'a*) contracts. The proposed alternative is unrealistic and is not likely to attract either the financier or the entrepreneur because of the high risks and uncertainties. For example, in the case of revenue sharing, the provider of finance may not get back its principal sum in full. Because of this uncertainty and risk, few financiers would want to provide money on the basis of revenue sharing. On the other side, the entrepreneur, after sharing revenue with the financier, may be left with revenue that does not even recover the costs. Because of this few entrepreneurs would like to avail themselves of finance on a revenue-sharing basis. The proposal attracts the same objection that orthodox economists and scholars raise against interest. According to some scholars the rationale for prohibition of interest is high risk and uncertainty (*gharar*). Revenue sharing can lead to a situation of high risk and uncertainty (*gharar*) for one or both parties. It is for this reason that some classical jurists, like Imam Abu Hanifa (703–67), opposed crop sharing, as it involved high risk and uncertainty for the farmer (*gharar*). Al-Suwailem is aware of this feature of revenue sharing but still recommends it as the best alternative to PLS.

18.9 CONCLUDING REMARKS

We have tried to enumerate the various problems that the profit–loss-sharing system creates for banking and finance in the present age. Muslim economists are aware of the various tricks and ruses that present-day Islamic financial institutions have devised to accommodate interest. They insist that Islamic financial institutions should adopt profit–loss sharing so that interest is effectively eliminated in all financial transactions. However, the present chapter has illustrated that profit–loss sharing is not practicable. There are several insurmountable obstacles that make Islamic financial institutions act cautiously towards it.

NOTES

1. This is equally applicable to a *murabaha* contract.
2. [As in original] See Umer Chapra, The prohibition of *riba* in Islam: An evaluation of some objections, *American Journal of Islamic Studies* (I, 2) (August) (1984), p. 34.
3. [As in original] See Masudul Alam Choudhury, *Contributions to Islamic economic theory: A study in social economics* (New York: Palgrave Macmillan, 1986), ch. 6; see also Zubair Hasan, Determination of profit and loss sharing ratios in interest-free business finance, *Journal of Research in Islamic Economics*, 3 (1) (Summer) (1985), pp. 13–29.
4. [As in original] See Mohsin Khan, Islamic interest-free banking, *IMF Staff Papers* 33 (1986), pp. 19–20. Khan also takes issue with the suggestion that profit and loss sharing would promote equality, indicating that this is not self-evident.
5. [As in original] A mechanism employed to determine the market interest rates for various borrowers based on credit-worthiness and security of posted collateral.
6. The present writer came across a difficult situation in 2000 when, in a seminar, a Christian bishop asked a question about budgeting for a charitable educational

institution being financed by interest income from trust funds. At that time Islamic banks had not yet devised methods to pay a fixed return on deposits as they are doing now. He said that a Christian welfare organization operating in Pakistan was running 40 schools. It had invested trust funds in banks as fixed-term deposits and knew the income that would accrue during the year. It was able to prepare its budget in light of the expected income. However, if it were to deposit these funds on the basis of profit–loss sharing it would only come to know its income at the year-end. How would it prepare its budget, he asked? Naturally, it was not possible for me to answer this question satisfactorily, as PLS banking does not allow any such method of forecasting and budgeting.

7.   For a comprehensive survey of the views of such scholars see Nyazee (1998).

8.   *The Economist*, London (22 January 2009) sums up the point succinctly: 'Rather than being victims, shareholders may well have driven managers on. Hans-Werner Sinn, the head of Ifo, an economic research institute in Munich, argues that limited liability gives them a reason to flirt with disaster. The creditors of a failed firm have no claim on the personal assets of its shareholders. So if the bank takes big risks that promise big profits, its shareholders stand to enjoy the full gains but to bear only part of the losses. By contrast the shareholders of low-risk, low-return banks that never collapse have to bear all the losses.'

19. Practice of Islamic banking and finance

The Islamic banking and finance sector is growing at a fast pace globally. Information on the exact status of Islamic financial institutions, products and services becomes outdated on a daily basis. Although we have tried our best to present the latest information at the time of writing this chapter, yet readers may find some of it out of date. But that does not defeat the objective of this chapter. Our objective is not to present up-to-the-minute information on the status of Islamic banking and finance. We aim to present a general overview of the industry as it existed at the end of 2011. The focus of the chapter is to highlight various issues that have emerged in the practice of Islamic banking and finance.

The dream of Islamic banking became a reality in the early 1960s as a result of the zeal and charismatic leadership of certain individuals. In 1961, S.A. Irshad[1] started an Islamic bank in Karachi (Pakistan) and in 1963 Ahmad al-Najjar started an Islamic bank at Mit Ghamr (Egypt). Neither bank survived for more than a couple of years. However, the candles lit by them left trails in the minds of various influential Muslims until in 1974 an Egyptian study under the auspices of OIC proposed the blueprint of the Islamic Development Bank, which was established in 1975 at Jeddah. In 1975, the Dubai Islamic Bank started up in the private sector, followed by the Bahrain Islamic Bank in 1979. At about the same time, the Ziaulhaq government (1977–88) in Pakistan set up a task force to propose measures for transforming the entire financial system of the country on an interest-free basis. The Iranian Revolution under Imam Khomeini (1902–89) also took place in 1979. The new Iranian leadership showed a lot of zeal in abolishing interest from the economy. The Sudanese government was equally enthusiastic in enforcing the Islamic financial system. As a result of these moves, Iran, Pakistan and Sudan announced plans for abolishing interest and transforming their public financial systems on Islamic lines. In the private sector around the Muslim world at about the same time a movement started to establish Islamic banks, Islamic investment companies, Islamic equity funds and Islamic insurance companies. The 35 years from 1975 to 2010 saw a movement of Islamic finance which has spread over the entire globe.

The GCC countries, Malaysia, Indonesia and now Pakistan and Sudan, are experimenting with a dual banking system. They are trying to have Islamic financial institutions along with conventional financial institutions. In practice, Islamic financial institutions have taken the following three forms:

a.   full-fledged Islamic financial institutions;
b.   Islamic windows in conventional financial institutions;
c.   Islamic subsidiaries of conventional financial institutions.

19.1   SIZE OF THE ISLAMIC FINANCE INDUSTRY

There are no final and universally accepted figures for various aspects of Islamic banking and finance in the world. Different writers and reports present different estimates. Part of the reason lies in the lack of complete transparency in the data published by various Islamic financial institutions. In the following paragraphs we present some estimates to give the reader a broad idea of the size of the Islamic finance industry.

Dar, Rahman, Malik and Kamal (2012: 44) report that, by the end of 2011, the size of the industry had reached US$1.357 trillion. This is also endorsed by *Global Islamic Finance Magazine*[2] (April 2012), which reports on the basis of TheCityUK's Islamic Finance Secretariat (UKIFS) report that Islamic finance assets reached a mark of $1.3 trillion in 2011, which was 150 per cent over the previous five years. Warde (2010: 1) reports that Islamic financial institutions are operating in 105 countries. Five countries dominate Islamic banking: Iran, with $345 billion in Islamic assets; Saudi Arabia, $258 billion; Malaysia, $142 billion; Kuwait, $118 billion; and the UAE, $112 billion. Islamic banks have been established in non-Muslim countries with Islamic minorities (e.g. the Islamic Bank of Britain). Islamic branches of the Western banks are offering Islamic products (for instance, HSBC Amanah, the global Islamic finance services arm of the HSBC Group).

Agha (2012) says that the Islamic finance industry is growing despite its inherent problems, and some market analysts project that it will be valued at anywhere from $3 trillion to $5 trillion by 2016. Schoon (2011: 1) reports that there are 700 listed funds in the major databases, with estimated funds under management of around $70 billion. Akkizidis and Khandelwal (2008: xviii) write:

> Nowadays, in European, American and Westernized markets, financial institutions such as Credit Swiss, Deutsche Bank, HSBC, the Islamic Bank of Britain,

etc. are offering more products and services for Islamic finance (it is estimated that only Arab investors have more than US $800 billion on deposit in overseas banks, much of which is secured in Swiss and European banks). Moreover, a great number of financial institutions in GCC countries and Asia are managing funds of over US $300 billion and are encouraged from their markets to provide Islamic financial products.

Iqbal and Mirakhor (2008: 27) report:

[About Islamic windows] several leading conventional banks, such as Hong Kong and Shanghai Banking Corporation (HSBC) are pursuing this market very aggressively. Citibank was one of the very early Western banks to establish a separate Islamic bank – Citi Islamic Investment Bank (Bahrain) in 1996. More recently Union Bank of Switzerland (UBS) established Noriba Bank. . . . The list of Western banks keeping 'Islamic windows' includes, among others, American Express Bank, American Bank, ANZ Grindlays, BNP-Paribas, Chase Manhattan, UBS, and Kleinwort Benson. The leading non-Western banks with a significant size of 'Islamic windows' are national Commercial Bank of Saudi Arabia, United Bank of Kuwait and Riyadh Bank.

Hasan (2010: 3–4) reports that, though the total assets of Islamic banks were expected to cross the one-trillion-dollar mark by 2010, yet the ratio of assets of conventional banks with Islamic banks was 80:1. Some of the conventional banks individually were larger than all the Islamic financial institutions put together. For example, the total assets of UBS of Switzerland alone amounted to $1533 billion in 2005, Citigroup came to $2.2 trillion on 31 March 2008, and Mizuho Financial Group of Japan was $1296 billion in 2006 (Visser 2009: ix). Iqbal and Mirakhor (2008: 155) write that more than 60 per cent of the Islamic banks were below the minimum assets size of US$500 million considered necessary for an efficient conventional bank, and the aggregate size of all Islamic banks was less than that of any bank on the list of 60 banks in the world.

19.2   ISLAMIC EQUITY FUNDS

Islamic equity funds are mutual funds that collect capital against share certificates and invest the funds in socially responsible and *Shari'ah*-compliant companies[3] with sound financial health. The funds could be closed-ended or open-ended. The closed-ended funds are illiquid, as the buyers of their certificates have to wait for a customer to sell them. But the open-ended funds buy their own certificates at the going market price quoted daily. Two institutes, namely the Dow Jones Islamic Fund Index and the FTSE Global Islamic Index, publish information on

Shari'ah-compliant companies, allowing the Islamic Equity Fund managers to benchmark their performance. Out of these, the Dow Jones is more comprehensive, as it has information on 34 countries and 18 market sectors.[4]

Schoon (2011: 51) writes:

> As of end of 2009, the number of funds listed in the Eurekahedge[5] database was nearing 700 with reported assets of just under $50 billion. Taking into consideration the fact that around 20 percent of the funds do not disclose their assets under management, the total assets is estimated to be around $70 billion. This implies an average size in assets under management of $100 million which, in comparison with the conventional fund market, is particularly small. In comparison, the Lipper[6] database contains in excess of 200,000 funds operating globally. . . . Out of the 700 funds only very few hold assets equal to or over $500 million, which is the benchmark size for conventional funds.

19.3   ISLAMIC BANKING IN SELECTED COUNTRIES

19.3.1   Islamic Banking in Bahrain

Bahrain Islamic Bank, the first full-fledged Islamic bank, was established in 1979. In 2011, there were 26 Islamic banks and 19 Islamic insurance companies (*takaful*) operating in Bahrain. Total assets and market share of Islamic banks in the banking sector was 11 per cent in June 2009. The Islamic banks provided finance on the basis of *murabaha, ijara, mudaraba, musharaka, salam* and *istisna'*, restricted and unrestricted investment accounts. In 2002, the Central Bank of Bahrain (CBB) was assigned regulatory responsibilities for the whole financial sector including banking, insurance and capital markets. CBB has issued rulebooks for Islamic banks and insurance companies that cover areas such as licensing requirements, capital adequacy, risk management, business conduct, financial crime, disclosure/reporting requirements, and *takaful* and re-*takaful* business. It requires all banks to establish an independent *Shari'ah* supervision committee complying with the Accounting and Auditing Organization for Islamic Financial Institutions (AAOIFI) Governance Standards for Islamic Financial Institutions. Bahrain is host to AAOIFI, the Liquidity Management Centre (LMC), the International Islamic Financial Market (IIFM) and the Islamic International Rating Agency (IIRA).

19.3.2   Islamic Banking in Bangladesh

Islamic banking started in Bangladesh in 1983 with the incorporation of Islami Bank Bangladesh Limited (IBBL) with an authorized capital of Tk10000 million (US$1 = Tk70). It had by 2010 invested more than Tk255178 million in various projects and businesses in the country. It has more than 500 branches in Bangladesh, with a number of overseas outlets in several Middle Eastern countries. Al-Baraka, often called the second Islamic bank of Bangladesh, commenced banking business on 20 May 1997. It is a joint-venture enterprise of Al-Baraka Investment and Development Company, a renowned financial and business house of Saudi Arabia, Islamic Development Bank, a group of eminent industrialists of Bangladesh, and the government of Bangladesh. The authorized capital of the bank is Tk600 million, and its paid-up capital is Tk259.55 million. The bank has now 35 branches in different parts of the country. In 1996, two more Islamic banks were given clearance to operate under Islamic banking principles. A number of private banks have also started Islamic banking. According to the Central Bank of Bangladesh, more than 45 per cent of the total financial institutions in the country have adopted Islamic modes of finance. Prominent Islamic banks in Bangladesh include Al-Arafah Islami Bank, First Security Islamic Bank, ICB Islamic Bank, Export–Import Bank of Bangladesh, Shahjalal Islamic Bank, Arab-Bangladesh Bank, Standard Chartered Bank (Saadiq Islamic Banking Branch), and Bank Asia (http://www.gatestoneinstitute.org/1470/sharia-banking-bangladesh, 16 August 2010).

Dar *et al.* (2012: 227) report that by the end of 2011 Bangladesh had made all the arrangements to launch the first Islamic money market in the country. The initiative was led by the Central Bank of Bangladesh. The money market would provide an avenue for the investment of surplus funds to Islamic banks, windows of conventional banks and non-banking financial institutions in the country. It is not yet clear how the money market will actually operate.

19.3.3   Islamic Banking in Egypt

Ahmad al-Najjar, a Muslim economist and activist, established the first Islamic bank in Egypt at Mit Ghamr in 1963. It functioned till 1968, when the government merged it with Nasir Social Bank. After that, the growth of Islamic banking in Egypt was quite slow until 1979, when Banque Misr started Islamic banking. In 2011, Banque Misr had 32 Islamic branches. The funds of such branches are completely separate from those of Banque Misr. These branches accept all types of deposits and offer certificates of deposit in Egyptian pounds and US dollars, besides banking services and project financing. In 2010 three major foreign Islamic banks operated in Egypt: Faysal Islamic Bank of Egypt (FIBE), International Islamic Bank for Investment and Development (IIBID), and Egyptian–Saudi Investment Bank (ESIB). The government of Egypt owns about 20 per cent of the capital of FIBE, 40 per cent of ESIB and 80 per cent of IIBID (Warde 2010: 220). IIBID and Nile Bank merged with the United Bank of Egypt. After merger, IIBID and Nile Bank lost their identity as Islamic banks. The Central Bank of Egypt owns 99.9 per cent of the shares of the United Bank of Egypt. By 2010, only 128 branches of banks offered Islamic banking services in Egypt, although the conventional banks had thousands of branches.

19.3.4   Islamic Banking in Indonesia

Indonesia adopted a dual banking system in 1998 by amending its banking law. Bank Muamalat Indonesia (BMI) was the first Islamic bank to be established, with a Rp3 billion deposit from Amal Bhakti Muslim Pancasila Foundation (of which Suharto was the chairman) in 1992. By 1999, only three Islamic banks, including BMI, existed in Indonesia. By 2009, 23 Islamic banks along with 456 Islamic windows at conventional banks operated in the country. Indonesia's Islamic banking industry represents only 5 per cent of the domestic bank assets (Warde 2010: 223). Indonesia does not have any law for asset securitization according to the *Shari'ah*. The law treats *sukuk* as debt instruments and allows their sale at a price other than the par value, which strictly speaking is not permissible under the *Shari'ah* law. Thus '*sukuk*' is only an Arabic name for interest-based bonds without using the term 'interest'. The Indonesian law relating to leasing also does not conform strictly to the *Shari'ah* requirements. The law does not cover *mudaraba* transactions (Djojosugito 2007: 493ff.). Siswantoro and Qoyyimah (2007: 471) have documented that about 71 per cent of the total financing by Islamic banks in Indonesia consisted of *murabaha*-based finance in 2004.

19.3.5   Islamic Banking in Iran

In 1983 Iran passed a law to transform its entire banking system to an interest-free basis. Dar (2010) reports that Iran has seven government-owned commercial banks, including Bank Melli Iran, which is the largest Islamic bank in the world in terms of assets under management. It has $59 billion of assets, over 3300 branches and more than 43 000 employees. Other commercial banks in Iran are Bank Mellat, Post Bank of Iran,

Bank Rafah, Bank Saderat Iran, Bank Sepah and Bank Tejart. Besides, there are five specialized banks that support agriculture, industry, mineral development, housing, small and medium-sized businesses, and exports. Dar (2010) reports that Iran follows a more liberal interpretation of the *Shari'ah* than even Malaysia, which itself is more liberal than the Middle Eastern countries. This is confirmed by other writers as well. For example, Ariff (1988) reports that Iran 'has decreed that government borrowing on the basis of a fixed rate of return from the nationalized banking system would not amount to interest and would hence be permissible'. Warde (2010: 121) reports about Iran:

> interest-based finance was not completely eliminated. Overseas banking operations, for example, continued to operate on the basis of interest, and . . . informal and semi-informal interest-based finance has thrived. . . . [A] much higher interest rate appeared in disguised form in informal markets. The world of Iranian finance became more speculative than it had ever been before.

Dar *et al.* (2012: 231) report that Iran is planning to issue *murabaha sukuk*, *ijara sukuk* and *istisna' sukuk* as fixed-rate instruments, which will be more attractive to risk-averse investors.

19.3.6   Islamic Banking in Malaysia

Bank Islam Malaysia Berhad (BIMB), the first Islamic commercial bank, commenced operations in 1983. Bank Muamalat Malaysia Berhad (BMMB) started operations in 1999. Both are registered under the Islamic Banking Act 1983. In 1993, Bank Negara Malaysia (BNM), the central bank, allowed conventional banks to offer Islamic banking services. The permission was a turning point for the growth of Islamic banking in Malaysia. In 2001, the central bank issued licences to foreign banks to provide Islamic banking services. Now almost every commercial bank in Malaysia offers Islamic banking services. In 2010 there were 17 licensed banks (six foreign) and ten *takaful* (Islamic insurance) operators (two foreign) in the country. Malaysia is an innovator of the concept of the dual banking system (Islamic and conventional banks operating side by side). In 1994 it became the first country to introduce Islamic mortgage bonds. The Arab–Malaysian Bank has also introduced an interest-free credit card on which the holder can spend equal to his or her deposit for a fee that is a certain percentage of the annual spending. Malaysia has also been home to the Islamic Financial Services Board (IFSB) since 2002. Since 2006, the Kuwait Finance House, al-Rajhi Bank of Saudi Arabia, and the Asian Finance House (a joint venture of Qatar Islamic Bank and other Middle Eastern investors) are also operating in Malaysia. Foreign banks are attracted to invest in Malaysia to tap the Islamic finance market. For example, Mizuho Corporate Bank of Japan has announced it will invest in Malaysia. The Elaf Bank Bahrain has got a licence to operate in Malaysia.

In 2011 total assets, total deposits and total financing of the Islamic banking industry constituted more than a 22 per cent market share of the overall banking industry (Dar *et al.* 2012: 236). Malaysia has several institutions that support the Islamic banking and finance industry. The most important of these are the Islamic Banking and Finance Institute (2002), International Centre of Leadership and Finance (2006), Malaysia International Financial Centre (2006), International Center for Education in Islamic Finance (2008) and International *Shari'ah* Research Academy for Islamic Finance (2008). On the academic front, in 2012 the International Shari'ah Research Academy (ISRA) announced publication of the first university-level textbook on Islamic finance (Dar *et al.* 2012: 236).

Mohamad and Yusoff (2008: 55) report that Malaysia had an impressive growth in the *sukuk* market. For example, by 30 June 2007, it had outstanding *sukuk* worth RM112 billion, which was 49 per cent of the total corporate bonds in the Malaysian economy. Dar *et al.* (2012: 236) report that Malaysia issued its third sovereign *sukuk*, worth $2 billion, in 2011. The Khazanah Nasional Berhad issued during 2011 the first three-year *sukuk*, worth 500 million yuan, denominated in Chinese currency. Senari Synergy, a local investment company owned by the Sarawak government, issued a 20-year RM380 million *sukuk* in August 2011 to finance the cost of Senari Synergy's industrial complexes of an oil terminal and a palm oil refinery. In 2011, Cagmas Berhad issued its third domestic *sukuk*, which was a one-year RM150 million commodity *murabaha sukuk*.

The government provided strong support to Islamic finance. For example, the 2012 budget provided a three-year deduction for expenses incurred on new *sukuk al-wakala* issuances in the country, extension of the income tax exemption on foreign-denominated *sukuk* and transactions until 2014, and establishment of a small and medium-sized enterprise (SME) *Shari'ah*-compliant financing fund (Dar *et al.* 2012: 236).

Despite rapid growth in Islamic finance, there are doubts about the 'Islamicity' of the Islamic finance practised in Malaysia. For example, Chong and Liu (2007) write about Malaysia:

> First . . . on the asset side, only 0.5% of Islamic bank financing is based on the PLS paradigm of *mudaraba* (profit-sharing) and *musharaka* (joint venture) financing. Islamic bank financing in Malaysia, in practice, is still based largely on non-PLS modes of financing that are permissible under the *Shari'ah* (Islamic law), but which ignore the spirit of the usury prohibition. On the liability side, however, *mudaraba* (profit-sharing) deposits, which account for 70% of total Islamic deposits, are more predominant.

Second ... the Islamic deposits are not really interest-free, but are very similar to conventional banking deposits. More specifically, we find that, contrary to expectation, the investment rates on Islamic deposits are mostly lower and less volatile than that of conventional deposits.

19.3.7   Islamic Banking in Pakistan

The demand for elimination of interest from financial institutions had been in the air since the very inception of Pakistan in 1947. However, the first serious effort was made by the government of Ziaulhaq (1977–88). On 29 September 1977, General Muhammad Ziaulhaq (1924–88) issued a presidential order asking the Council of Islamic Ideology, Pakistan (CII) to produce a blueprint for the Islamization of the financial institutions. The CII produced a blueprint in 1980, and the government announced its implementation from January 1981. The objective was to eliminate interest from the economy and to transform all existing financial institutions in the public and private sectors according to the *Shari'ah*. In 1981–85, the State Bank of Pakistan (central bank) issued a series of instructions.[7] Briefly, it prohibited the banks to deal in interest. For deposits, it introduced the concept of profit–loss sharing (PLS), besides current accounts as already practised. For financing, it prescribed 12 Islamic modes of finance.[8]

In practice, for term deposits, the banks substituted the phrase 'rate of interest' with 'expected rate of profit' and kept the entire regime of interest-based deposits intact. For financing, the banks adopted mark-up and buyback agreements as dominant modes. PLS financing was adopted only as an exception. The financial institutions continued trading in bills in exactly the same manner as under the interest-based system. Discounting of bills was done on the basis of mark-down, which was another name for interest. Leasing was another mode of finance. However, the banks developed a model of leasing that ensured them a fixed return without assuming any of the business risk of an operating lease. For long-term credit, and as a substitute for debentures, the banks introduced term finance certificates (TFCs). The clients issued TFCs to obtain finance on a mark-up calculated by using the compound interest formula.

The Islamization that started in 1981 soon dwindled into 'business as usual' as the financial institutions adopted various practices that retained the spirit of interest-based finance intact. The political instability and a constitutional bar on the *Shari'ah* Court did not allow any further action toward Islamization of the banks. However, in 1991 when the constitutional bar on the *Shari'ah* Court was lifted, the religious lobby took the case of elimination of interest from the economy to the Court. The Court ordered the government to undertake a complete transformation of the banking system in seven months. The government was lukewarm and hesitant, as it was not sure about its impact. The risks were high and the government did not have the will and capacity to obey the orders of the Court. However, to avoid the blame, it set up a permanent Commission for Islamization of Economy (CIE) and two task forces. The CIE and task forces issued several reports, but the government did not consider these reports practicable. In 1999, a private sector bank went to the Supreme Court of Pakistan (SCP) in appeal against the *Shari'ah* Court decision. The SCP upheld the decision of the *Shari'ah* Court and ordered the government to eliminate interest from the economy, again in a short span of 18 months. However, the government filed a review petition with the SCP. The SCP referred the case back to the *Shari'ah* Court for a second look on the definition of *riba* and various allied matters in June 2002. The matter was still pending with the *Shari'ah* Court as at the end of 2011. Practically, the banks adopted Islamic banking only in name by changing terminology and expressions. They kept interest-based dealings intact in spirit.

In January 2002, Pakistan issued a licence to Meezan Bank to operate as a full-fledged Islamic bank. Since then Pakistan has been following a dual banking system. Five dedicated Islamic banks and 12 conventional banks with a network of 799 branches in June 2011 offered Islamic banking services (State Bank of Pakistan *Islamic Banking Bulletin*, June 2011).

19.3.8 Islamic Banking in Saudi Arabia

In 1975, OIC established the Islamic Development Bank (IDB), an intergovernmental financial institution in Jeddah, Saudi Arabia. Despite the avowed objective of financing the development of member countries, the Bank was not a typical Islamic bank, though it took several initiatives subsequently to promote Islamic finance. IDB is steering the movement of Islamic finance around the globe. It has established the Islamic Research and Training Institute (IRTI), which is now a leader in promoting Islamic finance through research and training. King Abdulaziz University, Jeddah established the Centre for Research in Islamic Economics (CRIE) in 1976, which was the first formal organization in the world for promoting research and the dissemination of knowledge on Islamic economics and finance.

In 1985, the Saudi Arabian Monetary Agency (SAMA) granted a licence to al-Rajhi Banking and Investment Corporation to act as an Islamic bank. All banks in Saudi Arabia are supposed to function in accordance with the *Shari'ah*, though the sensitive question as to whether they actually do so is never raised and answered. The policy of SAMA toward Islamic banking was that of caution. Warde (2010: 216–217) writes:

the two largest Islamic banking groups, Dar al-Maal al-Islami and al-Baraka Bank, both owned by prominent Saudis, could not obtain licenses to operate commercial banks in the Kingdom. And when al-Rajhi Banking and Investment Company was authorized in 1985 to engage in interest-free banking, it was on the condition that it did not use the word 'Islamic' in its name. . . . Saudi Arabia does not officially recognize the concept of Islamic banking. The logic is that if one bank is recognized as an Islamic institution then all others, by implication, would be un-Islamic. The official line was that all banks operating in Saudi Arabia were by definition Islamic. In addition, the country's vast bank deposits and foreign holdings generated substantial interest income, and thus the Saudi authorities had to tread carefully around the issue of *riba*.

Dar *et al.* (2012: 241) report several large deals worth billions of dollars based on Islamic modes of finance transacted by various financial institutions in Saudi Arabia.

19.3.9 Islamic Banking in Sudan

Sudan announced it would Islamize its entire banking system in December 1983. Dealing in interest was prohibited by law. However, in 1986, Sadiq al-Mahdi's government suspended the Islamic laws. In 1991, the *Shari'ah* was introduced in northern parts of the country. From 2000 onward, the central bank worked with the IMF to create *mudaraba* and *musharaka* certificates. Dar (2010) reported that there were 32 Islamic banks in Sudan, some of which were foreign banks such as Qatar National Bank, Abu Dhabi National Bank, al-Salam Bank and al-Baraka Bank. The country followed the strictest interpretation of the Islamic law on *riba* and claimed to follow the purest form of Islamic banking. In 2006, after the Comprehensive Peace Agreement, Sudan adopted the dual banking system. The government of Sudan retracted from its original policy of transforming the entire financial system on Islamic lines. Conventional banks and Islamic banks are functioning side by side. Dar *et al.* (2012: 244) report that, in early 2012, the government of Sudan issued *sukuk* with a predetermined rate of return of 20 per cent to raise cash for the government, which was higher by 5 percentage points than the last such issuance.

19.3.10 Islamic Banking in Turkey

In 2007 Turkey had four Islamic banks, known as participation banks.[9] The most commonly used modes of finance were leasing, instalment sales, sale on mark-up and PLS. Alpay (2007: 373) asserts that the performance of the Islamic banks has been better as compared to conventional banks, especially during times of economic crisis. However, the share of deposits with the Islamic banks has reached only 2.6 per cent in 20 years (ibid.: 374). Wouters (2008) reports that in 2007 the participation banks had a meagre share of 3.5 per cent in terms of assets as compared to the banking industry of Turkey. Their deposits are now covered by the deposit guarantee fund of the banks. They do not have access to the money market. They face, like all Islamic financial institutions, the problem of non-existence of short-term investment opportunities. There are no Islamic windows and, therefore, foreign market players can only enter the market through shareholdings in the existing participation banks.

Dar *et al.* (2012: 245) report that Kuyet Turk issued a five-year term worth $350 million. There were expected to be more *sukuk* issuances during 2012, as the government changed the tax laws, applying the same tax rates and exemptions to *sukuk* as to conventional bonds.

19.3.11   Islamic Banking in the United Kingdom

The first wholly *Shari'ah*-compliant retail bank in the West, the Islamic Bank of Britain, was authorized by the Financial Services Authority (FSA) in 2004. The bank has seven branches, in London, Birmingham, Manchester and Leicester. By the end of 2010, the bank was serving more than 50 000 customers. However, the bank has not been a commercial success, making continuous losses since its launch.[10] The FSA also authorized the European Islamic Investment Bank, which is the first such investment bank. The UK now has five full-fledged Islamic banks, while another 17 leading institutions including Barclays, RBS and Lloyds Banking Group have set up special branches or subsidiary firms for Muslim clients. A report by International Financial Services, London reveals that Britain's Islamic banking sector is now bigger than that of Pakistan. The study says that the UK now has by far the largest number of banks for Muslims of any Western country. The $18 billion in assets of Britain's Islamic banks are more than the assets of the Islamic banks of Muslim states such as Pakistan, Bangladesh, Turkey and Egypt.

19.4   ISLAMIC MICROFINANCE IN SELECTED COUNTRIES

Obaidullah and Khan (2008) present a comprehensive survey of Islamic microfinance institutions across the globe. They mention microfinance institutions in Afghanistan, Lebanon, Malaysia, Northern Mali, Syria and Yemen. Surprisingly, they do not mention Pakistan, where several such institutions operate. In January 2011, Islamic microfinance organizations of Ghana, Iraq, Jordan, Kazakhstan, Mauritius, Pakistan and Yemen formed the Islamic Microfinance Network (IMFN). According to the IMFN website there are more than 300 Islamic microfinance institutions in 32 countries.[11] Karim, Tarazi and Reilli (2008: 1) report the results of a survey conducted by the Consultative Group to Assist the Poor (CGAP) in 126 microfinance institutions of 14 Muslim countries that Islamic microfinance had a total outreach of merely 0.5 per cent, that is, 380 000 from estimated total clients of 77 million.[12] The total outstanding loan portfolio for these institutions was about $198 million in 2006, with an average loan size of $541 (Karim *et al.* 2008: 8).

> According to the survey, Bangladesh has the largest Islamic microcredit outreach, with over 100,000 clients and two active institutions. However, Bangladesh is also the country where conventional microfinance products have the largest outreach – nearly 8 million borrowers – and Islamic microfinance represents only 1 percent of its microfinance market. (Ibid.: 7)

Dar *et al.* (2012: 184) report that Islamic microfinance represents less than 1 per cent of the global microfinance outreach despite the fact that almost half of the clients of microfinance live in Muslim countries and the demand for Islamic microfinance is very strong.

The CGAP survey results reported by Karim *et al.* (2008: 8) show that over 70 per cent of all financing by MFIs is on the basis of *murabaha*. Obaidullah and Khan (2008: 19) also confirm this finding on the basis of empirical evidence. Karim *et al.* (2008: 12) write about the cost of microfinance and its compatibility with the *Shari'ah* as follows:

> Critics of Islamic finance products suggest that the pricing of some products offered as *Shari'ah*-compliant too closely parallels the pricing of conventional products. For example, some institutions offer *murabaha* where interest appears to be disguised as a cost mark-up or administration fee. Islamic finance sometimes suffers from the perception that it is simply a 're-branding' of conventional finance and not truly reflective of Islamic principles.

The Asian Development Bank (2009: 35) reports that Islamic Relief UK has launched Islamic microfinance programmes in various countries, such as 'First Islamic' of Bosnia and Herzegovina, START of Kosovo, and Small Scale Enterprise Development, Pakistan (SSED). In Bosnia and Herzegovina and Kosovo, Islamic Relief provides financing through *murabaha* and *mudaraba*.

19.4.1   Islamic Microfinance in Bangladesh

In Bangladesh, the Social and Investment Bank, Islami Bank Bangladesh, and Alfalah and Rescue, an NGO, are the leading Islamic microfinance institutions. The Islami Bank Bangladesh (IBBL) launched the Rural Development Scheme (RDS) in 1995. By July 2009, it was providing microcredit to over 10 628 villages through its 139 branches. The microfinance provided was Tk21.76 billion to 319 230 clients. The average financing size was Tk15 369, and the average rate of return was 10 per cent, with 2.5 per cent rebate given for timely payment (H. Ahmed 2011: 205). However, Obaidullah (2008: 17) reports that the effective rate of interest (hidden in the form of *bai' mu'ajjal*) was 15 per cent per annum, which was lower than the 35 per cent that was the average rate of conventional microfinance institutions (Obaidullah 2008: 17, 21, 23).[13] Even at this level of interest, the scheme was supported by IBBL to absorb some overheads, like staffing and monitoring costs. But for the IBBL support, the operation would not have been sustainable at the existing rate of return (ibid.: 24).

19.4.2   Islamic Microfinance in Indonesia

Bank Muamalat Indonesia (BMI) has developed a model of Islamic microfinance. The bank operates through a network of cooperative organizations, known as Bait al-Maal wa al-Tamwil (BMT). Members of the local community, usually poor people who need financing for their microenterprises, form a BMT at the grassroots level. The BMI provides funds to BMTs on the basis of *ju'ala*, and the BMTs provide funds to members on the basis of *bai' mu'ajjal* (Obaidullah 2008: 56). In both cases, the basis of financing is a fixed return on capital.

Seibel (2005: 2) reports that Islamic microfinance in Indonesia started in 1991. By December 2003 assets of the MFIs were only 0.74 per cent of the total assets of the banking sector. The experience of Islamic rural banks was also not altogether successful. They started functioning in the early 1990s, but by 2003 their number was 4 per cent and their assets merely 1.4 per cent of those of the conventional rural banks. The experience of BMTs was equally discouraging. Not more than 20 per cent of these cooperatives were in good financial health. They required a continuous injection of fresh funds for survival. The main mode of finance was *murabaha* (86 per cent), with a fixed rate of profit for the bank (ibid.: 23). The average mark-up rate was 55 per cent per annum, which was close to the conventional rural banks' lending rate of interest (ibid.: 42). The Islamic rural banks gave a slightly higher return on deposits but charged a three to four times higher rate on financing as compared to the first Islamic commercial bank (BMI).

19.4.3   Islamic Microfinance in Iran

Sadr (2008) has given details of interest-free loan societies (*gharzul hasaneh* funds) in Iran. These are voluntary organizations which raise funds through donations and lend money to eligible needy persons on an interest-free basis. The organizations screen the clients on stringent criteria of eligibility. They extend credit at a nominal service charge of 1 per cent for meeting recurring expenses. The first such organization was established in 1969. By 2008, Iran had over 7000 such organizations (Bakhtiari 2009: 102). The government is supportive of this initiative. The central bank has also framed rules to oversee the organizations. However, these funds are for charitable institutions and not for microfinance in the usual sense. Besides, the law obliges the commercial banks to set aside 10 per cent of their saving account deposits to extend interest-free loans to cooperative societies to generate employment and to individuals for productive investment and personal needs.

About Islamic microfinance in Iran Seibel (2007: 2) says the following:

Let's have a look at the major government bank dealing with small clients.[14] In 2003–2004 the bank had about 2.5 million borrowers and 16.6 million deposit accounts (including current accounts); 2.7% of loans outstanding and 46% of deposit balances were unremunerated *qard al-hasan*:[15] a big discrepancy between *qard*[16] assets and liabilities. The depositors were attracted to the *qard* accounts by religious motives and by prizes at semi-annual draws, valued at 2% of deposits: very unwisely in economic terms. Inflation imposes a so-called inflation tax, to the benefit of the state. The biggest losers are the depositors. During the mid-1990s when inflation rates were around 50%, depositors lost about half the value of their deposits every single year. In 2003–2004 the inflation rate had dropped to 16%, which means that depositors still lost the equivalent of 14% of the value of their deposits. Accordingly, the state cashed in on what I would call the *usurious inflation* tax – very much in contrast to fairness and brotherhood as principles of Islamic banking. Religious authorities seem unconcerned. But on the lending side, aren't low profit-sharing rates beneficial to farmers, micro entrepreneurs and the poor? Unfortunately, experience has shown that they are not. The scarce resources flow disproportionately into the pockets of big borrowers, at the expense of small farmers and micro entrepreneurs. It is thus not surprising that microfinance institutions and programs are few and insignificant in Iran: a challenge to those in government who are in charge of *shari'ah* banking and finance!

19.4.4   Islamic Microfinance in Malaysia

Nine banks in Malaysia offer microfinance. Four of them offer conventional microfinance; two offer only Islamic microfinance. The three remaining offer both conventional and Islamic microfinance. Several NGOs offer Islamic microfinance. The most prominent, Amana Ikhtiar Malaysia (AIM), has been in microfinance since 1987. The *Shari'ah* Supervisory Board of Bank Negara Malaysia (the central bank) supervises Islamic microfinance (http://www.scribd.com/doc/50944105/Islamic-microfinance). As of September 2006, AIM had 157 787 members and had disbursed a total of RM1.8 billion loans. Basically, AIM followed the Grameen Bank, Bangladesh model for financing microenterprises.

19.4.5   Islamic Microfinance in Pakistan

The Asian Development Bank (2009: 36) mentions Islamic Relief Pakistan, Akhuwat, Karakoram Cooperative Bank, National Rural Support Programme and Muslim Aid as lead Islamic microfinance institutions in Pakistan. Except for Akhuwat, these organizations provide finance on the basis of *murabaha*. The Akhuwat loans have a negligible service charge. By 30 September 2011 Akhuwat had served 113 216 families, and disbursed a total of Rs1.3 billion, with an outstanding loan portfolio of Rs261 million in 35 cities and towns in Pakistan.[17] There was no collateral and no processing fee except an application fee of Rs100 and 1 per cent of the loan amount as an insurance charge, which was voluntary. The administrative expenses were minimal, as most of the operations were conducted in the local mosques. Akhuwat did not accept any donation from international donors. All funds were provided by private philanthropists. The rate of recovery reported by Akhuwat was 99.85 per cent. The central bank of the country had issued guidelines for Islamic microfinance.[18] Tameer Bank, Pakistan also claimed to be in the field of Islamic microfinance. Farz Foundation, an NGO, provided support at the grassroots level in the form of assets and not cash. In 2011 the Farz Foundation signed a memorandum of understanding with the World Congress of Muslim Philanthropists (WCMP) to foster collaboration in *Shari'ah*-compliant microfinance. The Huda Centre for Islamic Banking and Economics had set up an Islamic Microfinance Helpdesk for research, product development, training and education.

19.4.6   Islamic Microfinance in Syria

In Syria, UNDP has since 2000 supported the Sanadiq programme of Jabal al-Hoss, the poorest area of the country. The government of Syria was a key partner in the programme. The programme establishes village funds to provide finance to poor people to set up small businesses and for the broader objective of community development. The financing is on the basis of *murabaha* (with a profit margin of 0.75–1.25 per cent per month) in most cases. The fund uses personal and group guarantees to secure the funds. Besides microfinance, the programme also provides training and other ancillary services to the village. By 2002, UNDP had provided $370000 as equity, while the shareholders contributed $130000. During 2003–07, the Japanese government joined the programme. The management of the village funds was in the hands of village communities. The funds generate profit, which is partly distributed to shareholders and partly ploughed back. During 2001–05, the average dividend distributed among the shareholders was 31 per cent. However, the programme required additional equity for expansion and to cover additional villages (Al-Asaad 2008).

19.4.7   Islamic Microfinance in Sudan

Since 1983 when the Sudanese government announced the policy of transforming the entire public financial system, most of the microfinance has also been organized on Islamic lines. Several NGOs were involved in microfinance activity. For example, Port Said Association for Small Enterprise Development, El-Kifaya Bank, the Sudan Development Association, and the Women's Union of Khartoum were important NGOs in the field of microfinance. In 2009 the Central Bank of Sudan issued a policy that required all banks to allocate 12 per cent of their portfolios to microfinance. According to the policy the rate of mark-up should not be more than 9 per cent. The policy encouraged the banks to adopt modes of finance other than *murabaha* for microfinance business. No more than 30 per cent of the financing should be on the basis of *murabaha*.

The Sudanese Islamic Bank provided loans on the basis of *murabaha*, *musharaka* and *mudaraba* in rural areas. Other financial institutions such as Faysal Islamic Bank of Sudan, Islamic Cooperative Development Bank, Nelein Industrial Development Bank Group, Agricultural Bank of Sudan and Farmers Bank provide all their financing on the basis of *murabaha*, charging a margin of 15–25 per cent per annum or 3–4 per cent per month (Asian Development Bank 2009: 33). Islamic Relief UK, an NGO, has launched an Islamic microfinance programme in Sudan in collaboration with the Savings and Social Development Bank (ibid.: 35).

Kahf (2008: 59) reports that Diwan al-Zakah provides financial assistance to the non-poor but vulnerable small producers in rural areas who are hit by natural disasters such as drought or who face a shortage of fertilizers because of a lack of financial resources and so on. The average loan size was about $42, and the duration was six months. The loans were interest-free.

19.4.8   Islamic Microfinance in Afghanistan

Because of war in the last few decades, information on Afghanistan is scant. The following extract from a relevant website gives some information:

> There are currently 14 microfinance institutions in Afghanistan that are supported by the Microfinance Investment and Support Facility, Afghanistan (MISFA) – a multi-donor venture established in 2003. With just over 400,000 borrowers in Afghanistan, the popularity of Islamic loans has enabled Foundation for International Community Assistance to become Afghanistan's fastest-growing and second-largest MFI with nearly 60,000 clients. . . . The loans are provided to members of registered groups under collective guarantee of the group. The group members meet often to review the repayment situation of the loan. Once a loan is paid off, the group becomes eligible for another loan by a member of the group. (http://knowledge.insead.edu/islamicmicrofinance080205.cfm)

19.5   THE *SUKUK* MARKET

According to an International Islamic Financial Market (IIFM) report (2012: 3), the first *sukuk* were issued in Malaysia by Shell MDS, worth RM125 million, on the basis of *bai' bithaman ajil*. In 2000, the government of Sudan issued domestic sovereign short-term *sukuk* worth 77 million Sudanese pounds on the basis of *musharaka*. In 2001, the *sukuk* market went international with the issuance of the first US-dollar-denominated *ijara sukuk*, worth $100 million, by the Central Bank of Bahrain. Since then many sovereign and corporate *sukuk* issues have been offered in various jurisdictions.

Malaysia, Qatar, Bahrain, Pakistan, the State of Saxony in Germany, the Islamic Development Bank, several issuers in the US and Europe, multinational companies like Nestlé, and several oil companies in Dubai have issued *sukuk* in the international market. Dubai International Finance Exchange, the Labuan Exchange in Malaysia, and the Third Market in Vienna trade in *sukuk* (S.S. Ali 2008: 4). In 2005, the World Bank issued *sukuk* for 760 million Malaysian ringgits ($202 million). The London

Stock Exchange first listed *sukuk* in 2006 (Visser 2009: 64). In 2001–10, the total value of *sukuk* issued in various currencies worldwide was $197.642 billion, consisting of 2114 issues, out of which 1688 were corporate, 21 quasi-sovereign and 405 sovereign (IIFM 2012).

The IIFM report (2012: 12) notes a declining trend in international *sukuk* issuance during 2008 ($2.14 billion), 2009 ($7.47 billion) and 2010 ($5.35 billion) as compared to 2007 ($13.8 billion). According to Askari, Iqbal and Mirakhor (2010: 18, 25), it was mainly due to the shortcomings of Islamic finance relating to liquidity. Another possible reason, in the opinion of Taqi Uthmani, chair of the AAOIFI's *Shari'ah* Board, was that 85 per cent of the *sukuk* had questionable religious features (Warde 2010: 151). Salman Ali observes that many of the *sukuk* structures do not conform to the *Shari'ah* (2008: 9). Most of the *sukuk* replicate conventional debt instruments, with an effort to remain within *Shari'ah* bounds. They often combine more than one contract, which individually may be *Shari'ah*-compliant but when combined may defeat the objective of the *Shari'ah*. Besides, often the rate of return is tied to the London interbank offered rate (LIBOR) or the euro interbank offered rate (EUROBOR) rather than to the underlying business that the *sukuk* represent. This makes the *sukuk* so similar to conventional debt instruments that it is difficult to tell one from the other. That is the reason, perhaps, why the rating agencies, like Standard & Poor's, Moody's, Fitch and so on, apply the same methodology for rating the *sukuk* as for conventional debt instruments (Ali 2008: 10).

19.5.1 *Musharaka Sukuk*

Musharaka sukuk refer to certificates in evidence of investment on the basis of *musharaka*. Each certificate represents the share of assets of the company that the certificate-holder owns. There is a consensus that companies can issue *musharaka sukuk*. However, opinions differ about their sale in the secondary market, which is allowed only when the capital accumulated through *musharaka sukuk* represents non-liquid assets at least to the extent of 50 per cent of such capital. The reason is that, if the share certificates represent liquid cash or its equivalent (such as accounts receivable), their sale at a price other than the face value would involve *riba* according to the orthodox interpretation. However, contemporary *Shari'ah* scholars have allowed their sale if they represent a capital stock which has been converted into non-liquid assets at least to the extent of 50 per cent (M.A.I. Uthmani 2009).

The question arises: what difference does it make to an investor if the above restriction is imposed? Hardly anything positive can be thought of. This is obvious from the following example. Suppose an investor has bought *musharaka sukuk* of a company and the book value of the company's liquid assets is 51 per cent of the total assets. The investor is unable to sell the *sukuk* in the market because of the 50 per cent restriction. After a day or so, the company converts some more of its cash into non-liquid assets and crosses the limit of 50 per cent. It now has 51 per cent of its assets in non-liquid form. The investor can now sell the *sukuk* in the open market. In what respect does it affect the investor? It is an unnecessary condition that stops the investor from unloading the *sukuk* and introduces rigidity into the capital market, a negative factor from the investors' perspective. They will have less freedom to manage their investments because of the above restriction. The economy as a whole also does not gain in any way. There is no welfare gain in the whole process. It is a procedure for its own sake.

19.5.2   Hybrid *Sukuk*

Kamali (2007: 16) mentions a variation of *ijara sukuk* that combines *murabaha* and *istisna'* contracts. IDB issued these *sukuk* in 2004 in the name of *sukuk al-istithmar*. He writes:

> In July 2004, the Islamic Development Bank issued a US $400 million hybrid *sukuk* for the global market under a new name, *sukuk al-istithmar*. This was the first instance of Islamic securitization that comprised a plurality of instruments in its underlying pool of assets. Previous issues of global *sukuk* had relied on revenue from leases of real estate assets mainly in the form of *ijara* bonds. The IDB *sukuk* consisted of real *ijara*-based, and also debt-based assets (*murabaha* and *istisna'*). Yet the asset portfolio was structured so as to be dominated by the *ijara*-based portion which represented 66 percent of the total. It was also considered that *ijara* assets should always constitute more than 50 per cent of the portfolio. Due to the fact that the IDB portfolio comprises *murabaha* and *istisna'* receivables, the return on these certificates could only be pre-determined and fixed (at 3.625% per annum) payable at six monthly intervals until August 2008 when they will be redeemed in full.

19.5.3   Government Investment Certificates of Sudan

The government of Sudan has also issued bonds known as government investment certificates to meet its financial needs from the banking sector. These long-term bonds are issued on the basis of *salam, ijara and murabaha*. Another type of certificates issued by the government of Sudan is known as government *musharaka* certificates. They are issued for maturities of one year. The central bank of Sudan has also issued *ijara* bonds by securitizing assets owned by the central bank, such as the bank's building.

The central bank deals with the banks in these three types of bonds to manage the liquidity of the banks and the money supply in the economy (Solé 2007: 21).

19.5.4   *Sukuk*: Defaults and Challenges

Macfarlane (2009: 24) mentions a number of cases where the *sukuk* have defaulted or are in serious trouble. In May 2009, Investment Dar of Kuwait defaulted on \$100 million *sukuk*. Saad Group set up a committee to restructure \$650 million Golden Belt 1 *sukuk*. Standard & Poor's (S&P) cut the rating of the said *sukuk* owing to the non-availability of vital information. East Cameron Partners (ECP) issued a multiple-award-winning *sukuk* in 2006 but filed for bankruptcy in October 2008, prompting a legal dispute about the creditors' right to \$167.67 million in *sukuk* assets.[19] S&P downgraded the *sukuk* of Dubai Islamic Bank and Sharjah Islamic Bank. There was an estimate that 5–8 per cent of the *sukuk* in the market could default owing to the credit crunch in the global market. The total amount of the *sukuk* issued in 2008 fell by 56 per cent to \$14.9 billion as compared to 2007. As debt instruments, *sukuk* run the same risk as conventional debt instrument. Warde (2010: 152) writes:

> What is still unclear is what happens to *sukuk* when they fail – an issue that has not been tested in court. In Malaysia, some *sukuk* issues have junk status, and two other *sukuk* are already in default: the East Cameron Gas Company in the United States and Investment Dar of Kuwait. One of the unresolved questions is whether *sukuk* holders should stand in the line of creditors or in the line of owners of underlying assets.

19.6   SUPPORTING INSTITUTIONS AND INFRASTRUCTURE

19.6.1   International Islamic Financial Market

In 1999, Islamic Development Bank, Labuan Offshore Financial Services Authority (LOFSA) (Malaysia) and Bahrain Monetary Agency (BMA) signed an agreement to develop an International Islamic Financial Market. In 2000, the governments and central banks of Brunei, Indonesia and Sudan signed a memorandum of understanding to cooperate in establishing the IIFM. In November 2001, the IIFM came into being by the signing of a charter, and the aforementioned became the first members. The initiative led to the setting up of a board of directors, a secretariat, and a market and products committee. A *Shari'ah* advisory committee was set up simultaneously. The secretariat is located in Manama, Bahrain. The IIFM is a standardization body for Islamic capital market products and operations.[20] According to the IIFM website, it is supported by the State Bank of Pakistan and a number of regional and international organizations and financial institutions such as ABC Islamic Bank, Bank Islam Malaysia Berhad, Crédit Agricole CIB, Dubai International Financial Centre Authority, European Islamic Investment Bank, Kuwait Finance House, National Bank of Kuwait and Standard Chartered Saadiq, as well as other market participants as its members. The organization performs the following tasks:

- addressing the standardization needs of the industry;
- providing a universal platform to market participants through global working groups to develop the Islamic capital and money market;
- harmonizing documents, products and processes with reference to *Shari'ah*;
- ensuring wider acceptance of its products through the *Shari'ah* Advisory Panel.

IIFM is not a regulatory body. Its recommendations are not implemented by most of the Islamic banks.

19.6.2   Islamic Interbank Money Market (Malaysia)

Established by Bank Negara Malaysia on 3 January 1994, the Islamic Interbank Money Market (IIMM) develops instruments to manage the liquidity needs of the banks. The Islamic money market provides Islamic financial institutions with the facility for funding and adjusting portfolios over the short term. It is a channel for transmitting monetary policy. Financial instruments and interbank investment allow surplus banks to channel funds to deficit banks, thereby maintaining the funding and liquidity mechanism necessary for promoting stability in the system. Through the IIMM, Islamic banks and banks participating in the Islamic Banking Scheme are able to match funding requirements effectively and efficiently. Bank Negara Malaysia issued *Guidelines on the IIMM* on 18 December 1993 to facilitate proper implementation of the IIMM. It has developed the following products for use by financial institutions:

- *mudaraba* interbank investment;
- government investment issues;
- *wadi'a* acceptance;

- Bank Negara Monetary Notes-I;
- sell and buyback agreement;
- *when* issues;
- Cagmas *mudaraba* bonds;
- Islamic negotiable instruments;
- Islamic private debt securities;
- *Al-Rahnu* agreement-I.[21]

Malaysian scholars also look to concepts of *muqassa* and *rahn* as potential sources of liquidity management. *Muqassa* is a mechanism for debt settlement between two persons who are simultaneously debtors and creditors to each other. It is the setting off of each other's debt against the respective receivables. *Rahn* is a traditional mortgage where the creditor gets possession of an asset of the debtor. The creditor is allowed to make use of the asset for the duration of the debt. This interpretation of the concept of *rahn* is accepted in Malaysia. Jurists of other countries do not subscribe to it, as it is potentially an interest-based transaction.

19.6.3 Islamic Financial Services Board

On 3 November 2002, the central banks of Bahrain, Iran, Kuwait, Malaysia, Pakistan, Saudi Arabia and Sudan joined the Islamic Development Bank, AAOIFI and IMF to establish the Islamic Financial Services Board at Kuala Lumpur.[22] It started operations in March 2003. The membership consists of supervisory and regulatory bodies of a number of Islamic countries, the Asian Development Bank (ADB), Bank of International Settlements (BIS), IDB, IMF, World Bank and over 100 market players and professional firms. In its 14th meeting held in Riyadh (Saudi Arabia), it admitted two new regulatory and supervisory authorities as full members and eight new financial institutions as observer members, bringing its membership to 185 in 35 countries (Askari *et al.* 2010: 19). The main objective of the IFSB is to standardize and harmonize the operation and supervision of Islamic financial institutions. The IFSB sets standards on capital adequacy, risk management and corporate governance in consultation with a wide array of stakeholders and after following a lengthy due process. It complements the task of the Basel Committee on Banking Supervision. By the end of 2010, it had published 11 standards and five guidance notes. These documents are available on its website.

19.6.4   Liquidity Management Centre

The LMC was established by Bahrain Monetary Agency in 2002 to facilitate investment of the surplus funds of Islamic financial institutions into short- and medium-term financial instruments structured in accordance with *Shari'ah* principles. The LMC has been busy in developing a wide range of tools and instruments for the Islamic capital market. It has four shareholders with equal equity: Bahrain Islamic Bank, Dubai Islamic Bank, Islamic Development Bank and Liquidity Management House (a Kuwait Finance House subsidiary). On 31 December 2010, it had total assets worth about $236 million and equity worth $54 million. The LMC launched an open-ended short-term *sukuk* programme in January 2004. In September 2005, it had reached a size of $100 million. The LMC offers a broad variety of *sukuk* for various types of clients such as sovereign entities, financial institutions and other corporate entities. The purpose of issuance may be project finance, general corporate funding for working capital or expansion, corporate refinancing, asset securitization and asset acquisition. The LMC provides each and every one of its clients with *sukuk* structures and documentation tailored to meet its requirements. These may include, but are not limited to, the following:

- *murabaha sukuk* and post-dated sales;
- *salam* and *istisna' sukuk* development;
- *mudaraba* and *musharaka* and investment certificates;
- *ijara* and leased *ayan sukuk*;
- *istisna'* into *ijara sukuk*;
- investment agency *sukuk*.

The LMC aims to develop an active secondary market for all transferable Islamic investment instruments.[23]

19.6.5   International Islamic Liquidity Management Corporation

The International Islamic Liquidity Management Corporation (IILM) is an international institution established by central banks, monetary authorities and multilateral organizations to create and issue short-term *Shari'ah*-compliant financial instruments to facilitate effective cross-border Islamic liquidity management. By creating more liquid Islamic financial markets for institutions offering Islamic financial services (IIFS), IILM aims to enhance cross-border investment flows, international linkages and financial stability. Established on 25 October 2010, IILM has 14 founding members consisting of the central banks or monetary authorities of Indonesia, Iran, Kuwait, Luxembourg, Malaysia, Mauritius, Nigeria, Qatar, Saudi Arabia, Sudan, Turkey and the United Arab Emirates and two multilateral institutions, the Islamic Development Bank and the Islamic Corporation for the Development of the Private Sector (http://www.iilm.com).

19.6.6   Islamic International Rating Agency

The IIRA started operations in July 2005 in Bahrain.[24] It is sponsored by 17 multilateral development institutions and leading banks and other rating agencies. The rating system incorporates unique features of Islamic finance. The Rating Committee is completely independent of the board of directors. The IIRA is engaged in developing benchmarks and rating various Islamic financial institutions in light of efficient market principles. The IIRA assists the Islamic financial services industry gain recognition locally and internationally as strong and capable financial institutions, adhering to greater standards of disclosure and transparency. It aims to support the development of the regional capital market and improve its functioning.

19.6.7   Islamic Indices

Several Islamic indices have emerged to filter and find companies suitable for Islamic investment. The most prominent of these is the Dow Jones Islamic Market Index (DJIMI) established in 1996. The Index has been approved by Fiqh Academy of the OIC (McMillen 2008: 730). The Index uses three levels of screening. The first screen applies to those companies which deal in businesses not allowed by Islamic law such as alcohol, pork, gambling, prostitution, pornography and so on. The second screen applies to the level of debt. Companies whose total debts divided by their 12-month average market capitalization are 33 per cent or more of their total sources of funds do not qualify for Islamic investment. McMillen (2008: 730) notes that this screen has been revised to include new tests such as ratio of total interest income and expense to total revenue. The third screen treats those companies suitable for Islamic investment that have 'impure income or expenditure' (including, of course, interest) of 5–10 per cent of their income or expenditure. The reason for this benchmark is that it is virtually impossible to find companies that do not have interest income or expenditure. To the extent the Index relaxes the position on the taking or paying of interest, it is a compromise of the orthodox position that treats all types of interest as *riba*. The door has been opened to investment in companies which have some non-compliant activities. It is an attempt to live with interest-based business somehow.

In 2006, Citigroup launched the Dow Jones Citigroup Sukuk Index. The Index includes *sukuk* of a minimum size of $250 million, minimum maturity of one year and a minimum rating of BBB-/Baa3 by leading rating agencies. Further, the *sukuk* must be in conformity with AAOIFI standards for *sukuk*.

In 1998, the FTSE Global Islamic Index was launched. It has 15 Islamic indices. The classification is based on industry (ten indices) and region (global, the Americas, Europe, the Pacific Basin, and South Africa) (Askari, Iqbal and Mirakhor 2009: 250). Between these two main indices, over 100 style and regional indices have been created to track conformance of various stocks with the *Shari'ah* (Warde 2010: 152).[25]

In 2007, the MSCI Islamic Index series was launched.[26] The MSCI Global Islamic Indices are constructed from the conventional MSCI country indices and cover 69 developed, emerging and frontier markets, including regions such as the GCC and Arabian markets. A variety of indices are part of the series, including country, region and industry. The indices exclude companies that are directly active in or derive more than 5 per cent of their revenue from alcohol, tobacco, pork, conventional financial services, defence and weapons, gambling, music, hotels, cinema and adult entertainment (Schoon 2011: 80). In 2009, the Russell-Jadwa *Shari'ah* Global Index was launched. It consists of a set of indices grouped by region. It uses the Russell Global Index Universe as the underlying investible universe. The Index excludes companies dealing in conventional financial services, alcohol, tobacco, non-*halal* meat, pork, prostitution, pornography, restaurants and hotels that provide prohibited services and products, dealers in stem cell or human embryos, and anything determined as non-compliant with the *Shari'ah* (Schoon 2011: 81).

The Global Gulf Cooperation Council Index (GGCCI) is an index of 66 companies based in GCC countries. The countries included are Bahrain, Kuwait, Oman, Qatar and the UAE.

19.6.8   Islamic Interbank Benchmark Rate

In November 2011, Thomson Reuters launched the world's first Islamic finance benchmark rate. Established in cooperation with the IDB, AAOIFI, the Bahrain Association of Banks, Hawkamah Institute for Corporate Governance and a number of major Islamic banks, the IIBR harnesses Thomson Reuters' global benchmark fixing infrastructure, which is used to compile over 100 fixings around the world.[27] The rate is designed to provide an objective and dedicated indicator for the average expected return on *Shari'ah*-compliant short-term interbank funding: the Islamic Interbank Benchmark Rate (IIBR). The rate uses the contributed rates of 16 Islamic banks and the Islamic sections of conventional banks for pricing Islamic instruments to provide an alternative to the conventional interest-based benchmarks used for mainstream finance. Islamic financial institutions had been using LIBOR as a benchmark, which came under a lot of criticism, as it referred to market interest rates. IIBR can now replace LIBOR. Rates for *Shari'ah*-compliant US dollar funding will be contributed by the 16-member panel in the morning each business day and will be published daily on Thomson Reuters terminals and feeds at 11 a.m. Makkah time (GMT+3). The new benchmark can be used to price a number of Islamic instruments, including common overnight to short-term treasury investment and financing instruments such as *murabaha*, *wakala* and *mudaraba*, retail financing instruments such as property and car finance, and *sukuk* and other *Shari'ah*-compliant fixed income instruments. It can also be used for the pricing and benchmarking of corporate finance and investment assets. It is not yet clear how the benchmark achieves the original objective of relating the rate of return with actual performance of capital in the real sector.

19.7   ROLE OF *SHARI'AH* SUPERVISORY BOARDS

One of the primary justifications for establishing Islamic financial institutions was to ensure that their business complies with rules of the *Shari'ah*. The clients of Islamic financial institutions required independent verification of this fact. To achieve this objective, all Islamic financial institutions have to set up *Shari'ah* supervisory boards (SSBs). According to AAOIFI (2005):

> A *Shari'ah* Supervisory Board (SSB) is an independent body of specialized jurists in *fiqh al-mu'amalat*[28] (Islamic commercial jurisprudence) . . . it may include a member who should be an expert in the field of Islamic financial institutions and with knowledge of *fiqh al-mu'amalat*. The *Shari'ah* Supervisory Board is entrusted with the duty of directing, reviewing and supervising the activities of the Islamic financial institution. . . . The *fatwas* (legal opinions) and ruling of the Board shall be binding.

It is now a standard practice of every Islamic financial institution to have an independent SSB. In some countries the central banks or other supervisory authorities have created SSBs to oversee compliance with the *Shari'ah*. The confidence of the stakeholders of Islamic financial institutions rests on the avowed claim of the Islamic financial institutions that they are compliant with the *Shari'ah*. To ensure that this confidence remains intact, AAOIFI (2008) and Fiqh Academy of the OIC have issued guidelines and standards for *Shari'ah* compliance. In 2009 the IFSB issued guiding principles on *Shari'ah* compliance. However, Islamic financial institutions are not obliged to follow these guidelines and standards. Each Islamic financial institution has its own SSB, making compliance a private sector matter. Another difficult issue emanates from different interpretations of the *Shari'ah* on different issues,[29] leaving an unwary observer wondering which one of the various interpretations can be considered as truly compliant. There is a need for coordination among various standard-setting and regulatory bodies. Preferably, there should be a centralized SSB responsible for issuing uniform guidance.

Gradually, the work of the SSB is moving toward standardization. For example, the regulators in Bahrain, Indonesia, Jordan, Kuwait, Lebanon, Malaysia and Pakistan have developed guidelines for SSBs in their respective jurisdictions. Some countries, like Indonesia, Kuwait, Malaysia, Pakistan, Sudan and the UAE, have centralized SSBs (Askari *et al.* 2010: 21). Grais and Pellegrini (2006: 7) enumerate the following five functions for an SSB:

a.   certifying financial instruments for their compliance with the *Shari'ah*;
b.   verifying transactions for compliance with the *Shari'ah*;
c.   calculating *zakah* payable by Islamic financial institutions;
d.   disposing of non-*Shari'ah*-compliant income;
e.   advising on the distribution of income among investors and share-holders.

The members of an SSB are employed by the respective board of directors on behalf of the shareholders. The remuneration of SSB members is fixed by the board. These arrangements compromise the independence of the SSB (Warde 2010: 236). Grais and Pellegrini (2006: 12) report their analysis about transparency with respect to SSBs. They conclude that most Islamic financial institutions do not have practices which ensure transparency in the role and functions of the SSBs. In theory, the members of an SSB should be well versed in Islamic commercial law as well as contemporary financial practices. However, in practice, the number of such competent persons is extremely limited, compelling Islamic financial institutions to engage scholars who sit on the SSBs of their competitors as well. For example, Unal (2011) has analysed 1141 positions of SSB scholars as on 31 July 2010. His conclusion is that the busiest scholar among the top 20 holds 85 positions in Islamic financial institutions and 12 positions in standard-setting bodies. The least busy *Shari'ah* scholar among the top

20 had 14 positions in Islamic financial institutions and two positions in standard-setting bodies. That compromises the independence, competition and confidentiality of the Islamic financial institutions sharing the members of SSBs. It can also create situations of conflict of interest. The few scholars who are available are in great demand. It has pushed up their remunerations and perquisites. Khan and Bhatti (2008: 71) write:

> the small group of *Shari'ah* experts is serving on several *Shari'ah* boards of Islamic financial institutions worldwide. These experts earn as much as US $88,500 per year per bank. In some cases, they charge up to US $500,000 for advice on large capital market transactions.[30]

Abdul-Rahman (2010: 241) says:

> A typical *Shari'ah* Board member commands an annual retainer of approximately $50000 (or more) and a first-class plane-ticket and accommodations when he travels. Scholars with superstar status sit on the *Shari'ah* Boards of an average 50 to 70 banks. This raises very serious conflict of interest, confidentiality, and insiders' concern issues.

Kahf (2004: 26) writes:

> This alliance also gives the *Ulema* (religious scholars) a new source of income that by far exceeds what they were used to earning. It gives them an opening to a new lifestyle that includes air travel, sometimes in private jets, staying in five-star hotels, being under the focus of media attention and providing their opinions to people of high social and economic ranks, who are anxious to listen. In addition, they are frequently commissioned to undertake paid-for *fiqh* (jurisprudence) research and to find solutions to problems that the new breed of bankers face.

Farooq (2005) writes:

> This new lifestyle of the Islamic banks' *Ulema* (religious scholars) has resulted in certain changes in viewpoint as well. Many of them are now accused of being bankers' window-dressers and of over-stretching the rules of *Shari'ah* to provide easy *fatwas* (opinions) for the new breed of bankers.

19.7.1 Performance of the *Shari'ah* Supervisory Boards

Siddiqi (2009-a: 218) recognizes the contribution of the SSBs in terms of the colossal amount of literature produced by them on financial issues.[31] It is a valuable contribution and deserves due compliments. However, he also observes that the SSBs are often manned by scholars who are by training not aware of broader macroeconomic issues and do not have the capacity or ability to analyse matters beyond the level of the institution for which they are working. Some SSBs have issued decrees which may be justified from the perspective of an individual Islamic financial institution or within narrow legal constraints but are in conflict with broader objectives of the *Shari'ah*. He quotes the example of *tawarruq*, which has been justified and approved by several SSBs without recognizing that the instrument defeats the broader objectives of the *Shari'ah* (ibid.: 232, 235). In an earlier study Siddiqi (2006-a) points out that the job of *Shari'ah* scholars while on SSBs requires knowledge of the contemporary sciences of economics, finance, statistics, sociology, psychology and management. They must be proficient in the English language as well. Most of the scholars on SSBs do not meet these knowledge requirements. Other scholars have also criticized the performance of SSBs for a lack of independence and transparency. For example, Foster (2008: 12) writes:

> One of the main weaknesses with Islamic finance is there are not enough *Shari'ah* scholars to go around. If one looks at the proposals of most Islamic financial instruments that are approved for sale, one will find a cadre of the same names appearing on the boards of products from the US to Singapore, Nigeria to Pakistan, and the UK to GCC. The scholars are few and far between, and in much demand. . . . This sometimes means that the charge of '*fatwas* for rent' is leveled at scholars, with critics claiming that if enough money exchanges hands, then a *fatwa* will be passed. In effect it is taking a duck, sprinkling holy water on it and calling it chicken. The fact that in some cases this does occur is supported by Mahmoud El-Gamal, who said product designers and financial institutions they represent were capitalizing on people's religious insecurities.

Warde (2000: 227) writes: 'The reality, however, is more complicated. Interviews revealed that in many cases the review [by *Shari'ah* boards] is perfunctory, with Boards "rubber stamping" decisions already made by the bank's management or shunning controversial issues.'
Farooq (2005) writes:

> Furthermore, the routinely-used expression '*Shari'ah*-compliant' is often misleading. . . . So, by *Shari'ah*-compliant generally what is meant is not that it is necessarily compliant with the Islamic rules, but that it is considered acceptable by a Board of *Shari'ah* experts that is often handpicked and employed by these institutions with quite a high level of monetary compensation. Such experts often resort to *hiyal* (legal stratagem) that is used to pronounce such transactions as *Shari'ah*-compliant.

Siddiqi (2006-a) enumerates the following outcomes of the situation:

a.   The Islamic financial institutions treated the advice of the experts as their property and felt they were under no obligation to share with others what exactly the experts told them. Transparency of the advice was reduced. Traditionally Islamic religious opinion (*fatwas*) had been a public good, but in the context of Islamic financial institutions it has become a private good.

b. There is a tendency to duplicate conventional financial instruments with certain modifications in terms and phrases, creating a semblance with interest-based instruments and bringing a bad name to Islamic finance. Examples are *sukuk* and *tawarruq*. The *Shari'ah* experts do not have the expertise and training to understand all the consequences of the new instruments that they approve.

c. The gamut of issues and the scope of Islamic economics are too vast to be mastered by any one *Shari'ah* expert. The challenge is to cope with the emerging new issues in light of the objectives of the *Shari'ah*. The existing education and training of scholars do not equip them to come up to that challenge. The Muslim global community (*ummah*) needs to consider this problem at the international level, not to mention the individual *Shari'ah* scholar level.

19.8   ISSUES IN THE PRACTICE OF ISLAMIC BANKING AND FINANCE

19.8.1   Governance Issues

Islamic financial institutions have two types of investment deposits:

a. Restricted investment deposits, where the Islamic financial institutions act on the instructions of the depositors and have no role in deciding the mode and outlet of the investment. All risks are borne by the depositors. The Islamic financial institutions charge a fee for their services.

b. Unrestricted investment accountholders (UIAs), which give full authority to the Islamic financial institution to place funds as it deems fit. The UIAs share the profits with the Islamic financial institution but bear all the losses.

This last feature of UIA deposits raises governance issues. As a matter of principle, the investors should be represented on the board of governors of the Islamic financial institutions so that they can have a say in the policies relating to the efficiency and productivity of their capital, share some of the responsibility for key decisions, and put the theory of risk sharing into practice. However, in practice, no such mechanism exists.

The management of an Islamic financial institution appointed by the shareholders commingles funds of the UIAs and invests these funds as it deems fit. The UIAs do not have any role in decision making. The Islamic financial institution can shield its poor performance behind profit equalization funds or investment risk reserves, which it creates out of profits during good times. FAS 11 of the AAOIFI requires the Islamic financial institutions to disclose the proportion of dividend met from current operational profits and the proportion met from profit equalization reserves. However, in practice, the Islamic financial institutions seldom disclose or register this information, as they find UIAs complacent, with a regular and almost fixed return on their deposits. It is only when an Islamic financial institution approaches insolvency that the UIAs come to know that their deposits have eroded over the period. Since the Islamic financial institutions do not have any stake in protecting these deposits, they can also adopt a carefree attitude in investing these funds. A further concern is added by the ownership structure of most of the Islamic financial institutions in the Middle East, which are owned by rich families with a tendency to confidentiality and secrecy (Iqbal and Molyneux 2005: 122).

Tahir (2009: 69) finds that the governance and control of Islamic financial institutions is quite similar to those of conventional financial institutions. He writes:

> The governance, supervision and control matters for Islamic banks are being handled in the same way as those for interest-based banks. There is no evidence that the arrangements for the Islamic banks have been developed on some *Shari'ah* basis. For example, the formulas for SLR (statutory liquidity requirements), capital adequacy ratio, and risk management standards are same for Islamic banks as those for interest-based banks.

The Islamic financial institutions have not devised any institutional mechanism for involving the UIAs in decision making, for sharing performance information with them on a timely basis and for overseeing the performance of the Islamic financial institutions. The UIAs have neither the rights of shareholders nor those of debtors. In fact, they are as helpless or irrelevant as the depositors of a conventional bank.

19.8.2 Divergence of Practice from Theory

In theory, the Islamic banks should collect savings on the basis of profit sharing (*musharaka* and *mudaraba*) and invest these funds on the same basis. During the early days of Islamic banking some banks were enthusiastic about PLS. However, soon their enthusiasm faded away. They discovered that the investment of depositors' funds on a PLS basis was highly risky. The banks also did not have experience of business in the real sector. The likelihood of loss was quite high, and prudence would not recommend investing the funds on the basis of PLS. That prompted the banks to search for modes of finance that would bring a safe and fixed predetermined return on their funds. They were able to find a set of such modes in the form of mark-up, leasing, *salam, istisna'* and their various combinations. The investments through these modes bring a fixed return. The asset side of the balance sheet of a typical Islamic bank, therefore, appears very much similar to that of a conventional bank. On the liability side, the Islamic banks claim to practise *mudaraba*. Under this mode, the depositors are owners of the capital (*rabb al-mal*), and the bank is the entrepreneur (*mudarib*). As owners of the capital, the depositors are supposed to bear all risk of loss on the bank's investment operations. Thus the Islamic banks have shifted all risk of loss to depositors on the liability side of the balance sheet.

It is now a situation where the banks have an assured return on their investments, but should there be losses after meeting the overheads and operational expenses such losses are passed on to depositors. The depositors are thus exposed to the risk of loss while the banks are able to protect themselves through various fixed-return investment modes. Warde (2010: 164) aptly describes the situation as 'Islamic moral hazard' in which the banks are able 'to privatize the profits and socialize the losses'.

In practice, since the Islamic banks may thus face a problem of attracting deposits, they have created various schemes that offer a predetermined fixed rate of profit on deposits in a similar manner to that of conventional banks. The situation boils down to banking business that is quite similar to conventional banking business. It is difficult to tell one from the other. The Islamic banks charge a fixed return on the funds provided by them and pay out a fixed return to depositors. The paper work, though, shows that they are doing this business on the basis of various Islamic modes of finance. From the perspective of a client it hardly matters (Warde 2010: 164).

The practice of Islamic banking is removed from its theory in several ways. El-Hawary, Grais and Iqbal (2004: 15–16) point out several features of Islamic financial institutions that clearly indicate that practice diverges from theory. The income of Islamic financial institutions is not related to performance of finance in the real sector. It is based on contractual terms that bring a fixed return. Thus the very rationale of Islamic banking has been defeated. Similarly, the theory of Islamic banking pleaded for keeping distinct accounts for various types of deposits so that the return can be assigned to each type on an actual basis. In practice, Islamic financial institutions pool all types of deposits. The investment accountholders' deposits are commingled with other deposits and also with equity-holders' funds. It is not possible to determine the performance of each type of funds separately. It is possible that the Islamic financial institutions invest current accountholders' funds as well without giving them any share from the earnings. It is also possible that the investment accountholders' funds bring in a higher return than the investment of equity-holders' funds. But the Islamic financial institutions do not keep separate accounts for various income streams. Thus the whole rationale of regulating different types of funds separately is lost. Moreover, the Islamic financial institutions promise and actually pay a fixed return on term deposits. They never charge losses to the fixed-term deposits but absorb any losses on these funds in income derived from other sources. The result is that a term deposit with an Islamic financial institution has the same features with respect to income stream as a term deposit in a conventional bank. These practices have made Islamic financial institutions quite similar to conventional banks.

Several Muslim scholars have criticized the situation. For example, Siddiqi (1983-a: 52) writes on this:

> we cannot claim, for an interest-free alternative not based on sharing, the superiority which could be claimed on the basis of profit-sharing. What is worse, if the alternative in practice is built around predetermined rates of return to investible funds, it would be exposed to the same criticism which was directed at interest as a fixed charge on capital. It so happens that the returns to finance provided in modes of finance based on *murabaha, bai' salam* (a forward sale, whereby payment is made at time of contract and item delivered at later), leasing and lending with a service charge, are all predetermined as in the case of interest. Some of these modes of finance are said to contain some elements of risk, but all these risks are insurable and are actually insured against. The uncertainty or risk to which the business being so financed is exposed is fully passed over to the other party. A financial system built solely around these modes of financing can hardly claim superiority over an interest-based system on grounds of equity, efficiency, stability and growth.

Khan and Bhatti (2008: 73) write:

> One of the pioneers of Islamic banking and finance, D.M. Qureshi (2005),[32] has described the whole Islamic banking and finance affair in the following words: 'Islamic banking as it stands today is with all due respect and humility, a labeling industry. Everything that is conventional is being labeled and you say it is Islamic.'

Dusuki and Abozaid (2007: 146, 147) write:

> Observers point out that the use of PLS instruments, namely *mudaraba* and *musharaka* financing have declined to almost negligible proportions (Iqbal and

Molyneux 2005;[33] Kuran 2004;[34] Lewis and Algaud 2001;[35] Yousef 2004[36]). In many Islamic banks' asset portfolios, short-term financing, notably *murabaha* and other debt-based contracts account for the great bulk of their investments. Yousef (2004) refers to the strong and consistent tendency of Islamic banks to utilize debt-like instruments in the provision of external finance as the '*murabaha syndrome.*' . . . The only difference the examiner may find is in the technicalities and legal forms, while in essence, the substance is the same. . . . In fact Islamic bankers use the same financial computation just like other bankers to calculate present and future values of investments. Hence, at the end of the day, unconvinced Muslims and other critical outsiders, observe that Islamic banks in reality keep interest but just call it by another name, such as commissions or profits (*riba*).

Asutay (2007: 173) quotes Hasan[37] that in Malaysia the share of *musharaka* financing declined from 1.4 per cent in 2000 to 0.2 per cent in 2006. Major forms of Islamic finance in 2006 were with a fixed return: *bai' bithaman 'ajil*[38] (55.9 per cent) and *ijara thumma al-bai'*[39] (25.2 per cent). This is only one example of a Muslim country. The same trend is discernible in all Islamic banks around the globe. Khan and Bhatti (2008: 49) present a sample of leading Islamic banks and their modes of finance for 2000–06. They conclude that only 6.34 per cent of the total financing of these banks was on the basis of PLS, while the same percentage was 17.34 in 1994–96. It means that over the years the trend has been towards a declining use of the PLS mode of finance. As compared to PLS, the sample showed that 54.42 per cent of financing was on the basis of *murabaha*, 16.31 per cent on the basis of *ijara* and 5.60 per cent on the basis of *salam* and *istisna'* during 2004–06.

Briefly, Islamic financial institutions do not like to finance undertakings that will expose them to indeterminate loss. As passive equity investors the banks may be subjected to unacceptable losses. On the other side, clients of the banks also do not like to compromise their sovereignty in decision making. They do not like banks interfering in their business as partners.

The question arises: why have Islamic financial institutions deviated from PLS, which was the main justification for their establishment? The question has been variously answered by different scholars. For example, Dar and Presley (2000–01: 5–6) summarize the reasons as follows:

a. There is an inherent incentive for the bank's client to report less profit. The higher the declared profit, the higher will be the bank's share. That is a deterrent against honest reporting.
b. The property rights in most Muslim countries are not properly defined. That makes the practice of profit–loss sharing difficult.
c. Islamic banks face severe competition from conventional banks which are firmly established and have centuries of experience. The

Islamic banks are not yet sure of their policies and practices and feel restrained in taking unforeseen risks.

d. The PLS is not suitable or feasible in many cases such as short-term resource requirements, working capital needs, non-profit-generating projects such as in the education and health sectors, and so on.

e. In some countries interest is accepted as business expenditure and given tax exemption but profit is taxed as income. The clients of the business who obtain funds on a PLS basis have to bear the financial burden in terms of higher taxes. That deters them from PLS.

f. There are as yet no secondary markets for Islamic financial products based on PLS.

g. *Mudaraba*, one of the forms of PLS, provides limited control rights to shareholders of the bank and creates an imbalance in the governance structure of PLS. The shareholders like to have a consistent and complementary control system, which is missing in the case of *mudaraba* financing.

Iqbal and Mirakhor (2008: 144–147) note the following additional points:

a. informational asymmetry due to inefficient financial markets, resulting in costly delegated monitoring;

b. fiscal imbalance of the governments, forcing them to borrow at cheaper rates from banks, thus not allowing the Islamic banks to realize their full potential;

c. lack of a strong supervisory and regulatory prudential framework.

Iqbal and Molyneux (2005: 136) give further reasons as follows:

a. It is difficult to expand a business financed through *mudaraba* because of limited opportunities to reinvest retained earnings and/or raise additional funds.

b. The entrepreneur cannot become the sole owner of the project except through diminishing *musharaka*, which may take a long time.

c. On the liabilities side, the structure of deposits of the Islamic banks is not sufficiently long-term, and therefore they do not want to get involved in long-term projects.

d. PLS contracts require a lot of information about the entrepreneurial abilities of the customer. This may not be easily available.

Chapra (2008-a: 9) thinks that the reason for not practising profit–loss sharing is the absence of the necessary institutions to minimize the risks associated with anonymity, moral hazard, principal/agent conflict of interest, and late settlement of financial obligations. The required institutions are: a centralized *Shari'ah* board, *Shari'ah* clearance and *Shari'ah* audit, credit rating agencies, Islamic chambers of commerce and trade, *Shari'ah* courts and banking tribunals, depositors' associations, a qualified pool of talent, an Islamic financial market, a lender of last resort and an Islamic stock exchange. Obviously, this is a long-term process and it may take decades before the real potential of Islamic banking is actualized.

The *Shari'ah* scholars and pioneers of Islamic finance like Siddiqi, Chapra, Taqi Uthmani and Khurshid Ahmad are quite critical of the Islamic financial institutions' mass-scale adoption of fixed-return modes of finance. They have argued quite vehemently that moving away from *musharaka* and *mudaraba* would simply defeat the very purpose of the Islamic finance movement. Their most commonly recommended advice is that Islamic financial institutions should gradually move toward PLS and minimize reliance on fixed-return modes of finance. However, they remain oblivious to the fact that the reason for not adopting PLS lies in its inefficiency. Nawab Haider Naqvi (2000: 42) sums up the enigma of this point of view as follows:

> The almost 'universal' recommendation still is that the PLS principle to be observed faithfully, even exclusively, because it is hoped – presumably by some variant of Say's Law – an ample supply of such instruments will create their own demand. But this argument comes dangerously close to circular reasoning: it makes the desired efficiency and equity outcomes of Islamic banking contingent on the adoption of PLS principle, which is prejudged as the only one which is Islamically just! The possibility that the PLS principle, if implemented universally and without any safeguards, may itself lead to inefficiency and inequity is totally alien to this antiseptically 'consequence-insensitive' procedural way of thinking.

19.8.3   Islamic Banks Seeking Financial Guarantees

In theory, Islamic financial institutions are partners of their clients. As partners they should not ask for any collateral or financial guarantees from their clients. However, in practice, most of the Islamic banks require financial guarantees or collaterals. Aggarwal and Yousef (1996: 11) reported that, besides the goods purchased or assets leased, Islamic financial institutions required additional financial guarantees. They quoted Kazarian[40] that the size of collateral for Islamic banks in 1990 in Egypt was between 40 and 85 per cent of the funds provided. They reported that, in 1979–90, secured loans by commercial banks were 60 per cent and by investment banks 78 per cent in Egypt. But in the same period the percentage of secured loans by Islamic banks was over 90 per cent (see also Zarrokh 2007: 22). This is another example where the practice of Islamic banking has deviated from its theory.

19.8.4 *Shari'ah* Arbitrage: The Deadweight of Islamic Finance

Islamic banks provide the same services as conventional banks do. However, they cause a social deadweight in terms of additional costs that users of Islamic banking services have to pay. Fadel (2008: 656) writes:

> Many scholars have attacked the schizophrenic relationship of Islamic finance vis-à-vis conventional finance as little more than crass exploitation of religious sentiment. One leading scholar coined the term '*shari'ah* arbitrage' to describe Islamic finance as little more than the extraction of fees simply for transforming a conventional product into one that seems to comply with the formal requirements of Islamic law, while retaining all the economic features of that conventional product.[41]

In a footnote to the above he adds (ibid.):

> To the extent Islamic financial products merely replicate already existing financial instruments, the costs generated by Islamic finance are simply dead-weight losses from a social perspective. To the extent that Muslim investors or end-users of financial products are unwilling to avail themselves of conventional financial products, however, the existence of an Islamic financial sector could nevertheless be socially efficient, even if suboptimal. For this to be true, one would have to assume that social gains in the form of increased savings and investment arising out of the existence of Islamic investment and credit alternatives exceed the dead-weight losses arising out of *Shari'ah* arbitrage.

In practice, there is no conclusive evidence that adopting Islamic modes of finance is more profitable for clients of the Islamic financial institutions. Nor is there any evidence to prove that depositors of the Islamic financial institutions are better off in financial terms as compared to clients of the conventional banks. In both cases, clients of the Islamic banks may be worse off, as they have to bear the additional legal and documentation costs that the Islamic financial institutions incur. That is the cost of trying to comply with the *Shari'ah*!

19.8.5 Liquidity Management

Islamic financial institutions have to manage funds to ensure liquidity on one hand and a maximum return on surplus funds on the other. In conventional banking, the banks are able to optimize their earnings by borrowing and investing for any duration including short periods such as a day or so. The rate of interest can be calculated for any period of time. However, when it comes to PLS the banks cannot place funds for short periods, as profit or loss cannot be determined for short periods. Since they cannot place funds for short periods, Islamic financial institutions often face a situation of surplus funds. They cannot compete with the conventional banks, which can invest their funds optimally for any duration.

Khan and Bhatti (2008: 710) quote Hakim[42] that on average Islamic financial institutions carry 40 per cent more liquidity than their conventional counterparts, because of a serious dearth of long-term *Shari'ah*-compliant investment tools. Islamic financial institutions cannot obtain funds for short periods from the interbank market, nor are they able to offer these funds on a conventional basis. This has led to chronic difficulties for the Islamic financial institutions. The Islamic Financial Services Board (2008: 8–9), on the basis of 2006 data of six countries, concludes that the average daily volume of interbank transactions among Islamic financial institutions, between Islamic financial institutions and conventional banks, and between Islamic financial institutions and central banks is very low compared to the trades in the conventional money market. Similarly, it notes that Islamic financial institutions are forced to place a much higher percentage of funds with central banks as compared to conventional banks because they do not have profitable investment avenues. Some countries such as Bahrain, Iran, Malaysia and Sudan have taken the initiative of developing and issuing securitized papers on the basis of *musharaka*, *mudaraba* and *ijara*, but the relative volume of these securities is much smaller than on the conventional capital market because of lack of an appropriate and efficient secondary market (ibid.: 13).

Lack of a developed money market in Islamic financial products has forced Islamic financial institutions to use benchmarks of an interest-based money market, such as LIBOR, for various transactions which otherwise are not based on interest.[43] Not only does it defeat the very purpose for which the Islamic finance movement started, but it also deviates from the basic premise that the rate of return should be based on the actual results of investment in the real sector rather than with reference to interest rates in the money market. Absence of a developed money market also creates constraints for Islamic financial institutions when it comes to dealing with central banks. Islamic financial institutions do not have a suitable mechanism to benefit from open market operations or to take advantage of the lender-of-last-resort facility.

19.8.6 Internal Controls: Frauds in Islamic Financial Institutions

Clients of financial institutions deal in an environment of mutual trust and sincerity. They expect that the financial institutions will safeguard their savings and provide funds on fair and just terms. These expectations rise to greater heights in the case of Islamic financial institutions, which are backed by a sense of religiosity and piety. But in practice they have not fared better than conventional financial institutions. They are also not immune to fraud and embezzlement. Ali (2006–07: 26) notes that Ihlas Finans of Turkey indulged in fraud by showing some of the finance used for internal problem solving as *mudaraba* financing. Abdul-Rahman (2010: 248) cites the example of Sunrise Equities, a Chicago-based company that offered its Islamic investors a return of 15–20 per cent per annum. The major clientele of the company consisted of Indian Muslims of Hyderabad. In September 2008, the 'turban-dressed and bearded' leaders of the company disappeared, with unwary Muslim investors losing all their investments. Such episodes have also been experienced in Egypt, Turkey and many other places.

Warde (2010: 78–80) narrates extensively the fraudulent operation of about 200 Islamic management companies in Egypt during 1985–88. By some estimates, frauds resulted in some $3 billion, or 15 per cent of Egyptian GNP, evaporating into thin air. In 1991 the Bank of Credit and Commerce International (BCCI) scandal further tarnished the image of Islamic finance, and unfairly so, as BCCI was not an Islamic bank but had an Islamic banking unit in London and used the Islamic rhetoric extensively. Warde (2010: 162) quotes an example of fraud of $50 million in 1998 committed by an employee of Dubai Islamic Bank (DIB), leading to a run on the bank and withdrawal of $138 million (or 7 per cent of the bank's deposits) in one day. In another case DIB filed a lawsuit in Miami, Florida against a West African tycoon, Foutanga Dit Babani, for $242 million swindled by him through collaboration with the bank staff. In 2009, seven employees of DIB defrauded it of $500 million via CCH, its trade finance subsidiary. Warde (2010: 121) reports about Iran as follows:

> Fraud is rampant and seldom sanctioned, and one of the more curious elements of the official banking system is proliferation of lotteries and randomly fixed gifts (thus raising religious issues related to *maysir*[44]) as a means of encouraging savings. . . . Some 1300 Islamic credit funds have become essentially 'usury stores'. Under the aegis of the Bazaar, they were federated into an 'Organization of the Islamic Economy', offering 'annual profit participation' rates in the 25 to 50 percent range. . . . Abuses have been common, and a number of financial scandals have been discovered. The most massive fraud occurred between 1992

and 1996. Some \$4 billion disappeared and the primary suspect was Morteza Rafiqdust, younger brother of the head of the Bonyad Foundation.

19.8.7 Efficiency of Islamic Banks

Several people have conducted studies about the efficiency of Islamic banks. They have consistently found that Islamic banks are less efficient than conventional banks. For example, Hassan (2006: 63) studied 43 Islamic banks in 21 Muslim countries over the 1996–2001 period: 'The results indicate that, on average the Islamic banking industry is relatively less efficient compared to their conventional counterparts in other parts of the world.' Mokhtar, Abdullah and al-Habshi (2007: 5) studied the efficiency of full-fledged Islamic banks and Islamic windows in Malaysia during 1997–2003. They found that the full-fledged Islamic banks were more efficient than the Islamic windows but less efficient than conventional banks. Ali (2006–07: 16) studied the performance of Islamic banks in Turkey (known as special finance houses or SFHs). He found that the performance of SFHs on various indicators was lower than that of conventional banks in 1999–2001. Bader, Mohamad, Ariff and Hassan (2008) measured the cost, revenue and profit efficiency of 43 Islamic and 37 conventional banks over the period 1999–2005 in 21 countries. They found that there were no significant differences between the overall efficiency results of conventional versus Islamic banks. Hasan and Dridi (2010: 6–7) presented perhaps the most comprehensive review of the performance of Islamic banks during the global crisis of 2008–09. They covered 120 Islamic banks in eight countries (accounting for 80 per cent of all Islamic financial institutions worldwide). Their conclusion was that Islamic banks performed better than conventional banks during 2008 in terms of profitability because of a better business model, but in 2009, owing to weaker risk management, their profitability was lower than that of conventional banks. The credit and asset growth of Islamic banks during the crisis period was at least twice higher than that of conventional banks. These studies do indicate that Islamic financial institutions are decidedly not more efficient than conventional institutions. At best, they are similar to conventional institutions.

19.8.8 Stability of Islamic Financial Institutions

In theory Islamic financial institutions are supposed to be more stable than conventional banks. Islamic financial institutions have two main types of depositors: current account and investment account. Islamic financial institutions are not supposed to use current account deposits to finance the investment needs of their clients. Therefore they can always meet any demand for withdrawal of these deposits. As regards investment deposits, the depositors share the risk of the entrepreneurs. If the return of the bank goes down because of losses suffered by the entrepreneurs, the depositors also share those losses. The liabilities of the bank also go down. Theoretically, there cannot be a situation where the Islamic financial institution has to pay out a higher return to its depositors even if its own income goes down. This is as against the situation in the case of conventional banks which are committed to pay a fixed rate of interest on deposits even though their own earnings go down. Theoretically, the question of bank failure under the Islamic finance regime does not arise, as the investment depositors know that their return is variable and can also be negative. However, in practice some Islamic banks have failed. For example, Ihlas Finance House, an Islamic financial institution in Turkey, closed its operations in 2001. Similarly, Bank Taqwa closed in 2001. The regulatory authority closed Faisal Bank UK for regulatory reasons. The reasons for such failures could be unique to Islamic financial institutions,[45] but also similar to conventional banks, because the former have adopted similar modes of finance. For example, poor credit risk assessment may lead to excessive exposure in the case of conventional banks. The same is possible in the case of Islamic financial institutions if they adopt a lax standard for risk assessment. The chances of overextension of finance remain high in times of boom. Similarly, the business of Islamic financial institutions creates vulnerabilities not present in the business of conventional banks. For example, since Islamic financial institutions are supposed to participate in various lines of business, they may have equity exposure in various enterprises. Losses in some of these can have a knock-on effect in other businesses and the bank may get an adverse reputation, leading to instability in its business (Ali 2007-a: 115).

Internal control failures can lead to bank failure in the case of conventional banks. Similar risk exists in the case of Islamic financial institutions. Warde (2010: 89) tries to paint a realistic picture about the stability of Islamic banks against the backdrop of the 2007–09 global financial crisis. While in the beginning Islamic banks were unscathed, gradually the effect of the financial downturn got translated into the real sector. The asset-backed real economy also got hit by the financial tsunami, though its inherent conservatism somewhat mitigated the effects of the downturn. 'This showed that Islamic finance was not after all a panacea, and that a faith-based system is not automatically immune to the vagaries of the financial system.'

In brief, it is an oversimplification to claim that Islamic financial institutions are more stable than conventional banks. Both have their risks and vulnerabilities. It is as yet too early, in the absence of empirical evidence, to claim that Islamic financial institutions are more stable than conventional banks.

19.8.9 Islamic Financial Institutions and the Objectives of the *Shari'ah*

One of the objectives for the establishment of Islamic financial institutions is to promote the socio-economic objectives of the *Shari'ah*. In fact, the very first Islamic bank at Mit Ghamr (Egypt) (1963–68) aimed at promoting community and social banking to help poor farmers. However, in practice, Islamic financial institutions are mainly motivated by profit maximization and have hardly played any significant role in promoting the socio-economic objectives of the *Shari'ah*. Sairally (2007: 287) quoted several studies that highlighted the failure of Islamic financial institutions in promoting these objectives. For example, most of the Islamic financial products focused on high-net-worth individuals or institutions and paid scant attention to the needs of an ordinary investor. There is no significant effort by Islamic financial institutions to provide interest-free loans (*qard hasan*) to the needy and the poor (Warde 2000: 174).

Islamic financial institutions have professed their support for such elegant concepts as corporate social responsibility (CSR) and have tried to read it as reinforcement of their commitment to the objectives of the *Shari'ah*. However, the actual practice departs from the lofty claims. Sairally (2007: 299) concluded after a questionnaire survey of 48 Islamic financial institutions in 19 countries that the practice of Islamic financial institutions fell short of their avowed support for CSR. For example, they did not reveal information on ethical screening criteria of their investments. There was little concern for criteria for investment relating to sustainability of the environment. Reported practices showed scant support for ethical employment policies and community involvement. The budget for CSR ranged between nil and 2 per cent of profits of the Islamic financial institutions under study, despite oral commitment to socially responsible policies. There was a lack of transparency about funds spent for charitable purposes (ibid.: 302). These examples show that Islamic financial institutions took a peripheral approach to CSR. By and large, they neglected the comprehensive social objective of welfare.

Another method to assess the contribution of Islamic financial institutions toward the overall objectives of the *Shari'ah* is to evaluate their contribution to the economic development of the host countries. Several authors have analysed this aspect of Islamic finance. For example, Warde (2010: 179–183) writes:

Banking in much of the Islamic world also tends to epitomize 'crony capitalism'. . . . Rather than going to worthwhile investment projects, financing goes primarily to 'well-connected' borrowers or 'politically-exposed persons' (PEP). . . . Most evidence highlights the tendency of Islamic banks to invest in short-term commercial transactions as opposed to industry or agriculture. In Sudan, an agricultural country, only 4 percent of the investments were allocated to agriculture, while 90 percent went to import–export operations. . . . There are no comprehensive or comparative surveys on the subject, but anecdotal evidence as well as a number of case studies suggests that the promise of bringing the system a heretofore neglected segment of the market has not been fulfilled.

El-Gamal (2006: ix–x) writes:

This supposed Islamization of contemporary financial practice is accomplished by means of modified pre-modern financial contracts (such as sales, leases, and simple partnerships). . . . By attempting to replicate the substance of contemporary financial practice using pre-modern contract forms, Islamic finance has arguably failed to serve the objective of Islamic law (*maqasid al-Shari'ah*): Wherever the substance of contemporary financial practice is in accordance with Islamic law, adherence to pre-modern contract forms (with or without modification) leads to avoidable efficiency losses, thus violating one of the main legal objectives that defined classical Islamic jurisprudence.

Zaman and Asutay (2009: 77) conclude that Islamic banking and finance are not economically feasible and efficient. If preservation of wealth is an objective of the *Shari'ah*, existing Islamic financial institutions certainly fail on this count. Secondly, very little wealth has actually reached the most needy societies of the Muslim world. Instead it circulates among corporate interests in the oil-rich states. The whole enterprise of Islamic finance revolves around technical and procedural issues of Islamic law (*fiqh*) and ignores the broad developmental policy issues faced by the Muslim world. Islamic financial institutions and their *Shari'ah* boards are occupied with meeting certain procedural requirements irrespective of whether they are able to respond to the broader macroeconomic needs of the Muslim people. Siddiqi (2008: 19) criticizes the current practice and evolution of Islamic banking and finance on another ground as well. He argues that Islamic finance has provided the means of making more money for the rich and wealthy of the Muslim countries but has nothing to offer to the poor. Moreover, he argues, the existing practice of Islamic finance has not focused on the establishment of justice and equity in Muslim societies, where it is glaringly absent.

19.9 SUMMING-UP ON THE PRACTICE OF ISLAMIC BANKING AND FINANCE

The general evolution of Islamic banking has been unidirectional. It has been moving toward convergence with conventional banking. Islamic banks took the easier path of imitating conventional banks in product development rather than innovating completely new products. They have evolved as a subset of conventional banks. Islamic finance has become more of a supplement to conventional finance than a competitor. Several Muslim scholars have expressed their dissatisfaction with the evolution of Islamic financial institutions. For example, Siddiqi (2009-a: 214ff.) says that Islamic banks have joined the race to be equal or similar to conventional banks, providing services and products that are the same as, or similar to, those of conventional banks. Thus they have arrived at a destination which is exactly the opposite of what they had aimed at. The whole rationale of Islamic banking was to establish a different type of banking which was aligned to fairness, equitable income distribution, and ethical modes of investment supportive of the broader social objectives of Islam and conducive to development that is aligned to environmental protection, inter-generational equity and the greater common good. Leaving aside all these lofty ideals, Islamic banking in practice is trying to pursue the same goals as conventional banking. If it does not carry out major rethinking and restructuring, it will lose the very purpose for which it came into being. In an earlier paper Siddiqi (2006: 8) wrote as follows:

> While theory aspired to prove Islamic finance was *different* from the conventional one, practitioners were busy searching for ways to make it *similar* to it. Convergence rather than divergence was order of the day. Starting sometimes during nineteen eighties, *Shari'ah* advisors focused mainly on designing 'Shari'ah-compliant' substitutes for financial products with which market was familiar.

While commenting on Masudul Alam Choudhury's paper (2007), Ariff (2007: 1033) summarizes the position of Islamic banking and finance in a precise and crisp manner. His conclusions are that: (a) elimination of interest has become the be-all and end-all of Islamic finance to the neglect of the other social objectives of Islam; (b) Islamic banking has been instrumental in adding a few more instruments to the global financial market; (c) elimination of interest is more apparent than real, as Islamic financial instruments are 'overtly interest-free' but remain 'covertly interest-based' to the extent that cost of funds and return on deposits are guided by prevailing interest-rate structures in the conventional banking market; (d) Islamic banks have been unwittingly admitting interest through the back door. Chapra (2007: 111) arrives at a similar conclusion when he says that, if Islamic banking and finance do not change their present direction of relying on fixed-return-based modes and various contrivances, people will lose all faith in them and the whole enterprise will suffer a severe setback.

Saleh Kamel, a pioneer Islamic banker, says in his IDB prize-winning speech (1998: 11ff.) that Islamic banks have not moved away from the concept of financial intermediary. This has led to the fact that the preferred modes of investment of Islamic banks are a mix of loan and investment. It is a mix with most of the characteristics of a *riba*-based loan and the flaws of capitalism. The documentation of Islamic banks is very similar to that of *riba*-based banks. As a result, the dominant finances of Islamic banks flow to well-to-do people who have all the guarantees to offer. Islamic banks have not gone into the promised field of the development of Muslim communities. If Islamic banks continue on the present pattern where they do most of their business on the basis of fixed rates of return, they will lose all theoretical and practical justification. Abdul-Rahman (2010: 255) cites the ruling of the Office of the Comptroller of Currency, UK on the application of the United Bank of Kuwait to allow Islamic banking on the basis of *murabaha* and lease-to-own models that these products were the same as interest-based financing. Hasan (2010) argues that the objectives of Islamic finance as envisaged by its pioneers were greater growth, distributional parity and the alleviation of poverty. For this purpose, interest was to be replaced by *musharaka* and *mudaraba*. However, in practice, the structure adopted by Islamic financial institutions was that of the conventional banks, which was not suitable for achieving the objectives the early writers thought of realizing from Islamic finance.

NOTES

1. He also wrote a book: S.A. Irshad, *Interest-free banking* (Karachi: Orient Press of Pakistan, 1964).
2. www.globalislamicfinancemagazine.com.
3. The screening criteria for *Shari'ah* compliance is as follows: (i) the stocks invested in or scrutinized should not involve companies engaging in any forbidden trade; (ii) there should not be an unbearable amount of debt (debt-to-capital ratio under 33 per cent); and (iii) there should not be excessive profit from interest income (non-operation interest income under 5 per cent).
4. For more information on the Dow Jones visit http://www.investaaa.com/.
5. [As in original] 'Eurekahedge is a subscription-only database provider which collates and publishes data on hedge funds, private equity funds and a number of specialist funds including *Shari'ah* compliant ones. Individual share classes are incorporated as a separate entry. Http://www.eurekahedge.com/specialfunds/index.asp.'
6. [As in original] 'Lipper, which is Thomsons Reuters Company, provides a subscription-only service listing conventional funds.'

7.	For the step-by-step detail of the instructions issued by the State Bank of Pakistan, see Zaidi (1991).
8.	For a list of the Islamic modes of finance, see Chapter 17.
9.	Prior to 2005, they were known as special finance houses (SFH).
10.	Wikipedia: Islamic Bank of Britain.
11.	http://imfn.org/.
12.	These figures do not include clients of cooperatives in Indonesia, which were estimated at 80 000 and also exclude statistics about Iran, where a sizeable number of people get help from institutions that provide interest-free loans.
13.	Obaidullah (2008: 25) remarks that the method of *bai' mu'ajjal*, which is the only mode used by the scheme, is in name only, as the basic *Shari'ah* controls to make it distinct from *riba* do not exist in practice. *Bai' mu'ajjal* is only a cover for interest-based lending (ibid.: 26).
14.	Seibel does not mention the name of the bank in his paper.
15.	Lit. good loan. It refers to an interest-free loan.
16.	*Qard* means a loan.
17.	www.akhuwat.org.pk.
18.	www.sbp.org.pk.
19.	For an explanatory note on the issuance of *sukuk* by ECP see Jobst (2008: 112).
20.	www.iifm.net.
21.	For more information visit http://iimm.bnm.gov.my.
22.	See the IFSB home page: www.ifsb.org.
23.	For more information visit www.lmcbahrain.com.
24.	http://www.iirating.com/home.asp.
25.	For example, included in the Islamic family of indices are the broad Dow Jones Islamic Market Index, the Dow Jones Islamic Market US Index, the Dow Jones Islamic Market Technology Index, the Dow Jones Islamic Market Extra Liquid Index, the Dow Jones Islamic Market Canadian Index, the Dow Jones Islamic Market UK Index, the Dow Jones Islamic Market Europe Index, and the Dow Jones Islamic Market Asia/Pacific Index.
26.	http://www.mscibarra.com.
27.	http://digbig.com/5bfdep.
28.	Islamic law of commercial transactions.
29.	For example, on the question of '*tawarruq*' or '*bai' al-inah*'.
30.	Hasan (2009: 96) also confirms the statement.
31.	A collection of *fatawa* issued by various *Shari'ah* boards is available at the ISRA website (http://www.isra.my/).
32.	D.M. Qureshi, Vision table: Questions and answers session. In *Proceedings of the First Pakistan Islamic Banking and Money Market Conference*, 14–15 September 2005, Karachi.
33.	Munawar Iqbal and Philip Molyneux, *Thirty years of Islamic banking: History, performance and prospects* (New York: Palgrave Macmillan, 2005).
34.	Timur Kuran, *Islam and mammon: The economic predicaments of Islamism* (Princeton, NJ: Princeton University Press, 2004).
35.	M.K. Lewis and L.M. al-Gaud, *Islamic banking* (Cheltenham, UK and Northampton, MA, USA: Edward Elgar, 2001).
36.	T.M. Yousef, The murabaha syndrome in Islamic finance: Laws, institutions and policies. In *Politics of Islamic finance*, ed. C.M. Henry and Rodney Wilson (Edinburgh: Edinburgh University Press, 2004).
37.	[As in original] Z. Hasan, Fifty years of Malaysian economic development: Policies and achievements, *Review of Islamic Economics* 11 (2) (2007).
38.	Credit sale with a mark-up.
39.	Lease-purchase agreement.
40.	[As in original] E.G. Kazarian, *Islamic versus traditional banking: Financial innovation in Egypt*. Boulder, CO: Westview Press (1983).

41. He cites Haider Ala Hamoudi, Jurisprudential schizophrenia: On form and function in Islamic finance, *Chicago Journal of International Law* 7 (2007), pp. 605, 606.

42. [As in original] S. Hakim, *Islamic banking; Challenges and corporate governance*, paper presented at the LARIBA 2002 conference, Pasadena, CA, 30 March 2002, retrieved 24 August 2007 from https://www.lariba.com/knowledge-center/articles/pdf/LARIBA%20 2002%20-%20Islamic%20Banking%20-%20Challenges.pdf.

43. The exact mechanics of the Islamic Interbank Market Rate (IIMR), launched in November 2011, are not yet known. It is also too early to make an assessment.

44. Lit. gambling.

45. For example, Islamic financial institutions cannot reprice or resell their *murabaha* financing at a premium or discount at a time of liquidity crunch.

20. A trajectory of legal tricks (*hiyal*)

The journey of Islamic finance in the second half of the last century commenced with the search for an alternative to commercial interest as the basis for banking and finance. Behind this search was the orthodox interpretation that equated interest with *riba* and applied the Qur'anic prohibition to all transactions involving interest. Theoretical literature on the subject pleaded for the adoption of profit–loss sharing (PLS) as the basis for modern banking in the Islamic framework. However, as we have shown in previous chapters, PLS was not an easy concept in practice in banking and finance. Though a large number of Islamic financial institutions sprang up in the short span of three decades and dealt in trillions of dollars yet most of them shied away from PLS.[1] However, pressure from the religious lobby pushed these institutions to adopt methods and procedures that appeared to comply with the *Shari'ah* though they did not adhere to its spirit. The *Shari'ah* supervisory boards (SSBs) helped Islamic financial institutions to devise these methods and procedures. They justified various solutions on the basis of the apparent legitimacy of each segment of the procedure without considering the impact of the transaction as a whole. Incidentally, this type of conciliatory attitude had some mention in Islamic legal literature. In the past, certain scholars had tried to devise mechanisms to give an apparent semblance with the word of the law even though its spirit was defeated. They justified it in the name of legal stratagems (*hiyal*; singular, *hila*). According to Schacht (1964: 78–79):

> *hiyal* . . . can be described, in short, as the use of legal means for extra-legal ends, ends that could not, whether they themselves were legal or illegal, be achieved directly with the means provided by the *Shari'ah*. The 'legal devices' enabled persons who would otherwise, under the pressure of circumstances, have had to act against the provisions of the sacred law, to arrive at the desired result while actually conforming to the letter of the law.

Some scholars accepted the methodology of *hiyal* in good spirit. For example, Saeed (1995: 513) says:

> While it is no secret that *hiyal* was practiced by Muslims with the blessings of many jurists, the schools of law are not in agreement about its permissibility, at least in its most extreme forms, which are used to evade the clear prohibitions

of the *Shari'ah*. The Hanafis and the Shafi'is are the most favourably inclined to accept its legality. Among the Hanafi authorities who wrote works on *hiyal* are Abu Yusuf (d. 182 AH), al-Shaybani (d. 189 AH), and al-Khassaf (d. 261 AH) and among Shafi'is are Muhammad al-Sayrafi (d. 330 AH), Yahya ibn Suraqah al Amiri (d. 416 AH) and Muhammad ibn Husayn al Qazwini (d. 440 AH).[2] The Hanablis and the traditionalists (*ahl al-hadith*) are its most vocal opponents.

The argument, briefly, in support of the *hiyal* is that the use of *hiyal* is an indicator that the person wants to adhere to the *Shari'ah* but is finding it difficult to do so. He or she, therefore, is trying to find a way out without violating its apparent form. However, most of the religious scholars in the past objected to such mechanics. Even some contemporary scholars have objected to the *hiyal* devised by Islamic financial institutions to accommodate interest in a hidden form.

The present chapter will present some of the *hiyal* developed by Islamic financial institutions with the blessing and approval of SSBs. It is not possible to list all *hiyal*, as they are too numerous to be counted and the number is increasing by the day. Our objective is to show that Islamic financial institutions were not able to follow the orthodox interpretation of *riba* in its true spirit. An oft-repeated observation by the religious lobby is that Islamic financial institutions have not followed the injunctions of the *Shari'ah* sincerely and that they should gradually move in that direction. However, they refuse to consider the alternative suggestion that the orthodox interpretation of *riba* that prohibits commercial interest may itself be in need of further review. As we have shown in previous chapters, there are still several unresolved issues in the orthodox interpretation. PLS-based banking is also not practicable. The Muslim intelligentsia have failed to think outside the box. A prime example of that came to light in the case of Pakistan, where the government announced in the early 1980s that interest would be eliminated from all public and private transactions. However, the effort failed badly. We have briefly documented the milestones in this effort elsewhere in this book.[3]

Seen from hindsight, one can observe that the best brains consisting of economists, financial experts and *Shari'ah* scholars from Pakistan engaged themselves in preparing a report issued by the Council of Islamic Ideology (1980). The best judges wrote judgments of the *Shari'ah* Court (Federal Shari'at Court of Pakistan 1991) and the Supreme Court (Supreme Court of Pakistan, Shari'ah Appellate Bench 1999) and the best economists with strong religious commitment presented the *Blueprint* of the IIIE (Tahir, Atiquzzafar, Ali and Waheed 1999). All these efforts clearly professed that the ideal system for replacing interest was PLS. However, all of them acknowledged that PLS had certain inherent weaknesses and practical difficulties. Although they were unanimous in treating all forms of interest as *riba*, yet while finding themselves unequal to the task they proposed several alternatives that concealed interest in some form. They did not recognize that PLS, which all of them considered to be the 'Islamic' alternative, was a human construct and did not have any divine basis. PLS is as much a human solution to the problem of finance as interest is, to the extent that both are human ideas and do not have any divine basis. If we can criticize interest, there is also nothing sacrosanct about PLS. It is amazing when all the best brains were facing a stone wall while moving toward PLS that none of them took a pause to reconsider the definition of *riba*, which incidentally is also a human understanding of the concept. Although they were accommodating interest in the guise of various modes of finance yet they were unwilling to re-examine the definition of *riba*, which could have spared them a lot of unnecessary effort in devising various ruses and stratagems.

Bangladesh, Malaysia, Pakistan, Sudan and Turkey have ultimately settled with a model of a dual banking system: Islamic banking and conventional banking living side by side. It is a clear departure from the earlier enthusiasm for transforming the entire economy on Islamic lines. However, Islamic economists are afraid of Gresham's law working here too. Conventional banking can engulf Islamic banking, as it has certain advantages. It is easy to understand; rights and obligations are clearly defined; it can handle all types of financial needs and for all durations; it has a practice of centuries; and it is supported by a sound regulatory and supervisory apparatus. Islamic banking as developed is still in its infancy and is weak in all these respects; the bank and the client are unsure of results; it cannot handle transactions of various types; it cannot provide viable and profitable investment avenues for savings of financially vulnerable segments of society; and it does not have a well-developed apparatus for supervision and oversight. The central banks do not have satisfactory tools for managing monetary policy within the Islamic framework. Islamic financial institutions do not have recourse to a lender of last resort. To overcome these shortcomings, Islamic banks are forced to use various stratagems. Consequently, Islamic banking has not been able to win the hearts and minds of people even in Muslim countries. For example, in countries where the experiment of dual banking is in vogue, the percentage of people actually dealing with Islamic banks is very low. Whether Islamic economists call it Gresham's law or recognize the limitations of Islamic finance, the fact remains that the efforts to devise a fundamentally different system of finance have not borne fruit in practice.

In the following discussion we shall present a summary of various stratagems and legal tricks devised by Islamic financial institutions to appear to be *Shari'ah*-compliant. A deeper look into these stratagems will show that 'prohibited interest' has been retained intact in some hidden form.

20.1   *MURABAHA* AND ITS VARIATIONS

Murabaha is the most dominant form of financing practised by Islamic financial institutions. Technically, it means selling something on a pre-determined mark-up on cost. Originally, *murabaha* was necessitated by the desire of a buyer to buy something at less than the market price. The buyer would negotiate with the seller to reduce the price and agree to pay a given percentage over the seller's cost. It was generally a cash transaction. But *murabaha* as practised by Islamic financial institutions combines the classical cost-plus (*murabaha*) contract with credit sale (*bai' mu'ajjal*) (Uthmani n.d.-a: 2). *Murabaha* was not a financing contract at all, as the classical jurists did not perceive any situation when the price of the commodity sold on the basis of *murabaha* could be delayed (Nyazee 2009: 12, 29). However, proponents of Islamic finance have commissioned this concept to their service by making it a mode of finance. Its application by Islamic financial institutions is as follows.

The operation of *murabaha* is quite similar to that of credit sale (*bai' mu'ajjal*). In the case of credit sale the bank as seller is not required to disclose the cost to the client (buyer) and can add a mark-up to the price, again not to be disclosed. In the case of *murabaha*, the law requires the bank to disclose the cost and also the rate of mark-up. In both cases the added rate is usually the going rate of interest on capital. In practice, *murabaha* is a paper transaction. The client buys on the bank's behalf with cash from the bank, which sells these goods back to the client immediately, on a deferred term basis, after adding a mark-up to the cost of the goods. In the process, the client gets cash and agrees to repay it with a mark-up in the future. Uthmani (1999-b: 50–51) explains how it is practised in Pakistan:

> What was done was to change the name of interest and replace it by the name of mark-up. The mark-up system as in vogue today has no concern with any real commodity whatsoever. In most cases there is no commodity at all in real sense; if there is any, it is never purchased by the banks nor sold to the customers after acquiring it. In some cases this technique is applied on the basis of buyback arrangement which means that the commodity already owned by the customer is sold by him to the bank and is simultaneously purchased by him from the bank at a higher price which is nothing but to make fun of the original concept. In many cases it is done merely on papers without a genuine commodity to be sold and purchased. Moreover, this technique is applied indiscriminately to all the banking transactions having no regard whether or not they involve a

commodity. The procedure is being applied to all types of finances including financing overhead expenses, payment of bills etc. The net result is that no meaningful change has ever been brought about to the system of interest on the assets side of the banks.

Khan and Bhatti (2008: 111) give a similar account about Pakistan as follows:

> In actual practice, clients were not given the right to refuse the goods after making a promise to purchase them from banks. The State Bank of Pakistan (SBP) allowed banks to include an additional mark-up for 210 days in the original price of the mark-up contract as a cushion against any likely delay or default in the repayment of the loan. If the client repaid the mark-up loan on time, banks returned the extra mark-up amount to him by calling it a 'rebate' for prompt payment or timely payment. If the client delayed the repayment of the mark-up loan but repaid it within 210 days, the banks used to reduce the amount of the rebate proportionately.

Tahir (2009: 68) explains the practice of *murabaha* in the South-East Asian region as follows:

> In the *murabaha* financing . . . the Islamic banks create a similar effect by first appointing the client as agent to buy the thing and then i.e. after the client has acquired the things, complete an offer and acceptance formality to actualize the *murabaha*. Apparently, this is done in order to ensure that Islamic banks sell what they have. It is indeed a very complex arrangement toward compliance with the Prophet's directive on not selling what one does not have. An interesting thing about the *murabaha* financing is that the original seller's invoices are not made in the name of the Islamic bank and the transaction is not shown in the accounts of the Islamic bank as a purchase and a sale. On the whole, apart from documentation, financing under . . . *murabaha* resembles interest-based loan financing.

For further discussion, also see Sairally (2002: 83) and Vogel and Hayes (1998: 8–9).

Beyond this obvious similarity, the *murabaha* contract resembles interest-based finance in other respects as well. For example, in both cases, the bank assesses the creditworthiness of the client; the underlying asset is treated as collateral; the relationship of the client and the bank is that of a debtor–creditor; and in the case of delay or non-payment comparable recourses are available. The Islamic banks have devised various versions of *murabaha* to provide cash loans and finance for imports and to pay profit on deposits, to name a few (Nyazee 2009: 39ff.).

While practising *murabaha*, Islamic financial institutions make sure that all trade risks are transferred to the client. For example, the time period between ownership of the bank and transfer of ownership to the client could be reduced to minutes, if not seconds. The insurance cost of goods can be transferred to the client by raising the mark-up rate. The banks can cover themselves against defective goods by returning the goods to the original seller or by making the client accept them. The banks undertake only the credit risk, which is what conventional banks also undertake. Islamic banks now have juristic approval to charge a mark-up with reference to the market interest rate (El-Gamal 2006: 67). In addition, the banks do not follow the conditions of the contract faithfully. For example, the banks do not follow the fundamental condition of *murabaha*, that is, inform the client about the purchase price (i.e. the cost of funds) and the profit they will make on those funds (i.e. the spread between the two rates of interest).[4] (Also see El-Gamal 2006: 43.)

In practice, Islamic financial institutions make the promise to buy the ordered goods binding on the client to protect themselves against the risk of buying goods which they could not offload. It means that, once the promise to buy becomes binding, the banks do not have any risk in this trade. They shift the entire commercial risk on to the client and earn an assured profit. The final outcome of the transaction is quite similar to lending money on interest. The practice has raised controversy among jurists considering whether the banks can make the promise binding on clients. The strict legal position is that the clients make a promise to buy something from the bank. Legally, they cannot be forced to honour this promise (Uthmani 1999-a: 137). It is only their moral responsibility to honour it. Since this is a commercially weak position and the bank cannot rely on it, some jurists have created space to make the promise binding if the bank has incurred some liability (Sairally 2002: 81). Even this is not acceptable to all banks. Some jurists have suggested that each bank take its own decision whether to make the promise binding or not (Sairally 2002: 82[5]). The fact is that the theoretical basis for *murabaha* in which the client promises to buy something from the bank is weak, and the banks have sought to violate this legal position by making the promises binding. The practice does not adhere to the theory.

In sum, the contract of *murabaha* is a clear case of deviation from the orthodox interpretation of *riba*. *Murabaha* as a financing technique has degenerated into a method of borrowing funds from Islamic financial institutions on the basis of interest under the guise of Islamic legal contracts. The transaction resembles interest-based financing to such an extent that it is difficult to tell one from the other. Several writers have pointed out the similarity of *murabaha* with *riba*-based transactions. For example, Siddiqi (1983-a: 139) says about *murabaha* that 'for all practical purposes this will be as good for the bank as lending on a fixed rate of interest'. (Also see Nyazee 2009: 39.) Some contemporary jurists, notably Taqi Uthmani, have expressed their reservations about *murabaha* as a regular alternative for interest-based financing. They consider it a transitory measure till financing on the basis of *mudaraba* and *musharaka* are firmly established in practice (Uthmani n.d.-a: 7).

20.1.1   Buyback Agreements

A variation of *murabaha* is financing through buyback agreements. The practice of Islamic banks is as follows. A client approaches the bank to get finance to purchase a durable asset like a machine. The bank, after determining the amount involved, buys from the client the machine (which the client also does not have) and pays the sum needed by the client. Immediately, the client buys back the machine from the bank on a deferred payment basis but for a higher price. In this way, the client gets cash with an agreement to repay with an increment in the future. All this happens in one sitting by filling in various forms. It obviously is a ruse to borrow money on interest and tantamount to *bai' al-'inah*. Out of four *Sunni* schools of law, only Shafites accept it as lawful. Following this school, contemporary Malaysian jurists have legitimized it (Nagaoka 2007: 7–8). Dusuki and Abozaid (2007: 155–156) write:

> Perhaps the most controversial product of Islamic banking and finance is *bai' al-'inah* (buyback sale) which is widely practiced in Malaysia. Many financial applications are based on *bai' al-'inah* such as *bai' bi thaman ajil* (deferred cost-plus sale), Islamic credit card (*bai' al-'inah* model), Islamic private debt securities (IPDS) and Islamic overdraft facility. In all these applications the Islamic bank is supposed to act as a trader selling or buying as the word *bai'* suggests, but in reality, we find the Islamic bank merely acting as a financier who provides money without taking any risk and without being involved in the investment process, if any.
>
> *Bai' al-'inah* here is resorted to as a legal device (*hila*) to circumvent *riba*-based financing, but as far as the substance is concerned *bai' al-'inah*-based financing and the conventional *riba*-based financing are the same. They serve exactly the same purpose, and share exactly the same economic substance and consequences, albeit their form may be different.

20.1.2   *Bai' Bithaman 'Ajil* (Deferred Payment Sale)

A slightly different version of *murabaha* is prevalent under the terms of *bai' bithaman 'ajil* (deferred payment sale) or *bai' mu'ajjal* (credit sale). The bank agrees to provide goods and services to a client and receive the price later. While doing so, the bank fixes the price of the goods in such a manner that it includes the profit (or interest) of the bank up front. On paper, however, the bank buys and sells these goods with an increase in the cash price that is commensurate with the period of payment by the client. The bank may also seek collateral to protect its interests. Islamic law allows the bank not to get into the actual buying and selling of goods. The bank can designate the client to do this on its behalf. The bank does not run any commercial risk. However, the bank cannot increase its claim if the client delays the payment beyond the due date. The client cannot claim a rebate if the payment is made earlier than the due date (Tahir *et al.* 1999: 49ff., 69; also Uthmani n.d.-a: 25). At the end of the day, the client gets finance from the bank to purchase goods from the market. The transaction is quite similar to interest-based finance. The only feature that differentiates it from interest-based finance is that the bank cannot increase the financial claim if the client delays the payment. Muslim scholars emphasize this feature to argue that the deal is not exactly similar to interest-based finance (e.g. Chapra 2007-a). However, the banks protect themselves against this risk by inflating the original price for an additional period from the date promised by the client. In Pakistan it is six to seven months. If the client pays on time, the bank gives a rebate for the additional period charged earlier.

Dusuki and Abozaid (2007: 147) explain how it is merely a ruse to hide interest:

> *Bai' bithaman 'ajil* (deferred sales contract) which is widely practiced by Islamic banks in Malaysia and Brunei is an example of such an abuse of sale contract. While *Shari'ah* requires a selling party to hold all liability arising from all defective goods sold based on *khiyar al-'aib*[6] rules, in practice, the Islamic bank holds no such liability. Apparently, the Islamic bank transfers all the risks and liabilities to the customer, thereby leaving the bank with practically no risk to bear while securing profits which are fully guaranteed by way of executing a sale contract i.e. *bai' bithaman 'ajil*.

In brief, the mechanism of credit sale is a method of borrowing funds on interest in a disguised manner.

20.1.3   Flexible-Rate Financing

Murabaha financing requires that the rate of mark-up is fixed once and for all. It introduces a sort of rigidity into the contract, as both parties remain exposed to credit risk should the market interest rate fluctuate during the period of the contract. Classical jurists, however, allowed renegotiation of long-term lease contracts on a monthly basis, subject to the mutual consent of the parties. The technique is applied to contemporary *murabaha* financing, allowing both parties to agree on a different rate of mark-up during the period of the contract at different points of time. However, this exposes both parties to the risk of 'mutual consent' should one of the parties refuse to adjust the rate. To overcome this constraint, contemporary jurists have allowed agreement on a mark-up rate that is flexible *ex ante*, such as LIBOR plus or minus some basis points (El-Gamal 2006: 100). The jurists have taken yet another step toward convergence with contemporary finance.

20.1.4 Applying the Technique of the Un-commissioned Agent (*Fuduli*)

Islamic law requires that the seller must possess the article before selling it (except for *salam* and *istisna'*). The requirement makes it essential for banks to get into the real sector and buy an article before they can sell it under *murabaha*. However, it entails extra cost. To avoid that cost, some banks have invoked the unusual form of sale where an un-commissioned agent (*fuduli*) enters into a sale agreement subject to final approval by the owner of the article.[7] By using this mechanism, a bank assumes the role of un-commissioned agent and sells the article to the client without possessing the article, as the article remains the property of the original seller and the bank acts as the agent of the seller and sells the article.

20.1.5 Islamic Floating Rate Note (IFRN) under *Murabaha*

Iqbal (2002) has proposed the model of an Islamic floating rate note which can substitute for a conventional note for risk-averse investors.

A floating rate note is a fixed-income security used by institutional investors in the conventional interest-based financial system. It is an investment instrument where the rate of interest is not fixed but is determined at the beginning of each coupon period with reference to a pre-agreed index. The objective of the IFRN is to devise a mechanism that provides a stable stream of income to risk-averse investors like pensioners, widows and orphans and with low transaction costs. Such an instrument can be attractive to entrepreneurs as well. The mechanics of the IFRN are as follows.

Suppose a firm requires funds for its working capital. It deals with an investor to obtain funds against an IFRN on the basis of *murabaha*. The investor provides the funds for the purchase of raw material, supplies and so on at a fixed mark-up, and the firm issues the IFRN. At the end of the first period, the firm pays the investor the mark-up and both parties agree to reinvest the original principal. They can also agree to reinvest the original sum as well as the mark-up, which will be tantamount to compounding the mark-up.

Once the basic instrument is developed it can be used for other types of investments such as *ijara, mudaraba, salam, istisna'* and so on. These instruments can be made tradable in the secondary market. To manage the whole system of IFRNs, investment trusts can come into being as financial intermediaries which hold these notes as assets and issue *mudaraba* certificates to collect funds from investors (which will be the liability of the trust fund). The trust funds will buy various types of IFRNs from the primary as well as the secondary market and pass on the profits, after deducting their service charges, to the holders of the *mudaraba* certificates. Since the price of the IFRNs will fluctuate in the secondary market and since the aggregate of the returns flowing from them will also differ, the trust will be able to offer a variable rate to *mudaraba* certificate-holders, very much similar to the holders of units of investment trusts in the conventional market. In this way a floating rate of return will emerge from the pool of IFRNs, which will be channelled to the investors by the trust funds.

A closer look into the mechanics of the proposal will show that it is a roundabout method of earning a rate of return on one's capital, quite similar to that of the conventional system. The only difference is that the proposed system is more complicated and entails untested ground with unknown risks as well as undeveloped infrastructure to regulate and oversee the system. The investor is exposed to higher risks and greater vulnerabilities in these untested waters. It need not be said that, from the *Shari'ah* perspective, it would also be impermissible, as it involves the sale of debt (in particular in the case of *murabaha*, which is a debt agreement).

20.2 *SALAM* AND ITS VARIATIONS

20.2.1 Value-Based *Salam*

Salam is a method of sale practised in agricultural commodities. The farmer agrees to deliver a commodity after harvest at a price that is fixed in the present. The buyer pays the price in full in cash and waits for delivery of the crop in the future. The farmer gets finance immediately. Financing on the basis of *salam* is unanimously acceptable according to all schools of Islamic law. One of the binding conditions of *salam* is that the financier pays the full price of the commodity in advance. The risk in the deal is that the price of the commodity when delivered may go down and the financier is unable to recover its principal or to get the expected return on its capital. Al-Suwailem (2006: 132) has suggested a way out to cover this risk. The contract should fix the value rather than the quantity of the commodity to be delivered. The quantity of the commodity would be determined in light of the prevailing market price at the time of delivery. For example, if the *salam* finance is Rs100 000 for wheat to be delivered after three months, the repayment could be in the form of wheat which would be equal to Rs110000. At the time of delivery, the market price of the wheat will be ascertained and the quantity of wheat for Rs110000 calculated. In this manner, the financier is hedged against possible market fluctuation. In the proposed solution the financier provides Rs100000 and is assured of getting back Rs110000. The rest is only a procedure, which is much more complex and riskier than for a conventional interest-bearing loan.

20.2.2   Parallel *Salam*

In a typical *salam* contract, the financier expects to get the commodity after a certain time. However, it can pose problems of liquidity for the financier who may be keen to realize the amount earlier than the maturity date. For such situations, Al-Suwailem (2006: 135) proposes parallel *salam*. The financier of the original *salam* contract, who is expecting to receive the commodity after some time, can enter into a contract with another party and sell the commodity in a parallel *salam*. The sellers in both contracts are bound by law to deliver on the due date. If the first seller fails, the second seller remains responsible for the delivery. The mechanism does overcome the liquidity problem. However, Al-Suwailem has not clarified whether or not the second buyer can establish another parallel *salam*. If so, then what is the difference between the existing futures market and parallel *salam* contracts? If the answer is in the negative, then we need to specify why it is acceptable for the first buyer to sell something that he or she does not possess but unlawful for the second, third and subsequent buyers.

20.3   LEASE FINANCING (*IJARA*) AND ITS VARIATIONS

20.3.1   The Financing Lease

Islamic financial institutions, with the help of SSBs,[8] have devised the mechanism of the financing lease in which they provide cash to clients to purchase assets. The client simultaneously takes the asset on lease from the bank and agrees to pay rent. The contract is designed in such a manner that the Islamic financial institution transfers most of the business risks to the client while keeping its right to receive a predetermined stream of income in the future. The asset remains the property of the Islamic financial institution but the client uses the asset and pays regular rent (M.A. Khan 1994). When requesting finance the client agrees to accept the specified asset. The client does not have the option to reject the asset or to return it before expiry of the lease term. At the end, the Islamic financial institution only gets back its money with a predetermined increment.

Tahir *et al.* (1999: 54) consider the financing lease to be contrary to Islamic law. They think (ibid.: 67) that Islamic financial institutions should have their own subsidiaries which deal in leasing business. These subsidiaries should deal in machinery and equipment, which business firms can get on lease for a limited period on an operating lease. The idea is perfectly in line with the Islamic legal requirement. But is it also good banking? Will the banks get into this type of business, departing from their usual role as financial intermediaries? Moreover, what will be the method to finance these subsidiaries? How will banks match the maturities of the depositors' funds and the income streams of these subsidiaries? It also raises the broader issue of economic power. Once the banks got into the leasing business in the real sector, smaller firms in this business would not be able to compete with them. Does it match the objectives of the *Shari'ah* over the long run?

20.3.2   Lease Purchase (*Ijara wa Iqtina'*)

A variation of the simple financing lease is the lease purchase agreement (*ijara wa iqtina'*). El-Gamal (2006: 23) illustrates the similarity of lease purchase to interest-based financing as follows:

> The Islamic financial institution buys the financed object, and retains the title through the life of the contract. The customer makes a series of lease payments over a specified period of time, and may have the option at the end to buy the item from the lessor (and owner) at a pre-specified residual value. The period of the lease and the rent payments may be made such that the final payment is only symbolic. It is no secret (at least it should not be a secret) that the Islamic bank or financial institution will take into consideration the same factors when determining the rental payments and residual value that a regular bank would consider. . . . Of course, an implicit 'interest rate' can trivially be calculated from the price, residual value, term of the lease and the lease payment. There is no need to hide this fact, and indeed, the intelligent Muslim customer (as Muslim customers should always be) must be encouraged to 'shop-around' and ensure that the Islamic financial institution is not implicitly charging an interest rate which is not in line with the conventional market. *However, in the final analysis, the difference will be in the form of the contract.*[9]

The mechanics of this deal leave little doubt that it is quite akin to interest-based conventional finance. El-Gamal also agrees about the similarity of the contract with interest-based finance. However, he thinks that in so far as the 'form' of the contract is in accordance with the juridical rules it should be acceptable to the Muslim user of the financial services.

In a typical *ijara wa iqtina'* contract the residual value of the asset or its sale price to the lessee is fixed at the time of signing the contract, but the quality of the asset and market conditions at the end of the contract are unknown at this stage. The lessee, however, undertakes to buy it at a price defined in the contract. It involves uncertainty that borders around the prohibited *gharar*. Moreover, if the lessee is unable to make the lease payment at some stage it loses the payments already made as the price of the asset. The lessor takes back the asset irrespective of the value of the asset at that stage. As a result of this action, the lessee could suffer an undue loss. As compared to a situation where, for example, the lessee had taken an interest-bearing loan, the payments made toward the principal sum of the loan would still be counted in determining the final liability of the lessee. Even simple *ijara* contracts put the lessee in a worse condition as compared to a person who buys an asset with an interest-bearing loan. Suppose, for example, a person takes a five-year interest-bearing loan to buy a car. After two years, if he finds that keeping the car and the loan is uneconomical, he can sell the car in the market and repay the loan. This is not so in the case of *ijara*. *Ijara* finance cannot be terminated prematurely (Visser 2009: 60).

Abu Ghuddah (n.d.-a: 115) raises and answers a question about the legality of the compulsory sale of an asset at the end of the lease term. The way out is that the lessee should promise in the lease contract to purchase the asset on termination of the lease. The lessee should pay a cash guarantee to express the seriousness of this promise. In the case where the lessee fails to honour the promise to purchase the asset, the bank should confiscate the cash guarantee. If, as a result, the bank has to dispose of the asset itself, the bank can recover its loss from the cash guarantee and return the balance, if any, to the lessee. The solution is nothing short of coercion and a forced sale and raises a question about the justification for such a sale in the Islamic law of contracts. Kamali (2007: 8) has another suggestion. The Islamic financial institution should sign two separate contracts with the lessee: the first one to lease the asset and the second one to sell it on termination of the lease. In essence the contract remains the same. The technicality overcomes the legal hitch.

20.3.3   The Floating Lease

In the case of secular inflation, the Islamic financial institution can suffer in real-value terms in the amount of rent if it is fixed for the period of the lease. To protect Islamic financial institutions against this loss, jurists have proposed the solution of floating *ijara*. The contract of *ijara* should provide that the rent will be reviewed after fixed predefined intervals.

20.3.4   Forward *Ijara*[10]

Abu Ghuddah (n.d.) explains the mechanism of forward *ijara* through which the Islamic bank can minimize its risk and yet have a completely fixed rate of return. He defines the contract as follows (p. 6):

> A forward *ijara* contract can be defined as commitment of the lessor to provide a benefit that has been thoroughly described (to the standards required in *salam* sales) such that potential conflict is eliminated, whether the benefit is from an object, such as rental of a car of certain specifications or from a human service, such as tailoring or teaching. It is not a condition that the lessor possesses the benefit when sealing the contract. Rather, the benefit can be fixed at a future date to enable the contractor secure the means of providing it at the appointed time.

The contract has been justified on the analogy of the *salam* contract. Hanafite jurists prohibit this type of contract, while the majority of *Sunni* jurists allow it. The question of whether the payment of rent should be up front or delayed is also controversial (Nassar n.d.: 14). Briefly, the procedure works as follows.

The Islamic financial institution enters into a contract with a builder to lease a building on a certain date in the future at the rate of rent agreed in the present. It is not necessary to pay any advance rent. Simultaneously, the bank enters into a second contract with another client to lease out the same building on a future date at a specified rent. Obviously, the rent in the latter case would be higher than in the former, leaving a margin for the bank. Since both contracts are binding, the risk of a vacancy period (which happens in the case of an operational lease) does not arise. Practically, the bank's risk is reduced to nothing, but it gets a fixed return for acting as an intermediary, which service it provides only once, but the return continues till the two contracts are in force. At the end of the day, it may be more exploitative than a conventional lease where the bank finances the property as well.

Theoretically, forward *ijara* can be applied in medical, educational and other services. Islamic financial institutions also provide medical and educational services to their clients by agreeing to pay for these services up front to hospitals or educational institutions and accepting repayment from clients in instalments later on. In the process, Islamic financial institutions charge a rent for the services provided. It is assumed that these institutions have agreed to provide certain services to the Islamic financial institutions, which are subleasing these services to their clients. Similar arrangement can be made with enterprises providing tourist services for *umra* and *hajj* packages, and so on. All this is legal rigmarole that brings a fixed return to the Islamic financial institutions for the funds they provide to hospitals, educational institutions or tour operators on behalf of their clients. The rest is legal jugglery.

Another application of forward *ijara* is through the securitization of lease benefits. The investors can buy securities issued as a source of income in the form of the rent of a certain property which the lessor will buy with the money collected through the sale of securities. The security-holders are entitled to receive the rent periodically. They can also sell the securities at whatever price they like (Nassar n.d.: 28).

20.3.5 Subleasing

A variation of the finance lease has emerged in which a financial institution leases a property for a specified period and pays its rent to the owner. The financial institution then subleases the property to one or more lessees for limited periods against a rental which is usually higher than the rent paid by the financial institution. It is also possible that a client requests the financial institution to acquire rights of use for it in a certain hotel or apartment building for a specified period. The financial institution acquires these rights and then sells these rights to the client on the basis of *murabaha* to be paid in instalments. The mark-up on the original lease between the owner and the financial institution is the profit of the financial institution (Abu Ghuddah n.d.: 137). How does it differ from the situation where a client obtains finance on interest to pay advance rent and then repays the financial institution with interest later on?

20.4 *MUSHARAKA* AND ITS VARIATIONS

20.4.1 *Musharaka* as a Fixed-Return Contract

Musharaka (partnership) is one of the two primary modes of finance (the other being *mudaraba*) on which an ideal Islamic banking system is justified. Theoretically, in a *musharaka* contract the bank provides part of the capital of a firm and participates in its management in return for a share in profit or loss. However, the banks have devised various schemes to ensure a fixed return on their capital in some kind of clandestine manner. For example, in Pakistan the banks implemented *musharaka* contracts in the following manner (Khan and Bhatti 2008: 113):

a. The client who obtains finance under *musharaka* is allowed to charge a fixed predetermined 'good management fee' as an expense before arriving at the net profit to be shared with the Islamic financial institution. However, the bank has the authority to waive this right or reduce the rate of the fee if the profit declared is not as expected by the bank. If the bank is able to get its 'expected' share, the client is also allowed to keep the 'good management fee'. The mechanism allows the bank to ensure that its share of the profit does not fall below the market interest rate.

b. The central bank prescribes minimum and maximum profit-sharing rates to ensure that the share of the bank remains within the range of the market interest rate. The profit rate is kept variable (to satisfy the religious lobby) but contained within a range. The bank openly uses these rates on a predetermined basis, remaining within the range prescribed by the central bank. Apparently, a range of profit rates replaces the interest rate, but the substance of conventional finance is kept intact.

c. Non-banking financial institutions, such as small business finance corporations, provide in their contracts that they will accept the financial statements of the client if the declared profit is above a certain minimum, but they will have the right to scrutinize the accounts if the profit is less than the minimum limit. That ensures that the clients do not declare profits below the market interest rate.

d. The banks do not pick up losses of the client according to the contract. If the client declares a loss, he or she absorbs it in future profits. The bank does not take any losses. However, if the loss is more than the total capital of the client, the bank shares the residual loss.

20.4.2 Converting *Musharaka Mutaniqsa* (Diminishing Partnership) into Shares

Arbouna and el-Islamy (2008: 193) refer to a technique of converting diminishing partnership into shares of the client company. This can happen as follows. Suppose a company acquires finance on the basis of diminishing partnership (*musharaka mutaniqsa*) and starts repaying profit as well as a part of the principal sum to reduce the share of the bank in the company. At some time, it is unable to continue repaying the bank's share. The company issues shares to the bank equivalent to the value of its outstanding capital. The bank sells the shares on the open market and realizes its principal sum. The practice is similar to the arrangement where a bank lends money against collateral and the client is unable to pay on time. The bank then sells the security, realizes its capital and adjusts it against its claim from the client. The diminishing partnership as discussed above does not remain a partnership in a real sense. It is effectively converted into a loan agreement without saying so.

20.4.3 Third-Party Hedging

Al-Suwailem (2006: 124) suggests an interesting mechanism to hedge against the loss of capital in *musharaka* financing. According to this mechanism, the bank provides capital to a company on the *musharaka* basis. Subsequently, it sells the bulk, say 95 per cent, of its share to a third party on a deferred payment basis at a price that allows it to recover all of its capital while still retaining a small part in the company for sharing profits. The third party pays the bank in instalments while sharing the profit and loss in the company for its share of the capital. In this case, the author asserts that all parties gain. The bank gets back its capital while it still has a right to share the profits on the residual amount that it holds, the third party becomes entitled to profits at a low cost of mark-up, and the company does not incur any debt.

The mechanism is interesting. In the process of making everyone happy, it involves selling a financial stake at a price that is higher than its nominal value. For example, if the bank has invested Rs10 million and it sells capital worth Rs9.5 million for Rs10 million to the third party, is it not a transaction of hidden interest? Secondly, it is complicated. The mechanism requires a third party that is willing to buy the bank's share at a price at which it still expects to make a gain in the transaction. The mechanism does not indicate the implications of any expected loss or the willingness of the bank as well as of the third party to get into this deal in the first place.

20.5 INVESTMENT IN EQUITIES

The most appropriate method of investment from the *Shari'ah* point of view is to buy common stock of joint stock companies. However, in practice, this also poses certain problems. For example, some of the companies may be engaged in unacceptable businesses such as liquor, gambling, pornography, torture equipment and so on. The other problem could be transactions of companies in interest-based finance, either by borrowing from banks or by investing surplus funds on interest. These problems made *Shari'ah* scholars think more deeply about investment in the equity of companies. The immediate reaction was that there should be some mechanism to distinguish companies in which a Muslim can invest from those in which he or she cannot. This gave rise to the need to define filters for deciding acceptable companies. While doing so, *Shari'ah* scholars have made several compromises. El-Gamal (2000: 28–29) summarizes the compromises as follows:

The following is the list of rules/compromises used by DJII [Dow Jones Islamic Index]:

1. Exclude companies with a debt to total asset ratio of 33% or more.
2. Exclude companies with 'impure plus non-operating interest income' to revenue ratio of 5% or more.
3. Exclude companies with accounts receivable to total assets ratio of 45% or more.

Those rules are virtually identical to those used by other indices, e.g. the FTSE Global Islamic Index Series, http://www.ftse.com/ebox/TII.html. However, I can point out that the cut-off-rules on financial ratios used in this area seem extremely arbitrary, and potentially rigid. In this regard, even if they are indeed justified, it is very unlikely that fixed cut-off ratios will be appropriate for all circumstances and all pools of equities!

20.6 ISLAMIC PAWNBROKING

Habib Ahmed (2011: 204) explains the mechanism of the Islamic pawnbroking scheme of Bank Rakyat Malaysia (BRM). The bank provides loans for up to six months against gold jewellery. Generally, the value of the loan is between 65 and 70 per cent of the assessed value of the jewellery. The bank charges safekeeping charges, which are about 13.8 per cent per annum. The fact that the safekeeping fee is related to the value of the loan and the period for which the loan remains outstanding leaves little distinction between the fee and an interest rate. In the case of the loan not being returned on time, the bank waits for about seven months and then auctions the gold. The price obtained is adjusted against the bank claim and the balance, if any, is given to the client. Dusuki and Abozaid (2007: 148) write:

> In this transaction, the Islamic bank will provide its customer with a so called benevolent loan on condition that the latter provides a *rahn*; e.g. valuable jewellery to be kept by the bank as collateral; however, the problem arises when the Islamic bank charges this customer the custodianship fee of this jewellery. The amount of this charge is subject to the amount of the loan and, in practice, equivalent to the bank rate of profit.

20.7 THE OVERDRAFT AND ITS VARIATIONS

20.7.1 Overdraft on Current Accounts

Like conventional banks, Islamic banks also accept current account deposits and do not pay interest on them. The problem of overdraft is, however, quite tricky. In principle, there cannot be any overdraft, as the Islamic bank will not be able to charge any interest on such amounts. Some banks, however, allow it for a fixed fee (Visser 2009: 83). A fixed charge on overdraft is open to misuse from both sides. The client may delay repayment without any additional charge and thus have a free ride. Alternatively, the bank may charge a fee that is higher than the conventional interest rate.

Conventional banks provide short-term finance by allowing the client a limit for the overdraft. Of course, the facility is interest-based. In Islamic finance, it cannot be handled in so simple a manner. Islamic financial institutions have devised certain ways to deal with this as stated below:

a. *Mudaraba*-**based facility:** The client gets finance on the basis of *mudaraba* on the conditions that: (i) if the profit is lower than the expected profit (specified in a pre-finance feasibility study submitted by the client), the client will purchase the *mudaraba* assets at a pre-specified price (usually with a mark-up); (ii) if the actual profit is higher than the expected profit, the bank will give a bonus to the client to restrict its own share to the expected profit. Thus the bank is assured of a fixed return at the going market interest rate as in conventional finance (Habib Ahmed 2011: 174).

b. *Ijara*-**based facility:** The client presents a fixed asset to the bank. The value of the asset is split into shares of equal value. For example, the client's building, with a value of Rs10 million, is split into 100 shares of Rs100000 each. When the client requires the overdraft, it sells shares of its fixed assets equal to the value of the overdraft to the bank. For example, it requires an overdraft of Rs1 million. Ten shares of the building will be sold to the bank. The bank will lease this part of the building back to the client at a specified rent. Once the contract is over, the bank sells back the shares of the asset to the client at the previous price. For the period of the overdraft, the bank receives rent for the portion of the asset owned by it (Habib Ahmed 2011: 175).

c. **Diminishing partnership facility:** The bank and the client join in a partnership agreement to own an asset. When the client withdraws funds, it is assumed that the bank is selling part of the asset to the client. The client pays rent to the bank on the share of the asset thus purchased. Once the contract period is over, the partnership is dissolved (Habib Ahmed 2011: 175).

d. *Tawarruq*-**based facility:** The bank creates a debt against the client through *tawarruq* (which includes the principal sum plus mark-up). The client is allowed to overdraw from its normal current account by linking the debt with the current account. For example, a client requires an overdraft limit of Rs1 million, and the rate of mark-up is 10 per cent. A debt of Rs1.1 million will be created. The client will be allowed to overdraw up to Rs1 million and repay Rs1.1 million. The actual charges for the overdraft will be determined with reference to the actual use of the limit. For example, if the overdraft used is half of the limit, the bank will give a rebate to the client for the other half that has not been used (Habib Ahmed 2011: 175).

It is obvious that all these methods are indirect means to provide an overdraft facility on interest.

20.8   *SUKUK* AND THEIR VARIATIONS

In conventional finance if a business firm requires medium-term or long-term finance, it can issue debentures with a fixed rate of interest. However, since the orthodox interpretation disallows interest business firms had to find a solution for medium- and long-term financing in the Islamic framework. The most popular method for raising finance adopted by Islamic firms is issuance of medium-term and long-term certificates (*sukuk*) as the price of a real asset. The *sukuk*-holders are entitled to receive lease money on the asset periodically, which is considered legitimate as compared to interest on debentures that is received for merely providing the finance, not backed by any asset. Actually, conventional finance securities are also backed by assets, but mostly the assets are debts and receivables, which are not accepted as a legitimate base for earning income in the *Shari'ah* framework. Balala (2011: 32) delineates the difference between *sukuk* and conventional finance debt securities as follows:

> *Sukuk* are even distinguished from their conventional asset-backed securities (ABS) counterparts in that conventional ABS may have as their underlying assets different types of loans,[11] all of which are interest bearing and, therefore, may make the product fundamentally different from *sukuk*,[12] and given that debts are not deemed proprietary under the *Shari'ah*, they are not legally permissible securities. The key distinction, therefore, between Islamic finance and conventional finance is not whether the finance is asset backed or not but rather the Islamic finance does not yet recognize debt rights (receivables) as proprietary whilst conventional finance does.

In practice, a special purpose vehicle (SPV) manages the process of issuing certificates, and collecting and distributing the lease money among the *sukuk*-holders. The SPV issues a guarantee, out of sheer benevolence, to the *sukuk*-holders to return the principal sum in full. Since the

guarantee is issued by the SPV, an independent entity, and not the originator, it is considered lawful in the *Shari'ah* parlance. By making the SPV
the guarantor and avoiding issuance of a guarantee directly, the originator
complies with the *Shari'ah* regulation that prohibits a guarantee of the
full repayment of the invested funds. Although intrinsically the *sukuk* are
quite similar to conventional bonds, splitting the whole deal into three
segments makes it comply with the *Shari'ah* apparently. Yean (2009: 4)
reports:

> According to Moody's report,[13] many *sukuk* structures applied have been
> effectively 'reduced' to a form that is identical to conventional unsecured bond.
> Most 'asset-based' *sukuk* may have the 'form' of 'asset-backed' *sukuk*, but not
> in substance. In other words, while most *sukuk* have assets in their structures,
> they were only considered as 'asset-backed' or 'asset-secured' if key securitiza-
> tion elements are present to ensure that holders enjoy beneficial title and realiz-
> able security over the assets and associated cash flows.[14]

Theoretically, *sukuk* have justification in the *Shari'ah*. However, since
the issuance of *sukuk* and their subsequent sale and purchase involve
several risks, Islamic financial institutions have devised several methods
to ensure that the risks are transferred to third parties and they earn a
fixed return on their capital, very much like interest income on conventional finance. Dusuki and Mokhtar (2010) assess that out of 560 *sukuk*
issues only 11 qualify as asset-backed and thus strictly according to the
Shari'ah requirement. That comes to only 2 per cent of total *sukuk* issues.
AAOIFI also took notice of the situation and issued a clarification in
March 2008. McMillen (2008: 740ff.) has discussed in detail the AAOIFI
Sukuk Clarification. The Clarification addresses several concerns relating to disclosure, tradability, regular payments as a percentage of capital
value, projected payments to *sukuk*-holders, setting aside profits for
future payments at equal rates, guarantee of principal, nature of assets
valid for investment, possession and disposition of assets, and so on. The
Clarification is an attempt by AAOIFI to regulate the *Shari'ah* boards in
their process of *sukuk* approvals and to ensure that rigorous standards,
Shari'ah-compliant in fact and not just in name, are applied.

In the following discussion we shall discuss various methods adopted by
Islamic financial institutions to ensure that they get a fixed predetermined
income stream on the funds deployed through the sale of *sukuk*.

20.8.1 Substitution of the Original Asset

Theoretically, the distinctive feature of the *sukuk* is that they are backed
by a real asset. In practice, the originator agrees with the issuer that at any

time the originator will have the option to substitute the underlying asset with another asset of equivalent value. The need for this arises from the fact that assets which can be made the basis for issuing *sukuk* are in limited supply and the originator may require the same asset for further lots of *sukuk* to be issued. Once the originator exercises the option to substitute the underlying asset, the issuer is obliged to accept the second asset and release the previous one. The originator can then use the first asset for issuing another lot of *sukuk*. The original concept that a specific asset, which is expected to bring a certain amount of rent, backs the *sukuk* is replaced by a concept of any asset. The original asset, supposedly having a higher rental value, is reused to issue further lots of *sukuk*. Since the rate of rent is also linked to LIBOR, it hardly matters to the originator, issuer and *sukuk*-holders as to which asset is underlying the issue. Thus the whole concept of *sukuk* being backed by a specified asset becomes perfunctory (al-Amine 2008: 10–11).

20.8.2   Return on *Ijara Sukuk* Linked to LIBOR

In theory, *ijara sukuk* are issued by purchasing a property and then leasing it to third parties. The lease income is to be distributed among the *sukuk*-holders. In practice, the return on *ijara sukuk* is linked to LIBOR and not to the rental value of the underlying asset.[15] Thus if in a locality where the *sukuk*-related property is located the rents are going up but the interest rates are going down, the return to the *sukuk*-holders also goes down, although in theory they should be getting a better return. In this manner, the whole exercise of issuing *sukuk* and relating it to the real sector becomes a farce (al-Amine 2008: 8).

Jabeen and Khan (2008: 75–77) illustrate the issuance of *ijara sukuk* by the Water and Power Development Authority (WAPDA) of Pakistan in 2006. The *sukuk* were issued for Rs8 billion for seven years at a floating rate of six-month KIBOR[16] plus 35 basis points with the sovereign guarantee of the government. The capital was raised to strengthen the capacity of the Mangla power station by installing new turbines. On the face of it the *sukuk* substituted the fixed interest rate with a floating *ijara* rate of KIBOR plus 35 basis points and made it appear compliant with the *Shari'ah*. But in actual practice it did not apply the spirit of the *Shari'ah* in determining the rate of return on the capital. The *ijara* rate had no relationship with the actual return on capital. If, for example, the actual return on capital by WAPDA was less than the contractual *ijara* rate, the difference was to be met by subsidy from the government, which would be a burden on the taxpayer, thus defeating the objectives of the *Shari'ah*. The fact is that the whole mechanism of issuing *sukuk* and making them look *Shari'ah*-compliant was nothing but a stratagem to raise capital on interest but under a different garb. (Also see Tahir 2009: 69.)

20.8.3   The Secondary Market for *Ijara Sukuk*

Can *ijara sukuk* be sold at a price different from the face value? Contemporary Muslim jurists think it is possible to do so, as each certificate represents a certain portion of the property that the holder of the certificate owns. While selling that portion of the property, the price could be more or less than the face value of the certificate (McMillen 2008: 750). The answer satisfies the legal requirement of the *Shari'ah*. However, it makes the *sukuk* look quite similar to conventional bonds which can be bought and sold on the secondary market. With reference to the question that the *ijara sukuk* have a fixed rate, how could they operate in the secondary market where rates fluctuate? Kamali (2007: 17) provides the answer as follows:

> Until a few years ago, floating rate *ijara* was not seen to be *Shari'ah*-compliant as it was thought that the originator could only guarantee rents or returns or fixed return on underlying assets. But fixed rate *sukuk* face many market risks. To match the market requirement of *sukuk* to be a floating rate on one hand, and the *Shari'ah* requirement of rents to be fixed rate on the other, a solution was found, which was to base the *ijara* bonds on a master *ijara* agreement with several subordinate *ijara* agreements. In the subordinate *ijara* contracts the rents were revised semi-annually in accordance with the market benchmark. This method ensured that the rent was fixed for six months and floating at the same time. Major *ijara* bond issues in the Middle East, Gulf and Malaysia are based on this variant. This method abated, partially at least, the market risks concerning the fixed rate *ijara* bonds.[17]

The method creates conditions in which debt can be traded at any price. This is an obvious departure from the generally accepted position in the *Shari'ah* that debts cannot be traded except at face value.

20.8.4   *Musharaka Sukuk*

Musharaka sukuk are quite similar to *ijara sukuk*. The originator contributes capital in the form of land, building, vehicles and so on, and the special purpose vehicle, fully owned by the originator and created for this very purpose, contributes cash collected from the sale of the *sukuk*. The profit is shared in agreed ratios. The loss is shared according to the ratio of capital contributions between the SPV and the originator. To this extent the arrangement is distinct from interest-based bonds. However, it is also provided in the contract between the SPV and the originator that the latter will gradually purchase a share of the SPV (or will purchase at the maturity date) at the original price which will be paid to the *sukuk*-holders as the principal sum of their investment. Thus the return of the original price to the *sukuk*-holders is guaranteed. This last point transforms the entire arrangement into an interest-based bond deal (al-Amine 2008: 14).

A variation of the *musharaka sukuk* is as follows. The entrepreneur (usually a company) that needs funds forms a joint venture (*musharaka*) with a bank, which agrees to provide the funds. The equity interests of the *musharaka* (called *hissas* or *sukuk*) are sold to the bank for cash at face value. Subsequently, the entrepreneur purchases the shares of the bank on the basis of *murabaha* at a price higher than the face value but to be paid on a deferred basis. As the entrepreneur pays the price of the shares held by the bank, it becomes the owner of the equity capital of the *musharaka* to that extent. The process continues until the entrepreneur purchases all the shares of the bank. The *musharaka* comes to an end at that point (McMillen 2008: 767). The structure is simple. There are two contracts: *musharaka* and *murabaha*. Even conventional banks can join hands in the *musharaka* along with the Islamic bank. However, the whole arrangement is quite similar to providing finance on the basis of interest. The banks get a fixed return as a mark-up on the face value of the shares. The entrepreneur pays the price of the shares on a deferred basis. Thus it gets long-term funding at a cost. Except for the legal terms, there is no difference between this arrangement and interest-based borrowing from conventional banks.

Another mechanism specifies a hurdle rate (or fixed amount), and any earnings above that are paid to the manager/obligor as an incentive. If the earnings are lower than the hurdle rate, various types of arrangements protect the profit share of the investor. These include income-smoothing reserves, a borrowing facility from the obligor, advances to be adjusted against future payments, and so on. In brief, the whole arrangement boils down to a fixed rate of return to the investor, but the name used is *musharaka* or *mudaraba sukuk* (S.S. Ali 2008: 10).

20.8.5   Tricks in *Mudaraba* and *Musharaka Sukuk*

Dusuki (2010) has documented various tricks followed by the Islamic financial institutions in issuing *mudaraba* and *musharaka sukuk*. These tricks aim at guaranteeing the principal sum and a constant stream of income on the *sukuk* for the provider of the funds. The tricks are as follows:

a.   **Liquidity facility arrangement:** According to this arrangement the originator guarantees that the *sukuk*-holders will get income from the

sukuk. Should there be a shortfall in the actual profits the originator undertakes to make up the shortfall from its own resources. For
example, if the expected return on the *sukuk* is 7 per cent and the
actual return is only 5 per cent, the originator will contribute 2 per
cent to ensure that the *sukuk*-holders get the promised return.

b. **Purchase undertaking on a fixed formula:** According to this arrangement, the originator guarantees the principal sum plus accrued profits
at face value at the time of maturity or when there is a default. For
example, if the expected rate of return is 7 per cent and the maturity
date is five years, the originator guarantees to buy the *sukuk* at face
value plus accrued profit at the expected rate of 7 per cent for five
years on maturity.

c. **Capping of profit:** The *sukuk*-holder pays back any excess of the actual
return over the expected return to the originator. For example, if the
expected rate of return is 7 per cent and the actual rate of return is 10
per cent, the *sukuk*-holder will accept only 7 per cent and forgo 3 per
cent in favour of the originator as a good management fee.

20.8.6   *Bai' Bithaman 'Ajil (BBA) or Murabaha Sukuk*

The issuer of the *sukuk* collects money from investors and sells an asset at
a predetermined price. The issuer promises to buy back the asset from the
investor in the future at a predetermined price at a profit. The issuer gets
immediate cash against the promise to buy back the asset, which creates
an obligation to be released over an agreed period (Iqbal and Mirakhor
2008: 184). As these *sukuk* are purely debt instruments, they cannot be
traded in the secondary market except at the original price. However,
Malaysian scholars have permitted their sale at a price other than the
original price, which makes them, for all practical purposes, conventional
interest-bearing bonds (Visser 2009: 65).

20.8.7   Term Finance Certificates

The banks in Pakistan issue term finance certificates (TFCs) to substitute
for the debentures of conventional finance. Client enterprises issue TFCs
to obtain finance from banks at a mark-up that includes a safety margin
for realizing the expected rate should the client fail to repay on time.
For example, if the market rate of interest is 15 per cent, the TFCs may
be issued at 22 per cent. If the client repays on time, the bank will give
a rebate of 7 percentage points to match the cost of the TFCs with the
market rate of interest. The only difference between conventional finance
and TFCs is that there is no mark-up on mark-up, in the latter case,

should the client delay the payment beyond the due date (M.A. Khan 1994).

20.8.8 Participation Papers

Since 1993, Iran has been issuing participation papers (PPs) to finance specific investment projects. A credit committee determines the guar anteed minimum rate to be paid to the investor after due diligence and analysis. The borrower may pay a higher return, depending upon its own profits. However, the guaranteed minimum has to be paid in any case. Government bodies, religious foundations and private sector enterprises issued five PPs in 1995–97 for terms ranging from 2.5 to 5 years and set a minimum return. The purchaser can resell the PP to the agent bank at face value plus accrued return. The bank is expected to resell the bond at face value less accrued return to the public on demand. No fee is charged for these secondary market transactions. The minimum return is generally kept slightly above the bank deposit rate with similar terms to ensure marketability and to compensate for a 5 per cent tax applied to the return from PPs but which is not applied to earnings from bank deposits (Sundararajan, Marston and Shabsigh 1998: 21).

20.8.9 Overall Assessment on *Sukuk*

Several authors have criticized the mechanism of *sukuk*. Briefly, their argument is that, in practice, it is difficult to differentiate between interest-based debentures and Islamic *sukuk*. We shall present only a few comments to illustrate the point.

M.T. Uthmani (2008: 4, 13), an authority on Islamic finance, laments as follows:

> virtually all of the *sukuk* issued today guarantee the return of principal to the *sukuk*-holders at maturity, in exactly the same way as conventional bonds. This is accomplished by means of a binding promise from either the issuer or the manager to repurchase the assets represented by the *sukuk* at the stated price at which these were originally purchased by the *sukuk*-holders at the beginning of the process, regardless of their true or market value at maturity. . . .
>
> Then, by these complex mechanisms, *sukuk* are able to take on the same characteristics as conventional, interest-bearing bonds since they do not return to investors more than a fixed percentage of the principal, based on interest rates, while guaranteeing the return of investors' principal at maturity. . . .
>
> However, if we consider the matter from the perspective of the higher purposes of Islamic law or the objectives of Islamic economics, then *sukuk* in which are to be found nearly all of the characteristics of conventional bonds are inimical in every way to these higher purposes and objectives. The noble objective

for which *riba* was prohibited is the equitable distribution among partners of revenues from commercial and industrial enterprises. The mechanisms used in *sukuk* today, however, strike at the foundations of these objectives and render the *sukuk* exactly the same as conventional bonds in terms of their economic results.

The above opinion was widely reported in the international press. *The Economist*, London (10 March 2008) reported as follows:

> It [the debate] was sparked by chairman of the board of scholars at the Bahrain-based Accounting and Auditing Organization for Islamic Financial Institutions, Sheikh Mohammed Taqi Uthmani, who said in November that some 85% of *sukuk* issues in the Gulf Cooperation Council (GCC) member states failed to comply with *shari'ah* principles owing to the repurchase undertaking attached to the notes. This entails the borrower guaranteeing repayment of the securities at face value on maturity or in the event of default – violating, according to Sheikh Mohammed, the risk and profit-sharing requirement.

(Also see Yean 2009: 9–10.)

M.N. Siddiqi, the founding father of Islamic economics and finance, writes (2006: 13):

> [T]he whole procedure [is] akin to lending a sum of money for an annual payment till the capital is paid back. With an asset in between, fixed or variable return *sukuk* (of the type currently in practice) replicate the conventional bond based on lending and borrowing relationships. The fact that the paper results from a series of distinct but stitched together contracts of sale and lease makes a difference in law. But it is hardly of any effect in economics. The economic role of *sukuk* would be similar to that of conventional bonds. The difference in economic consequences, if any, has to come from involvement of real assets in the process.

20.9   *TAWARRUQ* AND ITS VARIATIONS

Business firms require finance for working capital needs. In conventional finance it is possible to get loans on interest for any duration. However, in the case of Islamic finance, there is no easy way to do so. Clients cannot get into *murabaha*, as they do not need to buy anything immediately. They cannot adopt *ijara* (leasing), as they do not require any fixed asset. They cannot adopt *salam* and *istisna'* techniques either, because these techniques are not relevant for working capital needs. They require cash to meet various immediate requirements. Islamic financial institutions have commissioned the classical concept of *tawarruq* to their service to provide short-term finance. The technical definition of *tawarruq* given by Al-Haddad (n.d.: 2–3) is as follows:

> *Tawarruq* means to purchase a commodity at deferred price, either by nego-tiation or *murabaha*, and then sell the commodity to a third party, in order to obtain liquidity. In this sense, *tawarruq* is a mutual trade, because there is no difference between buying at cash and selling at cash or deferred price. Moreover, there is no difference between buying at deferred and selling at cash or deferred price.

While Malaysia does not use *tawarruq*, the Islamic financial institutions in Saudi Arabia, the UAE and other GCC countries practise it quite exten-sively for extending cash to clients. The mechanism is as follows. Suppose a client wants to have cash worth $5000 and the bank wants to charge interest at 9 per cent. The bank would buy platinum worth $5000 from a dealer and transfer it to the client at $5450 on a deferred payment basis. The client would immediately sell back the platinum to the bank at $5000 and get cash. The client gets the cash. The platinum goes back to the bank, which returns it to the dealer. In the process, the bank earns interest at 9 per cent from the client for extending the $5000 cash. In practice, the bank need not contact the platinum dealer. The mechanism has become simpler than this, as explained below by Siddiqi (2006: 15–16):

> The client approaches the Islamic financial institution with a wish and col-lateral and comes back with the desired cash after signing a number of papers. One signature would attest his or her purchase on credit, through the agency of Islamic financial institution, a motor vehicle or a certain quantity of precious metal. A second signature will assign the Islamic financial institution the task of selling that same vehicle or metal on behalf of the client. The third signature will witness that sale has been affected and the proceeds handed over to the client. As we observed in case of a certain type of *sukuk*, it is money obtained now for more money to be paid later. The real asset involved in the process is no more than a dummy. In actual practice too, the same asset facilitates numerous such transactions with no depreciation suffered.

Several contemporary jurists have questioned the legality of *tawar-ruq*. M.T. Uthmani (n.d.: 15ff.) has expressed his reservations about the legality of *tawarruq*. He thinks that the contemporary practice of *tawar-ruq* is nothing but lending on interest. Regarding *tawarruq* through the international stock exchange, he says: '*Tawarruq* carried out through international stock exchange markets is vulnerable to many violations, because of the loss of Islamic legal conditions for the validity of the con-tract' (ibid.: 26). Al-Haddad (n.d.: 6) argues that, although *tawarruq* is a legal device (*hila*), yet it is lawful, as it helps people to overcome certain difficulties in everyday life. One common difficulty is that a person may be hard pressed financially and unable to get an interest-free loan. He can resort to *tawarruq* to overcome this difficulty. However, Al-Haddad thinks that *tawarruq* as practised by Islamic financial institutions is not permissible (ibid.: 13, 20) because: the commodity is not actually specified and possessed; the seller is financier, agent for sale, agent for holding the commodity, and agent for taking the price all at the same time; and the mark-up on the price of the commodity is determined by the market interest rate. El-Gamal (2007: 12) reports two legal opinions issued by the Fiqh Council of the Muslim World League. The first opinion, issued in 1998, allowed *tawarruq*, but the second, issued in 2003, disallowed it. However, Islamic financial institutions mainly followed the first opinion. The OIC Islamic Fiqh Academy, in its 19th session held in Sharjah, United Arab Emirates in April 2009, reiterated its ban on organized *tawarruq*, because simultaneous transactions occur between the financier and the *mustawriq*[18] (customer or an agent of the customer), whether it is done explicitly or implicitly or based on common practice, in exchange for a financial obligation.[19]

Bouheraoua (n.d.: 30ff.) summarizes all the juristic arguments against the permissibility of *tawarruq*. Beside a purely legal case against *tawarruq*, he also mentions that the cost of funds in this case is higher than for interest-bearing loans for similar durations because of the multiplicity of contracts and legal fees. In terms of exploitation, it is even worse than the interest-bearing loans of conventional banks. (Also see Al-Suwailem 2009.)

Siddiqi (2009-a: 228) laments that, despite the fact that the distinctive feature of Islamic finance is to keep the financial structure aligned with the real sector, in practice there is a superactive market in *tawarruq*. However, he does not delve deeper into the question: why has this happened? What compulsions have led the players of Islamic finance to adopt *tawarruq* as a financial instrument? An answer to this question would lead us to conclude that Islamic financial theory has yet to find a solution for the working capital cash facility. The techniques and stratagems for covering up interest under various modes such as *murabaha*, *salam*, *istisna'* and so on cannot work where a client requires cash for a short duration. *Tawarruq* is an answer to that. Until a truly Islamic solution is presented, Islamic financial institutions will perforce adopt *tawarruq* or something similar to that to meet the working capital cash needs of their clients. Since most of the contemporary scholars have declared it to be unlawful the question of short-term finance remains unresolved. Salman Khan (2010) has faced this question. He suggests that, if *tawarruq* is phased out as non-compliant with the *Shari'ah*, then the need for cash advances may be met through a contract of *salam*. Another suggestion by him is that mini-*mudaraba* and -*musharaka* projects may be presented by the client and the bank agrees to finance those projects. These suggestions look good and acceptable on paper. However, whether they will find favour with the banks remains to be explored.

20.9.1   *Tawarruq* as a Proxy for Term Deposits

Islamic financial institutions also practise *tawarruq* to substitute for the term deposits of conventional banks. The procedure is as follows. Suppose a customer has Rs1 million that he wants to deposit with the bank and earn some return on it. He approaches the bank with the money. The bank buys a commodity with the money for cash on behalf of the client. Once the client owns the commodity, the bank buys that commodity from the client at a higher price (say Rs1.1 million) on credit to be paid after, say, one year. The bank then sells the commodity in the market for Rs1 million. The transaction is variously known as 'inverse *murabaha*', 'reverse *tawarruq*', 'proxy investment' or 'direct investment'. The net result of the transaction is that the bank gets cash for a fixed period and the client gets a return on that cash after the agreed period. The whole process of buying and selling the commodity is done on paper and not in the real market. It is difficult to tell the difference between the above procedure and term deposits of conventional banks. Al-Suwailem (2009: 37ff.) has documented the legal decrees of various jurists condemning this type of transaction and declaring it a ruse to hide *riba*. The most prominent of these opinions is the legal edict of the Fiqh Academy of the OIC resolution passed in its 17th session at Makkah (November 2007).[20]

20.9.2   *Tawarruq* as a Tool for Foreign Exchange Swaps

Islamic financial institutions face similar risks from foreign exchange fluctuations as conventional banks, which minimize the risk by foreign exchange swaps. The mechanism for the conventional swap involves two transactions. The first is an exchange transaction at the spot rate and the other is the reverse of this transaction at a forward rate in the future. For example, if a Pakistani bank (A) has Rs85 million and wants to buy dollars at a spot rate of $1 equal to Rs85, it will change Pakistan rupees for 1 million dollars from a US bank (B). Simultaneously, in another contract the two banks agree to reverse the above transaction at a future date, say in one year's time, and the forward rate is Rs87 for a dollar. After one year, bank A will pay back $977011 (85000000/87) and get its Rs 85 million back from bank B. Since the *Shari'ah* does not allow a forward contract in monetary exchange, Muslim scholars have deployed the concept of *tawarruq* to handle the situation. Dusuki (2009) has explained the mechanism as follows:

a. A, a business firm, approaches bank B, to convert Rs85 million at the spot rate and reconvert the sum at a forward rate after one year, but in accordance with the *Shari'ah*.
b. The bank arranges for A to purchase a commodity, say oil, worth $1 million, at Rs85 = $1, through a broker.
c. A pays Rs85 million as the price of the oil in cash.
d. B buys the oil from A for Rs87 million credit payable after one year.
e. B sells the oil to the same or another broker for Rs85 million cash.
f. B changes Rs85 million into dollars at the spot rate of $1 = Rs85. With $1 million B buys oil from the said broker.
g. B sells the oil to A for $1 023 529 ($1 = Rs87) at the forward rate, payable after one year.
h. A sells the oil to the broker for $1 million.
i. In the process A changes Rs85 million to $1 million at the spot rate. It will also earn Rs2 million as profit from the bank (Rs87 million − Rs85 million) after one year. Bank B pays $1 million but will get back $1 023 529 and earn a profit of $23 529 on $1 million invested.

In summary, A was able to get $1 million for its Rs85 million at the spot rate but was able to reverse the transaction after one year at the forward rate of Rs87 for a dollar. After one year, A was able to sell the dollars it bought a year ago at a pre-fixed price, irrespective of the spot rate of the dollar at that time. This is exactly what happens in the case of a conventional swap transaction. The involvement of commodity purchase and sale only adds to the cost and complexity of the transaction.

Dusuki (2009) also mentions a variant of the foreign exchange swap through *waa'd* (promise), which has been declared binding by Saudi *Shari'ah* scholars. According to this mode, the investor and the banker promise to exchange currencies at the spot rate now and reverse the transaction in the future at a forward rate. Since it is only a promise, it has been accepted as permissible. But, through another edict, this promise has been made obligatory, overcoming the original prohibition on forward contracts in the exchange of currencies. Dusuki (2009: 17) also quotes AAOIFI Resolution 25, which allows the amalgamation of more than one contract into one if all the contracts are permissible independently. Thus the legal hurdle is removed by the AAOIFI. But most of the *Shari'ah* supervisory boards of the Islamic financial institutions levy strict conditions to regulate the swap of currencies. There is no evidence that Islamic financial institutions actually adhere to these conditions or whether they are mere paper documents to protect the integrity of the *Shari'ah* boards.

20.9.3 Hedging against Currency Risk

The Islamic bank may provide *murabaha* finance in euros, but the capital of the bank is in US dollars. The bank will want to take back the money in US dollars. However, during the course of time, the dollar–euro rates may move adversely for the Islamic bank. Al-Suwailem (2006: 130) suggests a way out of this difficulty. To overcome such loss, the Islamic bank may require the client to provide a bank guarantee from a conventional bank securing its amount in US dollars. The conventional bank may issue such a guarantee for a fee or on the basis of interest. The cost of this finance will be embedded into the *murabaha* transaction of the Islamic bank. Again, this is only hiding interest behind the veil of the *murabaha* price.

20.10   *SHARI'AH* CONVERSION TECHNOLOGY

DeLorenzo (2007) has described and criticized strongly a stratagem by which some Islamic banks have opened a back door for un-Islamic business with the approval of *Shari'ah* boards. A gist of his paper is given below.

The *Shari'ah* supervisory boards of some Islamic banks have approved a stratagem to convert a *Shari'ah*-compliant investment into another investment, which may or may not be *Shari'ah*-compliant. The investor is assured that his funds will be invested in the *Shari'ah*-compliant business; the funds will be protected over the period of the investment; and he is promised he can swap the return on his funds by the return on the other investment if the return on the other investment is higher than that of the *Shari'ah*-compliant investment. For example, suppose an Islamic pension fund wants to invest $100 million in a *Shari'ah*-compliant business for three years through an Islamic bank. The Islamic bank guarantees that these funds will be protected; the investor's funds will be invested in *murabaha* on which it will get, let us say, 5 per cent per annum as return. The Islamic bank also promises that, if the return on its other investment is higher than 5 per cent, the investor will get the higher return. The precise mechanics of the deal are as follows.

The Islamic bank passes the funds of the investor to a structuring bank (which is usually a conventional bank) that issues a note ensuring that the funds will be invested in a *Shari'ah*-compliant business and the investor will get guarantees for return of the principal and the rate of return. It will also get a promise that the structuring bank will swap the return on the *Shari'ah*-compliant investment with its return on the other investment, provided the return on the latter is higher than on the former. The structuring bank charges a fee for issuing such a note. The structuring bank invests these funds with an asset management bank (again a conventional financial institution) on the basis of *murabaha* or *salam* at a specified rate of return. Subsequently, the structuring bank swaps the *murabaha* or *salam* contract investment into a loan to the asset management bank, against the collateral of the *murabaha* or *salam* contract. The asset management bank agrees to pay the same rate of interest on this loan that it had agreed for the *murabaha* or *salam* contract. Once the funds are with the asset management bank, it lends these funds to one or more fund management companies, which invest these funds on the stock exchange on any business they find profitable. The fund management companies earn interest or dividends on these funds and pay interest to the asset management bank at pre-agreed rates; the asset management bank pays interest to the structuring bank. The structuring bank pays interest to the Islamic bank if it is higher than the *murabaha* or *salam* rate agreed to in the first instance; otherwise it pays the *murabaha* or *salam* rate. At each stage the principal sum and the rates of return are guaranteed. The investor has the incentive of getting a higher return than that of the *Shari'ah*-compliant investment. All the financial institutions in the chain get their differential of interest rate plus fees for agency services and other legal charges. The whole chain of transactions is a highly profitable business for all, with the least risk at each stage, except that it is difficult to distinguish from conventional bank business.

DeLorenzo observes that it is a mechanism to wrap non-*Shari'ah*-compliant investment with *Shari'ah*-compliant contracts and is illegal (*haram*). The first leg of the whole deal is supposedly 'Islamic', but all the other links in the chain leave the door open for 'un-Islamic' business. The fund managers, the last link in the chain, which are responsible for actual investment, may invest these funds in any business, such as dealing with liquor, gambling, prostitution, pornography or weapons of mass destruction, or in interest-bearing bonds, securities and so on. The chain of transactions would not come into being if there were no initial investment by the *Shari'ah* investor. Its funds are swapped from a *murabaha* or *salam* contract into loans of various types and ultimately lead to any type of investment whether compliant or non-compliant with the *Shari'ah*.

20.11   HOUSING FINANCE AND ITS VARIATIONS

Housing finance is a primary need of every person. The Muslim religious lobby has effectively pleaded for an abandoning of conventional mortgage-based finance, as it involves interest, which is prohibited. That posed a serious challenge to Muslim thinkers. In response they have come up with various methods that enable ordinary consumers to avail themselves of housing finance without entering into interest-based transactions. However, the methods devised are close cousins of conventional finance. Their appearance is distinct, but their substance is similar to interest-based finance. Besides, the Islamic methods of buying a house put the consumer at a greater disadvantage in terms of costs, risks and uncertainties as compared to conventional finance. In the following discussion we shall show various tricks and ruses devised for avoiding interest in form only.

20.11.1   Housing Finance on the Basis of *Murabaha*

Visser (2009: 106) has referred to Ramadan[21] for a *fatwa* by the European Council for Research and *Fatwas* and the League of Scholars of *Shari'ah* in the USA that allows borrowing from conventional banks on the basis of necessity. Some American organizations[22] have developed methods, allegedly *Shari'ah*-compliant, for the purchase of houses. In the UK, housing finance is provided in a similar manner (Dar 2002). One of the most popular methods for housing finance is through *murabaha*. The method operates as follows (Thomas 2001: 6). The consumer selects a house and applies for funding to the financier, who approves the house, pays the price to the seller directly and obtains title. The financier sells the house and transfers the title to the consumer on a deferred payment basis by adding a mark-up on the purchase price. The consumer starts paying instalments. When the contract ends the financier has already got back, through instalments, the price of the house with a mark-up. The mark-up is usually the market interest rate on funds provided by the financier. The house remains under mortgage with the financier until the consumer pays off all the instalments (Dar 2000: 5).

Abdul-Rahman (2010: 210–211), after explaining the mechanics of housing finance on the basis of *murabaha*, concludes as follows:

> there is no mention of the method that is used to calculate the mark-up (profit) in the *murabaha* model. The fact of the matter is that they use the prevailing interest rate used by all banks in the conventional *riba*-based system, call it rent or profit, and claim that this interest (usually LIBOR-based) is looked upon as an index. . . . [I]t is troubling to see the bank . . . form a special purpose vehicle with the intention of abandoning it just to make the deal look compliant with

Shari'ah. . . . [S]uch an approach stands in fact as a mockery of the real purpose, intent, and wisdom of the prohibition of *riba* or the culture of renting money.

Meera and Abdul Razak (n.d.) have concluded after analysis that, in the case of default or early redemption, the cost of *murabaha* financing is always higher than that of conventional finance for housing. Habib Ahmed (2011: 194) points out that, in the case of early payment by the client, *murabaha*-based home finance is more expensive than conventional finance. For example, if a person buys a house through an Islamic financial institution on the basis of *murabaha* for 15 years, the price will include interest for 15 years. If the buyer comes back after one year to repay the whole amount, the Islamic financial institution will charge the entire amount settled in advance, which includes interest for 15 years. In the case of conventional finance, in a parallel situation, the client will pay one year's interest and a penalty for breaking the contract. The economic implication of *murabaha*-based finance is that it deters clients from settling accounts early even when they can. Overall, it is an inefficient arrangement where the bank's funds are tied in a transaction and the client is also burdened with an avoidable cost. Another problem is that the financier would not extend the loan period, as there would be no way to compensate it for the extension (Visser 2009: 108). From the perspective of the financier, the transaction is inflexible. The financier cannot securitize the debt and get it discounted to realize early cash. There is no way that you can sell a debt except at par under the *Shari'ah* (Visser 2009: 109). El-Gamal (2007: 6–7) highlights the disadvantage of *murabaha*-based financing for purchasing a house. He writes:

[A]ll that is accomplished in *murabaha* home financing is to replicate a conventional mortgage, at payments approximating those of a conventional one, with some added cost for spurious trading and various fees. At a recent conference in Toronto, Canada, it was reported that the 'Islamic mortgages' cost the mortgagors roughly an extra 100 to 300 basis points in Canada, and 40 to 100 basis points in the U.S. . . . Unfortunately, whatever the economic harm, it appears that the 'Islamic' *murabaha* mortgage will result in a larger debt with a higher interest rate. . . . One is then forced to conclude based on the economic analysis that if the Islamic mortgage is permitted, then so must the conventional mortgage, and vice versa. . . . The substance-oriented jurists would . . . ask what benefits the 'Islamic mortgage' has produced relative to the conventional one. In fact, they would argue, if one had to choose between the two of them, one may be forced to choose the conventional *riba* as the lesser of two evils. . . . As far as the mortgagor is concerned, his involvement in the transaction is based on debt, and the debt is higher for the ostensibly 'Islamic' transaction than for the conventional transaction to finance the same property.

20.11.2   Housing Finance on the Basis of *Ijara*

Another method of housing finance popular among Muslim buyers is through the lease purchase method (*ijara wa iqtina'*). It works as follows. The financial institution provides finance to buy a property jointly with a client. The client pays the down payment and becomes a partner. The financial institution and the client jointly own the property in proportion to their investments. On purchase, the client rents the property and pays rent for the portion owned by the financial institution, with an additional sum to buy its share in instalments. Gradually, ownership of the financial institution is transferred to the client. Monthly payment of the rent is adjusted periodically to represent the percentage of ownership of the respective parties. The contract is designed in such a manner that the client bears all registration and maintenance costs. In some cases, the client also pays insurance costs. However, where the financial institution shares the insurance costs, the rent is so determined that the bank recovers its insurance cost as well. Some orthodox scholars like Taqi Uthmani and Zuhayli insist that these rates must be specified at the outset and not left ambiguous till a later period. They also consider application of LIBOR, as a benchmark for rent, impermissible. However, other contemporary orthodox jurists allow the linking of rent with LIBOR or any such index. The formula for working out the monthly instalment remains the same as under conventional mortgage contracts. Islamic financial institutions can also revise the rent periodically to match the cost of funds (Meera and Abdul Razak, n.d.). Al-Baraka Bank, London devised this model in 1990. Taqi Uthmani refined it further the same year (Thomas 2001: 9; Abdul-Rahman 2010: 215). Substantively, the method is quite similar to the traditional method of housing finance, with a few additional disadvantages, risks and costs. Abdul-Rahman (2010: 217, 221) explains as follows:

> However, the customer has to go through a number of extra steps without reaping any economic or religious benefits – like joint venturing with a limited liability company (LLC), paying extra costs, and accepting a joint title ownership that may result in future undefined risks . . . the risk carried by the company is even less than the risk assumed by a conventional bank . . . the method exposes the consumer to many risks, especially the risk of getting involved in nonstandard mortgage structure with nonstandard contracts and notes that has not been tested in the courts.

This obviously is a contract in interest-based finance. However, El-Gamal (2000: 24) says that this should not be of concern to Muslim clients so long as the contract is written according to the rules of the *Shari'ah*. He says:

As for the correspondence of the 'rental' portion of payments to what would be an interest payment on the principal balance in a conventional mortgage, this should afford the intelligent Muslim customer an opportunity to ensure that he is not being charged excessively relative to the conventional market. As far as compliance with the Islamic *Shari'ah* is concerned, the form of the contract is what matters. To keep the Islamic financial industry from reaping excessive profits at the expense of devout Muslims with few alternative sources of financing, this comparison to conventional market trends is very valuable.

The American Finance House (popularly known as Lariba Bank) has introduced a variation of the lease-to-own contract. The bank provides finance for purchase of an agreed property jointly. The property is registered in the name of the client. The bank gradually sells its share to the client on payment of instalments. The agreement provides the bank with a lien on the property. However, the agreement restrains the client from selling the property until it acquires full ownership by paying all the instalments. The bank also acquires a right to earn rent on the property. The agreement can use the word 'interest' to satisfy the requirements of US laws. The costs, including fees, maintenance and other fees, are charged to the customer. The insurance cost is also borne by the client. The agreement is quite similar to a diminishing partnership. The client pays a monthly instalment that consists of two components: the purchase price of a segment of the property and rent (or interest) on the investment by the bank. According to this model, the rent of the asset purchased and leased to the client is marked to the market. It varies according to market conditions, the location of the asset and an independent assessment of the fair value of the rent. It is not fixed as with conventional banks' mortgages. The bank reviews this rate periodically and adjusts it upward or downward. One of the challenges for this model is to remain competitive with conventional rates of interest. For this purpose, the Islamic bank adjusts its assessed rates of rent in the locality in such a manner that they are closer to the conventional rates of interest on mortgages of houses in that area (Abdul-Rahman 2010: 258ff.).

Besides the shareholders and a few high-worth individuals, Freddie Mac and Fannie Mae, two US home finance organizations, are other major sources of funds for Lariba Bank. They invest part of their funds through Lariba Bank and indicate the expected rate of profit. Lariba Bank uses that rate as a benchmark and, based on its evaluation of the market, assesses the possibility of accepting their funds. Once Lariba Bank finds a property profitable on this benchmark, it buys the property with its own funds but gets reimbursement from these organizations within a week or so.

The difference between the Lariba model and other Islamic models for housing finance is that, in the former case, the rent is determined with reference to the market rates of each locality. In the case of other Islamic models, the rents are calculated at a predetermined rate, usually with reference to the interest rate. In both models, the client pays for using the capital of the bank in the form of rent. However, in the case of the Lariba model, the rent liability remains unknown till the end. It can move upward or downward according to market conditions. From the perspective of the client, the Lariba model entails greater uncertainty and risks as compared to other Islamic models.

In addition, the whole scheme of the Lariba model is procedure-oriented. From the perspective of the bank, certain legal formalities are fulfilled which enable it to claim that the return it is getting is not traditional interest (or *riba*). But, from the perspective of the client, it hardly matters what legal procedures are adopted. He or she is getting finance and is paying an extra sum on that. It is consistent with the orthodox definition of *riba*. If we insist on the orthodox definition of *riba*, we have to adopt this roundabout procedure, but it does not change the essence of the matter.

A variation of the *ijara* scheme was started by the House Building Finance Corporation, Pakistan (HBFC) in 1979. The HBFC provided funds to construct or purchase a house and share the notional rent of the property with the owner in proportion to its investment in the total cost. The rents were assessed every three years. Since more than 80 per cent of the users of the funds constructed houses in localities where rents were comparatively low, the rent share of the HBFC was also lower as compared to market interest rates. By 1987 the average rate of return of the HBFC was 4.8 per cent, while about Rs10 billion were in arrears. In 1988, yielding to the pressure of international donors to reform the financial sector, the government directed the HBFC to abandon the rent-sharing scheme in favour of a fixed rate of interest on funds provided by it (M.A. Khan 1994: 23).

20.11.3 *Bai' al-Wafa* Accommodated in Lease Purchase Agreements

Bai' al-wafa was a technique practised in medieval times (after the fifth century of *Hijra*) and since then to the present day under various guises to bypass the prohibition of *riba*. The technique was as follows. An owner would sell his real estate for ready cash with a binding promise by the buyer to return the property after a fixed term when the seller would return the original price. During the interim period the buyer could derive any benefit from the property by way of leasing, residing, farming and so on. The benefit derived from this property was a proxy for the *riba* which the buyer could not charge on the cash advanced to the seller, as it was prohibited by the *Shari'ah*. The contract was considered a stratagem to conceal *riba* but was allowed by some jurists.

In the modern age, Islamic financial institutions have adopted a similar technique under a different title. The client agrees to sell a property to the Islamic financial institution (buyer) for ready cash and agrees to take it back on rent for a specified period. The rent is fixed in such a manner that the client repurchases the property in instalments, part of which is applied toward the purchase price of the property. It is a modern version of the *bai' al-wafa*. The difference between the two is that the Islamic financial institutions do not have to look for a lessee. The seller himself becomes the lessee. In the case of *bai' al-wafa*, the buyer may have to find a third party to rent the property. Alternatively, the buyer may decide to use it directly. From the perspective of the financier the modern version is more beneficial and easier to practise. In essence both are stratagems for concealing interest. Rafic al-Masri (2006) has discussed the issue in detail and concludes that the technique of sale with a lease-back agreement is nothing but a stratagem to accommodate *riba* in a concealed form.

20.11.4   Parallel *Istisna'*

Another method, not widely used but accepted as Islamic, is application of the principles of *istisna'*. In this method, the bank agrees to get a house or some other asset built for a client through a construction company and then sell it to the client by using any of the permissible modes of finance such as *murabaha, ijara* or lease purchase which we have discussed earlier (Thomas 2001: 10). A variation of this technique is parallel *istisna'*, which is more popular in industrial finance. The exact mechanics of the technique are as follows. The bank enters into two parallel contracts. The first contract is between the bank and a client who requires the end product, such as a building, a ship or an aircraft. The second contract is between the bank and a manufacturer for construction or manufacture of the product. Both contracts are on the basis of *istisna'*. However, the mode has at least three limitations. First, it is usually applied for the production or manufacture of a single major product but does not cater for other industrial needs. Second, the bank's role as a manufacturer in the first contract and as a supplier of products in the second is artificial. In reality, the bank is neither a supplier nor a consumer of the products. It is only a financial intermediary, and the whole façade of parallel *istisna'* is created to overcome a legal requirement without adding any utility to the process of financing. Third, it involves intrusion by the bank in the technical operations of the manufacturer through a complicated contractual process. Most manufacturers would not like such intrusion. They would like to have financing in a straightforward manner.

20.12   CONSUMER CREDIT: THE CASH NEEDS OF INDIVIDUALS AND BUSINESS

20.12.1   Finance for Durable Consumer Goods

Tahir *et al.* (1999: 66) propose that finance for durable consumer goods can be made available either on the basis of credit sale (*bai' mu'ajjal*) or, in the case of cars, for example, on the basis of leasing. In both cases, the bank charges a fixed amount for the finance provided. The amount charged by the bank is related to the period for which the bank's funds remain locked. The solution may meet the legal requirements, but from the perspective of the client it is quite similar to borrowing money on interest from a conventional bank. It is possible that in the case of Islamic finance the cost and risks are higher as compared to conventional finance.

20.12.2   *Qard Hasan* (Interest-Free Loans)

In theory, Islamic financial institutions should provide interest-free loans to needy persons for education, health care, marriage and so on. They can levy a one-time fixed charge to meet the administrative expenses. Muslim economists are aware of the fact that there does not exist any satisfactory method of providing interest-free loans by Islamic banks (Siddiqi 2009-a: 73). Siddiqi (2009-a: 236) suggests a way out. Islamic financial institutions should set aside a portion of current account deposits for lending on an interest-free basis. Deposits of trust funds (*awqaf*) or *zakah* funds can also be partly used to provide interest-free loans. He has also given the example of Iran, where savers are encouraged to open interest-free deposit accounts with Islamic banks. The banks utilize the funds in these accounts to provide interest-free loans. Interestingly, he mentions that the depositors are compensated by the banks through prizes or bonuses, which are not predetermined. This last point brings the whole question of interest on savings accounts closer to interest-free deposit accounts except that the conventional banks are more transparent and fairer toward depositors than Islamic banks. Islamic banks treat depositors in a similar manner to conventional banks but without disclosing in advance the rate of return. That provides Islamic banks with the power to deal with depositors in any manner they like.

20.13   ISLAMIC CREDIT CARDS

There is no easy way to handle the use of credit cards in an interest-free environment. Despite that, some Islamic financial institutions have issued credit cards. For example, Bank Islam Malaysia Berhad has issued credit cards. The mechanics are as follows. The customer of the bank uses the card to buy a piece of land on credit from the bank, which he or she sells back to the bank at a lower price immediately for cash. The bank deposits the cash in the account of the client, who can draw it to meet his or her needs. The difference between the sale and purchase prices is the profit of the bank. The other income of the bank arises from the terms of repayment, which oblige the customer to pay certain fees determined with reference to the period of repayment and the number of instalments. In this mechanism, there is no difference between interest on a conventional credit card transaction and the fees of the Islamic credit card, except that the latter is more expensive, as it involves legal charges for sale and purchase of land in addition to all the other charges of a conventional bank (Visser 2009: 67).

Prabowo (2009: 12) writes:

> In Malaysia, the development of *Shari'ah* credit card was firstly done by AmBank in December 2001. The bank launched *Al Taslif Credit Card* using *akad bai' inah* with the margin of 1.25% per month or 15% per year from the total buying. In the first transaction, the bank agreed to sell certain good to the cardholder with certain price. In the second transaction, the cardholder agreed to resell the good with lower price. Such credit card using cannot be accepted by the *Ulema*[23] from the Middle East and Indonesia because it is considered as fake transaction. In the development, in July 2002, Bank Islam Malaysia Berhad (BIMB) also launched *Shari'ah* credit card. This bank claimed that their product was the first pure *Shari'ah* credit card. This BIMB product used three different *akad*s (contracts) i.e. *bai' inah*, *wadi'ah* (deposit), and *qard hasan* (goodness loan). At present, Bank Muamalat Malaysia Berhad (BMMB) still uses *akad bai' inah* to fund the *Shari'ah* housing program. The recent data up to 2007 show that the housing fund composed about 70 to 80% from the total fund of BMMB noted, up to 5.6 billion Ringgits Malaysia (RM).

Another version of the credit cards charges a fixed annual fee. However, it also charges a monthly fee for the outstanding balance against the client. A variation of the fee-based card is that the bank, besides the annual fee, charges a monthly fee for the limit of the card. If the customer does not use the card to its limit, the bank gives a rebate for the unused part of the limit (Habib Ahmed 2011: 177).

The Kuwait Finance House has issued the al-Tayseer card, which can be used as both a Visa card and a MasterCard. It requires monthly balance repayments amounting to one-third of the balance. Cardholders also pay an annual fee and a fee for withdrawal of cash (Visser 2009: 67). Some Islamic financial institutions have issued *tawarruq*-based credit cards. They create a debt against the cardholder to the extent of the card limit plus the charges on the limit and deposit that amount in a special account in the name of the client. If the client uses the entire limit, she pays the whole amount. However, if she does not use the entire limit, the bank gives a rebate in its charges on the unused part of the limit (Habib Ahmed 2011: 178).

20.14 DEBT GUARANTEES

The question of guarantees issued by banks for a fee has been under discussion among Muslim jurists. The majority opinion is that conventional banks issue such guarantees for a fee, which, in fact, is another form of charging interest on the sum being guaranteed. However, Hammad (1997) has argued that this fee is not interest and can be charged and paid under the *Shari'ah*. His argument, briefly, is that the commitment to pay a debt is different from the paying of the debt itself. Although it is commendable if a person gives such a commitment as a gesture of goodwill, the *Shari'ah* has not forbidden the charging of a fee for such a commitment. It is only when the guarantor actually meets the obligation because of the default of the debtor that another contract comes into being. That other contract is a loan contract between the guarantor and the debtor. Charging any excess on this would become *riba*. However, he does not face the question about the amount of the fee which may subsume a charge for a possible subsequent debt default that the guarantor was guaranteeing. For example, the guarantor may calculate that, if the debtor defaulted, he would have to meet the obligation and would not be able to charge any interest explicitly. To meet such an eventuality, the fee for the guarantee is decided in such a manner that a charge for interest on the debt is also included in it. In that case, though the word 'interest' is not used, the guarantee fee hides in it the element of interest. Hammad does not face this ultimate question.

20.15 GOVERNMENT FINANCE

Islamic financial institutions and governments committed to the Islamization of public finance have devised various stratagems to bypass the strict orthodox interpretation of *riba*. In the following discussion we shall highlight some of these stratagems.

20.15.1   *Shari'ah* Alternatives to Government Bonds

Abdul Latif Rahim Janahi (2005) discusses s*alam* bonds (*sukuk al-salam*) and leasing bonds (*sukuk al-ijara*) issued by the government of Bahrain through the Bahrain Monetary Agency (BMA). He argues that these bonds are innovative Islamic financial instruments. Let us see how they work. The BMA issued *salam* bonds at par value for the sale of aluminium by the government of Bahrain. The bond-holders paid cash to the government with a promise to receive the aluminium later through a third party, created by law, which guaranteed a profit of 3.67 per cent on the purchase price. The question is: how does it differ from lending on interest? It is more complex and roundabout and ends up at the same destination. The situation of leasing bonds is similar. The BMA issued leasing bonds to buy a capital asset. The asset is purchased in the name of the bond-holders. Then the asset is leased by the bond-holders to the government of Bahrain. The government guarantees the leasing of the asset, payment of rent and also repurchase of the asset after the lease period at par value of the bonds. What is the summary result? The bond-holders provide cash to the government, get a fixed sum of money as 'rent' for a fixed period and then get back their principal sum. How does it differ from an interest-based loan?

20.15.2   Government Investment Issues (GII)

In 1983 the government of Malaysia introduced Government Investment Issues (GII), a type of sovereign bonds on the basis of interest-free loans (*qard hasan*). The banks were provided with an opportunity to place funds in these bonds. The government may give some return as a gift to the investors based on its calculations relating to the rate of inflation, real growth rate of the economy and existing yields on other financial instruments. The rate of return is fixed by a government committee which cannot be termed as transparent (Sundararajan *et al.* 1998: 7). The bonds were not tradable on the interbank market. To overcome this difficulty, in 2001 the Malaysian government permitted the sale and purchase of these bonds as well. It has opened the door to the sale of debt, which by a consensus is not permissible under the *Shari'ah*. That is why most Middle Eastern scholars do not approve of these bonds (Solé 2007: 21).

20.16   INVESTMENT OF SURPLUS FUNDS

20.16.1   Islamic Real Estate Investment Trusts (I-REITs)

Since 2006, Malaysia has innovated Islamic real estate investment trusts (I-REITs). The Securities Commission of Malaysia has issued guidelines for floating and managing the trusts. The trusts raise capital by issuing units which represent the capital value of the real estate in which these funds are invested. A company manages the trust and performs such functions as acquisition, sale and lease of properties. In actual practice, the trust acquires the property of a business concern and leases it back to the same business at a fixed rent. In the process, the business concern gets working capital and agrees to pay rent on the leased property. The income of the trust is divided among unit-holders on a pro rata basis after deducting the fees of the trustee company. If the properties are given on lease to a third party, a contractor company provides maintenance and allied services. The maintenance expenses are charged to profit before distribution. Besides the leasing and resale of properties, the trust fund can also engage in financial intermediation by providing finance to various property developers on a mortgage basis. In that case also the income of the trust consists of rent and not interest. The Securities Commission guidelines also provide for the screening of the income of the trust if the lessee is engaged in a business which is not wholly compliant with the *Shari'ah*.

In actual practice, the business concern that sells the property to the REIT and leases it back is only availing itself of an 'Islamic' veil for an interest-bearing loan from the trust. The business concern already owns the property, which remains with it. To use the funds of the REIT, it agrees to pay a fixed 'rent' on its own property. The difference between straightforward borrowing on interest and this roundabout method of getting finance is that, in the case of taking funds from a REIT, the business concern also hands over ownership of its property to the trust, while in the case of interest-based finance it would only offer this property as a mortgage. There is no substantial difference. The client who takes finance from a REIT on an Islamic basis is, perhaps, worse off in real terms as compared to the situation if she borrowed on interest from a conventional bank. The Islamic trust exercises greater economic power over the client than the conventional bank would do. Which of the two methods is closer to the objectives of the *Shari'ah*?

20.16.2 Real Estate Investment: Innovative Practices

McMillen (2008: 718–728) has discussed in detail the mechanism for real estate investment by Muslim investors from the Middle East in the markets of the US and Europe. The prime concern of the investors was to find some *Shari'ah*-compliant avenue for the investment. Since it was difficult to find a wholly *Shari'ah*-compliant avenue elsewhere, the investors looked for opportunities in the real estate sector. The first innovation was to accept the possibility that the investor had to be *Shari'ah*-compliant but the other party need not be. That opened the way for the creating of intermediate companies which would accept the investors' funds as equity but were free to contract interest-based loans to supplement their resources. These companies could then purchase buildings which could be leased, and rent received could be paid, on a pro rata basis, to investors on their equity capital. However, one further problem was that the tenants of these buildings could be engaged in prohibited businesses, such as interest-based banking, ATM machines, restaurants selling alcohol and pork, cinemas, grocery stores with gambling machines, and so on. Finding tenants who were 100 per cent compliant with the *Shari'ah* was difficult. This was overcome by accepting the principle that the overall or main business of the tenants should not be prohibited or the amount of rent from, or the space occupied by, such activities should be minimal. For example, in a residential apartment building, an ATM machine might be allowed as an exception. *Shari'ah* scholars examined such cases and gave verdicts on a case-by-case basis. But the end result was that some compromise had been allowed to increase the opportunities for investment of surplus funds.

20.16.3 Conditional Rate of Return Investment in *Mudaraba*

Arbouna and el-Islamy (2008: 194) also mention a technique where, in a contract of *mudaraba*, the *mudarib* is bound by the contract to invest the *mudaraba* funds only if they can earn a certain predetermined rate of return. Some juristic schools allow this restricted form of *mudaraba* with certain conditions. If the *mudarib* is unable to generate the minimum profits, he or she is required to compensate the financier (*rabb al-maal*) for the difference.

20.16.4 Negotiable Islamic Certificates of Deposit

Finding profitable avenues for the surplus wealth of high-net-worth individuals has been a great attraction for Islamic financial institutions. They were able to find a solution in the form of the negotiable Islamic certificate of deposit (NICD), which appeared to comply with the *Shari'ah*. Dusuki (2007-a: 9) explains the mechanism of these certificates as follows:

> A high net-worth individual client who wishes to deposit RM 1 million in NICD with an Islamic bank would normally expect a fixed return from the bank. The bank sells its asset (i.e. its shares certificate) worth RM 1 million to the client and gets paid on cash basis. The bank now secures RM 1 million deposits. Subsequently, the client sells back the share certificates to the bank at a deferred price, which is based on a profit rate; say 7.5 percent for duration of six months ($7.5\% \times 6/12 \times 1,000,000 = 37,500$). The bank now issues the client NICD worth 1,037,500 as the nominal value. The issuance of the NICD is undertaken as evidence of the RM 1,037,500 debt that the bank owes to the client. At maturity, the NICD are redeemable at par value where the client gets back the RM 1 million deposits plus RM 37,500 as profit. More importantly this NICD is tradable in the secondary market for liquidity purposes.

Most contemporary jurists object to this type of mechanism, as it allows the entry of *riba* through the back door. However, Malaysian jurists have permitted the transaction.

20.16.5   Interest on Current and PLS Deposits

Islamic financial institutions accept current, savings and term deposits. However, they use different terms such as interest-free loan (*qard hasan*) or trust (*wadi'a*) to denote current or saving deposits. Like conventional banks, they also offer some return on savings account deposits, in the form of profit, dividend, gift or bonus. For term deposits, they use the expression 'expected return' or 'estimated return' rather than a predetermined fixed rate of interest, although both the customer and the Islamic financial institution understand that the return is predetermined and fixed. However, the mechanism may leave depositors worse off in some way as compared to the situation with conventional bank depositors. Farooq (2006-a) quotes Sudin Haron as follows:

> Unlike savings account facilities at conventional banks, where depositors are automatically rewarded upon placement of their funds, rewards to savings account holders are dependent on the *Shari'ah* (Islamic laws) principles which are adopted by Islamic banks when offering this facility. When *wadi'a* (trusteeship) or *qard hasan* (benevolent loan) are used, the returns are entirely at the discretion of the banks.[24]

The above position gives an extra handle to Islamic financial institutions to exploit the depositors, if they so choose, as the rate of return is entirely discretionary and not mandatory. Islamic financial institutions treat current deposits as loans and only the principal sum is guaranteed. But, in the absence of any deposit insurance, depositors of Islamic financial institutions are subject to greater risk than depositors of conventional banks (Iqbal and Molyneux 2005: 121). For example, in extreme cases, the losses suffered by Islamic financial institutions on their investment accounts may eat away their reserves and investment capital, and the losses may spill over to current account deposits. In such cases, the current deposits run an additional risk (Chapra and Khan 2000: 13).

Khan and Bhatti (2008: 94–96) show how the Council of Islamic Ideology, Pakistan proposal in 1980 came quite close to what conventional banks were doing to pay interest on deposits. It provided a mechanism by which depositors would get a return in proportion to the length of period a deposit remained with the bank. This was exactly parallel to the interest-based system of paying a return on term deposits. Only the nomenclature of the rate was changed from 'interest' to 'PLS'. Tahir (2009: 68) says:

> Exactly the same thing happens in Islamic banks in lieu of term-deposits. In both cases (i.e. Islamic and conventional finance) all funds are pooled together, profits are assigned to different categories of the deposits according to their maturity period, and finally distributed among the respective class of depositors according to the daily-product method. . . . Islamic banks are using the same covers for their financing as the interest-based banks: mortgage, guarantees and promissory notes. . . . The Islamic banks are using more or less the same accounting and balance sheet conventions that have been developed for interest-based banks. For example, despite the fact that *murabaha*-based deposits involve sharing of the ownership (not lending) by the depositors with the Islamic banks, all deposits are routinely reported on the liabilities side of the Islamic banks.

20.16.6 Fixed Income Investment for Those Who Cannot Earn Actively

Another problem that Islamic finance had to face was to provide an avenue for a continuous stream of risk-free income for those who cannot engage in any active service or business such as pensioners, widows, orphans or disabled persons. In an interest-based economy, this need is met by various types of saving schemes which offer risk-free streams of income. Since the orthodox interpretation of *riba* treated this type of return as prohibited, there was a need to find a method to cater for the requirement of these segments of society. Again, the ingenuity of Muslim scholars came to the rescue. The concept of the *ijara* fund has been launched, where a financial institution, mutual fund or bank can accumulate people's savings, buy properties and put them on lease. The income appropriated from rentals of the properties is apportioned, after deducting expenses, among depositors of the funds on a pro rata basis. The question arises: from the perspective of the savers, how does this arrangement differ from the term deposit of an interest-based bank?

20.16.7   Return-Protected *Waqf* Fund

This is a mechanism by which the bank creates a *waqf* (trust) fund where a part of the profits are allocated every year. The *waqf* fund is used to equalize the fluctuating rates of return to depositors. In the case of liquidation of the bank, the *waqf* fund balance is donated to a charity. This is a mechanism for giving a fixed or expected rate of return to depositors without being exposed to the fluctuations of profit–loss shares.

20.17   THE MONEY MARKET

20.17.1   Creation of a Secondary Market for Financial Instruments

Balala (2011: 122) argues that the orthodox position about the prohibition of a secondary market for financial instruments is not legally tenable. She differs with the orthodox interpretation of the legal maxim that prohibits the sale of debt for debt (*bai' al-kali' bil kali'*). Her main point is that the legal maxim presumes excessive uncertainty (*gharar*) when a debt is sold for another debt. However, she argues, in a secondary market when a person buys a certificate on credit he or she is actually buying property rights. Selling those rights further and on credit cannot be treated as the sale of debt for debt. Selling property rights at any price and on credit is permissible by a consensus (ibid.: 124). Thus the whole foundation of orthodox opinion that disallows the sale of financial instruments on credit and at a price other than the face value is dismantled. This is the straightforward acceptance of a secondary market in financial papers in the conventional sense. Some writers have presented more roundabout methods for creating the secondary market in financial papers. One such method is as follows.

Arbouna and el-Islamy (2008: 191) suggest the creation of a secondary market through a receivables trading house (RTH) that accepts the receivables and uses them to pay for the purchase of commodities. The sellers of commodities (for example, crude oil) accept the receivables and provide the commodities that the RTH will sell for cash immediately and pay the original owners of the receivables after charging a commission. The original holders of receivables get cash immediately. The sellers of the commodities hold the receivables and wait till maturity to realize the cash. The authors also mention a slightly modified form of this mechanism and note that it is approved by some *Shari'ah* boards with certain conditions (ibid.: 192). However, the mechanism does not give all the details. For example, it is possible that the price of the commodity the RTH gets is significantly lower than the value of the receivables. Will the RTH or original owners of the receivables want to take this risk? What will happen if the RTH is loaded with commodities that do not sell readily? What compensation will the secondary holders of the receivables get for the time lag? The secondary holders of receivables may also not be able to collect all the receivables on time. Will such business houses that primarily deal in commodities want to get into the business of collecting receivables and assume all the concomitant risks? Even if we accept there is a legal way through the RTH, the efficiency of the mechanism is questionable. It is a roundabout method of doing the same thing, though at a higher cost, that conventional finance does.

20.17.2   Secondary Market for *Mudaraba* and Other Types of *Sukuk*

Hakim (2007: 269) suggests a way out for creating a secondary market for *mudaraba* bonds (*mudaraba sukuk*). The suggestion paves the way for selling bonds at whatever price the market fetches. He argues that the *mudaraba sukuk* represent the assets in which the funds collected through these bonds are invested. The *sukuk* holders as owners of these assets are free to sell the assets at any price for cash or credit. Therefore the orthodox interpretation that prohibits the sale of *sukuk* in the secondary market requires review, which should focus on redefinition of *mudaraba sukuk* from being debt instruments to being asset instruments. Once that is done, the sale and purchase of *mudaraba sukuk* at any price become legitimate.

20.17.3   Islamic Interbank Market Malaysia

Ibrahim and Mokhtar (2010: 134) discuss the experience of Malaysia in developing an interbank secondary market for Islamic financial institutions. Bank Negara Malaysia (BNM) has sponsored the following instruments for Islamic financial institutions. Although the *Shari'ah* advisory board of BNM has approved these instruments, yet a closer scrutiny of the precise mechanism is required to determine their compatibility with the orthodox definition of *riba*-free transactions (ibid.: 136ff.):

a.   Bank Negara Monetary Notes–Islamic (BNMN-I): These notes are issued either on a discounted value or with coupons.
b.   Negotiable Islamic debt certificates (NIDCs): The NIDCs are issued on the basis of *mudaraba*. The financial institution sells NIDCs to its

customers at an agreed price on a cash basis. It agrees to purchase back the certificates at a profit for a price which is to be settled at an agreed future date.

c.   Islamic negotiable instruments of debt (INIDs): INIDs are issued on the basis of *bai' al-'inah*. The INIDs are short-term deposit/finance certificates which are issued on the basis of a sale-and-buyback agreement.

d.   Bank Negara Malaysia Notes–*Murabaha* (BNMNs-M): BNMNs-M are mark-up-based sale transactions. They are debt instruments arising out of the sale of an asset such as palm oil on the basis of *murabaha*. The instruments are used for short-term finance/deposit needs.

e.   *Mudaraba* interbank investment (MII): MII provides a mechanism for surplus banks to place funds with deficit banks for a short term with a maximum of three months. The cost of funds is usually lower as compared to conventional finance.

f.   *Wadi'a* acceptance: Bank Negara Malaysia accepts the surplus funds of Islamic financial institutions on the basis of interest-free deposits (*wadi'a*) as a tool of monetary policy.

The BNM has ensured that the transactions are transparent and fair. It has launched the Islamic Interbank Money Market (IIMM)[25] and regulates it. It has introduced an online tendering system,[26] which provides pricing information in real time, and also an automated settlement system.[27]

20.17.4   Interbank *Mudaraba* Certificates

Bangladesh, Indonesia and Malaysia have designed interbank *mudaraba* certificates for short-term investment of funds. According to the Islamic Financial Services Board (2008: 17):

> [It is an] investment facility where interbank placement of funds for a period ranging from overnight to 12 months produces returns based on an agreed profit ratio, with the formula for profit computation typically being based on that used for *murabaha* investments of one year, or *murabaha* investments of comparable maturity, in the bank receiving the interbank funds.

How does this differ from calculating the return on the basis of interest?

20.18   DISCOUNTING OF TRADE BILLS

20.18.1   Sale of Debt

Muslim economists are gradually conceding ground to the institution of interest under various excuses. So far they have been arguing vociferously that Islam does not tolerate the sale of debts for cash or on credit, as it would involve *riba*. But some ground has been conceded on this account as well. Habib Ahmed (2006: 91) writes:

> The majority of the Islamic jurists forbid the sale of debt other than at its face value based on classical injunctions. Chapra and Khan (2000: 77–78)[28] distinguish between debt arising from borrowing money and debt created from transactions of contemporary Islamic financial institutions. In the latter case, debt is created by selling goods and services using sale-based modes of financing like *murabaha*. Arguing that the price in these transactions is profit and not interest, and also the availability of credit ratings that reveal information of the issuing institution thereby eliminating *gharar*, may form different bases compared to the case where the original rules on sale of debt applied. Given the changed realities, they argue for the reconsideration of the verdict on the sale of debt originating from sale-based modes of financing in contemporary Islamic financial markets.

(Also see Visser 2009: 68.)

Khan and Bhatti (2008: 93–94) paraphrase the technique proposed by the Council of Islamic Ideology, Pakistan (1980: 37–38) for the discounting of bills as follows:

> The Council of Islamic Ideology proposed that the conventional techniques be replaced by commission fee. The bank would charge a variable commission on the basis of the amount rather than the bill's maturity period. The client would enter into two separate agreements with the bank. In the first agreement, the client would appoint the bank as its agent for collecting the bill from the drawee. In the second agreement, the client would receive a cost-free loan from the bank, equal to the face value of the bill, for the duration of its maturity. The bank would charge a commission for collection of the bill from the client in advance. It would use the proceeds from collecting the bill for settling the interest-free loan made to the client against the bill. If the bill were dishonoured, the client would be personally liable to repay the interest-free loan to the bank immediately.

Another roundabout method is Islamic factoring. The factor does not discount the client's receivables. Instead, it acts as an intermediary between sellers and buyers. The sellers sell the products to the factor for cash and the factor sells it to the ultimate buyers on credit and collects the sale proceeds in due course of time (Visser 2009: 99).

20.18.2   Sale of Debt (*Bai' al-Dayn*)

Bai' al-dayn refers to the sale of debt either for immediate cash or for another debt. In conventional finance, the most prevalent form is the sale of accounts receivable or the discounting of negotiable bills for immediate cash. This is a form of getting a loan on interest. According to Hanafite *fiqh*, the transaction is prohibited, as it involves *riba*. The Islamic Fiqh Academy of the OIC in its 11th meeting at Manama (1998) categorically prohibited all forms of *bai' al-dayn* (Nagaoka 2007: 9). However, the *Shari'ah* Advisory Council of Malaysia has ruled that the transaction is permissible, as it overcomes the real difficulty that lies in safeguarding the interests of both parties through regulation and supervision by the Securities Commission and the central bank. The ruling has opened the door to legitimizing the issuance of *sukuk* (Mohamad and Yusoff 2008: 64). Kamali has defended the legitimacy of the transaction (Nagaoka 2007: 10). His argument is that the debt sold is not currency but a real asset and can have a varying price when sold. There is nothing wrong in selling accounts receivable at a lower price than their face value.

20.18.3   Discount on Early Repayment

One of the ever-nagging problems of Islamic finance has been to find a solution to the universal commercial practice of cash discount on early settlement. Its varied application is found when a credit card company reduces its claim on early payment. The practice has been in vogue since ancient times but is controversial in Islamic law. Any reduction in the debt due to early payment is clearly a concession for the time and is a form of interest forgone. Recently, this has been accepted as legitimate by various juristic bodies (El-Gamal 2000: 13). Nyazee (2009: 76) after extensive discussion on the question concludes that, if the claim consists of a single amount (without saying what the price of the commodity is and what the mark-up portion in the claim is), there is nothing against reducing the claim for early payment. He thinks that discounting is related to reduction of the mark-up and not to the claim as such and if the mark-up is not distinctly stated then the reduction in the claim would be permissible. We think this is based on a faulty understanding of the concept of discounting. Discounting is not the reduction of interest; it is the reduction of the financial claim, whether of the principal sum or of interest (mark-up) in lieu of early payment.

20.18.4   Converting Long-Term Debts into Short-Term Debts

Islamic financial institutions can face liquidity problems when funds are tied up in long-term debts. Since Islamic financial institutions cannot sell debt for cash, Al-Suwailem (2006: 126) has proposed a way out to overcome the liquidity problem. The Islamic financial institutions can use their long-term debt 'appropriately discounted' to pay for commodities that they want to finance on the basis of *murabaha*. In this manner, the debt will be converted into commodities and not cash and will overcome the *Shari'ah* objection to converting debt for cash. The proposal is in its bare bones and does not explain what is meant by 'appropriately discounted' and how this will differ from conventional discounting of bills. Although from a legalistic point of view there is no exchange of cash for debt, yet the procedure does involve conversion of long-term debt into the equivalent of cash, which is used to pay for the price of the commodities that the bank is financing on a *murabaha* basis. Cash has not changed hands explicitly, but everything else is the same as conversion of a higher amount of long-term debt into a smaller amount of short-term debt. It does not require much acumen to understand the trick.

Another method to ease the liquidity problem is to combine long-term debt with real assets in such a manner that the percentage of debt in the whole package is less than 50 per cent. The portfolio can then be securitized and sold at whatever price. In the process, the debt will be converted into new securities, providing ready cash in the form of the sale of securities. Again, the process does overcome the legal objection of converting debt into cash, but in economic terms we are, in fact, converting our debt into cash at a price other than its nominal value. The process of securitization is only a veil to hide the discounting process.

20.19   INTERNATIONAL TRANSACTIONS

20.19.1   Exchange of Currencies

Tahir *et al.* (1999: 103) contend that the present currencies are paper currencies and do not have any intrinsic value like coins of gold and silver. The *Shari'ah* injunctions relating to exchange of currencies (*bai' al-sarf*) do not apply to present-day currencies. One of the key injunctions is that both currencies should change hands simultaneously. There should be no delay in delivery of one or both currencies in the transaction. Once this restriction is removed, forward trading of currencies also becomes permissible, as the authors have also contended. However, the position requires reconsideration. For all practical purposes we treat paper currencies as having a value. That is why *zakah* is payable on rupee balances as well. But when it comes to exchange we take another position and contend that paper currencies do not have any intrinsic value. How do we reconcile the two positions?

The fact is that the condition of simultaneous exchange of currencies was levied only to minimize risk and fraud in the exchange of currencies. Now that the foreign exchange markets are highly regulated, exchange rates are transparent and the commitments are binding on both sides, with the risk of heavy penalties for violation, the need for spot exchange has minimized. It is because of these changes in circumstances that we need to have innovative thinking (*ijtehad*) in this area and allow forward transactions in foreign exchange. However, if we refuse to review our position, we shall have to find lame excuses and invent roundabout methods to go along with the commercial practices of the world.

20.19.2   Letters of Credit for Imports

Tahir *et al.* (1999: 105, 6.2–ix) suggest that Islamic banks should issue letters of credit without any fee. It is a simplistic suggestion. Despite that, we would say that practising bankers should examine the suggestion. Can they issue letters of credit without any fee, which will become binding on them once the goods are dispatched by the exporter? They would be tying their funds with the contingency of the importer's failure to honour his or her commitment. Would they be willing to do that? If so, what would their interest in it be?

20.19.3   Financing Imports on a Deferred Payment Basis (*Bai' Mu'ajjal*)

Tahir *et al.* (1999: 105–106) have also suggested that Islamic banks can act as importers on behalf of their clients. The bank should pay the foreign exporter but sell to the local client on a deferred payment basis (*bai' mu'ajjal*). The price of the goods will include the bank's profit and other expenses incurred by the bank. The bank has safeguards against the default of the client, including down payments, third-party guarantees, and options to sell the goods on the open market. Besides the question of whether banks would want to get into this type of business (moving away from their role as financial intermediaries to actual traders), the whole transaction is a complicated way of earning interest on finance provided by the bank.

20.19.4   Financing Exports on an Advance Payment Basis (*Bai' Salam*)

Tahir *et al.* (1999: 106) have proposed that for confirmed export orders the bank can buy goods from local exporters and pay them cash. It can then enter into agreements with foreign importers and agree on supplying the goods at a price that includes the bank's profit and other expenses. Does it differ from conventional interest-bearing finance except in complexity?

20.19.5   Pre-shipment Export Finance on the Basis of *Murabaha*

Islamic financial institutions use a variation of *murabaha* to provide pre-shipment finance to exporters. The technique is as follows. The exporter finalizes the transaction of sale with an importer abroad and informs the Islamic bank about the price agreed between the exporter and the foreign importer. The bank and the local exporter sign two agreements. In the first agreement, the client appoints the bank as agent and in the second agreement the client agrees to sell the goods to the bank for immediate cash at a price that is lower than the price agreed between the local exporter and foreign importer. The difference between the two prices is the income of the Islamic bank (M.A.I. Uthmani 2009). The two prices are fixed in such a manner that the bank earns the market rate of interest on funds provided to the local exporter. It is obviously a roundabout method of legitimizing interest.

20.19.6   Pre-shipment Export Finance on the Basis of *Musharaka*

Islamic banks can provide export finance on the basis of *musharaka*. The client exports the goods and shares the profit, which is known in advance, with the bank. However, a problem can arise when the foreign importer fails to make the payment. The banks are averse to taking such risks. For such situations, contemporary scholars have suggested a way out. The *musharaka* agreement can provide that the bank will not share such a loss. The basis for this opinion has been found in a legal ruling that the owner of capital will not suffer if the loss is due to the negligence of the *mudarib*. This ruling can be invoked if it is certain that the importer is defaulting on payment only because the goods delivered were not according to the agreed specification (M.A.I. Uthmani 2009). The solution does not tell, however, about the situation when the importer defaults for other reasons.

20.19.7 Post-shipment Export Finance

M.A.I. Uthmani (2009) explains the mechanics to get *Shari'ah*-compliant finance after a local exporter has shipped goods and is waiting for payment. The foreign importer, in this case, would have issued a bill receivable. The local exporter approaches the Islamic bank with the bill. The Islamic bank signs two agreements with the exporter. In one agreement the exporter appoints the bank as agent to collect dues from the foreign importer for a fee. The fee is the bank's income. In the second agreement, the bank provides finance equal to the amount of the bill receivable as an interest-free loan to the local exporter with permission to the bank to adjust the proceeds of the bill against the interest-free loan. The net result is that the local exporter gets the amount of the bill receivable minus the collection fee (which is usually equal to the market rate of interest on an interest-free loan provided under the second agreement). This is a roundabout method of discounting bills receivable at a hidden rate of interest.

20.20 STOCK EXCHANGE TRANSACTIONS

20.20.1 Options Trading

The conventional stock exchange provides a mechanism for dealing in stocks and bonds on the basis of margin trading and short selling. Margin trading enables a buyer to pay a small percentage of the sale price as a token of intention to purchase the stock. The payment of a margin provides an option to the buyer to purchase the stocks and bonds at the agreed price or let the option lapse. In the latter case, the margin paid is forfeited to the seller. Conventional stock exchanges have evolved into complex trading places where option-holders can sell an option at a price different from that which the option-holder had paid. Gradually, a market of options has emerged where options are traded irrespective of the underlying asset. The question whether options can be a valid subject of sale from the Islamic legal point of view has been under debate among Muslim scholars. The dominant opinion is that the sale of options is illegal, as it is the sale of something that does not exist (see e.g. Obaidullah 2006: 57). However, some contemporary scholars have expressed a different opinion. For example, Forte and Miglietta (n.d.: 8) quote Kamali, as follows:

> As for options contracts, a number of scholars have found such contracts objectionable, but ultimately Kamali (1995)[29] concluded that 'there is nothing inherently objectionable in granting an option, exercising it over a period of

time or charging a fee for it, and that options trading like other varieties of trade is permissible and as such it is simply an extension of the basic liberty that the Qur'an has granted'.

20.20.2 Short Selling

Dusuki and Abozaid (2008: 66, 74) write:

[T]he Securities Commission of Malaysia has recently legalized short-selling transaction, under strict securities borrowing and lending (SBL) regulations. The *Shari'ah* Advisory Council (SAC) of Securities Commission at its 69th meeting held on 18th April 2006 resolved that regulated short-selling (RSS) is in compliance with *Shari'ah*. . . . In other words, the introduction of SBL can increase the probability that the shares sold will be delivered. When the probability of delivery is high, then the element of *gharar* will no longer be significant. . . . Therefore, short selling of items that are not owned by the seller takes place in the share market with the assurance by the exchange authority (Securities Commission) that can remove the excessive risk and uncertainty (*gharar*) with respect to its delivery. Even if the short seller does not own the item when selling the shares, his ability to make delivery is nevertheless assured beyond doubt.

After considering the utility of the short selling of stocks for the efficient and smooth working of the capital market, Dusuki and Abozaid get stuck in the orthodox interpretation that treats all forms of interest as *riba*. Despite their best effort, they are unable to find a solution to this problem. They write:

It is known that in the application of short selling the lender, i.e. the stock owner, stipulates a gain in return for lending the stocks. However, as we have already concluded that any gain stipulated by the lender is deemed *riba*. Therefore, the issue of the lender stipulating a return for lending the stocks becomes the fundamental factor in determining the legality of the whole trans- action, this is regardless of the original ruling concerning stocks trading, as this is an issue in itself that necessitates a careful study and its legality cannot be taken for granted, especially in the light of the recent economic and social negative implications. (Ibid.: 77)

In sum, Muslim scholars are gradually conceding ground to conven- tional finance for various types of transactions. The trend calls into question the rationale for devising Islamic financial institutions and instruments in the first place.

20.20.3   Forward Trading

Since orthodox scholars do not allow forward trading, Islamic financial institutions have invented an intricate method to deal in forwards. The method involves five sale transactions (two *murabaha*-based, two spot sales and one *salam*-based), as explained below.

Suppose the spot price of a ton of silver is Rs10 million. A and B want to construct a forward trade contract. A promises to sell B one ton of silver with delivery after one year for Rs10.1 million on a deferred payment basis and settlement after one year. To achieve this objective, A sells the silver on a *murabaha* basis to a special purpose vehicle, SPV-1, for Rs10.1 million to be paid after one year. SPV-1 sells one ton of silver to B for Rs10.1 million on a *murabaha* basis to be paid by B in one year. B sells the silver to SPV-2 at the spot price Rs10 million. SPV-2 sells the silver back to A on a spot basis for Rs10 million. The result of these transactions is that B gets Rs10 million cash to be paid back to SPV-1 as Rs10.1 million after one year. Further, A and B enter into a *salam* contract. B pays Rs10 million as the price of one ton of silver cash in advance to A, who agrees to deliver the silver to B after one year under the *salam* contract. The net result of all the transactions is that A will deliver one ton of silver to B after one year in exchange for Rs10.1 million to be paid by B through SPV-1. A and B were able to deal in a contract of forward trade without being blamed for violating the *Shari'ah* rules. In conventional finance, this is done in a straightforward single contract (Habib Ahmed 2011: 180).

20.20.4   Futures Trading

Most of the orthodox *Shari'ah* scholars consider futures trading to be against Islamic law. However, Kamali (1996) has given a verdict that legitimizes futures trading as in vogue. According to him, futures trading reduces risk. Futures trading does not come under the purview of the famous Tradition of the Prophet that forbids the sale of something that one does not possess, as the Tradition pertains to unique goods and assets and not to generic (fungible) goods or assets. The example of *salam* being permissible is a proof of this understanding of the Tradition. The objective of this prohibition is to safeguard against deception and fraud, which in the case of modern futures exchanges are minimal. He further contends that the conventional view that forbids postponement of both the price and the goods does not have any basis in the Qur'an or *Sunnah* of the Prophet (Visser 2009: 74).

20.21   CENTRAL BANKING OPERATIONS

20.21.1   *Murabaha* for Liquidity Management

Dusuki (2007-a) discusses the commodity *murabaha* programme (CMP) introduced by the central bank of Malaysia. CMP is a cash deposit product which is based on the principle of *tawarruq*. The underlying commodity is palm oil. It is also a popular scheme in Gulf countries and in Saudi Arabia. It was approved by the *Shari'ah* Advisory Council of Malaysia on 28 July 2005. It involves the following steps:

a.   The bank that faces a problem of excess liquidity can buy a commodity, say palm oil, for cash from broker A for Rs10 million, for example.
b.   The bank sells the commodity to the central bank at a mark-up of 10 per cent per annum to be paid in six months, for example. The price of the commodity would be Rs10.5 million in this case.
c.   The central bank sells the commodity to broker B at Rs10 million for cash.
d.   After six months, the central bank pays the investing bank Rs10.5 million as originally agreed.
e.   The mechanism provides an avenue to banks with excess liquidity to place their funds with the central bank and earn some profit as well. The Islamic Financial Services Board (2010: 4) terms it commodity *murabaha* financing (CMF) or commodity *murabaha* for liquid funds (CMLF). These are investments of surplus funds and are shown as assets of the Islamic financial institutions.
f.   In the case where the bank faces a shortage of liquidity, the process can be reversed. The Islamic Financial Services Board (2010: 4) terms it commodity *murabaha* for obtaining funds (CMOF). Some Islamic financial institutions call it reverse *murabaha*. This is a liability of the Islamic financial institutions.

In a subsequent paper (2009-a) Dusuki has criticized the technique, arguing that it adheres to the form and ignores the substance of the *Shari'ah*. He argues that the contract undermines the objectives of the *Shari'ah*. From a prudential point of view the Islamic Financial Services Board warns against excessive use of commodity *murabaha* transactions for liquidity management. The Board considers that the excessive use of *murabaha* is both risky and inconsistent with the *Shari'ah* principles (Islamic Financial Services Board 2010: paragraph 25).

A closer look at the above mechanism indicates that the management of liquidity through *murabaha* is a technique that does exactly the same thing that conventional banks do but in a roundabout manner. An Islamic financial institution which has surplus funds provides funds to the central bank or to another Islamic financial institution on a fixed profit for investing these funds on *murabaha*. The central bank or the other Islamic financial institution, as the case may be, buys a commodity on credit and sells it on spot for cash. The surplus Islamic financial institution is able to place its surplus funds for a profit fixed in advance. It gets back the funds with profit after the agreed period. The commodities are usually standardized and there is no physical delivery in most cases (Islamic Financial Services Board 2010: footnote 7). The whole process is similar to a normal *murabaha* process. Substitute a client for the central bank or other Islamic financial institution and it would become a normal *murabaha* transaction except that in this case, on both sides of the transaction, there are financial institutions that actually do not trade in commodities.[30] The process involves a rigmarole of paper work and efforts to bypass the law. There is nothing that has changed in essence. The bank with surplus cash invests the funds for a short period on a fixed-term profit in the name of *murabaha*. The rest is only procedure.

20.21.2 *Tawarruq* as a Monetary Policy Tool

Solé (2007: 22–23) notes that *tawarruq* can be used as a monetary policy tool. To absorb excess liquidity of Islamic financial institutions, the central bank can take two steps as follows:

- **Step 1:** Suppose the central bank desires to absorb excess liquidity from the market. For this, it will approach Islamic banks and ask them to purchase some commodity on its behalf. The banks, in turn, will contact commodity brokers and agree on a specific price. At this point, the Islamic banks do not transfer funds to the broker. The central bank agrees to repay the Islamic banks at a future date the cost of purchasing the commodities plus a margin (as in *murabaha* contracts).
- **Step 2:** Subsequently, the central bank requests the Islamic banks to resell the commodities – typically at the same price and to the original commodity broker, who will cancel the debt acquired in step 1 by the Islamic banks. The Islamic banks, however, make a payment to the central bank, out of their own treasury, equal to the value of the spot sale of the commodities. This payment is what constitutes the liquidity withdrawal, while the cost of the monetary operation is determined by the future instalment payments over the spot payment.

Solé (2007: 21) illustrates the above procedure in the case of Bahrain:

> Mirroring the use of treasury bills in conventional systems to manage systemic liquidity, the Central Bank of Bahrain uses *al-salam sukuk* to engage Islamic banks in its monetary operations. Under *al-salam sukuk*, the government agrees to sell forward to the Islamic banks a commodity (typically aluminium in the case of Bahrain) against spot payment. Simultaneously, the Islamic banks designate the Bahraini Government as their agent to sell the commodity to a third party upon delivery. The price of the future sale determines the return on the *sukuk*, while the initial spot payment from the Islamic banks to the central bank constitutes the liquidity withdrawal.

To increase the liquidity of banks, the above process can be reversed. A closer look at the entire scheme will show that the procedure is mere eyewash. The Islamic financial institutions will place their surplus funds with the central bank, which will repay with a mark-up (or interest) later. In the process the central bank sucks up the excessive liquidity of the Islamic financial institutions. This is exactly what happens in conventional finance. The Islamic procedure is cumbersome and costly.

The Islamic Financial Services Board (2008: 21) explains how Islamic financial institutions invest their surplus funds with the Saudi Arabian Monetary Agency (SAMA) through a *murabaha*-based transaction. At the end of the day, the Islamic financial institutions place surplus funds with SAMA for a fixed period and get these funds back with a premium (or mark-up). The question arises: what is the difference between the above transaction and a transaction based on interest? Perhaps the interest-based transaction is simpler and more economical.

20.21.3   Central Bank Participation Papers

The central bank of Iran issues participation papers on the basis of *musharaka*. The yield on the papers is guaranteed and linked to the central bank's profit excluding the cost of monetary operations. The government of Iran also issues similar papers to finance budget deficits with a guaranteed return on the principal linked to the government's share in its investment in public sector enterprises (Islamic Financial Services Board 2008: 25). How does it differ from interest-based finance?

20.21.4   Central Bank *Wadi'a* Certificates

Bahrain, Indonesia and Malaysia use central bank *wadi'a* certificates. The return on these certificates is linked to the average return on interbank *mudaraba* investments (Islamic Financial Services Board 2008: 25). At the end of the day the certificates earn a return without actual investment in the real sector, which is the main plank of the orthodox interpretation of *riba*.

20.21.5   A *Shari'ah*-Compliant Alternative to REPO (Sale and Buyback Agreement)

Malaysia uses an alternative to conventional REPO transactions. According to the Islamic Financial Services Board (2008: 26):

> [It] involves one contract to sell a security outright at an agreed price, with a second contract for a forward purchase of the security at a specified price and on a specified future date. The undertaking made by both the buyer and the seller to sell and buyback the instrument, respectively, at the maturity date is based on promise.

There is hardly any difference between such transactions and interest-based REPO deals.

20.22   OVERALL ASSESSMENT

To be fair to proponents of contemporary Islamic banking, we should admit that some soul searching has already started. After three decades of practical Islamic banking, Muslim economists and scholars have started realizing that the original hopes of founding an Islamic banking and financial system were merely a fond hope. Islamic financial institutions have not been able to find a viable substitute for interest. They have devised various modes of 'Islamic' finance which are so akin to interest-based modes that it is difficult to tell one from the other. For example, Boudjellal (2006: 27, 31) says:

> Despite this encouraging progress, Islamic banks have not succeeded in formulating into practice the principle of profit and loss sharing stated above. . . . There is a need to invert the reasoning and admit that the Islamic banking practices incite us to rethink our effort of theorization in light of the constraints encountered on the ground. Fixed return modes of finance comply with *Shari'ah* rules. Its excessive use by Islamic banks should not be the subject of critics. In fact, we need to castigate our incapacity to think about another institutional setting where other non-monetary financial intermediaries would be best placed to use PLS modes of finance.

He further proposes that Islamic banking should be reorganized in two streams. Retail banking should accept deposits on fixed return and extend credit through fixed-return modes of Islamic finance. The other stream should be investment banking that accepts long-term investment funds on a profit-sharing basis and extends finance on the basis of *musharaka* and *mudaraba* for the long term. This type of reorganization would reduce the risks of Islamic banks, which are now constrained to short-term deposits and long-term financing demands.

However, these scholars are still clinging fast to the orthodox interpretation of the term '*riba*'. They are still trying to do some patchwork to accommodate the definition of *riba* in the contemporary banking system and find a compromise. These efforts are far from satisfactory. For example, Boudjellal (2006) thinks that we can continue with the fixed-return modes of financing for short-term financing but resort to profit–loss sharing for long-term financing. Thus he is pleading for the creation of two types of Islamic financial institution. However, it is not known whether even this compromise would be practicable and acceptable to practising bankers. It need not be said that this compromise retains the fixed modes of return as 'Islamic' for short-term financing needs.

Taqi Uthmani (2008) says:

> Undoubtedly, *Shari'ah* supervisory boards, academic councils and legal seminars have given permission to Islamic banks to carry out certain operations that more closely resemble stratagems than actual transactions. Such permission, however, was granted in order to facilitate, under difficult circumstances, the figurative turning of the wheels of those institutions when they were few in number [and short of capital and human resources]. It was expected that Islamic banks would progress in time to genuine operations based on the objectives of an Islamic economic system and that they would distance themselves, even step by step, from what resembled interest-based enterprises. What is happening at the present time, however, is the opposite. Islamic financial institutions have now begun competing to present themselves with all the same characteristics of the conventional banks. Often times these products are rushed to the market using ploys that sound minds reject and bring laughter to enemies.

El-Gamal (2007: 9–10) has ably summarized all that has happened to Islamic finance during the last three decades. Muslim scholars and economists and Islamic financial institutions joined hands in fabricating a series of stratagems and ruses to accommodate interest in financial transactions. They did not realize that the need for this activity was uncalled for to begin with. Had they looked back at the definition of *riba*, which they expanded to cover financing and investment transactions, they would not have required any of these tricks. In fact, the whole enterprise of creating Islamic financial institutions was unnecessary. The original definition of *riba* which can be distilled from the primary sources of Islam applies to interest on loans. Muslim scholars of the nineteenth and twentieth centuries tried to extend its meaning to all financing and investment transactions besides loans. Unwittingly, they landed themselves in unremitting trouble to find a solution to replacing interest with another device in all financial transactions. Had they remained content within the original boundaries of *riba* as defined by the Qur'an or various Traditions of the Prophet, they would not have got into the effort of finding alternatives to conventional financial institutions. That does not mean that conventional financial institutions do not have any problems. They have various shortcomings and require reforms to achieve broader social and human objectives. But that would not require elimination of interest from conventional financial institutions. Instead, it would require reforms within the existing framework. Muslim economists and scholars have not succeeded in eliminating interest from financial transactions. They have supported the creation of Islamic financial institutions, which are struggling hard to come closer to conventional financial institutions, retaining interest in a concealed manner and rejoicing in a framework of hypocrisy that entails higher costs, bigger risks and greater inefficiency.

NOTES

1. A good summary of the state of the art is available in M.N. Siddiqi (2006).
2. [As in original] Subki Mahmasani, *Falsafa al-tashri' fil Islam*, trans. Farjat Ziyadah (Leiden: E.J. Brill, 1961), p.122.
3. See section 19.3.7.
4. In 1976, Sami Hamoud, a Jordanian scholar, proposed the innovative idea of using *murabaha* as a financing technique (Visser 2009: 52). He got the IDB Prize for Islamic Banking in 1987, presumably for pioneering this concept (Nyazee 2009: 15).
5. [As in original] A.S.A. Ghuddah, Juridical aspects of application of profit sharing contract in contemporary society, in *Investment strategy in Islamic banking: Applications, issues and problems*, ed. N. El-Din El-Assad (Amman: Al Albait Foundation, 1992).
6. Lit. option to return the goods bought if the buyer notices a defect.
7. For example, *fatwa* 62 for Dalla al-Baraka and *fatawa* 17 and 24 for Kuwait Finance House allow this technique (El Gamal 2006: 67).
8. Translation of Selected Fatwa of Al-Baraka Seminars, Seminar 6 (pp. 77–78), Algeria, 5–9 Sha'baan, AH 1410, 2–6 October 1990 CE, www.lariba.com.
9. Emphasis added by the present writer.
10. In the terminology of Islamic jurisprudence, it is known as *al-ijara al-mawsufa fil dhimma*.
11. [As in original] Business loans, consumer loans, student loans, credit card receivables, etc.
12. [As in original] Adam and Thomas, *Islamic bonds*, p.77.
13. [As in original] Khalid Howladar, *The future of sukuk: Substance over form? Understanding Islamic securitisation, asset-backed and AAOIFI principles*, Moody's Investors Service, 6 May 2009.
14. [As in original] Asian *sukuk* market faces new but familiar challenges, *Islamic Finance News* 6 (16), 24 April 2009.
15. For example, McMillen (2008: 751) mentions that the Malaysian government's *sukuk* trust certificates issued in 2002 were based on LIBOR.

16. Karachi interbank offered rate.
17. [As in original] Ali Arsalan Tariq, Managing financial risks of sukuk structures, unpublished, M.Sc. dissertation, Loughborough University, UK, 2004, n. 16, 50.
18. Also termed '*mutawarriq*' in literature on Islamic finance. See for example Al-Suwailem (2009: 22).
19. Refers to Resolution no. 179 (19/5), OIC Islamic Fiqh Academy, available at www.isra.my.
20. Available at Al-Suwailem (2009: 49).
21. Tariq Ramadan, *Western Muslims and the future of Islam* (New York: Oxford University Press, 2004).
22. For example, Al-Manzil (New York), the Council of American Islamic Relations Minnesota, and Lariba.
23. Lit. religious scholars.
24. Sudin Haron, The effects of management policy on the performance of Islamic banks, *Asia Pacific Journal of Management* (Singapore) 13 (2) (October 1996), pp. 63–76.
25. http://iimm.bnm.gov.my.
26. Fully Automated System for Tendering (FAST).
27. Real Time Electronic Transfer of Funds and Securities (RENTAS).
28. M.U. Chapra and Tariqullah Khan, *Regulation and supervision of Islamic banks*, Occasional paper 3 (Jeddah: Islamic Research and Training Institute, Islamic Development Bank, 2000).
29. M. Hashim Kamali, Islamic commercial law: An analysis of options, paper presented at the conference of SPTF/Islamic Banking Products, Kuala Lumpur, December 1995.
30. Normal *murabaha* may actually involve some trading with commodities changing hands. In the case of commodity *murabaha* for liquidity management, on both sides of the transaction are financial institutions. There is a little likelihood that actual trade will take place. Most of the work will be on paper.

21. Islamic insurance (*takaful*)

21.1 THE ORTHODOX POSITION ON CONVENTIONAL INSURANCE

There is hardly any difference of opinion among Muslim scholars on the need for managing, redeeming and mitigating general, business and life risks covered by the insurance business. However, orthodox scholars have two main concerns about conventional insurance. First, it is uncertain if and when the insured event will take place and, if it does take place, what would be the relationship of compensation to the insurance premium paid. It is possible, in the case of general insurance, that the event will never take place and the policyholder will forgo all sums paid as premiums. In the case of life insurance, death can take place even after the first instalment of the premium, in which case the nominated person gets the entire insured sum immediately and the insurance company suffers a significant loss on this contract. In brief, the occurrence of the insured event and the amount of compensation are highly uncertain. That makes the insurance business similar to gambling, where the gambler does not know about the fate of the game. The uncertainty in the insurance business is excessive and borders on prohibited *gharar* (excessive uncertainty). Second, insurance companies invest surplus funds on the basis of interest and pay out a part of such earnings to policyholders as bonuses. According to the orthodox interpretation, interest income of the company is *riba*, and so are bonuses that the policyholders get. In brief, according to the orthodox opinion, elements of gambling, *gharar* and *riba* make conventional insurance unacceptable from the *Shari'ah* perspective (Mulhim and Sabbagh n.d.: 36–37). This is a bare summary of the orthodox position on present-day insurance. For details see: Fazlur Rahman (1960), Tonki (1965), Muslehuddin (1969), Shafi (1972), Sanbhali (1973), Council of Islamic Ideology, Pakistan (1984), Hassan (1985), Vogel and Hayes (1998), Al-Suwailem (2006) and Al-Dhareer (1997).

The orthodox position on present-day insurance is weak and unpersuasive. First, it is not true to say that the insurance contract involves gambling. In a gambling situation, the casino does not cover any risk. The gamblers play a game of chance in which they can win or lose. No risk is covered and no damage is mitigated. In the case of insurance, the company provides cover against defined risks. Second, it is an overstatement to say that insurance involves excessive uncertainty. The statistical techniques and actuarial sciences have progressed to a stage where the insurance company can calculate its risks and benefits with great precision and cover the element of excessive uncertainty. The company does not, in normal circumstances, take any excessive risk. Third, the extension of the definition of *riba* to insurance bonuses or to interest on investment of surplus funds involves the same mistake that the orthodox school has committed in the case of other financial transactions. We have demonstrated in the previous chapters that the orthodox definition of *riba* is untenable and has created insoluble problems.

21.2   THE MODERNIST VIEW ON INSURANCE

Although orthodox opinion on conventional insurance considers it unlawful under the *Shari'ah*, yet even among orthodox scholars some have adopted a more positive attitude and accept insurance under certain conditions. For example, the Syrian jurist Mustafa al-Zarqa (1904–99) argued that insurance companies sum up the risk of large numbers and redistribute it in a manner that makes it bearable. It is a form of cooperation and is compatible with the *Shari'ah*. Of course, the general conditions of the Islamic law of contract would apply anyway (Visser 2009: 103). Similarly, Siddiqi (1985), the father of Islamic economics, has argued that the contemporary concept of insurance is in conformity with the *Shari'ah*. Several other scholars have also supported the conventional concept of insurance. For example, see Mulhim and Sabbagh (n.d.), Klingmuller (1969), Irfani (1984) and Mortuza Ali (1986).

In the case of insurance, as with commercial banks, orthodox opinion prevailed, and a movement for Islamizing the contemporary insurance business started in the last quarter of the twentieth century. The basic premise of this movement was that the insurance business should be organized on principles of brotherhood and fraternity where all policyholders join hands to cover the risks of one another. Insurance should be a fraternity where all members provide security to one another in the group. For that reason insurance was translated into the Arabic term '*takaful*', which stands for mutual guarantee. There is a consensus among Muslim scholars about the legitimacy of this type of insurance (Mulhim and Sabbagh n.d.: 14, 33–36). The Islamic Fiqh Academy of the OIC also approved *takaful* as a legitimate form of business in 1985 (Ernst & Young 2008).

Takaful has emerged as an alternative to conventional insurance business. The basic concept of *takaful* is seductively persuasive. A group of persons (legal or natural) join hands to form solidarity. They contribute small amounts of money to create a fund, generally known as a participants' *takaful* fund (PTF). The nature of these contributions is a donation (*tabarru'*) and not a business deal. The purpose of the fund is to cover general business and life risks to any member of the solidarity. Each member insures the other members and remains eligible for the benefit of similar coverage, should there be a need. Mutual help and not the profit motive is the driving force of *takaful*. It covers the objection of *gharar* in conventional insurance, since it is not a business deal to begin with.

Conceptually, *takaful* has to be a company that is owned and managed by all the policyholders. If a person of the solidarity suffers loss, others make it up by providing financial support that is accumulated in the form of insurance premiums. If the loss exceeds the accumulated fund, the policyholders should provide additional resources. This pristine concept of *takaful* has been put into practice in a modified form where a *takaful* company is set up very much like a conventional insurance company. The policyholders, known as *takaful*-holders, pay the premium. The company pays the claims of the *takaful*-holders. Any shortfall in the fund for meeting all the claims is made up by the *takaful* company from its own resources. The business of a *takaful* company is quite similar to the business of a conventional insurance company. For example, the *takaful* company also provides insurance cover for damage to property, civil and vocational liabilities, life assurance, transport risks, engineering risks and so on. However, there are differences in the organizational set-up of the *takaful* company and the conventional insurance company, as explained below.

21.3   MODELS OF THE *TAKAFUL* BUSINESS

21.3.1   *Mudaraba*-Based

The members (or *takaful*-holders) contribute toward a fund, which is invested on the *mudaraba* basis. The profits are accumulated to individual accounts after the *takaful* operator (TO) has charged its underwriting fee and investment fee, which are specified percentages of the underwriting surplus and investment profits respectively. The losses of any member are met from the profit of the fund. The members are allowed to withdraw the accumulated investments. If there are no accumulated profits, the losses are passed on to the *takaful*-holders, as they are owners of the capital (*rabb al-mal*) in the *mudaraba* contract.

21.3.2 *Tabarru'*-Based

The premiums paid by members are accumulated into a donations (*tabarru'*) fund. The fund is used for meeting the losses of any member. The fund is invested and profits are added to the primary fund. The members are not allowed to take back their contributions, nor are they entitled to any profits. Justification for non-entitlement to profits emanates from the fact that the members never donated to the fund to earn a profit. However, in some cases, the members can agree to distribute part of the profit among themselves if the profit ensues as a result of good financial management (Mulhim and Sabbagh n.d.: 26). The *takaful* operator acts as agent of the members and charges a fee (*wakala* fee) for its services before the surplus is credited to the primary fund.

21.3.3 *Waqf*-Based

Members contribute funds to create and register a trust (*waqf*). The *waqf*, by definition, is a permanent body, with a distinct entity, and is a legal person for all business purposes. The members also pay a regular premium to get the insurance coverage. A *takaful* operator acts as agent of the members and charges a fee (*wakala* fee) for its services. The funds are invested and the benefits are distributed to the intended beneficiaries. It is like a public foundation and strictly speaking an insurance business. Any residual profits are accumulated in the primary fund and not distributed among the members. Similarly, the members do not pay anything in addition to the policy premium, should the total claims exceed the available fund. The *takaful* company (*waqf*) is assumed to make up the shortfall.

21.3.4 Combination of *Tabarru'* and *Mudaraba*

A combination of *tabarru'* and *mudaraba* is possible where the participants donate funds on the basis of *tabarru'* (first contract) but the *takaful* operator invests these funds on the basis of *mudaraba* (second contract). The two contracts are governed by their respective *Shari'ah* rules.

21.4 THE DIFFERENCE BETWEEN COMMERCIAL INSURANCE AND *TAKAFUL*

Al-Suwailem (2006: 117) explains the difference between commercial insurance and *takaful*. Commercial insurance involves the payment of insurance benefits to the insured irrespective of the premium paid and availability of funds with the insurance company. In theory, *takaful* is not a business but a form of mutual cooperation. Compensation is limited to the extent of the available funds contributed by the participants. If losses exceed the available funds, either the participants contribute more funds or the benefits are reduced to match the available funds. In practice, the *takaful* is run as a business and the *takaful* company remains responsible for making up any shortfall in the funds. The amount of premium in the case of *takaful* is set in a very similar manner to how it is set in commercial insurance with reference to the value of the goods or property insured or the life risks involved (Mulhim and Sabbagh n.d.: 18ff.). Theoretically, the premium provided by policyholders in commercial insurance is the property of the insurance company. In the case of *takaful*, the premium remains the property of the members. The *takaful* company is only an agent of the members. The *takaful* company is supposed to invest the funds of the members in *Shari'ah*-compatible channels. There is no such restriction on commercial insurance companies.

21.5   REINSURANCE AND RE-*TAKAFUL*

Khan and Bhatti (2008: 62) mention that *takaful* companies do not have a satisfactory arrangement for reinsurance. As a result, they reinsure 80 per cent of their risk with conventional reinsurance companies. Akoob (2009: 162) says:

> Most of the *re-takaful* contracts in operation are still based on the mechanism and wordings applicable to conventional reinsurance. These wordings are unsuitable for *takaful*. The basic principle of *tabarru'*, or mutual help, among participants, is not clearly defined in such contracts, nor is the segregation of *re-takaful* (participants') fund and *re-takaful* operator's fund defined.

The above criticism is valid to the extent that we review the practice of re-*takaful* on the benchmark of *takaful* theory. However, the actual practice of *takaful* and re-*takaful* is very much similar to conventional insurance and reinsurance in essence, as we discuss in section 21.7.

21.6   UNRESOLVED ISSUES IN *TAKAFUL*

The *takaful* company or *takaful* operator underwrites the risks of *takaful*-holders. However, some issues relating to their respective rights and obligations are nebulous. Haron and Taylor (2009: 187) point out the following questions relating to the underwriting of risks which require clear answers in all *takaful* contracts:

a. In the event of heavy losses which cannot be met from the *takaful* fund, do *takaful*-holders have recourse to the assets of the TO or have priority over other creditors?
b. Is it obligatory upon the TO to provide interest-free loans if there is a shortfall in the PTF? If so, what are the terms of the loans?
c. What happens if there is a heavy loss and the TO is unable to meet it?
d. What if the TO is guilty of misconduct, negligence or fraud? What recourse do the *takaful*-holders have?
e. Can the TO use the PTF for its own benefit? If not, what controls are necessary? If yes, on what terms?
f. If the TO is wound up, what immunity does the PTF have against the claims of the TO's creditors?

21.6.1 Is *Takaful Gharar*-Free?

One of the primary objections raised by Muslim scholars against conventional insurance is that it involves excessive uncertainty (*gharar*). Although there is a difference of opinion about the exact extent at which uncertainty becomes *gharar*, opponents of conventional insurance argue that a contract of insurance involves *gharar*. They argue that it is possible in conventional insurance contracts to pay all the premiums, but if the insured event does not take place you lose all the premiums, or in life insurance it is possible that a policyholder might have paid only one premium before he or she dies, and thus the entire amount of insurance will become due to the nominated person. Thus the uncertainty could be very great. The criticism is valid to the extent that the actual facts are like those that have been stated here. But the question arises: does not *takaful* have a similar nature to *gharar*? Is it not true that a *takaful*-holder is entitled to similar benefits or risks to those to which a conventional insurance policyholder is entitled? There is an additional dimension of *gharar* in the case of *takaful*. In the case where the losses are more than the available PTF and the TO is not able or willing to provide an interest-free loan to bridge the gap, the unmet losses are passed on to the *takaful*-holders. It increases their risk to an extent which can be termed *gharar*, as they do not know what their liabilities will be at the end of the day.

21.7 *TAKAFUL* IN PRACTICE

The Islamic Insurance Company of Sudan was the first *takaful* company, and came into being in 1979. Dar al-Maal al-Islami, Luxembourg started *takaful* business in 1983. However, the business could not capture any significant segment of the market. Mulhim and Sabbagh (n.d.) enumerate some of the oldest *takaful* companies as follows:

a. Islamic Insurance Company of Sudan, Khartoum (1979);
b. Arab Islamic Insurance Company, Dubai (1979);
c. National Cooperative Insurance Company, Riyadh (1981);
d. *Takaful* Malaysia (1984);
e. Islamic Insurance and Reinsurance Company, Bahrain (1985);
f. International Islamic Insurance Company, Bahrain (1992);
g. Islamic Insurance Company, Jordan (1996).

In 1997, Asean Re-*takaful* International Limited (ARIL) entered the market as a reinsurance company. In 2006, worldwide reinsurance operators (such as Hannover Re-*takaful*, Bahrain and Munich Re, Malaysia) started dealing with re-*takaful* business as well (E & Y *World Takaful Report* 2008). According to *World Takaful Report 2010* (Ernst & Young 2010) the size of *takaful* business in terms of total contributions rose from $1.384 billion in 2004 to $5.318 billion in 2008. In 2005 there were 82 companies worldwide engaged in *takaful* business, 77 of which were dedicated *takaful* companies, and five were offering *takaful* products through Islamic windows. In 2006, the number of *takaful* operators rose to 133 (Ernst & Young 2008). At present Malaysia and the Gulf countries are leaders in *takaful* business, but even in these countries it was a small segment of the total insurance business (Visser 2009: 104). Staib (2011: 4) reports that the average annual growth rate of *takaful* was 30 per cent in 2007–10. By the end of 2011, total *takaful* contributions amounted to $12 billion (as compared to $4 trillion for conventional insurance) and are expected to touch $25 billion by 2015 (Dar, Rahman, Malik and Kamal 2012: 57).

21.8 ASSESSMENT OF *TAKAFUL* IN PRACTICE

Despite the fact that the basic concept of *takaful* is attractive, the way it is practised leaves an objective observer less than satisfied and gives birth to several questions. The first problem arises from the need to have a legal structure for the proposed solidarity. The laws of most countries require that the solidarity should be registered in some legally acceptable form. It cannot remain an informal group of members. The *takaful* companies have generally complied with this requirement by registering under the relevant insurance laws of each country. For this purpose, the insurance company assumes the role of *takaful* operator. Thus members of the solidarity actually become policyholders of the TO and do not remain members of a solidarity, as originally conceived. However, to maintain the distinction, they are termed *takaful*-holders. A *takaful* organization is similar to a conventional insurance organization in other respects as well. For example, it is the TO which establishes the business and not the *takaful*-holders, who in theory are supposed to form a solidarity group. The TO makes all the crucial decisions, such as rate of premium, risk strategy, asset management and allocation of surpluses and profits. The TO shareholders, and not the *takaful*-holders, appoint and dismiss managers of the *takaful*. The *takaful*-holders do not have any 'voice' regarding management of the TO. For all practical purposes, they are like policyholders of a conventional insurance business company.[1] In conventional insurance, the company's income consists of the underwriting surplus and interest income from the investment of surplus funds. In *takaful* it consists of *wakala* fees (agency fees) and the sharing of profit from the investment of PTF funds. Except for the method of investment of surplus funds the sources of income in both cases remain the same or similar.

The second problem arises from the possibility of the PTF falling short of the actual losses suffered by the *takaful*-holders. In the case of conventional insurance, the insurance company absorbs these losses. In the case of *takaful*, a provision is created whereby the PTF accumulated by the *takaful*-holders borrows on an interest-free basis (*qard hasan*) from the TO enough money to meet any shortfall. The loan is supposed to be, in theory, a loan to members of the solidarity from the TO to cover the risks. The loan is interest-free in theory but in practice the TO may provide the loan for a fee (Visser 2009: 105). This would cause no problem if the members of the group remained static and those who borrowed now remained liable to repay later. However, in practice, members keep on entering and leaving the organization. The members who actually borrow may not be the members who have to repay the loan. The future *takaful*-holders may, quite fairly, be loath to repay the loans taken by past members who have left the solidarity. Conceptually, this creates a problem. There is as yet no general solution to the problem. However, in Pakistan, a practical way out has been found to overcome this difficulty. The insurance premiums of the *takaful*-holders are used to create and register a *waqf* (trust) fund. The *waqf* is a legal entity and can borrow and lend. The fund is responsible for borrowing funds from the TO if there is a shortfall. It also can retain any profits if the funds are invested and there is net income after meeting all the insurance claims. In the case of conventional insurance too, that is what happens in practice. The company is responsible for meeting all the claims and has the right to retain all the residual profits. Since the TO has full control of the operations of the *takaful*, it can determine its agency (*wakala*) fee and its share of profit from investment (as a *mudarib*) in such a manner that it is able to earn a competitive return on its funds. It can thus compensate itself, in a non-transparent manner, for any interest-free loans provided to the PTF. The mechanism of *takaful* through *waqf* gets so close to conventional insurance that it is difficult to tell one from the other. Except for names and terms, the essence of the business in both cases is the same. For this reason, it has come under a lot of criticism from *Shari'ah* scholars (Archer, Karim and Nienhaus 2009).

Perhaps the only difference between conventional insurance and *takaful* is on investment of surplus funds on a fixed-interest basis, which is termed *riba* in the orthodox understanding. As this book has consistently argued that the orthodox understanding of the concept of *riba* is not well founded and requires review, the last objection to conventional insurance also goes. At the end of the day, the *takaful* and the conventional insurance businesses are similar in essence but different in appearance. Some Muslim scholars have pointed out this similarity and have expressed dissatisfaction about the manner in which the concept of *takaful* is being practised. For example, Siddiqi (2006: 18) writes:

> In order to avoid endorsing contingent payments which obviously involve *gharar* (albeit of a special kind) they have tried to model insurance (*takaful*) on altruistic giving (*tabarru'*). *Takaful* companies have filled the gap by rejection of commercially organized life insurance. But reciprocity (give in order to take) is so obvious in *tabarru'* (donation) based mode of *takaful*/insurance, that it runs the risk of losing credibility as a clean Islamic contract, joining the ranks of *Tawarruq* and the newest Islamic bonds/*sukuk*. As a matter of fact, the property of our environment which makes *takaful* possible and effective is the same as behind all kinds of insurance (i.e. the kind of cooperation relied upon in *takaful* would not solve any problem without the property of human environment conceptualized by the law of large numbers). The form of organization chosen to take advantage of the law of large numbers does not change the reality. We can make insurance a not-for-profit activity (provided we can ensure efficient management), but that does not change the essential nature of what is being done.

In brief, the whole movement toward developing a distinct form of Islamic insurance has dwindled to conventional insurance with Arabic terminology and language of contract. The original objections against the conventional insurance business could not be handled in the *takaful* business as well. *Takaful* also entails similar uncertainty to that of conventional business. It manages the entire business in a similar manner to that of a conventional insurance company. The *takaful* company, except for its Arabic name, does not have much difference in the essence of its business when we compare it with a conventional insurance business.

NOTE

1. An exception can be found in Sudan, where the *takaful*-holders have more say in the management of the *takaful* business. See Archer, Karim and Nienhaus (2009: 63–64).

PART IV

Zakah in the present age

22. Contemporary application of the law of *zakah*

Muslims have an obligation to pay a certain percentage of their wealth as *zakah* every year. The Arabic root of the term '*zakah*' refers to the dual meanings 'to grow' and 'to purify'. The *zakah* thus means something that *purifies* (human soul) and something that leads to *growth* (in wealth). The *zakah* as a tax purifies the wealth of any social, moral and spiritual failings in earning it. Besides, after paying the *zakah* the wealth grows in the future through blessings (*baraka*) of God – a spiritual concept that still requires authentic interpretation in a cause–effect framework. It is generally agreed that an Islamic government has an obligation to collect and distribute the *zakah* according to the divine law (Q. 9:60). Primarily, proceeds of the *zakah* are meant for alleviating poverty and providing a social security net. However, the *zakah* can also be spent on the general and broad objective 'in the way of God' (*fi sabil Allah*), which according to some scholars covers a wide range of socio-economic objectives. The present chapter deals with the *zakah* law and its application in the present age. We shall show the problems created by the orthodox interpretation of the law and how it has led to non-achievement of its original objectives.

22.1 ORTHODOX INTERPRETATION OF THE LAW OF *ZAKAH*

The Qur'an mentions the *zakah* at several places. A number of authentic Traditions of the Prophet give instructions about its collection and distribution. The practice of the Prophet and first four caliphs provides further rules. Jurists have elaborated the law over the centuries. The orthodox position is that such matters as the rates, exemption limits (*nisab*) and expenditure heads of the *zakah* as specified in the primary sources are immutable. The opinion does not give much credence to changes that have taken place in the creation and distribution of income and wealth over the centuries, because doing so would take us away from the divine law. As illustrated below, a number of ambiguities stem from a literal application of the law in the present age.

22.1.1　*Zakah* as a Form of *'Ibadah* (Devotional Law)

Orthodox scholars argue that since *zakah* is a form of devotional law (*'ibadah*) its provisions are applicable in letter and spirit in the same form as received from the Prophet and his companions. For example, al-Qardawi (1969: I, xxxiii) argues that the rates and exemption limits (*nisab*) of *zakah* are 'clearly defined in the texts and the Muslims have no disagreement on them through history'. The *zakah* is like the five daily obligatory prayers. For devotional practices Muslims must keep the form and procedural details intact as handed down from their ancestors. Ibn Ashur (2006: 220) explains the rationale for keeping the form and content of devotional laws intact and the reason for allowing changes in social transactions as follows:

> [T]hat acts of ritual worship concern the realization of unchanging purposes, whose permanence and uniform obligation on people throughout the ages do not result in any harm except in very rare situations that are dealt with by the rule of license (*rukhsah*). In contrast, social transactions require explanation according to the changes in circumstances and eras. Therefore, binding people with fixed and uniform rules entails great difficulty and inconvenience for many sections of the community. Accordingly, analogical reasoning operates very rarely in matters of ritual worship in contrast with social transactions where it operates on a very wide scale. Because of this, we find that in the Qur'an the commands regarding transactions are mostly framed in general and universal terms.

A question arises: how do we decide that a particular law is devotional and not transactional? There are no hard-and-fast rules, and jurists have differed through the ages in interpreting the various Islamic laws. In fact, a large number of difficulties in implementing Islamic laws have emerged from this confusion about the nature of a particular law. Ibn Ashur (2006: 65) says:

> In fact, the scholars of Islamic jurisprudence should not have accepted the existence of devotional commands in the legislation of human dealings and transactions (*mu'amalat*). Instead, they should have insured that what was asserted to be devotional rather consists of rules based on subtle and hidden reasons. Many of the rules concerning transactions that some jurists interpreted as merely devotional have been the cause of numerous difficulties for Muslims in their dealings. Indeed, the Muslim community has suffered severely because of this, whereas God says: 'and [He] has laid no hardship on you in [anything that pertains to] religion' (Q. 22:78).

We think the law of *zakah* is one such law on which orthodox scholars have erred by declaring it a devotional law (*'ibadah*) and then insisting on its implementation in a literal sense. If we classify *zakah* as a transactional law and not a devotional law, there does not remain any obstacle in resorting to *ijtehad* in implementing it. Several scholars have emphasized the need for *ijtehad* in the law of *zakah* (e.g. Sadeq 2002; al-Jarhi and Zarqa 2007: 63). They point to the need for the redefinition of exemption limits (*nisab*), recognition of new forms of income and wealth, definition of the poor and needy, meanings of 'in the way of God' (*fi sabil Allah*), methods of distribution of *zakah* proceeds, role of government in *zakah* collection and distribution, application of *zakah* on public assets and financial assets represented by the shares and certificates of companies, rates of *zakah*, and so on.

Orthodox scholars oppose any reconsideration of the *zakah* law. The maximum concession they make is to accept *ijtehad* in cases that are not explicitly covered in the Qur'an or Traditions of the Prophet. While there is no doubt that the Traditions have sanctity, the Prophet made some decisions as head of state in a certain temporal context.[1] As a first step we should carefully identify the context of the Prophet's decisions. For decisions taken in the context of his own time, we should think of present-day solutions even though we find explicit Traditions of the Prophet available on the subject. This may appear iconoclastic but is necessary in achieving the overall objectives of the *Shari'ah*. A blind application of the Traditions can defeat the objectives of the *Shari'ah* itself. The following discussion illustrates the nature of the conflict with the objectives arising from a literal application of the law.

22.1.2 *Zakah* on Income

According to the orthodox interpretation, the *zakah* is payable on year-end savings in terms of cash, jewellery and stock-in-trade. Income from business, salaries and other means is exempt. However, in the case of agriculture the *zakah* is payable on the gross yield of land for each crop. That introduces a sort of inconsistency. While farmers have to pay *zakah* on their income, other professions pay *zakah* only on their savings. The implication could be that a poor farmer may have to pay 5 or 10 per cent[2] of the land's produce as *zakah*, while a rich person, earning through salary, rents and dividends, living in a vast mansion, driving a luxurious car, spending holidays at expensive resorts but saving nothing, may not pay any *zakah*. Besides the fact that it discriminates between two segments of society, it also makes the poor farmer pay the *zakah* but leaves the rich rentier exempt if he or she is spendthrift also. Obviously, this could not be the objective of the *Shari'ah*.

22.1.3   Exemption Limit (*Nisab*) and Distribution of Wealth

There has been a consensus since the times of 'Umar b. Abdulaziz (d. 720) among jurists that the exemption limits (*nisab*) of the *zakah* for gold and silver used to be 20 *dinars* and 200 *dirhams* respectively in the days of the Prophet. It seems that in those days the prices of these two metals had a ratio of 1:10. By the time Ibn Khaldun (1332–1406) wrote his *Muqaddima* the ratio had become 1:7.[3] This ratio has been followed by jurists since then. For example, al-Qardawi (1969: I, 130) has concluded that the *nisab* of gold and silver would be 85 and 595 (ratio of 1:7) grams respectively, if we translate 20 *dinars* and 200 *dirhams* into present-day weights. He also suggests that we should adopt gold as the basis for determining the *nisab* in this age, as the *nisab* in terms of silver would be harsh on the *zakah*-payers.

For livestock, after a lengthy discussion, al-Qardawi (1969: I, 112) has deduced a general principle that the *nisab* is double that of gold and silver. It means the *nisab* for livestock would be 400 *dirhams* in monetary terms. For the *nisab* of agricultural produce, al-Qardawi (1969: I, 186) concludes that, in the present age, it would be equal to 653 kilograms of wheat. For other crops, it would be equal to the price of 653 kilograms of wheat. For liquids such as honey and oils, the *nisab* is 825 litres, although al-Qardawi thinks it should be equal to the average price of 653 kilograms of grain such as wheat (ibid.: 217).

Let us, first, examine the *nisab* for gold and silver. Since the time of the Prophet the exchange rate between these two metals has varied widely and changes on a daily basis. If we adopt the above-stated values of gold and silver as the *nisab* it can create situations which will not be acceptable, even to orthodox scholars. For example, in October 2010 the rate of gold per ounce (troy) was $1381 (or $1381 / 31.10 = $44.41 per gram) and that of silver $24.45 or ($0.79 per gram). The ratio of gold and silver prices was 56:1,[4] while the ratio of the classical *nisab* for these two metals is 7:1, as stated above. It means if a person has gold worth $3330 (i.e. 75 grams, which is less than the 85-gram orthodox limit for gold) he can accept *zakah* as a needy person from someone who has silver worth $513 (650 grams, which is more than the 595-gram orthodox limit for silver) and would be considered rich. Does it make sense? Similar anomalies can be shown if we compare and analyse the *nisab* of livestock and agricultural produce. For example, the retail price of 653 kilograms of wheat in Pakistan during October 2010 was about Rs15000, while the retail price of 825 litres of honey was Rs32000 in that month.

Second, if we insist on keeping the *nisab* limits of the days of the Prophet, we need to face a valid question about discrimination among various categories of income and wealth. For example, according to al-Qardawi, the *nisab* limit for livestock is double that of cash and jewellery. There should be some rationale for continuing with this discrimination in this age. When it comes to *zakah* on agricultural produce and livestock, jurists face a difficulty in sticking to the principle of the sanctity of *nisab*, as the Prophet did not cover all types of rural wealth in his injunctions. The types and varieties of agricultural produce and the nature of livestock farming have undergone significant changes since then. These occupations have become businesses, and calculation of *zakah* on agricultural produce and the number of livestock is not straightforward. The owners have costs to bear, liabilities to pay, incomes to receive in the short and long term, and so on. These elements make it necessary that the *zakah* on agricultural produce and livestock should be assessed as for a business. It further means all discussion on *nisab* of *zakah* in the classical texts on agricultural produce and animal wealth has become redundant. In brief, it is difficult to reconcile such differences. We have no option except to undertake *ijtehad* in defining the exemption limits.

22.1.4 *Zakah* Rates

Muslim scholars generally agree that the rate of *zakah* on gold and silver is 2.5 per cent on year-end balances (al-Qardawi 1969: I, 125). There is also consensus that the rates of *zakah* on agricultural produce are 10 per cent of *gross* produce if the crop is irrigated by rainfall and 5 per cent if it is irrigated manually (ibid.: 178–182). The rate for honey is 10 per cent after deducting expenses (ibid.: 217). The rates for livestock differ according to the type of animal. However, al-Qardawi (ibid.: 112) generalizes the rate at around 2.5 per cent for all types of animals. The rate for animal products like milk, eggs, honey, silk and so on is 10 per cent of the *net* value unless the animals themselves are subject to *zakah* (ibid.: 218). Regarding the *zakah* on minerals, making an analogy with agricultural produce, al-Qardawi thinks the rate should be 10 per cent or 5 per cent depending upon the extraction costs. If, for example, the minerals are on the surface of the earth and do not require arduous work, the rate could be 10 per cent. If, however, extraction requires digging and significant costs, the rate could be 5 per cent (ibid.: 228).

The above rates create problems on criteria of equity and the incidence of taxation. For example, the rates of *zakah* on gross produce make sense if farming requires only seed and water. In the present day, a number of inputs like fertilizers, pesticides and machinery are needed to grow crops. Ignoring these expenses could render the net yield equal to or even less than the *zakah* payable. For example, if we levy *zakah* on gross yield we would take away the entire surplus if the net yield is equal to the rate of *zakah*. We would force the farmer to borrow to pay the *zakah* if the net yield is less than the *zakah* payable. Obviously, such could not be the objective of the *Shari'ah*. The implication is that we need to rethink the rates and apply them to net rather than to gross yield; otherwise we can end up at a totally meaningless system of taxation.

There is a need to rationalize the rates of *zakah* for other agricultural products such as honey and milk. People producing different agricultural products should pay *zakah* on their respective products at similar rates if we want to minimize distortions in economic activity. The same is the case for minerals. There is a need to review the rates of *zakah* on minerals. There could be hardly any income from mines without involving significant costs. It would be fair if we treated mining as a business and distributed the net profits among owners who would pay the *zakah* as applicable to them on their income and wealth. On an analogy with agricultural income, in a case where the owner of a mine has not worked actively, the rate should be 10 per cent. If, however, the owner has worked to generate the income, the rate should be 5 per cent. This approach does away with such subjective questions as whether the costs are significant or mining is an arduous activity or the mineral wealth is on top of the earth or is buried, and so on. All these subjective questions are taken care of in this approach.

A similar readjustment of rates is desirable in the case of livestock. For example, the rates of *zakah* on sheep start at 2.5 per cent and regress to less than 1 per cent as the flock exceeds 500 sheep (al-Qardawi 1969: I, 98). The same is the case for rates on cows and camels. Table 22.1 (Abu Saud 1988: 34) illustrates the point further. The rates get lower as the number increases. We cannot at this stage explain the rationale for such rates. One possibility, which Abu Saud has indicated, is that these rates did not have the divine sanction (Abu Saud 1988: 2). The Prophet's letter from which they were taken was never issued by him. Maybe these rates did not have any divine sanction but were considered in the conditions of Arabia at the time. (God knows the best.) However, in this age we do not find any rationale to apply them, firstly because they are regressive and secondly because they apply to cattle freely grazing in wild land where there are no overheads on their grazing (al-Qardawi 1969: I, 83). The second condition has also changed materially. Cattle are now reared on farms, and farmers have to incur significant expenses which cannot be ignored. In brief, application of these rates would lead to several anomalies. The rates should be the basis for further thinking and review.

Table 22.1   Rates of zakah *applicable on sheep*

Range	Rate (no. of sheep)	Incidence (%)
1–39	0	0
40–120	1	2.5 – 0.83
121–200	2	1.65 – 1.00
201–399	3	1.49 – 0.75
400–499	4	1.00 – 0.80
500–599	5	1.00 – 0.83
Over 600	One extra sheep for each 100	<1

22.1.5   *Zakah* on Fixed Assets

The orthodox position is that fixed assets of a business firm, not meant for trade, are exempt from *zakah* on the analogy with the tools of a crafts-man which are exempt by a consensus (see e.g. al-Qardawi 1969: I, 170; Rahman 2006–07: 92). The position ignores the fact that the fixed assets of a business firm are not the same thing as the tools and implements of a workman. Large-scale industrial concerns own fixed assets worth huge amounts. Considering these assets as analogous to the tools and imple-ments of a workman is nothing but naivety. Business firms generate profits by using all their assets including fixed assets. Giving exemptions to fixed assets would mean that factories, machines, equipment, cars, planes, ships, buildings, real estate and fixtures were exempt from *zakah* regardless of their value, earnings or size. However, al-Qardawi, after a lengthy discus-sion (1969: I, 246 and II, 250), concludes that *income* from factories, rented buildings and other fixed assets should be taxed but the assets themselves should be exempt. He adds that a certain percentage of income can be set aside for depreciation of assets so that replacement is possible at a later date. Subject to this, the *zakah* on fixed assets should be treated like *zakah* on agricultural income.

22.1.6   *Zakah* on Stock-in-Trade

Jurists have discussed the question of stock-in-trade or inventory from different angles. Al-Qardawi (1969: I, 61, 169) discusses the issue at length. He concludes that the firm should pay *zakah* on cash, receivables and inventory after deducting any liabilities and bad debts. The approach does not handle the issue of *zakah* on business firms in a comprehensive manner and leaves several questions unanswered. For example, how do we determine the value of inventory? There are several methods familiar to accountants (such as LIFO, FIFO, average and so on), and the room for manipulation is great. Second, it introduces a dichotomy between *zakah* on agricultural produce and *zakah* on business. On agricultural produce the tax is on the produce (output or income), but in the case of business the *zakah* is on current assets irrespective of whether the business is profitable or not. Should the business's current assets be taxed even though the business is in loss? Third, the approach ignores the fact that the business concern generates profit by use of all resources and not by current assets alone. Fixed assets also contribute to the profitability of the firm. Is it fair to ignore fixed assets when taxing the business firm? Fourth, a business firm may also use third-party resources in the form of long-term and short-term liabilities, which contribute to its profitability and should be considered while determining the *zakah*. Fifth, the business firm may have old, unsold inventory or bad and doubtful debts. Levying *zakah* on such assets year after year would be unfair to the business firm. Focusing only on cash, receivables and inventory is a truncated view of the *zakah* on the business entity. The business concern should pay *zakah* on its net income at the year-end.

The form and size of a business have undergone a tremendous change since the early days of Islam. In a situation where a business meant buying or selling on the spot or at the most having a shop with a small amount of fixed assets, we could think of levying *zakah* on cash and whatever was the year-end balance of stock-in-trade, because that would be the entire wealth of a businessman. But in the present day the business involves large amounts of capital invested in fixed assets such as land, buildings, machinery and fixtures, with large amounts of short- and long-term liabilities. In this situation, taxing merely the cash and stock-in-trade leaves the bulk of the wealth untaxed, and we might end up taxing the poor and exempting the rich. Such cannot be the objective of the *Shari'ah*. Moreover, new forms of business have emerged which were not in existence in seventh-century Arabia. For example, leasing, financial services, professional practice, consultancy, publication of newspapers, TV channels, e-commerce and so on are new forms of business. Many of them do not have any stock-in-trade in the traditional sense. If we stick to the principle that a business means cash and stock-in-trade, a large number of wealthy people will pay very little *zakah*, as they will not have much stock-in-trade or cash in hand.

22.2   ISSUES IN *ZAKAH* APPLICATION

22.2.1   Exemption Limit (*Nisab*) of *Zakah*

We have discussed above the need to revise the orthodox approach towards *nisab*. Some other scholars have also realized the need to revise the *nisab* in this age. For example, Sadeq (2002: 33) mentions Kahf arguing for devising a formula for determining the *nisab* in light of the prices of commodities in the days of the Prophet and then adjusting it for prices in the present time. Sadeq (ibid.: 35) refers to Raquibuzzaman, who suggests that the *nisab* should be equivalent to an amount which is adequate to maintain a reasonable standard of living and should be revised as prices change. Sadeq (ibid.) also mentions Abu Saud, who pleads for a change to *nisab* limits. It should be enough for the sustenance of an average family for a year and should be reviewed regularly according to changing circumstances. Shah Waliullah (2003: 298) also thinks that the *nisab* is meant to suffice for a small family for the whole year.

Al-Qardawi (1969: I, 136) presents the opinions of Malikite and Hanafite jurists that the *nisab* should be over and above the basic needs. He does not elaborate the point any further. However, while discussing the *zakah* liability of rental income from fixed assets (ibid.: 248), he concludes that the gross income should be reduced by the minimum living expenses required by the owners, and the residual, if equal to or more than the *nisab*, should be taxed. In this manner he maintains the classical *nisab* limits for judging the status of the person only. The status defines whether a person is subject to *zakah* or not. It does not define the amount on which the *zakah* is payable. Once a person is defined as subject to *zakah* (*sahib al-nisab*), he or she should be given an allowance for living expenses. The exemption for living expenses is besides the *nisab*. Thus he pleads for two exemptions: (i) exemption of *nisab*; and (ii) exemption for living expenses (al-Qardawi 1969: II, 276). In our opinion, this is unnecessary. Al-Qardawi has tried to make room for an additional exemption because he does not dare to depart from the traditional *nisab* limits. At the same time he is uncomfortable with the classical law that would tax even the income that is necessary for basic living. To solve the problem he introduces two exemptions and labours hard to justify them. A simpler solution could be to revise the *nisab* limit, make it equal to the basic needs of the poorest segment of society and deduct the *nisab* from the income. The balance should be subject to *zakah*. It would take care of basic living expenses and also rationalize the system.

The following questions require the attention of scholars in this age if they agree to undertake *ijtehad* to revise the *nisab*:

a.   If the rationale for the *nisab* is to give exemption for personal
     expenses, should we define its limits differently for different income
     groups? If the answer is 'yes', the method of categorizing people and
     deciding *nisab* for each category would invite value judgements which
     cannot be reconciled easily. If the answer is 'no', then we have to
     define a single *nisab* for all types of income and wealth. In that case,
     how do we define that limit?
b.   Once the limit of the *nisab* is defined (somehow), do we levy *zakah*
     on the balance of the wealth after deducting the *nisab*, or is it only a
     defining limit for the *status* of the person and, once a person exceeds
     that limit, should his or her entire income/wealth be taxed?

Contemporary jurists have not addressed these questions adequately.
Our opinion is as follows:

a.   The *nisab* should be equivalent to the aggregate minimum wage for
     a year as defined in each country by its government or parliament.
     The limit should be valid for all categories of income and wealth. This
     should also be the *nisab* for livestock wealth. However, if a person has
     a short-term debt to be paid within the next 12 months, the amount
     of the debt should be deducted from the closing cash balance to deter-
     mine whether the wealth or income of the person is equal to *nisab* or
     not.
b.   Regarding deduction of the *nisab* from income, our opinion is that
     it should be deducted from the gross income and *zakah* should be
     payable on the balance. Those who have income equal to the *nisab*
     will have zero *zakah* liability. However, when calculating *zakah* on
     personal wealth (as opposed to income) there should be no deduction
     of the *nisab*, because the wealth consists of accumulated savings which
     are over and above current consumption.

There are several advantages in the above approach. First, it does not
leave definition of the *nisab* in the hands of individuals or any specific
income category. Second, it is better to adopt the needs of the poorest
segment as the basis for defining the *nisab* than to consider various segments of society, each of which will have a different set of basic needs.
Third, it is applicable across the board on all persons and all types of
income and wealth. The literature on *zakah* delves into the question of
nisab and rates in great detail and tries to determine the *nisab* for each
type of wealth and income separately. Besides being cumbersome, it
introduces anomalies. The above proposal streamlines the limit for all
types of income and wealth. Fourth, the proposal exempts the poor and

achieves the egalitarian objective of the *Shari'ah*. Fifth, it levies *zakah* on a higher proportion of income as the income level goes up. Thus the incidence of *zakah*, which otherwise is a proportional tax, tends to be progressive. Since the *nisab* would be fixed for at least one year, the impact of deducting the *nisab* on the incidence would be progressive. As a person earns more income, the deduction of *nisab* being the same, it would leave a higher percentage of income available for tax. Thus the higher income groups will pay *zakah* on a higher percentage of their income.

The above principle implies that the *nisab* for livestock and agricultural produce will also be the same as above. Obviously, those who think that the *nisab* limits prescribed by the Prophet are sacrosanct and applicable for all times to come cannot accept this idea. However, their position raises some questions. First, the Prophet has prescribed *nisab* limits for camels but not for cows (al-Qardawi 1969: I, 92). Obviously, we need to do some thinking if the livestock consists of cows. It means we agree to open the door to *ijtehad* in some cases. If that is so, why do we not open it in other cases as well in the interest of greater transparency, fairness and consistency?

Al-Qardawi (1969: I, 168) has raised another issue. Should we consider the *nisab* at the beginning or the end of the year or at both points in time? After lengthy discussion his conclusion is that the *nisab* is relevant for the amount of wealth or income at the year-end, irrespective of the financial position at the beginning of or during the year. He supports this position on analogy with the Prophet's own practice of levying *zakah* on livestock if the number was above the *nisab* at the year-end. It is a rational approach, but it does not specifically mention the *nisab* for wealth and *nisab* for income separately. Our opinion is that, if the closing balance of wealth is above the *nisab* limit, the person becomes liable to *zakah*. Similarly, if the aggregate income of the whole year, calculated at the year-end, is above the aggregate of the annual minimum wage, the person will be liable to pay *zakah*.

22.2.2   One-Year Term

We agree with the principle of a one-year term for calculating the *zakah* payable by a person or a business entity. The important accounting implication is that once a person pays *zakah* he or she does not pay it again on the same wealth in the same year. But the wealth will be subject to *zakah* in subsequent years if it exceeds the *nisab*. The condition of one year is fulfilled if the person or the business entity had income or wealth above the *nisab* (i.e. *sahib al-nisab*) at the beginning of the year and also at the year-end, no matter what happened during the year. However, we need to explain it further. In the case of income, the *zakah* will be payable on total income minus the *nisab*. For wealth, the *zakah* will be payable on total wealth minus any increase due to income on which the *zakah* has already been paid during the year. The *zakah* will not be payable on the closing balance but on the opening balance of the wealth, since the closing balance may have increased due to any savings from the current year's income, on which *zakah* has already been paid. There could, however, be a situation where a person may have spent some of his or her savings. In that case, the closing balance of the wealth may have gone down as compared to the opening balance. In that case, the *zakah* would be calculated on the lower of the opening and closing balances. In sum, the general principle is that the *zakah* on the wealth of an individual would be payable on the lower of the opening and closing balances without deducting the *nisab*.

While applying this principle across the board on the entire population, the *zakah*-collecting authority has to define the *zakah* year and cut-off dates for determining the *zakah* liability of every person. It may create problems in individual cases. For example, it may be possible for a person to obtain some cash only a few days before the cut-off date and the *zakah* may become payable on it. Similarly, it is possible for a person to receive a deposit by way of trust or loan that is part of the closing cash balance. To solve these and similar problems, our opinion is that, when calculating individual liability on cash balances, the *zakah* should be payable on the lower of the opening and closing balances. To understand this principle we need to analyse reasons for movements in the opening cash balances. Increase in opening cash balances could be the result of one of the following:

a. sale proceeds of a capital asset;
b. dividends or profits from investment;
c. income from wage or salary income, agricultural income, professional services and so on;
d. gifts, bonuses, royalties, inheritance, unusual incomes and so on.

We will treat the above one by one:

a. The sale proceeds of a capital asset will be taken into account to calculate net profit from the asset. The *zakah* will be payable on the net profit, and the balance of the proceeds will become part of the cash and bank balances.
b. The dividends and profits from investment will be subject to *zakah* as they accrue. The balance, after paying the *zakah*, will become part of the cash balances.

c. The *zakah* on income from wages and salaries will accrue as the income is received. Any savings from the income will become part of the cash balances.

d. The *zakah* will also be payable on gifts, bonuses, royalties, inheritance and other incomes as they accrue. The balance will become part of the cash balances. It is obvious that, if the cash balance of a person increases during the year for any of the above reasons, he or she has already paid *zakah* on the income before the residue was added to the increase in the cash balances. Therefore now the *zakah* is due only on the opening balances. That is why we have argued that the *zakah* on cash balances will be on the lower of the opening and closing balances.

Similarly, the opening cash balances can decrease by the year-end for the following reasons:

a. equity investment/financial assets;
b. purchase of durable assets;
c. excess of current expenses over current income;
d. emergencies;
e. repayment of liabilities.

In all such cases, the closing cash balances will be lower than the opening balances, assuming there is no increase in the opening cash balance from any other source. In all fairness, the person should pay *zakah* on the closing cash balance, which is the lower of the opening and closing balances.

The above discussion has not taken into account any increase in the cash balances due to temporary deposits, loans or trust funds. These funds will be deducted from the closing balances to determine the net closing balance before it is compared with the opening cash balance to determine the *zakah* liability because the person does not own these balances.

To understand the principle, let us take an example. Suppose Mr A has Rs500 000 as a closing balance, which includes Rs200 000 as dividend income from investment in shares of a company. He is liable to pay *zakah* on Rs200 000 at 10 per cent as he receives this income. The balance of Rs180 000 will have become part of the closing balance. Suppose further that the opening balance was Rs350 000. In this case, the *zakah* will be payable on Rs350 000 and not on Rs500 000. If, for example, the closing balance includes a sum of Rs200 000 as a trust deposit from a friend or a short-term loan, his actual closing balance will be Rs300 000. The *zakah* will be payable on Rs300 000, which is the lower of the opening and closing balances. However, if the opening balance is Rs750 000, the *zakah* will be payable on Rs500 000 or Rs300 000 (assuming a trust deposit of Rs200 000). By adopting this method we can observe the true spirit of the principle of the passing of a year on the wealth.

Regarding *zakah* on livestock, we should conceive livestock rearing as a business. Each livestock farmer's business should be assessed for profit or loss at the year-end, and the *zakah* should be payable on the profit if the owner of the business has income above the *nisab* or his or her assets are above the *nisab*. The livestock kept for personal use or for agricultural use will be exempt like other personal assets. In this proposal we are trying to harmonize the law of *zakah* for all types of income and wealth.

22.2.3   Rates of *Zakah*

There are four sets of rates available in the primary sources of Islam. The first set relates to cash, jewellery and business stock-in-trade. This is 2.5 per cent of the capital value. The second set relates to agricultural produce. The rates are 10 per cent on the produce of land irrigated by rainfall and 5 per cent on the produce of land irrigated artificially. The third set is applicable to livestock and is a detailed code. The fourth set relates to wealth found as treasure trove. The rate is 20 per cent. We need to decide on the rate of *zakah* for various types of income and wealth in the present age so that all taxpayers are treated equitably and the objectives of the *Shari'ah* are also met.

Sadeq (2002: 33) mentions Kahf pleading for revision of the rates but does not suggest new rates. He refers to Mannan, who wants to make household durable assets subject to *zakah* by redefining the *nisab* limits. Mannan also suggests having different rates of *zakah* except for gold and silver, which are fixed by the Traditions. We find a lot of hesitation among Muslim scholars when suggesting a change in the rates. Most of them emphasize adopting the rates of *zakah* found in the Traditions of the Prophet, since a change would be sacrilege. However, the problem has become serious because of the change in the nature of wealth. Of many changes that have taken place, the general acceptance of the concepts of stock and flow of wealth is the most prominent. Classical jurists considered *zakah* a tax on the wealth of a person at the year-end. But in this age we can imagine situations where wealthy people, earning fabulous amounts of income from salaries and past investments, either spend their income on luxuries or reinvest those incomes in a manner that leaves little in their cash balances. To bring this category into the tax net, wealth should be recognized both as a flow and as stock. The flow of wealth should be subject to *zakah* as the income accrues, and the stock should be subject to *zakah* at the year-end. This is in conformity with what the

Prophet himself ordained in the case of *zakah* on agricultural produce and *zakah* on cash. If a farmer has to pay *zakah* on his or her produce, why should not other people also pay on their incomes and profits? Once we accept this general principle, the application of *zakah* in the contemporary age becomes simple and straightforward.

To levy the *zakah* on flows of wealth, we can adopt the same rates as the Prophet prescribed for agriculture. For income earned through active work the rate should be 5 per cent and for income gained without work the rate should be 10 per cent. For stocks of wealth, we can adopt the rate of 2.5 per cent on the 'lower of the opening and closing balance' once a year. The rates of livestock need to be analysed in this age in light of the prevalent prices. The given rates were rational in the times of the Prophet. They require reconsideration in light of current market conditions to achieve the objectives of the law.

Al-Qardawi (1969: I, 90–91), while stating the law of *zakah* on camels, mentions that the Prophet himself equated the price of sheep with 10 *dirhams* on one occasion and with 20 *dirhams* on another. It shows that rates during the time of the Prophet were rational in light of market prices. Instead of insisting on retaining these rates as they were, we need to re-examine them in light of present-day conditions and rationalize them. Al-Qardawi (1969: I, 108) suggests that the rate of *zakah* on horses should be 2.5 per cent of the value on the basis of the opinion of 'Umar b. Khattab (d. AH 23), who levied *zakah* on horses at one *dinar* per horse. Nowadays, the value of horses is not the same, and nor do the *dinars* of those days exist. We should decide the matter in light of contemporary conditions. The rate should be decided by people of wisdom (ibid.: 231). It affirms the principle that revision of the rates is possible if the socio-economic conditions so require.

We think the most appropriate basis for analogical reasoning is *zakah* on agricultural income. For agricultural income, the *Shari'ah* has kept in view the degree of human effort in generating the income. We can use the same rationale for further reasoning. However, in this age, since agriculture involves significant expenses, the *zakah* rate should be applied on the net income rather than on the gross yield. This general principle can be applied across the board for all types of income. We can say that the *zakah* rate on the yield of assets will be 10 per cent if there is no human effort in earning the income and 5 per cent if there is human effort. It means that the rate on net income from business, salaries or professional practice will be 5 per cent. But the *zakah* rate on income from *mudaraba*, dividends, rents, interest on deposits, and so on will be 10 per cent. However, in each case direct expenses in generating the income will be deducted from the gross yield before applying the rate. Abu Saud has recommended the rate of *zakah* on salary income as 2.5 per cent. We do not agree with it. If we apply 2.5 per cent on salary income, it will introduce an inconsistency in the whole system. In that case, the rate of professional income may also have to be revised. So we do not see any reason why we should treat salary income differently from other income.

22.2.4 Condition of Growth

Al-Qardawi (1969: I, 59) explains the reason for the condition of 'growth' in wealth for *zakah* to be applicable:

> Ibn al Humam[5] writes, '*Zakah* is legislated to help and relieve the poor without impoverishing the rich, by having the rich pay from their surplus, taking a little from the plenty. Imposing *zakah* on wealth that does not, by definition, grow, reverses this purpose, since *zakah* is paid year after year, in addition to living expenses.'

Al-Qardawi (1969: I, 60) adds: 'What is important, however, is the growth potential of the assets and not actual growth, because actual growth can hardly be measured and is subject to differences in measurement.' Al-Qardawi (ibid.: I, 62) has further taken up the issue of wealth which was not invested by its owner. His opinion is that such wealth should be subject to *zakah* even if the owner was unable to invest it. Generally, this opinion makes sense, because it will encourage people to invest their surplus wealth. However, it does not consider the special case of old-age pensioners who have some wealth to fend for their old-age expenses. They are themselves unable to do any business, and handing over this wealth to another person for business entails significant risks. What is the obligation of *zakah* for such persons? In particular, we should also keep in view that this wealth is already subject to reduction by inflation. Contemporary jurists have not discussed this question. Our opinion is that such wealth should be declared exempt from *zakah*. If we do not do that we risk pushing the self-sufficient into dependency over time as their past savings deplete through inflation and *zakah*. Obviously, that would defeat the objective of the *Shari'ah*.

Sadeq (2002: 37) refers to Kahf and Abu Saud. Both of them consider the condition of growth (*mal nami*) as ill-founded and superfluous. However, orthodox scholars consider it a necessary condition and because of that exclude fixed assets from the application of *zakah*.

22.2.5 *Zakah* and Income Tax

The introduction of *zakah* laws in some Muslim countries has brought to the forefront a problem for ordinary taxpayers. As Muslims they are obliged to pay *zakah* and as citizens of the state they have to pay income tax. Some people feel they are subject to dual taxation for the same income and wealth. Orthodox scholars insist that the *zakah* must be paid, as it is an obligation from God and no one can waive it. The state requires that the income tax must also be paid under the law of the land, which does not recognize any exemption for the *zakah* paid.[6] There is no final solution to this dichotomy. However, Iqbal and Lewis (2009) have made a reasonable suggestion. They think that the income tax law should allow every taxpayer to declare the amount of tax to be adjusted against the *zakah* liability. The amount of *zakah* declared should be accounted for distinctly and used for objectives of the *zakah*. In brief, they have recommended a rebate for the *zakah* paid by an individual provided the state collects it. The solution solves the problem of dual taxation and also empowers the state to recognize *zakah* as regular revenue for social security and poverty alleviation programmes.

22.2.6 *Zakah* on Agricultural Produce

Agricultural produce is subject to *zakah* by a consensus if the production is over and above the *nisab*. However, there is some difference of opinion about whether the *zakah* is payable on the gross or net value of the produce. Al-Qardawi (1969: II, 276) contends on the authority of various classical jurists that production expenses must be deducted before assessing *zakah* on agricultural produce. This implies that the net value and not the gross value of the produce is subject to *zakah*.[7] We support this opinion, as it resolves a potential situation of levying tax even when the net value is below the *nisab*.

Another issue about agricultural produce pertains to estimation of the crop before harvesting. The officer deputed for estimation is advised to determine the average and not the maximum value of the crop. Jurists have recommended that persons responsible for estimation should be honest and just. However, this is a weak area of practice. It opens the door to discretion and corruption. The government should develop procedures for fair and equitable estimation and leave minimal discretion to public functionaries.

Yet another important question relating to *zakah* on agricultural produce pertains to the status of land. Islamic jurisprudence treats distinctly the lands on which Caliph 'Umar (AH 12–23) levied *kharaj* (land tax) after the conquest of Iraq, Syria, Egypt, Iran and so on (Abu Yusuf 1966). Since then these lands have been considered as *kharaji* lands, that is, lands on which *kharaj* is payable. The lands of Arabia which came under Muslim rule earlier by conversion of the owners are considered *ushri* lands, that is, lands on which *ushr* (10 per cent or a part thereof) is payable. It is generally agreed that the classification of lands into *kharaji* and *ushri* categories is eternal. To the extent that the tillers of the *kharaji* lands were non-Muslims, it was a simple tax regime. The tillers paid *kharaj* as rent because the land belonged to the Islamic state. Since they were non-Muslims, they were not subject to *ushr*, which is a religious tax. However, the situation became fluid when the tillers started converting to Islam or the Muslims started purchasing the *kharaji* lands. The question arose: what should be the tax on these lands?[8] One opinion was that the owners or tillers as Muslims should pay *ushr* only. However, this created discrimination on the basis of faith. For two persons with land side by side, one Muslim and one non-Muslim, the Muslim would pay 5 or 10 per cent tax, but the non-Muslim would pay *kharaj*, which was usually higher (20 per cent or more). That created dissatisfaction and was also obviously unfair. The other opinion was that Muslims should pay both *kharaj* and *ushr*. They should pay *kharaj*, since they were tilling state lands and the state should get a share of the produce as rent. They should also pay *ushr*, since all Muslims are required to pay *ushr* on their crops. However, it created discrimination against Muslims. It became a disadvantage to be a Muslim. The tax regime defeated the objectives of the *Shari'ah*. A third opinion was that conversion to Islam should not matter. Tillers of the *kharaji* lands should pay *kharaj*, and owners of the *ushri* lands should pay *ushr*. The opinion was an obvious amendment to the *Shari'ah* rule that all Muslims must pay *ushr* on agricultural produce. The confusion about the final position with reference to the status of the land persists to this day. Muslim scholars are not unanimous about the tax rate with reference to the status of the land and the faith of the tiller.

Our opinion is that the confusion has arisen by treating the classification of *kharaji* and *ushri* lands as eternal. The decision of Caliph 'Umar at the time was most appropriate in light of the objectives of the *Shari'ah*. With the passage of time, the ground reality has changed. Muslims are no longer conquering new lands, and conversion is also not that rapid. Besides, there are developments in human thinking on fiscal management as well. It is now generally accepted that the citizens of a state should not be discriminated against on the basis of faith. Even the Qur'an (Q. 11:15) makes an oblique reference to the general principle that people must not be discriminated against while being rewarded for their efforts in worldly affairs because of their faith. For these reasons, the most appropriate approach is to review the question of land tax afresh. There should be only one tax regime, which should not discriminate against faith. The tax regime should be based on the system of *ushr* on net value of the land produce. The general rates of *ushr* (10 per cent or a proportion of that) as applicable to Muslims should also be payable by non-Muslims. If, however, they have an objection to the use of religious terms such as *ushr* and half-*ushr*, the nomenclature of the tax can be changed, but the rates should remain universal for all irrespective of faith.

22.2.7   Disbursement of *Zakah*

The Qur'an has prescribed eight broad categories of people who are entitled to receive *zakah* funds (Q. 9:60): the poor (*fuqara'*); the needy (*masakin*); *zakah* collectors; those whose hearts have to be won over; those who are freeing human beings from bondage; those who are over-burdened with debts; those who are struggling in the cause of God; and wayfarers. Muslim scholars have discussed and elaborated these categories at length. We shall not reproduce the discussion here to avoid digression, but a relevant question for the present age is about spending the proceeds of the *zakah* on development projects for the welfare of the common man. Some scholars allow it, others allow it with some restrictions and still others disallow it. There is no consensus on the issue. Sadeq (2002: 40) has summarized various opinions on the subject. The *zakah* law of Pakistan allows loans from the *zakah* fund for constructing hospitals for the poor (ibid.: 47). Al-Qardawi (1969: II, 53) supports use of the *zakah* fund for loans to the needy.

Spending from *zakah* funds in the way of God (*fi sabil Allah*) has been a point of controversy among contemporary and earlier generations of Muslim scholars. Al-Qardawi (1969: II, 71) discusses it at length and con-cludes that it pertains to the struggle for Islam (*jihad*) in its broader mean-ings. In this age, it will include all intellectual, cultural and informational activities for spreading the message of Islam. Of course, it does include, as a priority, any armed struggle to defend Muslim lands against foreign aggression or to liberate the Muslim population from the colonial yoke. However, fighting for mundane purposes or to usurp other people's lands or to secure the wealth of other countries is not *jihad*, and *zakah* cannot be spent for such armed adventures. It also does not include activities of general welfare, which should be financed from other taxes and not from *zakah* funds. We tend to agree with al-Qardawi on this conclusion.

22.2.8 Incidence of *Zakah*: Progressive or Not?

An objection to the orthodox interpretation is that the *zakah* is regressive and causes a higher burden on the poor as compared to the rich (e.g. Saleh and Ngah 1980). The concept of progressive taxation is a later development in public finance and is in line with the egalitarian stance of Islam. However, the orthodox interpretation does not reconcile with the egalitarian nature of Islam. The problem arises from the belief that the rates of *zakah* are immutable and cannot be changed. However, when the question of incidence of taxation crops up, the Muslims have lame excuses. For example, Abu Bakar and Rahman (2007: 30) say:

> Comparing *zakah* with progressive taxation, *zakah* was claimed as having a wider base than progressive taxation; it is imposed not only on income, but also on idle assets. The proceeds of *zakah* will benefit mainly and directly the poor and the needy. Hence, it will consequently raise the propensity to consume.

The rates of *zakah* are proportionate and not progressive. However, the rationale behind progressive taxation is also quite compelling. Consequently, some Muslim economists tend to accept progressive taxation while others, who insist on keeping the rates of *zakah* intact, argue for proportionate taxation. Kuran (1989: 179) sums up the confusion as follows:

> There is a similar controversy over the method of financing public projects. '. . . A progressive taxation system', says one prominent Islamic economist, 'seems to be perfectly in harmony with the goals of Islam.'[9] Another sharply disagrees: 'Progressive taxation assumes illegitimacy of the income of the rich. The rising slabs represent taxation with vendetta. Only a proportional tax at a fixed rate (on the pattern of *Zakat*) is to be levied on the accumulated wealth of the capable taxpayers without any distinction.'[10] Yet another Islamic economist sees merit in both positions: 'Proportional taxation becomes Islamic if income and wealth are already distributed according to Islamic economic egalitarian criteria. . . . However, in the existence of mal-distribution of income and wealth . . . a progressive system of taxation should be invoked.'[11]

We have argued in this chapter that the orthodox interpretation of the *zakah* law requires reconsideration. We have proposed certain changes in the exemption limit and rates of *zakah*. The effect of these changes will be that people with higher income will pay *zakah* on a higher proportion of their income as compared to people with lower income, though the tax rates remain proportionate. It would make the *zakah* progressive to some extent but not in the usual sense understood by this term. It may require some further thinking.

22.3   *ZAKAH* AND POVERTY

There is hardly any need to discuss the importance of poverty alleviation. It is now generally accepted as the most serious problem of humanity. Besides, Islam treats poverty as an enemy of spiritual progress as well. The Prophet once prayed for God's refuge against poverty and disbelief and clarified that both are equally undesirable.[12] The Qur'an emphasizes distribution of income and wealth and encourages Muslims to ensure that wealth does not keep circulating among wealthy people only (Q. 59:7). The fight against poverty has a spiritual dimension also. It is a religious duty of the Islamic state to alleviate poverty, mainly through *zakah*, though Islam prescribes other means as well. Shirazi (2006: 19) says:

> Most of the African Muslim countries are very poor and they need large funds for meeting their resource shortfall. *Zakah* proceeds from these countries, even collected to its potential, are not sufficient. Therefore, other sources of transfers are needed. These countries need the help from other rich countries. Some countries are able to overcome shortfall of their core poor from the potential *zakah* collection. Therefore, a system of *zakah* should be introduced in its true spirit in all Muslim countries, where resource surplus countries could help resource-deficit countries.

However, despite his concern for poverty, Shirazi does not go far enough to suggest a review of the contemporary interpretation of the *zakah* rules, including the possibility of revising the *zakah* rates, applying *zakah* on flows of capital (like current incomes) besides stock of capital (like savings), investing *zakah* proceeds for the benefit of the potential beneficiaries, and so on. Leaving out all such possibilities of *ijtehad*, his lament about the inadequacy of the *zakah* proceeds for fighting poverty is not well founded.

The literature on Islamic economics is replete with romantic visions of social insurance established during the period of the Prophet and the first four caliphs. The state at that time actually took care of the poor and the indigent through the proceeds of the *zakah*. We think the system of social insurance started by the Prophet and continued by the first four caliphs was the beginning of an institution. With the passage of time, the institution of *zakah* has decayed. Muslims did not develop it further and left the work unfinished. There is a need to develop the system of social insurance latent in the law of *zakah* according to the needs of the twenty-first century. That would require not only rethinking some elements of the law but also tailoring the administrative and governance structures of the *zakah* to suit present-day needs.

22.3.1 Proposed Poverty Alleviation Model

Poverty alleviation with *zakah* and charitable spending has a romantic appeal among Muslims. However, in actual practice, they are unable to solve two problems:

a. All schemes of poverty alleviation which aim to provide assistance in cash or kind run the risk of the undeserving non-poor queuing up for assistance. It is usually very difficult to determine who deserves and who does not except at the cost of violating the personal privacy of the poor and at the risk of injuring personal dignity. Organizations doing this work have tried various methods that are either expensive or ineffective.
b. The other problem is the reverse of the above. Some deserving people hesitate to line up for help for reasons of self-respect and personal dignity. There is no satisfactory method of bringing such people into the social safety net.

There is a general environment of mistrust and potential corruption in welfare schemes run by the government or public sector organizations. Philanthropists who have the means to fund government-run welfare programmes have mistrust. Moreover, the administrative cost and inefficiency of the government-run programmes leave much to be desired. The following proposal can help overcome these problems:

a. Poverty alleviation should be made a private sector project. The government should operate through the private sector and not undertake any direct role. The main role of the government should be in creating an enabling environment for the private sector. It should encourage philanthropists to organize themselves in NGOs, enact enabling statutes, issue guidelines, and create a system of record keeping and a mechanism for oversight and accountability.
b. The law relating to poverty alleviation should define various categories of the poor and the nature of assistance for each category. It should also define the source of funds for each category. For example, it should clarify if a certain category of the poor should be given a grant or a loan, and so on. Such details can be defined in the law relating to poverty alleviation.
c. The law should provide incentives for NGOs to register with the government to play an effective role.
d. The government should undertake independent poverty surveys of the entire country and produce data on profiles of the poor in each

area. The data should be available online and updated regularly. The survey should be a continuous activity.

e.   It should be possible for NGOs to check from the government database the profile of every person who has applied for help from charity funds.

f.   It should also be possible to draw data about persons who deserve charity but have not applied for help and thus are not registered as applicants.

g.   The government should create a complaint-handling mechanism to redress any abuse or misuse of public donations by private sector bodies.

h.   The government should have a mechanism for protecting whistle-blowers to minimize abuse of public donations by organizations involved in poverty alleviation work.

i.   The private sector bodies in the business of poverty alleviation should be entitled to receive grants from the government, *zakah* funds or various *waqf* funds but should be subject to audit and oversight. These organizations must adhere to open and transparent systems and publish their performance reports for public information on their websites and in hard copies as well.

j.   Deserving persons should consist of two main categories: (a) permanent; and (b) temporary. The permanent category would consist of those persons who are unable to earn owing to age, health, gender or other disabilities. They need cash grants or food subsidies or other help on a permanent basis. The temporary category will consist of those poor who can help themselves with some temporary assistance. This category would consist of persons who require help in education, training, temporary finance or some assistance in setting up a small enterprise for self-employment, and so on. This category can get help in the form of grants or even as interest-free loans from *zakah* and other charitable funds.

22.4   A RATIONALIZED SYSTEM OF *ZAKAH* FOR THE PRESENT AGE

The above discussion amply justifies the need for *ijtehad* for implementing the law of *zakah* in the present age. In the following discussion we shall submit a proposed system of *zakah* for the present age. As a first step, we shall discuss some basic premises on which the rest of the proposal holds. We shall also explain why we think these premises are important for implementing the *zakah* law in present-day society.

22.4.1 *Zakah* on Cash and Cash Equivalents

There is a consensus that cash or cash equivalents are subject to *zakah* at 2.5 per cent of the value. Cash is the only asset which is taxed as it is, because it has no yield until invested. For other assets, the yield and not the asset is taxed. Perhaps the intention of the *Shari'ah* is to force unproductive wealth into circulation. The penalty for holding it in the form of cash is to pay a fixed sum as *zakah*. Mahmud Abu Saud has vehemently argued on this premise and we tend to agree with him (Abu Saud 1988: 71–72). We should like to clarify that the *zakah* on cash or its equivalents is applicable if it is held idle. Mostly, it will mean cash or bank balances held by individuals. It will also include cash held in terms of foreign exchange or in the form of gold and precious metals even with the intention of investment. Cash or its equivalents as assets of a business will be treated separately, as discussed below.

22.4.2 *Zakah* on Other Assets

All other assets except finances provided to others for a long period and that are not likely to be recovered within the coming 12 months will be taxed on their yield and not on their capital value. Any asset which is unproductive or leads to a loss will not be subject to *zakah*. Any interest-free loan provided to others and that is not likely to be recovered within the next 12 months will be exempt from *zakah*. While calculating the *zakah* of a business, we shall take into account all assets, fixed or current, except any loans, advances or pre-payments the benefit of which will accrue in more than a year. It means that the debate about applicability of *zakah* on machinery or other fixed assets is also settled once and for all. These assets will also be taken into account. In the case of business the cash and bank balances or cash equivalents will become part of current assets and will not be kept separate, since they are not taxable on their capital value as in the case of an individual. Instead, they are included in the total value of assets for calculating the net worth of the business, as is done in the case of other assets.

22.4.3 Loans and Advances

Loans, advances or accounts payable are sources of funds except that they are repayable within the coming 12 months. In the latter case they will be treated as short-term liabilities and deducted from total assets, because they may become due even a day after the *zakah* date. It seems unfair that one should pay *zakah* on such income or wealth. Similarly, loans, advances or accounts receivable should be deducted from total assets, as their benefit will not accrue, except that amounts due are expected to be received in the coming 12 months, because the amount may be received the very next day after the *zakah* date. It is unfair, again, to leave such income or wealth untaxed. We think short-term liabilities and short-term receivables should be taken care of at the time of calculating *zakah*. The long-term portions of liabilities and receivables can be ignored. From out of long-term liabilities, the amount payable in the next 12 months should be deducted from the total assets. The same is true for long-term receivables. The amount expected to be received in the coming 12 months should be part of the total assets. Accounts receivable not expected to be recovered in the coming 12 months should be deducted from the total assets.

22.4.4   Consumption Loans

It need not be said that loans taken out for consumption purposes do not form part of one's assets, whatever the length of the period for which the loan is taken. But for a person who gives a loan, it will be part of his or her wealth if the loan is recoverable within the coming 12 months. Although lending money on interest is unlawful in Islam, yet if a person has interest income it will be subject to *zakah* anyway. The fact that such an act is reprehensible in the *Shari'ah* will remain, and one will have to account for it in the hereafter, but for the present purpose one will have to pay the *zakah* on this income as well.

22.4.5   The Concept of Net Yield or Net Income

We have argued that the *zakah* should be levied on the net yield or net income of assets and not on the capital value of assets (except for cash or cash equivalents of individuals). Now we need to define the concept of 'net yield' or 'net income'. We use these two terms interchangeably in this chapter. Traditionally, business firms arrive at the value of income by the following formula:

$$\text{Net income} = [\text{Total assets}] \, (-) \, [\text{Total equity} + \text{Total reserves and provisions} + \text{Total liabilities}]$$

The value of total liabilities can be arrived at fairly easily. The value of equities is also known. It is the valuation of assets which creates a problem. The generally accepted principle is that the accounting should follow conservatism. The valuation of assets and liabilities should take into consideration all risks and uncertainties. The valuation of assets involves an estimation of depreciation of fixed assets, amortization of intangible assets, bad debts, and so on. A higher rate of depreciation will reduce the value of fixed assets and consequently that of the value of net income. A lower rate will do the reverse. The same is the case for the bad debt estimation. Thus the valuation of assets can be a source of serious difficulty in assessing the *zakah*. FAS 9 (AAOIFI 1998), paragraph 5 recommends that, for purposes of *zakah*, the valuation of assets should be on the basis of cash equivalent value. It means that, for the purpose of *zakah*, the business entity should recast its accounts on the basis of cash equivalence and discard the principle of conservatism. Profit or loss by this method means any increase or decrease in the current cash equivalent of assets at the end of the accounting period over the beginning of the accounting period. If we adopt this methodology, it will be difficult to apply this method immediately, as there is no ready market for determining the current cash equivalent value of all types of assets. It may become possible gradually, as such professional firms will come into being, which will determine the current cash equivalent value of all types of assets independently. If this method is adopted, it will overcome the subjectivity of depreciation rates and bad debt rates.[13] This will mean major changes in accounting concepts. For example, we are implicitly moving away from the historical cost concept and incorporating inflation accounting into the model. We are also doing away with the concept of the going concern, which is a basic assumption of capitalist accounting theory.

However, if for any reason one is uncomfortable with such major changes in accounting concepts, one can still work out the *zakah* by using the conventional capitalist accounting theory concepts. In that case we shall have to live with subjectivity in the values of the assets. Whatever basis of valuation is adopted, the following adjustment in determining net income will have to be done anyway:

Net income = [Total value of assets (−) Value of long-term loans, advances and provisions (−) Investments in stocks and shares or loans on interest] (−) [Total value of equity (+) Reserves and provisions (+) Retained incomes (−) Long-term liabilities]

The following explanations are in order:

a. The reason for deducting long-term loans and advances from total assets is that these are finances which the business has provided to others, and the business is not earning anything on them. These are usually accounts receivable in over one year's time. They could also be pre-paid charges like insurance premiums for periods longer than a year. They could also be advances given to employees.

b.   The reason for deducting investments and interest-bearing loans is that they are a separate category of income, and *zakah* on them will be payable at 10 per cent, as it is earned without active labour.

c.   The reason for deducting long-term liabilities from total liabilities is that they are not payable in the next *zakah* year. They are in fact a resource on which the business is earning money through investment in the business. Any interest paid or payable in the coming *zakah* year on these liabilities will be duly accounted for as an expense or a short-term liability.

22.4.6   Capital Gains

Capital gains from the sale of durable assets, including any assets held in the form of foreign exchange or precious metals, need special treatment. It is difficult in every case to determine exactly the amount of capital gain or loss on the sale of a durable asset because of changes in the price levels between the time an asset was purchased and the time it is sold. For the sake of simplicity we propose that all such differences in price levels be ignored. The difference between the sale price and the book value of the asset will determine the capital gain or loss. The *zakah* at a rate of 10 per cent will be payable on the capital gain because it is earned without labour. There will be no effect of a capital loss on the *zakah* liability.

A related question pertains to the manner in which the seller handles the sale proceeds. Suppose a person sells a plot of land. After paying *zakah* at 10 per cent on any capital gain, the balance of the cash proceeds, if deposited in the bank, will become part of the cash balance and will be taxed as a cash balance. The individual will pay *zakah* on the lower of the opening and closing cash balances at the year-end. In the case of a business firm, the cash balance will be part of the total assets and will change the value of the net income at the year-end. However, if the sale proceeds are invested in another income-generating investment, after paying *zakah* on the capital gain, the balance of the sale proceeds will not be taxed. Income from the new investment will be subject to *zakah*. If it is invested in another asset that does not generate any income (e.g. a plot of land), it will remain exempt until it becomes productive or is resold and generates a capital gain.

22.4.7 Provisions and Reserves

Generally, business firms allocate a part of profit for the creation of provisions to meet specific future needs and obligations. Common examples are provisions for depreciation, bad debts, provident funds, social security payments, pension benefits and so on. The provisions can be either of the two following types:

a. provisions created from profits but ploughed back into the business, that is, no separate funds are created;
b. provisions created from profits but invested in separate funds.

In the latter case, firms often invest the provisions outside the business, and any gains or losses are adjusted in the fund's value itself. Our opinion is that provisions pertaining to the former category should be added back into the net worth calculations as for long-term liabilities. However, for the second category, we should treat each fund as a separate entity, and its accounting should also be disclosed separately. The funded provisions should be deducted from the value of the business assets. However, the *zakah* should be paid on the income of these funds at 10 per cent separately. If the funded provisions have subsidiary ledger balances of individual beneficiaries, the *zakah* paid on the funded provisions should also be debited to the individual entitlements. Simultaneously, the individuals should be intimated of the *zakah* paid on their behalf in the accounts of these funds, so that they are able to carry out the necessary adjustments in their individual *zakah* accounts.

22.4.8 Research and Development Costs

Some business firms spend significant amounts on research and development. If they decide to capitalize these expenses, the unamortized value of the asset will remain part of total assets for calculating the *zakah*. The exact treatment of the research and development costs should be decided in light of the applicable accounting standards followed by the business entity.

22.4.9 Intangible Assets

The treatment of intangible assets like goodwill, patents, copyrights and so on will depend on disclosure of these assets in the balance sheet. If a firm invests in the acquisition of these assets, it will decide whether the assets should be charged to the period in which expenditure was incurred or whether they should be capitalized and amortized over a number of years. In the first case, it will be an expense and will not appear in the balance sheet. In the second case, the net unamortized value will appear in the balance sheet. For calculating *zakah*, the net unamortized value of intangible assets will be part of total assets. The decision about the treatment of intangible assets should be made in light of the applicable accounting standards.

22.4.10   Foreign Currency Balances

Any foreign currency balances on the date of the balance sheet should be translated at the prevalent market rate of exchange.[14] The same will be the case for any foreign currency account receivables and payables. Any hypothetical or unrealized gains or losses on account of foreign currency transactions will be ignored when calculating the *zakah*. Similarly, if a firm spends money to hedge against any future foreign currency losses, this will be treated as an expense. Any notional gain in the absence of this hedge will be ignored for calculating the *zakah*.

22.4.11   Assets of Foreign Subsidiaries

There are two methods of accounting for the assets and liabilities of foreign subsidiaries. The first is known as the temporal method. Under this method, all items quantified in terms of past transactions (such as inventory, plant, equipment, common stock, depreciation, cost of goods sold, etc.) are translated at historical cost. The items quantified as future events (such as cash, receivables, short-term payables, etc.) are translated at the current market exchange rate on the date of the balance sheet. The second method is the current rate method. Under this method all assets and liabilities are translated at the current rate of exchange on the date of the balance sheet. In our opinion, for calculating the *zakah* we should adopt the all-current method. This is consistent with our approach for all other assets and liabilities. This is also in line with the guidance of IAS 21.

22.4.12   Shares and Bonds

Al-Qardawi (1969: I, 271) argues that shares and stocks of a business entity should not be taxed. Instead, the net profit of the business entity should be taxed at 5 or 10 per cent as applicable. The owners should pay *zakah* on the income earned on this capital. Regarding *zakah* on bonds, al-Qardawi (ibid.) thinks that the bonds should be subject to *zakah* on their capital value, like assets, even if they are earning interest. He treats the capital value as taxable, leaving the question of *zakah* on interest income out of the discussion. In our opinion, shares and bonds should be treated in a similar manner. In both cases, income from the investment should be subject to *zakah* and not the capital sum itself. As al-Qardawi has said, the fact that a capital sum has been invested on interest should not lead to an exemption from *zakah*. We think income from interest should not be exempted because it is interest income. For a consistent application of the law, all income, including interest income, should be subject to *zakah*.

22.4.13 *Zakah* on Earned Income

Al-Qardawi (1969: I, 259–260) has discussed the question of *zakah* on earned income at length. Departing from the orthodox interpretation, he concludes that income from wages, salaries and other professional services should be subject to *zakah* as it accrues, without the condition of one year, on the analogy of *zakah* on agricultural produce. The rates of *zakah* should also be similar to *zakah* on agriculture. However, he does not discuss the question of deducting living expenses from these incomes. Our opinion is that all earned income should be reduced by the *nisab* limit, which should be equal to the minimum wage of a worker, and the balance should be subject to *zakah* at 10 or 5 per cent as applicable.

Al-Qardawi (1969: II, 269) argues that the rates of *zakah* differ for different sources of income. In general, where the income is generated by a trade or work, the rate is 2.5 per cent and, where the income is generated by a natural activity such as agriculture, the rate is 5 or 10 per cent, depending upon the method of irrigation. While we agree with the general position taken by al-Qardawi that income should also be subject to *zakah*, we do not think it is rational to levy a 5 per cent tax on agricultural income and half of that on salary and trade incomes. For the sake of consistency and fairness, income from trade, salaries and other sources should also be subject to the 5 per cent rate if it involves active work and the 10 per cent rate if it accrues without work, such as pensions, rental income or certain unusual income from rewards or bonuses for which no specific work was done by the individual.

22.4.14 Treatment of *Zakah* in the Accounts

The question of how *zakah* should be treated in the accounts of a business is important for various reasons. The government, financial institutions, shareholders and the general public will want to know about it. In our opinion, the *zakah* should not be treated as a business expense, because it will mean the business firm will recover the expense from its customers through the prices of its products. It will convert *zakah* into an indirect tax. Ultimately, poor people may be paying it back, and the whole purpose of *zakah* will be lost. Thus we think that the *zakah* should be treated as part of the appropriation account. It should remain a direct tax on the business.

22.5   CALCULATING THE *ZAKAH* LIABILITY OF AN INDIVIDUAL

In light of the above discussion we shall now illustrate the calculation of *zakah* for an individual. Let us take the following example.

Mr A has the following assets and sources of income for the financial year ending 31 December 2011:

a.   Salary income Rs10 000 per month.
b.   Annual income from tenant-cultivated agricultural land Rs100 000. *Ushr* (crop value worth Rs10 000) has already been paid on it.
c.   Annual rental income of a house Rs200 000. The repairs and taxes are Rs37 000.
d.   Cash balances in the bank on 31 December 2011, Rs45 700; on 31 December 2010, Rs57 800.
e.   Market value of the stocks and shares, Rs345 000. Dividend and interest income during the year, Rs49 700.
f.   A plot of land bought for Rs480 000; loan for purchase of the plot, Rs400 000. Instalments payable during the coming 12 months, Rs40 000.
g.   Loan given to brother, Rs50 000; no return expected during the next 12 months.
h.   Provident fund balance, Rs86 900, which includes interest Rs17 400 accrued during the current financial year.
i.   Jewellery worth Rs120 000, which according to his *fiqhi* school is taxable.
j.   *Nisab* limit, Rs35 000.

What will his *zakah* liability be on 31 December 2011?

According to our model, the *zakah* payable by Mr A on 31 December 2011 would be as shown in Table 22.2.

If we synthesize these calculations we find the interesting results shown in Tables 22.3 and 22.4.

According to orthodox interpretation of the *zakah* law, Mr A should pay *zakah* only on his cash balance and jewellery, which comes to Rs4143

Table 22.2   Calculation of zakah of Mr A on 31 December 2011

Particulars	Total value (Rs)	Zakatable value (Rs)	Rate of *zakah*	Zakah (Rs)	Notes
Salary income	120 000	85 000	5%	4 250	1
Agricultural income	100 000	0	0	0	2
Rent income	200 000	163 000	10%	16 300	3
Income from shares and stocks	49 700	49 700	10%	4 970	4
Loan to brother	50 000	0	0	0	5
Provident fund	86 900	17 400	10	1 740	6
Cash	45 700	5 700	2.5%	142	7
Jewellery	120 000	120 000	2.5%	3 000	8
Plot of land	480 000	0	0	0	9
Total	1 252 300	440 800		30 402	

Notes:
1. Salary being earned income will be taxable at 5%, as it involves human effort. *Nisab* will be deducted before levying the *zakah*.
2. He has already paid *ushr* on it. No further tax on this income during this year.
3. *Zakah* payable at 10% on gross income, Rs200 000 minus taxes and repairs, 37 000. Since human effort is not involved in generating the income the rate is 10%.
4. Income from shares and stocks involves no human effort; the rate is 10%. The capital value of the shares is exempt.
5. The loan to his brother will not be included anywhere, since no recovery is expected.
6. Interest income of Rs17 400 is taxable at 10%, since no human effort is involved in earning it.
7. The closing cash balance was Rs45 700, from which is deducted the loan instalment of Rs40 000 payable during the coming financial year, leaving a net balance of Rs5700. The *zakah* is payable on the lower of the opening and closing balances (lower of Rs57 800 and Rs5700), i.e. Rs5700.
8. *Zakah* on jewellery is at 2.5%.
9. The plot of land whatever its value will not be subject to *zakah*, as it is not generating any income. Once it is sold, the decision about *zakah* on the sale proceeds will depend on the manner in which the proceeds are handled. If the proceeds become part of the cash balance, they will be taxed at 2.5%. If the proceeds are invested in an income-generating investment, the net income of the new investment will be taxed.

[(45 700 + 120 000) / 40]. According to our model the *zakah* of Mr A is Rs 37 260, which is 9 times the *zakah* calculated on the basis of the orthodox interpretation. If we add *zakah* on wealth too, the total *zakah* of the individual would be 9.75 times (40 402 / 4143) the *zakah* payable by the orthodox formula. The illustration supports our basic assertion that a revision of the *zakah* law would increase *zakah* proceeds significantly.

Table 22.3   Total income of individual in the illustrated case

Particulars	Amount (Rs)
Salary	120000
Agricultural income	100000
Rent	200000
Dividends	49700
Provident fund interest income	17400
Total	487100

Table 22.4   Effective rate of zakah *(Rs) of individual in the illustrated case*

Particulars	Amount (Rs)	Total (Rs)
Total income	487100	
Total *zakah* as per Table 22.2	30402	
Add *ushr*	10000	
Total *zakah* paid/payable (subtotal 1)		40402
Less *zakah* on cash and jewellery	(−) 3142	
Zakah on income (subtotal 2)		37260
Effective rate of *zakah* on income	(37260 / 487100) × 100	7.65%

22.6   CALCULATING THE *ZAKAH* LIABILITY OF A BUSINESS ENTITY

In this section we shall illustrate how the *zakah* of a business entity would be calculated in light of our proposed model. The profit or loss figure in the financial statements will change after adjustments for the *zakah* calculation. Suppose Alpha Limited has the balance sheet shown in Table 22.5 as at 31 December 2011.

The net income for the purpose of the *zakah* calculation will be as shown in Table 22.6.

Based on the above calculation of net income, the *zakah* payable will be as shown in Table 22.7. The effective rate of *zakah* on Alpha Limited for the year ending 31 December 2011 = [Zakah payable / net profit as in the balance sheet] = 300000/2000000 = 15%.

According to the orthodox interpretation, the *zakah* of Alpha Limited would be only on cash and inventory, which comes to Rs175000 [2000000

Table 22.5   Balance sheet of Alpha Limited as at 31 December 2011

Equities	Amount (million Rs)	Assets	Amount (million Rs)
Share capital	10	Cash	2
Net profit	2	Accounts receivable	1
Short-term liabilities	2	Long-term advances	2
Long-term liabilities	4	Stock-in-trade	5
Unfunded provisions	1	Investment on the stock exchange*	3
General reserve	1	Fixed assets	7
Total	20	Total	20

* Investment income of Rs0.5 million is included in the investment on the stock exchange.

+5 000 000) / 40]. The *zakah* calculated through our model would be about 1.7 times the *zakah* calculated on the basis of the orthodox interpretation. It supports our overall assertion that a revision in the *zakah* law would increase total *zakah* proceeds significantly.

22.7   SUMMING UP

The present chapter has highlighted the need for rethinking on the law of *zakah*. The chapter also discusses several issues which require the attention of Muslim scholars. As a first step, we have also proposed a rationalized system of *zakah* for the present age. Through two illustrations we have tried to show how *zakah* would be calculated for an individual and for a business entity. Both illustrations show that *zakah* proceeds would increase significantly by revising the *zakah* law. Until we do that, the intended benefits and objective of the *zakah* law will not be achieved. The problem of poverty and social security through *zakah* in Muslim countries can be adequately addressed by reviewing the orthodox interpretation of the law.

Table 22.6   Calculation of net income for the zakah *of Alpha Limited for the year 2011*

	Amount (million Rs)	Amount (million Rs)	Notes
Total assets	20		
Less: Total liabilities	(−) 6		
Net worth as per balance sheet (Subtotal 1)		14	
Add: Long-term liabilities	(+) 4		1
Less: Long-term advances	(−) 2		2
Less: Investment on the stock exchange (Subtotal 2)	(−) 3	(−) 1	3
Add: General reserve		(+) 1	
Add: Unfunded provisions		(+) 1	
Net worth for *zakah* (Subtotal 3)		= 15	
Less: Share capital		(−) 10	
Net profit for *zakah*		= 5	4

Notes:
1. Long-term liabilities are added back, since they are resources of the business.
2. Long-term advances are deducted, as the business will not use these funds during the coming year.
3. Investment on the stock exchange (including dividend income capitalized) is deducted, as *zakah* on it is payable at 10% separately.
4. The balance sheet net profit is now Rs5 million, because long-term liabilities and general reserve and unfunded provisions have been added to it. It means that, for the purpose of *zakah*, any past savings of the business will become part of the net worth and thus affect the net profit.
5. The rate of *zakah* on the business profit will be 5%, as this is being earned by human effort. But once an individual who has only purchased its shares receives them, he or she will have to pay the balance of the *zakah* on his or her share of dividends at 5%. His or her rate of *zakah* on such income is 10%, except for the proportionate share of dividend income from the stock exchange on which 10% has already been paid. In practice, firms will be required to deduct *zakah* at source and give a certificate to each shareholder to this effect. The shareholders when determining their personal *zakah* liabilities will claim a rebate for any *zakah* deducted at source.

Table 22.7   Zakah payable by Alpha Limited for the year 2011

	Amount (Rs)
Zakah on business income: 5% of Rs5.0 million	250 000
Zakah on investment on the stock exchange: 10% of Rs500 000	50 000
Total *zakah* payable	300 000

NOTES

1. Mahmoud Abu Saud has very strongly argued that the law of *zakah* that is mainly based on a letter of the Prophet, which the first caliph Abu Bakr discovered after the death of the Prophet and then implemented, was a document containing his instructions on *zakah* as ruler of the Islamic state and not as Apostle of God. These instructions were temporal in context. Now that this context has changed, we should do *ijtehad* on various provisions of the *zakah* law (Mahmoud Abu Saud 1988: 1–27).

2. The *zakah* law prescribes that the produce of land irrigated by rain will pay 10 per cent, while produce from land irrigated by an artificial method will pay 5 per cent.

3. Quoted by al-Qardawi (1969: I, 129).

4. http://money.cnn.com/data/commodities/ (accessed 17 October 2010).

5. [As in original] *Fath al Qadir*, Vol. 11, p.482.

6. As an exception, Malaysia allows a tax credit for *zakah* paid (Habib Ahmed 2008: 106).

7. It need not be said that, for the sake of consistency, the government or some other neutral body will have to standardize the expenses for each crop per acre. This would take care of the problem created by economies of scale that benefit big farmers as compared to small farmers.

8. There is a lot of literature on the subject. It is not feasible to summarize the whole literature here. However, the interested reader may like to refer to a select list: Mawdudi (1950); M. Abu Saud (1952); Aghnides (1961); Shafi (AH 1383); Shemesh (1967); Abu Ubaid (1969); Haque (1977); Johansen (1988).

9. [As in original] M.U. Chapra, *The economic system of Islam* (London: Islamic Cultural Centre, 1970), p.245.

10. [As in original] S.M. Yusuf, *Economic justice in Islam* (Lahore: Sh. M. Ashraf, 1971), p.67.

11. [As in original] S. Waqar Ahmed Husaini, *Islamic environmental systems engineering* (London: Macmillan, 1980), p.135.

12. Abu Abd al-Rahman bin Shu'aib al-Ash'ath Nasai', *Sunan*, Kitab al-ist'dhan (Cairo, AH 1312), ch. 29.

13. For a detailed treatment of the subject see any text of accounting theory, e.g. Camber (1966); Henderiksen (1990); Schroeder (1990).

14. This is in line with IAS 21, effective from July 1983 and as revised in 1993 and effective from 1 January 1995. See Haskins, Ferris and Selling (1996), p.368. IAS 21 has been updated several times since then. The business entity should translate its balances in light of the latest applicable standard.

Bibliography

AAOIFI. 1998. *Financial accounting standard 9*. Manama, Bahrain: Accounting and Auditing Organization for Islamic Financial Institutions.

AAOIFI. 2005. *Accounting, auditing and governance standards for Islamic financial institutions*. Manama, Bahrain: Accounting and Auditing Organization for Islamic Financial Institutions.

AAOIFI. 2008. *Governance standards: Shari'a supervisory board: Appointment, composition and report*. Manama, Bahrain. Accounting and Auditing Organization for Islamic Financial Institutions.

Abderrezak, Farid. 2008. The performance of Islamic equity funds: A comparison to conventional, Islamic and ethical benchmarks. MA dissertation. University of Maastricht, http://www.failaka.com/downloads/AbderrezakF_Perf_IslamicEquityFunds.pdf.

Abdul-Rahman, Yahia. 2010. *The art of Islamic banking and finance*. Hoboken, NJ: John Wiley & Sons.

Abu Bakar, Nur Barizah and Abdul Rahim A. Rahman. 2007. A comparative study of zakah and modern taxation. *Journal of King Abdulaziz University: Islamic Economics* 20 (1): 25–40.

Abu Ghuddah, A.S. n.d. Practical application of al-ijara al-mawsufa fil dhimma (forward ijara). Presented at Al-Baraka 30th Symposium for Islamic Economics, http://www.Isra.my.

Abu Ghuddah, A.S. n.d.-a. *Ijara (leasing)*. Al-Baraka Group, Department of Research and Development, http://www.albaraka.com/media/pdf/Research-Studies/RSIJ-200706201-EN.pdf.

Abu Saud, M. 1952. The exploitation of land and the Islamic law. *Islamic Review* 40: 9–10.

Abu Saud, Mahmoud. 1988. *Contemporary zakah*. Cincinnati, OH: Zakat and Research Foundation.

Abu Ubaid, al-Qasim bin Sallam. 1969. *Kitab al-amwal* [Book on finance]. Urdu. Trans. A.R. Surti. Islamabad: Islamic Research Institute.

Abu Yusuf, Imam. 1966. *Islam ka nizam e mahasil* [Taxation system of Islam]. Urdu. Trans. M.N. Siddiqi. Karachi: Maktaba Chiragh e Rah.

Addas, Waleed A.J. 2008. *Methodology of economics: Secular vs. Islamic*.

Kuala Lumpur: International Islamic University Malaysia Press. Online at http://mpra.ub.uni-muenchen.de/8264/, MPRA Paper no. 8264, posted 5 May 2008, 14:43.

Adnan, M. Akhyar and Muhamad. 2007. Agency problems in mudaraba financing: The case of sharia (rural) banks, Indonesia. *IIUM Journal of Economics and Management* 15 (2): 219–243.

Aggarwal, Rajesh and Tarik Yousef. 1996. *Islamic banks and investment financing*, http://ssrn.com/abstracts=845.

Agha, Oliver. 2012. *Is Islamic finance a failure? An assessment*, http://www.reuters.com/article/2012/01/27/islamicfinance-future-idUSL5E8CR0FV20120127.

Aghnides, Nicholas. 1961. *Muhammadan theories of finance*. Lahore: Premier Book House.

Ahmad, A.R. Yusri. 2002. Methodological approach to Islamic economics: Its philosophy, theoretical contribution and applicability. In *Theoretical foundations of Islamic economics*, ed. Habib Ahmed, pp. 20–60. Jeddah: Islamic Research and Training Institute, Islamic Development Bank.

Ahmad, A.R. Yusri. 2009. *Tawarruq, its concepts, its practices, and its economic implications on its promotion by Islamic banks*. Kuala Lumpur: International Shari'ah Research Academy, http://www.isra.my/articles/islamic-banking/tawarruq.html.

Ahmad, Abu Umar Faruq and M. Kabir Hassan. 2006. The time value of money concept in Islamic finance. *American Journal of Islamic Social Sciences* 23 (1): 66–90.

Ahmad, Khurshid. 1980. Economic development in Islamic economic framework: Some notes on the outlines of a strategy. In *Studies in Islamic economics*, ed. Khurshid Ahmad, pp. 171–190. Leicester: Islamic Foundation.

Ahmad, Khurshid. 2007. *Capitalism, socialism, the welfare state, and Islam*. IDB/IRTI lecture. Jeddah: Islamic Research and Training Institute, Islamic Development Bank.

Ahmad, Manzur. 2008. Credit cards ki shari'i hathiyat [Legal position of credit cards]. Urdu. *Fikro Nazar* (Islamabad) 45 (4) (April–June): 83–125.

Ahmad, Sheikh Mahmud. 1952. *Economics of Islam*, 2nd edn. Lahore: Sh. M. Ashraf.

Ahmad, Sheikh Mahmud. 1989. *Towards interest-free banking*. Lahore: Institute of Islamic Culture.

Ahmad, Syed. 1977. Reflection on the concept and law of riba. In *Outlines of Islamic economics*, pp. 26–34. Indianapolis, IN: Association of Muslim Social Scientists.

Ahmad, Ziauddin. 1989. *Public finance in Islam*. Working paper WP/89/68, 6 September. Washington, DC: International Monetary Fund.

Ahmed, Habib, ed. 2002. *Theoretical foundations of Islamic economics*. Jeddah: Islamic Research and Training Institute, Islamic Development Bank.

Ahmed, Habib. 2002-a. Analytical tools of Islamic economics: A modified marginalist approach. In *Theoretical foundations of Islamic economics*, ed. Habib Ahmed, pp. 125–145. Jeddah: Islamic Research and Training Institute, Islamic Development Bank.

Ahmed, Habib. 2006. Islamic law, adaptability and financial development. *Islamic Economic Studies* 13 (2) (February): 79–101.

Ahmed, Habib. 2008. Zakah, macroeconomic policies and poverty alleviation: Lessons from simulations on Bangladesh. *Thoughts on Economics* 18 (3) (July): 83–112.

Ahmed, Habib. 2009. Financial crisis: Risks and lessons for Islamic finance. *ISRA International Journal of Islamic Finance* 1 (1): 7–32.

Ahmed, Habib. 2011. *Product development in Islamic banks*. Edinburgh: Edinburgh University Press.

Ahmed, Wahabalbari Amir. 2010. The concept of scarcity and its implication on human behavior: Searching the Qur'anic perspective. *Review of Islamic Economics* 14 (1): 147–171.

Akhtar, Muhammad Ramzan. n.d. Definition, nature, and scope of Islamic economics. *Journal of Islamic Banking and Finance* (online), http://www.financeinislam.com/.

Akhtar, Muhammad Ramzan. 1993. Modeling the economic growth of an Islamic economy. *American Journal of Islamic Social Sciences* 10 (4) (Winter): 491–511.

Akhtar, Waheed, Nadeem Akhtar and Khurram Ali Jaffri. 2009. Islamic microfinance and poverty alleviation: A case of Pakistan. *Proceedings of 2nd CBRC Lahore*, 14 November, http://www.ciitlahore.edu.pk/pl/ abrc/Proceedings/All%20papers/ISLAMIC%20MICRO- finance%20 and%20poverty%20alleviation%20a%20case%20of%20pakistan%20 (dr%20waheed).pdf.

Akkizidis, Ioannis and Sunil Kumar Khandelwal. 2008. *Financial risk management for Islamic banking and finance*. Houndmills, Basingstoke: Palgrave Macmillan.

Akoob, Mahomed. 2009. Reinsurance and re-takaful. In *Takaful Islamic insurance: Concepts and regulatory issues*, ed. Simon Archer, Rifaat Ahmed Abdel Karim and Volker Nienhaus, pp. 143–168. Singapore: John Wiley (Asia).

Al-Amine, M.B. Muhammad. 2008. Sukuk market: Innovations and challenges. *Islamic Economic Studies* 15 (2): 1–22.

Al-Asaad, M. 2008. Village funds: The experience of rural community development at Jabal al Hoss, Syria. Paper presented at the First International Conference on Inclusive Islamic Financial Sector Development: Enhancing Islamic Financial Services for Micro and Medium Sized Enterprises, 17–19 April 2007, Brunei. In *Islamic finance for micro and medium enterprises*, ed. Mohammed Obaidullah and Hajah Salma Haji Abdul Latiff, pp. 197–210. Jeddah: Islamic Research and Training Institute, Islamic Development Bank.

Al-Dhareer, S.M. al-Ameen. 1997. *Al-Gharar in contracts and its effects on contemporary transactions*. Jeddah: Islamic Research and Training Institute, Islamic Development Bank.

Al-Haddad, A.A. Aziz. n.d. *Tawarruq, its essence and its types: Mainstream tawarruq and organized tawarruq*. Trans. and ed. Khalil Mohammed Khalil and Mohammad Ashadi Mohd Zaini. Kuala Lumpur: International Shari'ah Research Academy, http://www.isra.my/articles/islamic-banking/tawarruq.html.

Al-Jarhi, Mabid A. 2002. Transactions in conventional and Islamic economics. In *Theoretical foundations of Islamic economics*, ed. Habib Ahmed. Jeddah: Islamic Research and Training Institute, Islamic Development Bank.

Al-Jarhi, Mabid A. and Munawar Iqbal, eds. 2001. *Islamic banking: Answers to some frequently asked questions*. IDB Occasional Paper 4. Jeddah: Islamic Research and Training Institute, Islamic Development Bank.

Al-Jarhi, Mabid Ali and Muhammad Anas Zarqa. 2007. Redistributive justice in a developed economy: An Islamic perspective. In *Advances in Islamic economics and finance: Proceedings of 6th International Conference on Islamic Economics and Finance*, Vol. 1, ed. Munawar Iqbal, Salman Syed Ali and Dadang Muljawan, pp. 43–74. Jeddah: Islamic Research and Training Institute, Islamic Development Bank.

al-Kassim, Faisal A. 2005. *Profitability of Islamic and conventional banking in GCC countries: A comparative study*, http://www. failaka. com/ research/php.

al-Masri, Rafic Yunus. 2004. Are all forms of interest prohibited? *Journal of King Abdulaziz University: Islamic Economics* 17 (1): 37–41.

al-Masri, Rafic Yunus. 2006. Renting an item to who sold it: Is it different from bay' al-wafa' contract? *Journal of King Abdulaziz University: Islamic Economics* 19 (2): 39–42.

al-Qardawi, Yusuf. 1969. *Fiqh al-zakah: A comparative study of zakah regulations and philosophy in the light of Qur'an and Sunnah*, Vols 1 and 2. Trans. Monzer Kahf. Jeddah: Scientific Publishing Centre, King Abdulaziz University.

al-Sadr, S.M. Baqir. 1971. *Iqtisaduna* [Our economics]. Urdu. Trans. Zeshan Haider. Lahore: Maktaba Ta'mir e Adab.

Al-Suwailem, Sami. 1999, 2000. Towards an objective measure of gharar in exchange. *Islamic Economic Studies* 7 (1–2) (October, April): 61–102.

Al-Suwailem, Sami. 2006. *Hedging in Islamic finance.* Jeddah: Islamic Research and Training Institute, Islamic Development Bank.

Al-Suwailem, Sami. 2009. *Tawarruq banking products.* Presented at the 19th Seminar of the OIC International Fiqh Academy, Sharjah, UAE, April. Kuala Lumpur: International Shari'ah Research Academy, http://www.isra.my/articles/islamic-banking/tawarruq.html.

al-Zuhayli, Wahba. 2006. The juridical meaning of riba. In *Interest in economics*, ed. Abdulkader Thomas. London: Routledge.

Ali, K.M. Mortuza. 1986. Insurance in Islam. *Thoughts on Economics* 7 (4): 1–37.

Ali, S. Nazim. 2008. Islamic finance and economics as reflected in research and publications. *Review of Islamic Economics* 12 (1): 151–168.

Ali, Salman S. 2006–07. Financial distress and bank failure: Lessons from closure of Ihlas Finans in Turkey. *Islamic Economic Studies* 14 (1–2) (August, January): 1–52.

Ali, Salman S. 2007-a. Financial distress and bank failures: Relevance for Islamic banks. In *Islamic banking and finance: Fundamentals and contemporary issues*, ed. Salman S. Ali and Ausaf Ahmad, pp. 99–120. Jeddah: Islamic Research and Training Institute, Islamic Development Bank.

Ali, Salman S. 2008. Islamic capital markets: Current state and developmental challenges. Introduction to *Islamic capital markets: Products, regulation and development*, ed. Salman Syed Ali, pp. 1–19. Jeddah: Islamic Research and Training Institute, Islamic Development Bank.

Ali, Salman S. and Ausaf Ahmad, eds. 2007. *Islamic banking and finance: Fundamentals and contemporary issues.* Jeddah: Islamic Research and Training Institute, Islamic Development Bank.

Alpay, Savas. 2007. The evaluation of special finance houses: A case study on Turkey. In *Advances in Islamic economics and finance: Proceedings of 6th International Conference on Islamic Economics and Finance*, Vol. 1, ed. Munawar Iqbal, Salman Syed Ali and Dadang Muljawan, pp. 369–386. Jeddah: Islamic Research and Training Institute, Islamic Development Bank.

Anjum, M. Iqbal. 2007. An inquiry into alternative models of Islamic banking. In *Advances in Islamic economics and finance: Proceedings of 6th International Conference on Islamic Economics and Finance*, Vol. 1, ed. Munawar Iqbal, Salman Syed Ali and Dadang Muljawan, pp. 419–458. Jeddah: Islamic Research and Training Institute, Islamic Development Bank.

Ansari, M.I. 1994. Islamic perspective on sustainable development. *American Journal of Islamic Social Sciences* 11 (3): 394–402.

Arbouna, Mohammed Burhan and Hurriyah el-Islamy. 2008. Rate of return risk management in Islamic finance: Challenges and propositions. In *Islamic capital markets: Products, regulation and development*, ed. Salman Syed Ali, pp. 179–199. Jeddah: Islamic Research and Training Institute, Islamic Development Bank.

Archer, Simon, Riffat Ahmed Abdel Karim and Volker Nienhaus, eds. 2009. *Takaful Islamic insurance: Concepts and regulatory issues.* Singapore: John Wiley & Sons (Asia).

Ariff, Mohamed. 1988. Islamic banking. *Asian-Pacific Economic Literature* 2 (2) (September): 46–62.

Ariff, Mohamed. 2007. Comments on 'Islamic economics and finance: Where do they stand? by Masudul Alam Choudhury'. In *Advances in Islamic economics and finance: Proceedings of 6th International Conference on Islamic Economics and Finance*, Vol. 1, ed. Munawar Iqbal, Salman Syed Ali and Dadang Muljawan, pp. 103–105. Jeddah: Islamic Research and Training Institute, Islamic Development Bank.

Ariffin, N. Mohd, Simon Archer and Rifaat A.A. Karim. 2007. Transparency and market discipline in Islamic banks. In *Advances in Islamic economics and finance: Proceedings of 6th International Conference on Islamic Economics and Finance*, Vol.1, ed. Munawar Iqbal, Salman Syed Ali and Dadang Muljawan, pp. 153–173. Jeddah: Islamic Research and Training Institute, Islamic Development Bank.

Asad, Muhammad. 1947. Towards an Islamic constitution. *Arafat* I (9). In *Muhammad Asad: Europe's Gift to Islam*, Vol. II, ed. M. Ikram Chaghatai. 2006. Lahore: Truth Society and Sang-e-Meel Publications.

Asad, Muhammad. 1980. *The message of the Qur'an.* Gibraltar: Dar al-Andalus.

Ascarya and Diana Yumanita. 2008. Comparing the development of Islamic financial/bond markets in Malaysia and Indonesia. In *Islamic capital markets: Products, regulation and development*, ed. Salman Syed Ali, pp. 375–409. Jeddah: Islamic Research and Training Institute, Islamic Development Bank.

Asian Development Bank. 2009. *Islamic Republic of Pakistan: Improving access to financial services – Islamic finance component*, November, http://www.adb.org/Documents/Reports/Consultant/39492-PAK/39493-PAK-TACR-Vol6.pdf.

Askari, Hossein, Zamir Iqbal, Noureddine Krichene and Abbas Mirakhor. 2010. *The stability of Islamic finance: Creating a resilient financial environment for a secure future.* Singapore: John Wiley & Sons (Asia).

Askari, Hossein, Zamir Iqbal and Abbas Mirakhor. 2009. *New issues in*

Islamic finance and economics: Progress and challenges. Singapore: John Wiley & Sons (Asia).

Askari, Hossein, Zamir Iqbal and Abbas Mirakhor. 2010. *Globalization and Islamic finance: Convergence, prospects, and challenges.* Singapore: John Wiley & Sons (Asia).

Asutay, Mehmet. 2007. Conceptualization of the second best solution in overcoming the social failure of Islamic banking and finance: Examining the overpowering of homoislamicus by homoeconomicus. *IIUM Journal of Economics and Management* 15 (2): 167–195.

Asutay, Mehmet. 2010. An introduction to Islamic moral economy. Paper presented at the Durham Islamic Finance Summer School 2010, School of Government and International Affairs, Durham University, 5–9 July.

Ayub, Muhammad. 2002. *Islamic banking and finance: Theory and practice.* Karachi: State Bank of Pakistan Printing Press.

Ayub, Muhammad. 2007. *Understanding Islamic finance.* Chichester: John Wiley & Sons.

Azid, Toseef. 2008. *Appraisal of the state of research on labor economics in the Islamic framework.* Paper presented at the 7th International Conference on Islamic Economics, King Abdulaziz University, Jeddah, 1–3 April, http://islamiccenter.kaau.edu.sa/7iecon/index.html.

Azid, Toseef, Mehmet Asutay and Umar Burki. 2007. Theory of the firm, management and stakeholders: An Islamic perspective. *Islamic Economic Studies* (July): 1–30.

Bacha, Obiyathullah Ismath. 1999. Derivative instruments and Islamic finance: Some thoughts for reconsideration. *International Journal of Islamic Financial Services* 1 (2) (July–September).

Badawi, Zaki al-Din. 2000. *Theory of prohibited riba.* Arabic. Trans. Imran Ahsan Khan Nyazee. Islamabad: Advanced Legal Studies Institute (ALSI), www.nyazee.org.

Bader, M.K.I., Shamsher Mohamad, Mohamed Ariff and Taufiq Hassan. 2008. Cost, revenue and profit efficiency of Islamic vs. conventional banks: International evidence using data envelopment analysis. *Islamic Economic Studies* 15 (2) (January): 23–77.

Bakhtiari, Sadegh. 2009. Islamic microfinance, providing credit to the poor: A case study of Iran. *International Economics Studies* 34 (1) (Summer): 99–107.

Balala, Maha-Hanaan. 2011. *Islamic finance and law.* London and New York: I.B. Tauris.

Ballantyne, W.M. 1986. *Commercial law in the Arab Middle East: The Gulf States.* London: Lloyds of London Press.

Bashir, M. Abdel Hameed. 2001. Assessing the performance of Islamic banks: Some evidence from the Middle East. Unpublished. Prepared for the MEEA/American Economic Association Annual Meeting, New Orleans, LA, 4–7 January.

Beik, Irfan Syauqi and Didin Hafidhuddin. 2008. Enhancing the role of sukuk on agriculture sector financing in Indonesia: Proposed models. In *Islamic capital markets: Products, regulation and development*, ed. Salman Syed Ali, pp. 85–96. Jeddah: Islamic Research and Training Institute, Islamic Development Bank.

Blaug, Mark. 1992. *The methodology of economics or how economists explain*. Cambridge: Cambridge University Press.

Böhm-Bawerk, Eugen von. 1890. *The positive theory of capital*. London: Macmillan.

Boudjellal, M. 1982. The business of interest-free banking with special reference to Kuwait Finance House. M.Sc. dissertation. Heriot-Watt University, Edinburgh.

Boudjellal, M. 2006. Three decades of experimentation: Rethinking the theory of Islamic banking. *Review of Islamic Economics* 10 (1): 23–39.

Bouheraoua, Said. n.d. *Tawarruq in the banking system: A critical analytical study of juristic views on the topic*. Presented at 19th Seminar of the International Islamic Fiqh Academy of the OIC. Kuala Lumpur: International Shari'ah Research Academy, http://www.isra.my/articles/islamic-banking/tawarruq.html.

Cakir, Selim and Faezeh Raei. 2007. *Sukuk vs. eurobonds: Is there a difference in value-at-risk?* Working paper WP/07/237. Washington, DC: International Monetary Fund.

Camber, R.J. 1966. *Accounting, evaluation, and economic behaviour*. Englewood Cliffs, NJ: Prentice-Hall.

Chachi, Abdelkader. 2005. Origin and development of Islamic banking operations. *Journal of King Abdulaziz University: Islamic Economics* 18 (2): 3–25.

Chachi, Abdelkader and Salma Abdul Latiff. 2008. Islamic marketing ethics and its impact on customer satisfaction in the Islamic banking industry. *Journal of King Abdulaziz University: Islamic Economics* 21 (1): 23–40.

Chapra, M.U. 1982. Money and banking in an Islamic economy. In *Monetary and fiscal economics of Islam*, ed. M. Ariff. Jeddah: Islamic Research and Training Institute, Islamic Development Bank.

Chapra, M.U. 1985. *Towards a just monetary system*. Leicester: Islamic Foundation.

Chapra, M.U. 1996. *What is Islamic economics?* Islamic Development Bank, Jeddah in IDB Prize Winner's Lecture Series no. 9. Jeddah: Islamic Research and Training Institute.

Chapra, M.U. 2001. *What is Islamic economics?* Jeddah: Islamic Research and Training Institute, Islamic Development Bank.

Chapra, M.U. 2006. Why has Islam prohibited interest? Rationale behind prohibition of interest? In *Interest in Islamic economics*, ed. Abdulkader Thomas. London: Routledge.

Chapra, M.U. 2007. Comments on 'Islamic economics and finance: Where do they stand? by Masudul Alam Choudhury'. In *Advances in Islamic economics and finance: Proceedings of 6th International Conference on Islamic Economics and Finance*, Vol. 1, ed. Munawar Iqbal, Salman Syed Ali and Dadang Muljawan, pp. 107–117. Jeddah: Islamic Research and Training Institute, Islamic Development Bank.

Chapra, M.U. 2007-a. The case against interest: Is it compelling? In *Islamic banking and finance: Fundamentals and contemporary issues*, ed. Salman S. Ali and Ausaf Ahmad, pp. 35–59. Jeddah: Islamic Research and Training Institute, Islamic Development Bank.

Chapra, M.U. 2008. *Muslim civilization: The causes of decline and the need for reform*. Leicester: Islamic Foundation.

Chapra, M.U. 2008-a. *Forum speech*. Presented at 8th Harvard University Forum on Islamic Finance, 19–20 April, Harvard Law School, Cambridge, MA, http//:ifp.law.harvard.edu.

Chapra, M.U. 2008-b. *The Islamic vision of development in the light of the maqasid al-Shari'ah*. Jeddah: Islamic Research and Training Institute.

Chapra, M.U. 2008-c. The global financial crisis: Can Islamic finance help? *IIUM Journal of Economics and Management* 16 (2): 118–124.

Chapra, M.U. 2009. Ethics and economics: An Islamic perspective. *Islamic Economic Studies* 16 (1&2) (January): 1–21.

Chapra, M.U. and Tariqullah Khan. 2000. *Regulation and supervision of Islamic banks*. Occasional paper 3. Jeddah: Islamic Research and Training Institute, Islamic Development Bank.

Chong, Beng Soon and Ming-Hua Liu. 2007. *Islamic banking: Interest-free or interest-based?*, http://papers.ssrn.com/sol3/papers.cfm?abstract_id=868567.

Cizakca, Murat. 1997. Towards a comparative economic history of the waqf system. *Al-Shajara* II (1). Kuala Lumpur: International Institute of Islamic Thought and Civilization.

Cizakca, Murat. 2000. A history of philanthropic foundations: The Islamic world from the seventh century to the present. Eighth draft, http://www.mcizakca.com/.

Cizakca, Murat. 2007. Democracy, economic development, and maqasid al-shari'ah. *Review of Islamic Economics* 11 (1): 101–118.

Choudhury, Masudul Alam. 2007. Islamic economics and finance: Where do they stand? In *Advances in Islamic economics and finance: Proceedings* of 6th International Conference on Islamic Economics and Finance, Vol. 1, ed. Munawar Iqbal, Salman Syed Ali and Dadang Muljawan, pp. 75–98. Jeddah: Islamic Research and Training Institute, Islamic Development Bank.

Commission for Islamization of Economy. 1992. *Report on banks and financial institutions.* Islamabad: Government of Pakistan.

Cornell, Vincent J. 2006. In the shadow of Deuteronomy. In *Interest in Islamic economics*, ed. Abdulkader Thomas, pp. 13–25. London: Routledge.

Council of Islamic Ideology, Pakistan. 1980. *Elimination of riba from the economy and Islamic modes of financing.* Islamabad: CII.

Council of Islamic Ideology, Pakistan. 1983. Eliminating interest from the economy. In *Money and banking in Islam*, ed. Ziauddin Ahmad *et al.* Jeddah: International Centre for Research in Islamic Economics, King Abdulaziz University; and Islamabad: Institute of Policy Studies.

Council of Islamic Ideology, Pakistan. 1984. *Bima wa qawaneen e bima* [Insurance and contemporary insurance laws]. Urdu. Islamabad: CII.

Dabu, Ibrahim Fadhil. n.d. *Tawarruq, its reality and types.* Kuala Lumpur: International Shari'ah Research Academy, http://www.isra.my/articles/islamic-banking/tawarruq.html.

Dar, Humayon A. 2002. Islamic home financing in the United Kingdom: Problems, challenges and prospects. *Review of Islamic Economics* 12: 47–71.

Dar, Humayon A. 2010. Islamic banking in Iran and Sudan. *Business Asia*, 27 June, http://www.humayondar.com/businessasia4.pdf.

Dar, Humayon A. and J.R. Presley. 2000–01. *Lack of profit loss sharing in Islamic banking: Management and control imbalance.* Economic research paper 024. Leicester: Loughborough University.

Dar, Humayon A., Rizwan Rahman, Rizwan Malik and Asim Anwar Kamal, eds. 2012. *Global Islamic finance report 2012.* London: Edbiz Consulting.

DeLorenzo, Yusuf Talal. 2007. *The total returns swap and the 'Shari'ah conversion technology' stratagem*, http:// www.failaka.com/research.php.

Department of the Treasury. 2009. *Financial regulatory reform – a new foundation: Rebuilding financial supervision and regulation.* Washington, DC: US Government.

Djojosugito, R. 2007. Necessary legal reforms to create legal basis for effective Islamic asset securitization (sukuk) in Indonesia. In *Advances in Islamic economics and finance: Proceedings of 6th International Conference on Islamic Economics and Finance.* Vol. 1, ed. Munawar

Iqbal, Salman Syed Ali and Dadang Muljawan, pp.489–502. Jeddah: Islamic Research and Training Institute, Islamic Development Bank.

Dusuki, A.W. 2007. The ideal of Islamic banking: A survey of stakeholders' perceptions. *Review of Islamic Economics* 11: 29–52.

Dusuki, A.W. 2007-a. Commodity murabaha programme (CMP): An innovative approach to liquidity management. *Journal of Islamic Economics, Banking and Finance* 3 (1): 1–22.

Dusuki, A.W. 2008. Banking for the poor: The role of Islamic banking in microfinance initiatives. *Humanomics: International Journal of Systems and Ethics* 24 (1) (February): 1–21.

Dusuki, A.W. 2009. *Shari'ah parameters in Islamic foreign exchange swap as hedging mechanism in Islamic finance.* Presented at International Conference on Islamic Perspective on Management and Finance. Kuala Lumpur: International Shari'ah Research Academy, http://www.isra.my/articles/islamic-banking/tawarruq.html.

Dusuki, A.W. 2009-a. *A critical appraisal on the practice of commodity murabaha transactions from maqasid al-shari'ah (objectives of Shari'ah) perspectives.* Presented at Insaniah-IRTI International Conference on Islamic Economics, Banking and Finance, Langkawi, Malaysia, 18–19 August. Kuala Lumpur: International Shari'ah Research Academy, http://www.isra.my/articles/islamic-banking/tawarruq.html.

Dusuki, A.W. 2010. Do equity-based sukuk structures fulfill the objectives of Shari'ah (maqasid al-Shari'ah)? *Review of Islamic Economics* 14 (2): 5–30.

Dusuki, A.W. and Abdelazeem Abozaid. 2007. A critical appraisal on the challenges of realizing maqasid al-shari'ah in Islamic banking and finance. *IIUM Journal of Economics and Management* 15 (2): 143–165.

Dusuki, A.W. and Abdelazeem Abozaid. 2008. Fiqh issues in short selling as implemented in the Islamic capital market in Malaysia. *Journal of King Abdulaziz University: Islamic Economics* 21 (2): 65–80.

Dusuki, A.W. and Humayon Dar. 2007. Stakeholders' perceptions of corporate social responsibility of Islamic banks: Evidence from Malaysian economy. In *Advances in Islamic economics and finance: Proceedings of 6th International Conference on Islamic Economics and Finance*, Vol. 1, ed. Munawar Iqbal, Salman Syed Ali and Dadang Muljawan, pp.249–277. Jeddah: Islamic Research and Training Institute, Islamic Development Bank.

Dusuki, A.W. and Shabnam Mokhtar. 2010. *Critical appraisal of Shari'ah issues on ownership in asset-backed sukuk as implemented in the Islamic debt market.* Research paper 8/2010. Kuala Lumpur: International Shari'ah Research Academy, http://www.isra.my.

El-Ashker, Ahmed. 2006. Rethinking Islamic economics: A vision to the future. *Islamic Business and Finance* 12, 13 (October, November).

El-Din, Seif el-Tag. 2004. The question of an Islamic futures market. *IIUM Journal of Economics and Management* 12 (1): 1–19.

El-Din, Seif el-Tag. 2008. Review of *Introduction to microeconomics: An Islamic perspective* by Zubair Hasan. *Muslim World Book Review* 28 (4): 73–76.

El-Din, Seif Tag. 2008-a. Income ratio, risk-sharing and the optimality of mudaraba. *Journal of King Abdulaziz University: Islamic Economics* 21 (2): 39–62.

El-Diwani, Tarek. 1999. *Fractional reserve banking and the interest bearing money supply*. Paper presented at meeting of the Association of Muslim Social Scientists, London School of Economics, October, http://www.islamic-finance.com.

El-Diwani, Tarek. 2003. The great Islamic mortgage caper? *Journal of Islamic Finance* (April), http://www.islamic-finance.com.

El-Diwani, Tarek. 2003-a. *The problem with interest*. UK: Kreatoc.

El-Gamal, Mahmoud A. 2000. *A basic guide to contemporary Islamic banking and finance*. Houston, TX: Rice University, http://www.ruf.rice.edu/~elgamal.

El-Gamal, Mahmoud A. 2001. *An economic explication of the prohibition of riba in classical Islamic jurisprudence*, http://www.ruf.rice.edu/~elgamal.

El-Gamal, Mahmoud A. 2001-a. *An economic explication of the prohibition of gharar in classical Islamic jurisprudence*, http://www.ruf.rice.edu/~elgamal.

El-Gamal, Mahmoud A. 2006. *Islamic finance: Law, economics and practice*. Cambridge: Cambridge University Press.

El-Gamal, Mahmoud A. 2007. *Incoherence of contract-based Islamic financial jurisprudence in the age of financial engineering*, http://www.ruf.rice.edu/~elgamal.

El-Hawary, Dahlia and Wafik Grais. 2005. The compatibility of Islamic financial services and microfinance: A little-explored avenue for expanding outreach. *United Nations Capital Development Fund: Microfinance* 14 (July), http://www.uncdf.org/english/microfinance/newsletter/pages/2005_07/news_compatibility.php.

El-Hawary, Dahlia, Wafik Grais and Zamir Iqbal. 2004. *Regulating Islamic financial institutions: The nature of the regulated*. World Bank policy research working paper 3227. Washington, DC: World Bank.

Ernst & Young. 2008. *World Takaful Report*, www.ey.com.

Ernst & Young. 2010. *World Takaful Report*, www.ey.com.

Fadel, Mohammad. 2008. Riba, efficiency, and prudential regulation:

Preliminary thoughts. *Wisconsin International Law Journal* 25 (4) (April): 655–702, http://ssrn.com/abstract=1115875.

Farook, Sayd. 2007. On corporate social responsibility of Islamic financial institutions. *Islamic Economic Studies* 15 (1) (July): 31–45.

Farook, Sayd. 2008. A standard of corporate social responsibility for Islamic financial institutions: A preliminary study. Paper presented at the First International Conference on Inclusive Islamic Financial Sector Development: Enhancing Islamic Financial Services for Micro and Medium Sized Enterprises, 17–19 April 2007, Brunei. In *Islamic finance for micro and medium enterprises*, ed. Mohammed Obaidullah and Hajah Salma Haji Abdul Latiff, pp. 37–52. Jeddah: Islamic Research and Training Institute, Islamic Development Bank.

Farooq, Muhammad O. 2005. The riba–interest equation and Islam: Reexamination of the traditional arguments. Draft, http://www.globalwebpost.com/farooqm/writings/islamic/I_econ.fin/.

Farooq, Muhammad O. 2006. Self-interest, homo Islamicus and some behavioral assumptions in Islamic economics and finance. Draft. http://www.globalwebpost.com/farooqm/writings/islamic/I_econ.fin/homo-Islamicus.doc.

Farooq, Muhammad O. 2006-a. Qard al-hasana, wadi'ah/amanah and bank deposits: Applications and misapplications of some concepts in Islamic banking. Draft, www.globalwebpost.com/farooqm/writings/islamic/I_econ.fin/.

Farooq, Muhammad O. 2006-b. Riba, interest and six hadiths: Do we have a definition or a conundrum? Draft, http:// www.globalwebpost.com/farooqm/writings/islamic/I_econ.fin/.

Farooq, Muhammad O. 2006-c. *Stipulation of excess in understanding and misunderstanding riba: The al-Jassas link*, www.globalwebpost.com/farooqm/writings/islamic/jassas_stip.doc.

Farooq, Muhammad O. 2006-d. The riba–interest equivalence: Is there an ijma (consensus)? Draft, www.globalwebpost.com/farooqm/writings/islamic/I_econ.fin/.

Farooq, Muhammad O. 2007. Exploitation, profit and the riba–interest reductionism. Draft, http://www.globalwebpost.com/farooqm/writings/islamic/I_econ.fin/.

Farooq, Muhammad O. 2007-a. Partnership, equity-financing and Islamic finance: Whither profit–loss sharing? *Review of Islamic Economics* 11: 67–88.

Farrell, M.J. 1957. The measurement of productive efficiency. *Journal of the Royal Statistical Society* 120: 253–281.

Federal Shari'at Court (FSC) of Pakistan. 1991. *Judgment on riba (interest)*. Islamabad: Pakistan Legal Decisions.

Forte, G. and F. Miglietta. n.d. [2007?] *Islamic mutual funds as faith-based funds in a socially responsible context*, http://www.failaka.com/downloads/Forte&Miglietta_SocialResp.pdf.

Foster, John. 2008. Curb your enthusiasm. *Islamic Business and Finance* 28 (March): 11–13.

Foster, John. 2008-a. Cover interview: Indexing Islam. *Islamic Business and Finance* 33 (August): 8–10.

Friedman, Milton and Rose Friedman. 1980. *Free to choose*. New York: Harcourt Brace Jovanovich.

Ghamidi, Javed A. 2008. Sud ka mas'ala [The problem of interest]. Urdu. *Monthly Ishraq* 21 (10) (October): 2–3.

Ghazi, Mahmud A. 2008. *Mahadirat e fiqh* [Proceedings of seminar on fiqh]. Urdu. Lahore: al-Faisal Nasharan.

Gilani, S.M. Ahsan. 1947. *Islami ma'ashiyat* [Islamic economics]. Urdu. Karachi: Sh. Shaukat Ali and Sons.

Grais, Wafik and Matteo Pellegrini. 2006. *Corporate governance and Shari'ah compliance in institutions offering Islamic financial services.* Policy research working paper 4054, November. Washington, DC: World Bank.

Grais, Wafik and Matteo Pellegrini. 2006-a. *Corporate governance in institutions offering Islamic financial services: Issues and options.* Policy research working paper 4052, November. Washington, DC: World Bank.

Hakim, Cecep M. 2007. Islamic bonds: Indonesian experience. In *Islamic banking and finance: Fundamentals and contemporary issues*, ed. Salman S. Ali and Ausaf Ahmad, pp. 260–275. Jeddah: Islamic Research and Training Institute, Islamic Development Bank.

Hameedullah, Muhammad. 2009. *Le prophet de l'Islam*. Trans. from Urdu by Khalid Pervaiz (Paighamuber e Islam). Lahore: Beacon Books.

Hammad, Nazih Kamal. 1997. Charging fees for debt-guarantees: Extent of permissibility in Islamic fiqh. *Journal of King Abdulaziz University: Islamic Economics* 9: 95–121.

Hammad, Zaki Ahmad. 2007. The Gracious Qur'an. Lisle, IL: Lucent Interpretations.

Haneef, Mohamed A. 1995. *Contemporary Islamic economic thought: A selected comparative analysis*. Kuala Lumpur: S. Abdul Majeed & Co.

Haneef, Mohamed A. 2005. Can there be an economics based on religion? The case of Islamic economics. *Post-autistic Economics Review* 34 (October).

Haneef, Mohamed A. 2008. *Funding research in Islamic economics and finance*. Paper presented at 7th International Conference on Islamic

Economics, King Abdulaziz University, 1–3 April, Jeddah, http://islam-iccenter.kaau.edu.sa/7iecon/index.html.

Haneef, Mohamed A. 2009. *Research in Islamic economics: The missing fard 'ayn component.* Paper presented at 3rd Islamic Economics Congress, 12–14 January, Kuala Lumpur. [An earlier draft was presented at the 7th International Conference on Islamic Economics and Finance, Islamic Economics Research Center, King Abdulaziz University, Jeddah, 1–3 April 2008.]

Haneef, Mohamed A. 2010. Islamic economics, banking and finance in the 21st century: Selected issues in curriculum/human capital development. *Thoughts on Economics* 20 (1) (January): 25–40.

Haneef, Muhammad A. and Emad Rafiq Barakat. 2006. Must money be limited to only gold and silver? A survey of fiqhi opinions and some implications. *Journal of King Abdulaziz University: Islamic Economics* 19 (1): 21–34.

Haque, Ziaul. 1977. *Landlord and peasant in early Islam.* Islamabad: Islamic Research Institute.

Haque, Ziaul. 1992. *Nature and methodology of Islamic economics: An appraisal.* Paper presented at the 8th Annual General Meeting of the Pakistan Society of Development Economists, Islamabad, 7–10 January, http://www.financeinislam.com/.

Haron, Abdullah and Dawood Taylor. 2009. Risk management in takaful. In *Takaful Islamic insurance: Concepts and regulatory issues*, ed. Simon Archer, Rifaat Ahmed Abdel Karim and Volker Nienhaus, pp. 169–191. Singapore: John Wiley (Asia).

Haron, Sudin and Wan Nursofiza. 2008. Creating a dynamic Islamic capital market: The essential role of innovation. In *Islamic capital markets: Products, regulation and development*, ed. Salman Syed Ali, pp. 23–32. Jeddah: Islamic Research and Training Institute, Islamic Development Bank.

Hasan, Maher and Jemma Dridi. 2010. *The effects of the global crisis on Islamic and conventional banks: A comparative study.* IMF working paper WP 10/201, September. Washington, DC: International Monetary Fund.

Hasan, Zubair. 1998. Islamization of knowledge in economics: Issues and agenda. *IIUM Journal* 6 (2): 1–40.

Hasan, Zubair. 2002. Mudaraba as a mode of financing in Islamic banking: Theory, practice and problems. *Middle East Business and Economic Review* 14 (2): 41–53.

Hasan, Zubair. 2005. Treatment of consumption in Islamic economics: An appraisal. *Journal of King Abdulaziz University: Islamic Economics* 18 (2): 29–46.

Hasan, Zubair. 2006. Sustainable development from an Islamic perspective: Meaning, implications, and policy concerns. *Journal of King Abdulaziz University: Islamic Economics* 19 (1): 3–18.

Hasan, Zubair. 2009. Islamic finance education at the graduate level: Current state and challenges. *Islamic Economic Studies* 16 (1, 2) (January): 77–102.

Hasan, Zubair. 2010. *Islamic finance: What does it change, what it does not? Structure–objective mismatch and its consequences*, http://mpra.ub.uni-muenchen.de/21224/.

Hasan, Zubair. 2011. Scarcity, self-interest and maximization from Islamic angle. Unpublished. Online at http://mpra.ub.uni-muenchen.de/29414/, MPRA Paper no. 29414, posted 8 March 2011, 06:20.

Hasanuzzaman, S.M. 1984. Definition of Islamic economics. *Journal of King Abdulaziz University* 1 (2).

Hasanuzzaman, S.M. 1989. Limited liability of shareholders: An Islamic perspective. *Islamic Studies* 28 (4): 353–361.

Haskins, M.E., Kenneth R. Ferris and Thomas I. Selling. 1996. *International financial and reporting analysis*. Chicago: Richard D. Irwin.

Hassan, H.H. 1985. *Bima ki shari'i hathiyat* [Legal position of insurance]. Urdu. Trans. A.R. Ashraf Baloch. Islamabad: Islamic Research Institute.

Hassan, Muhammad K. 2006. The x-efficiency in Islamic banks. *Islamic Economics Studies* 13 (2) (February): 49–77.

Hassan, Muhammad K. and Rasem N. Kayed. 2009. The global financial crisis, risk management and social justice in Islamic finance. *ISRA International Journal of Islamic Finance* 1 (1): 33–57.

Hassan, Muhammad K. and Mervyn K. Lewis. 2007. Ends and means in Islamic banking and finance. *Review of Islamic Economics* 11: 5–28.

Hassan, Muhammad K. and Mervyn K. Lewis, eds. 2007-a. *Handbook of Islamic banking*. Cheltenham, UK and Northampton, MA, USA: Edward Elgar.

Hausman, D.W. 1985. Is falsification unpracticed or unpracticable? *Philosophy of the Social Sciences*, 15: 313–319.

Heck, Gene W. 2006. *Charlemagne, Muhammad, and the Arab roots of capitalism*. Berlin and New York: Walter de Gruyter.

Henderiksen, E.S. 1990. *Accounting theory*. Homewood, IL: Richard D. Irwin.

Homoud, S.H. 1985. *Islamic banking*. London: Arabian Information.

Hussain, Ishrat. 2007. The surge in Islamic financial services. *Daily Dawn* (Karachi), 11 September.

Hussein, Khaled A. 2008. *Islamic economics: Current state of knowledge and development of the discipline*. Paper presented at 7th International

Conference on Islamic Economics, King Abdulaziz University, 1–3 April, Jeddah, http://islamiccenter.kaau.edu.sa/7iecon/index.html.

Ibn Ashur, Muhammed al-Tahir. 2006. *Treatise on maqasid al-shari'ah*. Arabic. Trans. Mohamed el-Tahir el-Mesawi. Herndon, VA: International Institute of Islamic Thought.

Ibrahim, Muhammad and Hamim Syahrum Ahmad Mokhtar. 2010. Islamic liquidity management: The Malaysian experience. *ISRA International Journal of Islamic Finance* 2 (2): 130–157.

Imadi, Tamanna. 1965. Riba aur bai'. [Riba and trade]. Urdu. *Fikro Nazar* (Islamabad) 2 (7): 429–434.

International Islamic Financial Market. 2012. *Sukuk report: A comprehensive study of the global sukuk market*, http://iifm.net/media/pdf/IIFM_sukuk_report_2.pdf.

Iqbal, Munawar. 2008. *Contributions of the last six conferences*. Paper presented at 7th International Conference on Islamic Economics, King Abdulaziz University, 1–3 April, Jeddah, http://islamiccenter.kaau.edu.sa/7iecon/index.html.

Iqbal, Munawar and Salman Syed Ali, eds. 2007. Introduction to *Advances in Islamic economics and finance: Proceedings of the 6th International Conference on Islamic Economics and Finance*, Vol. 1. Jeddah: Islamic Research and Training Institute, Islamic Development Bank.

Iqbal, Munawar, Salman Syed Ali and Dadang Muljawan, eds. 2007. *Advances in Islamic economics and finance: Proceedings of the 6th International Conference on Islamic Economics and Finance*, Vol. 1. Jeddah: Islamic Research and Training Institute, Islamic Development Bank.

Iqbal, Munawar and Philip Molyneux. 2005. *Thirty years of Islamic banking: History, performance and prospects*. New York: Palgrave Macmillan.

Iqbal, Zafar and Mervyn K. Lewis. 2009. *Islamic perspective on governance*. Cheltenham, UK and Northampton, MA, USA: Edward Elgar.

Iqbal, Zamir. 2002. Portfolio choices and asset pricing in Islamic framework. In *Theoretical foundations of Islamic economics*, ed. Habib Ahmed, pp. 167–189. Jeddah: Islamic Research and Training Institute, Islamic Development Bank.

Iqbal, Zamir and Abbas Mirakhor. 1987. *Islamic banking*. Occasional paper 49. Washington, DC: International Monetary Fund.

Iqbal, Zamir and Abbas Mirakhor. 2004. The stakeholders' model of governance in an Islamic economic system. *Islamic Economic Studies* 11 (2): 43–63.

Iqbal, Zamir and Abbas Mirakhor. 2008. *An introduction to Islamic finance*. Lahore: Vanguard Books.

Irfani, A.M. 1984. Bima ki shari'i hathiyat [Legal position of insurance]. Urdu. *Fikro Nazar* (Islamabad) 21 (7) (February): 6–23.

Islahi, Abdul Azim. 2011. *A study of Muslim economic thinking in the 11th a.h./17th c.e. century.* Jeddah: Islamic Economics Research Centre, King Abdulaziz University.

Islahi, Abdul Azim and Mohammed Obaidullah. 2004. Zakah on stocks: Some unsettled issues. *Journal of King Abdulaziz University: Islamic Economics* 17 (2): 3–17.

Islahi, Amin Ahsan. [1955–85] 1999. *Tadabbur e Qur'an.* Lahore: Faran Foundation.

Islamic Economics Research Centre. 2008. *A proposed strategic vision for future research in Islamic economics.* Paper presented at 7th International Conference on Islamic Economics, King Abdulaziz University, 1–3 April, Jeddah, http://islamiccenter.kaau.edu.sa/7iecon/index.html.

Islamic Financial Services Board. 2006. *Issues in regulation and supervision of takaful (Islamic insurance).* IFSB, http://www.ifsb.org.

Islamic Financial Services Board. 2008. *Technical note on issues in strengthening liquidity management of institutions offering Islamic financial services: The development of Islamic money markets.* IFSB, http://www.ifsb.org.

Islamic Financial Services Board. 2010. *Guidance note in connection with the risk management and capital adequacy standards: Commodity murabaha transactions.* IFSB, http://www.ifsb.org.

Jabeen, Zohra and Memoona Rauf Khan. 2008. An inquiry into the usage of real assets in Islamic transactions and their benchmarking: The implications for Islamic capital markets. In *Islamic capital markets: Products, regulation and development,* ed. Salman Syed Ali, pp. 69–84. Jeddah: Islamic Research and Training Institute, Islamic Development Bank.

Jalal, Ayesha. 2008. *Partisans of God: Jihad in south Asia.* Lahore: Sang-e-Meel Publications.

Janahi, A.L. Rahim. 2005. Shari'ah alternatives to government bonds. In *Financial engineering and Islamic contracts,* ed. Munawar Iqbal and Tariqullah Khan. Houndmills, Basingstoke: Palgrave Macmillan.

Jobst, Andreas A. 2007. The economics of Islamic finance: Securitization. *Journal of Structured Finance* 13 (1). Electronic copy available at: http://ssrn.com/abstract=970682.

Jobst, Andreas A. 2008. Derivatives in Islamic finance. In *Islamic capital markets: Products, regulation and development,* ed. Salman Syed Ali, pp. 97–124. Jeddah: Islamic Research and Training Institute, Islamic Development Bank.

Johansen, Baber. 1988. *The Islamic law on land tax and rent.* London: Croom Helm.

Kahf, Monzer. n.d. *Introduction to the study of economics of zakah*, http://monzer.kahf.com/.

Kahf, Monzer. n.d.-a. *Non-tax private financing of government in Islam*, http://monzer.kahf.com/.

Kahf, Monzer. n.d.-b. *Budget deficit and public borrowing in an Islamic economic system*, http://monzer.kahf.com/.

Kahf, Monzer. 1982. Fiscal and monetary policies in an Islamic economy. In *Monetary and fiscal economics of Islam*, ed. M. Ariff. Jeddah: Islamic Research and Training Institute, Islamic Development Bank.

Kahf, Monzer. 1997. The use of assets ijara bond for bridging the budget gap. *Islamic Economic Studies* 4 (2) (May).

Kahf, Monzer. 2004. Islamic banks: The rise of a new power alliance of wealth and Shari'ah scholarship. In *The politics of Islamic finance*, ed. Clement Henry and Rodney Wilson, pp. 17–36. Edinburgh: Edinburgh University Press.

Kahf, Monzer. 2005. *Islamic banking and development: An alternative banking concept?*, http://monzer.kahf.com/.

Kahf, Monzer. 2007. *Islamic finance: Business as usual*. Lecture at Muslim Community Association of San Francisco Bay Area organized by Hambaba, 22 May, http://hambaba.com/discover/islamic-finance-business-as-usual.html.

Kahf, Monzer. 2008. Role of zakah and awqaf in reducing poverty: A proposed institutional setting within the spirit of Shari'ah. *Thoughts on Economics* 18 (3) (July): 40–67.

Kahf, Monzer and Tariqullah Khan. 1992. *Principles of Islamic finance: A survey*. Jeddah: Islamic Research and Training Institute, Islamic Development Bank.

Kamali, M. Hashim. 1995. Islamic commercial law: An analysis of options. Paper presented at the conference of SPTF/Islamic Banking Products, Kuala Lumpur, December.

Kamali, M. Hashim. 1996. Islamic commercial law: An analysis of futures. *American Journal of Islamic Social Sciences* 13 (2): 197–212.

Kamali, M. Hashim. 2007. A Shari'ah analysis of issues in Islamic leasing. *Journal of King Abdulaziz University: Islamic Economics* 20 (1): 3–22. [Revised and improved version of the paper presented at the International Islamic Leasing Conference in Kuwait, 24–25 April 2005.]

Kamel, Saleh. 1998. *Development of Islamic banking activity: Problems and prospects*. Jeddah: Islamic Research and Training Institute, Islamic Development Bank.

Karim, N., Michael Tarazi and Xavier Reilli. 2008. Islamic microfinance: An emerging market niche. *Consultative Group to Assist the Poor (CGAP) Newsletter Focus* 49, http://www.cgap.org/p/site/c/.

Kayed, Rasem N. 2008. *Appraisal of the status on research on labor economics in the Islamic framework*. Paper presented at 7th International Conference on Islamic Economics, King Abdulaziz University, 1–3 April, Jeddah, http://islamiccenter.kaau.edu.sa/7iecon/index.html.

Kazmi, Aqdas Ali. 1992. The non-equivalence of interest and riba. *Business Recorder* (Karachi), 14 May.

Khalil, Emad H. 2006. An overview of the Shari'ah prohibition of riba. In *Interest in Islamic economics*, ed. Abdulkader Thomas. London: Routledge.

Khalil, Emad H. and Abdulkader Thomas. 2006. The modern debate over riba in Egypt. In *Interest in Islamic economics*, ed. Abdulkader Thomas. London: Routledge.

Khan, I. 2010. Role of Islamic finance in developing the Muslim world. Paper presented at the Durham Islamic Finance Summer School, School of Government and International Affairs, Durham University, 5–9 July.

Khan, Javed A. 1995. *Islamic economics and finance*. London: Mansell Publishing.

Khan, M. Mansoor and M. Ishaq Bhatti. 2008. *Developments in Islamic banking: The case of Pakistan*. Houndmills, Basingstoke: Palgrave Macmillan.

Khan, M.S. 1986. Islamic interest-free banking. *IMF Staff Paper* 33 (1) (March).

Khan, Muhammad Akram. 1994. *Islamic banking in Pakistan: The future path*. Lahore: All Pakistan Islamic Educational Congress.

Khan, Muhammad Akram. 1994-a. *An introduction to Islamic economics*. Islamabad: International Institute of Islamic Thought and Institute of Policy Studies.

Khan, Muhammad Akram. 2000. Some accounting issues relating to zakah. *Islamic Studies* 39 (1): 103–120.

Khan, Muhammad Akram. 2001. Eliminating interest from the economy. *New Horizon* (May–June).

Khan, Muhammad Akram. 2003. *Islamic economics and finance: A glossary*, 2nd edn. London: Routledge.

Khan, Muhammad Fahim. 1991. The value of money and discounting in the Islamic perspective. *Review of Islamic Economics* 1 (2): 35–45.

Khan, Muhammad Fahim. 2002. Fiqh foundations of the theory of Islamic economics: A survey of selected contemporary writings on economics related subjects of fiqh. In *Theoretical foundations of Islamic economics*, ed. Habib Ahmed, pp. 61–85. Jeddah: Islamic Research and Training Institute, Islamic Development Bank.

Khan, Muhammad Fahim. 2003. Guaranteeing investment deposits in

Islamic banking system. *Journal of King Abdulaziz University: Islamic Economics* 16 (1): 45–52.

Khan, Muhammad Fahim. 2007. Comments on *Towards a new paradigm for economics* by Asad Zaman (JKAU: Islamic Economics, 18(2). 2005). *Journal of King Abdulaziz University: Islamic Economics* 20 (1): 65–72.

Khan, Salman. 2010. Organized tawarruq in practice: A Shari'ah non-compliant and unjustified transaction. *New Horizon* (177): 16–21.

Khan, Waqar Masood. 2002. *Transition to a riba-free economy.* Islamabad: International Institute of Islamic Thought and Islamic Research Institute.

Kholis, Nur. 2008. Murabaha mode of financing for micro and medium sized enterprises: A case study of Baitul mal wat tamwil (BMT), Yogyakarta, Indonesia. Paper presented at the First International Conference on Inclusive Islamic Financial Sector Development: Enhancing Islamic Financial Services for Micro and Medium Sized Enterprises, 17–19 April 2007, Brunei. In *Islamic finance for micro and medium enterprises*, ed. Mohammed Obaidullah and Hajah Salma Haji Abdul Latiff, pp. 161–184. Jeddah: Islamic Research and Training Institute, Islamic Development Bank.

Klingmuller, E. 1969. The concept and development of insurance in Islamic countries. *Islamic Culture* (Hyderabad) (January): 27–37.

Kuran, Timur. 1983. Behavioral norms in the Islamic doctrine of economics: A critique. *Journal of Economic Behavior and Organization* 4: 353–379.

Kuran, Timur. 1989. On the notion of economic justice in contemporary Islamic thought. *International Journal of Middle East Studies* 21 (2) (May): 171–191.

Kuran, Timur. 1996. The discontents of Islamic economic morality. *American Economic Review* 86 (2) (May): 438–442.

Kuran, Timur. 2004. *Islam and mammon: The economic predicaments of Islamism.* Princeton, NJ: Princeton University Press.

Leibenstein, H. 1966. Allocative efficiency vs x-efficiency. *American Economic Review* 56: 392–415.

Lewis, M.K. and L.M. al-Gaud. 2001. *Islamic banking.* Cheltenham, UK and Northampton, MA, USA: Edward Elgar.

Lings, Martin. 2005. *Muhammad: His life based on the earliest sources.* Lahore: Suhail Academy.

Lone, F. Ahmad. 2009. The modern challenges of Islamic banks. *Islamic Business and Finance* 45 (September): 36–37, www.cpi.financial.net.

MacFarlane, Isla. 2009. Sukuk slide. *Islamic Business and Finance* 43 (June), http://www.cpifinancial.net.

Mannan, M.A. 1992. *Islamic economics: Theory and practice.* Cambridge: Islamic Academy.

Mannan, M.A. 2008. Comments on *Islamic economics: Current state of knowledge and development of the discipline* by Khaled A. Hussein. Paper presented at 7th International Conference on Islamic Economics, King Abdulaziz University, 1–3 April, Jeddah, http://islamiccenter. kaau.edu.sa/7iecon/index.html.

Mannan, M.A. and M. Ahmad, eds. 1996. *Economic development in an Islamic framework.* Islamabad: International Institute of Islamic Economics.

Mardhatillah, Amy and Ronald Rulindo. 2008. Building capacity of micro and medium enterprises through spirituality training. Paper presented at the First International Conference on Inclusive Islamic Financial Sector Development: Enhancing Islamic Financial Services for Micro and Medium Sized Enterprises, 17–19 April 2007, Brunei. In *Islamic finance for micro and medium enterprises,* ed. Mohammed Obaidullah and Hajah Salma Haji Abdul Latiff, pp. 323–338. Jeddah: Islamic Research and Training Institute, Islamic Development Bank.

Masud, M. Khalid. 2007. *Taqdeem* [Prelude]. Urdu. *Ijtehad* (Journal of the Council of Islamic Ideology, Pakistan) 2 (December): 1–3.

Mawdudi, Abu al-'Ala. 1950. *Mas'ala milkiyyat e zamin* [The problem of land ownership]. Urdu. Lahore: Islamic Publications.

Mawdudi, Abu al-'Ala. 1961. *Sud* [Interest]. Urdu. Lahore: Islamic Publications.

Mawdudi, Abu al-'Ala. 1969. *Ma'ashiyat e Islam* [Economics of Islam]. Urdu. Lahore: Islamic Publications.

McMillen, Michael J.T. 2008. Asset securitization sukuk and Islamic capital markets: Structural issues in these formative years. *Wisconsin International Law Journal* 25 (4) (Winter): 703–772.

Meera, A.K.M. and Dzuljasri Abdul Razak. n.d. *Home financing through the musharaka mutaniqsa contracts: Some practical issues.* Kuala Lumpur: International Shari'ah Research Academy, http://www.isra. my/articles/islamic-banking/tawarruq.html.

Mehmood, Aurangzeb. 2002. Islamization of economy in Pakistan: Past, present and future. *Islamic Studies* 41 (4): 675–704.

Mersch, Yves. 2009. *About the role of central banks in financial stability and prudential liquidity supervision and the attractiveness of Islamic finance.* Kuala Lumpur: Islamic Financial Services Board, www.ifsb.org.

Mills, Paul and John Presley. 1999. *Islamic finance: Theory and practice.* Houndmills, Basingstoke: Macmillan.

Ministry of Finance, Government of Pakistan. 2002. *Report of the task force for Islamization of the economy,* 3 June.

Mirakhor, Abbas. 2007. *A note on Islamic economics.* IDB prize series 20. Jeddah: Islamic Research and Training Institute, Islamic Development Bank.

Mirakhor, Abbas. 2007-a. Globalization and Islamic finance. In *Advances in Islamic economics and finance: Proceedings of 6th International Conference on Islamic economics and finance*, Vol. 1, ed. Munawar Iqbal, Salman Syed Ali and Dadang Muljawan, pp. 19–40. Jeddah: Islamic Research and Training Institute, Islamic Development Bank.

Mirakhor, Abbas and Noureddine Krichene. 2009. *The recent crisis: Lessons for Islamic finance.* Kuala Lumpur: Islamic Financial Services Board.

Moghul, Umar F. 2007. No pain, no gain: The state of the industry in light of an American Islamic private equity transaction. *Chicago Journal of International Law* 7 (2) (Winter): 469–494.

Mohamad, Shamsiah and Mohd Fadhly Md Yusoff. 2008. Key Shari'ah rulings on sukuk issuance in the Malaysian Islamic capital market. In *Islamic capital markets: Products, regulation and development*, ed. Salman Syed Ali, pp. 55–68. Jeddah: Islamic Research and Training Institute, Islamic Development Bank.

Mokhtar, Hamim S.A., Naziruddin Abdullah and S. Musa al-Habshi. 2007. Technical and cost efficiency of Islamic banking in Malaysia. *Review of Islamic Economics* 11 (1): 5–40.

Mulhim, A.S. and Ahmad M. Sabbagh. n.d. *The Islamic insurance: Theory and practice*, http://pdfszone.com/pdf/Ahmed-Salem-Mulhim-;-Ahmed-Mohammed-Sabbagh-;-The-ISLAMIC-INSURANCE-THEORY-and-PRACTICE-;pdf.html.

Muqorobin, Masyhudi. 2008. *Journey of Islamic economics in the modern world.* Paper presented at 7th International Conference on Islamic Economics. King Abdulaziz University, 1–3 April, Jeddah, http://islamiccenter.kaau.edu.sa/7iecon/index.html.

Muslehuddin, M. 1969. *Insurance and Islamic law.* Lahore: Islamic Publications.

Muslim, A.G. 1974. The theory of interest in Islamic law and the effect of the interpretation of this by the Hanafi school up to the end of Mughal empire. Ph.D. dissertation. University of Glasgow.

Nagaoka, Shinsuke. 2007. Beyond the theoretical dichotomy in Islamic finance: Analytical reflections on murabaha contracts and Islamic debt securities. *Kyoto Bulletin of Islamic Area Studies* 1 (2): 72–91.

Nagaoka, Shinsuke. 2010. *Islamic finance in economic history: Marginal system or another universal system?* Presented at Second Workshop on Islamic Finance: What Islamic Finance Does (Not) Change, 17 March, EM Strasbourg Business School.

Naqvi, S.N.H. 2000. Islamic banking: An evaluation. *IIUM Journal of Economics and Management* 8 (1): 41–70.

Nasr, S.V.R. 1986. Whither Islamic economics? *Islamic Quarterly: A Review of Islamic Culture* 30 (4).

Nassar, A.M.M. n.d. *The parameters of forward ijara and its application in financing services in Islamic financial institutions.* Kuala Lumpur: International Shari'ah Research Academy, http://www.isra.my/articles/islamic-banking/tawarruq.html.

Ngadimon, Md Nurdin. 2008. Intangible asset: A new asset class to structure Islamic financial products. In *Islamic capital markets: Products, regulation and development,* ed. Salman Syed Ali, pp. 125–146. Jeddah: Islamic Research and Training Institute, Islamic Development Bank.

Nienhaus, V. 1995. Searching for alternative paths to development: Islamic economic theory of development. *Thoughts on Economics* 5 (1–2) (January–June): 7–16.

Nomani, Farhad. n.d. *The interpretative debate of the classical Islamic jurists on riba (usury),* http://www.luc.edu/orgs/meea/volume4/NomaniRevised.htm.

Noorzoy, M. Siddiq. 1982. Islamic laws on riba (interest) and their economic implications. *International Journal of Middle Eastern Studies* 14 (1): 3–17.

Nyazee, I.A.K. 1998. *Islamic law of business organizations (corporations).* Islamabad: International Institute of Islamic Thought, www.nyazee.org.

Nyazee, I.A.K. 2000. *The rules and definition of riba.* Islamabad: Advanced Legal Studies Institute, www.nyazee.org.

Nyazee, I.A.K. 2000-a. *Excerpt on riba from Ahkam al-Quran by al-Jassas.* Islamabad: Advanced Legal Studies Institute, www.nyazee.org.

Nyazee, I.A.K. 2009. *Murabaha and the credit sale.* Islamabad: Advanced Legal Studies Institute, www.nyazee.org.

Obaidullah, Mohammed. 2006. *Teaching corporate finance from an Islamic perspective.* Jeddah: Centre for Research in Islamic Economics, King Abdulaziz University.

Obaidullah, Mohammed. 2008. *Role of microfinance in poverty alleviation: Lessons from experiences in selected IDB member countries.* Jeddah: Islamic Research and Training Institute.

Obaidullah, Mohammed. 2008-a. *Introduction to Islamic microfinance.* India: International Institute of Islamic Business and Finance, Islamic Banking and Finance Education and Charitable Trust, http://www.iiibf.org.

Obaidullah, Mohammed and Tariqullah Khan. 2008. *Islamic microfinance development: Challenges and initiatives*. Jeddah: Islamic Research and Training Institute.

Omar, M. Azmi, A. Noor, A.K.M. Meera, T.A.A. Manap, M.S.A. Majid, S.R.S. Zain and M.A. Sarif. 2010. *Islamic pricing benchmark*. Research paper 16/2010. Kuala Lumpur: International Shari'ah Research Academy for Islamic Finance, www.isra.org.my.

Oran, Ahmad F. 2010. An Islamic socio-economic public interest theory of market regulation. *Review of Islamic Economics* 14 (1): 125–146.

Oran, Ahmad Farras and Ghaida Khaznehkatbi. n.d. The economic system under the Abbasid dynasty. In *Encyclopedia of Islamic Economics and Finance*. Leicester: Islamic Foundation.

Pal, Izzud-Din. 2006. *Islam and the economy of Pakistan: A critical analysis of traditional interpretation*. Karachi: Oxford University Press.

Philips, Abu Ammeenah Bilal. 1990. *The evolution of fiqh (Islamic law and mad-habs)*. Riyadh: International Islamic Publishing House.

Phulwari, M.J.S., ed. 1959. *Commercial interest ki fiqhi hathiyat* [Commercial interest in Islamic law]. Urdu. Lahore: Idara Thaqafat e Islamiyya.

Pickthall, Marmaduke. 2008. Muslim education. *Islamic Studies* 47 (4): 527–536. (Reproduced from *Islamic Culture*, 1 (1), 1927, pp. 100–108.)

Prabowo, Bagya Agung. 2009. The practice of murabaha scheme in syariah banking: Critical analysis towards the application of murabaha scheme in Indonesia and Malaysia. *Journal Fakultas Hukam* 16 (1).

Purcell, Noel. 2008. The survival of capitalism: Supporting communities to stare down national and global threats. In *Commentaries on financial crisis October 2008*, ed. Stephen Young, 16 June, http://www.cauxroundtable.org.

Qadri, G. Sarwar. 1978. *Ma'ashiyat nizam e Mustafa* [Economics of the system of Mustafa]. Urdu. Lahore: Mustafa Academy.

Qureshi, D.M. 2005. Vision table: Questions and answers session. In *Proceedings of the First Pakistan Islamic Banking and Money Market Conference*, 14–15 September, Karachi.

Rahman, A.R.A. 2006–07. Pre-requisites for effective integration of zakah into the mainstream Islamic financial system in Malaysia. *Islamic Economic Studies* 14 (1–2) (August and January): 91–107.

Rahman, Fazlur. 1960. Bima e zindagi mumtaz ulema e misr ki nazar men [Insurance in the opinion of eminent Egyptian scholars]. Urdu. *Al-Furqan* (Lucknow) (April–May): 35–56.

Rahman, Fazlur. 1964. Riba and interest. *Islamic Studies* 3 (1) (March): 1–43.

Rahman, M. Miazur. 2010. Islamic micro-finance programme and its impact on rural poverty alleviation. *International Journal of Banking and Finance* 7 (1): 123–145, http://epublications.bond.edu.au/ijbf/vol7/iss1/7.

Rosenberg, R., Adrian Gonzalez and Sushma Narain. 2009. Are microcredit interest rates excessive? *CGAP Brief*, February, http://www.cgap.org/p/site/c/.

Saad, Norma M., M. Shabri Abdul Majid, Rosylin Mohammad Yusof, Jaria Duasa and Abdul Rahim Abdul Rahman. 2006. Measuring efficiency of insurance and takaful. *Review of Islamic Economics* 10 (2): 5–25.

Saadullah, Ridha. 1994. Concept of time in Islamic economics. *Islamic Economic Studies* 2 (1): 1–15.

Sachedina, Abdulaziz. n.d. *The issue of riba in Islamic faith and law*, http://people.virginia.edu/~aas/isislam.htm.

Sadeq, Abu al-Hasan. 1990. *Economic development in Islam*. Selangor, Malaysia: Pelanduk Publications.

Sadeq, Abu al-Hasan. 2002. *A survey of the institution of zakah: Issues, theories, and administration*. Jeddah: Islamic Research and Training Institute, Islamic Development Bank.

Sadr, Kazem. 2008. Gharzul-hasaneh financing and institutions. Paper presented at the First International Conference on Inclusive Islamic Financial Sector Development: Enhancing Islamic Financial Services for Micro and Medium Sized Enterprises, 17–19 April 2007, Brunei. In *Islamic finance for micro and medium enterprises*, ed. Mohammed Obaidullah and Hajah Salma Haji Abdul Latiff, pp. 149–159. Jeddah: Islamic Research and Training Institute, Islamic Development Bank.

Saeed, Abdullah. 1995. The moral context of the prohibition of riba in Islam revisited. *American Journal of Islamic Social Sciences* 12 (4): 496–517.

Saeed, Abdullah. 1996. *Islamic banking and interest: A study of prohibition of interest and its contemporary interpretation*. Leiden: E.J. Brill.

Sairally, Salma. 2002. Murabaha financing: Some controversial issues. *Review of Islamic Economics* 12: 73–86.

Sairally, Salma. 2007. Evaluating the 'social responsibility' of Islamic finance: Learning from the experiences of socially responsible investment funds. In *Advances in Islamic economics and finance: Proceedings of 6th International Conference on Islamic Economics and Finance*, Vol. 1, ed. Munawar Iqbal, Salman Syed Ali and Dadang Muljawan, pp. 279–320. Jeddah: Islamic Research and Training Institute, Islamic Development Bank.

Saleem, M. Yusuf. 2008. *Methods and methodologies in fiqh and Islamic economics*. Paper presented at 7th International Conference on Islamic

Economics, King Abdulaziz University, 1–3 April, Jeddah, http://islam-iccenter.kaau.edu.sa/7iecon/index.html. [Also published in *Review of Islamic Economics* 14 (1), 2010, pp. 103–123.]

Saleh, Ismail Muhd and Rogayah Ngah. 1980. Distribution of the zakat burden on padi producers in Malaysia. In *Some aspects of the economics of zakah*, ed. M. Raquibuzzaman, pp. 80–153. Gary, IN: Association of Muslim Social Scientists.

Sanbhali, M.B. 1973, 1974. Insurance fiqhi nuqta e nazar say [Insurance from a juridical point of view]. Urdu. *Islam aur Asr Jadeed* (New Delhi) (October, January).

Schacht, J. 1964. *An introduction to Islamic law*. Oxford: Oxford University Press.

Scharf, T.W. 1983. *Arab and Islamic banks*. Paris: Organisation for Economic Co-operation and Development.

Schoon, Natalie. 2011. *Islamic asset management: An asset class on its own?* Edinburgh: Edinburgh University Press.

Schroeder, R.G. 1990. *Accounting theory: Text and readings*. New York: Wiley & Sons.

Seibel, Hans Dieter. 2005. *Islamic microfinance in Indonesia*. Cologne: University of Cologne Development Research Center.

Seibel, Hans Dieter. 2007. Islamic microfinance: The challenge of diversity. *ICMIF Takaful* 12 (October), www.takaful.coop.

Sen, Amartya. 1991. *Money and value: On the ethics and economics of finance*. First Paolo Baffi Lecture on Money and Finance. Rome: Banca d'Italia.

Sen, Amartya. 2000. *Development as freedom* (14th impression 2008). New Delhi: Oxford University Press.

Seoharvi, M. Hifzur Rahman. 1959. *Islam ka iqtisadi nizam* [Economic system of Islam]. Urdu. Delhi: Nadvatul Musanaffin.

Shafi, Mufti Muhammad. AH 1383. *Islam ka nizam e aradi* [Land management system of Islam]. Urdu. Karachi: Idaratul Ma'arif.

Shafi, Mufti Muhammad. 1972. *Islam aur bima* [Islam and insurance]. Urdu. Karachi: Dar al-Isha'at.

Shafi, Mufti Muhammad. 1973. *Provident fund ki zakat aur sud ke masa'il* [Zakah on provident fund and questions relating to interest]. Urdu. Karachi: Dar al-Isha'at.

Shah, S. Yaqub. 1967. *Chand ma'ashi masai'l aur Islam* [Islam and some economic problems]. Urdu. Lahore: Idara Thaqafat e Islamiyya.

Shams, Rasul. 2004. *A critical assessment of Islamic economics*. Discussion paper 281. Hamburg: Hamburg Institute of International Economics (HWWA), http://www.hwwa.de.

Shemesh, Ben. 1967. *Taxation in Islam*, 2 vols. Leiden: E.J. Brill.

Shihab, Rafiullah. 1966. Bankari aur us ka munafa' [Banking and its profit]. Urdu. *Fikro Nazar* (Islamabad) 4 (12) (July–August): 51–58.

Shirazi, Nasim Shah. 2006. Providing for the resource shortfall for poverty elimination through the institution of zakah in low income Muslim countries. *IIUM Journal of Economics and Management* 14 (1): 1–27.

Siddiqi, H.Z. 1950. *Islam ka ma'ashiyati nizam* [Economic system of Islam]. Urdu. Lahore: Kitab Manzil.

Siddiqi, M.M. 1955. *Islam ka ma'ashi nazariya* [Economic concepts of Islam]. Urdu. Lahore: Idara Thaqafat e Islamiyya.

Siddiqi, M.N. 1970. *Some aspects of Islamic economy*. Lahore: Islamic Publications.

Siddiqi, M.N. 1982. Economics of profit sharing. In *Monetary and Fiscal Economics of Islam*, ed. Mohammad Ariff. Jeddah: International Centre for Research in Islamic Economics.

Siddiqi, M.N. 1983. *Banking without interest*. Leicester: Islamic Foundation.

Siddiqi, M.N. 1983-a. *Issues in Islamic banking*. Leicester: Islamic Foundation.

Siddiqi, M.N. 1985. *Insurance in Islamic economy*. Leicester: Islamic Foundation.

Siddiqi, M.N. 1996. *Teaching economics in Islamic perspective*. Jeddah: King Abdulaziz University, Centre for Research in Islamic Economics.

Siddiqi, M.N. 1999. Islamic finance and beyond: Premises and promises of Islamic economics. *Proceedings of the 3rd Harvard University Forum on Islamic Finance: Local Challenges, Global Opportunities*, 1 October, pp. 49–53. Cambridge, MA: Harvard University.

Siddiqi, M.N. 2002. *Comparative advantages of Islamic banking and finance*. Presented at Harvard University Forum on Islamic Finance, 6 April, http://www.siddiqi.com/mns.

Siddiqi, M.N. 2004. *What went wrong with Islamic economics?* Paper presented at Roundtable on Islamic Economics: Current State of Knowledge and Development of Discipline, Islamic Research and Training Institute, Jeddah and Arab Planning Institute, Kuwait, 26–27 May, Jeddah, http://www.siddiqi.com/mns/.

Siddiqi. M.N. 2004-a. *Riba, bank interest, and the rationale of its prohibition*. Jeddah: Islamic Research and Training Institute, Islamic Development Bank.

Siddiqi, M.N. 2006. Islamic banking and finance in theory and practice: A survey of the state of the art. *Islamic Economic Studies* 13 (2) (February): 1–48.

Siddiqi. M.N. 2006-a. Shari'ah, economics and the progress of Islamic finance: The role of Shari'ah experts. Presented at the Pre-Forum

Workshop on Select Ethical and Methodological Issues in Shari'ah-Compliant Finance, 7th Harvard Forum on Islamic Finance, Cambridge, MA, 21 April.

Siddiqi, M.N. 2007. *Economics of tawarruq*, http://www.siddiqi.com/mns/.

Siddiqi, M.N. 2007-a. Maqasid shari'at ki roshani men ijtehad ki halia koshishen [Recent efforts of ijtehad in light of Shari'ah objectives]. Urdu. *Fikro Nazar* (Islamabad) 44 (4) (April–June): 3–24.

Siddiqi, M.N. 2007-b. *An approach to Islamic economics*, http://www.siddiqi.com/mns/.

Siddiqi, M.N. 2007-c. *Future of Islamic finance*. Presented at the Conference on Leadership in Global Finance: The Emerging Islamic Horizon, organized by the International Centre for Education in Islamic Finance, Kuala Lumpur, 30 August, http://www.siddiqi.com/mns/.

Siddiqi, M.N. 2008. *A note on sukuk and their role in Islamic finance*, http://www.siddiqi.com/mns/.

Siddiqi, M.N. 2008-a. Maqasid e Shari'at: fahm o tatbique [Objectives of Shari'ah: Understanding and reconciliation]. Urdu. *Fikro Nazar* (Islamabad) 45 (3) (March): 3–23.

Siddiqi, M.N. 2008-b. *Obstacles to Islamic economics research*. Paper presented at 7th International Conference on Islamic Economics, King Abdulaziz University, 1–3 April, Jeddah, http://islamiccenter.kaau.edu.sa/7iecon/index.html.

Siddiqi, M.N. 2008-c. The current financial crisis and Islamic economics. *IIUM Journal of Economics and Management* 16 (2): 125–138.

Siddiqi, M.N. 2009. *Risk management in an Islamic framework*, http://www.siddiqi.com/mns/.

Siddiqi, M.N. 2009-a. *Maqasid e shari'at* [Objectives of the Shari'ah]. Urdu. Islamabad: Institute of Islamic Research, International Islamic University.

Siddiqi, Muhammad Saad and Salman Ahmad Khan. 2010. Iltizam bit tassaduq: fiqhi wa shari'i hathiyat [Compulsory charity: Juridical and legal position]. Urdu. *Fikro Nazar* (Islamabad) 48 (2) (October–December): 3–33.

Siddiqi, Naeem. 1958. *Ma'ashi nahumwariyon ka Islami hall* [Islamic solution to economic inequalities]. Urdu. Karachi: Maktaba Chiragh e rah.

Siddiqui, Shamim A. 2008. *An evaluation of research on monetary policy and stability of the Islamic economic system*. Paper presented at 7th International Conference on Islamic Economics, King Abdulaziz University, 1–3 April, Jeddah, http://islamiccenter.kaau.edu.sa/7iecon/index.html.

Siswantoro, Dadik and Hamidah Qoyyimah. 2007. Analysis on the feasibility study of musharaka mutaniqsa implementation in Indonesian

Islamic banks. In *Advances in Islamic economics and finance: Proceedings of 6th International Conference on Islamic Economics and Finance*, Vol. 1, ed. Munawar Iqbal, Salman Syed Ali and Dadang Muljawan, pp. 471–488. Jeddah: Islamic Research and Training Institute, Islamic Development Bank.

Solé, Juan. 2007. *Introducing Islamic banks into conventional banking systems*. IMF working paper WP/07/175. Washington, DC: International Monetary Fund.

Soros, George. 2008. The crisis and what to do about it. *Real-World Economics Review* 48 (6 December): 312–318, http://www.paecon.net/PAEReview/issue48/Soros48.pdf.

Staib, Daniel. 2011. *Islamic insurance revisited*. Kuala Lumpur and Zurich: Economic Research and Consulting, Swiss Reinsurance Company.

Sufian, Fadzlan. 2006. The efficiency of the Islamic banking industry in Malaysia: Foreign vs. domestic banks. *Review of Islamic Economics* 10 (2): 27–54.

Sufian, Fadzlan. 2006–07. The efficiency of Islamic banking industry: A non-parametric analysis with non-discretionary input variables. *Islamic Economic Studies* 14 (1–2) (August, January): 53–91.

Sundararajan, V. 2007. Risk management and disclosure in Islamic finance and the implications of profit sharing investment accounts. In *Advances in Islamic economics and finance: Proceedings of 6th International Conference on Islamic Economics and Finance*, Vol. 1, ed. Munawar Iqbal, Salman Syed Ali and Dadang Muljawan, pp. 121–152. Jeddah: Islamic Research and Training Institute, Islamic Development Bank.

Sundararajan, V. and Luca Errico. 2002. Islamic financial institutions and products in the global financial system: Key issues in risk management and challenges ahead. Working paper WP/02/192, November. Washington, DC: International Monetary Fund.

Sundararajan, V., David Marston and Giath Shabsigh. 1998. *Monetary operations and government debt management under Islamic banking*. Working paper, September. Washington, DC: International Monetary Fund.

Supreme Court of Pakistan, Shari'ah Appellate Bench. 1999. *Judgment on riba*. Lahore: Shariat Law Reports.

Supreme Court of Pakistan, Shari'ah Appellate Bench. 2002. *Judgment on riba case review*. Lahore: Shariat Law Reports. [Also in *Islamic Studies* 41 (4): 705–724.]

Tahir, Sayyid. 2007. Unresolved issues in Islamic banking and finance: Deposit mobilization. In *Islamic banking and finance: Fundamentals and contemporary issues*, ed. Salman S. Ali and Ausaf Ahmad, pp. 80–98.

Jeddah: Islamic Research and Training Institute, Islamic Development Bank.

Tahir, Sayyid. 2009. Islamic finance: Undergraduate education. *Islamic Economic Studies* 16 (1&2) (January): 53–77.

Tahir, Sayyid, Atiquzzafar, Salman Syed Ali and Atif Waheed. 1999. *IIIE's blueprint of Islamic financial system including strategy for elimination of riba*. Islamabad: International Institute of Islamic Economics, International Islamic University.

Thomas, Abdulkader. 2001. Methods of Islamic home finance in the United States: Beneficial breakthroughs. *American Journal of Islamic Finance*, http://www.failaka.com/downloads/Methods%20of%20Islamic%20 Home%20Finance%20-%20AST%202002.pdf.

Tonki, Walihasan. 1965. Islam aur bima [Islam and insurance]. Urdu. *Bayyenat* 5, 6 (March, April): 18–40, 17–33.

Toutounchian, Iraj. 2009. *Islamic money and banking: Integrating money in capital theory*. Singapore: John Wiley & Sons (Asia).

Unal, Murat. 2011. *The small world of Islamic finance: Shari'ah scholars and governance – A network analytic perspective*, v. 6.0, 19 January. Funds@Work; Zawya Shari'ah Scholars, www.shariahscholars.com.

Uthman, Usama A. 2001. Money, interest and an alternative macroeconomic system. *IIUM Journal of Economics and Management* 9 (1): 101–114.

Uthmani, M.A. Imran. 2009. *Meezan Bank's guide to Islamic banking*. Trans. Zeenat Zubairi, www.meezanbank.com.

Uthmani, Muhammad T. n.d. *Verdicts on at-tawarruq and its banking applications*. Trans. and ed. Yahya T. Muritala and A. Ashadi M. Zaini. Kuala Lumpur: International Shari'ah Research Academy, http://www. isra.my/articles/islamic-banking/tawarruq.html.

Uthmani, Muhammad T. n.d.-a. *Murabaha*, www.accountancy.com.pk.

Uthmani, Muhammad T. 1992. The principle of limited liability for the Shari'ah viewpoint. *New Horizon* (August–September): 21–22.

Uthmani, Muhammad T. 1995. *Islam aur jadeed ma'eeshat wa tijart* [Islam and modern economy and trade]. Urdu. Karachi: Idaratul Ma'arif.

Uthmani, Muhammad T. 1999. Futures, options and swaps. Interview. *International Journal of Islamic Financial Services* 1 (1) (April–June), http://islamic-finance.net/journals/journal1/art4.pdf.

Uthmani, Muhammad T. 1999-a. *An introduction to Islamic finance*. Karachi: Idaratul Ma'arif.

Uthmani, Muhammad T. 1999-b. Text of the Supreme Court Shari'ah Appellate Bench decision on riba written by Taqi Uthmani, www.al-Balagh.net.

Uthmani, Muhammad T. 2000. *The historic judgment on interest delivered in the Supreme Court of Pakistan*. Karachi: Idaratul Ma'arif.

Uthmani, Muhammad T. 2007. *Introduction to Islamic finance*. Karachi: Qur'anic Studies Publishers.

Uthmani, Muhammad T. 2008. *Sukuk and their contemporary application*, http://www.muftitaqiusmani.com/Downloads/Publications/Articles/Sukuk.pdf.

Uzair, Muhammad. 1980. Some conceptual and practical aspects of interest-free banking. In *Studies in Islamic Economics*, ed. Khurshid Ahmad. Jeddah: International Centre for Research in Islamic Economics; and Leicester: Islamic Foundation.

Visser, Hans. 2009. *Islamic finance: Principles and practice*. Cheltenham, UK and Northampton, MA, USA: Edward Elgar.

Vogel, Frank and Samuel Hayes. 1998. *Islamic law and finance: Religion, risk and return*. The Hague: Kluwer Law International.

Waliullah, Shah. 2003. *The conclusive argument from God*. Trans. Marcia K. Hermansen. Islamabad: Islamic Research Institute.

Warde, Ibrahim. 2000, 2010. *Islamic finance in the global economy*. Edinburgh: Edinburgh University Press.

Williams, Orice M. 2009. *Hedge funds: Overview of regulatory oversight, counterparty risks, and investment challenges*. Washington, DC: Government Accountability Office.

Wilson, Rodney. 2007. Making development assistance sustainable through Islamic microfinance. *IIUM Journal of Economics and Management* 15 (2): 197–217.

Wilson, Rodney. 2009. Shari'ah governance for Islamic financial institutions. *ISRA International Journal of Islamic Finance* 1 (1): 59–75.

Wouters, Paul. 2008. *Islamic banking in Turkey, Indonesia and Pakistan*, January, http://www.bener.av.tr/docs/en/Islamic%20Banking%20In%20Turkey,%20Indonesia%20And%20Pakistan.pdf.

Yean, Tan Wan. 2009. *Sukuk: Issues and the way forward*, http://ebook browse.com/. [Also at *Islamic Economics and Finance Pedia*.]

Yousef, T.M. 2004. The murabaha syndrome in Islamic finance: Laws, institutions and policies. In *Politics of Islamic finance*, ed. C.M. Henry and Rodney Wilson. Edinburgh: Edinburgh University Press.

Yudistira, Donsyah. 2004. Efficiency in Islamic banking: An empirical analysis of eighteen banks. *Islamic Economic Studies* 12 (1) (August): 1–19.

Yusuf, Hafiz Ghulam. 2009. *Ghair Muslim mumalik men sudi lain dain se muta'allaq fuqahay Pak o Hind ki ara' ka jai'za* [A review of the opinions of the jurists of the Indo-Pak subcontinent regarding dealing in interest in non-Muslim countries]. Urdu. *Fikro Nazar* (Islamabad) 46 (4) (April–June): 3–49.

Yusufali, Abdullah. 1988. *The holy Qur'an: Text, translation and commentary*. New York: Tahrike Tarsil e Qur'an.

Yusufuddin, M. 1950. *Islam ke ma'ashi nazariye* [Economic concepts of Islam], 2 vols. Urdu. Hyderabad, Deccan: Matba'a Ibrahimiyya.

Zaidi, N.A. 1991. Islamic banking in Pakistan. *Pakistan Banker* (July): 16–22.

Zaim, Sabah el-din. 1989. Islamic economics as a system based on human values. *Journal of Islamic Banking and Finance* 6 (2): 13–21.

Zaman, Arshad and Asad Zaman. 2000. Interest and the modern economy. *Lahore Journal of Economics* 6 (1): 1–12.

Zaman, Asad. 2005. Towards a new paradigm for economics. *Journal of King Abdulaziz University: Islamic Economics* 18 (2): 49–59.

Zaman, Asad. 2008. *Islamic economics: A survey of the literature*, http://mpra.ub.uni-muenchen.de/11024/, MPRA paper no. 11024.

Zaman, Asad. 2009, 2010. Islamic economics: A survey of the literature. *Islamic Studies* 48 (3) (Autumn): 395–424; 48 (4) (Winter): 525–566; 49 (1) (Spring): 37–63.

Zaman, Nazim and Mehmet Asutay. 2009. Divergence between aspirations and realities of Islamic economics: A political economy approach to bridging the divide. *IIUM Journal of Economics and Management* 17 (1): 73–96.

Zarqa, M. Anas. 1983. An Islamic perspective on the economics of discounting in project evaluation. In *Fiscal policy and resource allocation in Islam*, ed. Ziauddin Ahmed, Munawar Iqbal and M. Fahim Khan. Jeddah: International Centre for Research in Islamic Economics, King Abdulaziz University; and Islamabad: Institute of Policy Studies.

Zarqa, M. Anas. 1988. A note on Islamizing economics. In *Frontiers and mechanics of Islamic economics*, ed. Rafiq al-Islam Molla. Sokoto, Nigeria: Sokoto University Press.

Zarqa, M. Anas. 2008. *Duality of sources in Islamic economics, and its methodological consequences*. Paper presented at 7th International Conference on Islamic Economics, King Abdulaziz University, 1–3 April, Jeddah, http://islamiccenter.kaau.edu.sa/7iecon/index.html.

Zarrokh, Ehsan. 2007. *Islamic financing arrangements used in Islamic banking*, http://ssrn.com/abstract=978911.

Glossary of terms

Awqaf (sing. waqf)
Corporate bodies that manage funds generated from investment of dedicated property on behalf of defined beneficiaries. Generally, the beneficiaries are the poor and needy. The property is donated by wealthy individuals or groups.

Bai'
Sale of definite goods or property with free consent of the parties for a definite price.

Bai' al-dayn
Sale of debt either for immediate cash or for another debt.

Bai' al-'inah
A contract of sale where a person sells an article on credit and then buys back at a lower price for cash.

Bai' mu'ajjal
Credit sale.

Bai' al-wafa
A sales contract in which an owner sells real estate for ready cash with a binding promise by the buyer to return the property after a fixed term for the original price. The buyer derives benefit from the property which is a proxy for *riba* that the buyer could not charge under the *Shari'ah* law on the cash advanced to the seller.

Bai' bithaman 'ajil
A sale deal in which a person sells an article for cash but buys it back on deferred payment for a higher price. Thus he gets immediate cash to be repaid later with an increment. Also used for credit sale.

Baraka
God's blessing or bounty in relation to one's worldly pursuits. Qualitative growth in one's possessions. The notion refers to an invisible but concrete blessing resulting from a person's conduct including, and most importantly, his economic behaviour.

Fasad fil ard
Corruption on the earth such as highway robbery, arson, manslaughter, burning of crops and social destruction of any type. It also covers such individual economic behaviour or policies of the state that cause socio-economic imbalance, poverty, deprivation, economic backwardness and unemployment.

Fatwa (pl. *fatawa*)
A decree by a competent *Shari'ah* scholar on a matter in light of the *Shari'ah* rules and principles.

Fiqh
Science of deducing Islamic laws from evidence found in the sources; by extension the body of Islamic laws so deduced.

Gharar
Excessive uncertainty. Covers situations where the outcome of a contract could be highly risky.

Hadith (pl. *ahadith*)
Speech, action, habits and events of the Prophet's life codified by his companions and enlarged and revised by later Muslims.

Hisba
An institution that existed throughout Muslim history for implementing what is proper and preventing what is improper. The main role of *hisba* was to regulate markets and provide municipal services.

Hiyal (sing. *hila*)
Legal devices used to exploit that which is legitimate for an illegitimate purpose or end, or that which appears to be legitimate but is not.

Ijara
Sale of usufruct of an asset in exchange for definite reward. Also refers to a contract of land lease at a fixed rent payable in cash. It is an arrangement under which an Islamic bank leases equipment, a building or another facility to a client against an agreed rental. The rent is so fixed that the bank gets back its original investment plus a profit on it.

Ijara thumma al-bai'
A form of Islamic financing arrangement for infrastructure projects under which an infrastructure company sells an underlying project like a road to financiers for cash. The financiers, as owners of the project, then lease back the project (in this case the road) to the infrastructure company, which issues *ijara* certificates. The financiers can sell these certificates on

the stock exchange. After expiry of the lease, the infrastructure company can repurchase the asset from the financiers.

Ijara wa iqtina'
A contract under which the Islamic bank finances equipment, a building or another facility for a client against an agreed rental together with an undertaking from the client to make additional payments into an account which will eventually permit the client to purchase the equipment or the facility. The rental as well as the purchase price is fixed in such a manner that the bank gets back its principal sum along with some profit which is usually determined in advance.

Ijtehad
Process of arriving at reasoned decisions to suit new circumstances. The decisions themselves are also referred to as *ijtehad*.

Israf
Intemperance, immoderateness, exaggeration, waste. Covers (a) spending on lawful objects but exceeding moderation in quantity or quality; (b) spending on superfluous objects while necessities are unfulfilled; (c) spending on objects which are incompatible with the living standard of the majority of the population.

Istihsan
Relating to the sources of Islamic law, it is a deviation on a certain issue from the rule or a precedent for a more relevant legal reason.

Istisna'
A contract of sale whereby a purchaser asks a seller to manufacture a clearly defined product at a given price. The price could be paid in advance, in instalments or at the time of delivery.

Jahbadh
Financial administrator in the Abbasid period (AD 750–945) responsible for maintaining prescribed standards of fineness and quality of gold content and equivalence of various currencies. He acted like a banker to collect government dues and also provided loans to the government when needed.

Ju'ala
Literally, the stipulated price for performing any service. An agreement to pay a specified fee or compensation for getting a specified service.

Kharaj
Land tax on state-owned lands whether the cultivator is a leaseholder or a permanent tenant.

Maslaha mursala
Interest or benefit that has not been regulated or qualified by a specific text and is based on a general principle of the *Shari'ah* or its spirit.

Mudaraba
A partnership contract between the capital provider (*rabb al-mal*) and an entrepreneur (*mudarib*) whereby the capital provider contributes capital to an enterprise or activity that is to be managed by the entrepreneur. Profits generated by the enterprise or activity are shared in accordance with the contract while losses are borne solely by the capital provider unless caused by misconduct, negligence or breach of contract by the entrepreneur.

Muqassa
A mechanism for debt settlement between two persons who are simultaneously debtors and creditors to each other, setting off each other's debt against their respective receivables.

Murabaha
A contract to sell a specified asset at an agreed profit margin on cost whereby the cost and profit margin must be disclosed. The asset must be under complete ownership of the seller.

Musharaka
A contract between two or more people for participating in capital and profits and losses or for participating in transactions in someone else's capital and its profits and losses or for participating in profit and losses without participating in capital or transactions but in consideration of the work effort or goodwill.

Musharaka mutaniqsa
A diminishing partnership. A partnership arrangement whereby one or more partners undertake to gradually purchase the share of the others. The share of the selling partner continues to diminish in the joint venture till it is completely bought off.

Muzara'a
A contract for tilling the land of another person in consideration for a part of the produce of the land or a fixed cash contract.

Nisab
Exemption limit in the law of *zakah* that defines the status and obligation of a person.

Rahn
To pledge or lodge a real or corporeal property of material value in accordance with the law as security for a debt or pecuniary obligation so

as to make it possible for the creditor to regain the debt or some portion of the goods or property in case of default by the borrower.

Riba
An increase in a loan transaction that accrues to the lender over time without giving an equivalent counter-value or recompense to the borrower.

Rizq
All tangible and intangible resources at the disposal of a person. God speaks of these resources as one of His blessings. Man is accountable to God for his share of the *rizq*, i.e. how he acquired these resources and how he utilized them.

Sadaqa
In its widest sense an attitude of mutual appreciation, affection, assistance, an act of loyalty to God and to one's fellow beings, a sense of true humanness. At the material level it consists of two kinds: voluntary (*al-sadaqa al-tatawwu*), given by the free will of the donor; and obligatory (*zakah*), imposed by the Qur'an on Muslims having wealth beyond a certain limit.

Salam
A sale agreement that involves advance payment for goods which are to be delivered later. The objects of the sale are mostly fungible things and cover almost all things which are capable of being definitely described as to quantity, quality and workmanship. One of the conditions of this contract is advance payment of the full price of the product. It is usually applied in the agricultural sector where the bank advances money and agrees to receive a share in the crop later.

Sarf
Sale of a monetary value for monetary value or exchange of currencies.

Shari'ah
The sum total of Islamic laws which were revealed to the Prophet Muhammad and are recorded in the Qur'an as well as deducible from the Prophet's lifestyle (called the *Sunnah*).

Shari'ah supervisory board
Specific body set up or engaged by an institution offering Islamic financial services to carry out and implement its *Shari'ah* governance system.

Suftajah
A type of banking instrument used for delegation of credit during the Abbasid period (AD 750–945). It was used for collecting taxes, disbursing government dues and transferring funds by merchants.

Sukuk (sing. *sakk*)
Certificates that represent a proportional undivided ownership right in tangible assets, or a pool of assets.

Sunnah
Practices, actions, omissions, lifestyle and way of the Prophet Muhammad as transmitted authentically to later generations through traditions or historical records.

Sunni
One of the two major sects of Muslims. The other is the *Shi'a* sect.

Tabdhir
Extravagance and waste of resources; also covers spending on objects which have been explicitly prohibited by the *Shari'ah* irrespective of the quantum of expenditure.

Takaful
An Islamic form of insurance where everyone in a group of persons agrees to support the others against defined losses. All members of the group contribute a sum of money to cover the risk of loss suffered by any member.

Taqwa
God-consciousness or piety. In particular, being conscious of God's presence everywhere and trying to adhere to the norms of the *Shari'ah* in all matters voluntarily and with the hope of getting a reward in the hereafter.

Tawarruq
A financing technique adopted by Islamic financial institutions to provide liquidity to customers, in which they immediately receive an amount of money and commit to repay a deferred amount that is more than the cash received. This deferred payment is established via an agreement to buy a commodity on a deferred basis and then sell it for cash to a third party who is not the first seller at a lower price than the initial selling price.

Ummah
The global Muslim community based on unity of faith.

Ushr
A tax on the agricultural produce of land levied on Muslims at 10 percent if the land is irrigated by rainfall and at 5 percent if the land is irrigated otherwise.

Wadi'a
A contract whereby a person leaves valuables as a trust for safekeeping.

Zakah

A tax levied on all persons having wealth above an exemption limit (*nisab*). The objective is to take away a part of the wealth of the well-to-do and distribute it among the poor and needy.

Index